Women in Early America

Women in Early America

Struggle, Survival, and Freedom in a New World

Dorothy A. Mays

A B C CLIO

Santa Barbara, California   Denver, Colorado   Oxford, England

Library of Congress Cataloging-in-Publication Data
Mays, Dorothy A.
    Women in early America : struggle, survival, and freedom in a new world / Dorothy A. Mays.
        p. cm.
    Includes bibliographical references and index.
ISBN 1-85109-429-6 (hardback : alk. paper)
ISBN 1-85109-434-2 (e-book)

1. Women—United States—History—17th century—Encyclopedias.   2. Women—United States—History—18th century—Encyclopedias.   3. Women—United States—Social conditions—Encyclopedias.   4. United States—History—Colonial period, ca. 1600–1775—Encyclopedias.   5. United States—Social conditions—To 1865—Encyclopedias. I. Title.

HQ1416.M395 2004
305.4'0973'09032—dc22

                                                                          2004019721

07 06 05 04   10 9 8 7 6 5 4 3 2 1

This book is also available on the World Wide Web as an eBook.
Visit http://www.abc-clio.com for details.

ABC-CLIO, Inc.
130 Cremona Drive, P.O. Box 1911
Santa Barbara, California 93116-1911

This book is printed on acid-free paper ∞ .
Manufactured in the United States of America

Contents

Topic Finder

Preface and Acknowledgments

Early American women rarely played a direct role in landmark events of the time, but the establishment and survival of the colonies could not have occurred without women. These women did not invent the smallpox vaccine. They led no battles during the Revolution, nor did they participate in drafting the Declaration of Independence. However, a vivid example of the difference women made in early American society is demonstrated by comparing the initial settlements at Jamestown, Virginia, and the Massachusetts Bay Colony. In Jamestown there were very few women, but the gender ratio was roughly equal in the Massachusetts Bay Colony. The Jamestown settlers were disorganized and chose to hunt for gold and plant cash crops rather than establish self-sufficiency. The early years of Jamestown are typically described as disastrous. By contrast, the settlers in Massachusetts immediately constructed their homes, planted crops, and established viable forms of government, education, and satisfactory relations with the Indians. The presence of women and families has frequently been cited as a major factor for the improved conditions and progress of the Massachusetts Bay Colony.

Students often develop a fascination for history through identification with a time period, an individual, or a historical event. Those seeking information about women in early America can become frustrated by the sparse amount of research that has been done on the subject. Most history textbooks treat women with little more than an occasional sidebar or footnote. This is not done deliberately to slight women's experience, but is a reflection of the fact that history has tended to record the activities of male-oriented events. Women did not leave as many traces in the historical record and are thus harder to weave into the narrative of a standard history text.

In recent decades, historians have used innovative research methods to gain insight into the life of ordinary women in early America. Their scholarship reveals a world remarkably different from the Antebellum and Victorian eras that would follow. Early American women lived in a rougher, more dangerous world. They suffered from diseases for which immigrants from Europe and Africa had yet to gain acquired immunity. Communities were often vulnerable to crop failure or deteriorating relationships with Native Americans. Women of early America could not afford to live a life devoted primarily to motherhood and were required to play an active role in supporting the household. They had large families and developed unique systems of community support to assist women who were overwhelmed by caring for numerous small children.

The goal of this encyclopedia is to highlight the research that illuminates the world of early American women and make it available to the general reader. It is intended for precollegiate as well as college-level researchers. Like any developing discipline, women's history is rife with controversial issues and healthy academic debate. I have not attempted to present the nuances of such debate, but rather provide a clear introduction to the issues and events relative to women in early America. The lists of further readings at the end of each entry contain additional information for readers interested in exploring these issues in more depth.

I have defined the period "early America" as beginning in 1607, with the first permanent English settlement in America, and use the outbreak of the War of 1812 as the terminal date. The geographic focus is on the territory that later became a part of the United States. Because of my chronological constraints, most of the book is centered on the East Coast and the eighteenth-century frontier, an area rarely west of Ohio or Alabama. In the interest of readability appropriate to the book's intended audience, I have modernized spelling and punctuation in most of the historical quotations. The majority of the book addresses women of Anglo descent, but German, French, Dutch, African, Native American, and Spanish women are represented as well.

Entries for African and Native American women are particularly problematic. The immense ethnic diversity among these groups made generalizations about their life and culture difficult. It is easier to generalize about the African experience than that of the Native American. African women were transported from huge sections of Africa, with different religions, languages, and cultural norms. Although these women arrived with remarkably diverse traditions, they tended to adapt to American culture within a generation after arrival. African women of similar ethnic groups were often deliberately severed from each other upon their arrival in America. The conditions of slavery forced newly arrived women to learn a common language and share the same hardships. This fostered a sense of community that developed into an African American culture among subsequent generations of their descendents.

Native American women were deeply affected by European colonization, but they were rarely severed from their culture. They continued to nurture and adapt their way of life in the face of changing circumstances. The life of a Mohawk woman was drastically different from that of a Cherokee woman. I have focused on Indian women as they interacted with European or African settlers, in areas such as trade, interracial marriage, work, and religious conversion. The difficulty in making generalizations about Native American life is attested to by the few books that treat "Indians" as a group. Most books focus exclusively on a particular ethnic group or are arranged with chapters on noteworthy individuals. For students seeking more in-depth information on women of specific Indian groups, I have included references in the bibliography at the end of this book.

It is impossible to write a book about women in early America and not discuss extraordinary women such as Abigail Adams or Pocahontas. Such women represent only a tiny fraction of the millions of women who lived during this era, and their experiences were far from typical. Whenever possible, I have tried to highlight "ordinary" women and provide insight into the conditions of their lives. This presents a challenge, because surviving journals, buildings, and recorded history tend to be skewed toward those who lived a life of privilege. Every so often historians come across a windfall, such as the journal of Sarah Kemble Knight or the proceedings of Elizabeth Freeman's court case. These documents offer us a brief glimpse into the world of ordinary women, allowing us to see their living conditions and get a sense of their daily life. Entries documenting topical issues, such as aging, childbirth, or household responsibilities, use the experience of ordinary women as the norm and mention the experience of elite women when appropriate.

I hope readers will find this book useful for historical research, but also perhaps as an inspiration. Shakespeare's memorable line from *Twelfth Night* might be applied to countless women of early America. "Some are born great, some achieve greatness, and some have greatness thrust upon them." Many of these women lived in tough, dreary, and dangerous conditions. Some did not want to be in America at all. Most, however, rose to the occasion.

Acknowledgments

I want to give special thanks for support and assistance to: Jane Guthrie, John Auchter, and Kathleen Leighton, who read and helped with portions of the manuscript. Rollins College, for leave time and generous support through a Critchfield grant. Lisa Stronski for help tracking down a myriad of peculiar reference questions. All the librarians and archivists from the John D. Rockefeller Library at Colonial Williamsburg, especially Juleigh Clark. Patricia Grall and Shawne Keevan for good-naturedly supplying my incessant requests for odd resources. Melissa and Wendy Mays for their ideas, patience, and help keeping the home fires burning when I was too busy to do so. And my deepest thanks to Bill Mays, who was with me every step of the way.

Dorothy Mays
Rollins College

Introduction

The women's liberation movement of the 1960s and 1970s generated new curiosity about the history and accomplishments of women, resulting in a ground-swell of books and college courses. Although a wealth of excellent research on American women's history was produced, most of the scholarship has focused on women's unflagging crusade toward equal rights, the vote, and a variety of social concerns. Women of early America showed remarkably little interest in remedying gender inequalities. They were interested in survival. In the absence of women who broke new ground in areas of gender equality, women of the colonial era rarely attracted the attention of historians and remained in the shadows during the heyday of the feminist movement. As a result, many people's knowledge of women in early America begins and ends with Betsy Ross. This book hopes to address the lack of readily available reference material on women in early America.

In recent decades, scholars have addressed the shortfall of research on women in early America. Dozens of historians, such as Carol Berkin, Cornelia Hughes Dayton, Mary Beth Norton, and the Pulitzer prize–winning Laurel Thatcher Ulrich have mined the nation's libraries and archives to produce impressive works of scholarship. Each year sees the completion of new doctoral dissertations that piece together strands of historical data to create an ever-clearer picture of what life was like for women in early America. These historians rarely have the luxury of relying on memoirs written by women to record their thoughts or activities, as this type of journaling did not come into vogue until much later. Even more uncommon were colonial women who stepped outside their domestic sphere to leave a lasting impression in the public arena. In the absence of easily interpreted sources, historians have had to become far more resourceful in reconstructing the lives of early American women.

An example of the sort of meticulous original research that helps illuminate the lives of anonymous colonial women is historian Else Hambleton's study of illegitimacy in seventeenth-century Massachusetts. Using decades of church and court records to track dates of conception, marriage, and birth, she cross-referenced the data with prosecution of fornication and adultery charges. Analyzing the data allowed her to draw conclusions about the changing attitudes toward premarital sex and how the lingering taint of promiscuity marred a woman's ability to establish a respectable position in her hometown. In *A Midwife's Tale,* Laurel Thatcher Ulrich studied what appeared to be a bland, monotonous journal. Careful examination of the entries and chores recorded reveal an exhausting capacity for physical labor performed by an ordinary woman in her role as a housekeeper and midwife. Historian Carole Shammas studied probate inventories to learn what tools of home manufacture a typical colonial household possessed. Using such data, she was able to form a picture of what skills a colonial woman needed to have to support her household and which goods were likely to be purchased or traded. She found that contrary to the stereotypical belief that colonial women lived on entirely self-sufficient farms, most women specialized in a few skills and bartered for their other needs. This analysis provides us with greater insight into how colonial women actually used their daylight hours. These are but a few examples of the resourceful scholarship that allows us to reconstruct the lives of ordinary colonial women.

The women of early America lived very different lives from women in later centuries. The formative years of early settlement witnessed colonists who were struggling to define themselves as various cultures came together in a new and strange land. Some women immigrated to America motivated by a sincere desire to live according to deeply felt religious principles. Others came in search of land, wealth, or a legacy for their children. For countless thousands, the journey was forced upon them. African women were sent to answer the colonists' insatiable demand for labor. Indentured servants from Europe contracted themselves into temporary bondage in the face of dire economic circumstances. Whatever the cause of their immigration, women from a variety of religions, cultures, and economic groups converged in America.

In many ways, the lives of women living in early America mirrored the familiar patterns found in Europe. The majority of their adulthood was defined by pregnancy, nursing, and the rearing of children. Their chores were primarily domestic. They generally deferred to men in legal and business issues. But underlying these familiar routines were subtle differences. Women gave birth more often in America, averaging six to nine children per household, compared with three to five among women living in England. American women were richer in land but poorer in material goods. The American diet was more plentiful and varied than that commonly available in Europe. As a result, Americans were generally half an inch taller than their European counterparts. American women were scarce, and their value as workers and companions was more highly prized in the fledgling colonies. American women were more likely to sell or barter the products of their domestic labor than were European women. There was also a pervasive

sense of threat from the unknown in America. Indians who were once friendly might turn on settlers without warning. Strange diseases in the new environment struck with terrifying ferocity.

Our impressions of early American women have often been skewed by a few atypical examples. Perhaps the most famous piece of literature that continues to shape present-day thinking of early America is Nathaniel Hawthorne's *The Scarlet Letter* and its fictional heroine, Hester Prynne. Hawthorne was a progressive thinker who wrote during an era when the Puritan heritage was coming under criticism. Hawthorne's disapproval of Puritan austerity rings forth loud and clear, casting a shadow over present-day notions of women's life in seventeenth-century New England. Compounding Hawthorne's bleak view is the surviving literature of the era, much of which was written by ministers. Their published sermons exhorted women to embody a pious and submissive ideal. The resulting image is a dreary world awash in warnings, reprimands, and shades of gray.

Is this an accurate portrayal of how women in early America lived? For some it is. But in the raw, unsettled wilderness of America there was a huge range of experience for colonial women. The Anglican women of the Chesapeake had a vastly different life than the Puritan women of New England. Likewise, the women of the Dutch settlements lived under a legal system that granted them rights that were often comparable to the privileges enjoyed by men. Many of these Dutch women established thriving businesses and kept their maiden names after marriage. In recent decades, even the grim world of the Puritans has been reassessed by historians who assert that Puritanism accorded women a measure of respect unusual elsewhere in the early modern world. Although some Puritan women lived with oppressive husbands and fathers, others experienced deeply fulfilling marriages. In sharp contrast to the fictional oppressions of Hester Prynne, real-life Puritan Anne Bradstreet clearly adored her husband, when she wrote of him, "If ever two were one, then surely we. If ever man were loved by wife, then thee."

There was a tremendous diversity of experience in terms of racial, economic, and geographic regions. The women of the Chesapeake and southern colonies lived in steaming, unhealthy environments, where they were plagued by disease, tainted water, and crop failure. The resulting high rates of mortality played havoc on the traditional nuclear family. Parental death, remarriage, and stepfamilies were common. Many girls grew up with little parental supervision, which might have been a contributing factor to the higher rates of premarital pregnancy in the Chesapeake. Meanwhile, the comparatively healthy climate in New England led to far greater family stability. Children were more likely to know their grandparents. The longevity of parents had implications for the age of first marriage and inheritance patterns, as adult children were rarely able to afford to marry without parental consent and a substantial dowry or inheritance. Thus, greater familial stability sometimes came at a cost of intergenerational tension.

The experience of enslaved women varied dramatically, depending on whether they lived in town or in a rural region. The rural women tended to perform outdoor agricultural work and lived among large numbers of fellow slaves. This made finding a husband and living among an extended family far easier. Slaves who lived in towns led more isolated lives. Their work was primarily indoor domestic chores, and they were usually the only slave owned by their master. Although generally treated more humanely, urban slaves often led far lonelier lives than their rural counterparts. I have tried to be mindful of the diversity of women and their experience throughout this book.

Perhaps one of the most vivid differences between women of early America and those of later centuries was in their economic role. Early America was a world of few luxuries, and women needed to work in order for their households to survive. It was common to see women working side by side with their husbands in a variety of businesses. Farm women toiled in the fields; the printer's wife helped set type; the shopkeeper's wife tended the store. In the event of widowhood, a number of women assumed sole proprietorship of the family business.

Although gender dictated the sort of contributions women could make to society, without women's assistance the new settlements of America could not have flourished in the manner they did.

Beginning in the late eighteenth century, the Industrial Revolution brought great change to American society. Technological improvements resulted in a narrowing of women's economic roles. Once the population moved away from subsistence living and the purchase of manufactured goods became commonplace, a woman's labor was no longer as essential for the survival of her family. Her contributions to the household became less vital and less visible. Rising expectations for domestic comfort kept the housewife busy with meal preparation and ornamental domestic arts. Women's value became increasingly defined by their role as mothers. By the early nineteenth century, women who operated businesses outside the home were viewed as odd or neglectful of their motherly responsibilities.

The belief that the women of early America enjoyed a "golden era" when their labor was valued and they were free to seek employment outside the home is not without controversy. It appears to be true that most early American women who owned businesses were widows who were forced into the marketplace and often retired from the business upon remarriage or an upturn in their economic situation. Whereas a modern woman might regard the eighteenth-century woman who operated a printing press as remarkably liberated, the printer might have considered her life to be one of drudgery and struggle. Were these early American women drudges tied to their subsistence economy, or were they respected members of society who enjoyed the freedom to earn their own living? It is a controversial question that cannot be answered by this book and continues to be avidly debated by historians. What is certain is that women of the colonial era lived far different lives than the women of the nineteenth century. This book explores the social and cultural parameters of their lives, hoping to glean insight into the experiences of ordinary women who lived during an extraordinary time.

Abortion

Induced abortion has been practiced from ancient times, and the women of colonial America knew of various methods to end an unwanted pregnancy. Although not unheard of, abortions in colonial America were almost never performed by use of instruments or attempts to manually remove the fetus from the womb. The use of herbs was the most common technique for inducing a miscarriage.

Prior to any effective means of contraception, unwanted pregnancies were regular occurrences for both single and married women alike. Social stigmatization was obviously much higher for an unmarried woman, who could either quickly marry her lover or bring him to court to demand financial support for the child. Both were common practices, with as many as one-third of brides being pregnant in early eighteenth-century America. If a woman was unwilling or unable to marry her lover, she might have sought means to terminate her pregnancy through abortion.

Throughout most of the colonial period there were no explicit laws regarding abortion. Because colonial law borrowed heavily from England, it is worth examining the more fully developed laws of England regarding abortion. There were no sanctions against the deliberate termination of a pregnancy before the fetus had "quickened"—when a woman could first feel the fetus moving inside her. Quickening usually happened by the fourth month of pregnancy. Such feelings were the only concrete proof a woman was pregnant, as other medical

explanations could account for lack of menstruation. Because "blocked menstruation" was believed to be a sign of a dangerous medical condition, an attempt to remove a menstrual blockage was considered morally acceptable. Even if the blockage was later discovered to have been a pregnancy, there was no stigma or legal ramifications for clearing the blockage, as long as quickening had not occurred. Contemporaries did not believe that a fetus was a living child until it had quickened, and knowingly terminating an early pregnancy was not legally banned.

British jurist Edward Coke (1552–1632) formulated much of the English common-law tradition. Regarding abortion, he denied that it was possible for anyone to be accused of murder for ending a pregnancy, though any action taken against a child that has been born alive is clearly murder. He cited cases in which a pregnant woman was physically assaulted and lost a pregnancy as a result. Such cases could not be considered murder, since it was not conclusive that the woman would have successfully produced a living child.

Perhaps the best documentation of women's attempts to thwart the progression of a pregnancy can be found in medical books and herbals. Such texts contain repeated references to herbs that can be used to release "blocked menses" or serve as "menstrual stimulators." The most common herbs cited for such uses were pennyroyal, willow, and juniper leaves. Although rarely identified specifically as techniques to end a pregnancy, it is likely that midwives and physicians fully understood that blocked menstruation was usually the result of pregnancy. In some instances, the texts specifically identified which herbs should never be given to a pregnant woman, for they were known to bring on early labor. Vigorous exercises, such as horseback riding or jumping rope, were also suggested to induce menstruation or "remove a dead fetus."

It is difficult to determine how effective these techniques were, since successfully terminated pregnancies were unlikely to be documented in the historical record. Only in cases where the woman died or brought a malformed child into the world was there reason to note the attempted abortion. Cornelia Hughes Dayton documents a case from 1742, in which Sarah Grosvenor attempted several times to abort her pregnancy through the ingestion of herbs. After merely becoming sick, she resorted to a "physick" who used tools to induce a surgical abortion. Sarah sickened and died. The abortionist and Sarah's lover stood trial for Sarah's murder, but not that of the infant. Both were eventually acquitted. This is the only documented case in colonial America in which a surgical abortion was attempted, although there are occasional references to assault and punching in an attempt to terminate a pregnancy.

The use of herbs was problematic for women, because the dosage had to be precise. Although herbs such as pennyroyal could induce a miscarriage, too little merely sickened the woman, and too much could be toxic. Side effects from these herbs could cause liver damage, breathing difficulties, or convulsions. Herbs such as juniper leaves, pennyroyal, and rue were usually brewed into a strong tea that was orally ingested. In some cases women might have inserted the leaves into the vagina to induce a miscarriage. Although occasionally successful, it is unlikely that herbal techniques were very effective. Had herbal remedies been effective, there would have been no need to pursue the dangerous and chilling surgical techniques resorted to in later generations.

Despite the wide availability of herbs and texts that provided instruction on the termination of pregnancy, there were moral and ethical problems raised by the practice. Many herbals warn against tampering with the sanctity of life. William Buchan's 1769 text *Domestic Medicine* provided detailed instructions on how to cure menstrual irregularities and precautions that must be used by pregnant women. He acknowledges that these techniques can be used to wickedly procure an abortion and begs a woman considering such an act to "stop her murderous hand" by contemplating the child whom she might one day learn to cherish. Many herbals and medical texts carried such heartfelt exhortations, although they are absent from others. Thus, the writers of these texts knew that in instructing women which herbs to avoid during pregnancy, they had little control over how that information would be applied.

Perhaps the first attempt to prosecute someone for procuring an abortion occurred in 1650, when Captain William Mitchell attempted to force his twenty-one-year-old bond servant, Susan Warren, to abort the child he had fathered. He forced her to drink a noxious potion, which made her break out in boils and lose her hair but did not terminate the pregnancy. When she gave birth to a stillborn child shortly afterward, a Maryland grand jury indicted Captain Mitchell for having tried to force an abortion on Susan Warren. It was ultimately decided that the death of the child could not be conclusively traced to Mitchell, though he was fined five thousand pounds of tobacco for fornication. Susan Warren was flogged for fornication but released from further indenture to Captain Mitchell.

Over time the moral prohibitions against abortion gathered momentum. Most failed, but in 1821, Connecticut became the first American state to pass a law against the deliberate termination of a pregnancy after quickening. This law would become the model for other states, which enacted numerous laws against abortion over the next twenty years.

See also Gynecological Issues; Mothers, Single

Further Reading

Acevedo, Zoila. "Abortion in Early America." *Women and Health* 4 (1979): 159–176.
Dayton, Cornelia Hughes. "Taking the Trade: Abortion and Gender Relations in an Eighteenth

Century New England Village." *William and Mary Quarterly* 48 (1991): 19–49.

Klepp, Susan E. "Lost, Hidden, Obstructed, and Repressed: Contraceptive and Abortive Technology in the Early Delaware Valley." In *Early American Technology: Making and Doing Things from the Colonial Era to 1850,* ed. Judith A. McGaw. Chapel Hill: University of North Carolina Press, 1994.

Olasky, Marvin. *Abortion Rites: A Social History of Abortion in America.* Lanham, MD: Regnery, 1995.

Riddle, John M. *Eve's Herbs: A History of Contraception and Abortion in the West.* Cambridge, MA: Harvard University Press, 1997.

Tone, Andrea, ed. *Controlling Reproduction: An American History.* Wilmington, DE: Scholarly Resources, 1997.

Adams, Abigail Smith
First Lady (1744–1818)

Although she is most commonly remembered as the wife of President John Adams and mother of President John Quincy Adams, Abigail Adams is worthy of study on her own account. Her marriage to John Adams was an extraordinary partnership, which proved to be a practical and emotionally rewarding relationship for both parties. During her husband's long years of public service, Abigail managed their farm and finances. She was a sensible companion whom her husband used as a sounding board for many of his political ideas. In return, John Adams provided his curious and intelligent wife with entrée into a world of elite culture far beyond what most provincial women could have expected.

Abigail was born in Weymouth, Massachusetts, a town that was permeated by the Puritan standards of sober hard work, respect for education, and public service. Abigail inherited these traditional values that served her well as a household manager and wife of a politician whose salary was often slim. Abigail's father was a minister, who was able to provide her with a comfortable home, but the meager wages paid to ministers meant that she was expected to fully participate in household chores and appreciate the value of frugality. Although Abigail received no formal education, she had free use of her father's

Remember the Ladies

Perhaps the most often-quoted line from Abigail Adams's voluminous correspondence with her husband was her plea that he be mindful of women as he formulated ideas for a new form of government. Here is the context for that famous letter:

I long to hear that you have declared independency—and by the way in the new code of laws which I suppose it will be necessary for you to make I desire you would remember the ladies, and be more generous and favorable to them than your ancestors. Do not put such unlimited power into the hands of the husbands. Remember all men would be tyrants if they could. If particular care and attention is not paid to the ladies we are determined to foment a rebellion, and will not hold ourselves bound by any laws in which we have no voice, or representation.

That your sex are naturally tyrannical is a truth so thoroughly established as to admit of no dispute, but such of you as wish to be happy willingly give up the harsh title of Master for the more tender and endearing one of Friend. Why then, not put it out of the power of the vicious and the lawless to use us with cruelty and indignity with impunity. Men of sense in all ages abhor those customs which treat us only as the vassals of your sex. Regard us then as beings placed by providence under your protection and in imitation of the Supreme Being make use of that power only for our happiness.

Braintree, 31 March 1776

Source: Norton, Mary Beth, ed. *Problems in American Women's History: Documents and Essays.* Lexington, MA: D. C. Heath, 1996, p.77.

substantial personal library. When she was only sixteen, Abigail caught the eye of the ambitious young lawyer John Adams. The couple lived in different towns, and thus began their habit of writing letters to one another that would endure throughout their long marriage. In these early courtship letters Abigail playfully adopted the pen name "Diana," and dubbed John "Lysander."

The couple married on 25 October 1764 and moved to Braintree (which was later renamed Quincy), where John had inherited a farm. They had five children, four of whom survived into adulthood.

Portrait of Abigail Adams (1744–1818), American writer and wife of John Adams, second president of the United States (Library of Congress)

The first ten years of Abigail's marriage were dedicated to child rearing and tending the farm. It was during these years that John became increasingly involved in the political turmoil that simmered in Boston. In 1774 he was elected to represent Massachusetts in the First Continental Congress at Philadelphia. Throughout the next ten years John Adams was often away from his farm, leaving Abigail with primary responsibility for managing the home, farm, and the rearing of their children.

During the long years of John Adams's absences, Abigail stopped calling herself Diana and adopted the pen name "Portia" in her letters to John. Portia was the long-suffering wife of Brutus, and she kept the home fires burning while her husband served in the Roman Senate. During the American Revolution Abigail commented, "Patriotism in the female sex is the most disinterested of all virtues" (Abigail Adams to John Adams, 17 June 1782). She recognized that even if the American cause succeeded, it was men alone who would inherit the new political offices, the prestige, and the power.

Abigail Adams has often been credited with being an early feminist. Her frequently quoted "Remember the Ladies" remark has been said to be a plea to her husband to grant women greater political voice. Historians debate whether Abigail was truly in earnest or half-joking in her letter. Whatever her intent, her husband playfully dismissed her comments, and she did not reopen the subject. Although Abigail never established a record of advocating for women's inclusion in the political process, she demonstrated an unusual gender awareness for the eighteenth century. She was genuinely frustrated by the sad state of education for girls and believed they shared the same potential for intelligence as men.

Despite Abigail's respect for female abilities, she clearly accepted the eighteenth-century status quo regarding women's roles. She believed that men and women were to be true partners, having separate but mutually supporting spheres. A woman's sphere was in the home, and the male sphere was in the world of business and politics. A woman was to rear her children in a hardworking and godly environment, while creating a haven for her husband.

At the conclusion of the American Revolution, Abigail entered a different and more public role. No longer willing to tolerate years of uninterrupted separation, Abigail joined her husband in England in 1785 after he had been appointed the first U.S. minister to England. This position presented a number of challenges for Abigail. England was still smarting over the conclusion of the war, and she needed to present a gracious and conciliatory tone. The salary and entertaining allowance for U.S. diplomats was paltry. Rather than squander funds on lavish entertaining, Abigail hosted small informal dinner parties. Her gracious and intelligent conversation was generally well accepted among the diplomatic corps.

Abigail's years in England gave her a newfound appreciation for the United States. Although she reveled in the museums, splendid country estates, and other cultural attractions of England, she was shocked at the entrenched poverty of a large percentage of the population. England had a class of abject laborers who were at the mercy of an elite class prone to tyranny and insolence. Although America lacked the glamour and soaring riches found in England, there was opportunity available for people to create a healthy living. Her Puritan sensibilities were also rattled by the wantonness she believed to be rampant in English high society. On a 1787 trip to the resort town of Bath, she was disconcerted by the dissipation and gambling among the elite. She was relieved to return to the familiar comforts of the United States in 1788.

John Adams became the first vice president of the United States in 1789. During much of this time, Abigail chose to remain at home in Massachusetts rather than at the nation's capital in Philadelphia. Once again, their modest income could not support a home in the more comfortable part of Philadelphia, and the best they could afford was located two miles from the city. The climate of Philadelphia was not to her liking, nor did she particularly enjoy the public role associated with her position. During most of the time between 1791 and 1797, she lived on her farm in Massachusetts, and she only returned to Philadelphia when her husband was elected president. She agreed to come after receiving his plea, "I pray you to come on immediately.... I never wanted your advice and assistance more in my life" (Gelles 1999, 13).

For her position as first lady, Abigail followed the tone set by Martha Washington. She entertained in a gracious manner, but did not indulge in the lavish displays common in European courts. The Adams administration was marred by the development of increasingly bitter political factions. Publicly, Abigail did not voice political opinions, but in private, she was known to share her husband's ardent Federalist positions. When Adams lost the acrimonious election of 1800 to Thomas Jefferson, the couple retreated to Massachusetts.

The years following John's retirement from public office appear to have been the happiest of Abigail's life. Decades of carefully protecting their finances finally paid off, and John Adams was one of the few founding fathers to remain clear of debt after a life of public service. They built a new home named "Peacefield," and Abigail referred to herself as a "dairy-woman" and John as "the farmer." The home was not pretentious, but it was large and comfortable, with a spacious library and prosperous fields. They were surrounded by children and grandchildren. Abigail lived to see her son John Quincy attain the position of secretary of state, a stepping-stone to the presidency.

The Adams's fifty-four-year marriage was documented by an extraordinary series of letters exchanged between the couple, often separated because of John Adams's political commitments. Although the Adams's relationship has often been cited as an example of a profound love story and intense partnership, this is likely because of the voluminous correspondence that preserved the memory of the mutually rewarding nature of their marriage. The role Abigail played was no doubt shared by countless numbers of American women, whose husbands relied on their active support to operate the farm or business while they pursued other commitments.

See also Political Wives

Further Reading

Crane, Elaine Forman. "Political Dialogue and the Spring of Abigail's Discontent." *William and Mary Quarterly* 56 (1999): 745–774.

Gelles, Edith B. "Abigail Adams." In *Dictionary of Literary Biography: American Women Prose Writers to 1820*, ed. Cafla Mulford. Detroit, MI: Gale, 1999.

Morton, Joseph C. "Abigail Adams." In *Women in World History: A Biographical Encyclopedia*, ed. Anne Commire. Waterford, CT: Yorkin, 1999.

Withy, Lynne. *Dearest Friend: A Life of Abigail Adams.* New York: The Free Press, 1981.

Adams, Hannah
Writer (1755–1831)

Hannah Adams is remembered as a pioneer in the field of comparative religion and the first American woman to support herself through writing. Given her concern for the financial rewards of publication, it is not surprising that she was intimately involved in the advancement of a national copyright law. She was also distantly related to the Adams family of presidential fame.

Hannah was a shy and sickly child. Her mother died when Hannah was only ten, and her timidity and reluctance to mingle with others became ingrained from an early age. Reluctant to participate in normal childhood recreations, Hannah spent most of her youth exploring the volumes of her father's excellent library. Hannah's father, Thomas "Book" Adams, was a man of keen intellectual interests, as attested to by his nickname. Although Hannah was born into financially comfortable circumstances, her father decided to sell his prosperous farm and become a bookseller. This proved financially disastrous, and the family fell on hard times. Hannah was too sickly to obtain regular employment, but she attempted to supplement the family income by making bobbin lace. Book Adams resorted to taking in boarders and tutoring young men preparing for college. This proved unexpectedly beneficial for Hannah, for many of the people who sought out tutoring and lodging with her father were people of intellect and sophistication. Hannah's association with her father's pupils nourished her intellectual curiosity, and she began taking notes to record her thoughts on wide-ranging studies.

Hannah was especially interested in the study of theology, but could not help noticing that most of the published literature was disrespectful or dismissive of non-Christian religions. She recognized a need for an evenhanded and respectful survey of the world's religious traditions. *An Alphabetical Compendium of the Various Sects* (1784) explained the differences among various Christian denominations and provided an overview of other world religions. She suggested similarities among various religious traditions and rationalized many of the differences. In so doing, she reflected the liberal Unitarian philosophy that was beginning to take hold in New England.

Hannah's book was well received, but it proved unrewarding as a financial venture. Unfamiliar with the publishing business and relying on Book Adams's uninformed advice, she agreed to have four hundred fifty copies printed. Hannah's agreement only allotted her fifty copies to sell or dispose of as she saw fit, which brought her miniscule financial benefit. Although the book sold briskly and the printer profited greatly, this was Hannah's first experience with the difficulties of the book market. A subsequent edition was printed in 1791 that brought her a much better income.

Hannah's next project was to be a general survey of the history of New England. She traveled throughout the area for her research, nearly ruining her eyesight from the exhaustive research through old manuscript records. *A Summary History of New England* was published in 1799, but its sales proved disappointing. Hannah hoped an abridged version of the exhaustive work would have more popular appeal. If the book could be adopted as a text in schools, it would be especially profitable. While working on the condensed version of her work, Hannah learned that two other writers were collaborating on a similar project. The Reverends Jedidiah Morse and Elijah Parish were also in the midst of writing a textbook of New England history, and rumor accused them of heavy reliance on Hannah's work for their material. Hannah sought assurances from Reverend Morse that his book would not be in direct competition with her abridged version. Although Morse encouraged her to continue with her project, it soon became apparent that he was intending to directly compete with her and preempt her sales by publishing his work first.

Despite Hannah's timid and withdrawn nature, she had acquired a number of powerful friends in Boston's intellectual circles. These men were naturally inclined to be sympathetic to Hannah, for her liberal religious and intellectual positions were in accord with the progressive atmosphere of early nineteenth-century Boston. By contrast, the Reverends Morse and Parish were of the old school, viewing New England's history through the narrow lens of Puritanical orthodoxy. After the controversy became a public affair, the reverends were widely believed to have heavily plagiarized from Hannah's full-length work. Reverend Morse attempted to defend himself, asking if Miss Adams had the exclusive entitlement to write the history of New England. He pointed out that his work was heavily weighted to the religious history of the Puritans, whereas Miss Adams's focus was on the American Revolution.

Intellectual property and copyright law was not yet well defined, and Hannah could find no clear law to support her position. Nevertheless, the controversy would not die. In the interest of saving his reputation, Reverend Morse agreed to submit the matter before a board of three referees in 1809. The referees concluded that although the reverends were not guilty of violating any law, their actions had caused Miss Adams financial harm, and they had a moral obligation to provide her with recompense for their interference with her work. The decision was not legally binding, and there is no evidence that either coauthor ever paid any damages to Hannah.

By then Hannah was living independently. In 1805 her brother and his wife and children had returned to the family home to care for their aging father. It was too crowded for Hannah to remain, and she took independent lodgings, struggling to earn enough from her writing to pay her bills. Fortunately, a number of wealthy Bostonians who admired Hannah's work set up an annuity to supplement her income.

Hannah had a continuing interest in protecting the financial rights of authors. Although some states had passed copyright laws, there was no national system to protect the rights of authors. In 1790 she petitioned Massachusetts congressman Fisher Ames to introduce a national copyright law, which was passed later that year. She died in Boston, and her portrait hangs in the Boston Athenaeum, the library where she conducted much of her research.

Further Reading

Gleason, Gene. "A Mere Woman." *American Heritage* 24, no. 1 (1972): 80–84.

Vella, Michael W. "Hannah Adams." In *American Women Prose Writers to 1820,* ed. Carla Mulford. Detroit, MI: Gale, 1999.

———. "Theology, Genre, and Gender: The Precarious Place of Hannah Adams in American Literary History." *Early American Literature* 28 (1993): 21–41.

Wright, Conrad C. "Hannah Adams." In *Notable American Women, 1607–1950,* ed. Edward T. James. Cambridge, MA: Belknap Press of Harvard University, 1971.

Addictive Substances

Alcohol, tobacco, and narcotic drugs were available in colonial America, and the addictive qualities of these drugs caused some women to develop dependencies on them. Although the dangerous nature of alcohol was well known, neither tobacco nor the many varieties of opiates were clearly understood to be habit-forming or dangerous to the health. Other than drunkenness, there is little reference to drug abuse in colonial records.

Women drank, smoked, and took narcotic medications, but these were rarely considered to be harmful, scandalous, or even worthy of mention. With the exception of a handful of women who worked outside the home in urban areas, most women spent the overwhelming majority of their lives in their home. Within the privacy of their home or farm, unhealthful use of addictive substances would rarely cause comment, except in the few instances when courts interceded.

Alcohol

Early Americans had an enormous capacity for drink. A typical day started with a mug of hard cider or "small beer," a light lager that needed to be consumed within a few days of brewing. Water was shunned by early Americans, partly because of the bland taste, but also because of the health risks associated with the water supply. Well water could be easily tainted by animal or human waste. Settlers who lived near the ocean often had brackish water seep upstream during certain seasons, leading to dangerous levels of salt consumption for those who drank the water. The combination of the hearty British drinking tradition, the abundance of alcoholic beverages, and suspicion of drinking water led to high rates of alcohol consumption among all ages and sexes in colonial America. By 1770, the per capita consumption of hard liquor was 3.7 gallons per year, in addition to liberal amounts of cider and beer. Wine was rarely available in colonial America.

Families often had their own brewing facilities, and many women included the fermenting of small beer among their weekly chores. Women of the northern colonies would have known how to make the ever-popular apple cider, and southern women made peach brandy. Fermenting the fruit harvest was the only way to preserve the crop throughout the long winter season. The alcohol content of apple cider could be boosted by the addition of sugar or molasses. Imported molasses was abundant in colonial America, making rum one of the most common hard liquors. The classic mixed drink enjoyed by colonists was flip, a sweet drink made from beer infused with molasses, sugar, and perhaps a bit of dried pumpkin or apples. A shot of rum was added, and the drink was finished by plunging a red hot poker into it, causing the rum to foam and giving the drink a smoky, bitter flavor. Small beer was easy enough for the average farmer's wife to make, although brewing strong beer was left to the village brewer.

Alcohol was abundant and inexpensive. Even the poor could afford it, and they favored rum, because it was the most potent form of alcohol. The alcoholic content of colonial beverages was as follows: small beer 2 percent, regular beer 5 to 7 percent, hard cider 10 percent, wine 18 percent, and rum around 40 percent. Whiskey became affordable and widely available in the late eighteenth century, owing to the expansion of corn farming in the western frontier. Inadequate transportation meant that corn would spoil before arrival in the East. Farmers distilled their corn into whiskey, which was easier to transport and sell. The price of whiskey plummeted, making it a favorite among the working poor. There were no legal laws regarding the sale or consumption of alcohol, except that taverns must be licensed and public drunkenness was forbidden.

Colonial attitudes toward alcohol were influenced by the medicinal benefits alcohol was widely believed to possess. Strong drink was known to alleviate pain, and it was used for ailments as diverse as fevers, snakebites, nervous disorders, and the common cold. Although doctors often prescribed a bit of alcohol as a tonic, they were well aware of its detrimental effects. Overindulgence in alcohol was believed to have negative consequences on the entire body, resulting in harm to the digestive tract, a dangerous weakening of nerves, weakening of the bowels, and even making the blood "fizzy."

Although drinking was common in early America, drunkenness was disdained. Puritans disapproved of celebratory drunkenness, believing it led to sin, laziness, and the potential for lawlessness. Well-ordered family life was highly prized among the Puritans, and drunkenness led to the neglect of family, economic responsibilities, and a decline in godliness. Regulation of alcohol extended to the southern colonies as well. Drunkards were more likely to fall sick and become unable to support their families, leading to local laws that attempted to prevent drunkenness.

There was no prohibition against women drinking alcohol in colonial America. A large percentage of tavern keepers were women, indicating it was not unseemly for a woman to be associated with the selling or consumption of spirits. It was considered vulgar for women to drink in large quantities, but sipping small beer, or taking a bit of rum "for her health," was acceptable.

Most adult women of colonial America drank moderate amounts of alcohol, but some women

---

The Sad Demise of an Alcoholic Woman

The murder trial of Peter Lung recounted life in a chaotic household where alcohol contributed to domestic battery, the neglect of children, and the murder of his wife, Lucy Kelley Lung. The Lungs lived in a squalid house with their nine children, and Peter worked odd jobs when he could find them. What little money they had was quickly spent on rum or beer. Lucy was disinterested in most household chores, preferring drink and sleep. There was rarely food in the home, and it appears the family was often dependent on the charity of friends and neighbors. The children were generally unsupervised, because time and again when Peter returned home, his wife was sleeping off an alcoholic binge.

Lucy and Peter fought over the typical range of domestic issues. She accused him of dallying with other women; he accused her of refusing to cook for him. Arguments were often settled with fists. Peter freely admitted he beat and kicked his wife when he was angry. There is record of the children trying to comfort their mother, both after beatings and after she drank herself into insensibility. In August 1815 Lucy died after several days of binging and fighting with her husband. Peter was found guilty of murder and hanged for the crime. The fate of their children is not known.

Why Lucy chose to sink into inebriation is unknown. Marriage to an abusive man can only partly explain her despair. A battered woman had few options, and with four children under the age of ten, she could not afford to support her family without him. Her willingness to sink into an alcoholic stupor baffled those around her at the time, as does the behavior of alcoholics in contemporary society.

Source: Sherrow, Doris. "Murder in Middletown: Lower-Class Life in Connecticut in 1815." *Dublin Seminar for New England Folklife* 13 (1990): 38–47.

---

abused alcohol. When domestic disputes ended up in court, one or both parties were usually accused of drinking to excess. When neglected children were removed from homes, the parents were often noted as being too drunk to raise them. Public drunkenness was so disgraceful that repeat offenders were sometimes required to wear a *D* on their clothing.

There was no understanding of the correlation between drunkenness and alcoholism in early America. To drink in excess was viewed as a willful act, motivated by self-indulgence. Because the addictive nature of alcohol was misunderstood, early medical texts addressed drunkenness as a moral failing and sought to enlighten heavy drinkers by calling attention to how intemperance affected children and families. Drunkards were implored to simply stop drinking before they became drunk, much as they would be instructed to stop biting their fingernails.

Dr. Benjamin Rush was the first to enunciate the theory that drunkenness was caused by a pernicious craving for alcohol, acquired through an extended period of overexposure. He believed total abstinence was the only way to extinguish the insidious yearning for drink.

How many women were alcoholics in early America will never be known. Only infrequent references to women being prosecuted for public drunkenness or domestic squabbles cast light on what was probably a much more widespread problem. Children began drinking at an early age, and light alcoholic drinks were consumed throughout the day for many families. Some women doubtlessly developed a dependency on drink, even though it might not have been understood as a medical problem.

Tobacco

Although women never smoked as much tobacco as men, smoking in all forms was acceptable for women in early America. In the seventeenth century, the damaging health implications of smoking were little known. Doctors in the eighteenth century began to see tobacco as detrimental to both health and morality. They began documenting cases of people who became so attached to the use of tobacco they were unable to surrender their habit. Dr. Benjamin Rush believed people turned to tobacco during periods of stress or overwork. He reported one woman who became attached to smoking when she turned to it out of fear she would die in childbirth. Another woman became so attached she needed to get up two or three times a night to partake of more tobacco.

Tobacco Use: A Bewitching Thing It Is . . .

Mary Rowlandson was captured by Indians in the winter of 1676. She chronicled her three-month ordeal in a famous book, in which she recounted her struggle to survive. The following passage from her narrative provides us with insight into the comforts of pipe smoking:

> For though I had formerly used tobacco, yet I had left it ever since I was first taken. It seems to be a bait the Devil lays to make men lose their precious time. I remember with shame how formerly when I had taken two or three pipes I was presently ready for another, such a bewitching thing it is. But I thank God he has now given me power over it; surely there are many who may be better employed than to lie sucking a stinking tobacco pipe.

Source: Lincoln, Charles H. *Narratives of the Indian Wars, 1675–1699.* New York: Charles Scribner's Sons, 1913.

The pleasant sensation tobacco users testified to could not be dismissed. Many doctors believed there was some beneficial treatment offered by tobacco, but they were concerned that the habitual use of the drug negated its strength and resulted only in additional cravings. It was noted that people who attempted to stop their tobacco habit suffered from "uneasiness." Like those dependent on alcohol, women who appeared to be dependent on tobacco were perceived to be suffering from a moral weakness.

Fleeting references in diaries and court cases attest to the fact that women smoked both cigarettes and pipes. In 1668, a sixteen-year-old serving maid, Mehitable Brabrooke, was prosecuted for carelessly laying her pipe down and starting a fire at her master's house. The casual mention of female pipe smoking was alluded to in the rape trial of Thomas Hawes. The maidservant Sarah Lepingwell claimed she had been smoking a pipe when Hawes began forcing his advances on her. These chance references to women smoking reveal that such activities were in no way odd and would never have been preserved in the historical record but for the fact that a criminal act happened during a moment when the woman was smoking.

Opiates

Opium is one of the strongest painkillers known and has been used in various forms for thousands of years. English physicians began researching the medicinal use of opium in the seventeenth century, after imports of the drug were made available from Turkey, Persia, and Egypt. Opium was recognized as a miracle cure for pain, but scientists warned doctors against its use for minor conditions. One doctor warned that those who abuse the drug will forever after be made "troublesome and unhappy by the hurt it hath doth to their principal faculties" (Davenport-Hines 2002, 37). It was used to treat a variety of medical conditions in colonial America when pain management was difficult. It was used to treat women during childbirth, because it was believed not only to ease pain but also to speed delivery.

Although most of the potions sold by herbalists in early America were little more than colored water, many of them contained doses of opium. Known under various names, such as paregoric, laudanum, morphine, and tincture of opium, these drugs could be purchased by anyone willing to pay the price. They were recommended to treat conditions such as coughs, diarrhea, insomnia, heart problems, and dysentery. Women who suffered from irregular periods were also given opium.

Most medical literature regarding the use of opium was written by British physicians, upon which American doctors relied heavily for advice. George Young's *Treatise on Opium* (1753) recommended heavy use of opium for a wide range of female complaints. He instructed its use for easing menstrual cramps, calming the nausea of pregnant women, emotional problems, and as a sleeping aid. Young was not oblivious of the potential for misuse. He warned against giving opium to women in their late stages of pregnancy and had harsh words for mothers who fed it to calm their restless babies.

It was dangerously easy to slip into an opium dependency. Medical literature repeatedly warned of the dark side of opium use but rarely had recom-

mendations for a limit upon its use. Some women simply kept increasing the dosage, as their bodies grew accustomed to the drug's effects. When a patient ceased taking the drug, she usually experienced symptoms such as nervous tremors, aches, or vomiting. The withdrawal symptoms were often misconstrued as a reappearance of her original symptoms, so a renewed round of treatment might be ordered. Opium appeared to offer a quick and dramatic solution to pain, and many women developed dependence on the drug. Concern about excessive use of opium did not emerge until the mid-nineteenth century, when both its addictive qualities and its likelihood for overdose became understood.

See also Tavern Keepers and Innkeepers

Further Reading
Davenport-Hines, Richard. *The Pursuit of Oblivion: A Global History of Narcotics.* New York: W. W. Norton, 2002.

Jaffe, Jerome, ed. *Encyclopedia of Drugs and Alcohol.* New York: Macmillan Library Reference, 1995.

Rorabaugh, W. J. *The Alcoholic Republic: An American Tradition.* New York: Oxford University Press, 1989.

Zentner, Joseph L. "Opiate Use in America During the Eighteenth and Nineteenth Centuries: The Origins of a Modern Scourge." *Studies in History and Society* 5 (1974): 40–54.

Adolescence
See Girlhood and Adolescence

Adultery

Adultery was considered a different and more serious offense than fornication. Although all forms of sexual activity outside of marriage were frowned upon, adultery occurred when one or both of the participants were married. Thus, the offense was not merely a personal failing, but an offense against a spouse, children, and the entire community. Early Americans placed extraordinary importance on the

Did Puritans Really Use Scarlet Letters?

Perhaps the most famous shaming punishment used by the Puritans was the scarlet letter, immortalized by Nathaniel Hawthorne. Several New England communities passed laws requiring adulterers to wear letters signifying their crime. The Plymouth Colony statute of 1671 was typical. Adulterers were sentenced: "To wear two capital letters, A.D. cut in cloth and sewn on the uppermost garment on the arm and back; and if at any time they shall be found without the letters so worn while in this government, they shall be forthwith taken and publicly whipped." Such punishments were not limited to adultery. Drunkenness, Blasphemy, Theft, and Pauperism were all signified by forcing the offender to wear the initial of their crime.

The infamous case of Mary Batchellor (1650) was possibly used by Hawthorne as inspiration for *The Scarlet Letter.* Mary Batchellor was married to Stephen Batchellor, a minister more than eighty years old. The marriage was unhappy, and the reverend had long been living in another colony when his wife became pregnant. Mary was sentenced to thirty-nine lashes and to be branded on the flesh with the letter *A*. Although Mary Batchellor's sentence was unusually brutal, other adulterous women were threatened with branding should they appear in public without their letter.

Mary Batchellor's tribulations did not cease in 1650. Her husband returned to England without her, leaving her to care for her infant with no means of support. She applied for a divorce, but her petition was rejected. In 1652 she was once again publicly whipped for adultery. The historical record paints Mrs. Batchellor as a fortune hunter, schemer, and adulterer. From the scanty references to her story in court documents, it is difficult to determine if she was a scandalous villain, or merely a woman who had been ostracized from society and fended for herself as best she could.

Source: Newberry, Frederick. "A Red-Hot A and a Lusting Divine: Sources for the Scarlet Letter." *The New England Quarterly* 60 (1987): 256–264.

health of their community, which depended on the bedrock of stable and harmonious families. Adultery was not merely a moral failing, it was a serious legal infraction. Those suspected of adultery were put on trial and subject to severe financial and corporal punishment.

Adulterous affairs came to light through a number of avenues. In close-knit villages it was difficult to keep clandestine meetings secret. Homes lacked privacy, and women who spent too much time in the company of a man not her husband aroused suspicion. A woman who became pregnant while her husband was at sea or on another long journey was easily revealed as an adulteress. Other women were simply careless and gossiped about their affairs.

The punishment for adultery was more severe than that for fornication, which usually resulted in ten lashes and a fine of forty to fifty shillings. The standard punishment for adultery was a fine of up to £20 and thirty-nine lashes. Forty or more lashes was thought to be a life-threatening punishment, and adulterers were routinely sentenced to the maximum allowable thirty-nine lashes. Elements of public shaming were often included in order to warn others against slipping into temptation. In 1674 Ruth Read was punished for her adulterous affair by being forced to stand in the public square wearing a sign that read, "Thus I stand for my adulterous and whorish carriage." She received thirty lashes in addition to the public shaming (Koehler 1980, 144).

Adultery became a capital offense in 1632. Although dozens of adultery cases were subsequently prosecuted in New England courts, only three cases have come to light where the offending couples were put to death. The journal of Governor John Winthrop tells of the case of Mary Latham and James Britton, who were executed for adultery in 1643. Mary Latham had been spurned by the young man she hoped to marry and hastily married an elderly man out of revenge. She proceeded to have numerous affairs, but only her liaison with Britton had the required number of witnesses to prove adultery.

The Latham case was unusual, because Puritans were reluctant to punish adulterers by death in all

Illustration depicting a scene from *The Scarlet Letter*, by Nathaniel Hawthorne. Shows Hester Prynne—the famous literary adultress—enduring censure from the town's people. Seventeenth-century adultery was considered a crime against the stability of the community, rather than merely a personal failing. (Bettmann/CORBIS)

but the most egregious cases. It is likely that Mary Latham's confession to having more than a dozen affairs hardened the attitude of her judges. Although a couple might escape the death penalty, it was common for them to be subjected to the terrors of the gallows. Women were often sentenced to stand upon the gallows with a rope about their necks for a period of several hours, usually wearing a sign detailing their crime.

By the eighteenth century, one category of adultery became frequent enough that it was generally ignored. With divorce almost impossible to attain, it was not uncommon for unhappy marriages to end in abandonment. After a period of time, the abandoned spouse might take up residence with another partner and live in a common-law marriage. So long as the couple lived quietly and had the ability to provide support for children of the union, most people ignored the existence of the prior obligation. Although such couples were often shunned by polite society, there was rarely any attempt to initiate formal prosecutions for adultery.

Adultery in the Eighteenth Century

Adultery remained a criminal act in the eighteenth century, but the barbaric punishments and ritualized humiliations became a thing of the past. Over time, adultery was punished through lawsuits, divorce, and loss of reputation.

The crude punishments of the seventeenth century were generally inflicted in roughly equal measure to the offenders, regardless of gender. Women were sometimes disproportionately prosecuted for adultery, simply because pregnancy made their indiscretions more likely to be revealed. When guilty men could be identified, they were generally subject to the same measure of punishment as women. By the eighteenth century, a double standard in the treatment of adulterous couples began to emerge. Women were expected to tolerate their husbands' indiscretions, whereas men used their wives' adultery as grounds for divorce.

Some women sued for divorce because of their husbands' adultery, but their petitions were less likely to be granted. An adulterous woman represented a greater liability to the home, because her actions could result in a bastard child who might divert wealth and property away from legitimate heirs. Furthermore, sexual conquest was not seen as unmanly, but licentious behavior from a woman was considered contrary to all standards of femininity. Adulterous women were not considered fit wives or mothers. Should a man choose to pursue a divorce against a woman proven guilty of adultery, she risked losing her home, means of support, and children.

A marked difference in eighteenth-century cases of adultery is how they came to public attention. Most cases in the seventeenth century were reported by neighbors or ministers. By the eighteenth century it was almost always reported by the offended spouse. Adultery was no longer considered a threat to community well-being, and neighbors generally looked the other way. The occasional exception occurred when the woman became pregnant and it was feared she and the child would become a burden on the community unless provisions were made.

See also Divorce; Fornication

Further Reading

D'Emilio, John, and Estelle B. Freedman. *Intimate Matters: A History of Sexuality in America.* Chicago: University of Chicago Press, 1988.

Koehler, Lyle. *The Search for Power: The Weaker Sex in Seventeenth Century New England.* Urbana: University of Illinois Press, 1980.

Smith, Marril D. *Breaking the Bonds: Marital Discord in Pennsylvania, 1730–1830.* New York: New York University Press, 1991.

Thompson, Roger. "Sexual Mores and Behavior." In *Encyclopedia of the North American Colonies,* ed. Jacob Ernest Cooke. New York: Charles Scribner's Sons, 1993.

African American Women and Religion

The religion practiced by black women in early America was an amalgamation of African spirituality and Christianity. Women often had leadership roles in African society as priestesses or leaders of particular rituals. They came from a culture that was accustomed to deferring to women for particular aspects of spiritual leadership, a custom that was replicated in America. Black women were more likely than black men to be open to Christianity. After a woman had been converted, she shared her religion with her children and often persuaded her husband to partake in ceremonies.

Africans came to America from dozens of different ethnic traditions, but there were some similarities in their spiritual beliefs. They usually believed in one superior god, who was surrounded by a tremendous number of intermediary gods, disembodied spirits, and the spirits of ancestors. The sun, moon, wind, and thunder all had powerful spirits behind them. Specific religious rituals and beliefs varied among ethnic groups, and when one African tribe conquered another in warfare, there was generally a merging of the religious beliefs of both groups. Africans therefore had a long tradition of transforming their religious beliefs in the face of changing circumstances. For that reason, they were open to accepting new gods into their belief structure once they arrived in America. Basic beliefs of first-generation Africans lingered among their descendants. Most slaves who had been born in Africa believed that after death they would be transported back to Africa, where they would be reunited with the spirits of their ancestors. Some Africans reported that they longed for death and even committed suicide believing it was their only means of returning to Africa.

Although many aspects of African ritual and tradition were transported to the New World, it was difficult to sustain them over time. Aspects of African culture that could be easily practiced by individuals, such as magic practices, birthing customs, and prayers to ancestors, survived. The character of black American religion varied, depending on geographic location. Voodoo flourished in Haiti and New Orleans, Santeria in Cuba and Puerto Rico. African traditions did not remain so pronounced in British North America. Slaves came from dozens of different ethnic groups and were often deliberately divided by their captors, who knew they would adapt to America faster without compatriots to sustain them. Without strong concentrations of ethnically homogenous slaves to uphold a particular religious tradition, over time their native religions began to be supplanted by aspects of Christianity.

The first recorded baptism of a slave woman in Virginia was of "Isabel," who was baptized with her son William in 1624. Isabel was among the first African women shipped to the British colonies, and she arrived at a time when slavery was neither permanent nor well defined. Most of the slaves from this generation were freed after seven to ten years of service. It was not clear in the minds of the colonists if it was legal or moral to enslave a Christian. Some churches actively discouraged the conversion of slaves owing to the difficult moral dilemma presented by exploiting a slave who was a Christian.

Women such as Isabel might have believed that by accepting Christianity they added a veneer of protection to their situation. It might have resulted in slightly more humane treatment from her master and mistress, but over time it became clear that baptism conferred no legal protection on slaves. Between 1664 and 1706, Maryland, Virginia, North and South Carolina, New Jersey, and New York all passed laws that specifically denied the ability of a Christian slave to obtain freedom through their religious conversion.

The Church of England was slow to promote missionary activity among American slaves. Although in 1661, 1680, and 1681 various efforts were organized to encourage the conversion of slaves, these activities had little effect. Slaveholders generally consented to such activities, for it was believed that the brand of Christianity offered by the Anglican Church would inculcate docility. The early attempts to convert the slaves often resulted in rifts within the slave community, as those who clung to African religions looked at the newly converted Christians as traitors and weaklings.

It was not until the Great Awakening of the 1740s that Christianity took firm root among slave communities. This was a different brand of Christianity than the formal, mild-mannered teachings offered by the Anglicans. The Great Awakening depended on fiery preachers, whose passionate exhortations converted black and white alike. The Great Awakening promoted a brand of egalitarianism the slaves found welcoming. Blacks were welcomed into the churches with little regard for race or sex. Neither blacks nor poor whites had been made to feel welcome in the prim, orderly Anglican Church, where those who had not financially sponsored the church were relegated to the back pews. Baptist and Methodist preachers, who had lit the flames of the Great Awakening, were generally color-blind. Blacks themselves were allowed to become preachers. Contemporary observers noted the curious hand clapping, foot stamping, rhythmic preaching, hyperventilating, and shouting that was characteristic of black preachers. Old and young slaves alike participated in singing hymns, dancing to the music, and shouting affirmations to the preacher.

Following the Great Awakening a number of black churches were established that cultivated Christianity in the slave and free black population. Baptists and Methodists were most active in establishing black churches. The Bluestone Baptist Church was founded in 1758 on the plantation of William Byrd III. In 1794 a former slave, Richard Allen, founded the first black Methodist church in the North, the Bethel Church in Philadelphia. These churches provided a safe haven for black men and women who might not have felt comfortable praying in a segregated section of a white church.

What attracted black women to Christianity? Some scholars have speculated they believed they and their children would receive more favorable treatment if they shared the same religion as their master. Others point to the egalitarian nature of early Baptist and Methodist churches. Many of these biracial churches had slaves as their founding members, with the same voting rights and church authority as other members. It would have been unusual for a black woman to have been given such a place of responsibility and respect anywhere else in her world of labor and enslavement.

Another lure for slaves who accepted Christianity was the hope of learning to read. Although at various times teaching slaves to *write* had been outlawed, reading was considered less threatening. Reading and writing were taught as separate skills in colonial America, and many women were able to read without ever acquiring the subsequent skill of writing. A Christian slave could request reading instruction in order to study scripture. Although it is possible a hostile master might have prohibited this, reading the Bible was rarely considered threatening, and many slaves learned the skill. Having access to a Bible, with its stories of historic suffering, slavery, and ultimate redemption, would have had enormous appeal to many women.

The writings of some Christian slaves make it plain that their conversion was genuine and not a mere ploy to curry favor or bolster their status. Phillis Wheatley wrote a number of well-received poems about her love of Christ, and her letters testify to her deeply held convictions. It might be that the sufferings of Christ resonated with the slaves, who were willing to grasp on to the hope that their miseries on earth would be rewarded in a "mansion in the sky."

See also Education; Islamic Women; Wheatley, Phillis

Further Reading

Bradley, Michael R. "The Role of the Black Church in the Colonial Slave Society." *Louisiana Studies* 14 (1975): 413–421.

Laing, Annette. "Heathens and Infidels? African Christianization and Anglicanism in the South Carolina Low Country, 1700–1750." *Religion and American Culture* 12 (2002): 197–228.

Monaghan, E. Jennifer. "Reading for the Enslaved, Writing for the Free: Reflections on Liberty and Literacy." *Proceedings of the American Antiquarian Society* 108 (1998): 309–341.

Raboteau, Albert J. "The Slave Church in the Era of the American Revolution." In *Slavery and Freedom in the Age of the American Revolution*, eds. Ira Berlin and Ronald Hoffman. Charlottesville: University Press of Virginia, 1983.

———. *Slave Religion: The Invisible Institution in the Antebellum South.* New York: Oxford University Press, 1978.

African American Women and the American Revolution

The Revolutionary War brought a complex mix of fear and hope to American slaves. The economic and political implications of independence were of little interest to slaves. Time and again, evidence indicates that the primary factor in determining a slave woman's quality of life was her ability to establish a stable family. Most slave women had siblings, children, even husbands, living on nearby farms. Less than one-third of adult slave women lived with their husbands, so it was common to have families dispersed throughout the region. Although their ability to freely associate with family members was always constrained, the war brought a new level of insecurity to a slave woman's world. Fleeing white families often took their slaves with them, paying little attention to bonds of kinship that might be severed by removing a slave from her home. Promises of freedom dangled by the army tempted male slaves to leave home and take up arms. Slaves were considered property, and invading armies were known to confiscate slaves and press them into service. Even female slaves were liable to be kidnapped to work as cooks or laundresses for the army.

At the outset of the war, a typical female slave would have noticed a change in her work patterns. Shortages of male labor required that women put aside domestic chores such as baking and cleaning and take to the fields. Planting and harvesting crops became a priority in a world where troops needed to be fed and food shortages were rampant. One small mercy was that food crops were less labor intensive than tobacco. Manufactured goods from Britain, such as cloth, stopped being imported during the war. Larger plantations increased their production of cloth, affording some slaves the opportunity to learn new skills.

Black women were subject to most of the same fears, shortages, and disruptions that plagued all women during war. The food supply was not always plentiful. As armies or refugees crowded into towns, disease took a brutal toll, with outbreaks of smallpox, yellow fever, and typhoid attacking victims regardless of race or class. Anxiety for loved ones serving in the military increased with each reported battle. Slave women were not immune from rape by invading soldiers.

The British made overtures to the black population early in the war. Promises of freedom were extended to any person willing to serve the army for a set number of years. A number of male slaves heard the call and escaped behind British lines. Wartime disruptions and a safe haven increased the likelihood of a successful escape. Although some women tried to escape, their numbers were far fewer than men. It has been estimated that one-tenth of the male slave population served the British army, either by choice or by being pressed into service. Women were less likely to willingly serve the army. Most women had small children, which would have made following an army as a servant difficult and dangerous for the child.

Not all slaves supported the British cause during the war. Many of the largest estates in the country were owned by loyalists, and their slaves correctly believed that loyalist estates would be confiscated if the patriots won. Unfortunately, following the war the ownership of the slaves was transferred to new owners, and they were rarely set free.

Slaves who made no attempt to escape to freedom still sensed a slight increase in power during the war. As traditional markets evaporated and property became subject to the ravages of war, slave owners depended on the labor of their slaves as never before. With the country distracted by the war, traditional means for capturing escaped slaves disintegrated. Knowing that recovering an escaped slave would be difficult, many owners treated their slaves with greater care.

Masters were often absent from the plantation during the war, leaving their wives in charge. Many of these women reported increased disrespect and idleness among their slaves. Eliza Pinkney wrote to her son that she tried to relocate her slaves to her daughter's plantation during the war, but they refused to leave. She realized she had no power to force them to go, because escape to the British was an easy option for them. She concluded that her slaves "all do now as they please everywhere" (Norton 1980, 212).

Some black women clearly cast their lot with the British and escaped to service within the army. They washed clothes, cooked meals, and lived in the field with the soldiers as camp followers. After the war many of these women had the option of leaving the country with the departing British troops. It was a difficult decision. Leaving the country meant leaving behind family and friends forever. Although they faced an uncertain future in the United States, most African American women opted to stay in the new nation rather than venture into the unknown across the Atlantic.

A minority of escaped slave women refused to return to their former lives. Between escape and enlistment by the British, it is estimated that 55,000 men and women escaped slavery during the Revolution. Three thousand African Americans fled New

York City at the close of the war, 900 of whom were women. Most of the New York refugees went to Canada, but others ventured to England, the West Indies, or the fledgling colony of Sierra Leone in Africa.

The former slaves who went to England were required to find work immediately. Some white loyalists were successful in obtaining financial compensation for their wartime losses, but the British considered liberation from slavery to be reward enough for the service of black Americans. The adjustment for many of these former slaves was difficult. They were in a strange and urban environment, with no family or connections and few welcoming faces. In 1786 a plan to transport the African Americans from England to Africa began to take shape. The plan to create a colony in Sierra Leone of freed slaves was a well-intentioned but poorly planned undertaking. The hundreds of former slaves who made the journey to Africa were not fluent in native languages, had no knowledge of African agriculture, and were poorly funded. Many settlers sickened and died, and the colony floundered on the brink of disaster. In 1790 the colony was saved by the arrival of another 1,100 former slaves who were dissatisfied with their life in Canada.

Newly freed slaves who left the country faced challenges and heartache. Most emigrated with only a few close family members, leaving their extended families behind. Those who immigrated to the West Indies and Canada were not immune from racism, and establishing an independent homestead was difficult. Many former slaves had skills that did not transfer to their radically new environments, and men had difficulty obtaining employment. Fortunately for most women, their domestic skills were applicable wherever they went.

For the slaves who remained in the colonies, their lot depended on their geographic location. The irony of fighting for freedom while living in a slave society had not escaped the attention of abolitionists in the northern states. Immediately following the war, a number of New England states began investigating means of abolishing slavery. Some states, such as Pennsylvania, declared that all newly born African Americans would be born free. Others passed gradual abolition laws, which granted slaves their freedom by the time they reached a certain age. By 1804 all of the northern states had passed laws outlining a process for the abolition of slavery. Southern states were less interested in abolition, but most at least repealed the laws against the private manumission of slaves, allowing those who wished to set their slaves free the legal right to do so.

Slaves were also affected by the increasingly mobile society created by the Revolution. Migration westward accelerated rapidly. White families heading west uprooted their slaves, or sold them. In either case, it is likely that many slave families were torn apart by the westward migration.

The most important effect of the American Revolution for the black women who remained enslaved after the war was a raising of consciousness. Decades of rhetoric defining the nature of freedom had circulated widely before and during the war. It penetrated the consciousness of blacks and whites alike. A large and growing class of free blacks began to organize communities that would advance the cause of freedom for all in the coming decades. Aspects of African American life became more distinct and developed. Black churches, schools, and charitable organizations sought to ameliorate the condition of their enslaved brethren, but it would take several more generations before liberty would be extended to southern slaves.

Further Reading

Jones, Jacqueline. "Race, Sex, and Self-Evident Truths: The Status of Slave Women during the Era of the American Revolution." In *Women in the Age of the American Revolution*, eds. Ronald Hoffman and Peter J. Albert. Charlottesville: University Press of Virginia, 1989.

Newman, Debra L. "Black Women in the Era of the American Revolution in Pennsylvania." *Journal of Negro History* 61 (1976): 276–289.

Norton, Mary Beth. "The Fate of Some Black Loyalists of the American Revolution." *Journal of Negro History* 58 (1973): 402–426.

———. *Liberty's Daughters: The Revolutionary Experience of American Women, 1750–1800.* Boston: Little, Brown, 1980.

escaped slave, Virginia mandated that urban free blacks register with the state annually, and rural free blacks every three years. In many colonies, the "slave codes" applied to slave and free blacks alike. Although these codes varied from colony to colony, common restrictions included the inability to travel at night, buy or sell liquor, or possess firearms.

The increasing population of free blacks caused deep suspicion, especially in the South. In an attempt to discourage manumission, in 1806 Virginia passed a law in which newly freed slaves were required to leave the state within one year of emancipation or be reenslaved. Freed slaves who were subsequently convicted of a crime could be reenslaved in Louisiana.

Most states had antimiscegenation laws, which prevented marriage between blacks and whites. Many free women of color were in genuine relationships with white men, but were unable to enjoy the benefits of marriage or the protection for their children owing to such laws.

Despite the difficulties and discrimination faced by free women of color, they were able to find security and dignity impossible to their counterparts in slavery. African Americans developed extensive social and economic networks in urban environments that provided community aid and would later form the backbone of abolitionist movements. Black churches, schools, and charitable organizations were established to nurture the community. Women had the freedom to leave unacceptable working environments, and did not live in fear that their children would be sold away from them. Their material comforts often differed little from women in slavery, but their spiritual differences were profound.

See also Freeman, Elizabeth; Key, Elizabeth

Further Reading

Ashcraft-Eason, Lillian. "Freedom among African Women Servants and Slaves in the Seventeenth Century British Colonies." In *Women and Freedom in Early America*, ed. Larry D. Eldridge. New York: New York University Press, 1997.

Gilbert, Judith A. "Esther and Her Sisters: Free Women of Color as Property Owners in Colonial St. Louis, 1765–1803." *Gateway Heritage* 17, no. 1 (1996): 14–23.

Horton, James Oliver, and Lois E. Horton. *In Hope of Liberty: Culture, Community, and Protest among Northern Free Blacks, 1700–1860.* New York: Oxford University Press, 1997.

Ingersoll, Thomas N. "Free Blacks in a Slave Society: New Orleans, 1718–1812. *William and Mary Quarterly* 48 (1991): 173–200.

McNight, Andrew Nunn. "Lydia Broadnax: Slave and Free Woman of Color." *Southern Studies* 5 (1994): 17–29.

Newman, Debra L. "Black Women in the Era of the American Revolution in Pennsylvania." *Journal of Negro History* 61 (1976): 276–289.

Nicholls, Michael L. "Strangers Setting among Us: The Sources and Challenge of the Urban Free Black Population in Early Virginia." *Virginia Magazine of History and Biography* 108 (2000): 154–179.

Soderland, Jean R. "Black Women in Colonial Pennsylvania." *Pennsylvania Magazine of History and Biography* 107 (1983): 49–68.

Aging Women

Most women in colonial America did not expect to live beyond age seventy, although it is likely they would have led active and productive lives until their final infirmity. Women usually bore children until menopause put an end to their childbearing, which occurred sometime in their mid- to late forties. In colonial America, the fifties tended to mark a person's entrance into old age. As women in early America passed from an active midlife into their elderly years, there were changes in responsibilities, expectations, and physical abilities. The most noticeable difference between elderly women in contemporary society and early America is the different societal attitude toward advancing age. Elderly women in colonial America had important roles within their family and community, and there was little shame associated with the aging process. Aging women lived active lives and were held in veneration by most of society.

A number of explanations have been advanced to explain the esteem afforded to elderly women. One theory depends on the scarcity of elders in colonial society. Large families meant that more than half of the population was under twenty years of age, but only 4 to 6 percent of the population was over sixty. The rarity of elders made them worthy of respect, and they were looked to as sources of wisdom and experience. Another explanation credits the Puritan doctrine of limited election, which taught salvation was limited to those God had selected. Trying to determine who was among the elect drove Puritans to be on the lookout for signs of God's favor. Clearly, survival into old age was an indication of favor, so elderly people were considered worthy of reverence and sources of moral guidance.

Men experienced some decline in their social status as they aged, because much of their prestige was dependent on their physical strength and productivity. Women had no such deterioration of status. Their contribution to society was not predicated on physical strength or earning power. As women aged they moved into new roles as they assisted their daughters with motherhood, supervised young grandchildren, and provided much-needed advice on the complicated task of running a household. Older women were often the most active members of their church, and as such became highly visible examples of moral piety. Younger people in town often referred to any elderly woman as "grandmother," a sign of affection and respect automatically granted to a woman who reached such a venerable age. Elizabeth Drinker's famous diary of the late eighteenth century reflected on the sense of contentment she experienced as she moved into old age: "I have often thought that women who live to get over the time of child-bearing, if other things are favorable to them, experience more comfort and satisfaction than at any other period of their lives" (Drinker 1994, 175).

Women's clothing was expected to change as they aged. Older women wore dark colors and usually covered their heads with large, close-fitting bonnets with strings tied beneath the chin. Although these bonnets appear frumpy and unattractive to contemporary observers, there seems to have been no reluctance for women to adopt the official trappings of age. Indeed, women who attempted to cling to the fashions of youth were looked on as silly and lacking pride. The portraits of elderly women almost always include caps or bonnets, indicating it was unseemly to be seen without such a head covering.

Although elderly women are often associated with poverty, this was rarely the case in early America. Most elderly were able to continue living in their home and enjoyed a standard of living as good or better than the average young adult. The accumulation of assets took decades to achieve. Personal wealth was lowest for individuals in their twenties and gradually rose until it peaked when people were in their fifties. There was a gradual decline in income and assets as people moved into their sixties and seventies. This was offset by the lower expenses associated with age. It is likely that their loans would have been paid in full, there were fewer mouths to feed, and their grown children would have moved into their own homes.

Although most elderly women would not have feared poverty, some poorer families inevitably entered old age with few assets and a declining ability to earn income. If a poor woman was not able to support herself, the town usually intervened on her behalf. If there were no relatives in a position to help her, she would be lodged with a family that would be reimbursed by the community for her board. Few women wanted to become a public charge, and some attempted to remain living in their home by supporting themselves through begging. Although beggars were not welcome in colonial society, elderly or infirm women were usually considered among the "worthy" poor and had little trouble begging enough to meet their needs.

Despite the esteem in which elderly women generally were regarded, they confronted a number of problems associated with aging. Perhaps the most difficult would have been widowhood, for it struck women at both an emotional and a financial level. Under these circumstances, a woman's ability to remain living in her home was often called into question. A husband was a woman's legal and financial link to the world. Laws of coverture meant that while a woman was married, her entire legal identity was encompassed by her husband. She may have had no experience with managing money, maintaining the estate, or knowledge of how to assume responsibility for such things. Many widows were ill-equipped to become independent, and their first years of widowhood were likely colored by trepidation and insecurity. Although younger women might remarry, this was rarely an option for elderly women. It is likely that the woman's entire life would have been intimately tied to her home and family. To remarry would have required abandoning her home and orientation around her original family.

Law required that a widow be provided with at least one-third of her deceased husband's estate. Sometimes she would inherit the entire home, although it was quite common for a father to will the home and farm to a son, with provisions that his widow be allowed to remain living there. Wills often specified exactly how she was to be protected, such as stating which rooms of the house she would have exclusive right to use, assurances that she should have use of the kitchen, and which beds, equipment, or portions of the cellar she would be entitled to use. Many wills specified which portion of the fields she would receive the proceeds from, or which farmyard animals should be considered her property.

Physical problems would have emerged as a woman aged. Almost all colonial women lived active, physically demanding lives. It is likely that the daily exercise afforded women greater physical vitality as they moved into their middle and old age. The diaries of eighteenth-century women reveal that they performed an astonishing amount of work. The diary of Martha Ballard reveals that well into her sixties she rode horses, forded streams, and walked several miles through town in the course of her work as a midwife. Other diaries recount elderly women performing fieldwork, weaving at a loom, or working in a dairy throughout their old age. Despite the health benefits conferred by exercise, ailments inevitably took their toll. As women grew frail with arthritis or other chronic complaints, they would have felt the effects of aging as they hauled water, wrung out laundry, or stooped to milk a cow.

The daily demands of operating a household may have eventually become too much work for a woman, especially if she had no husband who could help with the more physically demanding chores. If

Portrait of Mrs. Richard Yates by Gilbert Stuart. Elderly women in colonial America had important roles within their family and community, and there was little shame associated with the aging process. (Francis G. Mayer/CORBIS)

she was fortunate she had children living nearby who could occasionally lend assistance. In other circumstances, she might be forced to move in with younger family members. Time and again diary passages of elderly women spoke of the sorrow they experienced when moving in with children. Taking in elderly parents was common in colonial society, and many children gladly accepted the responsibility. Older women had many useful services they could provide the family, including child care, cooking, mending, and household advice. But many women who had lived independently for decades found the transition difficult. Homes lacked privacy, and they would most likely have slept on a pallet in a room with several other family members. Sometimes permanent living arrangements were not possible, and a woman might be forced to move among the households of several relatives. Such was the case with Elizabeth Putnam, who wrote, "I am grown weary of my life. . . . This wandering about does not suit old folks" (Premo 1990, 36).

As women's health declined, they would have inevitably considered the prospect of death. Most of society was highly religious and took comfort in belief in an afterlife and reuniting with lost loved ones. They considered their elderly years a blessing from God that allowed them greater time to nurture their spiritual development. With their child-rearing years completed, their old age was to be devoted to spiritual exploration and imparting their wisdom to their family and community. The structure of religion provided many elderly women with comfort and a sense of purpose, but not all women could take reassurance from religion. Some women's diaries reveal they were uncertain about their salvation, or even doubted the existence of an afterlife at all. They expressed doubt and anxiety about their aging and lack of religious fervor. Time and again they claimed not to have been able to renounce worldly desires, or doubted they had achieved pure grace.

Respect for the elderly in early America was regarded a part of natural law. Old women were especially venerated for their wisdom on child rearing and dignified moral example. Most elderly women continued to actively participate in both work and family life throughout their final years. A shift in the attitude of respect of age occurred in the decades following the American Revolution, when the moral authority of old age began to be eroded, ushering in an era when youth would be glorified and rewarded.

See also Poverty; Widowhood; Wills and Inheritance

Further Reading

Demos, John. *Past, Present, and Personal: The Family and the Life Course in American History.* New York: Oxford University Press, 1986.

Drinker, Elizabeth, and Elaine Crane Forman, ed. *The Diary of Elizabeth Drinker: The Life Cycle of an Eighteenth Century Woman.* Boston: Northeastern University Press, 1994.

Fischer, David Hackett. *Growing Old in America.* New York: Oxford University Press, 1978.

Premo, Terri L. *Winter Friends: Women Growing Old in the New Republic, 1785–1835.* Urbana: University of Illinois Press, 1990.

Scott, Paula A. "'Tis Not the Spring of Life with Me: Aged Women in their Diaries and Letters, 1790–1830." *Connecticut History* 36 (1995): 12–30.

Agricultural Labor

The people of early America were land-rich, but labor-poor. Few of the settlers could afford so much as a single indentured servant or slave, meaning that except in the wealthiest families, farms were operated solely on family labor. England had a surplus of labor, and it was unheard of for a woman to toil in the fields. The early settlers in America could not afford the luxury of sparing women from manual labor. Women worked alongside their husbands and fathers to clear land, set fences, plant crops, and tend fields.

The enormous task of clearing fields was made easier by adopting a technique learned from the Indians. Rather than attempting the dangerous and difficult process of removing an entire tree, settlers "girdled" the tree by cutting deep notches into the trunk. After a few months the tree would wither, gradually losing all its leaves and then its branches. Sunlight could filter through the trees, providing enough light to support a crop of corn. The fields of deadened trees looked strange to European eyes, but it was the only way of quickly clearing enough land to plant crops in large quantity. After a few years the trees might be cut down for use as firewood.

Food to support the family was grown in a kitchen garden, and this was inevitably the domain of the farmer's wife. The gardens were always enclosed within a fence to protect them from hogs and other farmyard animals. Hogs had quickly become the staple form of protein in colonial diets, and they were allowed to forage for their own food in the woods. Rather than trying to enclose a large pasture for the voracious hogs, farmers opted for the easier route of merely enclosing their cultivated fields.

Work on farms was scheduled to make maximum use of sunlight. Days began by 5 A.M. at the latest. Farm labor usually stopped around 6 P.M., at which time supper was served. Candles were an expensive luxury, and people usually went to bed when the sun set.

Much of the labor on the farm was dictated by the seasons. During planting and harvesting time, it is likely most women would have worked in the fields. Throughout the summer a woman would tend the kitchen garden, which provided most of the family's immediate food needs. Fruit and herbs were dried so they might be used throughout the year. The autumn season was for slaughtering animals. The actual slaughtering and butchering was usually done by men, but some women did participate in these activities. Curing the meat, necessary to preserve it through the long winter months, was the task of women. Meat would be submerged in a heavily salted solution, which would draw out moisture and inhibit bacterial growth. Smoking meat could also help prevent spoilage and improve the flavor of the meat. Because no part of an animal was wasted, entrails would be gathered for making sausage. Hides were scraped, dried, and stretched to make leather.

Autumn was also the season for making cider. Tainted water was common in colonial America, and settlers preferred cider, beer, or ale to water. Farmwives usually had the ability to brew small beer, a malted drink of low alcohol content that could be brewed at home but had to be consumed within a week of brewing. Most farmwives also knew how to make cider, but the brewing of strong beer required greater skill and was usually left to a village brewer. Depending on the local climate, farmwives might have spent part of the autumn tending to fruit orchards, beehives, or gathering wild berries.

The short days of winter were a period in which maintenance issues that had been neglected during the busier months were addressed. Women made and mended clothing, repaired broken household tools, dipped candles, and spun thread. This would have been the time women would teach their children elementary reading skills and study of the Bible.

Spring-cleaning was a major event for colonial households. The house had sustained heavy use throughout the winter, making cleaning and repair necessary. Fires had been kept burning for months, and a layer of soot and ashes would have soiled most surfaces in the home. Most of the furnishings were moved outside to allow for thorough scrubbing of the floors and walls. Walls were often whitewashed with a solution of water, lime, and soap. Heavy fabrics, which could not be laundered during the winter because they would freeze before drying, were cleaned and set outside to dry in the sun.

Farmers who owned cows timed calving to occur in the spring. The dairy was usually the responsibility of the women, who cared for the calves, hand-feeding them as soon as possible, so as to be able to use the cows' milk to make butter and cheese. Other responsibilities were year-round tasks, which primarily centered around preparing food for the family, milking cows, making cheese and butter, and keeping the house clean. Aside from their work in the kitchen garden and tending to farm animals, a white woman's work in the fields was usually limited to planting and harvesting times. Such was not the case for female slaves or indentured servants, who were expected to toil alongside men throughout the season.

The major food crop in the Americas was corn, a crop that required little tending after planting and harvesting. It produced a higher food value per acre than any other grain the settlers were familiar with, and it could be easily grown in fields of girdled trees. Other traditional European crops, such as wheat, rye, and oats, did not fare as well. Rather than depend on these grains for food, early Americans only grew enough to support the brewing of beer.

Most farms of the middle and southern colonies planted tobacco, the gold standard of cash crops. Tobacco was a massively labor-intensive crop. After planting, the seedlings needed careful tending throughout the season, including transferring seedlings, maintaining mounds of soil around each plant, brushing off insects, pruning, weeding, and curing the leaves. The intensity of the work required to cultivate tobacco meant that wives and

Tending the Dairy

Most aspects of dairy work were under the purview of women in colonial America. They timed calving so that the calf would be weaned by late spring. This allowed the cow to have access to a good supply of grass throughout the summer, which prolonged lactation. Women milked a cow two to three times a day, developing strong arms during the twenty-minute process. They were responsible for the care of the cow, cleaning the animal's shelter, and feeding calves by hand until they were old enough to graze. Herbal remedies were used to cure digestive ailments and infections. Women were known to give their cows affectionate names, treating them more favorably than they did other livestock on the farm, which were seldom named.

Milk was rarely consumed by early Americans, but cheese, butter, and cream were valuable commodities. Women sold what their families could not consume, usually earning a healthy profit. Cheese was sometimes called "white meat," so important was it to the diet of early Americans. Transforming several gallons of milk into a small round of cheese was an art that required skill and patience. The pressing and curing of cheese could take weeks or months, depending upon the variety being made.

Source: Snow, Pamela J. "Increase and Vantage: Women, Cows, and the Agricultural Economy of Colonial New England." *Dublin Seminar for New England Folklife* 26 (2001): 22–39.

daughters might be recruited at various times throughout the year to tend the crop.

Life in a rural agricultural community would have been lonely for many women. Early communities built small farming plots in tightly defended clusters, but as the decades passed and adult children needed to create their own farms, holdings became ever more distant from the town center. On a typical day a woman living on an outlying farm would have no contact with people outside her immediate family. Church attendance was a welcome opportunity to touch bases with other adult women and have a respite from the physical toil of farmwork. Throughout the colonial period, the overwhelming majority of women lived on farms, and their daily life would be centered around the rhythms of the planting season.

See also Gardening; Household Responsibilities

Further Reading

Carr, Lois Green, and Lorena S. Walsh. "The Planter's Wife: The Experience of White Women in Seventeenth-Century Maryland." *William and Mary Quarterly*, 3d ser. 34 (1977): 542–571.

Cooke, Jacob Ernest, ed. *Encyclopedia of the North American Colonies.* New York: Charles Scribner's Sons, 1993.

Hawke, David Freeman. *Everyday Life in Early America.* New York: Harper and Row, 1988.

Jensen, Joan M. *Loosening the Bonds: Mid-Atlantic Farm Women, 1750–1850.* New Haven, CT: Yale University Press, 1986.

Spruill, Julia Cherry. *Women's Life and Work in the Southern Colonies.* Chapel Hill: University of North Carolina Press, 1938.

Alcohol

See Addictive Substances

American Revolution

The effect of the American Revolution on women has garnered substantial scholarly interest. The upheavals created by war and absent husbands plunged women into unfamiliar responsibilities, both on the home front and sometimes on the battlefield. There were no immediate changes in women's legal privileges following the war, although some scholars claim there were changes in women's self-perceptions that later evolved into constitutional rights. The issues addressing women and the American Revolution have been discussed under the following categories:

African American Women and the American Revolution

American Revolution and Its Effect on Women's Status

American Revolution on the Home Front

Boycotts

Camp Followers and Women of the Army

American Revolution and Its Effect on Women's Status

Because the American Revolution represented a profound shift in the political and economic organization of an entire nation, it is inevitable that historians would consider its effect on women. Did the celebrated ideology of liberation awaken a longing in women for similar emancipation? Or did the message fail to penetrate centuries of deeply engrained paternalism? The Anglo-American legal system assumed that women who shared their husband's social and economic position would automatically vote in lockstep with their husbands, rendering the need for women's suffrage irrelevant. The founding fathers made no provisions for women to maintain separate legal, economic, or social identities from their husbands. Women did not appear to protest. Was the American Revolution therefore irrelevant to women's rights? Despite the profusion of research on this topic, historians remain conflicted as to whether the Revolution had a positive or negative impact on women's status in society.

Complicating the question is the Industrial Revolution, ushered in on the heels of the American Revolution. The effect of greater industrialization doubtless had a far more profound impact on the daily lives of women than the political shift caused by the war. A typical day for a woman in seventeenth-century America would have been monopolized with an unrelenting round of food preservation, cloth production, sewing, washing, and cooking, just to meet the bare minimum needs of her family. With increased industrialization in the late eighteenth century, it was cheaper to purchase manufactured goods, freeing up an immense amount of time for other occupations. That women were alleviated from daily drudgery is without question. Where historians differ is on the meaning of how women used those newly liberated hours.

Many women placed renewed emphasis on home and hearth. Historians such as Mary Beth Norton cite the rise of "republican motherhood," which elevated motherhood to an issue of national virtue. If the young republic was to survive, their sons needed to be wise, well-educated, and morally upright citizens. The mother was the primary keeper of the flame for these ideals. Thus, through the glorification of the traditional feminine role, women were elevated in status, yet remained safely confined to the domestic sphere. Women were charged with increasing responsibilities to educate their children, establish a well-tended home environment, and provide her family with the civilizing influences of music, religion, and moral instruction. Gone was the Puritan's suspicion of women as "the weaker vessel," who needed protection from the temptations of the world. In its place was a newfound respect for feminine morality and the self-sacrificing nature of motherhood.

Historian Joan Hoff Wilson is skeptical about whether the American Revolution brought any concrete advantages to women's status. Although white, middle-class men benefited from the new political arrangement, Wilson could cite no new opportunities for women, minorities, or the poor. She acknowledges that in the frontier years of colonization, women's scarcity and economic value in the household made them prized. They were liberated from the traditional spheres of home and hearth and had the freedom to venture into nontraditional roles. During the Revolutionary War women were needed to keep the home fires burning and the crops in the fields alive. Once the war was over, prosperity was restored, and industrialization was under way, Wilson believes women's status declined, as traditional patriarchal values once again assumed ascendancy. Women's earlier "freedoms" during settlement and war were not a result of enlightened thinking, they were merely a practical necessity. As industrialization got under way, the need for women's household manufacture declined.

It is clear that women took pride in their activities during the war. Many participated in boycotts, fundraising, or performing small services for the troops. Others undertook the management of the family farm or business for years during their husband's absence. Yet after the war, these women seemed relieved to resume their prewar activities. It was as though they were seeking a sense of normalcy after the disruptive and stressful years of war. Compounding the issue was a flood of new literature from Europe that promoted the rise of sentimental romanticism. New standards of femininity were being set that glamourized romantic love, female delicacy, and elevated motherhood to an iconlike status. Despite Abigail Adams's celebrated letter to her husband, appealing that the new government "remember the ladies," there appears to have been little interest in challenging the assumption that only men were qualified to vote. Few women expressed a desire to maintain employment outside the home or to have the vote extended to women.

The decades following the American Revolution constituted a dynamic period that had different effects on women, depending on their race, class, and geographic region. The complexity of the issues rules out a simple answer to what effect the Revolution had on women's status as a whole.

See also African American Women and the American Revolution; Feminism; Suffrage

Further Reading

Grant, Linda De Pauw. "The American Revolution and the Rights of Women: The Feminist Theory of Abigail Adams." In *Legacies of the American Revolution.* Logan: Utah State University Press, 1978.

Huston, James H. "Women in the Era of the American Revolution: The Historian as Suffragist." *Quarterly Journal of the Library of Congress* 32 (1975): 290–303.

Norton, Mary Beth. *Liberty's Daughters: The Revolutionary Experience of American Women, 1750–1800.* Boston: Little, Brown, 1980.

Wilson, Joan Hoff. "The Illusion of Change: Women and the American Revolution." In *The American Revolution: Explorations in the History of Radicalism,* ed. Alfred F. Young. DeKalb: Northern Illinois University Press, 1976.

American Revolution on the Home Front

No one in the colonies could be insulated from the ravages of war. The most immediate effects of war confronted women whose husbands or sons enlisted in the army, leaving the women to run the family business on their own. Even women who had no family serving in the war felt its effects, as the economy, food supply, means of communication, and their sense of safety and security all wavered under the pressure of the war. Constant rumors of troop movements kept villagers on edge, never knowing when they might be forced to flee before a descending army. With troop movements came the spread of epidemic diseases. The war affected rich and poor, North and South, black and white. All women who lived through the American Revolution felt its force.

Wartime experiences were affected by regional differences. Women living in the middle colonies often endured the most traumatic effects of the war. Several cities in the middle colonies were occupied by English or Hessian troops for years. Women living in occupied territory were more likely to have their property confiscated, become subject to rape, and lose communication with family members serving in the military.

Many of the most destructive battles were fought in the southern colonies, damaging property, burning crops, and placing civilians in the path of danger. Fighting and occupation in the northern colonies, with the exception of the New York City area, was rare and sporadic after 1778. The families of New England suffered the least in terms of physical destruction of property and refugee problems.

Wartime Economy and Shortages

The economy of the American colonies had been entwined with England for more than a century. Colonists depended on England for manufactured goods, luxury items, and currency. With the outbreak of hostilities, this relationship came to an abrupt halt. Prices for formerly imported goods such as cloth, sugar, rum, and paper skyrocketed. A combination of war profiteering, hoarding, and scarcity led to runaway inflation. A woman buying a side of beef for her family paid 4 cents in 1777, but the price rose to $1.69 three years later. The price of rents, fuel, and grain underwent similar inflation. Congress attempted to control the situation by issuing currency, which rapidly lost its value. Problems

American colonists watch the Battle of Bunker Hill from the roofs of houses on Copp's Hill in Boston (painting by Winslow Homer). (Bettmann/CORBIS)

with the currency supply and inflation forced most people to turn to barter for their daily needs.

Merchants were often the targets of mob action by frustrated and hungry crowds. With some justification, it was widely believed merchants were hoarding goods or profiteering by price gouging. The names of profiteering merchants were printed and blacklisted. When this did not ease shortages, food riots and mob rule occasionally took over. Women took part in most of these riots and were the majority of the participants in roughly one-third of the documented food riots. In some cases they stormed merchants' shops, removing everything of value and leaving "a fair price" on the counter. In others, no payment was given.

The anger expressed toward the merchant class was especially difficult for female merchants. Usually operating smaller shops than men, female mer-

chants did not have the economic wherewithal to agree to the nonimportation resolutions passed in the years leading up to the war. They often found themselves on lists of shops to be boycotted. After the war began, these unpopular merchants were especially vulnerable to mob actions.

Shortages of luxury goods such as tea, coffee, and sugar were annoying, but easily endured. Women learned how to boil corn stalks to make a sugar substitute and brew tea from sage and checkerberries. The shortage of imported cloth was resolved by increasing home production. More difficult to cope with were shortages of immediate and necessary goods. The lack of salt escalated to a crisis point early in the war. Large supplies of salt were essential for the preservation of meat, and efforts to make salt through evaporation of seawater fell pitifully short of the required amount. Women finally resorted to an unsavory, but effective, substitute. Walnut ashes produced a lye extract that could be used to preserve meat, if not flavor it.

Women who had husbands or sons serving in the army faced especially difficult economic times. Not only did production at their family farm or business decline, but also they rarely received any economic support from the army. A soldier's pay was not intended to support a family. The Continental Army was notorious for failing to pay wages promptly, so even soldiers who could afford to send money home seldom had the opportunity to do so. For the most part, a soldier's wife was responsible for supporting herself and her children for the duration of her husband's service.

Volunteerism

Women were eager to lend support to the war effort and turned at first to traditionally feminine tasks. Knitting socks and making clothing were common contributions, usually performed spontaneously as women searched for something they could do to help. Denied a formal political vote, they voted with their purses by boycotting imported goods and denouncing those who patronized black-listed merchants.

Organized activities developed quickly. America had traditionally depended on England for manufactured cloth, but the war brought this trade to an abrupt halt. Women held "spinning matches" in patriotic efforts to fill the shortfall. Spinning matches began in response to the Townshend Acts of 1767, which taxed British manufactured goods, including cloth. In response, women vowed to boycott imported cloth and increase production of homespun fabric. They brought their spinning wheels to churches or taverns and held contests to see who could spin the most before sunset. The output was donated to the local minister, who sold or transferred the goods to the war cause. The Reverend Ezra Stiles hosted a spinning match in Newport, Rhode Island, every spring from 1769 through 1774, with more than ninety women participating in 1770. Dozens of other spinning matches were organized throughout the colonies.

A group of women in Philadelphia stitched more than 2,200 shirts to be donated to the army. The name of the lady who had made the garment was embroidered on the back of the shirts. Other women collected old clothes and mended them before shipping them off to the army.

Women also assisted in soliciting money and donations for the cause. They collected scrap metal, old pots, and the lead from windowpanes to be melted down for bullets. Lack of bandages prompted women to canvass their neighborhoods for old bed linen and cast-off garments that could be used at the hospitals.

Esther Reed of Philadelphia led the most highly organized charitable effort of the war. She divided the city into ten areas and assigned a volunteer to organize fund-raising activities in each area. They ultimately raised $300,000 to be used by General Washington. Women of other colonies organized similar fund-raising efforts, helping fill the coffers and raise the morale of the men in the army.

Many women provided medical care for wounded soldiers. Army hospitals were notoriously crowded and unsanitary. Wounded soldiers were often brought to homes located close to battlefields. Such soldiers usually needed recovery time, rather than the assistance of a doctor. Women nursed men back to health, sometimes in exchange for a stipend from the army, but many did so on a volunteer basis. Quaker women were especially noted for their nursing. Most Quakers were pacifists, an unpopular position during a war where neighbors looked with suspicion on people who were reluctant to take sides. Many Quaker women earned goodwill by providing medical care to wounded men without regard to the soldiers' political allegiance. Nursing was a dangerous service, because it had inherent risks of contracting communicable diseases. The Quaker women who selflessly nursed soldiers could no longer be branded as "cowards" for their refusal to support the war.

Keeping the Home Fires Burning

Women were usually partners in their family's business. Most families in the late eighteenth century supported themselves through agriculture. Farmers' wives understood the rudimentary aspects of planting, harvesting, and marketing goods. Knowing what needed to be done did not always mean a woman had the time and physical ability to carry out the tasks. A fortunate woman could hire assistance for the heavy labor she could not accomplish. Sometimes men serving in the local militia units could return during the heaviest work periods. Even the women with minimal assistance were usually able to keep the farms operating. Perhaps a few fields were left unplanted for a season, but most farmers' wives were able to keep their farms in operation.

Wives of urban professionals were in a different situation. The wives of merchants, printers, shop owners, and tavern keepers generally worked side by side in their husband's business. They were often able to shoulder the extra responsibilities without too much difficulty. The wives of lawyers, ministers, doctors, or other highly educated professionals enjoyed no such advantage. These women saw their family income grind to a halt when the breadwinner went to war. The case of Mary Fish Silliman is a classic example. Married to a wealthy attorney, Mary lived a privileged, upper-class existence. Her husband was absent for most of the eight years of the war, meaning all income from his law practice ceased. Because he spent several years as a prisoner of the British, he did not even draw an officer's salary during this time. Mary watched helplessly as her family's economic reserves dwindled away.

The nature of army life during the American Revolution allowed men to return home with some regularity. A large percentage of the soldiers who served were in militia units, which banded together for a few months at a time and rarely traveled far from home. The regular army allowed its enlisted soldiers to select one-year terms of service. Reenlistment was common, but if a soldier's family was in economic distress, he had the option of returning home until the situation improved. Because soldiers were often stationed nearby their homes, visits were not uncommon. A farmer might be able to help get crops in the ground before heading back to duty.

Women who took on their husband's business needed to do this in addition to their regular duties. Children still needed to be bathed and fed, meals needed to be cooked, and elderly parents had to be cared for. Productivity of the family business usually declined, but the wartime economy provided a ready market for whatever goods a woman was able to produce.

Letters between soldiers and their wives reveal an interesting pattern in the administration of the family business. Soldiers initially instructed their wives on what crops to plant, which merchants to conduct business with, what was to be done concerning the regular maintenance of the homestead, and other mundane tasks. Over time, a husband's knowledge of his business grew outdated and remote. Women began making decisions on their own, informing their husbands what actions had been taken. Over the years, women became better informed of the current state of affairs than their husbands, and needed little or no guidance. In their letters, women stopped referring to "your farm," but called it "our farm." Men no longer instructed their wives about specific actions to take, but told them to use their best judgment.

Some women suffered more profoundly from the loneliness and anxiety of separation than from the economic issues. Women who had loving marriages often came to depend on the camaraderie and moral support provided by a husband's presence. Diaries reflect the anxiety felt by women who were forced to make important decisions in their husband's absence. Mary Foster wrote to her husband "every trouble, however trifling, I feel with double weight in your absence." Some men served the entire eight years of the war with only sporadic visits home. Their wives essentially raised their children single-handedly. A child who was a toddler at the outset of the war was an adolescent by the end.

Communication with soldiers was erratic and inevitably traveled slower than news of recent battles. A woman who knew her husband's regiment had recently seen combat might have to wait months to learn his fate. Mary Slocum of North Carolina was not so patient. Learning of a recent battle, she had a premonition that her husband had been injured. She rode thirty miles to the scene of the conflict, inspecting the carts of the dead and wounded as she passed them on the road. As she tended to a group of wounded soldiers who had been moved under the shelter of a cluster of trees, her husband came upon her, bruised but unharmed. Most women did not have the ability to learn news so quickly and had to wait until news filtered down to them.

Safety and Security

As women found themselves in the path of the war, securing their immediate safety became paramount. Battles were usually fought in open fields, but invading armies occupied towns, ships fired cannons on harbor cities, and homes everywhere were likely targets for the looting that inevitably accompanied war.

Villages usually heard rumors of advancing armies well before the arrival of troops. The most important decision a woman had to make was whether to stay put or flee the town. Sometimes her decision depended on which sort of army was approaching. Hessian troops had a notorious reputation for looting, raping, and wanton destruction. Indians were just as feared, but were only a threat in the western frontier regions. English troops were generally better behaved, but their enlisted soldiers sometimes harassed women when officers were absent. Although American troops were also known to indulge in looting and rape, such behavior was an anomaly. Troops rarely released their hostility on their own population, which may account for the higher rates of lawlessness among the Hessian and English troops.

For those who remained at home, hearing the boom of distant cannons and gunfire created an ominous atmosphere. Terrifying as the sounds might be, most women learned they had little to fear from actual battlefield combat. Some women even became accustomed to battles. Sixteen-year-old Sally Wister wrote in her diary, "Tis amazing how we get reconciled to such things. Six months ago the bare idea of being within ten, aye, twenty miles, of battle would almost have distracted me. And now, though two such large armies are within

six miles of us, we can be cheerful and converse calmly of it."

The period immediately following a battle was when trouble was likely to begin for civilians. Wounded soldiers from either side were moved into private homes as soon as the inadequate regimental hospitals were full. Hungry soldiers might pillage and loot the town. A New York resident wrote of the destruction Hessian troops brought to her property. She reported they dismantled her fences for firewood, killed her cattle, and helped themselves to the contents of her kitchen. Although most British officers tried to prevent wanton looting, atrocities did occur, especially in the southern colonies. Plantation homes were burned, crops destroyed, and cattle stolen. Soldiers sometimes approached houses with empty carts and removed any furnishings, tools, animals, food, or clothing of value. Even slaves were liable to be taken. Women were forced to relinquish their wedding rings and shoe buckles to looting troops.

The pillaging by a victorious enemy army was threatening, but officers usually tried to keep the worst atrocities at bay. More menacing than the regular armies were groups of guerrilla units of dubious allegiance who roamed the countryside throughout the war. These units were sometimes no better than marauding bandits, intent on stealing whatever they could acquire under the guise of legitimate military operations. They stole cattle and horses to sell to whichever army would buy them. They kidnapped soldiers home on leave and ransomed them to whoever would pay the fee. When roving bands of criminals were known to be in the area, women without protection sometimes banded together at a single homestead, seeking safety in numbers. Following a terrifying experience with British raiders who descended upon her home in the middle of the night, Mrs. Eliza Wilkinson reported that she could not rest easy for months. She slept in her clothes, startled at the least sound, and lived in a state of constant anxiety and weariness.

Women sometimes became the target of sexual harassment and rape during the lawlessness that accompanied war. The risks were highest in areas occupied by Hessian or British troops. Troops sta-

Rape and the American Revolution

An anonymously written narrative of the Battle of Trenton contains reflections of the looting, arson, and harassment of women during the occupation of Princeton, New Jersey, by Hessian and British soldiers. Accounts of a number of rapes and attempted rapes were widely reported in the local newspapers, but many of the victims refused to be named. Only a handful of these women chose to report the offenses in an attempt to receive justice. Rarely were rapists tried or punished during the American Revolution. The following section of the account reflects on the shame that prevented women from coming forward:

> The damages done by these plunderings and desolations must amount very high and occasion much trouble to the sufferers. Yet they are vastly short of another horrid outrage that I have not yet mentioned, I mean the ravishing of women, which by a great defect in human nature that is against both justice and reason we despise these poor innocent sufferers in this brutal crime even as long as they live. In time of peace to avoid so miserable and lasting reproach I am of the opinion that many honest virtuous women have suffered in this manner and kept it secret for fear of making their lives miserable and so many of those capital crimes escape punishment. In time of war when those unnatural miscreants are sure of getting off with impunity they commit them the more frequently.

Source: Anonymous. *A Brief Narrative of the Ravages of the British and Hessians at Princeton, 1776–1777.* New York: Arno Press, 1968.

tioned for prolonged periods of time in the midst of a hostile population often asserted themselves by harassing women, grabbing at their clothing as they passed on the street, shouting offensive comments, and other threatening actions, including rape. Especially well documented were a series of rapes in New Jersey during the winter of 1776. Historian Mary Beth Norton speculates that the British were frustrated by a series of narrow American victories that made the possibility of a short war impossible, and the soldiers released their anger on the local population. Sixteen girls from Hopewell, New Jersey, were taken captive to a camp where they were raped over a period of several days by British troops. Thirteen-year-old Abigail Palmer was repeatedly gang raped in her own home by troops who harassed the family farm daily. Relatives who tried to protect her were either beaten or raped as well. The violence did not stop until the soldiers brought Abigail and her fifteen-year-old cousin to camp, where they were raped again until an officer took them to safety.

As was often the case with rape victims, many women chose not to report the crime. When the rape occurred by members of a passing army, a woman might not have known where to report the crime. Once the perpetrator was out of the vicinity, a woman might have chosen to preserve her reputation rather than launch an unlikely quest for justice. As mentioned previously, soldiers in the American army committed far fewer rapes, as soldiers rarely rape and harass their own people. When rape did occur by American soldiers, punishment was swift and severe, as when Washington ordered the execution of Thomas Brown for a second offence. General Washington knew the support on the home front would dissolve if his own troops were hostile to the population, prompting his 1777 order, which "strictly forbids all the officers and soldiers of the Continental army . . . plundering any person, whether Tory or others . . . it is expected that humanity and tenderness to women and children will distinguish brave Americans, contending for liberty, from infamous mercenary ravages, whether British or Hessians."

Of equal concern to the military and civilians was the fear of disease, which killed at least as many people as did battlefield fighting. Dysentery, smallpox, tuberculosis, and typhoid all played havoc on the population. Women often had lowered resistance to disease as a result of a poor diet, physical and emotional exhaustion, and exposure to troops. The cramped, unsanitary conditions of camp life were notorious for breeding disease among the soldiers. As they moved throughout the countryside, both British and American soldiers were often quartered with the civilian population. Thus, a woman might have been forced to accept a handful of soldiers into her home, who might soon show evidence of communicable disease.

Refugees

Rather than await the dangers of an invading army at home, some women opted to flee to safer environments. Refugees were usually only able to take a few baskets of provisions with them. Some left on horses or carts, but many were forced to walk. Most had a destination in mind, usually family or friends living in nearby towns. These arrangements were usually temporary. Rural women reported housing twenty or more refugees in their homes, a situation that could not last for months or years. Women living in the western frontier were sometimes repeatedly assaulted by Indian raids and chose to move to the nearest military fort. Anna Oosterhout Myers and her children lived at Fort Willett for two years until the Indians in this western New York region were no longer a threat.

Some women chose to follow their husbands into the army, especially women with loyalist sympathies. The military did not welcome refugees, but knew that in the interest of morale, they could not be peremptorily turned away. A soldier who knew his wife was not safe at home was likely to desert. In the interest of keeping men in the field, the army provided temporary safe havens for refugees. Officers tried to settle them in nearby towns when possible. Such was not often the case with loyalist refugees, who rarely found themselves welcome with any but close family. Thus, the British army always had a higher proportion of refugees among its ranks than the American army.

Life as a refugee was usually a temporary condition. Women fled oncoming armies, but rarely expected to abandon their home for the duration of the war. Most women chose to return home following a battle.

Aftermath and Recovery

Recovery after the war depended greatly on individual circumstances. Those whose husbands had been killed or wounded obviously had greater difficulty, as did those whose property had been pillaged or destroyed. Some regions had been devastated by fire, artillery bombardment, and looting. Even towns that remained physically unscathed knew the damage of war. They lived through a deranged economy,

A Refugee's Story

Ann Eliza Bleecker (1752–1783) lived a charmed life until the disaster of the American Revolution caused her to suffer a nervous collapse. She was married to John Bleecker, a kind, wealthy lawyer whom she adored. They established a prosperous farm in the rural community of Tomhanick, New York, where Ann raised her two daughters in a setting she described as happy and idyllic.

The war brought an end to Ann's peaceful life. In 1777 news of a British invasion prompted John Bleecker to go to Albany to secure a residence for his family should they need to evacuate. Shortly after he left, British troops began marching toward Tomhanick, and like other families in the area, Ann decided she and her family should leave immediately. With no means of transportation, she walked the eighteen miles to Albany with a baby in her arms and her six-year-old daughter at her side. The road was crowded with other refugees, all of whom were concerned with caring for their own families and not able to lend assistance to Ann. After two days of walking, Ann was reunited with her husband outside of Albany, which was no longer a safe haven. The family traveled down the Hudson River to seek shelter with Ann's mother. On the trip, Ann's infant daughter, Abella, contracted dysentery and died. The child was hastily buried beside the river. Although they safely reached her mother's home, in the coming months Ann endured the additional deaths of her mother and sister.

Two months later Ann returned to her home in Tomhanick, but suffered from severe depression and anxiety over the continued safety of her family. Her worst fears were realized in 1781, when her husband was captured. Although he escaped less than a week later, Ann was traumatized. She suffered a miscarriage and sank into a depression from which she never fully recovered before her death two years later.

Source: Giffen, Allison. "Ann Eliza Bleecker." In *American Women Prose Writers to 1820*, ed. Carla Mulford. Detroit, MI: Gale, 1999.

disrupted trade, and the loss of brothers and sons who would never return from the front lines.

Many personal fortunes were obliterated by the war. Mary Silliman's husband had been a successful attorney with a thriving practice prior to the war. When he became an officer for the patriots, he abandoned his business in lieu of a paltry officer's salary. After the war he was unable to produce detailed receipts for large requisitions he had made and was forced to reimburse the government for these immense purchases, leaving him in debt the remainder of his life. Elizabeth Drinker's merchant husband refused to accept the dubious continental bills of credit during the war and was blacklisted by the patriots. Such was the case for many women who were lucky enough to escape the physical devastation of war, but nevertheless endured economic upheaval.

In general, the southern states took longer to recover than the northern and middle states. After the first few years of the war, there had been little fighting in the North. The middle colonies had been occupied during much of the war, which was traumatic, but not destructive. The South had seen a number of battles, including substantial guerrilla warfare, which had resulted in destroyed barns, fences, and homes. Structures left standing suffered from disrepair and neglect. A large percentage of southern slaves had escaped, leaving the ranks of the traditional workforce decimated. Finally, southern crops, such as rice and tobacco, and naval supplies could no longer receive favorable trade status in England. New trading arrangements would take time to establish.

A number of returning soldiers came home maimed. There was no pension set up for the disabled or killed until 1818. Only the widows of officers received a slight payment, leaving the widows of working men with nothing.

We know from petitions to the British government by loyalist women that some of them suffered for years from nightmares and anxiety. Aside from these references, we know little of the lingering psychological effects of the war on women. The few eighteenth-century women who kept diaries rarely recorded personal emotions. Post-traumatic stress disorder was not recognized until the 1970s, but the condition has existed throughout the history of warfare, and there can be no doubt that women who experienced the havoc of the American Revolution felt the lingering effects of the war for decades.

Despite the difficulties of recovering from the horrors of war, the new nation had a sense of optimism and hope. Dr. Benjamin Rush noticed the sense of confidence experienced by the victors following the war. Even those who had lost property or suffered the death of family members enjoyed a sense of well-being. This curious phenomenon prompted him to write his *Account of the Influence of the Military and Political Events of the American Revolution upon the Human Body* (1812). Both supporters of the war and the loyalists suffered similar trauma during the war, yet loyalists seemed to have suffered more profound psychological and physical breakdowns in the subsequent years. Dr. Rush was one of the first to make a scientific study of how severe mental stress played havoc on physical health.

In the decades following the American Revolution, there was a sense of bonding among the revolutionary generation. The younger generation could not fully comprehend what it was like to experience eight years of anxiety, shortages, and disruption. As this revolutionary generation moved into old age, their accomplishments became more highly recognized and celebrated. Legends such as Molly Pitcher and Betty Zane's heroic dash to save Fort Henry became enshrined in the national memory. As the revolutionary generation aged, the contributions of wounded veterans and their widows were finally recognized, and a pension system was established in 1818.

See also Camp Followers and Women of the Army; Loyalist Women and the American Revolution

Further Reading

Bowman, Larry G. "The Scarcity of Salt in Virginia during the American Revolution." *Virginia Magazine of History and Biography* 77 (1969): 464–472.

Cometti, Elizabeth. "Women in the American Revolution." *New England Quarterly* 20 (1947): 329–346.

Gundersen, Joan R. *To Be Useful to the World: Women in Revolutionary America, 1740–1790.* New York: Twayne Publishers, 1996.

McCain, Diana Ross. "Spinning Matches." *Early American Life* (August 1990): 6–11.

Norton, Mary Beth. *Liberty's Daughters: The Revolutionary Experience of American Women, 1750–1800.* Boston: Little, Brown and Co., 1980.

———. "What an Alarming Crisis Is This? Southern Women and the American Revolution." In *The Southern Experience in the American Revolution,* ed. Jeffrey J. Crow. Chapel Hill: University of North Carolina Press, 1978.

Smith, Barbara Clark. "Food Rioters and the American Revolution." *William and Mary Quarterly* 51 (1994): 3–38.

Ward, Harry M. *The War for Independence and the Transformation of American Society.* London: UCL Press, 1999.

Anglican Women

The Anglican Church was also known as the Church of England in early America. Following the American Revolution it was renamed the Episcopal Church. The largest concentrations of Anglicans were in the colonies of Virginia, Pennsylvania, and South Carolina. The original settlers of these colonies were the Cavaliers, driven from England during the Puritan Revolution. These settlers did not come to America seeking religious freedom, they came to preserve their economic and social livelihood. The Anglican Church was the official church throughout much of the colonies. Although they did not mandate attendance or membership in their church, they commanded financial support from settlers in the form of mandatory taxation. Although almost all of the elite members of society from the middle and southern colonies were Anglicans, the church also attracted members from a healthy cross section of social classes.

Anglican religion did not permeate the daily existence of its practitioners. Anglican women believed in following moral precepts, attending Sunday services, and teaching their children to read the Bible. These basic tenets did not extend to their clothing, recreation, business dealings, or outlook on life in the same manner that Puritanism influenced almost every facet of daily life for its followers.

Perhaps the most fundamental difference between Anglicans and Puritans was their view on salvation. Puritans insisted that salvation was dependent on God's grace, and no course of moral behavior taken by an individual could "earn" salvation. They put great emphasis on spiritual thoughts and feelings. Any selfish or uncharitable thought was a sign of moral failing. Anglicans put more emphasis on actions rather than feelings. An upright person could be judged by respectable behavior and charitable actions. They mistrusted dramatic, public affirmations of faith. The weeping, trembling, and public exhortations displayed by Puritans and during other evangelical revivals were thought by Anglicans to be unseemly.

Anglicans favored beauty in both clothing and architecture. Intended to instill a sense of awe and piety, their churches were elegantly constructed with ornately decorated interiors. Women were likewise free to adorn themselves with vibrantly colored clothing, jewelry, and cosmetics for the more daring.

There were few formal roles for women in the Anglican Church. They were not permitted to preach as some Puritan women did, nor could they join formal holy orders, as was an option for Catholic women. An examination of sermons preached from Anglican pulpits reveals few references to the duties and responsibilities of wives and mothers. They were expected to be pious, raise their children in accordance with the values of their faith, be a helpmeet to their husbands, and attend church on Sunday. The Anglican Church as it was manifested in America was tolerant of diverse religious opinion and behavior. Women were not pressured to conform to a stereotypical ideal of a pious wife and mother. They had greater liberty to express their opinions and frustrations without fear of reprimand than did Puritan women.

The most substantial role of women in the Anglican Church revolved around the primary religious events in life: baptism, marriage, and funeral services. All of these activities took place in the home, rather than in a church. As such, women orchestrated the timing, scale, and preparations of the events. Although the minister presided over the ceremonies, it was the women who determined the character of the service.

The wives of Anglican ministers had unique responsibilities in maintaining the economic viability of their families. Ministers were not well compensated and tended to seek out wealthy brides. Because there was status associated with marriage to a minister of the Church of England, well-to-do families were eager for the alliance. Dowries were welcome, but not always sufficient to keep the rectory finances afloat. Most parishes were required to provide the minister with a small farm. It appears that many ministers' wives assumed management of the farm and sold its proceeds as a supplemental means of income. During the nineteenth century, the wives of ministers took on far more responsibility for organizing women's groups within the church.

The status of the Anglican Church was dealt a major setback during and after the American Revolution. Although people from Puritan traditions sided with the patriots, Anglicans leaned toward the loyalist cause. Many of the most ardent supporters of the English could be found among the Anglican hierarchy. The Anglicans were dealt a double blow in the wake of the American Revolution. With the disestablishment of the Anglican Church as the official church of the colonies, their financial base was undermined. Even more damaging was the characterization of Anglican ministers as traitors. A large percentage of their ministers either fled to Canada or returned to England. Some of their parishioners followed, but others were left without religious leadership. The taint associated with Anglicanism caused many of these people to seek out other Protestant denominations.

Anglicans seem pale and bland in comparison with the zealousness of the Puritans and the overt emotionalism of evangelical sects that flourished during the Great Awakening. Following the Revolution they lost members to other denominations, and their reputation suffered badly. They changed their name to the Protestant Episcopal Church in an effort to disassociate themselves from England. Many of the leading elite families maintained their affiliation with the church, but with the rise of Methodists, Baptists, and Pietistic sects, their membership would never again approach the dominance they had prior to the Revolution.

Further Reading

Gunderson, Joan R. "The Non-Institutional Church: The Religious Role of Women in Eighteenth Century Virginia." *Historical Magazine of the Protestant Episcopal Church* 51 (1982): 347–357.

Heyrman, Christine Leigh. *Southern Cross: The Beginnings of the Bible Belt.* Chapel Hill: University of North Carolina Press, 1998.

Appearance

See Body Image and Beauty; Clothing; Portraiture

Arnold, Margaret Shippen
Wife and accomplice of Benedict Arnold (1760–1804)

The reputation of Mrs. Benedict Arnold has evolved since the time of her husband's treason, when she was regarded as too innocent and simple to have participated in such a treacherous scheme. Most colonials, including General Washington, appeared to have believed that such a delicate, refined, and youthful lady could not have participated in duplicitous political schemes, despite the fact that Peggy's loyalist sympathies were common knowledge.

Peggy Shippen was born into one of Philadelphia's wealthiest families. The Shippen fortune had been acquired through international trade, and like most merchant families, they held conservative political views. Peggy Shippen had only one brother, who proved inept and disinterested in commerce. Her father decided Peggy had the greatest aptitude for business in the family and provided her with a fine education and mentored her in finances, real estate investments, and the principles of trade. Despite her interest in business, Peggy was also tutored in the arts typically expected of well-born daughters. She could sew, play musical instruments, and serve as a charming hostess. By the 1770s she had a reputation as the most beautiful and amiable debutante in Philadelphia.

The early 1770s was a turbulent time in the colonies. The presence of British troops escalated in response to political unrest, and the officers found a warm welcome in the Shippen home. The Shippen family made no secret of their loyalist stance, and Peggy appears to have shared her father's political allegiance. The adolescent Peggy Shippen came of age being entertained by British officers, and it is likely she shared a romantic liaison with John André, a key figure in the British intelligence network. Philadelphia was briefly occupied by the British army at the outset of the Revolution, and the Shippen home was a frequent meeting place and social center for British troops.

By May 1778, the British needed to make a strategic evacuation of Philadelphia, and the city was retaken by the patriots. General Washington appointed Benedict Arnold to serve as the military governor of the city. Arnold had a fascinating career. Having grown up in poverty, he made a fortune in trade through hard work and shrewd business acumen. He was forced to neglect his business after joining the army, and his personal fortune declined at the same time as his heroic military exploits made him a national celebrity. Having been gravely wounded during the Battle of Saratoga, General Arnold was given light duty in Philadelphia, attempting to keep peace in a city where tensions between loyalists and patriots were high.

Arnold tried to ease tensions in the city by inviting loyalist families to social events, and it was inevitable that Benedict Arnold would meet the Shippen family. He was quickly smitten by the eighteen-year-old Peggy, and the couple soon agreed to marry. Eager to rebuild his finances and impress his wealthy in-laws, Arnold engaged in some shady profiteering by taking payoffs from merchants desperate for his permission to do trade within the city. He also came under criticism from radicals who believed he was too lenient on loyalists. He eventually came under censure from Congress for his profiteering and other financial irregularities. Arnold was affronted by the implications

that he had illegally profited from the war and angered that his personal sacrifices were ignored by a government that had slighted him. Precisely when he began contemplating a shift of loyalties to the British is unknown, but it is certain he had the enthusiastic support of his wife.

Peggy Arnold had high connections with the British officers, and she reestablished contact with John André, sometimes described as the British spymaster. A system of coded messages was devised, which Peggy helped her husband compose and decipher. Peggy helped deliver the messages between André and Arnold, and ultimately a set of terms was agreed to for Arnold to switch allegiances. In exchange for £20,000, Arnold would permit the capture of West Point, the post to which he had recently been given command. The plot was sweetened when it was learned that General Washington would soon be visiting West Point. A flurry of messages was exchanged between Arnold and his British handlers to arrange for the simultaneous capture of West Point and General Washington. When these papers fell into American hands, both the plot and Arnold's treachery were exposed.

Arnold escaped West Point just minutes before he would have been arrested. Peggy and her infant daughter were left behind, because attempting to flee with them would have aroused the suspicion of West Point soldiers, not yet aware of Arnold's treachery. Thus, Peggy Arnold was left alone to confront General Washington and attempt to buy her fleeing husband more time. Her dramatic performance upon Washington's arrival has been the subject of much debate. She flitted from room to room, her baby clutched in her arms, crying and accusing Washington of having come to murder her child. General Washington, a longtime acquaintance of Peggy and her family, could not make sense of her behavior. He spent precious minutes trying to comfort the seemingly hysterical woman, who fainted, wept, and held the confused officers spellbound. By the time it was determined that Benedict Arnold was nowhere at the fort, he had made his escape aboard a British ship.

George Washington believed Peggy's hysterical outbursts to have been genuine. So did Alexander

Hamilton, who also witnessed the scene. Among those who knew her, Peggy Shippen Arnold was believed to be a refined, charming, but somewhat frivolous young lady. Neither loyalist nor patriot believed the twenty-year-old socialite could have been aware of her husband's treachery, or assisted in his escape through such an unladylike display. It is now apparent, through examination of papers in American and British archives, that Peggy Shippen was indeed aware of Arnold's activities and assisted him throughout his service to the British.

So convinced was General Washington of Peggy's innocence that he arranged for her to be escorted to her family home in Philadelphia. When the shocking news of Benedict Arnold's defection became known, her welcome in Philadelphia evaporated. She spent the remainder of the Revolution in New York, a stronghold of loyalist sympathy. Following the war she and Arnold immigrated to England, where they had a mixed reception. Benedict Arnold was mistrusted and disliked, but Peggy became an enormous favorite of Queen Charlotte. She received a pension of £1,000 per year, a welcome stipend in light of her husband's precarious finances. Peggy hoped one day to return to America, but it was apparent the Arnolds would never find welcome there. When she visited her dying mother in Pennsylvania years later, her reception was so cold she decided never to return.

Despite the tumultuous events of their marriage, Peggy and Benedict Arnold appeared to have been devoted to one another throughout their lives. They were often separated, as Benedict was forced to return to the sea to earn his living as a merchant and to serve in the war against France. His earnings were never good, and Peggy spent her last years fearing the queen would die, meaning an end to her much-needed pension. Benedict Arnold died in 1801, a bitter and disillusioned man. Peggy died three years later at the age of forty-four, from a tumor in her stomach. Her four sons all became British officers, and her daughter married a British general.

See also Spies and the American Revolution

Further Reading

Diamant, Lincoln. *Revolutionary Women in the War for American Independence.* Westport, CT: Praeger, 1998.
Randall, Willard Sterne. "Mrs. Benedict Arnold." *MHQ: The Quarterly Journal of Military History* 4, no. 2 (1992): 80–89.

B

Battered Women

See Domestic Violence

Beauty

See Body Image and Beauty

Benevolent Societies

Formal organizations for the relief of the poor were not established until the end of the colonial period. Prior to this, poor people sought temporary relief from members of their community. When possible, families were ordered to provide assistance to relatives who had fallen on hard times. Those without relatives in a position to render aid were either provided with provisions until their crisis had passed, or were housed at public expense with a member of the community. Such informal arrangements began to collapse by the end of the eighteenth century. Cities were growing larger, neighbors no longer knew one another, economic downturns increased the number of poor, and more internal migration meant many of the poor had no family structure to rely on. The population of New York City in 1790 was 33,131. Ten years later it was 96,373. Much of this expansion was the result of immigration and an influx of working-class people seeking employment.

Although many people in urban areas suffered from poverty, others in the merchant class were accumulating wealth at an unprecedented rate. This resulted in a class of people who had enough money to donate substantial sums to charitable organizations. It also freed wealthy women from the drudgery of housework. Some of those women sought to fill their days with meaningful activities to alleviate the suffering of the less fortunate.

Charitable work outside the home was viewed as a natural extension of the nurturing disposition of women. Many of the participants were motivated by religious considerations. Tending to the poor allowed them to demonstrate the twin Christian virtues of loving God and loving one's neighbor. Most women who became involved in social work were married. Some of the work, such as assisting poor women during their lying-in, was not considered suitable for unmarried women. Single women who did become involved usually participated in teaching Sunday school, sewing clothes for the needy, or visiting the aged and infirm.

Quaker women were especially active in benevolent societies. In 1795 a group of Philadelphia Quaker women founded the Female Society for the Relief and Employment of the Poor. Relief activities intensified during winter months, when employment became scarce because of the closing of the harbor and women without economic safety nets became vulnerable. The society divided the city into districts, with two volunteers assigned to each district. They canvassed their assigned area, distributing clothes, blankets, firewood, and food.

They also arranged for doctors and nurses to visit those in need. Sometimes the city of Philadelphia used the services of the society to distribute tickets to soup kitchens and firewood. Perhaps most importantly, they arranged employment for impoverished women. Knowing that many women were unable to work outside the home because of their small children, the society distributed spinning wheels and sewing projects for women to do in their homes. In 1798 they took this self-help concept further when they established the House of Industry, where poor women were provided with regular employment in the textile industry. Children were looked after in another room, where elderly women too infirm to spin provided care. The society provided the women and children with breakfast, lunch, and a heated environment in which to work.

Quakers were also great believers in the power of education to alleviate poverty. Organizations such as the Aimwell School Association (est. 1798) and the Society for the Free Instruction of African Females (est. 1795) provided instruction in basic literacy, mathematics, and sewing skills. These classes were immediately filled and usually had waiting lists. Volunteers provided instruction on a rotating basis, with two women teaching classes for a week at a time before another pair rotated in. Some women served as supervisors who monitored students throughout the year in order to provide consistency.

In 1797 Isabella Graham and Elizabeth Seton founded the Society for the Relief of Poor Widows with Small Children, located in New York City. The society's chief aim was to make these women self-sufficient. They canvassed neighborhoods looking for suitable employment for widows. They set up schools to look after the recipients' young children, usually taught by one of the poor widows. Although this was a noble experiment, the results were disappointing. The best jobs the society was able to obtain were usually sewing, laundry, or ironing. The wages generated were insufficient to support a woman and her children with no other means of income. It was necessary for the society to provide continuing relief in the form of food and provisions for these widows to make ends meet.

The poor women who received aid generally had to be the "deserving" sort. The society sought out women who were victims of circumstance, such as widowhood or illness. Such women could be rehabilitated to become productive members of society. Those who drank, gambled, panhandled, or prostituted themselves were turned away. There was a limited amount of aid to be spread among many, and women who were perceived as contributing to their debased condition were not considered worthy of assistance.

The role women played in organizing and managing charitable organizations may have inspired the development of feminist consciousness in the nineteenth century. Through providing assistance to women in need they became aware of the disabilities and inequities that prevented women from earning a living wage. They learned organizational skills and the effect of social activism. The leaders of benevolent societies interacted with city officials to work toward mutually beneficial goals. They learned to organize fund-raising drives, court wealthy benefactors, and manage accounts. This was a socially sanctioned way for women to channel their ambition, energies, and intellect into an activity outside the home. Women were barred from participating in elective government, but through work in benevolent societies they were able to become involved in their community's public sphere.

See also Graham, Isabella Marshall; Poverty; Seton, Elizabeth Ann Bayley

Further Reading

Boylan, Anne M. "Timid Girls, Venerable Widows and Dignified Matrons: Life Cycle Patterns among Organized Women in New York and Boston, 1797–1840." *American Quarterly* 38 (1986): 779–797.

———. "Women in Groups: An Analysis of Women's Benevolent Organizations in New York and Boston, 1797–1840." *Journal of American History* 71 (1984): 497–523.

Gilman, Amy. "From Widowhood to Wickedness: The Politics of Class and Gender in New York City Private Charity, 1799–1860." *History of Education Quarterly* 24 (1984): 59–74.

Haviland, Margaret Morris. "Beyond Women's Sphere: Young Quaker Women and the Veil of Charity in Philadelphia, 1790–1810." *William and Mary Quarterly* 51 (1994): 419–446.

Berkeley, Lady Frances Culpeper
Wife of three colonial governors (1634–c. 1695)

Although born in England, Frances Culpeper came to Virginia as a young girl. She was a member of one of the most powerful families in the colonies, and quickly made an advantageous marriage to Samuel Stephens, who ultimately became governor of the Carolinas and owner of Roanoke Island. The marriage endured for seventeen years, but it appears Frances was unable to have children. None of her lengthy three marriages resulted in any children, but Frances was nevertheless considered a major asset as an insightful and dedicated political wife.

Six months after the death of her first husband, Frances married the governor of Virginia, Sir William Berkeley. Frances was thirty-six, and her new husband was sixty-four. Despite the difference in age, the couple was a powerful force in Virginia society. Sir William had become governor of Virginia in 1641 as a charismatic and dynamic courtier only thirty-five years old. He inserted himself into the ranks of elite Virginia society and built an impressive mansion called Green Spring on a vast tract of land outside the capital. He was known for his generous hospitality and was popular among the tight group of wealthy plantation owners. Berkeley had immediately spotted a problem with the Virginia economy in its over-reliance on tobacco. He attempted to diversify crop production by encouraging the growing of flax, rice, and fruit, and the brewing of spirits. He sought to improve trade and relations with the Indians. He was a successful governor until 1652, when the Puritan Revolution brought a change of power to the colonies. Berkeley retreated to Green Spring, where he remained until the restoration of Charles II, who reappointed the aging Berkeley to power in 1660.

When Frances married Governor Berkeley, he was beginning to show the signs of age. He was going deaf and suffered from various illnesses. As he declined he grew to depend on Frances and a tight coterie of elite gentry dubbed the "Green Spring faction." Virginians who were not a part of this political cabal began to resent the governor, whose brusque temper increased as he aged. One of his foremost opponents was Frances's cousin Nathaniel Bacon. Frances had extended hospitality to Bacon when he first arrived from England. Opening her home to him and introducing him to elite society, she had helped him become established. When it became clear that Bacon was fomenting resentment toward her husband, Frances cut ties with her cousin, whose power grew as the governor's fell.

Although Berkeley wanted to trade with the Indians, Bacon wanted them removed from the state. Bacon led a revolt against the governor and launched a destructive series of assaults on Indian tribes throughout the colony. The colony descended into civil rebellion as colonists flocked to support Bacon. Governor Berkeley was driven from Jamestown, and Bacon burned the capital to the ground. Frances Berkeley was mortified by the actions of her cousin, whom she labeled a traitor and ingrate. She attempted to rally support among the gentry, but left for England when her husband requested she bring his appeal for aid to the Crown. She returned seven months later with one thousand English troops to help put down the rebellion.

By the time Frances returned to Virginia, Bacon had died of natural causes, and his rebellion sputtered to a halt. Berkeley and the Green Spring faction scrambled to confiscate rebel property. Although the immediate danger had passed, the Crown was furious with Berkeley for his heavy-handed measures used during the rebellion. He was temporarily removed from office, and Herbert Jeffreys was appointed to serve as lieutenant governor while Berkeley returned to London to defend his actions. Meanwhile, Lady Frances vigorously defended her husband's reputation and solidified as much power as possible in the Green Spring faction, of which she was now the central figure. Sir William died shortly after arriving in England, leaving

Frances to be the primary voice of opposition to the new administration. The Green Spring faction was successful in packing the Virginia Assembly with their supporters. Lieutenant Governor Jeffreys complained bitterly of Lady Frances's continued political activity, claiming she acted as though her husband was still living. Another of Frances's cousins, Thomas Culpeper, was appointed governor in 1680, and the tensions created by the Green Spring faction eased.

Frances suffered severe financial setbacks after Bacon's rebellion. Although the Green Spring mansion was still standing, many of the raids had destroyed her fields, livestock, and outbuildings. Out of financial desperation she rented her mansion to the colony to serve as an official governor's home, claiming it was the "finest seat in America." When her financial condition was restored, she once again moved into Green Spring.

In 1680 Frances married her third husband, Philip Ludwell, a member of the Green Spring faction. For several years Frances and Ludwell led the opposition to the royalist policies that sought to wrest control of Virginia from the local aristocracy. Despite Ludwell's turbulent relationship with the Crown, he was eventually appointed governor of North Carolina. Even while Ludwell was governor of North Carolina, Frances and her husband remained living at Green Spring, where she was still referred to as "Lady Frances."

Lady Frances continued to be active in the political affairs of Virginia and North Carolina until her death. As would be expected, she was a woman who aroused both fierce loyalty and bitter antagonism. Her opponents called her arrogant and devious, but her supporters considered her strong, courageous, and wise. Through a combination of family connections, advantageous marriages, and forceful personal character, Frances Berkeley was one of the most powerful women in early America. A fragment of her gravestone may still be seen at Jamestown.

Further Reading

Billings, Warren M. "Berkeley and Effingham: Who Cares?" *Virginia Magazine of History and Biography* 97 (1989): 33–47.

Carson, Jane D. "Lady Frances Berkeley." In *Notable American Women, 1607–1950*, ed. Edward T. James. Cambridge, MA: Belknap Press of Harvard University, 1971.

Snyder, Terri L. "Lady Frances Berkeley." In *American National Biography*, ed. John A Garraty. New York: Oxford University Press, 1999.

Birth Control

References of techniques for limiting family size are rare in colonial America. Folk wisdom was inherited from Europe, where a few techniques doubtlessly traveled with the immigrants to the New World. Demographers have traced a steady decline in American family size from the seventeenth century through the late nineteenth century. Although external factors such as war or the older age of brides at time of marriage might have influenced these declining rates, even studies that took these factors into account indicate that certain segments of the population seemed to have been able to reduce the number of their pregnancies.

Families in colonial America were large, typically averaging six to eight children. The number and spacing of childbirths among women who married young compared against those who delayed marriage until after the age of twenty-five reveals an interesting pattern. Both groups clustered their births toward the beginning of marriage, but the younger wives finished bearing their children at a much earlier age than the older wives. On average, the younger set bore their last child at age thirty-seven, whereas the older wives continued to bear children another four years. Given that both sets of women would still have been premenopausal, historians have concluded that women who had achieved the desired number of children were practicing some form of family limitation.

The primary technique used for discouraging conception was breastfeeding. Most women in colonial America breastfed their children and only turned to wet nurses should they be physically unable to nurse their own children. Among mothers who did not breastfeed their children, 20 percent would regain fertility within one month following

Mrs. Noah Smith and Her Children by Ralph Earl. Families in colonial America were large, typically averaging six to eight children. People of colonial America believed it was in accordance with God's will for a woman to be fruitful and multiply. (Geoffrey Clements/CORBIS)

childbirth. By the third month almost 80 percent of nonnursing mothers are capable of conception. Conversely, a nursing mother might not resume normal menstrual periods for almost a year. This drastic reduction in fertility was obvious to women, and nursing might have been deliberately prolonged by women choosing to delay conception.

Despite the effect nursing had on reducing a woman's fertility, it was not a guaranteed method of birth control. Abstinence was the only certain way to prevent conception, and this was widely used by women determined to prevent pregnancies.

Less reliable forms of birth control were known to exist, including crude condoms, made from animal intestine. Dating as far back as the sixteenth century, condoms were primarily intended to discourage the spread of venereal disease. Because the animal membranes were prone to tearing and slipping off during intercourse, they were an unreliable method of contraception until the vulcanization of rubber in the 1840s made a viable product. The expense and limited availability of condoms made them off-limits to any but the wealthy. Coitus interruptus, or male withdrawal before ejaculation, was also used. Abstinence, condoms, and withdrawal all depended on the willingness of the male and did not provide women with reproductive control.

Women were known to resort to barrier devices in an attempt to discourage conception. Crude pessaries, made of sponges and soaked in solutions such as lemon juice or honey, could be used in an attempt to block conception. Such devices lacked reliability, but were not completely ineffective. Douching, while not unknown, is rarely mentioned in colonial medical books as a technique for contraception.

Some herbal medicine books made reference to teas and medicinal brews that were intended to prevent conception. Some of these herbs, such as juniper, angelica, and pennyroyal, were known to provoke menstruation. Although in rare cases these herbs could be used as abortifacients, they were useless for preventing conception. Until the invention of the hormonal birth control pill in the twentieth century, there was no known form of oral contraception.

Superstition was also rampant in an era before full understanding of human anatomy. Folklore claimed that a woman who touched emeralds or sapphires would have temporary protection against conception. Drinking the tea of fruitless trees was said to render a woman sterile. Stranger beliefs, such as the suspension of hare's dung wrapped in a mule's hide over a bed, might have been perversely effective because they doubtlessly discouraged romantic encounters. Other folk beliefs relied on a woman tossing seeds into a river or turning the wheel of a grain mill backward at the midnight hour. Although such beliefs were based on superstition and were doubtlessly sneered at by many contemporaries as sheer nonsense, the frequency and persistence of rituals to prevent contraception can be seen as an indicator of the desire of women to control their reproductive lives.

We know less about techniques for preventing conception among Native Americans. Anthropological studies have revealed some Cherokee women chewed on the roots of certain plants to prevent conception, although there is no evidence that such a technique would have been effective. The lack of written records regarding contraception among Native Americans cannot be construed as evidence they did not have use of techniques, just that the historical record does not mention them.

Social acceptance of the use of contraception varied depending on geography and religion. In the late seventeenth century, Cotton Mather, a New England Puritan, expressed concern that women were prolonging breastfeeding as a way of delaying conception. Women who nursed babies past the first year might be looked on with disfavor, because such an action might be interpreted as detrimental to the colonial desire for large families. This concern over the use of contraceptive means was rooted in suspicion of sexuality. For a woman to willingly make use of contraceptives, she was interfering with God's plan for procreation in order to satisfy sexual desires. Although many colonial religions, including Catholicism and the Puritan sects, condoned healthy sexuality in marriage, the use of contraceptives implied wanton sexuality divorced from procreation. Suspicion of attempts to interfere with conception can also be detected in medical texts, which warn of the harmful effect of coitus interruptus.

Despite the suspicion of women who attempted to postpone or prevent conception, many women advised their daughters of the benefits of long periods of breastfeeding as a means of protecting their own health. The persistence of superstitious beliefs, however irrational, also reveals a deeply rooted desire to control fertility. The declining rates of childbirth, beginning in the eighteenth century and plummeting by the nineteenth century, reveal that fertility control was widespread.

See also Abortion; Breastfeeding

Further Reading

Gordon, Linda. *Woman's Body, Woman's Right: A Social History of Birth Control in America.* New York: Grossman Publishers, 1976.

Himes, Norman E. *A Medical History of Contraception.* New York: Schocken Books, 1936.

Klepp, Susan E. "Lost, Hidden, Obstructed, and Repressed: Contraceptive and Abortive Technology in the Early Delaware Valley." In *Early American Technology: Making and Doing Things from the Colonial Era to 1850,* ed. Judith A. McGaw. Chapel Hill: University of North Carolina Press, 1994.

Riddle, John M. *Eve's Herbs: A History of Contraception and Abortion in the West.* Cambridge, MA: Harvard University Press, 1997.

Treckle, Paula A. "Breastfeeding and Maternal Sexuality in Colonial America." *Journal of Interdisciplinary History* 20 (1989): 25–51.

Wells, Robert V. "Family Size and Fertility Control in Eighteenth-Century America: A Study of Quaker Families." *Population Studies* 25 (1971): 73–82.

Black Women

See African American Women, Free; Interracial Marriage; Islamic Women; Marriage and Family among Enslaved Women; Slavery

Body Image and Beauty

The size and proportion of a woman's figure has always been an important aspect of beauty. Many colonial women manipulated their figure through the use of corsets. Constructed of whalebone, horn, or other stiff matter, corsets molded a woman's shape into whatever the fashion dictated. Throughout much of the eighteenth century, women preferred the compressed, cone-shaped figure that narrowed the waist but flattened the bust. The hourglass figure, which allowed for fullness of the breasts, was not popular until well into the nineteenth century. Common to all corsets was an attempt to reduce the size of the waist. Such a feature was considered highly attractive and a mark of femininity.

The widespread use of corsets among middle- and upper-class women of colonial America might give the impression that they were preoccupied with maintaining a slim figure. Although obesity was considered unattractive to colonials, reed-thin women were not preferred either. The ideal female figure in the eighteenth century was strong and shapely, but equally important was excellent posture. The way a woman carried herself was a sign of health, class, and etiquette. A corset was indispensable for maintaining the faultless posture valued by early Americans.

Modern-day opinion of corsets associate them with feminine oppression, constricting women's freedom of movement, vitality, and comfort in the interest of satisfying a frivolous need to appeal to men. It is undeniable that wearing corsets was uncomfortable, even painful, but for centuries women chose to wear them. The appeal of corsets

Evelyn Byrd (1707–1737) was considered the most beautiful woman in Virginia. The ideal female figure in the eighteenth century was strong and shapely, but equally important was excellent posture. Corsets molded a woman's shape into whatever the fashion dictated. (Colonial Williamsburg Collection)

went far beyond mere fashion. The distinctive corseted silhouette was a sign of gentility and respectability. It connoted self-discipline and required excellent posture. Corsets restricted a women's freedom of movement. She could not reach her arms over her head, could not walk quickly without becoming out of breath, and could not allow her posture to slouch. Thus, a well-corseted woman carried herself with the utmost decorum. She walked slowly, made small, restrained gestures, and looked proud and elegant with her impeccable carriage. Eighteenth-century social philosophy valued discipline, grace, elegance, and self-control. The corseted figure evoked all these values.

Colonial corsets were not nearly as restrictive as the excruciatingly tight corsets of the Antebellum and Victorian eras. Corsets from the American colonial era reveal that most had waistlines ranging between twenty-four and thirty inches in diameter. These were small enough to require erect posture, but incapable of inducing the wasp-waisted silhouette made infamous in the late nineteenth century.

Colonial doctors bemoaned the dangerous health effects that corsets induced. A wide range of illnesses were attributed to tight lacing, including asthma, disease of the kidneys and liver, displacement of the ribs, fainting, unhealthy children, sterility, and lack of energy. It is likely that colonial corsets reduced a woman's waist approximately three inches. Modern medical studies reveal that even this modest reduction was enough to constrict a woman's lung capacity by 9 percent. Although corsets were uncomfortable and caused shortness of breath, it is unlikely the relatively modest corsets of the colonial era could cause the range of illnesses listed by doctors, who were also suspicious of the dangerous effects on women's health of swimming or excessive reading.

It is tempting to correlate colonial women's insistence on wearing corsets with modern-day illnesses such as anorexia. Although there are extremely rare cases of anorexia dating back to the Middle Ages, most of these women were fasting for religious reasons. Called *anorexia mirabilis*, this illness shared many of the same physiological characteristics of today's anorexia nervosa. The "miraculous anorexics" resorted to a rigid control of diet as a way of garnering attention through a display of self-denial and devotion to a higher ideal. There is no evidence that these women were motivated by a desire to attain a particular physical appearance.

Examination of the idealized female form in eighteenth-century paintings can give insight into what was considered fashionable for women's bodies. Although none of the goddesses and models appearing were fat, it is obvious that voluptuous, healthy figures were considered the most attractive female form.

Colonial writings indicate that the ideal woman should have evenly proportioned, well-chiseled features. The oval-shaped face was especially prized. Women were advised to practice moderation in all things, for too much or too little food, sleep, exercise, or worry would have a negative effect on appearance. Women with "pleasing demeanors" were praised for displaying good health, posture, and serenity. Beauty manuals told women to avoid bad tempers and "passions of the mind," because these destroyed her ability to convey a serene expression. The blank, expressionless appearance of many women in colonial portraits might have been a reflection of this beauty ideal.

In terms of beauty, the most important physical feature was a pale, smooth complexion. Smallpox ravaged a large percentage of the population, leaving survivors with disfiguring scars. Whiteness of the skin was also an indicator of class. The whiter the skin, the more likely the woman was wealthy enough to be spared from toil in the sun. Darker complexions were associated with manual labor, or perhaps mixed bloodlines. Although women of Indian and African descent could sometimes be considered "comely," the single feature repeatedly cited as unattractive was their dark, swarthy skin. White women wore bonnets and gloves to preserve their complexions from the damaging sun. There was no particular hair color that was considered more fashionable than others. Few women ever wore wigs or powdered their hair. Only upper-class women wore wigs, and then only on very special occasions.

The "high roll," a hairstyle so often seen in paintings of the late eighteenth century, was limited to formal occasions among the upper class. A tower of hair that was powdered stark white was a mark of leisure and status. A woman needed assistance in creating such an impractical hairstyle. The high roll was heavily associated with the British aristocracy, and during the American Revolution the style was ridiculed by male and female patriots as pompous and unattractive.

Although many Americans sought to emulate European fashions, what was considered beautiful in American women differed from European stan-

A Cure for Freckles

A clear, pale complexion was highly prized in colonial America. The following recipe was taken from an eighteenth-century book of beauty advice:

> Two drams honey of roses
> One dram oil of tartar
> Mix with rye meal and spread on a cloth. Place over your face, breasts or hands overnight. In the morning, rinse away with lemon juice.

Source: Beauties Treasury; or the Ladies Vade Mecum. London: S. Malthus, 1705.

dards. Upper-class European women wore whitening cosmetics, with heavy use of rouge, beauty spots, and powdered wigs. To American eyes, such devices appeared gaudy and pretentious. By the eighteenth century, Americans were turning away from European standards of beauty, which were associated with corruption and decadence. American women were more likely to shun cosmetics and wear their hair in natural styles.

See also Clothing; Hygiene

Further Reading

Baumgarten, Linda. *What Clothes Reveal: The Language of Clothing in Colonial and Federal America.* Williamsburg, VA: Colonial Williamsburg Foundation, 2002.

Brumberg, Joan Jacob. *Fasting Girls: A History of Anorexia Nervosa.* Cambridge, MA: Harvard University Press, 1988.

Haulman, Kate. "Object Lessons: A Short History of the High Roll." *Common-Place* vol. 2, no. 1. October 2001: Online. Available http://common-place.dreamhost.com/ (accessed 19 September 2003).

Steele, Valerie. *The Corset: A Cultural History.* New Haven, CT: Yale University Press, 2001.

Boycotts

Without a vote or the ability to serve in public office, women had limited ability to influence community decisions or behavior. One of their few ways to make their wishes heard was with their purchasing power—and their ability to withhold it. During the American Revolution, women's ability to organize and enforce boycotts was an effective means of lending support to the Revolutionary cause.

The colonies depended on Britain for the importation of manufactured goods and luxury items. In protest of the modest taxes that were levied on these goods, many communities vowed to boycott imported goods. Tea was the most obvious casualty of the boycotts. The sale of tea was highly profitable for the British, but hardly essential to daily survival of the Americans. Tea was thus an easy item to target for boycotts. Consumption of tea dropped from 900,000 pounds per year in 1769 to 327,000 pounds following the outbreak of the war. Boycotting tea became a public statement of support for the war. Women opted for substitutes such as "Liberty Tea," made of brewing lemon balm, rosehips, peppermint, and raspberry. Some women engaged in public demonstrations, such as when a group of women in Wilmington, North Carolina, burned their tea during a solemn procession.

Aside from the Boston Tea Party, the most famous boycott was referred to as the "Edenton Ladies' Tea Party," organized by a group of women from Edenton, North Carolina. The town had only 600 inhabitants, but 51 ladies signed a declaration in support of their husbands who were preparing to fight the British. Although they nowhere mention the word *tea*, the declaration quickly became associated with the widespread tea boycotts. The Edenton declaration was published widely in colonial newspapers, where it was praised as an example of feminine support and resolve. When news of the Edenton Ladies' Tea Party reached England, it was greeted with ridicule. It received satirical treatment in cartoons and political essays.

Tea was the most prominent, but not the only, luxury item that was boycotted. Imported fabric, brandy, and sugar all came under censure. Women were urged to increase their production of homespun fabric rather than buy imported cotton or silk. In order for the boycotts of imported goods to have any effect on British policy, leaders of the Revolution

British satire of American women from Edenton, North Carolina, pledging to boycott English tea in response to the Continental Congress resolution in 1774 to boycott English goods. (Library of Congress)

knew they needed the cooperation of women. Articles appeared in newspapers throughout the colonies urging women to support the boycott efforts.

Although boycotts served as a means for women to assert their political will, boycotts could also contain an element of coercion. In 1774 a group of ladies in Charleston announced they would be visiting households "to obtain the assent of every Mistress of a Family" in town so they could promise to reject the "baneful Herb." People who chose to purchase tea or silks might find a rock thrown through their windows. Merchants who chose to sell such goods risked a tar and feathering or watching their shop go up in flames. Many of the shopkeepers who refused to cooperate with the boycotts were women. With smaller supplies of locally produced inventories and a smaller financial base to cushion the economic downturn, many women

shopkeepers were unable to afford a boycott and were often blacklisted as a result.

See also American Revolution on the Home Front

Further Reading

Cumming, Inez Parker. "The Edenton Ladies' Tea Party." *Georgia Review* 8 (1954): 389–396.

Kierner, Cynthia A. *Beyond the Household: Women's Place in the Early South, 1700–1835.* Ithaca, NY: Cornell University Press, 1998.

Norton, Mary Beth. *Liberty's Daughters: The Revolutionary Experience of American Women, 1750–1800.* Boston: Little, Brown, 1980.

Bradford, Cornelia Smith

Printer, publisher, and editor (fl. 1740–1755)

Little is known of Cornelia Smith's early life, other than she came from New York and later moved to Philadelphia. In 1740 she married Andrew Bradford, the wealthy printer and publisher of the *American Weekly Mercury.* Cornelia became intimately involved with the operation of the newspaper, learning to set type, select stories for inclusion, and solicit advertising. By all accounts Cornelia had an abrasive and domineering personality, which caused dissention in the print shop. Andrew had taken his nephew William Bradford III as his apprentice shortly before he married Cornelia. Rumor claims Cornelia was attempting to divert the vast Bradford fortune into her family by arranging a marriage between William and her niece. When William refused, Cornelia proceeded to make life so miserable for him at the print shop that he abandoned his apprenticeship and moved to London. Cornelia later succeeded in persuading her husband to alter his will, diverting William's likely inheritance to herself.

It is impossible to tell from a distance of more than two hundred years if this avaricious picture of Cornelia is based on her actual behavior, or was rooted in mistrust of a forceful woman. In 1742 Cornelia became an extremely wealthy woman when her husband died following a lingering illness. In addition to inheriting the printing business, she received five hundred acres of land and a share of the Durham Iron Works. Andrew did not completely forget his nephew William, stipulating that upon Cornelia's death the printing press was to pass to him "if he shall behave himself handsomely toward her [Cornelia]."

Although most widows of printers who took up their husband's trade did so out of economic necessity, Cornelia obviously had no need to work. She chose to undertake editorship of the *American Weekly Mercury* because she enjoyed the work. Immediately following Andrew's death, the paper missed one weekly installment. When issue #1195 appeared one week later, it was bordered with black columns and the widow Bradford's solemn announcement she intended to carry on the business. In addition to editing the paper, she operated a stationery shop adjacent to the press.

The character of the paper altered after Cornelia assumed control. Andrew had been willing to publish politically controversial material and had served time in prison for circulating seditious writings. Cornelia opted for cautious, noncontroversial coverage of American and European news. She made liberal use of short, tabloidlike stories, covering stories of piracy, fires, epidemics, accidents, and murders. She also astutely used the paper to advertise the numerous wares she had for sale in her shop, including imported books, rum, herbs, and tobacco.

Cornelia had no children, and when she died in 1755, her considerable estate was divided among her nieces and nephews.

See also Printers and the Printing Trade

Further Reading

De Armond, Anna Janney. "Cornelia Bradford." In *Notable American Women, 1607–1950*, ed. Edward T. James. Cambridge, MA: Belknap Press of Harvard University, 1971.

Hudak, Leona M. *Early American Women Printers and Publishers, 1639–1820.* Metuchen, NJ: Scarecrow Press, 1978.

Bradstreet, Anne Dudley
Poet (1612–1672)

Anne Bradstreet was among the first generation of Puritans who left the security of England for the wilds of America. The daughter of Thomas Dudley, the steward for the Earl of Lincoln, Anne Dudley

---

To My Dear and Loving Husband

Anne Bradstreet's later poems are universally acknowledged to be better than her initial efforts. Deeply personal in nature, they reveal a tender and reflective perspective on the humble details of daily life rarely seen in poetry of the day. Her most often quoted poem was an ode to her husband, Simon:

> If ever two were one, then surely we.
> If ever man were loved by wife, then thee.
> If ever wife was happy in a man,
> Compare with me, ye women, if you can.
> I prize thy love more than whole Mines of gold
> Or all the riches that the East dost hold.
> My love is such that rivers cannot quench,
> Nor aught but love from thee, give recompense.
> Thy love is such I can no way repay.
> The heavens reward thee manifold, I pray.
> Then while we live, in love let's so preserver
> That when we live no more, we may live ever.

---

grew up in a vastly privileged environment. Most of her childhood was spent on the sprawling estate at Tattershall Castle, where she was permitted access to the earl's library. Although she was the product of a strict religious upbringing, Anne later confessed to an unwholesome desire for worldly things and frivolous pastimes. This changed in her sixteenth year, when she survived a bout of smallpox, experienced a religious conversion, and married Simon Bradstreet, a young man with whom she fell deeply in love.

By the late 1620s religious tensions in England were making life increasingly difficult and even dangerous for those of Puritan persuasion. The lure of a vast, pristine wilderness in which Puritans would be able to carve out their idealized vision of a godly kingdom tempted Anne and her parents to immigrate to America. They sailed aboard the *Arbella* in 1630, arriving in Massachusetts just a few years after the founding of the colony. The settlement had only forty dwellings, most of which were "English wigwams" modeled after the Indians' homes, or cavelike dugouts protected with timber and thatch roofs. About one-third of the houses were more substantial log cabins with oiled paper for windows. Anne acknowledged experiencing profound pangs of uneasiness when she saw the crude, rough-hewn town that was to be her home, but believing it was God's will for her, she reconciled herself to the idea and set up housekeeping with her husband.

In the following years she would move twice more, each time farther into the wilderness. She gave birth to eight children, all of whom except one survived into adulthood. In the midst of rearing children and the heavy duties required of a pioneering wife who lived in a raw, untamed wilderness, Anne Bradstreet sought comfort through writing poetry. Her early poems were stiff, elaborate imitations of the style of poetry popular in the seventeenth century, but her later poems show the warmth, humor, and sensitivity that has placed her among the most notable poets in American history. While her contemporaries were writing poems of weighty religious and historical nature, Anne wrote about the love she had for her husband and children, the despair she felt when her home burned to the ground, and other reflections on daily life.

In 1650 Anne's brother-in-law, the Reverend John Woodbridge, traveled to England on business. He brought copies of a number of Anne's poems and, without her knowledge or consent, he arranged for them to be published in book form. *The Tenth Muse, Lately Sprung Up in America, or Several Poems Compiled with Great Variety of Wit and Learning, Full of Delight,* was the first book of poetry written by an American. A later poem by Anne, "The Author to Her Book," reveals her mixed feelings on learning of Reverend Woodbridge's actions. She likened her poems to children and claimed embarrassment at their numerous errors that had been exposed to public view. She wished for a better opportunity to erase such blemishes, but overall she was clearly pleased with a sense of literary accomplishment at seeing her words in print. Indeed, Anne participated in a second edition of the work, in which she corrected such errors and added additional poems.

Despite surviving eight pregnancies and the rigors of living in the harsh New England wilderness, Anne was never a physically strong person. Sickly throughout much of her life, she died at age sixty after a prolonged illness.

Further Reading

Hensley, Jeannine. *The Works of Anne Bradstreet.* Cambridge, MA: Belknap Press of Harvard University, 1967.

Morrison, Samuel Eliot. *Builders of the Bay Colony.* Boston: Houghton Mifflin Co., 1930.

Rosenmeier, Rosamond. *Anne Bradstreet Revisited.* Boston: Twayne Publishers, 1991.

White, Elizabeth Wade. *Anne Bradstreet: The Tenth Muse.* New York: Oxford University Press, 1971.

———. "The Tenth Muse: A Tercentenary Appraisal of Anne Bradstreet." *William and Mary Quarterly,* 3d ser. 8 (1951): 355–377.

Brant, Molly

Mohawk leader and British loyalist (c. 1736–1796)

Although Molly Brant was a leader among the Iroquois people, she is primarily remembered for the influence she commanded as the mistress of the most powerful man in New England, Sir William Johnson. Molly was born near the Ohio River Valley and was a full-blooded Mohawk. It is believed her widowed mother married an English settler, which could account for Molly's Anglicized name and her familiarity with the English language and customs. Her brother Joseph Brant would also become an important leader among the Mohawk people. During the French and Indian War (1756–1763) Molly came into increasing contact with the English, because her people were important allies of the British. Folklore claims that Molly attended a regimental militia muster in Canajoharie, New York, where she first came to the attention of Sir William Johnson, the superintendent of Indian affairs. By 1759 she had moved into Johnson's house and was living openly with him as his housekeeper and mistress.

William Johnson was a fascinating man, having come from Ireland with no money and few prospects. Traveling to upstate New York to manage some property, he became enthralled by Indian culture. He lived among the Indians, adopted their dress and customs, and gained their trust. Moving freely between white and Indian culture, Johnson's aptitude for trade and negotiating alliances turned him into an exceptionally wealthy man. Having

Johnson Hall, the home Molly Brant shared with William Johnson. (Library of Congress)

gained the respect and trust of the Indians, Johnson became immensely influential during the course of the French and Indian War. He was appointed to be the Crown's chief negotiator with the Indian people. His success in military and diplomatic affairs earned him a baronetcy, a title, and massive award of land in upstate New York.

In 1759 the twenty-three-year-old Molly Brant joined Sir William's household. She bore him eight children and served as a common-law wife. She openly attended banquets, political discussions, and tribal councils. Although Johnson's relations with the Six Nations Confederacy of the Iroquois were strong, Molly's affiliation with Johnson provided the extra cement that would bind the Indians to the British cause in the coming turbulent years. For most of their years together they lived at Johnson Hall, a spacious Georgian mansion that served as both a home and headquarters. Here Indian councils were held, sometimes hosting as many as 900 Indians from various tribal delegations. In addition to presiding over such gatherings, Molly hosted meetings of British officers, nobility, and business traders. Activity at Johnson Hall was more like that of a small town, rather than a private home. Molly served as housekeeper, consort, hostess, and matron.

Molly's brother Joseph was assuming a principal leadership role within the Six Nations. Both Molly and Joseph were well acquainted with English norms, but they feared the brewing movement for political independence among the colonists. They were convinced that should America achieve independence from England, most Indian land would be consumed by the new nation. Although Molly and Joseph were advocates of certain aspects of European culture (Christianity, education, agriculture, and housing), they wished to retain distinctive Native American customs, territory, and power. Trying to take the best of the English world while still preserving native customs proved to be a balancing act that was impossible for the Brants to achieve.

In the summer of 1774 Sir William unexpectedly died at the age of sixty. Johnson had the unstinting loyalty of the Six Nations Confederacy of Iroquois, but this alliance began to fracture after his death. Although Molly still retained influence with the various tribal leaders, some tribes were seeking alliances with the American rebels in the brewing rebellion. Molly advocated continued loyalty to the British cause, but her efforts to hold the Confederacy together failed. Several of the tribes assumed a neutral or rebel stance, thus undermining British power in New England. Historians have often speculated at the outcome of the American Revolution had William Johnson lived, as he would doubtlessly have commanded the undivided loyalty of the Indian nations, thus dealing a powerful blow to the patriots' cause.

Following Sir William's death, Molly and her children moved to one of his other properties at Fort Johnson. From here she established a trading business and sheltered loyalists who were fleeing turmoil caused by the war. She also supplied arms and ammunition to the British. Tradition claims she provided intelligence to the British that helped them lead a successful rout of American forces at Oriskany in 1777.

Over the coming years Molly would be forced to flee advancing troops and finally immigrate to Canada following the war. The British government rewarded Molly with a fine home and a pension of £100 per year. Her children moved with her to Canada, where all of them married into wealthy British families. Although Molly retained Indian dress and identity, her children and descendants generally chose to live among white society.

Although she was a remarkable woman who lived through three wars, moved in the most elite circles, and wielded enormous influence in both white and Indian societies, a cloud hangs over Molly's legacy. Molly and her brother Joseph Brant's staunch loyalty to the British Crown cost their people greatly. They had hoped to bring the best elements of European society to their people without losing their ethnic identity. Their allegiance to the British accelerated the loss of the Six Nations' lands and subsequently much of their culture.

Further Reading

Allen, Robert S. "Molly Brant." In *American National Biography*, eds. John A. Garraty and Mark C. Carnes. New York: Oxford University Press, 1999.

Green, Gretchen. "Molly Brant, Catherine Brant, and Their Daughters: A Study in Colonial Acculturation." *Ontario History* 81 (1989): 235–250.

Johnston, Jean. "Molly Brant: Mohawk Matron." *Ontario History* 56 (1964): 105–124.

Breastfeeding

Studies of breastfeeding in seventeenth- and eighteenth-century America reveal fascinating insights into the attitudes toward religion, medical knowledge, and sexuality. Although there were no alternatives to breastfeeding during this period, the use of wet nurses and the duration of breastfeeding were matters a woman could control.

Most women of colonial America breastfed their children, although some were unable to do so because of medical complications, such as abscessed breasts or failure to lactate. "Milk fever," or an infection of the breasts that resulted in a high fever and even death, also prevented some women from breastfeeding. In such cases a wet nurse would be employed. Because lactating women continue to produce milk as long as they suckle a child, nursing other women's infants was a choice many women made to earn extra income. Colonial newspapers frequently carried advertisements from women willing to nurse children. The preference was usually for a woman who could visit the house regularly, although sometimes a wet nurse was willing to move in with the infant's family. Despite the necessity of wet nurses, women who did not personally nurse their children faced a stigma of laziness or lack of maternal affection. Doctors warned that wet nurses were careless and uncleanly. Other books directed toward women remind them of the warm and nurturing maternal bond that is created through personally nursing their children.

The one exception to the stigma of using a wet nurse was in the first week following birth, when almost all children received their initial nourishment from a wet nurse. Immediately following birth a woman produces colostrum, a clear substance highly rich in vitamins, minerals, and antiallergens. Early medical authorities were suspicious of colostrum, believing it toxic and even fatal to infants. Sadly, most infants were denied this rich source of nourishment and were entrusted to a wet nurse's care until the mother began producing normal milk, usually one week following birth. If a wet nurse was not available, women were advised to feed the newborns a dab of butter with sugar, or a little tea with a drop of gin. Less-educated families who lacked access to these medical books made due with a rag soaked in cow's milk, a much healthier alternative.

Early Puritans were strong advocates of maternal breastfeeding. They castigated women who chose to allow a servant to breastfeed their child, characterizing such women as vain and Eve-like. Observing that a woman's breasts were created to provide nourishment for a child, rather than to serve as an erogenous zone, a woman who chose not to breastfeed her child was suspected of laziness and self-indulgence. The famous Puritan minister Cotton Mather wrote "You will suckle your infant yourself if you can; Be not such an ostrich as to decline it, merely because you would be one of the careless women living at ease."

The demands of maintaining a household and rearing children kept most mothers at home while they nursed, although there was little stigma associated with women who nursed in public. Standards of privacy were different in colonial America, where homes often lacked partitions, hallways, and doors that could be closed. Large families, and the subsequent numerous years in which a woman nursed children, made it highly impractical for a woman to isolate herself during breastfeeding.

Medical texts of the era reveal that women were advised against resuming sexual activity while nursing, believing that such activities damaged the milk of the mother. Noticing that women rarely menstruated while nursing, it was believed that the blood of menstruation was diverted and converted into milk during lactation. If a woman resumed intercourse, it was feared that menstruation would be prompted, thus affecting the quality of the milk. One writer even warned that mere sexual thoughts could "infect the milk," although more lenient writers thought abstinence from intercourse for a few hours before nursing would preserve the milk.

Weaning usually occurred in the autumn or spring, as it was believed the summer heat and winter cold would add an additional burden to the difficulty of weaning. Between the ninth and twelfth months, the child's diet would be supplemented with foods like cornmeal, bread soaked in milk, and well-chopped fish. Various techniques were used to fully wean the child off breast milk, such as painting the nipples with a bitter tasting solution (mustard was preferred) to discourage nursing. Some mothers would place the child in another household for a few days until the child was adjusted to the new arrangement.

A major advantage of breastfeeding, clearly recognized by women, was the contraceptive effect breastfeeding had on their bodies. A nursing mother's fertility was usually suppressed for seven to eleven months after delivery. Most nonnursing mothers became fertile again within two months. Some women advised their daughters to extend nursing as long as possible, in order to give their bodies a reprieve from the exhausting cycle of pregnancy, birth, and tending an infant. Given that a colonial woman could expect to give birth eight times in her life, and nurse each child approximately one year, breastfeeding was an activity that dominated a large part of women's adult lives.

See also Birth control; Childbirth

Further Reading

Fildes, Valerie A. *Breasts, Bottles and Babies: A History of Infant Feeding.* Edinburgh: Edinburgh University Press, 1986.

Scholten, Catherine M. *Childbearing in American Society: 1650–1850.* New York: New York University Press, 1985.

Treckel, Paula A. "Breastfeeding and Maternal Sexuality in Colonial America." *Journal of Interdisciplinary History* 20 (1989): 25–51.

Ulrich, Laurel Thatcher. *Good Wives: Image and Reality in the Lives of Women in Northern New England, 1650–1750.* New York: Vintage Books, 1980.

Brent, Margaret

Estate owner and colonial leader (1601–c. 1670)

Margaret Brent was one of thirteen children from a wealthy English family. As Catholics, the Brents faced discrimination and limited opportunity in England. When Lord Baltimore obtained a charter for a colony open to Catholics, Margaret, her sister Mary, and two brothers immigrated to the fledgling colony of Maryland. Margaret and her sister were granted seventy acres of land they named "Sister's Freehold," and Margaret eventually acquired an additional thousand acres on Kent Island.

Although it was not the norm for women to manage estates and play active roles in local government, upper-class women of the seventeenth century often managed immense estates during their husband's absence. Prominent men could be absent for extended periods, whether due to government service, military duty, or death, and their wives were expected to know how to manage estates. Thus it was unusual, but not unheard of, for an upper-class woman to oversee large estates. Margaret Brent remained a single woman throughout her life and went about establishing her manor and farms with vigor and efficiency. Her brothers granted her power of attorney to manage their affairs during their frequent absences, and Margaret soon proved to have a keen legal mind. She was able to lend capital to other settlers and vigorously pursued her debtors and other affairs in court. Between 1642 and 1650 she appeared in court 124 times, either arguing her own cases or representing relatives and neighbors. In most cases she won her claim.

Throughout the 1640s Margaret had a close tie with the colony's governor, Leonard Calvert. It is possible that Calvert married one of Margaret's sisters, Anne, although no firm documentation has been found to prove this relationship. Calvert was also the Catholic brother of Lord Baltimore, who had been granted Maryland's charter. During the English Civil War of the mid-1640s, the colony's Catholic status was jeopardized as the king and other aristocrats appeared to be on the verge of losing power to their Puritan enemies. In Maryland, restless Puritan settlers launched an uprising against the Catholic-dominated government, and the governor fled to Virginia. He persuaded Virginia soldiers to defend Maryland against the uprising, promising to pay them out of his own purse. The soldiers quashed the uprising, although Governor Calvert unexpectedly died before he had discharged his debt. On his deathbed in 1647 he named Margaret his executor, charging her to "take all, pay all."

At forty-six, Margaret was unusually well prepared to handle such a task. She proceeded to liquidate the governor's assets to pay the soldiers. Further exacerbating Maryland's precarious situation was a food shortage and additional rumblings of rebellion. Margaret procured corn to feed the restless soldiers, and the colony settled into an uneasy peace. Despite her shrewd management of the affair, news of her actions reached Lord Baltimore in England, who berated her for selling his brother's goods.

The action for which Margaret Brent is best remembered occurred in January 1648, when she attended a meeting of the Maryland Assembly and demanded the right to vote. Noting her status as a substantial landowner and the deceased governor's attorney, she claimed to be entitled to *two* votes. Her claim was rejected, but it gave Margaret the distinction of being the first woman in the American colonies to demand the right to vote.

Despite the assembly's rejection of Margaret's petition, they vigorously defended her actions to Lord Baltimore. Baltimore was turning sharply against Margaret and the rest of the Brent family. Knowing that the Puritans were likely to gain ascendancy in England, Baltimore's Catholic heritage and his charter to the colony were vulnerable. By disassociating himself from the most prominent Catholic families in Maryland, Baltimore hoped to secure his position with the likely new leaders in England. The Maryland Assembly wrote to Lord Baltimore that in Margaret's hands the colony had fared well during the dangerous rebellion, and she deserved "favor and thanks from your Honor for her so much concurring to the public safety than to be liable to all those bitter invectives you have been pleased to express against her" (Spruill 1938, 240).

Despite the support of the Maryland Assembly, the Brent family sensed their preeminent position in Maryland was drawing to a close. In 1651 most of the Brents moved to Virginia. Margaret and her sister Mary established a plantation in northern Virginia named "Peace," where she lived the remaining twenty years of her life in relative tranquility.

Further Reading

Carpenter, Stephanie. "Margaret Brent." In *American National Biography.* New York: Oxford University Press, 1999.

Morello, Karen Berger. *The Invisible Bar: The Woman Lawyer in America, 1638 to the Present.* New York: Random House, 1986.

Spruill, Julia Cherry. *Women's Life and Work in the Southern Colonies.* Chapel Hill: University of North Carolina Press, 1938.

Bundling

See Courtship

C

Camp Followers and Women of the Army

To modern ears, the term *camp follower* implies a derogatory connotation far from the actual experience of camp followers during the American Revolution. It was common in eighteenth-century warfare for women to attach themselves to armies, either as paid employees, women accompanying their husbands, or refugees. Many of these women brought children with them. Although a small percentage of these women dabbled in prostitution, the army was vigorous about removing known prostitutes from their ranks. Prostitutes caused a breakdown in discipline and spread venereal disease among the troops. It is true that most camp followers came from the lowest ranks of society, but they were not prostitutes.

Camp followers had no legal obligation to the army. They signed no contracts, did not receive official wages, and were not subject to military discipline. Most followed the army for one of three reasons: They wished to be near their husband, they could not support themselves alone, or they desired adventure.

Both British and American armies had camp followers. Many of the women who followed the British army had come from England. English soldiers usually enlisted for life. Most were discouraged from marrying, because an enlisted soldier's salary was not adequate to support a wife and family. The women who did marry soldiers often traveled with the army. In exchange for rations and shelter, they cooked, cleaned, and mended. It is estimated that one in eight people living among the British army during the American Revolution was a woman. The number of women was fewer in the American army, where most men served only a brief term and their wives had responsibilities at home. It is estimated that the ratio of women to men in the American army was roughly one to forty.

General Washington was known to disapprove of camp followers and initially tried to forbid their presence. He quickly realized this was impossible. Not only were the unpaid housekeeping services of the camp followers essential, the women helped improve morale among the men. A price could not be put on the value of clean clothes, tents that did not leak, and socks that didn't have holes. Furthermore, many of the poorer soldiers could not afford to leave their wives at home. Had the presence of camp followers been forbidden, a small but significant percentage of the soldiers would have deserted or refused reenlistment.

Although most women living with the army were poor, the officers' wives represented a different sort of "women of the army." Usually from well-to-do families, these women followed their husbands out of choice, not economic necessity. They had few responsibilities in the camp other than to boost their husbands' morale. Unlike ordinary camp followers, who stayed with the army throughout the year, officers' wives usually stayed only while the army was camped in winter quarters, after the fighting season had ended.

Logistics

Living arrangements for camp followers varied depending on unit. Some officers insisted that women sleep in separate tents, while other units permitted wives to sleep in the same tent as their husbands. Most tents usually contained at least five men. Adding a woman and possibly children to the tent would have made for tight conditions. Few soldiers complained about the arrangement, because a woman's presence meant they would benefit from her housekeeping services.

Women and children were reluctantly tolerated by officers, but were expected to maintain pace with the army. Like most soldiers, they were expected to walk from camp to camp. Women, especially those with small children, were notorious for riding in wagons, despite a flurry of orders to ban this practice. The regularity of the orders forbidding women from riding in wagons indicates it was a rule that was regularly flouted. If the army was put on a brisk marching pace, women were ordered to remain behind rather than slow the pace.

Camp followers were expected to keep out of the way during battle. They traditionally took cover behind the baggage carts during military engagements, where they were safe except in the rare event the enemy attacked the supply train. Some women assisted during battle, either as nurses or in artillery units helping keep cannons in operation.

A typical woman who followed the army was there because her husband was in the regiment. If he was killed, his widow rarely chose to remain with the army. The British paid for return passage to England for all widows and orphans. No similar provisions were made for American widows, who might find themselves stranded with the army until the regiment moved to a place where they could get transportation home.

The average woman who followed the army was raised in hardscrabble conditions. The rigor of army life weeded out women who could not adapt to months of intense physical endeavors. These women worked hard in exchange for little more than a few rations and a spot of ground in a tent. Contemporary references to these women commented on their bedraggled and tough demeanor. Time and again it is noted that women and children following the army often had no shoes. Although the soldiers periodically received new uniforms, no provisions were made for supplying women with clothes or fabric. Camp followers usually mended their existing clothes until they literally fell to pieces, after which they modified cast-off clothing from the soldiers. As was true for men, war brought out both the best and the worst in a woman. Some women were known to engage in looting and pillaging following a battle. Others risked their lives to get a wounded soldier off the battlefield. Camp followers were routinely disparaged by their contemporaries, but were appreciated by the men on the front lines.

Chores and Responsibilities

Laundry was the primary service performed by camp followers. Although sanitary conditions in the army were poor, it was recognized that filth encouraged the spread of disease. Men were under orders to keep as clean as possible and locate latrines away from the drinking water. Any woman found washing upstream of drinking water, or disposing of wastewater within the camp, was punished. Some women charged soldiers a fee to do their laundry, although the army tried to regulate the fees to avoid price gouging. Because camp followers received daily food rations, they were expected to perform some laundry services to earn their keep. Women were free to perform additional laundry services for soldiers who requested it, but they were only allowed to charge a nominal fee.

Women also worked as sutlers, peddlers who sold provisions to the troops. Sutlers improved morale among the troops by selling basic quality-of-life items, such as soap, tobacco, sugar, and paper, but they also presented a host of problems for the military. Corrupt sutlers were willing to purchase goods that had been looted from civilians, and plundering frequently increased when a regiment had too many sutlers. The most lucrative item a sutler could peddle was liquor, which created drunkenness and disorder among the troops. Some regiments outlawed the sale of liquor all together, but sutlers could clandestinely sell it for almost any price they wished. Because of the problems associated with

Standard Fare in the Army

Camp followers spent much of their time cooking for the troops. They usually prepared simple, one-pot meals. Dried peas and heavily salted beef were common staples in both the British and American armies. The following recipe was a typical meal a woman would have prepared for six hungry soldiers:

Peas Porridge
3 loaves of hard bread
3 pounds salted beef or pork
3 cups dried peas
3 tablespoons of vinegar
Water

Cube the meat and brown it in the bottom of the pot. Stir in the peas, then stack the bread on top of the mixture. Add water and bring to a boil. Simmer until the peas are dissolved and the meat is tender.

peddling goods, most sutlers were required to register with a regiment's commanding officer. A woman had to be of good reputation to maintain her sutler privileges, and any hint of profiteering or illegal selling of liquor could result in her banishment from the camp.

All camp followers were expected to earn their keep. They cleaned, cooked, and mended garments. They were expected to cause no drain on the military, and they carted their meager belongings in packs on their back. They did their best to keep their children out of the way. Their primary form of compensation was rations, but when needed, they also received medical and legal assistance. Women who had been assaulted or robbed could appeal to the military for redress. They also needed a physician's care. The records of Revolutionary army doctors reveal the tough life these women lived. They suffered from occasional broken bones and fevers from living in cramped and unsanitary conditions, and they delivered babies in the midst of army camps.

Officers' Wives

The life of an officer's wife in camp differed drastically from that of an ordinary camp follower. Officers' wives followed the army out of choice rather than because of an economic necessity. These women tended to arrive for the winter season, when most of the fighting was over and the army settled into camp for the duration of the winter. Junior officers' wives could rarely afford to come, because they had substantial responsibilities at home. It was senior officers' wives, drawn from the upper crust of society, who could afford to leave home for lengthy periods of time.

The camps were usually situated near to town. Because most high-ranking officers moved into homes or taverns for their winter quarters, their wives were able to share these comforts. A handful of heartier women braved living in a tent with their husbands. Even for those living in a tent, life was far more comfortable than for ordinary camp followers. Officers' tents were larger and had cots for sleeping, tables, chairs, and a modicum of privacy.

Socializing was the primary occupation for officers' wives. Dinners and dances were held both in town and in the camp. Card games and teas also helped create a vibrant social circle for ranking army couples. When the women were not hosting social events, they knitted or stitched garments for the troops.

At the end of the winter season, the officers' wives were sent home, out of harm's way. These women created tight friendships with one another while they were at camp. They had a sense of camaraderie born of similar life experiences. Each knew what it was to support a husband through the difficulties of leadership during war. They did not endure the same physical or economic stress that ordinary camp followers were subjected to, but their willingness to come to camp at all was something beyond what was usually expected of a supportive wife.

See also Military Service and the American Revolution; Molly Pitcher Legend

Further Reading

Blumenthal, Walter Hart. *Women Camp Followers of the American Revolution.* Philadelphia, PA: George MacManus, 1952.
DePauw, Linda Grant. "Women in Combat: The Revolutionary War Experience." *Armed Forces and Society* 7, no. 2 (1981): 209–226.

Hagist, Don N. "The Women of the British Army during the American Revolution." *Minerva* 13, no. 2 (1995): 29–85.

Mayer, Holly A. *Belonging to the Army: Camp Followers and Community during the American Revolution.* Columbia: University of South Carolina Press, 1996.

Catholic Women

The first Catholic women who came to America were from Spain and France. A large part of the Spanish agenda for colonizing the New World involved spreading the Catholic faith as broadly as possible. To this end, Catholic nuns established convents throughout much of Latin America and the southern portions of what would later become the United States.

In England, simmering hostility toward Catholics made immigration to America a viable choice for adventuresome Catholic families. Maryland had been founded in 1632 by freedom-seeking Catholics, although the colony was open to any who wished to come. Established by Lord Baltimore as a Catholic haven, in 1649 the Act of Religious Toleration permitted freedom of worship for any Christian religion. Despite Maryland's reputation as a Catholic colony, Catholics never amounted to more than 10 percent of the population in the colonial period.

Jesuit missionaries provided most of the leadership to the Catholic population, and small chapels were established throughout Maryland. Liberty to practice Catholicism was challenged in 1688, when the Glorious Revolution ushered in a new round of anti-Catholic hostility in both England and America. Disgruntled Protestants ousted Catholics from positions of leadership and drove established churches underground. Ironically, this event resulted in increased standing for the Catholic women of Maryland. Churches were closed, but private chapels established in the homes of wealthy Catholics were permitted to operate. This elevated the status of the women who maintained the chapels. Because members of the community turned to these private chapels for marriages, baptisms, funerals, and weekly services, the mistress of the house became a central figure in the Catholic community. She would

have been responsible for preparing the chapel, maintaining the materials for the mass, and possibly serving as a hostess after services. She would have been in charge of religious instruction of her children and would plan meals around the feasts and fasts of the Catholic calendar. In a very real sense, these women helped preserve the Catholic faith during the years of persecution.

One of the challenges facing a Catholic woman in English America was finding a husband. The population of Catholics was small and scattered, and it was difficult to find a mate who was not disqualified as a marriage partner by the rules of consanguinity, which prohibited marriage within the fourth degree of kinship. Young Catholic women were facing spinsterhood unless they were permitted to marry outside of the faith, or marry a cousin. Believing that marrying outside the faith would quickly result in a diminished Catholic population, Catholics frequently requested, and were granted, dispensation to marry first and second cousins.

The American Revolution ushered in a new era of religious freedom, and Catholic women were once again free to worship in public. In 1790 John Carroll was consecrated the first Catholic bishop in America. He was eager to establish a series of convents throughout the new country, hoping that the nuns would provide spiritual guidance and practical public education for the poor. Most of the initial convents were established by French nuns, but soon immigrants from Ireland and Germany dramatically swelled the Catholic population. Archbishop Carroll had hoped the convents would be charitable institutions, whose sisters would actively engage the community through teaching, assistance to the poor, and medical care. When some of the initial convents made it plain they desired to become contemplative orders, Carroll reluctantly agreed, knowing that French Louisiana could attract contemplative nuns if he did not grant permission for them to found their orders in the United States.

One of the unexpected consequences of the establishment of Catholic convents was the surprisingly large number of Protestant women who chose to convert. A nun's life offered women an opportunity for personal satisfaction not available to them elsewhere. Many women took holy orders as a refuge from marriage. Others were seeking more meaningful lives of public service. Given the lack of options for a significant career in the secular world, women who took vows led active and engaged lives in their communities. They taught children, cared for orphans, tended the sick, and helped provide relief for the poor. It is a paradox that the immensely restrictive demands on their private life also brought nuns into greater public standing than what was available to most other women during this time.

Another substantial segment of the early Catholic population came from African American slaves. Catholic slave owners typically encouraged their slaves to convert. Surviving records from Maryland indicate that the number of slave baptisms outnumbered those of white Catholics. The 1790s witnessed an influx of slaves from Haiti, most of whom were already Catholic. Black Catholics also lived in the Spanish and French provinces. The oldest community of black Catholics was established in St. Augustine, Florida, in 1738, when the Spanish granted sanctuary to escaped slaves from plantations in Georgia and the Carolinas. In exchange for their freedom, the ex-slaves were charged with helping to build and fortify Fort Mose. Substantial numbers of slaves made it to Fort Mose, where the men served as garrison soldiers and the women and children lived inside the fort in family units.

The death of an owner was often a traumatic event for a slave. They were in danger of being distributed among the estate's heirs and thus uprooted from their families. A Catholic slave might become the possession of a new owner who was not Catholic and would not permit Catholic worship among his slaves. It is difficult to know if the conversions to Catholicism were genuine or were required of the slaves. Slaves in the French colonies were almost universally Catholic, because the *Code Noir*, the French rules that governed slaveholding, required baptism and Christian training for all slaves.

French Catholic women had established a strong presence in Canada, where convents were scattered throughout the colony. These communities were charged with converting the Native Americans, and indeed a number of Indian girls and women found Catholicism attractive. As the French moved south along the Mississippi River and to their outpost at New Orleans, Catholic women traveled with them. Some of the women wished for a devout life, but baulked at assuming formal holy orders and elected instead to join laywomen's confraternities. These Catholic associations were devoted to charitable works, prayer, and preservation of moral order. Most of the women who joined a confraternity were married women and mothers, but felt a spiritual calling to service not met through traditional roles available to women. These confraternities tended to be led by women from elite families, but members came from all walks of society, and it is possible that some women of color may have been members. The confraternities opened medical facilities, orphanages, and schools.

Although Catholicism grew in small, isolated pockets throughout the colonial period, after the American Revolution an influx of immigrants and the loosening of religious strictures swelled the church to around 30,000 members. Massive emigration from Ireland in the 1830s and 1840s pushed the number of Catholics in America into the millions. As the Catholic Church became more powerful, an increasingly patriarchal quality relegated women to supporting roles. The Catholic women of early America, possibly because of the persecution and the frontier nature of the environment, played a far more active and influential role than would be available to women until the twentieth century.

See also Brent, Margaret; Convents; Seton, Elizabeth Ann Bayley; Tekakwitha, Kateri

Further Reading

Clark, Emily. "By the Conduct of their Lives: A Laywomen's Confraternity in New Orleans, 1730–1744. *William and Mary Quarterly*, 3d ser. 54 (1997): 769–794.

Glazier, Michael, and Thomas J. Shelley, eds. *The Encyclopedia of American Catholic History.* Collegeville, MN: Liturgical Press, 1997.

Hardy, Beatriz Betancourt. "Women and the Catholic Church in Maryland, 1689–1776." *Maryland Historical Magazine* 94 (1999): 396–418.

Kenneally, James J. *The History of American Catholic Women.* New York: Crossroad, 1990.

Mannard, Joseph G. "Converts in Convents: Protestant Women and the Social Appeal of Catholic Religious Life in Antebellum America." *Records of the American Catholic Historical Society of Philadelphia* 104 (1993): 79–90.

Charitable Works

See Benevolent Societies

Childbirth

Childbirth was a painful and frightening experience for women in early America. Although the sad sight of mothers buried beside their infant children in colonial cemeteries testifies to the dangers of childbirth, maternal death in childbirth was uncommon. One maternal death per 200 births was typical in colonial America. If a woman delivered eight children in her life, she had less than a 5 percent chance of dying in childbirth. Statistics for infant survival are more difficult to determine, because stillborn infants and miscarriages were rarely recorded. An examination of diaries left by eighteenth-century midwives reveals an infant mortality rate of 2 to 3 percent.

Childbirth in colonial America was considerably safer than in Europe. America did not have the crowded urban conditions and its accompanying problems with sanitation that made medical conditions poor in much of Europe. A plentiful and varied diet improved the overall health among Americans, leading to a greater likelihood for a pregnancy to be carried to term and for a mother to have the strength to survive the rigors of delivery.

The average age of marriage for colonial women was twenty-two, and a typical woman could expect to give birth around sixteen months later. The next twenty years of her life would be interspersed with childbirth approximately every fifteen to twenty months. Colonial families were large, with six to eight pregnancies being typical.

Pregnancy

It was common for a woman to maintain her normal activities and workload in the months and weeks leading up to delivery. Unless a health crisis such as vaginal bleeding indicated danger, pregnant women engaged in household labor, travel, and even farmwork. Maternity clothes were an unknown luxury, with most women simply altering their normal clothing to accommodate their expanding bodies. Beginning around 1600 most pregnant women wore a skirt with a simple drawstring waist that was easily altered as the pregnancy advanced. The waistband of skirts and petticoats were tied up over the expanding abdomen, and no attempt was made to adjust hemlines to make the skirts hang evenly in front.

Folk remedies for the discomforts of pregnancy were many. A vinegar and rosewater solution was recommended to ease the swelling of feet and ankles. Swathing bands were tied around the bottom of the abdomen and back of the neck to ease the pressure of the growing child. It was widely believed that expectant mothers needed to remain calm and pampered throughout the pregnancy, for ungratified longings could mark the child in the womb with the color or shape of the food that had

---

Childbirth and Diaries

Diaries of early Americans recorded financial transactions and workaday events. The terseness with which the births of children are recorded might appear odd to present-day readers, who might easily misinterpret the brief entries as lack of interest. In 1755 Matthew Patten noted in his journal, "My wife was delivered about 8 in the morning of a Son and sold a cow to William Macmeal of New Boston." Joshua Hempstead noted on 30 July 1716, "I was all day getting waylogs and launching timber, my wife delivered of a daughter about sunset."

The brevity of these entries was consistent with the terse cultural style of eighteenth-century journal writing, rather than a sign of indifference.

Source: Ulrich, Laurel Thatcher. "Women's Travail, Men's Labor: Birth Stories from 18th Century New England Diaries." *Dublin Seminar for New England Folklife* 26 (2001): 170–183.

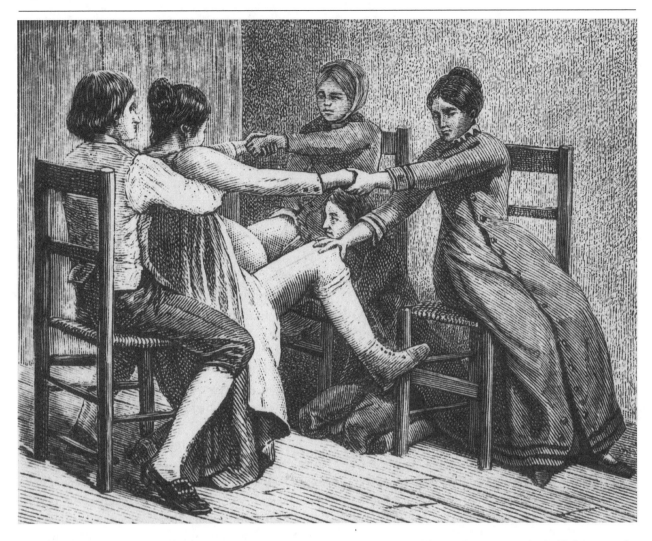

Colonial childbirth scene. Many women gave birth sitting on chairs or supported by another person who held them upright during the critical stages of delivery. (Bettmann/CORBIS)

been craved. Likewise, if a woman looked or stared at a deformed person, it was believed the deformity could be inflicted upon her own child.

Pregnancy was considered a normal part of a woman's life, and unlike in Victorian times, there were no social prohibitions against pregnant women appearing in public. As a practical matter, women in their later terms were reluctant to ride a horse or travel long distances, but medical books condoned moderate exercise.

In preparing for the arrival of a child, expectant mothers often traveled to their parents' home. This was possibly used as a respite from the work at home, as well as the pregnant woman's desire for

care and attention from her own mother. Another decision made by the expectant mother was the choice of who was to attend the birth. Midwives dominated the delivery of children in seventeenth- and eighteenth-century America. In the late eighteenth century, male physicians began to make inroads into the delivery of children, although modesty and cultural traditions made midwives the preferred practitioners.

Labor and Delivery
Other than providing a comforting reassurance, there was little midwives actually did during labor. In a normal labor midwives simply let nature take

its course, tied the umbilical cord, and helped deliver the afterbirth. In complicated cases they might attempt to turn a child that was not in the correct position. Hard liquor was usually the only drug used to comfort a woman in labor. Warm cloths on the stomach or an enema might be used to help open the vaginal passage.

In addition to a midwife or doctor, a series of neighboring women or female relatives would attend the birth. There was a strong taboo against husbands being present for the birth, and many diaries indicate that fathers were often tending fields or even asleep during their wife's labor. Neighborhood women provided the main source of comfort and moral support during the long hours of labor. They brought food for the woman to keep up her strength, with toast, broth, gruel, or eggs being the most commonly recommended food for a laboring woman. They also tended to any other young

---

Childbirth among Native American Women (1655)

Customs surrounding childbirth among Native American women varied across cultures. Here, Dutch surveyor Adriaen Van der Donck described the customs surrounding birth in the New York area.

> When the time of their delivery is near . . . they depart alone to a secluded place near a brook, or stream of water, where they can be protected from the winds, and prepare a shelter for themselves with mats and covering, where, provided with provisions necessary for them, they await their delivery without the company or aid of any person. After their children are born, and if they are males, although the weather be ever so cold and freezing, they immerse them some time in the water, which, they say, makes them strong brave men and hardy hunters. After the immersion they wrap their children in warm clothing . . .
>
> The native Indian women of every grade always nurse their own children, nor do we know of any who have trusted that parental duty to others.

Source: Van der Donck, Adriaen. *Description of the New Netherlands* (1655). Collections of the New York Historical Society, 2d series, v. 1.

---

children in the household that needed supervision. Midwive's manuals recommend the presence of these women, "their cheerful conversation supports [the patient's] spirits and inspires her with confidence" (Scholten 1977, 433).

Most women sat on birthing stools for delivery. These chairs were low to the floor, with props to hold the mother's extended legs. The seat was open, allowing for the midwife to have access. Other laboring women might kneel on a pallet or lie in the arms of another woman who would hold her upright during the worst of the labor pains. Few women chose to lie flat in bed.

In the early years of colonial America, doctors were called only in the most difficult of labors. If a woman appeared unable to deliver the child, physicians had tools for the extraction of the child. Use of these tools usually resulted in the delivery of a dead infant. Later, as the tools and medical skill improved, forceps were used to deliver living children. Thus by the late eighteenth century, doctors were being called on to assist in normal deliveries.

Folk remedies of dubious effectiveness were sometimes used to hasten a prolonged labor. Cinnamon tea or drinking water in which a swallow's nest had been dissolved was believed to ease a birth. Applying a magnet to the vagina was believed to help draw an infant out. It was commonly believed during the eighteenth century that women were more likely to begin their labor during a full or new moon. The reasoning was that these phases of the moons caused high tides, and might also result in a pull on blood pressure to bring about labor.

Dangers of Childbirth

Complications during delivery included tearing of the perineum and life-threatening hemorrhages. Eclampsia was a condition of dangerously elevated blood pressure that could sometimes occur during labor or the later stages of pregnancy. Symptoms were severe nausea, blurred vision, dizziness, and convulsions. The causes of eclampsia are unknown even today, but it could result in convulsions so severe they could be fatal to both mother and infant.

Often the most dangerous time for a woman was during the days following birth. Puerperal fever, also known as childbed fever, was caused by an infected wound in the uterine cavity. High temperature and pelvic pain were the first symptoms, but these were usually followed by delirium and death. Because it was caused by the streptococcus bacterium, colonial doctors had no way to treat the disease. Once it set in, puerperal fever was almost always fatal. Ironically, rates of puerperal fever were higher among births tended by doctors rather than midwives. A doctor's heavier reliance on medical instruments resulted in a greater number of maternal wounds and likelihood of infection. Puerperal fever could emerge any time within two weeks of delivery, but if a woman passed this stage without infection, she was likely to make a complete recovery.

Physicians who attended difficult births had a greater range of pain remedies than did midwives. Laudanum and opium might be used to ease pain, although too much of the drugs might cause a woman to lose consciousness and possibly even stop her contractions. The addictive nature of the drugs also caused some women to develop dependencies on them.

Lying-In

Midwives and physicians did not linger after delivery. If there were no signs of maternal danger, the midwife left once the afterbirth was delivered. The new mother was then in the care of her female relatives.

A newly delivered mother was confined to bed, ideally for three to four weeks. This lying-in period was to restore a mother's strength. She was to stir as little as possible for the first few days following birth. Over the next few weeks she was to be fed a diet of red meat, eggs, wine, and ale. The room was kept as warm as possible in order to prevent catching a cold. Hot drinks were recommended to ward off contagion. Although women who could not afford several weeks of idleness might rise from bed after a week, most new mothers were able to depend on the services of relatives and neighbors to relieve them of their chores and child care responsibilities.

The custom of a "groaning party" was used by New England mothers to mark the end of the lying-in period and to thank her attendants. The term is a

What to Name the Baby?

Parents in early America followed regional tradition in the selection of baby names. The Puritan parents of New England usually chose biblical names. The names Elizabeth, Mary, and Sarah accounted for more than half of all girl names in seventeenth-century New England. Girls were also given names that exemplified traditional virtues, such as Charity, Comfort, Deliverance, Hope, Patience, Peace, Silence, and Temperance. Settlers in the middle and southern colonies were more likely to name their children after English royalty or family names. Thus, Charles, Edward, William, Anne, Elizabeth, and Margaret were the most popular names.

Use of necronyms, or the names of recently deceased relatives, was enormously common throughout the colonies. In New England, when a child died, there was an 80 percent likelihood that the next child of the same gender born to the parents would be named after the dead child. The tragic case of Ephraim and Elizabeth Hartwell testifies to the comfort parents found in necronyms. In 1740 they lost all five of their children to throat distemper. In the coming years they had nine more children, five of who were named Ephraim, Samuel, John, Elizabeth, and Isaac after the children lost in 1740.

Source: Fischer, David Hackett. *Albion's Seed: Four British Folkways in America.* New York: Oxford University Press, 1989.

double entendre of "groaning" referring to both the agonies of childbirth and a table loaded with food.

See also Birth Control; Breastfeeding; Midwives; Motherhood

Further Reading

Leavitt, Judith Walzer. *Brought to Bed: Childbearing in America, 1750–1950.* New York: Oxford University Press, 1986.
Scholten, Catherine M. *Childbearing in American Society: 1650–1850.* New York: New York University Press, 1985.
———. "On the Importance of the Obstetrick Art: Changing Customs of Childbirth in America, 1760 to 1825. *William and Mary Quarterly* 34 (1977): 426–445.

Ulrich, Laurel Thatcher. *A Midwife's Tale: The Life of Martha Ballard, Based on Her Diary, 1785–1812.* New York: Vintage Books, 1991.

Wertz, Richard W., and Dorothy C. Wertz. *Lying-In: A History of Childbirth in America.* New York: Schocken Books, 1979.

Childhood

See Girlhood and Adolescence

Children, Custody of

There were a number of circumstances in early America that caused children to be placed outside of the legal control of their birth parents. Although in contemporary times we tend to associate custody disputes with divorce, marital breakdown accounted for only a tiny percentage of custody decisions in early America. More often, courts intervened to determine custody upon the death of a father, mental incompetence or financial inability of parents to support their children, or to arrange for the indenture or apprenticeship of children.

Children were regarded as economic assets in colonial America. In the labor-scarce American colonies, the work of a child between the ages of ten and eighteen was the most valuable economic commodity most families had at their disposal. There was little sentimentality about children, who could be indentured to perform labor as young as five years old. Childhood was not viewed as an independent, formative stage of development that must be nurtured with parental love. Rather, children were future workers who needed religious instruction, physical care, and training in an appropriate vocation. The law was tailored to protect the economic interest of the father and the state, rather than the best interest of the child.

Because children were viewed primarily as economic assets, fathers of legitimate children had almost unlimited legal authority over their children. Common law in England and America provided mothers with very little legal power to control their children's fate. A father could bind his child out for indentured servitude or apprenticeship without the mother's consent. He could likewise send the chil-dren to live in another household, if he thought it in their best educational or economic interest. Should a father die, the children's guardian was determined by the father's written will. Circumstances resulting in a loss of a mother's custody of her children are delineated below:

Death of a Father

The importance of a biological tie between parent and child was not of overriding interest in early America. Mothers were not automatically assumed to receive custody of their children following their husbands' death. Common law recognized the appointment of separate guardians for the child's physical custody and the administration of the child's inheritance. Father's wills usually granted physical custody of the children to the mother, but appointed another male relative to control the child's estate until sons reached the age of twenty-one, or until a daughter married. If a father feared his widow's ability to economically support his children, he had the right to request a court bind his children out for service.

It was not uncommon for a father to die before his children reached the age of maturity, and the chance his widow would remarry was high. Once a woman remarried she lost her independent legal identity and authority to act in the best interest of her children. As such, many men made provisions in their wills to safeguard their children's financial and physical well-being from a future stepfather.

Poverty and Indentures

The law in colonial America demanded that parents educate their children to read and train them in an appropriate vocation so they would not become a burden to society. Parents who failed in their duty to train their children to become economically productive members of the community risked losing custody. Terms such as *binding out* and *apprenticing* referred to the common custom of training children to become skilled workers. It was also a solution to the thousands of orphaned or impoverished children who had no other means of support. These arrangements were legally sanctioned and enforced by the courts. Once a child was bound out, surviving parents had no control over the care and treatment of their child. Binding out could be voluntary, as in cases where a household was too poor to support or train a child. Involuntary apprenticeships occurred when children were orphaned or their parents were judged too incompetent to raise the child.

In New England, town officials had the right to enter a household and question a child about his education and skills. Children found wanting could be removed from the home and apprenticed to another master. Extreme poverty also prompted the termination of parental rights. In a time when there was no economic safety net, some parents found themselves so poor that they were forced to give their children up. This was especially true of widowed mothers. Court records from children's indentures reveal the pitiful state that drove some mothers to give up their children. In 1661 Elenor Empson was so desperate she agreed to bind out her daughter Mary for two years. The unusually short period of service indicates Mrs. Empson intended only temporary relief until she was able to find means of supporting her child. "Note that I, the said Elenor Empson, am, constrained to dispose of the said child above specified for the present relief, otherwise it might have perished in the condition I am left in" (*Charles County Court Proceedings, 1658–1662*, 136–137).

Illegitimate Children

Fornication was a crime in colonial America, and children who were the product of illicit unions became the custody of the courts. Neither the mother nor the father was automatically entitled to custody of these children, because both were believed to be morally unfit individuals. The town where the child had been born was responsible for finding a home for the child. Because infants were a burden rather than an economic asset, most towns allowed the mother to care for the child at least until it had been weaned. Thereafter, illegitimate children were often bound out for service, the boys until age twenty-one, and the girls until age eighteen or marriage. These children bore a lifelong stigma as bastards and were not entitled to any inheritance or support from their parents. The mothers of these children were also stigmatized with public whippings, social shame, and the trauma of having a child taken from them. Such would be severe even if it occurred at birth, but because towns usually demanded the children be weaned, most mothers would likely have bonded to the child by the time it was taken from her.

Divorce or Separation

Only a tiny percentage of custody cases were the result of divorce or separation, but the shifting manner in the outcome of custody battles reflect important changes in how society viewed children and the importance of motherhood. Although divorce was rare in the colonies, it was legally sanctioned in most areas, especially in New England. Most of the documentation from divorce records address issues such as which partner was at fault and how the property was to be divided. Children were rarely discussed. In the 227 cases of divorce in eighteenth-century Massachusetts, children were mentioned in only one-third of the cases. These references were rarely in regard to custody, but were rather cited as evidence of infidelity (in the cases of long absent husbands whose wives bore children) or how the offending spouse has brought ruin to his or her children's home.

Common-law tradition granted fathers absolute right to custody of their children, even in cases where the husband was found to be the offending party in a divorce suit. Children were assets of an estate, totally owned and controlled by the father. Because their services and earnings belonged to the father, children were entirely under their father's control. A deeply ingrained prejudice common in colonial America held that mothers were naturally disposed to spoil their children. Fathers were responsible for the moral, religious, and physical training of their children. They were therefore better equipped to train children to be productive, skilled members of the community. There was no evidence that protecting the "best interest of the child" ever figured into eighteenth-century custody disputes.

Although custody of children became a hotly contested battle in nineteenth-century divorce cases, it is surprisingly absent from eighteenth-century divorces. There are two possible explanations for this phenomenon. Knowing that custody was almost automatically awarded to fathers, many women might not have even asked for it. Such a predicament can be illustrated by Nancy Shippen Livingston (1763–1841). At the age of sixteen, she was pressured by her parents to marry the dissolute Henry Livingston. By age seventeen she had a baby daughter and a miserably unhappy marriage. Her husband insisted the child be raised in a nearby home by his relatives, and Nancy had no legal authority to countermand this order. Limited to sporadic visits with her child, Nancy threatened to bring an action of divorce. Henry retaliated by absconding with the child. Nancy ultimately decided not to pursue a divorce in order to have the child brought back where she might visit with her. Nancy Shippen Livingston is likely one of many women whose fear of losing contact with their children dissuaded them from pursuing a divorce. Most women who filed divorce suits were either childless or were willing to surrender custody of their children.

Another explanation for the lack of custody battles in eighteenth-century divorces might be that the custody decisions were settled between the parties before the case ever came to court. In cases of mutually agreed marital separation, custody decisions were negotiated between the couple. Separations and divorces were rare owing to the expense of maintaining two households. More commonly, one spouse simply abandoned the home. In such cases, the fleeing spouse rarely brought their children along with them.

Custody became more contentious in the nineteenth century. As society became increasingly industrialized, the labor of children was no longer so crucial an issue in the home. The period of childhood was recognized as an independent, formative stage, in which the nurturing care of a mother assumed greater importance than the vocational training of the child. When determining custody of a child, courts began considering the qualifications and conduct of the parent, the age of the child, and the ability of the parent to provide a stable environment, all with the best interest of the child in mind.

In Connecticut, the case of *Nickols v. Giles* (1796) set a precedent when it granted custody to the mother. Mr. Nickols was a man of hot temper, little property, and no home. His wife had left him and moved in with her father, who was providing for both her and the child. Nickols sued the grandfather, Giles, for the return of his child. The court, ignoring hundreds of years of legal tradition, observed that in the grandfather's home the child was "well taken care of, and not likely to be so by the father." (*Nickols v. Giles*, 2 Root 461 Conn., 1796). Although the law was designed to favor fathers, judges began to exercise judicial discretion when they looked outside traditional common law to find justification for considering the best interest of the child over the rights of the father. Over the coming decades, mothers won occasional cases in which the fathers were clearly abusive or incompetent.

By the mid-nineteenth century, courts were predominantly operating with the child's best interest as their primary consideration. In the absence of mitigating factors such as alcoholism or adultery, children of "tender years" were almost always placed with the mother. Boys of older age were usually considered better off under the care of their fathers. In 1840 a New York court articulated the principle that all custody decisions should be made with no preference based on the sex of the parent. Other states soon followed suit, although in practice custody disputes were decided increasingly in favor of the mother, unless there was some grossly disqualifying factor.

See also Divorce; Orphaned Girls; Poverty

Further Reading

Dayton, Cornelia Hughes. *Women before the Bar: Gender, Law, and Society in Connecticut, 1639–1789.* Chapel Hill: University of North Carolina Press, 1995.

Goldstein, Jacob, and C. Abraham Fenster. "Anglo-American Criteria for Resolving Child Custody Disputes from the Eighteenth Century to the Present: Reflections on the Role of Socio-Cultural Change." *Journal of Family History* 19 (1994): 35–56.

Grossberg, Michael. *Governing the Hearth: Law and the Family in Nineteenth Century America.*

Chapel Hill: University of North Carolina Press, 1985.

Mason, Mary Ann. *From Father's Property to Children's Rights: The History of Child Custody in the United States.* New York: Columbia University Press, 1994.

Zainaldin, Jamil S. "The Emergence of a Modern American Family Law: Child Custody, Adoption, and the Courts, 1796–1851." *Northwestern University Law Review* 73 (1979): 1038–1089.

Church of England

See Anglican Women

Civil Disobedience

Although the term *civil disobedience* was not coined until the nineteenth century, women of early America were familiar with the concept of resisting authority. Civil disobedience implies public defiance of laws that govern society. In some cases, the acts were intended to call attention to perceived injustice, such as slavery or taxation without representation. Other uses of civil disobedience were intended to frighten passive citizens into action, such as during Bacon's Rebellion when western settlers used the threat of hostile Indians to try to force changes in colonial policies.

Many of the original settlers arrived in America after decades of opposition to the Church of England. Resisting religious authority was a well-established tradition among Puritans, and Anne Hutchinson stands as an example of a woman willing to continue her nonconformity in the face of extreme pressure. Anne Hutchinson attempted to shift theological interpretations of doctrine. Because her concerns were limited primarily to intellectual meanings of theology, the argument can be made that she was not engaging in true civil disobedience because she was not attempting to change society. Such cannot be said of her friend Mary Dyer, who repeatedly risked her life in her attempts to force concession for freedom of religious worship.

Women who rebelled against accepted norms were rarely welcome in colonial society. Ironically,

they had the greatest freedom to step outside their traditional domestic roles when they were advocating for the protection of home and hearth. Issues such as poverty, drunkenness, education, and the destructive forces of slavery on the family all provided women with socially acceptable avenues for civic activism. On a more fundamental level, they also became engaged in overt rebellion during times of crisis, such as Indian wars, political uprisings, and the American Revolution.

Early America was marked by a number of political revolts, including Bacon's Rebellion (1676–1677), Leisler's Rebellion (1689–1691), Shay's Rebellion (1786–1787), and the Whiskey Rebellion (1794). These insurrections shared the common trait of a breakdown of mechanisms for the redress of grievances. Although men led the charge during these revolts, there is substantial evidence that women supported their actions. Providing moral support, the provision of supplies, and acting as couriers were all part of women's roles in these rebellions.

Leisler's Rebellion was localized in New York, where leading Dutch citizens took the opportunity to seize power back from the English upon the dethroning of King James II. The response of women to the temporary change of government was curious. Some Dutch women eagerly embraced the Dutch cause, serving as couriers during the rebellion. Others were so hostile to the rebellion they resorted to physical violence. Mrs. Trijntje Jans helped instigate a riot and personally assaulted one of the provisional leaders of the rebellion. When the leader of the rebellion, Jacob Leisler, was hanged in 1691, it is said that his heart was cut from his body on orders of a woman who paid a bounty for it. Although they had few avenues for formal legal power, the passionate response of New York women to Leisler's Rebellion was a clear indicator that women were ardently concerned with matters that affected their communities.

Sometimes civil discord was sparked from fear. A shocking incident from 1677 records the violent reaction of women who had been living in fear of Indian attacks. The incident occurred near the conclusion of King Philip's War, the bloodiest conflict in seventeenth-century New England. In response to westward encroachment of white settlers, Indian tribes banded together and launched a series of raids, attacking more than half of the ninety fledgling settlements throughout New England. Citizens of Marblehead, Massachusetts, had been living in dread for more than two years, made worse by the periodic disappearance of fishing vessels and their crew. Most of the sailors never returned, but in the summer of 1677, a small band of captured fishermen managed to escape Indian custody and sailed back into town with two Indian hostages. The women of the town responded to the presence of the Indians with stark brutality. Despite the efforts of the fishermen to defend their hostages, a large throng of the town's women attacked the Indian captives. They alternately beat and stoned the Indians, causing their deaths, after which the women dismembered the corpses. This savage aggression among women was rare in colonial America, but it is proof that women were not immune from frontier vigilantism.

Bacon's Rebellion in Virginia was also sparked by the anxiety of frontier settlers who lived in fear of restless Indians. Women living in the remote western settlements of Virginia were often forced to seek temporary shelter with their neighbors in order to establish safety in numbers. Believing that the government officials, who lived safely ensconced in towns clinging to the eastern seaboard, had little concern for the safety of the frontier colonists, the settlers took up arms against the colonial administration. Years of trepidation marked by periodic attacks by Indians encouraged frontier women to eagerly support Nathaniel Bacon in his rebellion against the colonial government. As Bacon made his way toward Jamestown, women supplied the rebels with provisions and shelter. Some women carried letters between rebel forces.

After the defeat of the rebellion, government officials expressed frustration that these women could not be punished for their activities. The law of coverture made a woman's husband legally liable for her actions, with murder, treason, and maintaining a brothel the only exceptions to the law. Most of the aid rendered by the women was considered short of treason, and they could therefore not be

The Case of Lydia Chisman

Lydia Chisman was married to one of the leaders of Bacon's Rebellion, Major Edmund Chisman. Upon the conclusion of the rebellion, Major Chisman was captured and put on trial for his life. When Chisman was asked by Governor Berkeley to explain his treasonous behavior, Lydia Chisman unexpectedly stepped forward from the assembled observers. She claimed it was upon her insistence that her husband joined the rebellion, and had she not been so relentless in her appeals, Major Chisman would never have joined the rebels. She sank to her knees, confessed her own treasonous guilt, and asked that she be hanged in lieu of her husband. Contemporary observers attested to the power of her plea, but Governor Berkeley remained unmoved. Major Chisman died in prison while awaiting execution, and his estate was confiscated. Two years later, tempers had cooled and amnesty was extended to many of the rebels. Lydia Chisman succeeded in gaining the return of her estate and eventually remarried.

Source: Westbury, Susan. "Women in Bacon's Rebellion." In *Southern Women: Histories and Identities,* ed. Virginia Bernhard. Columbia: University of Missouri Press, 1992.

punished in the same manner as male supporters of the rebellion.

After the primary rebel leaders were executed, a general pardon was extended to other supporters of the rebellion. The governor specifically excluded Mrs. Sarah Grendon from the pardon, claiming she had played a great part in assisting and promoting the horrid rebellion. The governor attempted to put her on trial for treason, but was unsuccessful in convincing the attorney general of the colony to proceed against her. In order to prevent women from escaping justice so easily in the future, the Virginia Assembly passed legislation in 1677 to make women accountable for any future acts of rebellion. Specific penalties for women rebelling against the government were delineated, including stiff fines and public lashings.

In stark contrast to the contempt received by women who participated in unsuccessful rebellions, women were celebrated for their contributions to the American Revolution. Women took part in urban protests and boycotts and organized petition campaigns. They formed charitable groups to assist the families of men on active duty or the widows of soldiers. When storekeepers appeared to be profiting through price gouging, groups of women organized to force them to lower their prices. Women were also involved in violent mob action that resulted in the tar and feathering of merchants.

More than thirty food riots occurred between 1776 and 1779. Women were involved in and even instigated many of the riots. A typical example occurred in Fishkill, New York. When merchant Jacobus Lefferts received a large shipment of tea, for which he intended to charge premium prices, a band of women gathered in August 1776 to dissuade him. After unsuccessfully attempting to recruit some local men to assist them, the gang of women traveled en masse to Lefferts's store, where they informed him he would part with his tea for the "continental price" of six shillings per pound, the price recently passed by the Continental Congress as a fair charge. Lefferts refused, and the women appointed two of their members to serve as a clerk and a weigher. They seized the tea and carefully measured it into one-pound parcels. Rather than paying Lefferts, the departing women told him they would donate the proceeds from their tea sale to a Revolutionary county committee. Whether these rebellious ladies were true to their word is not recorded.

During times of severe political turmoil, it was natural for women to take a stance when they witnessed threats to their home or livelihood. In the absence of a crisis, most women opted out of public affairs. In times of danger and revolutionary turmoil, many women abandoned traditional norms and engaged in outright civil disobedience.

See also Boycotts

Further Reading

Axtell, James. "The Vengeful Women of Marblehead: Robert Roule's Deposition of 1677." *William and Mary Quarterly* 31 (1974): 647–652.

Meyers, Debra. "The Civic Lives of White Women in Seventeenth Century Maryland." *Maryland Historical Magazine* 94 (1999): 309–327.

Voorhees, David William. "How Ther [sic] Poor Wives Do, and Are Delt [sic] with: Women in Leisler's Rebellion." *De Halve Maen* 70, no. 2 (1997): 41–48.

Westbury, Susan. "Women in Bacon's Rebellion." In *Southern Women: Histories and Identities,* ed. Virginia Bernhard. Columbia: University of Missouri Press, 1992.

Cloth Making

See Textile Industry

Clothing

Children in colonial America wore loose-fitting, smocklike dresses until the age of four or five. These smocks were worn by both girls and boys, because they facilitated changing diapers and were easy to alter for rapidly growing bodies. Once children began wearing clothing specific to their gender, there was very little difference between the styles of children and adult clothing.

Daily wear for women consisted of a series of layers. A white linen shift was the first layer. Loose, with a wide neck and falling to the ankles, this served double duty as a nightgown and as the first layer of clothing. Next came a petticoat, which was fastened with a tie around the waist. The "gown" referred to the outer layer of clothing, consisting of a bodice sewn to yet another skirt. The skirted portion of the gown was often parted in the middle, to reveal the petticoats beneath.

The use of corsets and other garments used to reshape a woman's figure varied throughout the colonial period. A "stomacher" was a triangular piece of fabric stiffened with whalebone. It was worn over the stomach and breasts and was held in place through ties or pins. It had the effect of lifting the breasts and aiding in upright posture. Although not a comfortable garment, it was far less restrictive than a corset. Corsets wrapped around the torso, stiffened with whalebone, and tied in the back. Pulling the strings tight could exaggerate the natural

Why did Women Wear Long Skirts?

Requiring yards of expensive fabric, each dress was a major expenditure for women who could rarely afford luxuries. Although the dresses of colonial women appear attractive to modern eyes, the question of why women wore such seemingly impractical garments must be asked. Skirts impeded movement at a time when most women engaged in manual labor on farms or in kitchens. They were a fire hazard near open cooking fires that remained lit all day. They collected dirt as women worked in the gardens or walked along unpaved paths.

On the practical side, skirts allowed for easy expansion and contraction during the years a woman's body was changing size through frequent pregnancies. In an era when menstrual protection required bulky rags and ties, skirts conveniently hid evidence of any encumbrance. During most seasons, the warmth provided by layers of fabric would have been welcome.

American women were not alone in their preferences for skirts. Anthropological studies of cultures throughout world history show that women have a marked preference for long skirts, with trousers only becoming an acceptable alternative for women in the twentieth century. Anthropologists have identified an "ideal ratio" of skirt, waist, and bodice proportion. A study of female silhouettes over a period of several hundred years reveals a long-standing preference for full skirts and a defined waist. This feminine silhouette appears to be most pleasing to both men and women throughout cultures. Thus, American women were following in a pattern that had centuries of tradition behind it.

Source: Kroeber, Alfred, and Jane Richardson. "Three Centuries of Women's Dress Fashions: A Quantitative Analysis." *Anthropological Records* 5 (1940): 111–153.

The use of hoops to expand a woman's skirt came in and out of fashion throughout the early American period. Once again, hoops were a mark of the well-to-do. The larger the hoop, the more formal the occasion. Hoops not only exaggerated the hourglass shape of a woman, they required a greater outlay of expensive fabric in direct proportion to the size of the hoop, creating a grand display as a woman entered a room. The first mention of hoops in the American colonies dates to 1709. The earliest hoops created a modest cone shape, although by the 1720s, wealthy women wore outlandishly large bell-shaped hoops. By the 1740s styles had changed again, and the "pannier" was in style. The pannier consisted of a wire frame on each hip, giving enormous exaggeration to the hips but creating a flat stomach. The pannier shape and the bell shape came in and out of fashion throughout the eighteenth century. By the early nineteenth century, the simple, classical styles did away with hoops for several decades. Classical dresses were simple garments that dropped straight to the floor, displaying little shape and did not require a corset.

Hoops and corsets tended to be restricted to the wardrobes of prosperous women. The changing style of hoops necessitated clothes tailored to the current size and shape of the hoop. Ordinary women could not afford the luxury of short-lived clothing. The average colonial passed their clothes down to future generations. A suit of clothes might be used between two and four generations before finally becoming too threadbare for further use. The poorest of women might have only one or two sets of clothing, although most had more. The average woman was concerned with utility, rather than display. In hot weather women were known to toil outdoors in only their shift, petticoat, and apron. This was not considered to be immodest or a state of undress.

Most women would have had several gowns. The 1688 accounting from Jane Humphrey's estate of Dorchester, Massachusetts, illustrates that even working-class women would have a variety of clothing. At the time of her death, she possessed five petticoats (two in red, one black, one green, and one white), five gowns of corresponding colors, four

curves of the figure, giving the woman an unnaturally narrow waist with voluptuous hips and bust. Such corsets were in fashion by the 1670s. The popularity of corsets varied, depending on a woman's social class. Because they inhibited mobility, they tended to be worn only by women who did not engage in manual labor.

aprons, numerous silk and calico neck cloths, a shawl, a cloak and hood, and a muff.

There was great regional variation in the fashion of clothing. Heavily influenced by Puritanism, the women of New England tended to dress in conservative fashions and colors. Despite the stereotype of Puritans dressing from head to toe in somber black, they dressed with far more variety and style. It is true they shunned the outlandish and provocative styles popular in Renaissance England. They discouraged high heels, plunging necklines, and embroidering precious metals, jewels, and lace onto clothing. Puritan styles appeared drab in comparison to high-flying fashions of the English court, but were hardly the stark costume engraved in popular memory. Black, brown, gray, red, and russets were the primary colors worn by New England women. Earlier settlers selected clothes for durability and warmth over fashion. Later generations, removed from the zeal of their founding mothers, tended to prefer more daring styles.

Settlers in the Chesapeake Bay area were far more flamboyant than New Englanders. Carrying on the cavalier tradition, they had no qualms about displaying wealth on their person. They favored brighter colors, plunging necklines, and adornment with lace, buckles, and jewelry. The women of the Chesapeake area thought of themselves as the most stylish women in the colonies and regarded northerners as dowdy by comparison.

Perhaps the most austere fashions were those worn by the Quakers of the middle colonies. Taking pride in "going plain in the world," Quaker women wore stark, simple colors. They shunned brightly dyed fabric, especially indigo, knowing such dye was produced using slave labor. They believed that wearing highly tailored or fashionable clothing was designed to provoke lust, and, therefore, women should opt for simple styles. Quakers tended to be people of wealth, and despite the severity of style, their clothing reflected their status. They used the finest silks and calicos that could be found. Foreign visitors to the colonies remarked on the fashion of Quaker women, generally finding them attractive in their simple, well-made gowns.

Colonial gowns did not have pockets, and many women wore large, U-shaped cloth bags under the outer skirts of their dresses. They usually covered their heads, either with a simple cap to keep their hair clean during daily chores, or a hood for warmth. Older women wore more substantial bonnets, a sign of age and status. Other accessories worn by Quaker women were neckerchiefs, which could be beautifully embellished fabrics or simple white cloths. They were worn draped around the shoulders and tucked into the bodice and served a dual purpose. Much easier to wash, they protected the bodice of the dress from oils and perspiration. They were also more likely to be more comfortable against the neckline than the stiff fabric of the bodice.

Shoes were usually made with wooden soles and covered in leather. Most had a low or no heel. The body of the shoe was also usually made of leather, with laces to tie the tops together. Wealthy women had shoes made of silk, damask, or taffeta. All shoes were expensive, and only the wealthy could afford to indulge in shoes made of such insubstantial fabric.

See also Body Image and Beauty; Sumptuary Laws

Further Reading
Baumgarten, Linda. *What Clothes Reveal: The Language of Clothing in Colonial and Federal America.* Williamsburg, VA: Colonial Williamsburg Foundation, 2002.

De Marley, Diana. *Dress in America: The New World, 1492–1800.* New York: Holmes and Meier, 1990.

Earle, Alice Morse. *Two Centuries of Costume in America.* London: Macmillan Co., 1903.

McClellan, Elisabeth. *Historic Dress in America, 1607–1870.* New York: Benjamin Blom, 1969.

Colonization, Effect on Indian Women

As European settlement of the eastern seaboard became more established, the way of life for Indian women was permanently changed. Some died from disease, some chose resistance to encroachment, and others found ways to assimilate aspects of European culture into their lives. Their only other option was the disruptive and temporary solution of westward migration. By the time of the American Revolution, 35 percent of all Indians in Rhode Island were living as part of a white household, usually as servants. Many of the others were on Indian reservations, but virtually all were trading or interacting with Europeans.

Disease

The most immediate and devastating effect of European colonization was the spread of infectious disease to which Native Americans had no immunity. The English came from an environment with centuries of exposure to smallpox and the measles. Europeans were not immune to the ravages of these diseases, but after centuries of periodic exposure, they had inherited limited resistance to infection. This resulted in a shorter duration of the sickness that mitigated its lethal effects.

When Europeans arrived in America, that very acquired resistance to disease proved deadly to Native Americans. Many Europeans carried dormant viruses and infections, which were harmless to the carrier, but deadly to the Indian. Virgin soil epidemics are the most lethal and debilitating of infectious diseases. Smallpox, measles, bubonic plague, and scarlet fever all swept through the Indian communities with relentless intensity. (See the entry entitled Disease for more detail on Native Americans and disease.) Communicable disease spread most readily in heavily populated areas, and the catastrophic effects of smallpox were worse for Indians of the densely settled Latin American regions than in the sparsely settled villages of the northeastern woodlands. Nevertheless, the periodic outbreak of disease was enough to demoralize and weaken the Indians even before the arrival of the *Mayflower*.

The ravages of disease had important consequences for Indian response to the settlers of North America. By the time English settlers arrived in Virginia and New England, disease had already thinned the ranks of the Indians. Periodic Spanish explorers and French trappers had made their appearance decades earlier, planting the viruses that would prove to be so deadly. Epidemics had taken their toll on Indian populations of the Chesapeake in the 1580s, 1608, and 1617. They did not associate their illnesses with the arrival of the Europeans, because the outbreaks were too sporadic to be attributed to the colonists.

The Indians were physically and spiritually weakened by the time the colonists began settlement in earnest. Young people were particularly vulnerable to disease, and many Indian women would have suffered the loss of a child. Some villages were almost completely demolished, causing the few survivors to seek out new tribes. With morale low and their lives already in a state of flux, few Indian tribes were prepared to negotiate with European settlers from a position of strength.

Economic Power

The importance of agriculture to the economy of most eastern Indian tribes resulted in substantial power for Native American women. They controlled all aspects of agricultural production, deciding what should be planted, when it should be harvested, and how it was to be distributed. Women were self-sufficient members of their community, able to trade their produce for whatever items they needed. They could withhold food from raiding or war parties, essentially giving the women veto power over actions of which they disapproved.

The arrival of European trading practices disrupted this pattern by elevating the value of furs and introducing alcohol to the Indians. Alcohol quickly became a commodity the Indians craved, and they were willing to provide whatever goods the settlers wanted in exchange for it. Furs were what the settlers valued above all else, and Indian men increased their hunting activities to supply the insatiable demands of white traders. As men went farther into the wilderness in search of increasingly scarce game, their absences from the village elongated. Indian men and women lived increasingly separate lives. The village became the women's sphere, while men roamed the countryside.

After the men dragged deer and beaver carcasses home, women skinned the animals and prepared the hides. Their agricultural activities faded in importance, as the fur trade became the dominant economic activity. Women lost control over the primary food supply and became dependent on the meat brought home by men. The matrilineal organization of many tribes broke down at the same time agriculture was pushed aside in favor of the fur trade. Traditional skills, such as making pottery, baskets, and stone axes, faded from memory. Indian women lost much of their economic independence and ability to support themselves as a result of the fur trade.

Alcohol

Indians had no experience with alcohol prior to the arrival of Europeans, who began selling rum to the Indians in the 1650s as an offshoot of their Caribbean sugar business. With no cultural traditions to govern the consumption of alcohol, strong liquor was freely consumed by Indian men, women, and children. Indians were ill-prepared for the ways in which alcohol clouded judgment, and many made poor decisions such as selling a year's supply of furs in exchange for a few bottles of watered-down rum. Families were impoverished by such actions, and they had little to eat other than what was provided by the subsistence farming performed by the women.

Indian women played a key role in the liquor trade. In the matrilineal tribes of the northeast, women had traditionally played major roles in the distribution of crops and material goods within their community. Women controlled almost all aspects of agricultural production, and they had the ability to barter their crops to traders who needed the produce. Women often accepted rum in exchange for corn, maple sugar, and wild rice. Other Indian women resorted to prostitution in order to obtain rum, although most preferred to trade food rather than their bodies.

The consumption of alcohol was quickly incorporated into Indian ceremonial practices, especially mourning rituals. Both men and women became deliberately intoxicated in an effort to come in contact with the spirit world. Missionaries did their best to discourage drinking, and many Christian Indians abstained altogether. Although Indian males clearly consumed more alcohol than Indian women, there were no gender prohibitions among the Indians that made drinking socially unaccept-

able for women. Alcohol proved to be a major force of destabilization for Indian communities, creating poverty, physical debility, and a destructive reliance on trade with white settlers.

Following the American Revolution, the U.S. government made periodic attempts to ban the selling of liquor to Indians. It was almost impossible to regulate the dealings of backcountry traders, and alcohol continued to be a serious problem among Indian communities for generations.

Slavery

English colonists experimented with Indian slave labor on a small scale, but it never reached the immense proportions practiced in the Spanish colonies. Slavery was not an alien concept to Native Americans. They had a long tradition of using captives of war as slaves, although their economy never depended on slave labor to function. As such, slavery was small scale, and not always a lifelong condition. Among forms of slavery practiced by Native Americans, children born to slaves were usually considered free.

Several factors made the Spanish version of large-scale enslavement of Indians impossible for the English colonists. Although disease took an appalling toll on North American Indians, the crippling effects of disease had been far more ferocious among the densely settled Latin American Indians. The pitifully few survivors of Central American epidemics were easier for the Spaniards to enslave. The English colonists arrived in small groups of settlers, rather than larger armies of trained soldiers. Outnumbered and underprovisioned, the English attempted coexistence, rather than forced slavery. Only after relations with the Indians deteriorated and the English gained military superiority did small-scale enslavement of Indian prisoners of war begin.

The first English colonists were desperately short of labor on arrival in America. During the initial years of settlement, they occasionally hired groups of Indians for large projects such as clearing fields or constructing a meetinghouse. Such labor was helpful, but did not alleviate the burden of daily domestic chores that weighed down the colonists.

Indians appeared willing to be hired for a few weeks of labor, but had no intention of entering into the long-term commitments common among English wage laborers.

After friendly relations with the Indians collapsed, the English began contemplating using captured Indians as slaves. Following the Pequot War of 1637, New England settlers took approximately 300 Indians captive as slaves. King Philip's War (1675–1676) also resulted in another round of enslavement for hundreds of Native Americans. Most of the slaves were women and children. Few colonists living on isolated farms welcomed the prospect of having a healthy adult Indian man as a slave. Such men were either killed outright or transported to the West Indies for enslavement. The colonists believed female slaves would be more compliant and already accustomed to performing domestic chores.

Enslavement of Indian women failed on several counts. Colonists believed the women would be fairly docile and capable of work. It was commonly believed that Indian women lived a subservient, drudgelike existence in their villages, and they would embrace the material comforts of white civilization. Compared with the heavy physical demands of Indian labor, the colonists believed Indian women would find household chores a welcome relief.

Most of the enslaved women had recently suffered the loss of a husband, son, or brother through warfare with the colonists, which embittered them toward their captors. Although Indian women were skilled at domestic service, the work on English farms was unfamiliar to them. Churning butter, milking a cow, dipping candles, and a whole range of such tasks were alien to these women. Language barriers hindered teaching such skills, even if the Indian women were willing to learn.

Escape was a real possibility for enslaved Indians. Unlike African slaves who had been transplanted into an alien land with no chance of return to their homes, Indian women were in familiar territory and knew that remnants of their families lived within a few days of travel. Some escaping slaves made the mistake of trusting other Indian tribes to shelter them. Escaping Pequot women often sought shelter with Algonquian tribes, but the Algonquians typically returned escaped slaves to the English, fearing retaliation should they be caught sheltering fugitive slaves. Despite such betrayals, a high percentage of Indian women eventually succeeded in escaping enslavement.

After the slave trade from Africa gathered momentum, colonists lost interest in Indian slaves. African slaves were less likely to run away and were more willing to learn new chores than the Indian slaves were. Rather than release their Indian slaves, many colonists had them shipped to the West Indies, where their new owners would not be confronted with the problems of runaways. By the late seventeenth century, most white communities abandoned their attempts to keep Indians as slaves.

Indians were also subjected to periods of forced indentured servitude. As European towns flourished, many Indians elected to trade or do business with the white settlers. Often these transactions were mutually agreeable, but over time conflicts emerged. When Indians were accused of stealing, cheating, or assault, they were subjected to the English judicial process under the same conditions and punishments as white colonists. Involuntary servitude was a common punishment for those who were unable to pay fines assessed by the court. Indians rarely had the cash or goods to satisfy judgments and often found themselves sentenced to several years of involuntary service. Indian women made up a high percentage of these convicted servants. Many Indian women were living in towns as wage servants, but should they be convicted of a crime, their status was forcibly changed for a fixed term of indentured servitude.

Interracial Relationships

Indian women sometimes elected to form alliances with white men. Unlike the case with black slaves, they were not compelled into such unions. Indian women could freely enter and leave these relationships with little difficulty. Over time, a class of mixed-race children were born. These children almost always remained with their mothers, although notable exceptions occurred, such as in the case of Mary Musgrove.

Sex ratios among many Indian groups became unnaturally skewed following European conquest. Indian men died fighting in battle or were sent to the West Indies as slaves. As settlers consumed Indian land, hunting grounds became limited. Young men tried to adjust to new economic conditions, either traveling farther away to hunt or migrating to towns in search of work. The changing lives of Indian men had a ripple effect on Indian women.

The sex ratio among European settlers remained unbalanced throughout the seventeenth century. Although Europeans had cultural prohibitions against interracial relationships, these were put on hold during times when few white women were available. There was no stigma among Indians who chose to associate with white settlers, and many women saw such relationships as a positive way to form alliances with a powerful new group of people.

The children of these interracial relationships were called Métis. Over time, Métis girls tended to become more subservient than their full-blooded Indian sisters. They married at a younger age than Indian girls and were less likely to have the freedom to select their own marriage partners. They absorbed European norms regarding sex roles and were less likely to be self-sufficient. Full-blooded Indian women had the ability to leave unhappy marriages, but such was rarely the case for Métis women. If a marriage proved unhappy, a Métis woman was often unable to support herself and had fewer close ties within the Indian community where she could turn for support. Although some of the interracial marriages were enduring and loving unions, many Indian women might have experienced profound anxiety as they adjusted to the differing gender expectations common among their European husbands.

See also Disease; Fur Traders' Wives; Interracial Marriage; Musgrove, Mary

Further Reading

Fickes, Michael F. "They Could Not Endure That Yoke: The Captivity of Pequot Women and Children after the War of 1637." *New England Quarterly* 73 (2000): 58–81.
Lurie, Nancy Oestreich. "Indian Cultural Adjustment to European Civilization." In *Seventeenth Century America: Essays in Colonial History*, ed. James Morton Smith. Chapel Hill: University of North Carolina Press, 1959.
Mancall, Peter C. "The Bewitching Tyranny of Custom: The Social Costs of Indian Drinking in Colonial America." *American Indian Culture and Research Journal* 17 (1993): 15–42.
———. "Men, Women, and Alcohol in Indian Villages in the Great Lakes Region in the Early Republic." *Journal of the Early Republic* 15 (1995): 425–448.
Nash, Gary. *Red, White, and Black: The Peoples of Early North America*. Englewood Cliffs, NJ: Prentice-Hall, 1992.
Sainsbury, John A. "Indian Labor in Early Rhode Island." *New England Quarterly* 48 (1975): 378–393.

Contraception
See Birth Control

Convents

A small number of Catholic women turned to holy orders in early America. Although offering a daughter to the church had a long history in Europe, it did not take root in America until the late eighteenth century. Protestant sects had renounced religious cloisters for women, and because so few Catholic women immigrated to America, there was intense pressure for these women to marry and safeguard the survival of the faith by nurturing strong and large Catholic families.

Religious discrimination in the English colonies prevented Catholics from establishing healthy and self-sustaining religious communities until after the Revolution. In 1727, French Ursuline nuns founded the first community of Catholic nuns in what was later to become the United States. They opened an orphanage and established a small school in New Orleans to educate girls, black children, and Native Americans.

The first convent of Anglo-American nuns was established at Port Tobacco, Maryland, in 1790. Founded by Carmelite nuns, this order was devoted to prayer, contemplation, and isolation from the outside world. Bishop John Carroll was reluctant to support such an order, believing there was a desperate need for nuns to teach, provide care for the poor, and spread the Catholic gospel. He wrote that although he believed society benefited from the sister's prayers, he preferred to support convents that permitted more active involvement in the world. Apparently, this activist philosophy was more appealing to women, because the teaching orders of the Visitandines and the Sisters of Charity attracted far more members than their contemplative sisters.

The Sisters of Charity was the most popular Catholic religious order for women, attracting members throughout the United States and Europe. They engaged in health care, education, teaching, and social services. The Visitandines were a semi-cloistered order that placed meekness, humility, and charity among their highest values. Although they lived in a restrictive environment, the Visitandines believed that teaching the poor was an important calling. The first group of Visitandines was established in Georgetown in 1799 by three women who had emigrated from Ireland.

The life of a nun was a unique choice for women in early America. Although most women were destined to become wives, mothers, and helpers in their family's trade, nuns renounced romantic entanglements and the possibility of motherhood. In lieu of assisting in a family business, these women embraced one of the few avenues available to women who sought active engagement in worldly activities. The convent offered women professional opportunities, social respect, and a support network of like-minded women. Although they led enormously restrictive personal lives, they had greater freedom to become involved in society at large. The convents in North America differed markedly from those in Latin America, which were primarily contemplative and isolated from the rest of society.

The life of a nun proved surprisingly tempting to a number of Protestant women. It is estimated that one in nine nuns in nineteenth-century America were women who converted to Catholicism as adults. Surviving records indicate many of these women were prompted to take up holy orders because it provided an avenue for them to pursue social causes and a more active role in spiritual devotion than available in other religious denominations.

The choice of these Protestant women is especially surprising given the mistrust of Catholicism rampant in early American society. Catholics were considered to be loyal to the pope rather than their nation. Elizabeth Seton was ostracized from her family when she chose to convert to Catholicism. Exacerbating the problem was a widespread misunderstanding of convents and holy orders. Some Protestants looked upon women who entered a convent as unnatural or hostile to motherhood. An editorial in the *Virginia Gazette* (25 April 1751) claims that convents were mere covers for a "dissolute way of living."

All of the convents in early America had a difficult time becoming established, some surviving for years with fewer than a dozen members. It was difficult to find funding and resources needed to sustain them. In the 1790s, there were only 30,000 Catholics in a population of almost 4 million people. There were few Catholic families who could afford to financially support the establishment of convents, and many young women were discouraged by their families from taking the unusual act of renouncing marriage and motherhood. Short of both money and members, many fledgling convents folded after a few years of operation. The Poor Clares of Georgetown (established in 1794) and the Trappistine nuns of New York City (established in 1810) each survived only for a few years.

There was no specific age that dictated when a woman could enter a convent. Records indicate some women joined as young as sixteen years of age, while others were in their seventies when they entered the convent. Many widowed women elected to join a convent after raising their children to adulthood. The average age for joining tended to be in a woman's early twenties. Contrary to popular belief, there was nothing to prevent a nun from leaving the order should she no longer feel a calling. Most women who entered convents were satisfied with their choices, as more than 80 percent of the women who became nuns never left their orders.

See also Catholic Women; Seton, Elizabeth Ann Bayley

Further Reading

Kenneally, James J. *The History of American Catholic Women.* New York: Crossroad, 1990.
Mannard, Joseph G. "Converts in Convents: Protestant Women and the Social Appeal of Catholic Religious Life in Antebellum America." *Records of the American Catholic Historical Society of Philadelphia* 104 (1993): 79–90.
Misner, Barbara. *Highly Respectable and Accomplished Ladies: Catholic Women Religious in America 1790–1850.* New York: Garland Publishing, 1988.

Cooking

A large part of a colonial woman's day was spent in food preparation, both for daily consumption and the preservation of food for later use. The central feature in all early American homes was the kitchen fireplace. Although small and crude in the earliest cabins, fireplaces soon evolved into spacious, walk-in structures in which several small fires could burn at one time, each calibrated to the particular function it was serving. Smoldering embers were used for raising biscuits, while blazing flames heated oversized cauldrons of water for cleaning. (The fireplace was the heart of family life, providing hot meals, warmth, and the primary source of light after the sun set.) It was in this room that families gathered for meals, conversation, and evening activities. Only in the South did the heat of the fireplace cause well-to-do settlers to construct the kitchen in a separate building.

There were four primary methods of cooking in early America: boiling, roasting, frying, and baking. Boiling was the most common method, because it could yield the classic one-pot meal. Such meals were easy to prepare, required little in the way of cooking utensils, and allowed a woman to go about other chores while the meal cooked. Diced meat and a few vegetables would be left to simmer for

A Chowder Recipe

Four pounds of fish are enough to make a chowder for four or five people. Use half a dozen slices of salt pork in the bottom of the pot, and hang above the fire so the pork will not burn. Take it out when done very brown; put in a layer of crackers, small or sliced onions, and potatoes sliced as thin as a four-pence. Mix with the pieces of pork you have fried; then a layer of fish again, and so on. Six crackers are enough. Strew a little salt and pepper over each layer. Over the whole pour a bowl-full of flour and water, enough to come up even with the surface of what you have in the pot. A sliced lemon adds flavor. A cup of tomato catsup is very excellent. Some people put in a cup of beer. A few clams are a pleasant addition. It should be covered so as not to let a particle of steam escape, if possible. Do not open it, except when nearly done, to taste if it be well seasoned.

Source: Child, Lydia Marie. *The Frugal American Housewife.* London: Tegg, 1832.

hours and made the most common supper. Grain dishes were also prepared in a single pot. Cornmeal cooked with molasses or milk was a popular dinner dish. The large cooking pot was used for boiling almost any food, including fish, fowl, porridges, puddings, and vegetables.

Roasting occurred over an open fire and was used for preparing large cuts of meat. This method was less common, simply because it required constant attention to the turning and basting of the meat, as well as maintaining the heat of the fire at the correct temperature for a prolonged period of cooking. Spits of various lengths and weights were needed for different sizes of meat. Turning the spit was usually relegated to children, because it was a tedious, but important chore.

Frying became popular in America because of the abundance and ease of raising hogs. Unlike cows, which required fencing, tending, and quality grazing pasture, hogs were allowed to forage for their own food. They bred easily and required no tending. The ease of raising hogs caused pork to become a staple of the American diet. Pork, ham,

Typical colonial kitchen at the Joseph Gilpin House, Delaware County. (Library of Congress)

and bacon have high fat content, making it perfect for frying in a pan. Other foods could then be fried in the rendered fat. Pork, and the subsequent fondness for the frying pan, was not nearly so common in Europe.

Baking was by far the most difficult task for any colonial woman to master. The earliest settlers would have made do by baking over an open fireplace. A heavy pot would be filled with dough and covered with a lid. Hot coals were placed on the lid, and changed frequently in an attempt to regulate the heat. Over time the settlers were able to build

ovens. In the South, ovens were made of brick, stone, or clay and were usually outdoors to keep heat out of the house. In northern colonies ovens were built to one side of the enormous fireplaces. Ovens were heated by placing hot coals inside the chamber. When it was hot, the coals were removed using a long-handled paddle, and the dough was placed inside.

Regulating the heat of the oven was the first challenge of baking, but other things were even more problematic. Baking must be done in warm, draft-free spaces. Knowing how long to allow the dough

An Apple Tansey

Take three apples, slice them round in thin slices, and fry them with butter; then beat four eggs with six spoonfuls of cream, a little rosewater, nutmeg, and sugar; stir them together, and pour it over the apples; let it fry a little, and turn it with a pie plate. Garnish with lemon and sugar strewed over it.

Source: Smith, Eliza. *The Compleat Housewife.* London: Buckland, 1766.

to rise, when to punch it down, and at what temperature to bake it is challenging even for contemporary bakers. Women living in drafty houses with fire-heated ovens had an especially delicate balancing act to perform in baking bread. The oven must be warmed to the correct temperature at precisely the same time the dough had risen to the proper level. The mystery of baking bread is one that many colonial women were never able to accomplish. For those who could bake, selling loaves of bread was often a welcome form of supplemental income.

Food Preservation

Cooking for daily meals was only a portion of a woman's responsibility regarding her family's dietary needs. Food production was seasonal, and in order to avoid monotony and nutritional deficiencies, woman needed to preserve certain food

Winter Squash Pie

Core, boil and skin a good squash, and bruise it well; take 6 large apples, pared, cored, and stewed tender, mix together. Add 6 or 7 spoonfulls of dry bread or biscuit, rendered fine as meal, half pint milk or cream, 2 spoons of rosewater, 2 ounces wine, 5 or 6 eggs, beaten and strained, nutmeg, salt and sugar to your taste, one spoon flour, beat all smartly together, bake.

The above is a good recipe for pumpkins, potatoes or yams, adding more moistening or milk and rosewater ... a few black or Lisbon currants, or dry whortleberries scattered in, will make it better.

Source: Simmons, Amelia. *American Cookery.* Albany: Webster, 1796.

items for consumption later in the year. Fall was the busiest season for preserving. Summer crops had been gathered, and corn needed to be dried, milled, and stored. Throughout the summer wild fruit, such as blueberries, strawberries, grapes, apples, plums, and cherries, were gathered. That which could not be consumed was dried, turned into jam, or fermented. Early settlers eagerly tried to make wine of the wild grapes, but were disappointed with the results. Apples were abundant, and cider became a primary alcoholic beverage throughout the American colonies. Apples were also turned into applesauce, apple butter, and dried apples.

Other preservation tasks were not dependent on the season. Animals, especially deer, were hunted year round. As much fresh meat as possible was consumed, but the rest needed to be preserved. Organ meat was consumed immediately, because it could not be preserved. Intestines were used for sausage casings. During hard winters, large cuts of meat could be hung in cellars where it would keep cold. At other times of the year it would be smoked or heavily salted in a brine solution to prevent spoilage. It was also possible to preserve cooked meat by cutting it into small pieces and covering them completely in lard.

Lard could be used to seal partially cooked vegetables in crocks for use in the winter. Root vegetables could be safely stored in a cellar with little preservation, but pickling was necessary for softer fruits and vegetables. Pickling infused the food with acid, preventing the growth of harmful bacteria. Items would be partially cooked to draw out water. If this were not done, the water in the vegetable's cells would dilute the vinegar, rendering the pickling less effective. All manner of foods were pickled, including cabbage, fennel, mushrooms, asparagus, cucumbers, onions, walnuts, and parsley. Salt and spices might be added to improve the flavor.

Dairy products were preserved by turning them into cheese and butter. Cheese making was a difficult chore, involving tending milk over the fire while it curdles, separating the curds from the whey, and shaping the curds. A soft cheese, such as cottage cheese or cream cheese, can be made in a few hours. The more desirable cheeses require weeks of pressing, turning, and keeping at an evenly maintained temperature. The best colonial cheeses took months to prepare. Because making cheese was difficult and required special cheese presses, many women chose to buy it from people who specialized in making it. Indeed, cheeses were often used in lieu of currency and were a valuable commodity for women who could make them.

The best place to store preserved food was in a cool cellar. Before loading it with the winter's food supply, the cellar needed to be prepared. Men banked earth up around their houses to prevent the cellar from freezing, which would destroy root crops. Women thoroughly cleaned, aired, and whitewashed the cellar before stocking it for the winter. Disaster could strike if the cellar became flooded or infested with rats. Watchful guard was kept over the cellar throughout the winter months. Should a particular item begin to rot (cabbages were notorious for spoilage), it needed to be removed before it attracted pests. If circulation was inadequate, grains could begin to ferment. If moisture leaked in, it could create dangerous frosts that would spoil whatever it touched.

By late autumn animals had been slaughtered, cider had been brewed, vegetables had been pickled, and grain had been barreled. A typical family would have between ten and thirty barrels of cider alone. The house would be stocked from cellar to loft with supplies, to be gradually drawn on throughout the long winter months.

Serving Meals

Tableware and dining utensils were a luxury in early America. Possession of a wide variety of plates, saucers, dishes, cups, teacups, and tea saucers were a mark of wealth that few possessed. A typical farming family in seventeenth-century America would have eaten off of an all-purpose trencher, a carved out piece of wood that measured ten or twelve inches wide and a few inches deep. It served as both plate and bowl. It would have been common for two people to share a trencher of food, because there might not have been enough for each family member to have his or her own. More prosperous families might have plates of earthenware or pewter. China did not make an appearance until the eighteenth century, and then only for the wealthy.

Spoons would have been the most common utensils. Most early American dishes were one-pot meals. Fish or meat was diced into soups and stews. Porridge, hominy, oatmeal, and ragout were also common meals. Spoons were made of wood, pewter, or silver, depending on the wealth of the family. On rare occasions when meat was prepared by roasting, it would be cut by a knife, served on trenchers, and eaten with the hands. Forks were a curiosity. John Winthrop brought a fork to Boston in 1633, and he kept it in a leather case. By the late eighteenth century, forks were beginning to become more common, although they were usually two pronged and used only to hold meat while it was being cut. Sometimes people used the fork to eat with, but just as often the meat was brought to the mouth on the flat edge of the knife. Foreign visitors thought this uncouth, and by the early nineteenth century the three- and four-pronged forks were becoming the primary eating utensil.

Rituals for eating varied by region and class. Historian David Hackett Fischer concisely defined the regional difference: Virginians dined, New Englanders merely ate. In the middle colonies, the main meal of the day would have been served in the early afternoon. In all but the poorest families, men and women were expected to dress for dinner. Hair would be carefully arranged, and a change of clothing would be standard. Most families in the middle and southern colonies would have had a dining room apart from the heat of the kitchen. This might have added an additional layer of formality to the dining rituals of the South. By contrast, New England meals were usually served at the long kitchen table, usually by the light and warmth of the fire. Prosperous families had chairs, but most would have had benches alongside the table. Dinner was less formal in New England, but throughout the colonies, conversation was an important aspect of meals. It was a chance for the family to relax in the midst of daily activities and was often the primary social activity of a day.

See also Diet

Further Reading

Earle, Alice Morse. *Home Life in Colonial Days.* New York: Grosset and Dunlap, 1898.

Fischer, David Hackett. *Albion's Seed: Four British Folkways in America.* New York: Oxford University Press, 1989.

Hooker, Richard J. *Food and Drink in America: A History.* Indianapolis: Bobbs-Merrill, 1981.

McMahon, Sarah F. "Laying Foods By: Gender, Dietary Decisions, and the Technology of Food Preservation in New England Households, 1750–1850." In *Early American Technology: Making and Doing Things from the Colonial Era to 1850,* ed. Judith A. McGaw. Chapel Hill: University of North Carolina Press, 1994.

Ulrich, Laurel Thatcher. *Good Wives: Images and Reality in the Lives of Women in Northern New England, 1650–1750.* New York: Vintage Books, 1980.

Coosaponakeesa

See Musgrove, Mary

Corbin, Margaret Cochran

See Molly Pitcher Legend

Corsets

See Body Image and Beauty

Courtship

Courtship marked the beginning of a rite of passage when a girl was transformed from a child into a woman. The objective of courtship was to find a marriage partner. There was no understanding that courting could be a recreational activity or part of an exploratory phase during which young people learned about themselves and members of the opposite sex. A young woman could only be exposed to a limited association with young men before her reputation began to take on unflattering connotations of promiscuity or unreliability. The qualities most valued in a wife were steadfastness, chastity, and modesty. A woman could not afford to encourage too many suitors before the community per-ceived her as lacking these qualities. Because most communities in early America were small, young women would have already been familiar with the available pool of suitors, so they already knew which young men were likely to be compatible.

Most courtships in colonial America were initiated by the young couple, rather than being prearranged by their parents. Colonial Americans did not have the equivalent of modern-day dating. In the absence of dances or other forms of entertainment, most courting would have taken place in conjunction with everyday life. A couple might walk to church, tend animals, or perform other household chores together. Privacy was always at a minimum, so the opportunities for couples to stray from the farmyard to gather berries or tend far-off fields were eagerly sought.

Parents tried to keep a watchful eye on young adults as they courted, but many couples succeeded in evading supervision. A significant percentage of colonial brides were pregnant on their wedding day, proving that premarital sex was not out of the ordinary. Around 30 percent of brides in the Chesapeake region were pregnant on their wedding day, and the rates were substantially higher for vulnerable classes of women such as orphans and indentured servants. Court records from seventeenth-century fornication hearings reveal that the most common trysting places for unmarried couples were distant fields and haylofts.

During the early colonial period, most women were looking for safety and security in a marriage. It was hoped they would marry someone they *could* love, but romantic love was not a prerequisite for marriage. Colonists tended to be wary of romantic love, believing it to be a poor indicator of an enduring match. Romantic love was volatile and could warp judgment, and it was commonly associated with childish, uncontrolled, and unreliable attachments. Young women were advised to seek out sober, hardworking, and amiable companions. It was assumed that love could slowly develop in the coming years of marriage.

Although a couple might initiate a courtship, parents became directly involved if the relationship appeared to be progressing toward a marriage.

A Most Curious Advertisement

People often used newspaper advertisements to request assistance, advance personal vendettas, or make announcements. Sometimes these personal advertisements provide a captivating glimpse into a story that has long been lost. Such is the case of the amusing advertisement below. Although she disguised her identity with a pseudonym, the daring character of the author is apparent.

Whereas a Gentleman, who towards the latter end of Summer, usually wore a blue camel coat lined with red and trimmed with silver . . . has been observed by Miss Amoret to look very languishingly at her, the said Amoret, and particularly one night during the last season of Assembly at the Theatre, the said Gentleman ogled her in such a manner, as showed him to be quite far gone. The said Miss Amoret desires the Gentleman to take the first handsome opportunity that offers to explain himself on that Subject.

Note: She believes he has very pretty teeth.
Source: Virginia Gazette, 29 October 1736.

Most couples depended on a parent's blessing in order to marry. All colonies had statutes that required parental approval of a marriage, and a man could be severely punished if he courted a woman without her parents' knowledge and consent. These laws served a dual function of protecting the family resources from fortune hunters and a daughter's reputation from association with unsavory rogues. Beyond the baseline considerations of good moral and religious character, parents hoped their children would find a partner of similar economic stature. Both sets of parents customarily provided financial assistance to a couple on the verge of marriage. A son usually received land, farming tools, a house, or assistance in building a house. A daughter received movable goods, such as livestock, clothing, and money.

Parents who disapproved of their daughter's choice usually resorted to delaying tactics, hoping her fervor might cool with time. They withheld financial assistance as the primary means of delaying a marriage, but could not do so indefinitely. Colonial authorities wanted to encourage their settlers to marry and raise new families, but recognized that in labor-scarce America, desperate parents might seek to exploit their children's labor for as long as possible. Once a child reached the age of consent, usually age twenty-one, parents were required to allow them to marry. Parents still could influence the choice of a marriage partner by the generosity of the marriage settlement.

The children of elite families usually had more formal courtship practices. It was desirable for children to marry into families of similar economic stature, and they often needed to look outside the local area to find an appropriate match. The practice of extended house visits helped facilitate courtship among upper-class families. A mother might take her teenaged daughters on lengthy visits to relatives in nearby cities. The host family would try to arrange as many teas or other social functions, to which eligible young men would be invited. Parents tended to play a far greater role in facilitating these high-profile, long-distance courtships. The character of the suitor was especially important, because if a marriage resulted, their daughter would be required to move far outside the comfort zone of her hometown family and friends.

Some parents tried to promote marriages that would be socially or economically advantageous for the family. Beyond the prestige factor, advantageous marriages could bring an entire family better business connections, career appointments, or opportunities for expanded landholdings. With so much at stake, parents might exert strong pressure on a child to accept a match, but the prospective bride and groom always had veto power over a marriage. Ministers were forbidden to perform a marriage with an unwilling partner. Despite the prohibitions against forcing a marriage, it is doubtless that some parents could eventually wear down the resolve of their children.

By the end of the eighteenth century, love became a more important factor in courtship and marriage decisions. Whereas the selection of a spouse used to be a matter of economic and social concern, courtship soon became a private matter

Courtship via a courting stick near the fireplace on Halloween in colonial days. This quaint custom looms larger in folklore than ever actually occurred in colonial America. (North Wind/North Wind Picture Archives)

between potential partners. Parents were discouraged from meddling in the affections of their daughters. Stories in magazines displayed less suspicion of romantic love and even began encouraging it as a necessary precondition for couples contemplating marriage. Although economic matters were still considered, women were becoming convinced that the strength of affection within a marriage would be the most important factor in determining their future happiness.

Most Protestant and Catholic families allowed their children to take the lead in selecting a mate. Quaker and Moravian elders played a far more active role in the selection of marriage partners. Quaker couples needed to obtain permission from a council of Quaker women elders. The council was to determine whether both parties were in good standing in the church, both sets of parents approved of the match, and the match met with the general approval of the community. Moravian communities were even more interventionist. Moravian elders paired couples, then drew lots to see if God approved of the match. Couples had veto power over a match if they found it repugnant, but the selection of a marriage partner was initiated by the elders.

Courtships for second marriages had their own characteristics. Widows were free to court and contract their own marriages. In lieu of a property settlement from her parents, a widow needed to make legal arrangements to protect the inheritance of any children she might have from her first marriage. Premarital contracts were not uncommon among partners who had children from prior marriages. Although most wives were automatically entitled to at least one-third of their husband's estate, a widow embarking on a second marriage usually had no such expectation. Explicit agreements were signed that identified how property would be split between the surviving spouse and children from previous marriages.

Bundling

Bundling was a curious custom practiced in Europe and transported to America with the early settlers. Because privacy was difficult and the selection of a compatible mate was crucial for long-term happiness, bundling allowed young couples to spend the night in the same bed. Always conducted in the young woman's home, the controlled setting allowed couples privacy and limited intimacy. Sexual intercourse was off-limits, and given the persistence of bundling for several generations in early America, it is unlikely that the custom would have endured had the prohibition on sex not generally been respected. Lieutenant Thomas Anburey, an English officer in the colonies, wrote this description of the bundling

procedures: "When a man is enamored of a young woman and wishes to marry her, he proposes that affair to her parents, without whose consent no marriage in this colony can take place; if they have no objection, they allow him to tarry with her one night, in order to make his court. At their usual time the old couple retire to bed, leaving the young ones to settle matters as they can, who having sat up as long as they think proper, get into bed together also, but without putting off their under garments, to prevent scandal" (Stiles 1871, 48–49). Folklore tells of various devices used to ensure bundling did not stray into forbidden intimacy. Bundling boards (a long piece of wood that was placed between the couples) or large sacks were supposedly used to prevent intimacy. It was most common among the lower and middle classes of New England. In the 1750s and 1770s, some New England towns tried to outlaw the custom, but were met with resistance by families who approved of the practice. The custom appeared to have subsided on its own, sometime in the early nineteenth century. Its association with the lower classes and occasional premarital pregnancy caused the practice to fall out of favor.

Betrothal

Once a couple agreed to marry, they entered a precontract stage. The banns, an official notice of the impending marriage, was published in the local paper or announced during Sunday services. The purpose of publishing banns was to discover if there was any legal impediment to the proposed match. During this precontract phase, the couple was in an unusual state, neither married nor single. They were required to be completely loyal to one another, and should one partner stray, the offense was considered to be the crime of adultery. Although sexual intercourse was forbidden to betrothed couples, the high rate of bridal pregnancy makes it apparent this prohibition was widely ignored. In some eighteenth-century New England towns, as many as one-third of the brides were pregnant on their wedding day.

The breaking of a betrothal was a gravely serious offense. Perhaps because it was assumed a certain amount of sexual liberties had been taken, a woman's reputation was tarnished following a broken engagement. Even if no sexual indiscretion had occurred, the failure of a couple to marry revealed an unsteadiness of character at best, or a deeply rooted flaw at worst. Both parties emerged with damaged reputations, but long-term implications were far worse for the woman. Modesty and steadfastness were the most essential virtues for a colonial woman, and a broken engagement cast a shadow over her character that could affect her chances for finding another partner. The party abandoning the betrothal could be sued for all costs and was often fined for punitive damages as well.

See also Marriage

Further Reading

Ktorides, Irene. "Marriage Customs in Colonial New England." *Historical Journal of Western Massachusetts* 2, no. 2 (1973): 5–21.

Norton, Mary Beth. *Liberty's Daughters: The Revolutionary Experience of American Women, 1750–1800.* Boston: Little, Brown, 1980.

Rothman, Ellen K. *Hands and Hearts: A History of Courtship in America.* New York: Basic Books, 1984.

Stiles, Henry Reed. *Bundling: Its Origins, Progress and Decline in America.* Mount Vernon, NY: Peter Pauper Press, 1871.

Coverture

Coverture is defined as the legal status of a woman following marriage that sublimated her legal identity under the authority of her husband. Most early American law was imported from English common law, which severely restricted women's legal status following their marriage. Under English law, an *unmarried* adult woman was entitled to almost all the legal rights of a man. She could sue and be sued, make contracts, write a will, buy and sell property, and operate a business in her own name. Such legal privileges were lost to her upon marriage, when her legal identity became folded into that of her husband.

Sir William Blackstone's *Commentaries on the Laws of England* (1765) provided a clear reflection of the legal implications of coverture: "By marriage, the husband and wife are one person in law; that is, the very being or legal existence of the woman is suspended during the marriage, or at least is incorporated and consolidated into that of the husband; under whose wing, protection, and cover, she performs everything" (*Commentaries,* Book I, Chapter 15, 442).

All property a woman brought into marriage, including real estate, clothing, furniture, or money, became the property of her husband. If the woman was employed outside the home, her wages belonged to her husband. Because a woman was not free to enter contracts under her own name, she could not buy or sell property, establish a business, or write a will. Because she could not enter into a lease or purchase a home, should she choose to live separately from her husband, she could not legally do so without his assistance.

The law of coverture, while it relegated the wife to the legal status of a child, worked well if the husband respected his wife and consulted her on important decisions. If the husband provided for his wife and sought her consent before making decisions and the pair were able to come to amicable agreements, coverture was not likely to be a burden to most colonial women. The difficulty lay in that the law of coverture assumed all women to have a loving and considerate husband. There were no provisions for women who were in an unhappy marriage. If a man frittered away money, neglected to provide for his family, or deserted his wife, there was little a woman could do to prevent such actions or provide for her own economic well-being.

The only major protection women were provided by the law of coverture was that a husband could not sell real estate his wife brought into the marriage without his wife's consent. This was a legacy from the laws of England, where the importance of land to an aristocratic lineage needed protection from wastrel husbands. Colonial statutes recognized that a wife's consent to sell property could be coerced. The law required for a wife to be questioned by a judge outside the presence of her husband, in order to determine if she concurred with the proposed sale of property. This procedure was notorious for being neglected, but if a woman strenuously objected, she had the ability to render the transaction null if there was no proof she consented to the sale of the land. Even with this protection, it was acknowledged that a private interview with the wife was not a foolproof means to prevent coercion. Judges concluded that if a woman agreed to the sale of property in a private meeting with a judge, she must be taken at her word.

In an effort to protect a woman's property and well-being, a number of legal techniques were developed to skirt coverture. A concerned father might set up a trust for his daughter, which insisted that funds be paid directly to the daughter without interference from her husband. Prenuptial agreements might also set property aside for the exclusive use of the wife. Despite the autonomy conferred by such legal arrangements, the beneficiary still depended on the generosity and goodwill of others to ensure that the legal protections were enforced.

Women who were deserted by their husbands lived in an especially difficult position. Because of the difficulty of obtaining a divorce, many men in unhappy marriages simply abandoned the home, leaving their wives to fend for themselves. Likewise, the wives of mariners and soldiers might go years without seeing their husbands. Their husbands might have been lost at sea, but having a missing man declared dead was a long and difficult process. These women could petition to be allowed to enter into contracts and keep the proceeds of any earnings, but were not able to sell or dispose of their husband's property. They needed the assistance of a court administrator to dispose of a husband's goods, should it be determined that he was unlikely to ever return.

The law as it was structured clearly put women in a subordinate position, and women who married an abusive or neglectful husband had few options. However, in practice, many of the laws of coverture were ignored. Studies of businesswomen in New York and Virginia reveal that many married women maintained thriving businesses, entered into contracts, and initiated lawsuits, all contrary to the law of coverture. Likewise, women were routinely able to obtain credit at the marketplace unless their husbands had specifically warned a merchant he would

not honor the agreement. It appears that few objections were raised in relation to these activities. In rare instances, some Anglo-American women were able to obtain the legal status of *feme sole* trader, which allowed them the ability to conduct business without their husband's supervision. This status was usually granted to women who had been abandoned by their husbands or whose husbands spent extended periods of time away from home.

A unique exception to the laws of coverture existed in the Dutch colonies of New Netherlands until the 1660s. According to Dutch tradition, women could select an *usus* marriage, in which she retained her legal identity, maiden name, and ability to conduct business affairs independent of her husband. Alternatively, she could opt for a *manus* marriage, which was remarkably similar to the laws of coverture. Women of the Dutch colonies were able to make this choice for themselves until the colony came under the control of England in 1664.

Mississippi was the first state to begin reforming the law of coverture when the state code was modified in 1839. Coverture was not fully abandoned throughout the United States until the 1880s.

See also *Feme Sole* Trader; Legal Status of Women

Further Reading

Gunderson, Joan R., and Gwen Victor Gampel. "Married Women's Legal Status in Eighteenth Century New York and Virginia. *William and Mary Quarterly,* 3d ser. 39 (1982): 114–134.

Salmon, Marylynn. "Equality or Submersion? Feme Covert Status in Early Pennsylvania." In *Women of America: A History,* eds. Carol Berkin and Mary Beth Norton. Boston: Houghton Mifflin, 1979.

———. "The Legal Status of Women in America: A Reappraisal." *Law and History Review* 1 (1983): 129–151.

———. *Women and the Law of Property in Early America.* Chapel Hill: University of North Carolina Press, 1986.

Crime and Punishment

Each colony had discretion in establishing its own set of laws. Local courts handled nuisance complaints and less serious crimes, whereas capital offenses were always referred to the central court within each colony. The American colonies inherited their system of laws from England, but the legal process was administered by men who had little formal legal training. With almost no attorneys among the early settlers, any well-respected man might be called upon to serve as a judge or prosecutor. Until the mid-eighteenth century, it was the custom for defendants to face the court without the aid of an attorney.

Women were in a unique legal limbo. If a woman was married, the laws of coverture placed her legal identity under that of her husband. Although she was legally accountable for criminal acts she clearly committed of her own volition, such was not the case if she could prove the act was committed with the knowledge of, or in the presence of, her husband. If she wished her husband to speak for her at trial, she did not need to testify on her own behalf, although she usually had the option to do so. Most women accused of minor crimes opted to let their husbands represent them in court.

The American legal system was established and operated entirely by men. Judges, juries, prosecutors, and sheriffs were all men. The only time women were called on to assist in trials was in matters of irregular births. If an abandoned infant was found, midwives were called on to examine women suspected of being the mother. Midwives also offered testimony as to paternity issues or premature births. In an ideal legal system, people would have the ability to administer impartial justice regardless of gender. With women excluded from all aspects of making law, determining guilt, and administering punishment, it is difficult to imagine that gender bias was absent. Women were three times more likely than men to be accused of fornication in Massachusetts. A portion of this discrepancy was because fornication by a woman could be revealed by an inconvenient pregnancy, but that alone cannot explain such a disproportionate figure.

There was no police force during the colonial period. Towns had watchmen, and sheriff's constables occasionally patrolled rural areas. Most crime came to light through victims' reports or alert neighbors. Because communities were small, most

---

The First All-Woman Jury

Indentured servant Judith Catchpole was accused of witchcraft and infanticide during her 1656 ocean crossing from England to Maryland. Testimony from fellow passengers claimed Catchpole attempted to use witchcraft to cause the death of several men. She was also seen cavorting with a fellow servant under cover of darkness and accused of murdering her own illegitimate infant.

Upon arriving in Maryland, the witchcraft accusation was dismissed due to lack of proof, but a jury was convened to try Catchpole for infanticide. An all-female jury, composed of seven married women and four single women, were convened to examine Judith's body for evidence of a recent pregnancy. After the examination, the women agreed that it was unlikely that the accused had been pregnant, and the charges were dismissed.

Source: Rose, Lou. "A Memorable Trial in Seventeenth Century Maryland." *Maryland Historical Magazine* 83 (1988): 365–368.

---

people knew their neighbors, their possessions, and their history of personal disputes with other local people. As such, colonists were surprisingly effective in identifying suspects for criminal activity.

Types of Crime

Seventeenth-century laws in the American colonies drew little distinction between crime and sin. Blasphemy, drunkenness, and fornication were crimes that carried legal consequences. Among the crimes constituting misdemeanors were assault, rioting, vagrancy, slander, and regulatory infractions such as selling liquor without a license or overcharging for bread. In the colonies settled by the Puritans, crimes of immorality were considered serious criminal actions. Adultery, fornication, and single motherhood were all matters that were regularly prosecuted in New England courts. Crimes of sexual immorality were enough to create lifelong stigmatization for women in the seventeenth century. By the eighteenth century such offenses could still seriously

Young woman reading the Bible in a Puritan jail, New England, 1600s. (North Wind / North Wind Picture Archives)

damage a woman's reputation, but were rarely prosecuted in a court of law.

Women often committed different types of crimes than men. Most men brought before a criminal court were there for crimes committed away from home. They mixed with gangs, got drunk and disorderly in public, or stole merchandise. In contrast, the criminal activity of women usually took place in their home environment. A servant might steal from her mistress. A mother might abuse a child. A wife might violently assault her husband. The serious crimes committed by women included:

Arson: The deliberate setting of fires was deadly serious business in colonial America. It was presumed to be a crime of revenge against the victim, but because fires could easily spread and obliterate years of work and endanger the livelihood of the entire community, arson was among the most serious of offenses and was punishable by death. Arson required no physical strength, merely the ability to commit a secretive and vindictive crime. Unlike other violent crimes that required strength, women were considered capable of and likely to commit arson.

Crimes of Property: Theft, counterfeiting, forgery, and embezzlement were usually male crimes. Few women committed these crimes on their own account, but on occasion women assisted their husbands in such exploits. In 1766, charges of theft were dropped against Mary Hodges, because it was apparent she was acting in conjunction with her husband. Richard Hodges was held fully accountable for the crimes, but the law of *coverture* protected his wife. The case of Rachel Wall was slightly different. She and her husband engaged in piracy by luring ships toward their small boat while pretending to be in distress. After killing their would-be rescuers, they stole the goods and gutted the ship. Rachel's husband, George, met his death during a storm at sea, and she returned to Boston, where she continued small-scale thievery along the docks. When she was apprehended, her history of piracy was revealed. Although thievery was not a hanging offense, Rachel's history of murder and piracy came to light, and she was hanged despite having committed these crimes in the presence of her husband. The laws of coverture could only be stretched so far before women were held accountable for their actions. Coverture implied a passive role for women, but Rachel Wall was clearly no delicate woman who needed a man to protect and provide for her. Perhaps her brash and unfeminine behavior was so inconsistent with traditional Puritan goodwives that Massachusetts authorities had little difficulty setting coverture aside in her case.

Murder: Most murders committed by women were related to attempts to disguise illegitimate births. Some were cases of child abuse where a young child died after a battering. Of those cases where women were tried for murder, 85 percent of the victims were the women's own children. The most common weapons used by women in murder cases were, in order of frequency: drowning, beating, neglect, poison, knives or axes, and clubs. Other targets of murderous women were employers and disagreeable neighbors. Many of these crimes were committed spontaneously, as when Katherine Ford pushed her neighbor Pheby White down a flight of stairs in 1694 during a fit of anger.

A few rare cases have come to light in which women poisoned elderly relatives in hopes of gaining an inheritance.

Types of Women Who Committed Crimes

Women who committed crimes in colonial America came from all races and classes. They were more likely to be unmarried, possibly because the most prevalent crimes they were accused of related to extramarital sex or bastardy.

Identification of criminal suspects depended on the testimony of the victim and townspeople to reveal a suspect. In cases where no clear suspect emerged, certain categories of people were more prone to accusation. Indians, servants, outsiders, and unmarried women of questionable reputation aroused the most suspicion. People who were on the economic fringes, such as the very poor, or the non-English-speaking immigrant, likewise were liable to be accused.

Women never accounted for more than 10 to 20 percent of criminal defendants. Most women spent the majority of their lives in semiseclusion on farms or in small towns. With the opportunity to mix and interact with society limited, women had fewer opportunities for becoming entangled in criminal activity. When they did engage in crime, it was usually of a domestic nature.

Many females accused of crimes were young women who had not yet married. This was considered to be a dangerous age by Puritans. The young women were no longer protected by the innocence and isolation of childhood and were now capable of sexual impulse, temptation, and reckless behavior. Many of these girls were placed in other households as domestic helpers. They had neither a parent to shelter them, nor a husband who could protect them from sexual indiscretions.

During the seventeenth century, women on trial for serious offenses were more likely to be found guilty than men tried for the same offenses. It is possible that because criminal activity was so alien to the model of demure and wholesome womanhood, male juries reacted with punitive severity toward any woman even suspected of committing such an offense. Whatever the cause, by the eighteenth century, women were no more likely to be convicted than male defendants.

There are a few rare cases of female con artists in colonial America. Such women could not flourish until the anonymity provided by urban areas came into being in the late eighteenth century. Prior to this, people of small towns were suspicious of strangers, and the impossibility of disappearing into a crowd made con-artistry impossible. Ann Carson was typical of the con artists who took advantage of the growing wealth and urbanization in late eighteenth-century America. A basically intelligent and attractive woman, she was able to dress and comport herself like a well-bred member of the middle class. After gaining people's trust, she committed theft, passed counterfeit bank notes, and even engaged in a foiled kidnapping attempt. She was captured many times, occasionally sentenced to prison, and quickly moved to a new city upon release. She ended her days ignominiously by dying of typhus in a Philadelphia prison. Other con artists were more successful, but this sort of crime was almost unheard of among women in early America.

Punishment

Trial by jury was the norm in colonial America. The more serious the crime, the more likely the individual was to be found "not guilty." Serious crime was usually punished with the death penalty, and juries were reluctant to convict unless clear and indisputable proof from reliable witnesses was presented.

Long prison sentences were unheard of in colonial America. They did not have the facilities or desire to pay for long-term incarceration. Jails were most commonly used only to allow drunks to sober up and violent individuals to cool down. If a criminal suspect was considered dangerous or a flight risk, he or she was incarcerated until trial. The most severe penalty for the restriction on personal liberty

was being sentenced to indentured servitude for a period of seven to fourteen years.

Hanging was the most common method of execution. The hanging of a criminal was intended to serve not only as punishment, but also as a public lesson on the wages of sin. As such, hangings took place in the town center during daylight hours. The condemned were encouraged to make a confession and apology prior to their hanging. The character of public executions was markedly different in England than it was in America. English executions had a carnival-like atmosphere, with crowds thronging the streets, rotten vegetables hurled at the condemned, and raucous shouting from the spectators. In the smaller communities in America, the spectators were more likely to have known the condemned, and the mood was generally somber. Of the women who were hanged in America, almost 80 percent were for murder, with witchcraft accounting for most of the remainder.

See also Adultery; Civil Disobedience; Fornication; Infanticide; Mothers, Single; Slander; Spooner, Bathsheba

Further Reading

Branson, Susan. "Beyond Respectability: The Female World of Love and Crime in Late Eighteenth and Early Nineteenth Century Philadelphia." *Studies in Eighteenth Century Culture* 25 (1996): 245–264.

Hoffer, Peter Charles. "Crime and Law Enforcement." In *Encyclopedia of the North American Colonies*, ed. Jacob Ernest Cooke. New York: Charles Scribner's Sons, 1993.

Hull, N. E. H. *Female Felons: Women and Serious Crime in Colonial Massachusetts*. Urbana: University of Illinois Press, 1987.

Rowe, G. S. "Women's Crime and Criminal Administration in Pennsylvania, 1763–1790. *Pennsylvania Magazine of History and Biography* 109 (1985): 335–368.

D

Dame Schools

See Education

Dancing

As with many customs in early America, the type of dance women engaged in varied tremendously depending on her social class. For elite women, dance was a way to showcase their refinement and familiarity with European culture. For the majority of colonial women without access to expensive dance masters, dancing had fewer rules and was merely a form of entertainment, rather than display.

Most documentation of early American dancing is from dance manuals or letters written by observers. Both reflected dance among the upper class, which was not representative of what the average American woman would have experienced. For the typical woman, dancing occurred at celebrations such as weddings or holidays. Informal dancing also occurred in taverns or in barns after community events. A day of barn raising, a quilting bee, or a military muster often closed with dances in barns. The music was simple, usually played with only a fiddle or a bagpipe.

The most common dances at informal events were country dances, which involved partners standing in two lines facing each other. The leading couple performed a few simple steps, which were emulated by successive couples down the line. These dances were easy to learn and required no formal instruction. Informal dances in taverns might be performed in solo or duo jigs. Free-form dancing, involving elbow swings, foot stomping, and impromptu movement was a timeless form of dance that needed no instruction. These free style moves would never have been performed in elite ballrooms of colonial America. Dance manuals even warned against spontaneous swinging of arms as it was a mark of the untutored.

As colonial society became economically stratified, elites began seeking ways to display their wealth and cultivation. Emulating European high society became an important mark of social distinction. Class was much more than the possession of wealth, and the dance floor was a singular test of membership in elite society. A person's command of manners, movement, ease, and style were all put on public display on the dance floor. Although some men considered dance an effeminate pastime, it was acknowledged as a crucial component of a young person's education. Clumsy display on the dance floor was an indicator of a neglected education.

Formal dancing could not be improvised. The most important dance among the elites was the minuet. Although it was not a difficult dance to learn, it required training and practice. The minuet was a hierarchical dance that symbolized precedence and power. It was led by the most socially prominent couple in the ballroom, while the rest of the assembled guests watched. The couple performed several standardized step sequences, moving throughout the dance floor in a series of parallel passes and two-handed turns. The challenge was

How to dance the minuet: "Dance Manual with Instructions in the Southern Colonies." The most important dance among the elites was the minuet. Although it was not a difficult dance to learn, it required training and practice. (Library of Congress)

to appear focused on one's partner while smoothly executing the moves. After the lead couple finished their minuet, other couples danced in order of their social position. The minuet could be a nerve-racking event for people not well tutored in the dance, and many recount breathing a sigh of relief when the minuets were over and less formal reels could begin.

Among the elite, dance lessons were a rite of passage into adulthood. Dancing masters were hired to provide lessons to young ladies and gentlemen alike. Most dance masters came from Europe, where they learned the latest dances being performed in the fashionable ballrooms of France and England. They set up schools in towns and often hosted regularly scheduled balls in their school-

room where parents could monitor the progress of their children. Francis Christian was typical of the itinerant dance master who provided instruction to elite rural families. He traveled among a circuit of Virginia plantations, staying for two days at each plantation every three weeks.

Although dancing was important to all age groups prior to the Revolution, by the late eighteenth century it became the province of young, unmarried people. The minuet, with its hierarchical formality, fell out of favor amidst the democratic ideals of the new nation. Dances became associated with courtship, and after marriage women gradually eased out of public dancing.

Further Reading

Brooks, Lynn Matluck. "Emblem of Gaiety, Love, and Legislation: Dance in Eighteenth-Century Philadelphia." *Pennsylvania Magazine of History and Biography* 115 (1991): 63–87.

Hendrickson, Charles Cyril, and Kate Van Winkler Keller. *Social Dances from the American Revolution.* Sandy Hook, CT: The Hendrickson Group, 1992.

Kierner, Cynthia A. *Beyond the Household: Women's Place in the Early South, 1700–1835.* Ithaca, NY: Cornell University Press, 1998.

Dare, Virginia

First child born of English parents in the New World (1587–?)

Aside from the dates of Virginia Dare's birth and baptism, her life remains shrouded in mystery. Virginia's parents, Elenor and Ananias Dare, were among the group of settlers who intended to plant a permanent colony in British North America.

England wanted a colony in the New World in order to shore up its positions in its ongoing cold war against Spain. England wanted to establish a base from which to refit and supply privateer ships that struck at Spanish trading vessels. The first colony of one hundred men on Roanoke Island, today part of the outer banks of North Carolina, was a failure. Poorly supplied and with harbors too shallow to support their needs, the colony was abandoned after a year.

Baptism of Virginia Dare, the first European child born in North America. (Corbis)

The second attempt to establish a colony took a different approach. It was intended to be a self-sufficient agricultural community composed of families. Ninety-one men, seventeen women, and six children set off for America in the spring of 1587. For unknown reasons, they returned to the exact spot of the original failed colony, even though another location in the Chesapeake Bay had previously been surveyed and selected. A few of the cottages from the previous expedition were still standing, and these were repaired while others were constructed. It is believed that the colony merely planned to winter in the spot before moving farther north to the Chesapeake Bay.

The fact that Elenor Dare was willing to embark on a voyage when she knew herself to be five months pregnant testifies to the likelihood these colonists intended their voyage to be part of a permanent settlement in America. Many of the other women who made the voyage likewise had small children. The conditions into which Virginia Dare was born would have been most primitive. It is known she was baptized a week after her birth on 24 August 1587. This was the last firm documentation of her life.

Faced with a growing need for supplies, John White, the leader of the expedition and Virginia's grandfather, returned to England. The outbreak of hostilities with the assault of the Spanish Armada in 1588 blocked his return voyage. He was unable to return until three years later, at which point he found the colony abandoned. There was no sign of foul play, and it appears the colonists made an orderly and unhurried departure. The only clue as to their destination was the word *Croatoan* carved into a tree.

The Croatoans were a friendly group of Indians living to the south of the colony. It is possible they sought shelter with the Indians when faced with famine, a hurricane, or some other calamity. It is known that during the years 1587–1589 the Chesapeake Bay area suffered the most severe drought in almost 800 years. This, plus the primitive conditions facing the European settlers might have forced them to seek refuge with the Croatoans.

No sign of the colonists ever surfaced again. When the settlement at Jamestown was initiated in 1607, the settlers heard rumors of "white Indians" living to the south. Expeditions were made, but nothing was ever found. Rumors of the lost colonists having assimilated into Indians tribes continued to float around the area for centuries, but no concrete proof has surfaced. Most historians believe the colonists, including the infant Virginia Dare, assimilated with the Croatoan Indians living in the area. In 1606 Chief Powhatan launched a massacre of Indian tribes living near the outer banks. It is likely that the Roanoke colonists were slaughtered alongside these Indians.

The story of Virginia Dare captured a romantic spirit of early American pioneers and embodied the idea of peaceful relations between Europeans and Native Americans. In the eighteenth and nineteenth century she became featured in more than a dozen novels, idealized as a beautiful, half-wild daughter of the New World. The most popular of these works is Paul Green's outdoor drama, *The Lost Colony* (1937), which is performed annually on Roanoke Island.

Further Reading

Kupperman, Karen Ordahl. *Roanoke: The Abandoned Colony.* Totowa, NJ: Rowman and Allanheld, 1984.

Quinn, David Beers. *Set Fair for Roanoke: Voyages and Colonies, 1584–1606.* Chapel Hill: University of North Carolina Press, 1985.

Stahle, David, et al. "The Lost Colony and Jamestown Droughts." *Science* 280 (April 1998): 564–567.

Death and Funeral Customs

Death in early America was not limited to the elderly and a handful of unlucky accident victims. Most colonists would have experienced the death of a sibling or a parent in their early years. Fewer than one-third of seventeenth-century Virginians reached the age of eighteen with two living parents. Death was not a shocking and unnatural event, but rather, a depressingly common occurrence. There was little attempt to insulate people from the prospect of death. People died in their own beds and were cleaned and prepared for burial by family members. Children witnessed the solemn events, because the experience was believed to be important for their understanding that death could strike at any time.

The average life expectancy for a seventeenth-century woman was only 41.8 years, but this bleak figure is skewed by high infant mortality. Because so many babies and children fell victim to disease before age five, it creates unnaturally low life-expectancy figures. If a girl safely passed through the dangerous years of childhood, she could expect to live into her sixties. Women faced some unique health challenges. The dangers of childbirth were at the forefront of a woman's health concerns. Beyond this, she was also more susceptible to malaria and anemia than men.

Women needed to find both spiritual and practical coping mechanisms for death. When a young adult died, a cooperative network of family and friends intervened to care for the children of the deceased. Widowed women might remarry with shocking speed following the death of a husband, because the economic needs of herself and children took precedence over her need to grieve. The death of a child would have been among the most traumatic experiences for colonial women. There is some evidence that women were reluctant to immediately bond with their newborn children. The first few months of life were always the most precarious, and as many as 10 percent of children died before their first year. Mothers might have psychologically braced themselves by delaying the naming of a child until it was a few months old and

Rachel Weeping (1772–1776) by Charles Willson Peale. A portrait of the artist's wife mourning their daughter, Margaret. (Philadelphia Museum of Art/CORBIS)

referring to an infant as "it" or "the baby." When children died, it was usually interpreted as the will of God, and people believed that no actions on the part of the parent could have prevented the tragedy.

Women provided assistance to families who had suffered a death. As soon as news of a death spread, neighborhood women brought food and offered their services in minding young children in order to allow the family to grieve. They assisted in washing the body and dressing it for burial. The practice of embalming was rarely used in colonial America. For several days after a death, neighborhood women took turns performing household chores, preparing food, and providing moral support.

Attitudes toward death were strongly shaped by religion, with great regional variation occurring among northern Puritans, southern Anglicans, and pockets of Quaker denominations. The Puritans had the most elaborate preparations for death. They were taught from childhood to never be secure in their personal salvation and that Hell was a reality all but the few saved souls would confront. The custom of "daily dying" was a spiritual exercise encouraged by Puritan ministers. A person was to daily examine his or her soul, as if preparing to face judgment that very day. Cotton Mather wrote that a devout Puritan should hope "every time the clock strikes, it may strike upon our Hearts to think, thus I am one hour nearer to my last!"

Puritan children were conditioned to fear death through fiery sermons. They were required to look into the open caskets of the recently deceased and pray for the souls of the dead. Beyond the instructional value of confronting the body of a loved one who was now facing judgment day, the corpse was of little interest to Puritans. There were no elaborate rituals, wakes, or tomb art in seventeenth-century Puritan culture. Funerals were simple and austere. A few prayers were said at home prior to embarking on the burial procession. There were often two sets of pallbearers, depending on how far the casket had to be carried to the burial grounds. The procession would be led by the most prominent individual among the mourners, usually a magistrate or minister. He would lead the procession with the widow, or nearest relative, beside him. Caskets were rudimentary, and the grave would be marked with a simple granite rock. There were rarely sermons delivered at the burial site. Following the burial the mourners would return to the home of the deceased, where a meal was served accompanied by large quantities of alcohol.

By the end of the seventeenth century, Puritan funerals became more elaborate. Tombstones became opportunities to provide instruction with art and epitaphs. In keeping with the Puritans' gloomy attitude toward death, most early grave art featured carvings of skeletons, hourglasses, and winged skulls. Tokens, such as scarves or mourning rings, were given to mourners.

In contrast to Puritan fear and anxiety regarding death, the Anglicans of the middle and southern colonies had a far more nonchalant view of death and afterlife. They did not believe in a harsh, retaliatory God and rarely interpreted death as something that had been willed by God. Death was an occasion for mourning, but not a time to be in fear for the lost one's soul. Anglican ceremonies were more elaborate, with large, alcohol-soaked banquets following the funeral. In contrast to New Englanders, who interred their dead in public cemeteries, most southerners used private burial plots in a secluded section of the farm. A fusillade (a ceremonial firing of guns) was often performed at the grave site.

Quakers had a more optimistic view of death, and this was reflected in their funeral customs. Death was not an event to be feared, but rather was the culmination of a spiritual life. Excessive mourning was discouraged, because it was believed that the deceased had gone on to a better life. To openly mourn too rigorously was either a sign of vanity or lack of faith. Funeral processions were discouraged, and a small ceremony was held following the burial. Even marking graves with a tombstone was discouraged, and in 1766 a recommendation came from Quaker leaders to remove all existing gravestones.

A curious colonial funeral custom was the giving of gifts to mourners. Gloves and mourning rings were the most common items given. The item would often be sent as an elegant form of invitation to the funeral services. Mourning rings were usually gold, often with black enamel and an inscription, such as "Death parts united hearts." If a mourner lived too far away to attend the funeral, they would be sent a ring to be worn in memory of the deceased. Goldsmiths kept a constant supply of such rings. Gloves were the most common gift. In 1736, more than one thousand pairs of gloves were given away for the funeral of Governor Belcher's wife. This was an extraordinarily large number, but it was not uncommon for a typical family to send out a hundred gloves for a funeral. Remembrance tokens could be enormously expensive, consuming almost a quarter of a household's annual income.

Elaborate mourning customs did not apply to a huge segment of colonial society: the poor, those living in the frontier, and African Americans. Among these people, burying the body in a burial cloth was the custom. Among Christian slaves, death was viewed as a liberating experience. Their burial traditions were a mix of African and Christian influences. The funeral was highly emotional, with a good deal of exhortations, hymn singing, and expressions of grief mixed with praises to Jesus. The grave would often be marked with no more than some seashells or a carved piece of wood. In keeping with African tradition, a second set of funeral sermons were said a few weeks after the burial. It was believed that if the dead were not buried properly they could haunt the living.

Much study has been done on grave art and the use of epitaphs. Initially epitaphs were used for only the most prestigious members of a community, such as governors, mayors, or famous clergy. Women were almost never dignified with an epitaph in the seventeenth century, but by the close of the eighteenth century they represented 28 percent of people considered worthy of an epitaph. This could be a reflection of an increasing respect for the role of motherhood in the establishment of a new nation. Early epitaphs made little reference to biographical details other than the name and date of death. Rather, they focused on moralistic reflections such as the brevity of life, worldly vanity, or judgment. Details such as the deceased's moral qualities and family relation-

ships became more common by the end of the eighteenth century. Later tombstones were also less likely to feature morbid images of death heads and skeletons, but moved toward more reassuring symbols such as cherubs, urns, and willows.

A number of superstitions and local customs accompanied death. For example, corpses should never be carried out of the house headfirst, because if they looked backward into the home as they were leaving, they could beckon others to follow them in death. Many families placed fabric covers over mirrors, fearing that death would come to anyone who saw their own image while death was still looming fresh in the house. Any portraits of the dead person were turned to face the wall. The portraits could be turned around after burial, but would be draped in black fabric throughout the mourning period. In rural areas, plates of salt and soil were laid on the corpse to represent the spirit and the flesh. If the town had a church bell, it was tolled one time for each year of the departed's life.

See also Disease; Orphaned Girls; Stepfamilies; Widowhood; Wills and Inheritance

Further Reading

Earle, Alice Morse. *Customs and Fashions in Old New England.* New York: Charles Scribner's Sons, 1911.

Fischer, David Hackett. *Albion's Seed: Four British Folkways in America.* New York: Oxford University Press, 1989.

Howard, Ronald William. "Old Age and Death." In *Encyclopedia of the North American Colonies,* ed. Jacob Ernest Cooke. New York: Charles Scribner's Sons, 1993.

Ludwig, Allan. *Graven Images: New England Stonecarving and Its Symbols, 1650–1815.* Hanover, NH: University Press of New England, 1999.

Vovelle, Michel. "A Century and One-Half of American Epitaphs (1660–1813): Toward the Collective Attitudes about Death." *Comparative Studies in Society and History* 22 (1980): 534–547.

Depression
See Mental Illness

Diet

The famous "starving time" of early Virginia settlers still lingers in historical memory and has cast an impression of desperately poor and famished settlers. Although it is true the first few ships of settlers were confronted with dire circumstances, this was a result of bad weather and poor planning, rather than problems with the American food supply. The first settlers stocked their ships with salted bacon, dried fish, cheese, and root vegetables. Upon arriving in America their shipboard provisions were rarely adequate to sustain settlers until crops could be planted and harvested. Hunting and foraging were therefore essential. Women gathered clams, mussels, nuts, and wild berries. These foods were familiar to European settlers and were easy to prepare.

The early American diet centered around meat. It was easier to shoot a deer than clear, plow, plant, and harvest a crop of corn. Settlers brought some animals with them, such as goats, cows, and chickens, but these were used more for their dairy and egg produce rather than as a source of meat. Hunting and fishing brought a plentiful source of meat to colonists. Hunting was an entirely male activity, but women participated in skinning and butchering, and they were entirely responsible for cooking the meat.

Of the grain crops grown in America, corn was the most important. It yielded more food per acre than any of the imported European crops such as rye or oats. It was unfamiliar to colonists, so they needed to learn not only how to grow it, but how to prepare the grain into edible dishes. Through a combination of working with the Indians and experimentation, settlers learned how to grind cornmeal and make simple, unleavened cakes. They also made it into *supawn,* an Indian dish of cornmeal porridge served with butter, molasses, or milk.

The morning meal was a simple affair, because women rarely had time to prepare anything elaborate. Leftover bread, cheese, and cider usually sufficed. A typical day in agricultural communities began by 5 A.M., although breakfast was not served for a few hours. After breakfast a woman would begin preparing lunch, which was the primary meal of the day in agricultural communities. Almost always prepared in one pot, the meal usually consisted of simmering meat and vegetables. Dinner was once again a simple affair, possibly cornmeal cakes or stewed beans.

There was a great deal of regional variation in diet. Fishing was common everywhere along the coast, but especially in New England. The growing season was short in the northern colonies, which resulted in greater reliance on fish. They ate all manner of cod, herring, mussels, lobster, clams, and bass. Oysters were a favorite dish and were readily available in early America. The bounty of seafood made chowders and fish stews a staple of the New England diet.

Apples, cherries, plums, blueberries, and cranberries were also easy to obtain. Apples became a vitally important resource in the North, because they could be used to produce cider. Cider was easier to brew than beer, and apples were less labor intensive to cultivate than rye. Settlers quickly converted their rye fields to corn after they adopted cider as their primary beverage.

Although the middle colonies did not share in the bounty from the oceans that blessed the North, they had longer growing seasons and more fertile land. They grew corn and rye for consumption, but the veneration of tobacco resulted in that crop consuming most of the farmland in the middle colonies. Hunting for meat and raising hogs therefore provided an important source of food. A typical family would supplement their diet with a small garden plot for home consumption. Onions, leeks, carrots, beets, chives, lettuce, and asparagus all grew well in the middle colonies.

Settlers in the southern colonies made good use of seafood, but their diets also suffered a lack of diversity because of their desire to plant tobacco. Dairy products did not do well in the South. In order to produce enough rich milk for cheese and butter, cows needed large expanses of quality grazing pastures, which the South lacked. The hot climate made long-term storage of meat difficult, so meat consumption was limited to fowl, pork, and occasional wild game.

Wheat was scarce in the South, but corn was plentiful and heavily used in breads and hominy.

African American Influences on Cooking

Slaves were responsible for preparing their own meals, and many used techniques and food staples that were familiar to them from Africa. Okra, watermelon, black-eyed peas, and yams were all native to Africa. How these plants were brought to America is a matter of debate. Some claim the slaves themselves secreted seeds in their hair or clothing just prior to departing Africa. More likely, the European and African slave traders arranged for these durable crops to be sold and traded in the New World.

Slaves were usually permitted a small garden plot where they could grow produce to supplement their diet. They combined these vegetables with the standard weekly rations, which usually consisted of cornmeal or rice, a few pounds of pork, and perhaps some molasses. Women used these basic staples to create a variety of dishes, usually made in a single pot and requiring little tending. Soups and stews were made from slow-cooking vegetables with bits of meat and rice. Chunks of eggplant gave the dishes a meaty texture, and okra provided a thickening element.

In contrast to the diets of white settlers, which centered around meat and starch, slaves made fruits and vegetables a central part of their cooking, and they can be credited with introducing more fresh produce into American cooking. Slaves used all parts of the plant. Simmering the leaves of sweet potatoes, turnips, and collard greens with some oil, peppers, and spices resulted in a nutritious side dish.

Following West African tradition, beef was rarely a part of African American diets. Chicken was an expensive luxury reserved for special occasions, but fish was widely available. Fishing rods were easy to make, and catfish, trout, and butterfish became a common meal. Although there was little tradition for deep frying food in Africa, slaves of the American South relied on this technique to keep food from spoiling in the hot climate.

Source: Dilday, Kenya, and Jonathan Gill. "Food." In *Encyclopedia of African American Culture and History,* ed. Jack Salzman. New York: Macmillan Library Reference, 1996.

Hominy was produced by scalding corn in a kettle until the hull fell off. The grains were dried and could later be cooked to make grits. "Hog and hominy" was a favorite dish made of hominy fried with pork. By the end of the seventeenth century, rice had become an established crop in swampy areas of the South, and it was prominently featured in many southern dishes. Bread, cakes, and cookies could all be made with rice flour. Peaches were the other famous delicacy of the South. Peach trees thrived, and the fruit was used in sauces, fancy cakes, jellies, and peach brandy.

Although the diet of the early decades of settlement was highly regional, the ease and abundance of food resulted in surplus, which led to trade. Colonists soon had built ships and harbors, which made it easy to import beef to the South and brandy to the North. New England became heavy exporters of salted fish and cider apples.

As trade with the West Indies increased, so did all manner of sugar consumption. The well-to-do purchased imported white sugar from the Indies. Shaped into large, hard cones, each weighing between eight and ten pounds, the sugar cones were kept in specially designed locked boxes. Sugar sheers were used for the delicate task of cutting off pieces. Refined, white sugar was costly and affordable only to the wealthy. Honey and maple syrup were also used as sweeteners, but their use was rare because of the labor-intensive nature of collection. Molasses was the sugar of the masses. After the sugar was crystallized out of cane or beet juice, molasses was the by-product that still retained enough sweetness to be used in cooking. The dark syrup was used to sweeten all manner of foods, including mush, puddings, sweetbreads, and meat. It could also be fermented to make rum. Americans developed an enormous sweet tooth, and women were expected to be able to produce pies, candies, tarts, cookies, and cakes.

The most commonly used spices were salt, pepper, nutmeg, cloves, mace, and cinnamon, all of which had to be imported and were therefore sparingly used. Although some salt could be locally produced, an enormous amount was required for curing meat and fish, so salt was imported from the

West Indies. Herbs grew in abundance in America and were readily available everywhere. Parsley, thyme, marjoram, hyssop, and fennel were all common in kitchen gardens.

Much of American cooking was "yeoman food," simple meals with few ingredients simmered in a single pot. By the eighteenth century, a distinctive upper class was developing a more sophisticated appetite. Imported spices and wines were used to season dishes. The wives of the wealthy were more likely to have servants in the kitchen, allowing them to produce more sophisticated meals. No longer confined to the use of a single pot, a wealthy family might have several dishes served separately. Meat would be seasoned with rich gravies or sweet sauces made of currants, raisins, or apples and would be served alongside stuffing or steamed vegetables. The wealthy could afford expensive seasonings, such as vanilla beans, olive oil, Parmesan cheese, and flavored vinegars. The most elegant of meals would feature several meat dishes. Diarist Philip Fithian described a typical dinner at a Virginia plantation as consisting of beef and greens, roasted pig, boiled fish, cheese, pudding, tarts, beer, cider, and brandy. Although the average American woman could not turn out such a spectacular array for a single meal, most Americans ate very well when compared with their peers in Europe. Only the enslaved, indentured, or the poorest of Americans went without adequate food, and it is likely they ate better than their counterparts in other areas of the world.

See also Cooking

Further Reading

Carson, Jane. *Colonial Virginia Cookery: Procedures, Equipment, and Ingredients in Colonial Cooking.* Williamsburg, VA: Colonial Williamsburg Foundation, 1985.

Doyle, Marian I. "A Plentiful Good Table." *Early American Life* 32 (2001): 46–49.

Hooker, Richard J. *Food and Drink in America: A History.* Indianapolis, IN: Bobbs-Merrill, 1981.

McMahon, Sarah F. "A Comfortable Subsistence: The Changing Composition of Diet in Rural New England, 1620–1840." *William and Mary Quarterly,* 3d ser. 62 (1985): 26–65.

Spruill, Julia Cherry. *Women's Life and Work in the Southern Colonies.* Chapel Hill: University of North Carolina Press, 1938.

Disease

The containment and treatment of disease was hampered throughout the colonial period by the lack of understanding regarding germs and the spread of disease. Early Americans attributed disease to causes such as bad air, witchcraft, or the punishment of God. Medical science of the day ascribed disease to theory of humors: the belief that illness or disease was caused by an imbalance of the body's blood, yellow bile, phlegm, and black bile. It was believed that living in a radically hot environment or failure to ingest the proper foods could result in an imbalance in the body's humors. In reality, disease in early America was caused by factors such as poor sanitation, polluted drinking waters, and contact between populations that had been geographically isolated.

Infectious diseases arise and flourish in specific environments, and the people living in these environments develop levels of resistance and immunity to the diseases native to their locale. Immunity can be inherited or acquired. A child who is exposed to and survives smallpox will carry a lifelong immunity to the disease. Populations who have lived for centuries or millennia in a given locale will be less susceptible to the diseases native to their environment. Conversely, if they are transported to a radically different environment, they will have zero innate tolerance to the local disease environment. Europeans had virtually no exposure to yellow fever or malaria, but these diseases thrived in the hot climates of the American South. Native Americans and Africans had no exposure to European diseases before the mingling of the cultures in seventeenth-century America.

Diseases of Contagion

The Atlantic Ocean proved an effective barrier against the transmission of certain contagious diseases that ravaged Europeans, but had yet to infect the New World. The average sailing time across the ocean in the seventeenth century was eight to ten weeks. Since the incubation period for diseases such as measles was two weeks, most epidemics would have run their course during the voyage, and the infection would have burned itself out before the ship reached America. By the eighteenth century, sailing time had been reduced to six weeks, and this allowed for the transmission of measles to America. The population density in America had also increased, allowing for the spread of disease from community to community.

Many diseases were spread via mosquitoes. Yellow fever and malaria were both tropical diseases that periodically devastated the southern colonies during the summer months. Neither disease was native to North America and they were probably carried by Europeans and Africans coming from tropical locales. As such, these diseases did not pose major threats until the end of the seventeenth century, when they began appearing in the international ports of trade. There was little understanding of these diseases, except it was known that they were more prevalent in hot climates. Much contemporary speculation led people to believe it was the heat itself that caused these diseases.

Towns in low-lying and marshy areas were especially prone to the diseases, because mosquitoes thrived in such conditions. Doctors knew of no effective treatment for these diseases other than making the patient comfortable. Not understanding how the diseases were spread, mothers did their best to isolate infected persons away from other members of the family.

The most feared disease in early America was smallpox. It was highly contagious, lethal, and often left its survivors permanently disfigured. Survivors of smallpox developed lifelong immunity, and the regularity of outbreaks among European communities tended to make it a disease among children. As early as 1700, English doctors began noticing that those who had a mild exposure to smallpox suffered a slight case, but attained the benefits of lifelong immunity. Experimentation with inoculation began, and in 1721 Cotton Mather convinced doctors in

The Smallpox Inoculation Dilemma

Mothers in eighteenth-century America needed to make a wrenching decision regarding the inoculation of their children against smallpox. The disease was lethal, killing around half of all those infected. Children under five years old who contracted smallpox suffered an 80 percent mortality rate. Those who survived were left with disfiguring scars and possible blindness. It had long been noticed that smallpox survivors were subsequently immune to further infection from the disease.

In 1721 experimental inoculation began in Boston. A healthy person had a small cut made in the arm, into which was placed puss taken from the sores of a smallpox victim. If the procedure was a success, the patient experienced a mild form of the disease. After a few days of nausea and body aches, the patient was expected to make a full recovery and posses lifelong immunity. A small percentage of inoculation patients inevitably sickened and died. The prospect of inoculation created a psychological frenzy in the communities where it was practiced in the early eighteenth century. Was inoculation contrary to the will of God? Could inducing the infection among healthy people open a Pandora's box by spreading the infection among citizens who chose not to be inoculated? As a precautionary measure, those who received inoculation were quarantined while their symptoms ran their course.

Colonial newspapers published articles on the risks and benefits of inoculation, which were carefully considered by mothers contemplating their own and their children's immunization. Perhaps some were influenced by the words of Benjamin Franklin, who wrote, "In 1736 I lost one of my sons, a fine boy four years old, by the smallpox. . . . I long bitterly regretted and still regret that I had not given it to him by inoculation."

By the late eighteenth century, inoculation techniques had improved, which reduced the risks of the procedure, and most mothers in urban areas were willing to have their children undergo the treatment.

Source: Burton, John D. "The Awful Judgments of God upon the Land: Smallpox in Colonial Massachusetts." *New England Quarterly* 74 (2001): 495–506.

Boston to begin the practice. Suspicion of the practice was rampant, but as decades passed, the effectiveness of inoculation was proven.

By the time of the American Revolution, inoculation against smallpox was required of all recruits into the army. The decision was more difficult for civilians. Because inoculation itself carried risk, many mothers chose not to inoculate themselves or their children. Diaries reveal that when large numbers of soldiers moved into an area, many women chose to proceed with inoculations. Although American soldiers were required to be inoculated, such was not the case among the thousands of camp followers and foreign mercenaries that occupied towns. Disease traveled with armies, and their presence was often enough to persuade reluctant mothers to inoculate their children. The inoculations were performed at local hospitals, where women waited and prayed that the induced illness would not overcome their children.

Diseases of the Early European Immigrants

The misery of malnutrition and inadequate housing endured by the earliest settlers was often compounded by the ravages of disease. "Seasoning" was a grim period endured by most settlers during their first two years, in which they would be exposed to a variety of new diseases and mental challenges. New immigrants were repeatedly struck with malaria or other fevers. Strange foods caused difficulties as they adjusted to a new diet. It was generally agreed that if a settler survived this seasoning period, he or she stood a good chance of attaining a normal life span.

One of the most devastating diseases among the early settlers in Virginia was salt poisoning. The colonists depended on rivers for their drinking water. This served them well most of the year, but during July and August the water level dropped owing to a decrease in rainfall and an increase in evaporation. As the river level typically dropped ten to fifteen feet, seawater worked its way up the river, encroaching as far as thirty miles upstream. Colonists could taste the increasingly brackish water, but did not realize the dangers of saline contamination. Salt poisoning weakened their resis-

tance to other diseases such as dysentery and the effects of malnutrition. Contaminated water caused dysentery, which results in severe inflammation of the bowel, bloody diarrhea, and dehydration. Death could follow, caused by bacterial toxins.

The other major disease to confront the early settlers was typhoid, also caused by contaminated water or food. High fever, lassitude, and bodily aches would intensify over a period of up to two weeks and was fatal in about a quarter of the cases.

The shockingly high death toll in the mid-Atlantic colonies has caused many historians to speculate on the reasons. The theory that malnutrition caused the deaths has been rejected in the face of evidence that food was generally plentiful except during a few winters. Contemporary observers spoke of the lethargy, apathy, and laziness of the settlers, who strangely refused to eat or fend for themselves. Although colonists were assaulted by numerous physical challenges, none of them were severe enough to result in the shockingly high death toll, which some years claimed upwards of 60 percent of the population. It is likely that the colonists' limited diet led to debilitating but typically nonfatal diseases such as scurvy, beriberi, and pellagra. Salt poisoning further weakened their immune systems. Symptoms of salt poisoning include lassitude, irritability, and apathy, all symptoms that had been attributed to the settlers at Jamestown by contemporary observers. The psychological stress caused by isolation in a strange and hostile environment further eroded their ability to battle disease.

The massive impact disease had on settlers in the Chesapeake Bay area did not occur in New England. There, water supplies were healthier, the colder climate inhibited the spread of disease, and the immigration of family groups might have limited the depression that apparently affected immigrants in the southern colonies.

Diseases of Childhood

Certain diseases appeared to strike children in a disproportionate number. This was because a large percentage of adults had been exposed to viruses and developed immunity. Children had no such safeguard, and when a viral outbreak swept through a town, it struck children down in frightening numbers. Women tried to protect their children by keeping them indoors, but lacking a fuller understanding of the nature of contagion, there were few effective measures to shield their children. The childhood diseases that caused the most fear were diphtheria, dysentery, and smallpox.

Diphtheria was a bacterial infection that caused sore throat, fever, and rapid pulse. If it developed into a severe case it caused breathing difficulties, poisoning of the blood, paralysis of the throat, and heart failure. Death typically occurred within a week. Dysentery also had devastating effects on children. Its main characteristic was debilitating diarrhea, which adults are usually able to survive, but can quickly kill a child. Caused by contaminated water and food supplies, it could sweep through a household with devastating consequences. Newspapers report of the toll it could take on a town. Dysentery devastated Massachusetts's communities in 1756, when it claimed the lives of five Sheppard children, four Parker children, four Smith children, four Lealands, and four Robinsons. At least one hundred other families lost two or three of their children to the disease. A minister in Lancaster, Massachusetts, thought the problem so severe he addressed one of his sermons to the children: "I write unto you little children . . . because I am tenderly concerned for you, and pained at my heart for that dreadful destruction that God had made among you within a few weeks. . . . In this parish I have buried 42 in about seven weeks, 33 of them children" (Caulfield 1942–1946, 52).

Such statements reflect on the trauma that could descend upon a community when large segments of its children were wiped out by disease. No mother could assume that all her children would survive to adulthood. The loss of even one child was traumatic, but the cumulative effect of multiple deaths must have been harrowing. Given the prevalence of childhood mortality, women had to develop coping mechanisms. Women's letters and diaries rarely mention infants, even though they go into detail about other events of their day. It has been suggested that women in early America might have unconsciously chosen not to bond with their babies until they had passed through the most dangerous stages of infancy and developed into sturdy toddlers. As soon as possible, mothers gave their children religious instruction that stressed salvation. Such attention to a child's spiritual health was no doubt a coping mechanism for a mother who knew she might lose the child to "a better afterlife."

Aside from contagious disease, the world of early America was full of other dangers to children. Accidents frequently happened from the use of candles or falling into open fires. Children drowned from falling into wells, streams, or off of wharves. Death could happen from eating poisonous berries or mushrooms. Most children grew up around large farm animals or horses, which presented another substantial source of danger.

Diseases of the Native Americans

The contact between European and Native American cultures proved disastrous for the Indians. Having migrated to America across the Bering Strait thousands of years earlier, Native Americans had never been exposed to the diseases that flourished in the crowded urban areas of Europe or the tropics of Africa. Thousands of years of exposure had brought Europeans and Africans a measure of tolerance for these pathogens. When they contracted the disease, they had a fighting chance of survival. Native Americans had no such biological defenses. The "Virgin Soil" theory postulates that because Native Americas lacked the biological exposure to diseases common elsewhere in the world, they were defenseless in the face of these viral and bacteriological invaders. Diseases such as smallpox, measles, and malaria swept through their communities like wildfire. Although accurate statistics are impossible to generate, it is estimated that most tribes lost between 50 and 90 percent of their populations to these newly imported diseases.

The most dreaded disease in early America was smallpox, a highly contagious and disfiguring disease that killed 15 to 20 percent of all Europeans who contracted it. Death rates were considerably higher among Native Americans.

A common treatment practiced by Native Americans for serious ailments was to sit in a sweat lodge, where toxins were perspired through the skin, followed by a plunge into cold water. This therapy was ineffective against European fevers and tended to further weaken those who practiced it. The Indian custom of fasting through an illness also weakened the strength of the afflicted.

Many infectious diseases confer immunity to their survivors, but Native Americans lacked the centuries of exposure that protected large percentages of Europeans. Smallpox, measles, bubonic plague, and scarlet fever all swept through the Indian population of North America with ferocious consequences. From 1616 to 1619 a debilitating disease raged throughout the Indian populations of New England. Probably either bubonic or pneumonic plague, it is believed this epidemic might have killed up to 90 percent of the Algonquians living along the seacoast. Smallpox epidemics occurred in 1616, 1622, 1633, 1649, 1662, 1669, and 1687. Smallpox was believed to have killed roughly half the native population in the Great Lakes region during the 1640s and 1650s. Measles crippled native populations in 1658 and 1692.

Lack of systematic record keeping prevents us from knowing how badly and when most epidemics struck, but at least thirteen major epidemics decimated the native population of North America in the seventeenth century. These epidemics swept through the land wherever European colonists settled, leaving the native population weakened and demoralized at a time they needed their strength to defend their lands.

Diseases among the Enslaved

Many enslaved Africans had a measure of tolerance for contagious diseases that were indigenous to Africa, such as malaria and yellow fever. It is estimated that as many as 90 percent of the people coming from West Africa had some form of immunity to malaria. It is now known that certain forms of the sickle-cell trait carried by many Africans granted them immunity to malaria. Ironically, the greater health of Africans made their institutionalized slavery even more tempting to European settlers, whose attempts to enslave Indians had been a failure,

owing in large part to chronic disease among the Indians.

Africans suffered in disproportionately high numbers when exposed to diseases that originated in Europe, such as smallpox, measles, and diphtheria. It has been postulated that slavery did not flourish in the North because of the high mortality among the African slaves exposed to the European disease culture that flourished in the temperate climate of the New England and the middle colonies. Indentured servitude supplied by European immigrants became the preferred choice for unskilled labor in the North, whereas African slavery burgeoned in the South. Estimates of mortality rates among African Americans indicate that they lived shorter and less healthy lives the farther north they lived.

Although European respiratory diseases such as tuberculosis, influenza, and pneumonia were less common in the South, they nevertheless took their toll on the slave population. Heavy labor and dietary deficiencies made slaves more susceptible to these infections. Because most slaves performed agricultural labor, they were also more susceptible to diseases contracted through contact with animals, such as anthrax and brucellosis.

Poor housing conditions contributed to the spread of diseases among slaves. Slave cabins typically had dirt floors, lacked adequate ventilation, were damp, and housed many people in tight quarters. Dysentery, tetanus, and other diseases linked to unsanitary conditions affected the enslaved population to a greater extent than other peoples.

See also Gynecological Issues, Venereal Disease

Further Reading

Caulfield, Ernest. "Some Common Diseases of Colonial Children." *Publications of the Colonial Society of Massachusetts* 35 (1942–1946): 4–75.

Coelho, Philip R., and Robert A. McGuire. "African and European Bound Labor in the British New World: The Biological Consequences of Economic Choices." *Journal of Economic History* 57 (March 1997): 83–115.

Crosby, Alfred W. *The Columbian Exchange: Biological and Cultural Consequences of 1492.* Westport, CT: Greenwood Publishing Co., 1972.

Curtin, Philip D. "Epidemiology and the Slave Trade." *Political Science Quarterly* 83 (1968): 190–216.

Dye, Nancy Schrom, and Daniel Blake Smith. "Mother Love and Infant Death, 1750–1920." *Journal of American History* 73 (1986): 329–353.

Earle, Carville V. "Environment, Disease, and Mortality in Early Virginia." In *The Chesapeake in the Seventeenth Century: Essays on Anglo-American Society and Politics*, eds. Thad W. Tate and David L. Ammerman. New York: Norton, 1979.

Kiple, Kenneth F., ed. *The Cambridge World History of Human Disease.* Cambridge: Cambridge University Press, 1993.

Kupperman, Karen Ordahl. "Apathy and Death in Early Jamestown." *Journal of American History* 66 (June 1979): 24–40.

———. "Fear of Hot Climates in the Anglo-American Colonial Experience." *William and Mary Quarterly,* 3d ser. 41 (1984): 213–240.

Winslow, Ola Elizabeth. *A Destroying Angel: The Conquest of Smallpox in Colonial Boston.* Boston: Houghton Mifflin, 1974.

Divorce

Like other laws in colonial America, rules regulating divorce and separation were inherited from England. Owing to a number of legal, religious, and practical issues, these English laws were quickly modified to suit the conditions in the American colonies. Although divorce in early America was always a difficult and legally cumbersome undertaking, it was far easier to make legal arrangements for the termination of a marriage in America than it was in England. English divorce was governed by the Church of England, which regarded a valid marriage as indissoluble. Only if the marriage was found to be null from the outset, in cases such as bigamy or a close relationship by blood, could the marriage be found invalid. (In extraordinarily rare cases, a nobleman could appeal for a private act passed by the House of Lords to dissolve a marriage if it could be proven the wife was adulterous) Such were the stringent divorce laws inherited by the American colonists, but a liberalization of divorce law took root almost from the outset of the colonial period.

The religious dissidents who settled in New England had little respect for the laws of the Church of England. Looking to the spiritual leadership of Martin Luther and John Calvin, the Puritans of the northern colonies viewed marriage as a civil contract, rather than a spiritual sacrament. As such, it could be dissolved for breaches such as adultery, desertion, cruelty, or incorrigible enmity between the spouses. These actions constituted a breaking of the marriage covenant, and thus the offended party could look to a civil court for relief.

There were two types of divorce available, *divortium a vinculo,* or true divorce, was the most complete severing of ties. It allowed both parties the ability to remarry, but was only granted in cases in which the marriage was judged null from the outset. Massachusetts and Connecticut had the most liberal divorce laws of the colonies and extended the grounds for complete divorce to include adultery, abuse, and desertion. *Divortium a mensa et thoro,* or separation from bed and board, was more common. All the legal obligations of marriage were maintained with the exception of cohabitation. It did not allow for the remarriage of either party. If the wife was found to be the innocent party, she was generally provided with ongoing financial support.

The dissolution of marriage in the southern colonies was more consistent with English law. The South was settled by Anglicans, who maintained allegiance to the Church of England, and for whom marriage was considered sacred and could only be broken if proven invalid. Limited divorces (*a mensa et thoro*) could be granted in flagrant cases of adultery or abuse but required an ecclesiastical court to make the ruling. Because there were no ecclesiastical courts in the colonies, many of the southern colonies allowed civil courts to assume this power. Absolute divorces were not permitted in the southern colonies until after the American Revolution. In the years following the war, each of the states liberalized the conditions under which an absolute divorce could be granted. Only South Carolina refused to permit absolute divorce until 1868.

Cited Reasons for Divorce

Adultery: Adultery was generally the claim most likely to result in a successful divorce application. To obtain a divorce on grounds of adultery, the adulterous act had to be testified to by two eyewitnesses or a confession of the guilty spouse. Alternatively, a male petitioner could prove adultery if his wife bore a child during a period when the husband was on an extended absence. Divorces were almost always granted if the wife was found guilty of adultery. Very few women even attempted to file for divorce based on an adulterous husband, and those who did were rarely granted one. A double standard clearly existed, in which sexual infidelity was not to be tolerated in a wife, but was condoned when committed by a husband. Some of this double standard can be accounted for by the reluctance of the law to force a man to leave his estate to a child who might not be his own. Divorcing an adulterous wife was therefore considered a man's right to protect his bloodline and inheritance.

Cruelty: An eighteenth-century euphemism for physical abuse, cruelty by itself was rarely accepted as grounds for divorce. A successful appeal on grounds of cruelty had to prove the woman feared grave bodily harm or death. Occasional or slight acts of physical violence were not substantial enough to warrant a divorce. If the cruelty escalated to the point where a wife could prove she feared for life or limb, the courts were willing to intercede on her behalf and force the husband to provide for her maintenance in a separate household. Thus, divorce from bed and board could be obtained, but an absolute divorce, with privileges of remarriage, were less common if abuse was the only charge.

Marital rape was not regarded as a crime or grounds for divorce. Alcohol abuse was frequently cited by both husbands and wives seeking divorce. Unless the problem drinking was associated with infidelity or extreme physical violence, however, it was not considered a factor in divorce petitions.

Physical abuse of women in early America can be documented through almshouse entries, court documents, and newspaper stories. Although a husband could be arrested for physically abusing his wife, it rarely resulted in more than a few days of confinement. Despite the dire situation abused wives found themselves in, only about one-third of divorce applications citing abuse were granted. Time and again husbands defended themselves by claiming that a wife was not submissive, was neglecting her housekeeping duties, or was promiscuous. In light of the low percentage of abuse allegations that resulted in divorce, such defenses were obviously accepted by the courts.

Women who were the target of severe abuse and had failed to obtain a divorce might simply leave their marriage. When Charity Barr left her husband, the enraged Mr. Barr took out an advertisement in the paper claiming his wife had deserted him for no reason. Mrs. Barr replied with an advertisement of her own, claiming repeated beatings and being "sometimes almost strangled by him, at other times thrown to the floor and stamped on, [with him] swearing he would murder her" (*Pennsylvania Gazette*, 10 August 1785). Mrs. Barr was fortunate in her ability to leave, because women who left their homes had no right to financial support from their husbands. Some desperate women might find shelter in an almshouse, although charitable institutions would usually only provide shelter until the woman's physical wounds had healed. Other women turned to friends, family, or their church for temporary sanctuary until their husband's rage had subsided. Because no church and few families could afford to support a woman for the rest of her life, most women eventually returned home.

Desertion: Some unhappy spouses simply left home, leaving their partner abandoned yet unable to remarry while the marriage was still valid. Depending on the colony, a period between three and seven years had to expire before an abandoned spouse could file this claim. Colonies with a heavy seafaring population also permitted the "absent and presumed dead" category. A combination of factors in early America made desertion common. It was relatively easy for an unhappily married spouse to simply abandon his or her town and take up residence elsewhere. The lack of communication and any sort of unified record keeping made locating an errant spouse almost impossible. Because divorce law tended to be punitive, meaning the guilty party

Divorces Filed by Women in Pennsylvania, 1785–1815

Grounds	Total Filed	Number Filed by Women	Percent of Total Filed by Women	Number Granted	Percent Granted
Adultery	127	43	34%	26	60%
Cruelty	76	75	99%	23	31%
Bigamy	8	6	75%	3	50%
Desertion	75	54	72%	34	63%
Impotence	3	3	100%	0	NA
False Rumor	1	0	NA	NA	NA
Adultery/Bigamy	4	2	50%	1	50%
Adultery/Cruelty	12	12	100%	6	50%
Adultery/Desertion	32	16	50%	8	50%
Bigamy/Cruelty	1	1	100%	0	NA
Bigamy/Desertion	9	6	67%	3	50%
Cruelty/Desertion	14	14	100%	10	71%
Unknown	5	4	80%	NA	NA
Totals	367	236	64%	114	48%

Source: Smith, Merril D.: *Breaking the Bonds: Marital Discord in Pennsylvania, 1730–1830.* New York: New York University Press, 1991, p. 27.

received an unfavorable financial settlement, a spouse who had been unfaithful might have perceived desertion a more desirable option.

Women who were deserted by husbands were placed in an odd sort of limbo. Because married women had the *feme covert* status, meaning they had little legal identity, they had difficulty finding the means to support themselves. Married women were unable to sue, engage in or enforce contracts, or own a business. A woman who had been abandoned by her husband would almost certainly need the support of her family for her basic support. The difficulty of obtaining a divorce and the long waiting period required to prove desertion caused many abandoned women to ignore their married status. Deborah Franklin, Benjamin Franklin's wife, had unknowingly married a bigamous man in 1725. This union was short lived, and the man eventually fled to the West Indies. Unwilling to undertake the legally burdensome process of a divorce, Deborah simply moved in with Franklin, and the couple declared themselves to the world to be legally married. Although there was a social stigma associated with this sort of common-law marriage, it was not enough to prevent the Franklins from rising in Philadelphia society.

Men were not the only people likely to desert from a marriage, although economic realities made desertion difficult for women. If a woman were wealthy, she might be able to seek shelter with friends or family. Less well-to-do women who deserted a marriage probably did so in the company of a lover. Husbands sometimes placed advertisements looking for runaway wives. The greatest damage a runaway wife could inflict on her husband was the use of his name to acquire credit. The *South Carolina Gazette* (25 May 1765) placed a notice from one disgruntled husband warning those who had dealings with his wife: "Whereas my wife, Mary Oxendine, hath eloped from me, this is to forewarn all persons from harboring or entertaining her, day or night, or crediting her in my name, as I am determined not to pay any debts by her contracted." The placing of a public notice was usually sufficient to protect a man from debts incurred by a runaway wife.

Social Implications

Women who found themselves in unhappy marriages faced challenges on economic and social grounds. If she were found to be the "guilty" party in a divorce action, a woman was unlikely to receive any form of financial support. Records of divorce petitions initiated by women usually requested the less severe *divortium a mensa et thoro,* or separation from bed and board, which would ensure she had ongoing financial support. A complete divorce rarely required any form of alimony for the wife. Furthermore, the social stigma of being a divorced woman was severe. Respectable families would have discouraged any of their menfolk from marrying such a woman, and the stigma might even taint the reputations of the divorced woman's children.

Given the difficult and publicly humiliating nature of divorce, some couples opted for private separation. Such agreements involved a legal contract that divided property and allowed for support payments. Neither party had the ability to remarry, but it allowed them to maintain their privacy while extricating themselves from an environment that one or both found to be intolerable.

Rates of divorce were extremely low in the early colonial period, with many communities having a divorce filed only every few years. By the 1740s rates began to increase, with some communities having multiple divorce cases filed annually. Although the laws regarding divorce had not changed, there was a striking increase in the number of petitions filed. Historians have speculated that as people witnessed more divorce in their community, discontented spouses were more willing to consider the possibility of legal action. Whatever the cause, rates of divorce gathered momentum throughout the eighteenth century. In Massachusetts, only six divorce petitions were filed between 1705 and 1714. Between 1765–1774 that number had grown to forty-six, and it would almost double in the following decade. There was no lessening of the social stigma of divorce in the eighteenth century, but it is possible that as people witnessed members of their own community successfully obtain a divorce, a chain reaction of dissatisfied spouses began to make use of the law.

Child Custody

There is a surprising lack of documentation regarding women's attempts to gain custody of their children during a divorce. During the eighteenth century, custody was almost systematically granted to the father, with little regard for the child's best interests. There was little sentimentality about children, who were viewed as economic assets under the direction and guidance of their father. Although mothers were entitled to respect and reverence from their children, courts did not believe they were entitled to any legal control outside of that willingly granted by the father. It was believed that women's loving nature was liable to spoil children and fathers were best able to provide vocational training necessary to ensure that the children became productive members of society.

Women knew there were no legal or cultural traditions that would allow them to retain custody if the father wished to raise the children. It is possible that women who felt strongly about raising their children simply did not seek divorces, knowing they would almost certainly lose contact with the children. By the late eighteenth century, courts began to consider the best interests of the child when assigning custody. Previously, only criminally negligent and abusive fathers would have lost custody.

See also Children, Custody of

Further Reading

Cott, Nancy F. "Divorce and the Changing Status of Women in Eighteenth Century Massachusetts." *William and Mary Quarterly* 33 (1976): 586–614.

Dayton, Cornelia Hughes. *Women before the Bar: Gender, Law, and Society in Connecticut, 1639–1789.* Chapel Hill: University of North Carolina Press, 1995.

Hirsch, Alison Duncan. "The Thrall Divorce Case: A Family Crisis in Eighteenth Century Connecticut." In *Women, Family and Community in Colonial America: Two Perspectives.* New York: Institute for Historical Research in History, 1983.

Salmon, Marylynn. *Women and the Law of Property in Early America.* Chapel Hill: University of North Carolina Press, 1986.

Smith, Merril D. *Breaking the Bonds: Marital Discord in Pennsylvania, 1730–1830.* New York: New York University Press, 1991.

Domestic Labor

One of the common ways a girl or woman could earn a small income was through taking a position as a domestic servant. The enormous amount of work necessary to keep a home operating was usually beyond the capacity of a sole woman. Even humble households could afford to hire a girl for part-time domestic chores. Although it was certainly preferable to rely on children for domestic service, young children were more a burden than an asset, and the optimal sex ratio of children could not be arranged. The window of years in which children could be depended on for household labor was usually no more than a decade. Women frequently relied on domestic servants to maintain a household during their children's early years and once again after the children left the household.

Indentured servitude and slavery were among the options for domestic labor, although both of these involved a greater financial investment than most colonial households could afford. Unlike domestic servants of the nineteenth century, colonial servants rarely lived in the home of their employer. They were usually village girls who might help out a few days per week or during seasonal periods requiring heavy labor. Likewise, a young girl might be employed full time for a few months to help out after the birth of a child.

Before the age of industrialization, a great deal of manual labor was required to keep a dwelling habitable. Tasks assigned to servants might include chopping wood, building fires, lighting and tending stoves, hauling water, and washing clothes. If the household was in a town, it is likely that most household products, such as candles, soap, butter, and woven cloth, would have been purchased rather than produced at home. Despite the luxury of being able to purchase such goods, buying them required walking about town to various establishments in order to procure these goods. Shopping often fell to servants, while the mistress stayed home to care for children. Other common tasks performed by domestic servants included knitting, mending, laundry, weeding the garden, tending farm animals, cleaning out the fire grates, and cleaning house. Cooking was one of the most labor-intensive chores. Women slaughtered animals, plucked poultry, smoked meat, dried fruit, baked bread, and prepared meals. Because options for preservation were limited, the chore of food preparation was unending.

Domestic servants tended to be young, unmarried women. Throughout most of the colonial period, servants were in scarce supply. Women married young and were rarely available for paid employment outside the home or family business. In the handful of communities that had a surplus female population (usually seaports), women married later and were therefore available for service. Some girls went into service because they had too many sisters at home. Most came from middle-class homes, and domestic servitude was merely a temporary condition until they married and established their own household. This pattern of informal domestic service provided an important social function in colonial America. It broadened a girl's ties to the community, allowing her to form a close relationship with another family in her town. She learned additional domestic skills from her host family. These few years when she transitioned from a girl into a woman were usually followed with marriage. Within a few short years, this young woman would likely be taking in a local girl of her own to assist her through early years of motherhood.

Typical domestic servants in America lacked the deferential and subservient attitude common among European servants. Likely owing to the scarce supply of domestic servants, young women knew they could easily find employment elsewhere if they were abused, overworked, or disrespected. Despite the shortage of female servants, wages were low. Household maids typically earned 40 percent what unskilled male laborers earned.

Some women became domestic servants later in life, which was usually a sign of severe economic stress. Widows or the wives of disabled men might turn to domestic service after their traditional means of income was cut off. Such women rarely boarded with a family and usually provided only day service. Turnover for such work was high, with the average length of service lasting fewer than four months. Few women were likely to obtain long-term employment from a single family. People who desired long-term service could buy a slave or an indentured servant. Only those who had seasonal needs turned to hiring a free woman. Oftentimes these women would be hired by the day or by the week.

The status of "housekeeper" was reserved for domestics who had greater experience and age than typical domestic servants. Such a woman assumed higher responsibility for household management, freeing the mistress of the house for more leisure or entertaining. Housekeepers typically lived with the family, earned a better wage, and worked for a longer period of time than the transient domestic servant. They might have been given their own bedroom and even been considered part of the family. Only wealthy families could afford a housekeeper, who would most likely be a widow or a spinster.

Further Reading

Hammond, Charles A. "The Dilemmas of Domestic Service in New England, 1750–1850." *Dublin Seminar for New England Folklife* 13 (1988): 58–87.

Main, Gloria L. "Gender, Work, and Wages in Colonial New England." *William and Mary Quarterly*, 3d ser. 51 (1994): 39–66.

Salinger, Sharon V. "Send No More Women: Female Servants in Eighteenth Century Philadelphia." *Pennsylvania Magazine of History and Biography* 107 (1983): 29–48.

Spruill, Julia Cherry. *Women's Life and Work in the Southern Colonies*. Chapel Hill: University of North Carolina Press, 1938.

Ulrich, Laurel Thatcher. "Martha Ballard and Her Girls: Women's Work in Eighteenth Century Maine." In *Work and Labor in Early America*, ed. Stephen Innes. Chapel Hill: University of North Carolina Press, 1988.

Wulf, Karin A. *Not All Wives: Women of Colonial Philadelphia*. Ithaca, NY: Cornell University Press, 2000.

Domestic Violence

Violence within the home occurred in colonial society, although their level of tolerance for physical abuse differed from contemporary standards. Corporal correction of children, and occasionally servants, was accepted. Physical violence of a husband toward a wife was universally condemned, although it was outlawed only in a few colonies. People who used physical violence on family members or children were considered lazy, crude, drunken, and antisocial.

The study of domestic violence is always distorted by the knowledge that many, perhaps most, cases are never reported to authorities. Although colonial courts record numerous cases of abuse complaints, it is difficult to determine what percent never came to the attention of the court. In the case of wife abuse, we know that most incidents were never reported. Abused women often turned to almshouses for shelter when battering put them in serious physical danger. Rarely are there corresponding court records to indicate these women initiated legal action against their abusers.

The most effective weapon of any abuse victim in colonial America was publicity. Maintaining a respectable reputation in colonial society was immensely important. Most people in these small communities knew one another, and public humiliation was an effective means of correcting behavior. Beyond avoiding mere embarrassment, being of good standing in the community was essential for economic well-being. Most business was conducted by barter or credit. Trade people had to have faith that payment for services would follow when the crops were harvested or the ship came in. If a man's reputation had been clouded by rumors of drunkenness or intemperate behavior, few people would do business with him. Likewise, settlers depended on their neighbors for assistance in times of need. If a man fell ill during harvest, neighbors assisted in bringing in his crops. Neighbors banded together to rebuild a barn damaged by fire. They brought food and firewood during times of crises. A man of disreputable character could hardly depend on such goodwill.

Public censure was surprisingly effective when the abuser had control of his or her impulses. When alcohol or mental illness was involved, the abuser had little regard for rational decision making. In such cases the victim needed to either suffer in silence or depend on the community for assistance.

Spousal Abuse

The law on spousal abuse differed depending on the colony. Pennsylvania strongly disapproved of marital violence, but unless the woman was maimed or in fear of her life, there was no law against it. Massachusetts passed a law in 1641 that prohibited a husband from striking his wife or inflicting any "bodily correction" unless he was defending himself. Verbal abuse between spouses was prohibited and punishable by two hours in the stocks or a whipping. There was no concept of marital rape in colonial America.

Perhaps because battering was illegal in Massachusetts, there are more public records documenting such cases from Massachusetts than from other colonies that had no formal laws. Massachusetts punished offenders through a combination of admonition, fines, posting bond to ensure future good behavior, sitting in the stocks, and public whipping. Alcohol was cited time and again as a factor in domestic violence. Early Americans consumed an enormous amount of alcohol, usually beginning with a mug of beer at breakfast. With alcohol being ubiquitous in daily life, it is little wonder that some slipped into alcoholism and its associated reckless cruelty. Physical altercations were also prompted by arguments over money, infidelity, and jealousy.

Many men sought to justify their behavior by claiming it was their "prerogative" to correct and guide a spouse. In one 1790 divorce case, Michael Fisher went so far as to say, "beating [his wife] was necessary to make her a good housekeeper and that she must have more of it" (Smith 1991, 114). Other husbands trivialized their violence, claiming they were provoked or that the lack of lasting physical damage indicated it was not a serious matter.

Women who had supportive family members living nearby or had independent means of income were more likely to seek out help, either through a minister, legal action, or publicly discrediting their husbands. Openly proclaiming one's husband a wife beater was not only humiliating for the woman, it might open her to charges of slander. Nevertheless, publicly damaging a husband's reputation appears to have been a popular means of revenge and correction. Some women went so far as to place advertisements in newspapers explaining their dissatisfaction. In 1796 Phebe Darling posted an advertisement in the *Vermont Gazette*, claiming her husband was a drunkard and had "at sundry times used me in so improper and cruel a manner, as to destroy my happiness and endanger my life" (*Vermont Gazette*, 1 February 1796).

Women in desperate circumstances might turn to an almshouse for shelter. One Jane Kean was brought to an almshouse in 1797 after a beating so severe she attempted suicide by drowning. In 1803 one Ann Mayberry sought shelter because she feared for the safety of her unborn child. Such help was only temporary. As soon as the baby was born

---

Rule of Thumb

A popular but inaccurate attribution for the expression "rule of thumb" is that it refers to a standard for the severity of wife beating acceptable in colonial America. According to the myth, early American courts permitted a man to beat his wife so long as the width of the rod was smaller than a man's thumb. Diligent research by historians has been unable to locate any law or informal precedent to substantiate this claim. Wife beating was not acceptable in colonial America, and numerous statutes and sermons throughout the colonies condemned the practice. Moral and legal condemnation did not prevent wife abuse from occurring, but it was not casually accepted by courts or society. The earliest known reference in American legal documents is an 1868 decision by a North Carolina judge who refused to prosecute a case because he believed a man had the right to beat his wife so long as the switch was smaller than his thumb. The state supreme court rejected this logic as unfounded, but the existence of the case has given credibility to the misconception.

According to the *Oxford English Dictionary*, the phrase *rule of thumb* has been in common use for more than 300 years, used as a means to form an estimate based on experience, rather than scientific knowledge.

Source: Kelly, Henry Ansgar. "Rule of Thumb and the Folklaw of the Husband's Stick." *Journal of Legal Education* 44 (1994): 341–365.

or the injuries were healed, almshouses were forced to turn these women out.

In extreme cases a woman might have had no choice but to turn to the courts to protect herself or her children. When courts intervened, husbands were usually fined. A £30 fine would have been a typical punishment for a tradesman of average income. He was required to post a like amount to ensure good behavior for the coming year. Imprisonment was rarely used. A man might be jailed for a day until he sobered up or his temper cooled. Lengthy imprisonment was far too expensive for communities to routinely use unless the offense was so severe as to put the woman's life in danger.

The options for women in chronic abuse situations were few. Divorce was difficult to obtain and was rarely an option. Some women with no children simply fled to another town. These women either had to find means to earn a living or turn to sympathetic friends for support. This choice was not available to most women, and they simply had to endure their situation for the duration of their lives.

Although the majority of reported spousal abuse cases cite the husband as the abuser, around 20 percent of the cases indicate the wife as the initiator of the violence. Eighteen percent of the divorce cases filed by men in New England cited violent wives as the cause. Women were charged with drunkenness and physical attacks on their husbands. In 1641, in Massachusetts, one woman was ordered to be severely whipped for having attempted to poison her husband with mercury. Like abusive men, women who physically or verbally attacked their spouses were subject to fines, whippings, and sitting in the stocks.

Child Abuse

Unlike spousal abuse, there were few laws or social stigmas associated with corporal punishment of children. Physical assaults on a child were assumed to be a legitimate means of parental discipline. Colonial America was a society in which children were to be obedient, and strong discipline was met with approval. Many colonies had laws indicating that physical punishment of anyone (prisoner, child, or spouse) could not be inhuman, barbarous, or

excessively cruel. Such laws were usually the only protection a child had under the law. There seems to have been no understanding of the distinction between calmly dispensed physical punishment and the actions of an angered parent who vented his or her frustration on a child. In almost all such cases, a parent could safely claim to have been disciplining a rebellious child.

Children could be physically disciplined by a parent, schoolteacher, or an employer. Unless the child was in danger of maiming or death, it was unlikely the state would intervene in any punishment deemed appropriate. The major exception to the routine disregard of children's physical well-being was in sexual offenses. Men who had sexual relations with a girl under ten were punished by death.

Parents were far more likely to be accused of neglecting their children than abusing them. There are numerous cases of parents who were accused of letting their children beg in the streets because they were too drunk to mind the children. Likewise, if a parent neglected to teach a child useful skills, the child could be taken away and apprenticed to someone willing to undertake the responsibility.

A child's obligation to respect and obey a parent did not cease when they became adults. Adult children were prosecuted for striking a parent. Others could be prosecuted for verbal abuse or rebellion against a parent, even after the child was married and living in another home. At some point the question of elder abuse arises. In 1705 a young man was fined for "horribly" abusing his grandfather in addition to swearing and cursing (McDonald 1986, 60). Other adult children were prosecuted for depriving parents or grandparents of property. In addition to legal actions, churches often intervened to show their displeasure. Both children and parents were excommunicated because of slanderous or violent actions toward family members.

Servants and Slaves

Slaves had no personal freedoms except those allowed by their master. Many servants in colonial America were also under complete control of their master or employer. Indentured servants were required to serve a set number of years. Apprentices and bound servants were usually young children under the age of eighteen, but who had been contractually obligated to serve and obey their employer. Children as young as five could be bound out as servants. Corporeal punishment was well within a master's prerogative and potentially more dangerous to the child to whom he might have had little emotional empathy. If children were severely maltreated, the indenture could be dissolved and the child passed to the care of another master.

Servants were as likely to be in danger from fellow servants as they were from their master. In the middle colonies where there were few women, young indentured women often complained of sexual harassment by other servants. Especially on rural farms, servants who were sent to the fields had little supervision, and opportunity for sexual assault was high.

Female servants living in remote areas were exceptionally vulnerable. Their physical isolation made it difficult to appeal for help. Servants were prohibited from leaving plantations without written permission from their master. In cases of sexual abuse, a servant's plight often came to the attention of authorities only when she became pregnant. Even then, she risked being labeled a willing participant in fornication.

In some cases a mistress might have cause to fear her own servants. If she was a widow, or her husband was away for an extended period, household discipline was her responsibility. Discipline was often physical, such as a cuff on the side of the head or a smack with a rake. Servants were liable to resent such correction under any circumstances, but when it was administered by a woman, tempers sometimes snapped. In 1665 Anne Batten was in charge of the family's Virginia farm while her husband traveled to England. When disciplining her indentured servant Andrew Hill, he grabbed the stick from her and turned it on her. Another servant, Hannah Langley, joined in the fray and participated in beating their mistress. In 1679 a Mrs. Hyde struck her servant Mary Barrow, who impulsively struck her back. Although corporeal punishment was an accepted means of disciplining servants and children, it should not be unexpected that

such violence was occasionally turned on the abuser.

Slaves suffered immense physical cruelty at the hands of their masters. There were no social prohibitions against beating or whipping a female slave. Slaves who caught the eye of their master had little choice but to endure sexual violation. This form of sexual abuse could be ironically compounded if the mistress of the plantation vented jealous rage on the slave. Some slaves died as the result of severe beatings. Most colonies had laws prohibiting the killing of a slave, but these were routinely put aside if the abuser claimed the slave had become violent and needed correction.

See also Divorce; Infanticide

Further Reading

McDonald, Brenda D. "Domestic Violence in Colonial Massachusetts." *Historical Journal of Massachusetts* 14 (1986): 53–64.

Roth, Randolph A. "Spousal Murder in Northern New England, 1776–1865." In *Over the Threshold: Intimate Violence in Early America,* eds. Christine Daniels and Michael V. Kennedy. New York: Routledge, 1999.

Rowe, G. S., and Jack D. Marietta. "Personal Violence in a Peaceable Kingdom, Pennsylvania 1682–1801." In *Over the Threshold: Intimate Violence in Early America,* eds. Christine Daniels and Michael V. Kennedy. New York: Routledge, 1999.

Smith, Merril D. *Breaking the Bonds: Marital Discord in Pennsylvania, 1730–1830.* New York: New York University Press, 1991.

Snyder, Terri L. "As If There Was Not Master or Woman in the Land: Gender, Dependency, and Household Violence in Virginia, 1646–1720." In *Over the Threshold: Intimate Violence in Early America,* eds. Christine Daniels and Michael V. Kennedy. New York: Routledge, 1999.

Duston, Hannah Emerson

Colonial heroine who escaped captivity by Native Americans (1657–1736)

Most of Hannah Duston's seventy-nine years of life were consistent with that of a typical Puritan wife and mother in rural Massachusetts. Married to a bricklayer and farmer, Hannah and her husband,

Thomas, had thirteen children, eight of whom survived into adulthood. She lived in a cottage built by her husband a few miles outside the town of Haverhill, Massachusetts. Her days were spent caring for her children and assisting her husband by tending to their nearby fields.

The event that would shake Hannah Duston's world occurred in 1697 as a result of King William's War. Fought between France and England, this war spilled into the American colonies. French forces, under the command of Count de Frontenac, encouraged their Indian allies to attack and disrupt English settlements. Such an assault occurred on the town of Haverhill in March 1697. Thomas Duston was in his fields when he noticed a band of Abenakis Indians moving toward his home. Hannah had given birth to their eighth child, a girl, only five days earlier. Thomas gathered the older seven children and directed them to flee toward a nearby garrison. Still in bed following childbirth, Hannah begged her husband to leave and protect the other children on their flight to the garrison. Thomas left Hannah and the infant in the care of the midwife, Mary Neff. Unable to flee the house in time, the trio was taken captive by the Indians.

Hannah was forced to dress quickly and was able to find only one shoe before being forced onto her long march north. The infant soon became a burden to the Indians, and Hannah watched as her captors bashed her daughter's head against a tree. It is estimated that the band of Indians and the two captive women walked almost one hundred miles before Hannah and Mary were turned over to an Indian family on an island near present-day Concord, New Hampshire. There they met another English captive, a boy named Samuel Lennardson, who had been captured over a year earlier. The Indian family consisted of two men, three women, and seven children. These were "praying Indians," who had been converted to Catholicism by the French. Despite their shared Christian faith, Hannah and Mary Neff were abused by the Indians and taunted with the news that they were to be turned over to other Indians who would have them stripped, scourged, and forced to run a possibly fatal gauntlet.

On the evening of 30 March 1697, Hannah and Samuel planned an ambush on their captors. Using hatchets, they each killed one of the sleeping Indian men. Then Hannah proceeded to kill eight others. One wounded squaw and one child escaped. Before fleeing the island, Hannah scalped the dead Indians for proof of her story. Hannah, Mary, and Samuel used a canoe to escape the island, later called Dustin Island, and returned to Haverhill a few days later.

Hannah collected a bounty of £25 for her scalps. Mary and Samuel were each awarded £12 for bravery. For a year after her captivity, Hannah was a heroine in her Massachusetts community. Her ordeal became the subject of a sermon by Cotton Mather, and she was invited to dine with local dignitaries. She received gifts and accolades from people throughout the colonies, including the governor of Maryland. After the initial commotion faded, Hannah returned to her farm. She bore more children and lived out the rest of her days as an ordinary New England farmer's wife.

Although during her life Hannah was characterized as a self-reliant and heroic mother who avenged the death of her child, in the nineteenth century her reputation underwent a curious evolution. No longer viewing her as a heroine, writers such as Nathaniel Hawthorne began to portray her as a bloodthirsty virago who slaughtered innocent children. In 1836 Hawthorne published an article in which he suggested Hannah personified Puritan brutality that delighted in the destruction of the American Indian and the unspoiled American wilderness. Hawthorne even suggested that Thomas Duston chose not to rescue his wife because he knew her aggressive character would be more than a match "for a whole tribe of Indians." Many of the writers who condemned Hannah Duston seem to take offence at her unladylike behavior, which was at odds with the feminine, domestic ideal of Victorian America.

Other writers continued to defend Duston, claiming she had good cause to fear for her life and avenge the death of her child. In 1874 and 1879 monuments were erected in New England to commemorate her experiences. She continues to be a figure of ambiguous reputation, representing a combination of bravery, self-reliance, and vengeful brutality.

See also Indian Captivity

Further Reading

Hawthorne, Nathaniel, et al. *The Captivity Narrative of Hannah Duston, Related by Cotton Mather, John Greenleaf Whittier, Nathaniel Hawthorne, and Henry David Thoreau: Four Versions of Events in 1697.* San Francisco: Arion Press, 1987.

Morse, Mary Harrower. "Murderess or Heroine?" *New England Galaxy* 9 (1968): 40–45.

Ulrich, Laurel Thatcher. *Good Wives: Image and Reality in the Lives of Women in Northern New England, 1650–1750.* New York: Vintage Books, 1980.

Weis, Ann-Marie. "The Murderous Mother and the Solicitous Father: Violence, Jacksonian Family Values, and Hannah Duston's Captivity." *American Studies International* 36 (1998): 46–65.

Whitford, Kathryn. "Hannah Duston: The Judgment of History." *Essex Institute Historical Collections* 108 (1972): 304–325.

Dutch Settlement, Women's Life and Culture in

The Dutch colony of New Netherlands (later renamed New York) was created as part of the vast seaborne empire of the Dutch republic. With wealthy entrepreneurs, skilled artisans, and international trading connections, the Dutch empire sought to create an outpost in the American wilderness to exploit the natural resources of the New World. The Dutch had gained experience in the establishment of colonies in the Indies. In marked contrast to some of the disastrous English expeditions, the early Dutch settlements in America were well planned and fully supplied. Some of the initial Dutch families arrived in America with the raw materials for several houses, ready to be assembled upon arrival.

Established to become an outpost of international trade, the Dutch colony quickly established flourishing towns, harbors, trading centers, and a cosmopolitan air. Importing the styles of housing from Europe, the Dutch home was dominated by a large stone fireplace. Walls were whitewashed, with exposed beam ceilings. Windows were common, and the front doors had a hinge in the top portion, so it could be opened for light while the closed bottom prevented animals from entering the home. The Dutch took care to enhance their homes with paintings, decorative ceramics, and quality furniture. Dutch women gained a reputation as exceptional housekeepers, taking pride in establishing a clean and comfortable home, complete with hearty meals, flawlessly maintained clothing, and attractive gardens.

Despite the value placed on housekeeping, Dutch women had far greater opportunities in society than most other European or American women. Although Dutch law prevented women from holding public office, in most other legal privileges they were on a par with men. Women could own and inherit property, operate a business, sue an abusive husband, and keep their own names after marriage. Schooling was also important to the Dutch, whose women had a higher literacy rate (45 percent) than the women of Virginia (25 percent) or Massachusetts (33 percent).

Marriage was considered a partnership. Although men were the senior partner in a marriage, Dutch women enjoyed more legal and economic rights than women anywhere else in the colonies. Dutch wives often participated in the family business, which was usually located very near the home. Record keeping and accounting were taught to many Dutch girls, which became a useful skill if she participated in the family business. This advanced level of education and exposure to the family business gave Dutch women essential skills to maintain their standard of living if they become widowed.

Women had considerable freedom in selecting a husband, although the founding families of the colonies—the Philipses, Van Courtlandts, Van Rennselaers, and Schuylers—tended to intermarry with great regularity. A woman could select from either a *manus* marriage, in which her legal identity would be subsumed by her husband, or an *usus* marriage, in which she maintained all her legal rights. An *usus* marriage was usually accompanied by an antenuptial contract that spelled out and protected the bride's premarital property.

New Amsterdam (New York) was the most cosmopolitan town in seventeenth-century North America. Dutch women often played active roles in trade. (Bettmann/CORBIS)

The Dutch colonies had difficulty attracting settlers from Holland, where employment was high, the economy strong, and religious persecution almost nonexistent. They were therefore willing to accept settlers from England and France as well as Jewish immigrants. From the outset New Netherlands had a culturally diverse and cosmopolitan atmosphere. Although strengthened by these diverse settlers, it also proved a danger to the Dutch control of the colony. The excellent harbors and abundant natural resources made the colony desirable to the English, who succeeded in seizing the ill-defended colony in 1664.

Although the Dutch Reformed Church was the only officially sanctioned church in the colony, the pluralism of New Netherlands required some conciliation for outside religions. The Dutch showed tolerance for various forms of worship so long as it was done quietly and without outward attempts at evangelism. The English conquest in 1664 was accompanied by promises to continue to permit religious liberty for all, especially the Dutch Reformed Church, although these promises proved short lived.

The coming of English rule in 1664 also impacted the legal identity of women. Because women were no longer permitted independent legal rights, the unusually high rates of female participation in business and trade dwindled in the coming decades. By the eighteenth century most of the immigrants coming to New York were now English, rather than Dutch. New York was founded by the Dutch to become a commercial trading hub, and in that respect their influence lingers to this day.

See also Legal Status of Women, Dutch Colonies

Further Reading

Biemer, Linda Briggs. *Women and Property in Colonial New York: The Transition from Dutch to English Law, 1643–1727.* Ann Arbor, MI: UMI Research Press, 1979.

Cooke, Jacob Ernest, ed. *Encyclopedia of the North American Colonies.* New York: Charles Scribner's Sons, 1993.

Gherke, Michael Eugene. "Dutch Women in New Netherland and New York in the Seventeenth Century." Dissertation. West Virginia University, 2001.

Van Rensselaer, Mrs. John King. *The Goede Vrouw of Mana-ha-ta: At Home and in Society, 1609–1760.* New York: Charles Scribner's Sons, 1898.

Dyer, Mary

Quaker martyr (c. 1610–1660)

Little is known about Mary Dyer's early years, but by all accounts she was attractive, highly educated, and from a privileged background. In 1633 she married William Dyer, a successful merchant, in England. In 1635 they traveled to America where they joined the first generation of settlers in the Massachusetts Bay Colony. Although the Dyers considered themselves Puritans, Mary became close friends with Anne Hutchinson and was soon in sympathy with Hutchinson's radical religious beliefs that proclaimed the spirit of God dwelled within a saved person.

Mary Dyer and Anne Hutchinson's friendship was further solidified by the tragic events of 1637, when Mary went into premature labor. A skilled midwife, Hutchinson assisted at the delivery. A dead and terribly deformed baby girl was born. The superstitious nature of seventeenth-century colonists sometimes claimed that deformed children were either the judgment of God, the work of the Devil, or punishment for the sins of the parents. Anne Hutchinson quietly buried the child and bid the other attendants at the birth to remain silent about the details of the birth. The child's existence remained a secret for five months.

In 1638 Anne Hutchinson was formally excommunicated from the church. As she left the scene of her trial, Mary Dyer rose from the assembly and walked hand in hand with Hutchinson out of the building. Such a public act of support for a notorious woman was bound to rouse suspicion, and rumors of Mary's malformed child began to circulate. Church authorities ordered the infant to be exhumed, and an examination was performed. Horrific descriptions of the child were circulated, claiming the child had no head, had claws instead of feet, and scales instead of flesh. News of the "monstrous birth" was used as evidence of Mary Dyer's wickedness and the contaminating effects of associating with Anne Hutchinson.

A wave of excommunications followed Hutchinson's banishment, and the Dyers were eventually banished from the colony as well. Fleeing to the more tolerant colony of Rhode Island, William Dyer became one of the founders of Portsmouth and eventually served as attorney general of the colony. In 1652 Mary and her husband accompanied Roger Williams to England on a political mission. Although her husband soon returned to the colonies, Mary remained in England for five years, during which time she became exposed to the teachings of George Fox and the Quakers. Similar to Hutchinson's teachings, the Quakers believed that the spirit of God dwelled within an individual and that revelation was an ongoing process. This egalitarian philosophy undermined the authority of church leaders and respect for tradition.

Quaker missionaries were enthusiastic and eager to spread their doctrine. After successful missions to Rhode Island and Barbados, they began encroaching on the Puritan stronghold of Massachusetts. The Puritan leaders of the Massachusetts

Illustration entitled *Mary Dyer Led to Execution.* The illustration shows Mary Dyer holding a Bible surrounded by a crowd and, more closely, by soldiers with guns and drums. Dyer was a Quaker martyr who was hanged in 1660 in Boston. (Bettmann/CORBIS)

Bay Colony looked with horror on the zealous Quakers and quickly passed brutal laws to prohibit their proselytizing in Massachusetts. Whipping, mutilation, and banishment were all used in the attempt to eradicate the Quaker threat. In 1656 a law was passed that made it illegal for any commander of a ship or other vessel to transport Quakers into the colony. Anyone in possession of Quaker literature was to be fined.

Unaware of these laws, when Mary Dyer returned from England she landed in Boston on her way to Rhode Island. She was immediately identified as a Quaker, imprisoned, and held incommunicado. Upon hearing of his wife's imprisonment two months later, William Dyer came to her aid as soon as possible. Using his position, he was able to obtain a release for his wife on the conditions she be removed from the colony without attempting to preach and was never to return.

In 1658 Massachusetts passed a law that made preaching the Quaker doctrine punishable by death. Two earnest Quaker missionaries felt compelled to enter the colony and spread the word. They were immediately arrested and sentenced to a flogging. Upon hearing of the sentence, Mary went to visit them in prison and was herself arrested. The three were released with the admonition not to return to Massachusetts. Apparently determined to challenge the law, the three missionaries returned to the colony and once again began preaching. Authorities arrested all three and sentenced them to death by hanging.

It is difficult from a distance of more than three hundred years to understand the hostility the Quaker sect aroused in the Puritans of Massachusetts. Although Quakers would later be associated with pacifism and charitable works, the seventeenth-century Puritans viewed them as wild-eyed radicals, deluded by Satan, and bent on destroying the unity and sanctity of the perfect society the Puritans had carved out in the American wilderness. The persistence of Mary and her fellow missionaries gave fuel to this speculation.

Mary's husband appealed her sentence and enlisted the aid of the governors of Connecticut and Nova Scotia to seek clemency. These petitions were presented to the Massachusetts court, which publicly rejected them. On 27 October 1659 the three Quakers were led to the gallows. Mary was forced to watch her two companions be executed and was then bound hand and foot and had the noose placed around her neck. She was then told her sentence was to be commuted for forty-eight hours, during which time she was to remove herself from the colony forever.

Mary left Massachusetts and began preaching to the Indians on Long Island Sound. Apparently unable to reconcile herself to the laws of Massachusetts that strictly forbade any form of the Quaker faith, Mary once again felt compelled to return. Her arrest and trial were swift and severe.

Her husband once again appealed for mercy and even implied that his wife was suffering from madness. The pleas fell on deaf ears, and Mary Dyer was hanged on 1 June 1660. As she mounted the gallows she asked that the unjust laws against preaching be repealed, but forgave her judges as people who erred from the simplicity of their hearts and extended her forgiveness to them. Her last words spoke of her joy as she prepared to enter Paradise.

There would be one last Quaker martyr, William Leddra, executed in 1661. The Puritan ministers were slowly coming to the conclusion that the executions were not effective and in fact might have been elevating the Quakers to martyr status. Furthermore, as they were still answerable to the king of England, it was not clear they had the authority to execute anyone for religious beliefs that were recognizably Christian. In September 1661 King Charles II ordered the halt of Quaker executions.

Mary Dyer's memory would ultimately be commemorated by a statue erected outside the State House in Boston, not far from a statue of her friend Anne Hutchinson.

See also Hutchinson, Anne Marbury; Quaker Women

Further Reading

Myles, Anne G. "From Monster to Martyr: Representing Mary Dyer." *Early American Literature* 36 (2001): 1–30.

Pestana, Carla Gardina. "The City upon a Hill under Siege: The Puritan Perception of the Quaker Threat to Massachusetts Bay, 1656–1661." *New England Quarterly* 56 (1983): 323–353.

———. "The Quaker Executions as Myth and History." *Journal of American History* 80 (1993): 441–469.

Plimpton, Ruth. *Mary Dyer: Biography of a Quaker Rebel.* Boston: Branden Publishing Company, 1994.

E

Education

The primary motivation for teaching girls reading skills throughout most of the early American period was to promote religious instruction and the ability to read the Bible. Because women were responsible for educating their young children, it was important for them to have basic literacy and the ability to teach the scripture to their children. Educating women toward any professional capacity was almost unheard of, and a formal education was not required to perform other daily functions in a typical colonial household. Throughout most of colonial America, education for girls was limited to reading and learning practical household skills. Girls from wealthier families might attend schools where they learned refinements thought important for a social hostess, such as dancing, foreign languages, or embroidery.

The quality of education a girl received varied depending on the region of the colony she was being raised in and whether she lived in an urban or a rural environment. The religious nature of the New England settlements, combined with their greater population density, resulted in greater attention to education and an easier ability to provide for formal schooling. The sparsely settled southern colonies, with their populations scattered throughout rural farms, made the establishment of schools difficult and in many cases impossible. As a result, education in the southern colonies occurred almost entirely at home, with some wealthier planters being able to hire tutors and neighboring children often invited to attend a few hours of schooling per day.

Basic Literacy

The traditional view that most women in early America were illiterate has been overturned by recent scholarship, which draws the distinction between the ability to read and the ability to write. Although these skills are learned simultaneously in the contemporary era, it is clear that reading was taught well before writing instruction in colonial society. Thus, studies that estimate female illiteracy based on a woman's inability to sign her name (such as on a marriage license or a will) provide an inaccurate measure of women's reading skills.

Studies indicate that between 30 and 45 percent of American women were able to sign their names in the seventeenth and eighteenth centuries. Women unable to sign their name made a "mark," usually an *X* or the signer's initials, to stand in place of a signature. An explanation of why a woman might be able to read and unable to write can be found in the manner of early literacy instruction. Children learned their letters by using hornbooks, a single page tacked to a wooden paddle that contained the alphabet and possibly the Lord's Prayer. After mastering the basic letters, students graduated to primers, or small booklets for basic reading and religious instruction. They usually contained a section presenting syllable combinations, words of increasing difficulty, and short prayers, psalms, and a catechism.

Reading instruction was conducted orally. Students sounded out syllables, words, and strung sentences together. They were not required to write. It

A New England Dame School of the Colonial Period. Color engraving, 1713. The dame school was one of the few educational opportunities available for ordinary girls. (Bettmann/CORBIS)

is likely that most girls would have learned reading at home from their mother, who might not have possessed writing skills either. Learning to write required the purchase of paper and investing in a professional teacher. Only parents who envisioned a professional future for their child would have been likely to invest in such a luxury. This typically meant daughters were excluded from writing instruction, although money would be found for the education of sons.

The distinction between reading and writing skills was embodied in many laws. As early as 1642, Massachusetts required that all children be taught to read. Other New England colonies passed similar laws in the 1650s. Although these laws applied to all children, some colonies went further to insist that the "sons" also be given instruction in writing. Given the distinction between reading and writing instruction, it is safe to conclude that the typical colonial woman could read, even if she could not write.

The ability for women to write increased dramatically after the American Revolution. During the decade-long conflict, women had assumed men's duties while their husbands were away from home. It was no longer feasible to assume women's education should be limited to genteel arts, and the idea of female education gained wide acceptance. The growing acceptance of "republican motherhood" insisted that mothers needed to nurture values of civic virtue, honesty, and responsible citizenship in their children. A woman would be better able to raise the next generation of informed citizens if she could both read and write. Once motherhood was endowed with increasing responsibility for preserving the moral health of future generations, the education of young girls assumed greater importance.

Dame Schools

Although the colonies did an admirable job of establishing public schools soon after settlers arrived, most of these grammar schools were exclusively for boys. A small percentage also admitted girls, but most girls from this period would not have had formal schooling.

The dame school was one of the few educational opportunities available for ordinary girls. Similar to modern day care, a local woman would take neighborhood boys and girls, usually three to seven years old, into her home for a few hours per day. She provided rudimentary instruction in reading and some other practical skills. The major benefit of the dame school was no doubt for overworked mothers, who gained a few hours' reprieve from supervising their children. The dame who taught the school received a modest fee from the parents, which provided a supplemental income for her family.

Attendance at a dame school marked the only formal educational experience that many girls had. The boys typically moved on to town schools, which were only occasionally open to girls. When girls were permitted to attend town schools, they were usually segregated from boys. Girls were permitted to go to school at the end of the day or during the summer months, when boys were not in attendance.

Boarding Schools

An exceedingly small percentage of women obtained education beyond what could be found at the local dame school. By the mid-1700s boarding schools for young ladies came to be an option. Most of these boarding schools were run in the home of the schoolmistress and usually had no more than six to ten pupils. The students would have shared rooms with one another and assisted in food preparation, washing, and tending house. A few hours of instruction would have been fit in around such domestic education. Contemporary newspaper advertisements for female boarding schools mention sewing, embroidery, geography, languages, and perhaps music or painting as courses of instruction. Special instructors were brought in to provide lessons in dancing, drawing, and possibly arithmetic.

The clear emphasis in eighteenth-century schools was in the "ornamental arts." Such skills were prized among women who hoped to become prominent hostesses and housewives. Dancing, painting, needlework, and musical ability were all thought important skills for fashionable ladies. Only the wealthy could afford to indulge in such recreations. When a woman had time to embroider exquisite designs on pillows or indulge in playing an expensive musical instrument, it was a sign of exceptional wealth. By training their girls in these superfluous luxuries, Americans were seeking to emulate the signs of gentility found in Europe's finest families.

By the early 1800s a small movement for more meaningful higher education for girls began to gather momentum. Teaching was becoming a viable profession for women who chose not to marry, and such women needed an education beyond basic literacy and the ornamental arts. Some schools for ladies began offering more challenging subjects, such as composition, logic, mathematics, and foreign languages. Boarding schools, or academies as they were called at the time, became larger and were no longer confined to the home of the schoolmistress. Separate buildings were purchased specifically for use as schools, and additional staffing made a more comprehensive course of study possible. Such an education was costly. With annual fees of around £30, parents were investing a substantial sum on behalf of the daughters they sent to such schools.

A number of religious groups founded schools for young ladies. The Moravians opened several schools for girls, including the Bethlehem Female Seminary (1742), the Salem Female Academy (1772), and Linden Hall Seminary (1794). Quakers established a number of schools for both girls and young women, and established societies to fund the process. The Society for Free Instruction of Female

Children (1796) and Harmony Society both hired women to teach regardless of the pupil's religion or race. The Quakers established a number of boarding schools, including Westtown School, Kimberton Boarding School, and Sharon Female Seminary. Catholic convents in Maryland and New Orleans also provided education for girls.

Despite the increasing rigor of female higher education, its purpose was still primarily focused on the preparation of future wives and mothers. The ideal of republican motherhood stressed virtue, which was to be fostered through religious training, study of the classics, and awareness of the world through learning geography and current events. The purpose of female education was not self-reliance, but to rear the next generation of good and virtuous citizens. In her 1793 valedictorian speech from the Young Ladies' Academy of Philadelphia, Pricilla Mason commented that men had "denied us the means of knowledge, then reproached us for want of it." She went on to remind her fellow graduates that the church, the legal bar, and the Senate were still closed to women.

See also Literature; Young Ladies' Academy of Philadelphia

Further Reading

Eisenmann, Linda, ed. *Historical Dictionary of Women's Education in the United States.* Westport, CT: Greenwood Press, 1998.

Kerber, Linda K. *Women of the Republic: Intellect and Ideology in Revolutionary America.* Chapel Hill: University of North Carolina Press, 1980.

Monaghan, E. Jennifer. "Literacy Instruction and Gender in Colonial New England." *American Quarterly* 40 (1988): 18–41.

Spruill, Julia Cherry. *Women's Life and Work in the Southern Colonies.* Chapel Hill: University of North Carolina Press, 1938.

Woody, Thomas. *A History of Women's Education in the United States.* New York: Octagon Books, 1966.

Elite Women

Americans have historically struggled with the dueling concepts of democratic equality for their citizens and the notion of a privileged class. Many first-generation immigrants fled the calcified social hierarchies of Europe that thwarted upward mobility. Early settlements did not begin with communitarian principles, and it was considered natural for people who worked hard to be rewarded by material riches. Yet even in the wilds of America, a natural deference toward an elite class emerged early in the seventeenth century. Wealthy Virginia congressman John Randolph was famously quoted as saying, "I love liberty. I hate equality."

The elite class represented not only wealth, but power. Ambitious men who sought appointments as magistrates, governors, trustees, or even ministers, depended on access to the right connections. Once in power, these men controlled how land would be parceled out to the settlers, how taxation schedules would be set, and what moral values would hold sway in the community. Their wives set the standards for fashion and manners. Perhaps more importantly, these women engineered the marriages of their children into other well-connected families.

Wealth and status were never synonymous in either England or the American colonies. Although it was possible for an ordinary man to acquire riches through trade or banking, he and his family were not welcomed into the elite ranks of society without a measure of refinement and the trappings of culture. Great wealth needed to be accompanied by political influence, a cultured demeanor, and the appearance of leisure. To this end, a talented wife could prove enormously important. A skilled hostess created an air of gentility that could soften the uncouth edges of a newly rich husband. If she had a tasteful eye, she could dress the home with the trappings important to the elite class. Wellborn women knew how to raise children that displayed the manners, habits, and attitudes that bespoke privilege. Although it was possible for an ambitious but humble man to accumulate vast riches in America, his surest means of securing acceptance in high society was by marrying a blue-blooded woman. Should he marry the dairymaid or the blacksmith's daughter, all hope of genuine acceptance into the elite class was closed to him, despite his riches.

The creation of a classless society was never an objective of the founding settlers of America, although the experience of New England high society was markedly different than the elite world of the southern colonies. Well-heeled southern families attempted to emulate the manners and gentility of English aristocrats, whereas New Englanders deliberately shunned many of the trappings of vast wealth. The experience of elite women in both societies bore little resemblance to the life of average women throughout the colonies.

Elite Women of New England

From its earliest years of settlement, Puritan New Englanders flatly rejected the establishment of an aristocratic class. In 1636, a group of very wealthy Puritan families were planning to emigrate from England to America. Prior to their departure they sought assurance from leaders of the fledgling colony that they and their heirs would be accorded the rank of "gentlemen of the country," which would carry hereditary privileges of power and rank. The magistrates and ministers of Massachusetts were anxious for the influx of money and resources these settlers would bring, but refused to grant the establishment of any hereditary privileges. They believed the creation of an aristocratic class carried potential for abuse and indolence. They sought to preserve their godly kingdom by prohibiting such a privileged class from gaining hereditary authority.

Despite their disdain for the aristocracy, New Englanders were a class-conscious people who saw a difference between gentlemen, yeomen, and laborers. Gentlefolk were referred to as Mister or Mistress, whereas members of the working class were called Goodman or Goodwife, which was usually shortened simply to Goody. Wealthy New Englanders expected a natural deference to their positions of authority, although they acknowledged this did not absolve them from a mutual show of consideration to their social inferiors. Even servants and beggars were creatures of God and entitled to be respected as such.

Upper-class New Englanders tended to amass their fortunes through trade or mercantile enterprises. Their businesses kept them close to town, rather than isolated in the countryside. The wives

Ladies and gentlemen having tea in a drawing room, 1700s. The formal procedure for preparing, serving, and drinking tea was a finely tuned performance that separated the genteel class from the uninitiated. (North Wind / North Wind Picture Archives)

and daughters of such men shared in the material advantages of living in an urban environment. They not only had more opportunities to socialize, they benefited from access to imported goods and a readily available labor market.

Living in a town played an important role in the character of these women's lives. Visiting was common, as were trips to the market center to shop and socialize. Although they were spared the drudgery of manual labor, it would have been considered in poor taste to flaunt their leisure. Useful occupations, such as tending to children, sewing ornamental needlework, or assisting in religious activities, were marks of a devout and feminine woman. A leisurely trip to the marketplace might not be a necessity, but if it could be justified by, for example, the purchase of fresh cream for the family table, this was consistent with a good housewife's role. Sheer idleness was viewed as a trap in which sin could take root, and the pursuit of leisure was not valued as highly in New England as it was in the South.

Many of the wealthy New England families had known one another prior to emigration, and they had a natural bond among them after arrival in America. Their children tended to know and marry each other, further solidifying the bonds among elite New Englanders. Because these women grew up in towns, they likely had the opportunity to know and court their suitors, without relying on arranged marriages to distant partners. They were more likely to remain living in the same vicinity after marriage than were their southern counterparts.

Elite Women of the South

Members of the elite class in the southern colonies did their best to emulate the high society of the English aristocracy. Immense estates were presided over by men of great wealth and power. Many of these original land magnates had been the younger sons of English aristocrats. English inheritance laws precluded them from the family wealth, so they sought out new realms in America. Sometimes called the "Younger Son Syndrome," these men craved the same deference, wealth, and prestige enjoyed by their titled older brothers in England. Unlike the founders of Massachusetts, they did not shun hereditary power. Rather, they embraced the concept of a privileged elite and were protective of its trappings. Conspicuous consumption was valued, with enormous sums spent to host parties that stretched over several days. Elegantly dressed wives to host such events became an important asset for men who sought to secure their place in society.

The wives and daughters living on large plantations were often socially isolated, and many of them participated in the domestic responsibilities of plantation maintenance. In the seventeenth and early eighteenth centuries even elite women were active in daily oversight of practical matters. By the mid-eighteenth century, wealth and privilege began to take on more distinctively British characteristics on the southern plantations. Wealthy women were expected to engage in elaborate hospitality. Meals became extraordinarily complex affairs with multiple courses and varied menus. *The Compleat House-wife,* the classic cookbook in well-heeled homes, recommended the following menu for an everyday meal in winter: Chicken with bacon seasoning, roast beef with horseradish, pickles, oranges, savory pudding, and a buttered apple pie. The feast served at the 1789 wedding celebration for Richard and Judith Randolph was an excellent display of what Virginians considered high-class dining. The tables were laden with chicken, roast beef, pork, mutton, ham, venison, duck, goose, rabbit, pheasant, partridge, quail, eels, and oysters. Custard, plum pudding, wine, ale, and lemon punch rounded out the affair.

Many elite women would have participated in the menu planning and supervision of the kitchen during meal preparation. The more exotic the menu, the higher her status rose. Exquisite care in menu planning was a sign she had the leisure to tend to her family and guests with such extraordinary thoughtfulness and attention to detail. An artful presentation of meals was valued. Silver nutmeg grinders, china dishes for serving oysters, and other specialized tools denoted high class.

The courtship and marriage of elite southern daughters was more contrived than that of northern women. It was important to marry only someone of similar rank, and the isolation of women on rural plantations meant they were unlikely to meet eligible men in the normal course of their day. Mothers arranged to take their daughters on extended visits to town, where they attended as many balls and social events as possible in an effort to mingle with the correct sort of people.

An informal "season" of socializing was established in Williamsburg and Charleston that coincided with the meeting of the legislature and courts. While the men attended to political business, their wives and daughters engaged in rounds of afternoon teas. The evenings were densely scheduled with balls and formal dinners. This social season served a dual purpose. It allowed the women to escape the isolation of the countryside, but also further solidified the complex web of ties forged among the most powerful families of the colony.

Many elite southern women would have come into contact with their future husbands through arranged meetings during the season or on an extended visit to plantations in other areas of the colony. Upon marriage, most women would have moved away from their birthplace to a new part of the colony. A woman could maintain ties with her family members through extended visits, but her daily life after marriage would not include her mother and sisters, which was common for northern women.

The elite women of the South were noted for their splendid dress, sense of style, and gracious hospitality. Northern women were far less likely to conspicuously display their wealth. Beyond the material trappings of wealth, there was a psychological difference between southern and northern elite. It has been said that one of the greatest tragedies of American history was the sense of superiority southerners had toward people of the North. The upper-class southerners considered themselves scions of Old World nobility, and Yankees were merely jumped-up tradesmen who lacked the refinement of true class. It is difficult to determine if this sense of superiority was shared by southern women, but their lifestyle and material possessions more closely mimicked English aristocrats than did those of northern Yankee women.

Southern women were famous for their hospitality, whether it was in the form of a country barbeque, providing travelers with lodging, or hosting a formal dress ball. Genteel culture in the South was largely defined by how well a hostess could entertain her guests. This highly public function of a hostess helped position her family within the social hierarchy of her community. Entertaining was a high art, requiring money, sophistication, and connections. A southern woman's education was geared toward providing her with the skills necessary to host entertainment on a high scale.

The Ritual of Tea

Much of elite culture was defined by conspicuous display of luxury items, ease of social conventions, and leisure time for indulging in hospitality. Nothing embodied all elements better than the ritual of the tea ceremony. The formal procedure for preparing, serving, and drinking tea was a finely tuned performance that separated the genteel class from the uninitiated.

Tea drinking began as a trend among seventeenth-century elite who could afford this expensive import from China. By the early eighteenth century the price of tea had dropped so low that it was no longer an exclusive privilege of the rich. Rather than sacrifice the beloved drink now that it was all the rage among "common folk," wealthy elites endowed their ritual with extravagant luxuries that allowed them to maintain the identification of tea with refinement. Costly imported luxuries became essential for the proper hostess to serve tea. Tea sets were to be made of richly embellished silver and consisted of a teapot, sugar bowl, cream pitcher, strainers, platters, teaspoons, tea tongs, and a waste bowl. An assortment of china teacups, saucers, and serving trays were essential. Other accoutrements included special tea tables, serving trays, tea chests, tablecloths, and rooms large enough to accommodate several visitors. Tea was to be served in a parlor, never a kitchen. Adequate seating space and coordinated china was necessary for gatherings that could number up to a dozen people. Delicate pastry and baked goods should accompany tea, and servants in elite homes spent much of their day preparing an array of delicacies for teatime.

The proper serving and drinking of tea was taught to young ladies with as much care as they devoted to academic subjects. They needed to know the proper methods for straining the tea, how to send silent signals to refill a cup, and how to decline without offending. The placement of the teaspoon near the cup was an indicator of when the visitor wished no more tea. Tea parties could last several hours, with visitors coming and leaving throughout the gathering.

Hosting tea parties was a fundamental duty of an elite hostess. It was during this classic hospitality ritual that she demonstrated her social graces and displayed her fine material possessions. Reciprocity was an essential part of hospitality, so the tea drinking ritual was repeated regularly among the elite class. Recurrent socializing during teatime helped solidify ties among the upper-crust families.

Tea drinking took on a political overtone in the years leading to the American Revolution. Unpopular taxation of tea caused it to be a natural target for boycotts, although exceptions were made for ill or elderly people, who were believed to need tea for their health. During the Revolution, ladies brewed herbal tea as a sign of political affiliation with the patriotic cause.

Political Influence of Elite Women

Women were excluded from formal avenues of political power, but the wives and daughters of elite men might have exercised more real political power than many middle-class men of early America. The duty of a politician's wife was to preside over an array of social gatherings. By controlling the guest list for such an event, she shaped who had access to important people. She could promote a young man she favored, but who currently lacked connections, merely by inviting him to tea. Marriages among elite families were often arranged matches. A woman hoping to advance her son's career might cultivate a friendship with another powerful wife in hopes of pulling off such a match.

We will never be able to adequately determine how a wife might have influenced a governor or congressman. Only in a handful of cases do we have letters where wives pleaded a particular issue. In most cases letters between husband and wife were unnecessary because they shared the same home. To suggest that the absence of written documentation for women's influence on their husband's decisions meant they had none is naive, because whispers into a husband's ear leave no traces in the historical record.

See also Plantation Mistresses; Political Wives

Further Reading

Fischer, David Hackett. *Albion's Seed: Four British Folkways in America.* New York: Oxford University Press, 1989.

Kierner, Cynthia A. *Beyond the Household: Women's Place in the Early South, 1700–1835.* Ithaca, NY: Cornell University Press, 1998.

———. "Hospitality, Sociability, and Gender in the Southern Colonies." *Journal of Southern History* 62 (1996): 449–480.

Roth, Rodris. "Tea-Drinking in Eighteenth Century America: Its Etiquette and Equipage." In *Material Life in America, 1600–1860,* ed. Robert Blair St. George. Boston: Northeastern University Press, 1988.

Shammas, Carole. "English-Born and Creole Elites in Turn of the Century Virginia." In *The Chesapeake in the Seventeenth Century: Essays on Anglo-American Society and Politics,* eds. Thad W. Tate and David L. Ammerman. New York: Norton, 1979.

Wecter, Dixon. *The Saga of American Society: A Record of Social Aspiration, 1607–1937.* New York: Charles Scribner's Sons, 1937.

Elopement

See Marriage

Employment

See Agricultural Labor; Domestic Labor; Midwives; Milliners and Seamstresses; Printers and the Printing Trade; Science and Technology, Women in; Shopkeepers and Merchants; Tavern Keepers and Innkeepers; Teachers; Textile Industry

Episcopal Women

See Anglican Women

Equity Courts

See Legal Status of Women

Etiquette

Etiquette is a system of rules and conventions that guide social behavior. These rules are rarely codified in any law, but are informally enforced by group consensus. In highly stratified societies, elaborate etiquette conventions can be used to enforce a sense of exclusiveness that keeps the unworthy at a distance. Americans never developed the extraordinary degree of exacting rules practiced by European aristocracy, although manners became more elaborate over time. American etiquette evolved from helpful neighborliness in the seventeenth century, to highly formalized rituals in the late eighteenth century. The relative informality of manners in the seventeenth century can be attributed to the character of early immigration and frontier conditions. By the end of the colonial period, society had become far more socially stratified and concerned with emulating the qualities of gentility found in Europe.

The Early Years

The early settlers of America were not characteristic of the steeply hierarchical society of England, where the aristocracy controlled most of the land and wealth but represented only a tiny fraction of the population. Poor laborers and tenants made up the bulk of society in England, and a small but growing middle class stood between the vastly rich and the destitute poor. The middle class was composed of yeoman farmers, skilled tradesmen, artisans, and lesser gentry, many of whom were dissatisfied with their lot in England. They were forced to pay feudal dues to those who outranked them and also heavy poor taxes for those below them. Immigration to America offered them freedom from such crushing taxes, as well as liberation from the intensely deferential society they found overbearing. It was this middling class that made up the bulk of immigrants to the New England colonies. The southern colonies had a higher percentage of poor and indentured servants, but the middling class made up the majority of early landowners who would set the tone for social mores.

Etiquette in the seventeenth century revolved around the necessity for neighbors to coexist and support one another. Hospitality was to be offered to travelers and new arrivals. Women provided vital assistance to neighborhood women when they gave birth or were otherwise unable to tend their children. All members of a village assisted with logrollings and barn raisings. This system operated on the expectation of reciprocity.

Early American society lacked the stark social stratification of European society, but even in the humblest villages it was clear who were the town leaders. Ministers, large landholders, and skilled artisans naturally rose in prestige. It was customary for those of lesser rank to dip a light curtsy or bow to such people. Town leaders were addressed as Mister and Misses, and the rest went by the more common Goodman and Goodwife, usually shortened to Goody.

Etiquette in early America was relatively straightforward: respect for elders, neighborly helpfulness, and basic table manners. Such codes of conduct were easily learned through parental instruction without resorting to books. Elegant rituals and flowery manners were flatly rejected as pretentious. Few settlers came from the elite section of English society that indulged in stylish ceremony, and those who tried to ape such manners were scorned.

The Eighteenth Century

As wealth increased in America, a natural hierarchy of social class began to emerge. The desire to lead more elegant lives was reflected in the accumulation of material goods such as porcelain, portraits, fine fabric, and larger homes. As social stratification increased, old patterns of deference and ceremonial behavior began to reemerge. Expectations of mere neighborly friendliness gave way to more ritualized manners. Those climbing the social ladder needed more than mere trappings of fine clothes and consumer goods to signify gentility.

Mastering the rules of courtesy was essential to indicate good breeding. This is not to suggest that etiquette was purely a shallow endeavor employed by social climbers. Business deals made by the growing middle class were founded on trust. Manners and predictable rules of behavior helped forge such ties. American etiquette books universally insisted that respect and dignity needed to flow both ways. Those higher on the social scale, while expecting a degree of deference, were to be courteous to all.

By the eighteenth century, etiquette was no longer merely the exercise of common good judgment. Conduct books became a popular means of learning the rituals and rules of proper society. Such books went into great detail on how a woman should dress, carry on conversation, and comport herself in front of her family. Advice was given for keeping conversations pleasant. They were to avoid contradicting or reproving others. When dealing with casual acquaintances, serious subjects were to be avoided in favor of small talk. General topics like history, literature, and poetry were safe, but one must never attempt to display too much learning and make the listener feel inferior. Excessive use of wit might become offensive. Women were to avoid all expressions of anger, and their tone of voice should remain soft, mild, and courteous. A woman was to listen politely and never tell a speaker she had heard a story before.

Underlying much of good etiquette is the concept of self-control. Biting one's nails, scratching, drumming the fingers, and fiddling with one's hair or clothing all signified poor self-control. Slouching indicated poor posture, but sitting too rigidly erect conveyed unease. Women needed to seek a middle ground of graceful carriage without rigidity. They were instructed on how to walk in a dignified manner, as scurrying too quickly gave the impression of being a servant. Table manners were of great concern, and instruction was provided on proper use of utensils and the cutting of meat. They were not to help themselves to food until it had been offered. They were not to eat food too quickly, as it signified a ravenous appetite.

Ladies were advised as to what sort of friends they should select. They should not seek out the companionship of superiors, as it would make them servile to their betters, and contemptuous of their inferiors. They were to display modesty and deference, and should never brag, indulge in ostentatious displays of learning, or dress more elaborately than their station. Rules of etiquette became more elaborate and refined the higher one moved in society. Manners were less formal in the New England colonies, where society was never as hierarchal in nature as the gentrified Virginia and Carolinas.

Conduct books should not be used as a means of discovering how early American women actually lived. The books were to serve as a role model of the ideal woman, rather than as a descriptive account of their actual demeanor. As with much prescriptive literature, conduct books viewed the world as their authors would like it to be, rather than reporting on what they actually witnessed. Although etiquette became more formal in the eighteenth century, the manners of the eighteenth century would seem crude by comparison with the immensely exacting codes of conduct that came into vogue during the Victorian era.

See also Elite Women; Literature, Conduct Books

Further Reading

Fischer, David Hackett. *Albion's Seed: Four British Folkways in America.* New York: Oxford University Press, 1989.

Hemphill, C. Dallett. "Middle Class Rising in Revolutionary America: The Evidence from Manners." *Journal of Social History* 20 (1996): 317–344.

Schlesinger, Arthur. *Learning How to Behave: A Historical Study of American Etiquette Books.* New York: Macmillan Company, 1946.

Zuckerman, Michael. "Manners." In *Encyclopedia of the North American Colonies,* ed. Jacob Ernest Cooke. New York: Charles Scribner's Sons, 1993.

F

Feme Sole

Legal status that granted women legal identity independent of a male relative.

According to the laws of coverture that existed in the American colonies, once a woman entered a marriage, she and her husband were one person in the eyes of the law . . . and that one person was the husband. The wife could not enter into contracts, make a will, or buy or sell property without the consent of her husband. No such restrictions applied to the man.

Adult single women were not under any such paternalistic legal form. After attaining the age of majority, usually twenty-one, a single woman had an independent legal identity, meaning she was free to own and operate a business, obtain employment, retain the wages she earned, and purchase property. In short, she had all the legal rights a man had, with the exception that she could not vote. Such a status was known as *feme sole,* or "woman alone."

There is little in the historical record to indicate that women shunned marriage because it meant abandoning *feme sole* status. The world of a spinster was dismal and presented few opportunities for a satisfying life. Women with serious concerns about losing legal control over their property could initiate a prenuptial agreement, also known as a marriage settlement. These legal agreements preserved a limited amount of control for a woman over the property she brought into the marriage. The rarity of prenuptial agreements, whether from ignorance or disinterest, is an indicator that the loss of *feme*

sole status was rarely in the forefront of a young bride's mind.

If a woman became widowed, her status as *feme covert* was immediately switched back to *feme sole.*

See also Coverture; Single Women

Further Reading

Berkin, Carol. *First Generations: Women in Colonial America.* New York: Hill and Wang, 1996.

Salmon, Marylynn. "The Legal Status of Women in Early America: A Reappraisal." *Law and History Review* 1 (1983): 129–151.

———. *Women and the Law of Property in Early America.* Chapel Hill: University of North Carolina Press, 1986.

Feme Sole Trader

Legal status that granted married women the ability to conduct business independent of their husband's permission.

Under limited and unusual circumstances, a married woman could obtain a legal identity independent of her husband. Because of the difficulty in obtaining a divorce in early America, rates of marital desertion were high. An abandoned wife needed a means to support herself, and if she lacked the ability to enter contracts, many people would refuse to do business with her. Any transaction executed by the wife, such as sums paid for the purchase or rental of a home, purchase of goods, or sale of property, could all be rendered null and void if the absent husband emerged and objected. Likewise, a dishonest woman could claim coverture laws relieved her of the obligation to pay debts contracted outside of the presence of her husband. Because entering into any legal transaction with a married woman acting independently of her husband was risky, careful merchants and landlords often refused to deal with an abandoned wife.

Feme sole trader status was created to restore limited legal identity to wives who found themselves without a husband. The women had to publicly announce her intentions of adopting this status, and in some colonies she needed to register with officials as a *feme sole* trader. She thereafter was entitled to all the privileges and responsibilities of entering into contracts, buying and selling property, and operating a business. This status could also be conferred upon a woman whose husband was absent for years at a time, such as if he were a mariner or a soldier.

See also Coverture; *Feme Sole*

Further Reading

Norton, Mary Beth. *Liberty's Daughters: The Revolutionary Experience of American Women, 1750–1800.* Boston: Little, Brown and Co., 1980.

Salmon, Marylynn. *Women and the Law of Property in Early America.* Chapel Hill: University of North Carolina Press, 1986.

Feminism

Feminism, as it is understood today, did not exist in early America. Feminism affirms the value of women's contributions to society and expects parity for women in terms of economic, legal, educational, and social opportunities. With the exception of a few rare individuals, women had no expectation of equality in early America. Along with the physical weakness of women, it was widely assumed that women were not as mentally capable as men. Hundreds of years of tradition and biblical teaching taught that women were naturally subordinate to men, and there is little evidence that women resented the status quo. Women of seventeenth-century America were considered morally frail, susceptible to temptation, and in need of the guidance and protection of men.

It has been suggested that before women could mobilize for equality in the eyes of the law and society, they needed to develop a collective sense of feminine consciousness. A woman needed to recognize that her limited opportunities were not merely a unique personal problem, but a condition shared by all members of the female sex. Margaret Brent was notable for demanding the right to vote in 1648, but she based her claim on her status as a landowner, rather than on the inherent right of a woman to vote. Many women petitioned courts for the right to conduct business in their own name, but these petitions for *feme sole* trader status were based on their unique economic need, rather than on the right of women to independent legal identity. Not until group consciousness was established could a public debate regarding women's rights begin.

Mercy Otis Warren (1728–1814), possibly the most politically active woman of her generation, wrote to a friend that women ought to accept subordination not because they were inferior, but "perhaps for the sake of order in families." Other elite leading ladies of the colonial era, such as Abigail Adams, Judith Sargent Murray, Elizabeth Drinker, and Elizabeth Southgate Bowne, never aspired to complete equality with men, except for the possible exception of educational opportunities. Women were viewed primarily as either mothers or potential mothers, and there is scant evidence they were seeking opportunities for social or economic expansion outside their traditional domestic sphere. Abigail Adams's famous request to her husband to "remember the ladies" was not an appeal for female suffrage or any other form of social equality with men. Her requests were limited to protecting wives from complete economic and legal subordination to their husbands.

The eighteenth century witnessed a shift in attitudes about women, possibly sparked by their enthusiastic participation in church activities. Ministers could not help but note that membership in their churches were disproportionately female, and most volunteer activities were organized and led by women. Church activities were one of the few areas outside the home where it was socially acceptable for a woman to participate. No longer considered morally weak, women were now protectors of home and hearth.

Following the American Revolution, a few women noted the irony of the ability of men to throw off the shackles of tyranny, while women were expected to remain content in their subordinate position. Such concerns were usually limited to private correspondence. Although the vote was extended to women in some areas, a series of legislative acts systematically disenfranchised women in the coming decades. Although the role of motherhood was elevated and glorified, opportunities outside the home for women began to retreat.

The first glimmer of sustained, widespread concern for women's rights arose over the issue of education. Boys had a variety of educational opportunities, but girls rarely received formal academic instruction beyond basic literacy. Some enlightened parents allowed their daughters to partake in the same lessons provided to their sons, but they were the exception. During the years surrounding the American Revolution, heightened political awareness caused the role of motherhood to be treated with greater respect. Women were charged with rearing the leaders of a democratic nation, a task to be fostered through religious training, study of the classics, and awareness of the world. Mothers needed to understand world events, geography, and political concerns if they were to rear the next generation of leaders, businessmen, and inventors. The purpose of female education was not to train women in self-reliance, but allow them to excel as mothers and wives.

English author Mary Wollstonecraft's landmark book *A Vindication of the Rights of Women* appeared in 1792. Demanding national reform to provide equal educational opportunities for women, Wollstonecraft envisioned a world where women would have genuine parity with men. Despite the controversy that greeted the book in England, it aroused little interest in America, where public debate regarding the expansion of women's rights in legal and economic spheres would not begin in earnest until well into the nineteenth century.

English author Mary Wollstonecraft's 1792 landmark book, *A Vindication of the Rights of Women,* demanded national reform to provide equal educational opportunities for women. Despite the controversy that greeted the book in England, it aroused little interest in America. (Corbis)

The "Golden Age"
Theory of American Women

A number of historians have accepted the theory advanced by Elizabeth Anthony Dexter that women in early America enjoyed greater liberty than their descendants of the nineteenth century. During the initial decades of settlement, women were scarce and highly valued. Single women were eagerly sought as wives. They offered household help and companionship that was desperately sought in this labor-poor, male-dominated world. Women's scarcity made them valued. The need for people to perform labor allowed them access to wherever their talents and ambitions led them. By toiling alongside men on the edges of the wilderness, women earned respect that had been unavailable to them in Europe.

Even after the lopsided sex ratio came into balance, early American women were still valued for the crucial labor they provided. While men worked on the farm, their wives provided an immense amount of assistance cooking, cleaning, sewing, and rearing children. There was no stigma attached to women who worked outside the home. Women worked as shopkeepers, printers, shoemakers, tavern keepers, bakers, and almost any other profession they were physically capable of performing. Most took such jobs out of necessity, but it is clear from the number of wealthy female merchants and printers that some chose to work of their own free will.

The opportunities for work outside the home were rolled back in the nineteenth century, when trade and industrialization created a higher standard of living for Americans. Women were able to purchase products such as bread, cheese, candles, and soap. No longer tied to the drudgery of subsistence living, women had more time to devote to their children and maintaining a home. With higher expectations for women as mothers and homemakers, there was growing disapproval of women who chose to work outside the home. Women of the nineteenth century have been characterized as victims of industrialization, which confined them to the domestic environment.

The golden age theory of women in America is not without its critics. It has been characterized as simplistic in its emphasis on women's status being tied solely to economic opportunity. Although it is true that there were extraordinary cases of female blacksmiths, newspaper editors, and other skilled professionals, such women were anomalies. Most early American women lived a life of backbreaking labor on farms. They might have had the respect of their husbands and their communities, but they had few luxuries in life and even fewer choices in shaping their destiny.

There can be no doubt that early American women did not share the same legal advantages as men. English common law codified a wide array of gender inequities. Far more difficult to determine is how common law was played out in the colonies, where frontier conditions put standard operating procedures on hold, allowing strong women the opportunity to carve out choices for themselves.

The differences of opinion between golden age historians and those more pessimistic about early American women's place in society are still actively debated.

See also American Revolution and Its Effect on Women's Status; Brent, Margaret; Legal Status of Women; Suffrage

Further Reading

Dexter, Elizabeth Anthony. *Colonial Women of Affairs: Women in Business and the Professions in America Before 1776.* Boston: Houghton Mifflin, 1931.

Malmsheimer, Lonna M. "Daughters of Zion: New England Roots of American Feminism." *New England Quarterly* 50 (1977): 484–504.

Norton, Mary Beth. "The Evolution of White Women's Experience in Early America." *American Historical Review* 89 (1984): 593–619.

Wilson, Joan Hoff. "The Illusion of Change: Women and the American Revolution." In *The American Revolution: Explorations in the History of American Radicalism,* ed. Alfred F. Young. DeKalb: Northern Illinois University Press, 1976.

Femmes du Pays (Country Wives)

See Fur Traders' Wives

First-Generation Immigrants

A number of important characteristics differentiated women who immigrated to America from those who had been born in the New World (often called native-born Americans). Women who elected to undertake a dangerous and expensive voyage to America were usually motivated by dissatisfaction with life in Europe, whether it be from poverty, religious discrimination, or lack of a marriage partner. Few of them were well informed about the realities of life in America. Eager to increase the number of white women in the English colonies, sponsors of the colonization effort circulated rumors in English villages regarding the bounty of land, wildlife, and resources freely available in America. Indians were portrayed as noble savages who were helpful to settlers. It is possible many women were severely disappointed upon their arrival.

Virginia Seeks Brides

The colony at Jamestown began as a business venture settled almost entirely by men. Within a decade they recognized that women were needed if Jamestown was to become a permanent community, and arrangements were made for the transportation of single women to Virginia. In 1620, ninety young women boarded the *Jonathan* and the *Merchant of London* bound for Jamestown. The following year brought another fifty-seven young women.

Most of these women were from London and were between the ages of sixteen and twenty-eight. They were from good families, but were often orphaned or widowed. Most lacked a dowry that would have made them an attractive marriage candidate in London. All were required to submit letters testifying to their good character, and many of these references came from respectable merchants, ministers, and even members of the gentry.

The women were provided with a set of basic necessities, consisting of bedding, two pairs of shoes and stockings, a petticoat, waistcoat, two smocks, two head caps, a headscarf, a pair of gloves, a hat, and an apron. The men who married the women were expected to reimburse the Virginia Company with 150 pounds of tobacco, valued at £18. It appears that most of these women were immediately married upon their arrival in Virginia.

Many of these women came to untimely ends, because an Indian attack in 1622 killed hundreds of settlers and destroyed most of their crops. The surviving colonists faced disease and starvation the following winter. One can only speculate what these urban women thought of their new home in the rustic settlement at Jamestown. Their prospects had been poor in London, but it is doubtful any of the women had a full understanding of what to expect in America.

Source: Ransome, David R. "Wives for Virginia, 1621." *William and Mary Quarterly* 48 (1991): 3–18.

The voyage to America would have been a long and dangerous experience. After arrival, most women would have experienced a marked deterioration in their standards of living. Even the poor in England slept on beds that were raised off the floor, but the average American in the seventeenth century slept on a pallet on the floor. The poor of England usually had reliable shelter, whereas immigrants to America lived in hastily and crudely constructed huts and cabins that had leaking ceilings, dirt floors, and tiny or nonexistent windows. Even the poor in Europe had access to trade at shops, markets, and fairs. Early Americans needed to be largely self-sufficient. Imported luxuries such as shoes, glass, sugar, and books were scarce and beyond the economic reach of most immigrants.

Of immediate concern during the initial years of settlement was establishing a homestead. As towns formed, they developed different policies for parceling out land. Although land was usually "free," it took an immense amount of labor to clear raw forest and construct a dwelling. There was no attempt to be democratic in the distribution of land. Well-to-do families received large parcels of land, and poor immigrants received only small plots. Some towns freely gave away generous land grants to their early settlers. Watertown, Massachusetts, gave allocations of 700 acres, Salem gave 50 acres per household, while Derby, Connecticut, gave only 8-acre plots.

One aspect that would have been better for most women in America was their diet. Food was meager and expensive in Europe. With the exception of a few difficult years during the earliest stages of settlement, the food supply was exceptionally good in America. We know from skeletal remains that Americans were better nourished and grew taller than their European counterparts.

An immigrant woman's experience in America varied greatly depending on if she immigrated alone or as part of a family. Most women who signed on as indentured servants arrived alone. Without parental supervision, such women were more likely to enter into sexual liaisons, either willingly or through coercion. One in three immigrant women were pregnant on the day of their marriage. This is twice as high as the number for women in England and substantially higher than the number for women who were surrounded by their families in America.

Immigrant women married later in life than native-born women. Indentured servants were not

Puritan family on the English coast. Women who elected to undertake a dangerous and expensive voyage to America were unlikely to ever return to the place of their birth, and many suffered from profound homesickness. (Bettmann/CORBIS)

allowed to marry until they completed their term of service, usually five to seven years. They typically married in their mid-twenties, whereas native-born girls in the seventeenth century married around age seventeen. Even women who did not arrive as indentured servants married later. If they left Europe when they reached adulthood, they lost more years in travel time and the time it takes to settle and meet and marry a man. Because of their later age at marriage, immigrant women lost up to ten of their childbearing years. Women who married after age twenty-four averaged 4.5 children, those who married between age twenty and twenty-four averaged 7.1 children, and those who married between fifteen and nineteen averaged 7.5. Clearly, the delayed age at marriage would have affected the number of children a woman had, which in turn would have influenced the amount of labor available at her homestead.

Immigrant women without extended family surrounding them were also less likely to inherit money, land, or goods. It was difficult to accumulate surplus luxury items in early America, making the windfall of a parent's estate one of the few opportunities for a person to acquire additional land, bedding, utensils, and farm equipment. Immigrant women tended to have fewer luxuries than native-born women.

Immigrant families were more mobile than native-born families. It was not uncommon for an immigrant family to move two or three times before settling in a community. Some colonists probably moved from their first home because they had chosen it hastily. After living in an area for a while, they might have learned of more desirable locations and moved. They usually moved among settled communities. The vast, untapped wilderness was seldom tempting owing to the danger of Indians, the labor involved in clearing land from scratch, and the lack of community support. Women also moved when they married. It is likely that immigrant women would have experienced far more relocations than their native-born sisters, who probably moved only when they were married.

Native-born women knew little of the world except what they experienced in America. Immigrant women would have had another frame of reference to compare their American life with, whether it was London, Dublin, Rotterdam, or any of the numerous European port cities. The memories of cities with thousands of inhabitants, streets made of brick, shops laden with consumer goods, and cathedrals that reached into the sky would have been something native-born women would have scarcely been able to imagine. Although it is difficult to document because very few women left written records of their thoughts, the sense of loneliness and homesickness must have been profound. Anne Bradstreet wrote of her first impression of the Massachusetts Bay Colony as her ship lay in harbor in 1630, just two years after the founding of the settlement. Looking at the meager huts, dirt paths, and ominous forests, she felt overwhelming anxieties about her new life. Only her faith that immigration to America was God's will helped her to become reconciled to this new life.

Some immigrant women had the ability to write and receive letters from family members back home. Although it might take six months for letters to reach their destination, at least it was a tenuous link with home. Most women never made a return voyage to Europe and would never see their families again. Native-born women did not have to cope with the wrenching break with family and the comforts of familiar surroundings. We know of a few women who simply could not settle in America and made the return voyage to Europe. One woman held captive by Indians for almost two years returned to England upon her liberation, unwilling to continue living on the edge of "civilization." This was usually an option only for the very wealthy.

First-Generation African Women

The first women sent to the English colonies from Africa probably arrived in 1619, on the British ship *Treasurer.* Twenty slaves arrived on this ship, at least one of whom was a woman renamed Angela by her captors. Little is known of Angela's subsequent fate, but it is certain she was confronted with a strange language, new climate, and a drastically unbalanced sex ratio. Adjusting to the new environment would have brought anxieties on a daily basis. Strange and uncomfortable clothing, unfamiliar foods, the hostile environment, and the inability to communicate with the people who controlled her life would have been a constant source of apprehension for her.

Underlying these harsh conditions would be a profound sense of loneliness and isolation. Having been torn from families in their home countries, these women may not have been able to communicate with their fellow captives. Blacks were taken

---

Insight into the Sad Life of an Escaped Slave

The following advertisement was placed in a Williamsburg newspaper to alert the community of an escaped slave named Sarah. In all likelihood, Sarah was a first-generation slave who had endured the horror of capture and transportation on a slave ship. It appears she suffered from epilepsy, spoke only broken English, and had little hope of finding her way in the strange new world she found herself in.

There is now living in my family, adjoining to this city, a Negro girl called SARAH who is about 14 years old, near 4 feet 7 inches high, somewhat slender made, and is very black; she says she is a Mundingo, but cannot tell her owner's name. I have been informed she was purchased by some person of Carolina, at Suffolk in Nansemond, and that she was in jail there since, consequently must had been advertised, as she was taken out to be sold for prison fees, but turned loose at Smithfield, without any thing being further done. She was there taken in by sundry families, as an object, and maintained for what little service she could do, being often troubled with choking fits, which deprive her of the use of her limbs, as well as her senses. Her owner is desired to apply for her to me, at Whaley's free-school. Samuel Wallace

Source: Virginia Gazette, 20 July 1775.

from a large range of ethnic groups from Sierra Leone, Madagascar, Angola, Gambia, Congo, Benin, and the Gold Coast. The primary tribal groups were the Ibo, Ewe, Bakongo, Wolof, Serer, Fante, Yoruba, Mandingo, and Bambara. Given the huge ethnic diversity of the captives, it is possible a woman like Angela would not have been able to communicate with her fellow passengers. Even if the captives had been able to form bonds on the shipboard passage, it is likely they would have been dispersed upon arrival in America.

Africans arriving in the early seventeenth century came into a system in which the laws of slavery were not yet codified. Most were treated as indentured servants. After a period of several years of service, these earliest Africans passed into free society, with the ability to purchase land and sell goods. Their children would have entered the world as free blacks, able to participate in the scramble for land and the establishment of settlements. By the mid-seventeenth century, there were several hundred free blacks living in Virginia and Maryland.

By 1662 the tide turned, when Virginia passed a law making the enslavement of blacks perpetual. Although the blacks who had already attained a free status were allowed to keep their freedom, there would be no more Africans released from bondage. Any child born in Virginia was to assume the enslaved or free status of the mother.

Many of the first-generation slaves had not been sent directly to America. Most slave ships went to the Caribbean or West Indies. We know that many of the slaves arriving in the English colonies spent time in the Caribbean, as these slaves often could speak French or Spanish and had been exposed to Catholicism.

First-generation African women had few children, usually no more than two. A number of physical, social, and emotional reasons account for this. Most African women did not bear their first child until their late twenties, almost a decade later than other women in America. Poor physical health and psychological stress might have caused them to delay childbearing. The difficulty of finding a mate who they could communicate with might also have resulted in women hesitant to form bonds until they were able to speak a modicum of English. Finally, the tiny and scattered nature of settlements in early America meant that many of these women would have been living in isolated settings where finding a partner was not always easy.

First-generation slaves from Africa were often called "saltwater" slaves. They were distinctively different from those who had been born in America, which were known as "Creole" slaves. The Creole slaves had the advantage of never having gone through the traumatizing effects of capture, transportation, and the loss of freedom. Having been born into the American environment, they had better physical resistance to the viruses and climate of America. They learned the language and customs of America from infancy. On plantations that had both Creole slaves and saltwater slaves, there was often a marked divide between the groups. Separated by language, ethnic traditions, and possibly a profound depression, many first-generation women felt a cultural divide with the Creole, American-born slaves. On some plantations, first-generation slaves lived in single-sex barracks, whereas the Creole slaves were permitted to live in family groupings. First-generation slaves were subject to taunts from native-born slaves because of their awkward manners, language difficulties, and religious practices. Native-born slaves were more likely to practice Christianity and shunned the "tribal superstitions" of new arrivals. These differences were substantial enough to add another layer of stress onto the lives of first-generation African American women.

See also Diet; Travel

Further Reading

Breen, T. H., and Stephen Foster. "Moving to the New World: The Character of Early Massachusetts Immigration." *William and Mary Quarterly*, 3d ser. 30 (1973): 189–222.

Carr, Lois Green, and Lorena S. Walsh. "The Planter's Wife: The Experience of White Women in Seventeenth-Century Maryland." *William and Mary Quarterly*, 3d ser. (1977): 542–571.

Kulikoff, Allan. "The Origins of Afro-American Society in Tidewater Maryland and Virginia, 1700–1790. *William and Mary Quarterly*, 3d ser. 35 (1978): 226–259.

Stevenson, Brenda E. "Slavery." In *Black Women in America: An Historical Encyclopedia,* ed. Darlene Clark Hine. Brooklyn, NY: Carlson Publishing, 1993.

Fornication

Fornication was defined as voluntary sexual activity by an unmarried person. It was both a moral and a legal failing. All colonies had laws that prohibited extramarital sexual activity, although the severity of the penalty fluctuated greatly depending on geography. Fornication was considered a serious offense in the seventeenth century, but by the eighteenth century its primary consequence was a blow to a woman's reputation. Although a serious crime in early America, fornication was not as bad as adultery, which was sexual activity of a married person with someone other than his or her spouse. Early Americans were not the prudish, sexually repressed people often portrayed in modern-day representations. Early Americans drew the distinction between healthy sex confined within a marriage and dangerous fornication that threatened the stability of their society.

Most religious and social commentators in early America believed that the primary purpose of sex was for procreation by a married couple. Any sexual activity contrary to this was frowned on. There was no room for sexual experimentation between young, unmarried persons, because the consequences for illegitimate children were far too serious. Likewise, masturbation, homosexuality, and oral sex were all considered to be fornication, because conception was not possible from these acts.

Early Americans believed chastity was an indicator of a woman's moral quality. Women who indulged in lustful activities outside the bounds of marriage were viewed as harmful to a community's moral and economic well-being. They were temptations to honest men, bad examples for young girls, threats to stable families, and economic burdens should they conceive a child. Because the consequences of fornication were so dire to the well-being of the community, both social and legal ramifications were employed to discourage sex outside of marriage.

One of the factors working against chastity was the delayed age of marriage. Marriage in early America did not take place until a young couple was economically capable of supporting themselves, usually between the ages of twenty-two and twenty-five. Because marriage usually did not occur until a decade or more after puberty, many couples slipped into sexual dalliances, despite strong prohibitions against doing so.

Colonists did their best to discourage sexual temptation. Provocative dressing and mixed dancing were condemned in most areas. Puritans practiced "Holy Watchfulness," which meant keeping an eye on the young adults of the community to ensure they were not slipping into immorality.

Regional Variations in Premarital Sex

The ratio of men to women influenced premarital sexual activity during the seventeenth century. In New England there were three men for every two women, and in the southern colonies men outnumbered women by about five to one. With women in such high demand in the South, the shame associated with loss of virginity was easier for a southern woman to overcome than it was for her northern sisters. During the seventeenth century, most southern women who bore children out of wedlock succeeded in attracting a husband, but less than one-third of such women in New England ever married any man other than the father of the child.

Family structure also contributed to higher premarital sexuality in the South. Young children in New England were likely to have one or both parents still living when they reached adulthood. Parental supervision made it far less likely that New England girls would be led astray. In the southern colonies, high rates of parental death from childbirth and disease meant that 75 percent of southern children had lost at least one parent during their childhood, and a third of the children lost both parents. Orphaned children were usually raised by neighbors or placed into service. Such guardians were less vigilant than a parent would be in exercising close supervision of adolescent children. Additionally, many young women in the southern colonies arrived in America as indentured servants. Marriage was off limits to such servants until their terms of indenture were completed. With no hope of marriage and no family to provide a stabilizing force, servants had a high rate of premarital sexual activity. Some of this may have been basic human nature to seek out companionship, but female indentured servants were often the target of unwanted sexual advances.

There were fewer opportunities for sexual promiscuity in the closely settled regions of New England than in the sparse, rural communities of the South. Puritans believed a community had a responsibility for upholding the morality of its members. Homes were built closer together in the villages of the North than in the far-flung homesteads of the South. Puritans made it their business to know their neighbors' children and keep a watchful eye on their activities. Privacy was almost nonexistent in New England towns, and opportunities to slip away for clandestine sex were difficult, though not impossible, to find. Communities of the South were not so closely knit. The wide variety of social, religious, and racial backgrounds made people less interested in securing uniformity of culture. Widely scattered homesteads made it easier to find privacy, and neighbors had less opportunity and interest in monitoring the activities of others.

Regional variations in extramarital sex diminished by the middle of the eighteenth century. The New England colonies became more religiously diverse, and the increasing density of villages pressured children to move farther into the frontier to seek out homesteads. Without extended family to provide community control over sexuality, premarital pregnancy rates increased. In the southern colonies, a more balanced sex ratio had been achieved. By 1700 men outnumbered women only two to one. Reliance on African slavery led to a decline in the reliance on indentured servitude. Mortality rates improved as southerners developed immunities to disease, leading to greater family stability.

Urbanization played a role in evolving standards of sexual morality and extramarital sexual activity. Young adults migrated to larger towns seeking opportunity. Outside the realm of parental supervision and community pressures, young adults tended to be more sexually adventurous than they were at home. Mariners and soldiers often took up temporary residence in cities, and this gave rise to a small but growing base of prostitutes.

Legal Prohibitions

Legal penalties for fornication were set by individual colonies, and as such they reflect the religious character of each settlement. Laws were more likely to be rigidly enforced in Puritan New England than in the religiously diverse southern colonies. Higher rates of fornication in the South led to growing toleration, and some couples escaped punishment altogether if they proceeded to marry.

In the Plymouth Colony, punishment for fornication was a fine of £10, a considerable sum for cash-strapped colonists. The fee was reduced to fifty shillings if the couple married. Those unable to pay the fine were publicly whipped. Women convicted of fornication were less likely than men to be able to afford the fines. As such, women were more likely to endure the shaming punishments of time in the stocks and public whippings. Fifteen lashes was a typical sentence for a woman found guilty of fornication.

Public humiliation was sometimes considered adequate punishment. It was not unheard of for a woman to be stripped to the waist and forced to stand in public. Such public shaming was the sentence for Joan Cowdall, a widow found guilty of fornication in 1672. She was stripped to the waist and tied to the great gun at Newport for a period of fifteen minutes. Other shaming punishments included standing before a congregation in a white sheet and a sign indicating the specific offense, or standing in the public stockade for two to three hours.

Oftentimes fornication was discovered only on the birth of a child too soon after a wedding. A couple was subject to prosecution if their child was born within seven months of their marriage and the infant was not obviously premature. Punishment of the couple would occur a few months after the birth, which allowed time for the mother to recover and midwives to affirm that the child had indeed been conceived prior to marriage. The couple would usually be required to pay a modest fine and make a confession before their congregation. Whipping and heavy fines were reserved for couples who elected not to marry at all.

Fornication prosecutions diminished in the eighteenth century, not because the problem was becoming rare, but because it was apparent the laws were having little effect. Courts had already abandoned the practice of punishing married couples whose first child was born too soon. Fathers who refused to get married or to support their illegitimate children could still be punished by the court, but unless a person was guilty of repeated and flagrant offenses, fornication prosecution by the court became rare. Despite the easing of legal sanctions, social condemnation of extramarital sex remained high throughout the period.

Double Standard

Extramarital sex was discouraged for both men and women, but the consequences were sharply different between the sexes. Charges of fornication could embarrass a man and tarnish his reputation, but rarely would his business dealings or marital situation be damaged. If he were married, his wife's anger might have been profound, but it is unlikely the marriage would be terminated. Although infidelity was grounds for divorce in some colonies, divorce was rarely granted based on nothing more than a husband's infidelity. Conversely, a divorce petition was far more likely to be granted if it was the wife who committed adultery.

Young adults were expected to remain virgins until marriage, but a man caught engaging in premarital sex would suffer no more than a nominal fine or public whipping. After accepting his punishment, there were few lasting consequences. If a woman was convicted of fornication, she would accept the same punishment, but social consequences were far more severe. The most highly prized virtues in women throughout most of the colonial period were her modesty, chastity, and potential to be a good mother. Should a woman engage in premarital sex, she was considered a lustful bawd. She could not hope to portray herself as a modest or honorable person. Should she marry the

man she was known to have dallied with, her reputation might be gradually repaired. If her lover refused to marry her, her chances of finding a desirable marriage partner were usually destroyed.

Fornication was believed to leave an indelible imprint on a woman, possibly resulting in sterility or weakened children. A woman who held herself out to be a virgin, but was discovered upon marriage to have been previously deflowered, could have her marriage annulled because she entered the contract under fraudulent pretenses. There is no evidence there were any corresponding protections for a woman who found her husband to be "impure" on his wedding day.

Words used to describe an unchaste man in colonial America are almost nonexistent, but those for promiscuous women are extensive: whore, bawd, harlot, strumpet, trull, wench, slut, and jade, just to name a few. The worse thing a man could be called in colonial America was a cuckold, which was a slur upon the chastity of his *wife,* rather than his own character.

Sexual Assault

Men often felt they had a right to the sexual services of their female slaves and indentured servants. Although there was a taboo against interracial sex, the existence of a large class of mixed-race children prove this taboo was widely ignored. Racial stereotypes portrayed African women as highly sensual and willing to engage in sex. In actuality, neither slave women nor indentured servants had little choice should their master press his advances on them. In rural environments, there were few places a victimized woman could turn for assistance.

Slaves and servants were not the only women who feared sexual assault. Women from all walks of life were vulnerable, although those from poorer families were more likely to be exposed to violence. Girls from poor families were often placed in the homes of employers to perform domestic service. There they were vulnerable not only to male members of the family but to fellow servants as well. Female servants were more than three times as likely to complain of rape than other classes of women. Rape was difficult to prove in early America, because it required witnesses and evidence of fierce resistance. In many cases, women who attempted to bring rape charges were ultimately convicted of fornication when they failed to have irrefutable proof they had been unwilling participants.

See also Adultery; Birth Control; Sex and Sexuality

Further Reading

D'Emilio, John, and Estelle B. Freedman. *Intimate Matters: A History of Sexuality in America.* Chicago: University of Chicago Press, 1988.

Godbeer, Richard. *Sexual Revolution in Early America.* Baltimore: Johns Hopkins University Press, 2002.

Hambleton, Else K. "The World Fill'd with a Generation of Bastards: Pregnant Brides and Unwed Mothers in Seventeenth Century Massachusetts." Dissertation. University of Massachusetts, 2000.

Morgan, Edmund S. "The Puritans and Sex." *New England Quarterly* 15 (1942): 591–607.

Smith, Merril D., ed. *Sex and Sexuality in Early America.* New York: New York University Press, 1998.

Thompson, Roger. "Sexual Mores and Behavior." In *Encyclopedia of the North American Colonies*, ed. Jacob Earnest Cooke. New York: Charles Scribner's Sons, 1993.

Franklin, Ann Smith
Printer (1696–1763)

Little is known about the early life of Ann Smith, other than she was raised in Boston and had a solid education. At the age of twenty-seven she married James Franklin, a printer and publisher of the *New England Courant*. Their life together had an unpromising start, because James's hostility to church and government authorities resulted in his imprisonment for printing "scandalous libel." After his release, he complied with the order that he cease publishing the *Courant*. Publication of the newspaper was turned over to James's apprentice and younger brother, Benjamin Franklin.

James and Ann Franklin moved to Newport, Rhode Island, where they established the colony's first printing press. During this time Ann gave birth to five children, three of whom survived into adulthood. In addition to fulfilling the common domestic duties of raising and educating children, preparing meals, and tending the home, Ann was an active participant in her husband's print shop. She learned to set type and operate the press and assisted in their small shop, which sold papers, books, and the innovative product of fabrics upon which they printed images per the request of customers.

Ann's skills in the print shop proved essential, because her husband, James, died in 1735, leaving Ann with the responsibility of supporting four young children on her own. Concerned that she did not have enough business to support her family, Ann appealed to the General Assembly of Rhode Island, hoping to obtain a contract to print their official publications. In 1736 she sent the following petition: "Whereas your petitioner being left with several small children which is a great charge to her, and having not sufficient business at the printing trade, humbly prays your Honors will grant her the favor to print Acts of the Colony and what other things shall be lawful and necessary to be printed, in order for your Petitioner's support and maintenance of her family she having no other way to support herself" (Ford 1995, 3).

Ann won the contract and became the official printer of the General Assembly. Although she continued her work as the assembly's printer until her death, the relationship was not without controversy. Ann had attempted to supplement her slender income by printing additional copies of the laws and selling them for a profit from her own shop. She was severely reprimanded for this action, possibly because the assembly had provided the paper on which the surplus documents were printed. She was forbidden to sell these documents for one year, under threat of a £5 fine per item. In subsequent years, the printing contract issued by the General Assembly was modified to allow her to produce excess copies, provided she supply all materials: "The Printer shall have the liberty to make as many more copies as he or she shall think fit, and dispose of the same for his or her private profit or advantage" (Ford 1995, 4). Aside from printing law books, Ann's work as assembly printer also gave her work printing election ballots, legal forms, and the colony's currency.

Despite the importance of this contract to Ann's business, she supplemented her income with a variety of printing jobs. She was hired by ministers to print sermons, merchants to produce advertisements, and on her own accord printed a number of popular books. Ann printed highly popular British novels that were expensive to produce, but sold well and were ultimately a low-risk item. Perhaps among her most curious publications were her broadsides of private quarrels. Townspeople made use of the printing press to air their grievances of both a personal and a business nature. For example, the widow of a distiller printed a grievance against her late husband's business partner, claiming he had swindled her of the still and stock shares. Such personal attacks often prompted replies from the affronted individual, resulting in some quick and easy business for the printer.

Ann's most noteworthy production was five editions of the *Rhode Island Almanac*. Almanacs were popular in colonial America, containing a calendar of the year, astronomical phenomenon, weather predictions, short verses, and pithy quotations. Her husband, James, had initiated the *Rhode Island Almanac* under the pseudonym Poor Robin, and Ann followed closely in his format. Although Ann compiled the information that appeared in her almanacs, it is unlikely she wrote very much of the material. The workload necessary to compile an almanac was tremendous, and Ann had little enthusiasm for the project. In 1741 she ceased publication of the *Rhode Island Almanac,* but began selling her brother-in-law's more successful *Poor Richard's Almanac.*

Ann was greatly assisted in her print shop by her children. Her daughters, Mary and Elizabeth, were efficient in setting type, and her son, James, went to Philadelphia to apprentice with his Uncle Benjamin. In 1748 James returned to Newport and went into business with his mother, their firm henceforth known as "Ann and James Franklin." In 1758 the pair produced the *Newport Mercury,* the first newspaper in Rhode Island. As Ann grew older she began easing herself out of the printing business, assigning ever more responsibility to her son. Tragically, both Ann's daughters had died early, and her son, James, died in April 1762. At age sixty-five, Ann returned full time to her printing press. Despite her failing health, she did not miss a single issue of the *Newport Mercury.* Later that year she took Samuel Hall as a business partner, and the pair continued to operate the press until Ann's death in 1763.

Ann Franklin's career has been overshadowed by her brother-in-law. She is chiefly remembered as having owned the press on which Benjamin Franklin learned to set type. Her newspaper carried an obituary that paid tribute to her as a woman by whose "economy and industry . . . supported herself and her family, and brought up her children in a genteel manner." Little mention was made of her professional career, but in the late twentieth century, Ann became the first woman inducted into the Journalism Hall of Fame at the University of Rhode Island.

See also Printers and the Printing Trade

Further Reading

Ford, Margaret Lane. "Types and Gender: Ann Franklin, Colonial Printer." In *A Living of Words: American Women in Print Culture,* ed. Susan Albertine. Knoxville: University of Tennessee Press, 1995.

Gale, Robert L. "Ann Smith Franklin." In *American National Biography,* ed. John A. Garraty. New York: Oxford University Press, 1999.

Henry, B. Susan. "Ann Franklin: Rhode Island's Woman Printer." In *Newsletters to Newspapers: Eighteenth Century Journalism,* eds. Donovan H. Bond and W. Reynolds McLeod. Morgantown: School of Journalism, West Virginia University, 1977.

Freeman, Elizabeth
Successful plaintiff in a slavery lawsuit
(c. 1742–1829)

Elizabeth Freeman, also known as "Mumbet," was one of the first slaves to successfully sue for her freedom in colonial America. She was born to first-generation African slaves sometime in the early 1740s, and grew up in the household of Peter

The Ashley home in Sheffield, Massachusetts. While a slave in the Ashley household, Elizabeth Freeman had overheard the conversations of Colonel Ashley and fellow revolutionaries, in which they discussed a proposed bill of rights and the idea that all people were born free and equal. (Library of Congress)

Hogeboom. She did not have a last name growing up and was usually referred to as Mumbet, or simply Bett. When her owner died in 1758, Elizabeth and her sister, Lizzie, were transferred to the household of Mr. Hogeboom's youngest daughter, Hannah Ashley of Sheffield, Massachusetts.

Hannah Ashley was a woman of short temper. When she attempted to discipline Elizabeth's sister with a heated shovel, Elizabeth intervened and received the blow herself. She bore the scar on her arm for the rest of her life and later said it was this incident that triggered her desire to seek freedom.

She ran away from the Ashley household immediately after the event and never returned.

In 1781 Elizabeth sought shelter and legal help from a promising young attorney, Theodore Sedgwick. While a slave in the Ashley household, Elizabeth had overheard the conversations of Colonel Ashley and fellow revolutionaries, in which they discussed a proposed bill of rights and the idea that all people were born free and equal. Since such rhetoric did not exclude slaves, Elizabeth was prepared to sue for her freedom. Theodore Sedgwick was not only willing to take her case, but he granted her refuge in his home until the case could be heard. Elizabeth became a paid servant in the Sedgwick home, where she became well known for her skills as a nurse and a caring nanny for the Sedgwick children.

Elizabeth's suit was joined with another escaped slave from Ashley's household named Brom, and the case was subsequently known as *Brom and Bett v. Ashley.* The jury found in favor of the escaped slaves, claiming they had been illegally held in bondage, and ordered Colonel Ashley to pay thirty shillings in compensation. The colonel vowed to appeal the decision, but shortly after the *Brom and Bett* case, the Supreme Court of Massachusetts ruled that slavery was unconstitutional in Massachusetts, and Ashley decided to drop his appeal.

Elizabeth elected the surname "Freeman" following her successful suit. She continued to work as a paid housekeeper and nurse for the Sedgwicks for several decades and became a beloved figure in the Sedgwick home. Mrs. Sedgwick suffered bouts of severe depression that bordered on insanity. During the bad spells, Elizabeth was the only person able to comfort the distraught woman. In her old age Elizabeth retired to a small home she purchased with her own savings. Little is known of Elizabeth's personal life. It is believed she married at a young age, but her husband was killed in the Revolutionary War. She had at least one daughter and several grandchildren.

See also African American Women, Free

Further Reading

Dumas, Bethany K. "Elizabeth Freeman." In *American National Biography,* ed. John A. Garraty. New York: Oxford University Press, 1999.

Swan, Jon. "The Slave Who Sued for Freedom." *American Heritage* 42 (March 1990): 51–55.

Zilversmit, Arthur. "Quok Walker, Mumbet, and the Abolition of Slavery in Massachusetts." *William and Mary Quarterly* 25 (1968): 614–624.

French Colonies, Women in

France had control of vast expanses of American land in the eighteenth century. The Louisiana Territory included land from the Great Lakes all the way to the Gulf of Mexico. The upper portion of this land, the Illinois Territory, was closely connected to the cultural and economic concerns of French Canada. The character of settlement around the Gulf of Mexico had a different economy, steamy climate, and higher rate of sickness and mortality than the more northern part of the territory. The southern portion of French America developed a unique amalgamation of French, Indian, African, and English cultures.

The first French women to arrive in southern Louisiana arrived with the explorer La Salle in 1684. Although four shiploads of colonists arrived, within three years their population had been decimated by disease, hunger, and Indian attacks. Fewer than thirty colonists were alive by 1687, seven of whom were women. This tiny band of colonists struggled with diminishing supplies and tropical disease. All eventually perished except for a few who disappeared into the Indian communities.

Subsequent attempts to plant French colonies along the Gulf of Mexico were more successful. Fledgling colonies near present-day Ocean Springs, Mississippi; Mobile, Alabama; and New Orleans, Louisiana, all took root in the 1710s and 1720s.

Unlike the northern French colonies, which were dominated by the fur trade, these colonies were designed to become self-sufficient, agricultural communities. The overwhelming majority of settlers were male, and the founder of the colony appealed to France for young, marriageable women. The colony lacked stability, with men failing to establish productive farms and stay rooted in one community. It was believed that women and established families would give the colonists a sense of permanency they lacked.

In 1704 a group of twenty-three young women arrived in Biloxi, Mississippi, from France. These women were quickly married, and the 1706 census demonstrates that many of them soon became mothers. Other ships full of marriageable young women followed, the most famous of which was the 1721 arrival of the "casket girls." These seventy-eight women arrived with all their worldly possessions in small caskets. Many of them were orphans with no prospect of decent lives in France, but some were prostitutes or women of otherwise questionable reputation. Unlike the earlier groups of women who were quickly married, many of the casket girls remained single for a few years. Some male settlers complained of the women's poor character or even homely appearance. A few women became pregnant and refused to name the father of their child. Despite the checkered character of some of these women, the male population greeted most of the casket girls with enthusiasm.

Survival in the early years of the Louisiana Territory was daunting. Sudden hurricanes and floods buffeted the fledgling communities. The sweltering humid heat was a breeding ground for a variety of tropical diseases unknown to settlers from northern Europe. Settlers were forced to adjust to major dietary changes. Wheat, wine, and cheese, staples of the French diet, were almost nonexistent. They needed to learn the difficult art of rice cultivation, as well as become accustomed to a higher proportion of seafood than they were used to consuming.

Many of the first generation of French settlers did not flourish. In their efforts to encourage immigration to America, companies portrayed the Louisiana Territory as an idyllic, tropical paradise.

Many of the settlers arrived clearly unprepared for the rigors of frontier life. Most lacked adequate provisions to establish themselves, and many chose to return to France.

The women who remained and survived the initial years of illness and deprivation were likely to have greater legal rights than their sisters in France. The scarcity of women in the French colonies meant women could be selective when deciding on a marriage partner. Inheritance laws granted them the right to their husband's premarital property as well as half of everything that was acquired during the marriage. Widows in the French colonies therefore fared much better than their counterparts in English colonies, who were entitled to only one-third of their husband's estate. Women from the French colonies rarely remained widowed for long. Women were in demand, and widows tended to possess substantial assets, making them especially desirable as marriage partners. Although charivari and social hazing discouraged hasty remarriage in France, no such prohibitions were imposed in the colonies.

The sex ratio imbalance resulted in disparity in the ages of marriage partners. Women were known to marry as young as fourteen, although most married between the ages of fifteen and twenty-one. The average age difference between husband and wife was ten years. This age discrepancy also resulted in a higher proportion of widows and remarriage for women.

The nature of economic life in the French colonies meant that men were often away from home. Many of them were engaged in the fur trade, while others dealt in trading manufactured goods throughout the French and Spanish Territories. Hunters, sailors, soldiers, and traders all spent considerable time away from their homes. This meant wives assumed substantial responsibility for keeping the household and farm operating. Although French women were under the law of coverture, meaning their legal identity was subsumed under their husband, it appears the rules were rarely enforced. Women whose husbands were away managed and sold property, collected debts, and paid creditors. These activities provided women with the practical experience they needed should they become widowed at an early age.

French women who were unhappily married had few options. The only grounds for a separation was if the husband admitted heresy, refused to provide his wife with the necessities of life, or treated her with extreme cruelty. Even if she was able to prove these activities, divorce was not an option. She would have to petition a court for alimony payments in order to establish a separate residence.

Not all women chose to marry. Almost all of the French women settlers were Catholic, and there were numerous opportunities, especially in the northern settlements, for women to enter convents. Given the scarcity of women, there was social pressure to marry, but some opted for life within the church. An Ursuline convent was established in New Orleans specifically for the education of girls, the care of orphans, and the operation of a hospital. The Ursulines opened the school for girls in 1727. In addition to reading, writing, and mathematics, they taught practical skills such as sewing and knitting. They also established classes for African and Indian girls.

The French never settled their colonies as densely as the English. Small villages scattered across a vast territory meant that the settlers led fairly isolated lives. Upon the purchase of the Louisiana Territory in 1803 the colony became a part of the United States. Although French language, culture, and religion lingered in the few areas of dense settlement, English culture became dominant in most areas within a few generations.

Further Reading

Baker, Vaughan B. *"Cherchez les Femmes:* Some Glimpses of Women in Early Eighteenth Century Louisiana." *Louisiana History* 31 (1990): 21–37.

Boyle, Susan C. "Did She Generally Decide? Women in Ste. Genevieve, 1750–1805." *William and Mary Quarterly* 44 (1987): 775–789.

Hawthorne, Margaret. "That Certain Piece of Furniture: Women in Colonial Louisiana, 1685–1763." *Journal of Mississippi History* 53 (1991): 219–227.

Robenstine, Clark. "French Colonial Policy and the Education of Women and Minorities: Louisiana in the Early Eighteenth Century." *History of Education Quarterly* 32 (1992): 193–211.

Fur Traders' Wives

The trade in animal skins was vital for the economy of North American colonies. Lacking the gold that enriched the Spanish colonies, fur was one of the few exports that brought rich returns in the French and English colonies. Travel into the frontier would have been impossible for fur trappers and traders without the cooperation of the Native Americans. Alliances had to be brokered that granted traders the permission to hunt. The fur traders were also in need of insight into the local climate, hunting grounds, and survival skills. Marrying an Indian woman brought all those advantages. Indian women who formed alliances with fur traders entered into a unique society that was balanced between two starkly different worlds. Becoming the primary companion of a fur trader/hunter, the woman likely learned the language of her husband, and was thereafter able to serve as a translator. She was able to serve as a cultural mediator as her husband traveled into new areas. She was a helper in his business and the mother of his children. Although her life entailed a great deal of manual labor, she was welcomed into fur trading posts, where she would have access to material goods and comforts unknown to her Indian sisters. Many of these women were exposed to Catholic missionaries and embraced Christianity.

Advantages flowed to the Indians from the partnerships as well. Having a fur trader intimately allied with a tribe raised the group's prestige. The Indian family gained access to European trade goods, such as metal awls, copper kettles, hatchets, fishhooks, rope, and netting. These implements enabled Indian families to greatly improve the efficiency of their daily chores, leaving them more time for leisure or assisting in fur production, which would bring yet more resources to the tribe.

Alliances between Indian women and white traders were not marriages in the Christian sense of the word. Called *femmes du pays,* or "country wives," these women were intended to be the wife of a man during his time in the wilderness. There was no expectation on either side that the marriage was to be a lifetime commitment. Most fur traders intended to spend their working careers in the wilderness, but would retire to the "civilized"

Fur Traders Descending the Missouri by George Caleb Bingham. Becoming the primary companion of a fur trader/hunter, an Indian woman likely learned her husband's language, and was thereafter able to serve as a translator. She was able to serve as a cultural mediator as her husband traveled into new areas. (Geoffrey Clements/CORBIS)

colonies on the eastern seaboard, or perhaps even return to Europe at the end of their careers. Not many Indian women would have welcomed such a move, nor would they have been warmly embraced by European societies. A few women did return with their husbands to the East Coast, and some men elected to remain in Indian country, but they were the exceptions.

Once an Indian woman and a white hunter decided to enter into an alliance, the man would pay a bride price to the woman's parents. The substantial sum would be paid in goods such as rum, iron tools, or a horse. After the bride price had been paid, a

pipe was smoked to seal the agreement. The new bride usually continued to wear Indian clothing, although some accepted gifts of European clothing from their husband.

The fur trader's wife would have enjoyed an initial increase in prestige. Her alliance put her at a pivotal position as the Indian with the most influence over an important trading partner. Some women traveled with their husbands into the woods in order to hunt, but others would have lived at a company base, such as Cumberland House or the Hudson's Bay Company's trading fort. The job of the fur trader's wife involved dressing furs, making leather, cooking meals, making moccasins, and stringing the netting on snowshoes. Women collected and prepared spruce roots, used for sewing birch bark canoes, and pine resin for caulking canoes. If a woman lived at the trading post, she would have tended a small garden to supply herself and her family with food. Those who traveled with their husbands into the woods also set up camp and taught the trader valuable survival skills, which most of the European-born men lacked. As soon as the rivers were free of ice, most women joined their husbands on canoe trips east to deliver pelts to trading posts.

There were two primary companies that underwrote fur traders, and each created markedly different roles for Indian wives. The Hudson's Bay Company was a London-based company, and the North West Company was based in Montreal. The operating rules for the Hudson's Bay Company were formed by shareholders in London, who saw no need to expend resources for the support of Indian wives. From the 1740s through the 1760s they forbade marriage with Indian women and barred them from the forts. This rule was widely disregarded by the men in the field, who wrote to London that the Indian women were essential for the operation of the fort. In contrast, the Montreal-based North West Company believed that traders were more likely to renew their contracts if they had wives and families in the area. Traders had to apply for permission from the North West Company to marry an Indian woman, but it appears such permissions were routinely granted.

Over time a generation of mixed-race children were born to these couples. Called Métis, these children grew up with heavy exposure to both Indian and white cultures. Most were bilingual and had at least a rudimentary understanding of both cultures. As such, they served as cultural mediators between the groups as European settlement continued to move westward. Over time, fur traders appeared to prefer Métis women for wives rather than full-blooded Indian women.

Problems occurred for the fur trader's wife when it came time for her husband to retire. Most men opted to return to the East Coast, and few Indian women either wished, or were invited, to accompany their husbands. The practice of making arrangements for the care of the discarded wife was called "turning off." The retiring husband tried to find another protector (i.e., a new husband) for the woman, or at least make arrangements for her to live with another family. Sometimes a sum of money would be left to ensure any children would be provided for. In rare cases, the man simply abandoned the woman.

In the early years of the fur trade, a widowed or abandoned fur trader's wife was warmly welcomed back into her original tribe. Over time this repatriation became difficult. Tribal affiliations were disintegrating following sustained contact with white society, and it was possible the woman's family was no longer living in the area or had become economically incapable of supporting her. The mixed-blood children, many of whom knew little of life outside of a trading post, had difficulty assimilating into an Indian tribe. Sometimes the abandoned woman and her children were permitted to continue living and working at the fur trading post. Over time the population of such dependents became so large they were a burden to company finances. In the 1820s rules were passed that deducted a portion of the salary from all men married to Indian women. The money was placed in a fund to care for women should their husbands die or retire to the East. The arrival of priests and ministers in the 1820s also discouraged the creation of temporary, informal marriagelike alliances.

See also Interracial Marriage

Further Reading

Sleeper-Smith, Susan. "Women, Kin, and Catholicism: New Perspectives on the Fur Trade." *Ethnohistory* 47 (2000): 423–452.

Van Kirk, Sylvia. *Many Tender Ties: Women in Fur Trade Society, 1670–1870.* Norman: University of Oklahoma Press, 1983.

———. Women and the Fur Trade. *Beaver* 303 (Winter 1972): 4–21.

G

Gambling

Gambling arrived in America with the first ship of immigrants to Jamestown. The funding of the colony had been supplemented by a public lottery in London. Furthermore, many of the men who settled at Jamestown were notorious for indulging in frivolous pastimes, including gambling. Almost anything could have a wager placed on it, whether it was a card game, a horse race, or who could throw a knife the farthest. There are few vices exclusive to any one sex, and just as men indulged in gambling, so, too, did women. For a short time in colonial America gambling even became a socially condoned, elegant pastime for well-to-do ladies.

The Puritan founders of New England strongly disapproved of gambling, regarding it as squandering time that could be better spent in either productive employment or respectful worship of God. Social prohibitions against gambling were strong in New England, which had been settled by Puritan immigrants who fled from a dissolute English society. Gambling was socially acceptable in England, especially among the upper classes. Both men and women wagered enormous sums on card games and horse races. Social condemnation against gambling was so strong among the Puritan settlers they saw no initial need to codify restrictions against the practice. As the decades passed, the fervor of the first Puritan settlers became diluted by other immigrants who did not share their revulsion for gambling. Antigambling laws were passed in 1682 and 1740 in an attempt to uphold the moral superiority of the new American settlements.

The character of the settlements in Virginia was markedly different from that of Puritan New England. Virginia settlers shared the mother country's love of gambling and other recreational pastimes. Although the laboring classes were discouraged from gambling, it was considered a suitable entertainment for gentlemen and their wives. Women gambled at card games. The most popular card game in colonial America was whist, which is much like modern-day bridge.

Lotteries and raffles were the other popular forms of female wagering. Lotteries were held to gather funds for public works such as roads and buildings. Women could therefore justify the purchase of tickets as a patriotic gesture. Raffles were sponsored by private individuals to raise money for a specific cause, and shop owners frequently held them to raise funds for their business. In 1767 Sarah Garland Pitt sold tickets to a raffle, for which the prize was to be millinery goods from her store. The prizes offered were manufactured goods such as jewelry, shoes, and clothing, and women were Pitt's primary clientele for the raffle tickets.

The appeal of gambling might be credited to its ability to channel competitive instincts into a safe outlet. It was regarded as a vice only if it interfered with social stability or the financial well-being of the home. Stakes tended to be low, usually no more than half a British pound. Thomas Jefferson assiduously recorded his wife's winnings and losses, and these never amounted to more than a few shillings. The diaries of colonial women make reference to the collection of their winnings, perhaps a sign of pride in their triumph at the whist table. It is unlikely that women ever incurred serious financial losses from gambling. Gambling losses were usually recorded in a family's account books, and although we can find numerous records that document destructive gambling patterns among husbands and sons, there are no corresponding figures for women.

See also Hobbies and Games; Sports and Leisure

Further Reading

Findlay, John M. *People of Chance: Gambling in American Society from Jamestown to Las Vegas.* New York: Oxford University Press, 1986.

Sturtz, Linda L. "The Ladies and the Lottery: Elite Women's Gambling in Eighteenth Century Virginia." *Virginia Magazine of History and Biography* 104 (1996): 165–184.

Games

See Hobbies and Games

Gardening

Gardening was an essential element in the lives of most early American women. From the poorest farmer's daughter to the governor's wife, women were expected to have a knowledge of the cultivation of plants.

Gardening was considered a separate activity from farming. Farming demanded the participation of the entire family in the production of a large crop such as corn or tobacco, but gardening was usually the province of the woman. Early American gardening was strictly utilitarian, intended to provide supplemental vegetables and herbs for household consumption. As settlements developed, gardens were embellished with flowering plants and hedges for their aesthetic value. The concept of a *front yard,* with a lawn and ornamental plants, was almost unknown in early America. The time needed to construct and support a decorative feature was a luxury few could afford. The ground in front of a home might have been used to let chickens graze or for the storage of farming tools, or simply left wild. Gardens were almost always located behind the house. They consumed one to three acres for women living in rural environments, and perhaps no more than a quarter-acre for those in villages.

Early Americans were fascinated with the scientific aspects of botany in the New World. It quickly became apparent that America contained specimens of herbs, vegetables, and timber unknown in Europe. Naturalists from Europe visited America to gather saplings and seeds for scientific examination, eager for new herbal medicines and varieties of timber suitable for naval construction. The export of seeds between Europe and America met with mixed success. European varieties of grapes and wheat proved unsuitable for the growing conditions in the New World, and settlers traded seeds with other colonies and local Indians in search of plants that would flourish in their gardens.

Women took chief responsibility for their gardens and were known to trade seeds, cuttings, and advice with one another for making their gardens flourish. Some enterprising women even marketed strains of plants that were particularly vigorous. Martha Logan advertised in the *South Carolina Gazette* (15 February 1768) "A fresh assortment of very good garden seeds and flower roots, also many other sorts of flowering shrubs and box edging beds, now growing in her garden."

The nature of a woman's garden depended on her economic needs and interests. Some women were skilled in using herbs for the treatment of common maladies, others were interested in herbs for their culinary value. Most gardens were simply "kitchen gardens," used to supplement the family's diet.

Kitchen Gardens

For practical reasons, kitchen gardens were usually located behind the house, near the stables. This made manure for fertilization more accessible. The gardens inevitably needed fencing or a hedge to protect the plants from grazing livestock or wild animals. Split rail fences were the most common, because they were easy to construct and could be moved when the soil was exhausted.

The wealth of a family often determined the sort of produce found in their kitchen garden. The average family grew reliable and nutritious staples, such as corn, potatoes, carrots, turnips, and cabbage. Wealthier women had the luxury to include delicacies such as celery, asparagus, cucumbers, salad greens, and herbs. American kitchen gardens soon included vegetables from other cultures. For example, Indians introduced early American women to squash, corn, and sweet potatoes. African slaves brought knowledge of the cultivation of okra, black-eyed peas, and eggplant, and these vegetables were grown in kitchen gardens throughout the southern and middle colonies.

The standard kitchen garden was a rectangle, with a gravel path down the middle. Larger gardens were split with an additional crosswalk to divide the garden into quadrants. This made the wheeling of a barrel or transportation of water buckets easier to accomplish without damaging the vegetables.

Some women became very ambitious in growing exotic produce in their gardens. Eleanor Laurens of South Carolina experimented with growing lime trees, sugarcane, olives, and oranges. Eliza Pinckney was most famous for her research that made large-scale indigo production a viable endeavor, but she also experimented with figs and silkworms.

Herbal Gardens

Herbs had two important functions in colonial America. They formed the backbone of colonial medicines, and they aided in the seasoning of food that often tasted heavily of the smoke or salt used to preserve it. Early records indicate the herbs colonists considered essential for an herbal garden: angelica, basil, dill, fennel, hyssop, marjoram, parsley, rosemary, savory, tansy, and thyme.

Also called medicinal or physic gardens, herbal gardens often contained plants heavily relied on by doctors and housewives to treat common ailments. A typical housewife would have known the most common remedies, such as mixing hyssop with honey to make a cough syrup, or using oil of thyme for a toothache. Women who specialized in midwifery or nursing knew of more sophisticated uses for herbs, such as how to make an antidote for snakebites from marjoram or how to use pennyroyal and juniper leaves to hasten the labor of a pregnant woman.

Pleasure Gardens

Only women from wealthy families could afford the luxury of creating ornamental gardens. By the mid-eighteenth century, extensive pleasure gardens became a mark of genteel living. Gardeners imported from England assisted in the layout of formal gardens. Initially such gardens were highly stylized, along the French model. Beds were formed in geometric shapes, sometimes including hedges cut into knot-work designs. Trees and shrubs were pruned into elegant topiaries.

Over time, the highly manicured, French-style garden was surpassed by the popularity of the English garden. The hallmark of the English garden was a naturalistic style. English gardens still demanded extensive labor in planting, pruning, and designing, but the aim was to create an Eden-like impression of natural bounty. Further embellishments might include the construction of naturalistic waterfalls, small Greek temples, serpentine walkways, and a variety of elevations built into the landscape.

Unlike that of the utilitarian kitchen garden, the creation and maintenance of these elite pleasure gardens was often overseen by men. Many of the leading figures of the eighteenth century, such as Thomas Jefferson, George Washington, and Charles Wilson Peale, viewed horticulture as an extension of a classical education. The design of a magnificent garden was the quintessential endeavor that blended scientific inquiry, artistic beauty, and the patriotic celebration of the bounty of America. The gardens attracted educated visitors from around the world. Not all famous gardens were created by men. The chief force behind the magnificent garden at Nomini Hall was the mistress of the plantation, Francis Carter. Eleanor Laurens spent so much time in her gardens that her husband imported a landscape designer and gardener from England to carry some of the burden. Extensive work in a garden provided many wealthy women with an artistic and intellectual outlet for their creative energies.

See also Agricultural Labor

Further Reading

Leighton, Ann. *American Gardens in the Eighteenth Century: For Use or for Delight.* Amherst: University of Massachusetts Press, 1986.

McLean, Elizabeth. "Town and Country Gardens in Eighteenth Century Philadelphia." *Eighteenth Century Life* 8 (1983): 136–147.

Rogers, George C. "Gardens and Landscapes in Eighteenth-Century South Carolina." *Eighteenth Century Life* 8 (1983): 148–158.

Tucker, David. *Kitchen Gardening in America: A History.* Ames: Iowa State University Press, 1993.

German Women

Germans were by far the largest group of non-British, white settlers in America. By the time of the Revolution, one in ten colonists was of German descent.

Despite their numeric significance, Germans did not leave a distinctive imprint on American culture in the manner of the French, Spanish, or African immigrants. A number of factors account for the thorough assimilation of Germans into the fabric of American culture. The ethnic differences among the immigrants themselves gave them little sense of community. A number of them came seeking religious freedom, including the Mennonites, Jews, Dunkers, Lutherans, and Moravians. The diversity among these religious immigrants meant they had little in common with each other. Other Germans came in search of economic opportunity or were refugees from various wars that riddled the eighteenth-century German states. Their immigration rarely came in large waves, but was sporadic throughout the colonial period. Most importantly, there was never an official German colony in America. French, Spanish, and Dutch colonies resulted in large concentrations of immigrants who had the freedom to transplant their culture, law, and language in the New World. The Germans had no similar structure.

Most German immigrants came through the port at Philadelphia, although Charleston, Baltimore, and New York were other common destinations. The first large-scale immigration of Germans began in 1709, when 13,000 people fled southwestern Ger-

many because of overpopulation, heavy taxation, and the resultant wreckage of war with France. These Germans came in family groups, the majority of them either newly married couples or young families with one or two children. In this they were markedly different than English and Irish immigrants, who tended to arrive as single adults bound in indentured servitude. The German immigrants almost always paid their own passage or were funded by German societies. As such, they were usually able to immediately establish their own household, farm, or shop.

Many German women arrived in the colonies as newlywed brides. Marriage restrictions and inheritance customs in Germany made marriage difficult for younger sons and girls lacking dowries. These restrictions ceased to apply after leaving Germany, so many of these young adults were embarking on a joint marriage-migration venture. Migration from the German states was more difficult and expensive than from England because of the additional hundreds of miles of overland travel. This may have discouraged poor and unskilled immigrants. As a group, the German immigrants tended to have more skills, education, and resources than the average English immigrant.

German immigrants were known for their frugal households and strong work ethic. They emulated the small, compact-style homes they had been familiar with in southwest Germany, and they used minimal furniture and utensils. German enclaves formed in many towns, most notably, Germantown, Pennsylvania. Here they needed to know only a little English, and for a time, a distinctively German culture took root. German-language newspapers were established, butchers produced German sausages, and German-language churches flourished for centuries.

The life of a German American housewife differed only slightly from that of her English counterpart. German women did their cooking in iron stoves, whereas Anglo women continued to cook over open fireplaces for generations. Germans preferred brightly colored stoneware instead of the pewter the English used for serving meals. They drank coffee rather than tea. They prepared more vegetables and less meat than English housewives. Aside from these slight differences, the rhythm of their lives was remarkably similar.

Although many Germans chose to live in ethnic enclaves, they quickly adapted to English customs. They knew that if they did not leave a will, their property would be divided according to English law, which was less generous to widows than German law. As their businesses became more successful, they needed to trade with members of the dominant English culture. These factors required fluency with the English language, and most children of German immigrants were comfortably bilingual.

There was a long tradition of hostility among the English, the French, and the Spanish, but no such tension between the English and the Germans. As such, German families had greater ease integrating into Anglo-American society. German parents did not prevent their children from marrying outside the German community. They showed little interest in preserving the German language and unique traditions among subsequent generations. Although German culture was kept alive by a constant influx of fresh arrivals from Germany, within a few generations the children of such immigrants were not noticeably different from members of the dominant Anglo culture.

Further Reading

Grubb, Farley. "German Immigration to Pennsylvania, 1709–1820." *Journal of Interdisciplinary History* 20 (1990): 417–436.

Roeber, A. G. "The Origin of Whatever Is Not English among Us: The Dutch-Speaking and the German-Speaking People of Colonial British America." In *Strangers within the Realm: Cultural Margins of the First British Empire*, eds. Bernard Bailyn and Philip D. Morgan. Chapel Hill: University of North Carolina Press, 1991.

Wokeck, Marianne S. "German Settlements in the British North American Colonies: A Patchwork of Cultural Assimilation and Persistence." In *In Search of Peace and Prosperity: New German Settlements in Eighteenth Century Europe and America*, ed. Hartmut Lehmann et al. University Park: Pennsylvania State University Press, 2000.

———. *Trade in Strangers: The Beginnings of Mass Migration to North America.* University Park: Pennsylvania State University Press, 1999.

Girlhood and Adolescence

The term *adolescence* did not come into currency until the mid-nineteenth century. The physiological and hormonal changes associated with childhood and adolescence were not understood in early America. Present-day observers sometimes mistakenly construe this to mean there was no recognition of childhood and adolescence as unique phases of life. A common fallacy about early America is that as soon as children obtained the age of reason, usually around five or six, they were to be treated as miniature adults. This belief has been bolstered by portraits of early Americans, in which children are portrayed wearing adult clothing, with somber and stiff demeanors. Though the portraits appear strange to our eyes, too much has been read into this artistic convention. There has been growing research attempting to document a youth subculture in early America, which shared characteristics such as rebellion, anxiety, and sexual curiosity with today's youth.

The truth probably lies somewhere between these two views. The experience of girls in colonial America was vastly different than it is in the present day, and this carried through in their attitudes, behavior, and life expectations.

Girlhood

The experience of infancy was little different for healthy babies in the seventeenth century than it is today. The greatest difference would have occurred around age two, when almost all colonial toddlers would have witnessed the arrival of another infant sibling. Colonial households were large and were presided over by a mother who was distracted by an immense amount of household chores that usually took precedence over child care. Upon the arrival of a new baby, the toddler would most likely come under supervision of an older sibling or young servant. The main concern in the care of a toddler was to keep her safe, rather than amused. With unguarded fireplaces, farmyard animals, sharp tools, and open wells, the world was a dangerous place for a curious toddler. Strict discipline was used to teach children to obey rules. Securing a child's obedience was more important than amusing them or exposing them to developmental opportunities.

A girl's chores would have varied by the season. In the spring she would help plant the vegetable garden, and she would spend her summer weeding, tending orchards, and caring for animals, as shown here. (North Wind / North Wind Picture Archives)

Girls learned domestic chores from an early age. Around age five they were old enough to shell peas, pluck geese, and tend to chickens. At around age eight they started learning skilled chores: spinning thread, sewing, cleaning, and cooking. A girl's chores would have varied by the season. In the spring she would help plant the vegetable garden, and she would spend her summer weeding, tending orchards, and caring for animals. In the autumn a girl would help her mother with the salting and smoking of meat. Winter would be spent performing a variety of indoor chores, such as spinning and sewing. Her mother would probably teach her to read, but a colonial girl would receive little formal education.

Girls lived a life somewhat segregated from boys. Almost all chores were gender specific. Men and their sons would leave the home to tend fields and go hunting, whereas domestic chores kept girls close to home. If there was a school in the village, boys spent a few hours a day in class. Girls were rarely given the opportunity to go to school, but if they did it was during the summer months when the boys were not in attendance.

Despite heavy chores, girls would have had some time for recreation. There was no attempt to segregate the sexes during playtime, so this would have been among the few chances girls had to mingle with boys. Common games included hopscotch, blindman's bluff, flying kites, and jumping rope. Among a girl's toys would be cornhusk dolls, marbles, and a bilbo catcher (a cup and ball game). Almost all homes would have had several pets.

Dogs were especially common, because they provided help with hunting and helped protect the family from intruders. Cats were helpful in keeping down the number of mice and rats, which were numerous on most farms.

Adolescence

Most girls would leave home for service in another household between the ages of eight and fourteen. If the girl was from a poor family, she was often bound out as a servant between the ages of eight and twelve. She would likely spend the rest of her childhood at her master's home until she married in her late teens or early twenties. Girls from middle-class homes would leave to reside with a relative or neighbor in her early teens. No money traded hands, but the girl provided valuable assistance to her host family through child care and the performance of household chores.

The reasons for this custom were many. Families with only very small children were desperate for household assistance, whereas a family whose daughters were moving into their teenage years had more help than they needed. By sending her teenage girl to another home, a mother had one less mouth to feed, her daughter's housekeeping skills were enhanced by learning from another woman's instruction, and community bonds were strengthened through this reciprocal sending out of daughters. Almost all families took in neighborhood girls when they had small children, and likewise they made their daughters available for this valuable service when they were able to do so. Some historians have speculated that highly religious groups like the Puritans preferred this system because they feared parents were too lenient with their own children, but a neighbor could be relied on to provide the structure and discipline necessary for a young adult.

No matter what the motivations, the practical outcome of this quasi apprenticeship for girls was that most of them left their home by their early teens and would never return. Villages were small, affording girls the opportunity for frequent visits with their mothers, but girls also began forming close ties with other female members in their community. In their new family, girls assisted with sickness, childbirth, and death. The girl was likely the closest female in age to the new mistress, and it is likely she would have become quite close to this woman, her children, and her extended family members.

Young, adolescent girls were naturally curious about boys. The culture of romantic love had not become commonplace, and most girls were not raised to expect romance as a feature of their life, though the idea doubtlessly occurred to them. Although they would not have had opportunities for formal dating, we know from premarital pregnancy rates that young couples were successful in finding private places in barns or distant pastures to be alone together.

Although historians studying the culture of adolescence in early America have long been searching for traces of youthful rebellion, stress, and anxiety that is commonly associated with this transitional period, little evidence of these characteristics has been found. Juvenile delinquency is almost absent from court records, and parents did not record their frustrations with rebellious children in letters or diaries. Speculations for the cause of this calm adolescent period abound. Some point to the lack of life choices and their accompanying stress factors. Girls did not struggle with career options, the decision to have or forgo children, choices about where to live, or even finding fashions to express their personal identity. All such decisions were preordained. With alternative life choices not even a glimmer on the horizon, most calmly accepted the life that was laid out before them.

Much has been made of the strict conduct that was expected of children. Sermons and conduct books warn parents of the necessity of "breaking the will" of the child. If parents actually put these prescriptive techniques into practice, it is possible that rebellion was suffocated at an early age and replaced entirely by obedience. Patterns of inheritance might have affected children's behavior. In early America, fathers held rigid control of property, and children had little ability to earn money or establish an independent means of income without parental assistance. This dependence on parents might have resulted in long-term obedience on the part of children and young adults.

A distinct change can be detected in the developmental life course of children in the years following the American Revolution. With the birth of the industrial age, children could find wage-paying work outside the home. No longer entirely dependent on the goodwill of parents to provide a financial start in life, children had more options available to them. Greater educational opportunities for children of both sexes redefined the role of childhood and adolescence. Whereas seventeenth- and early eighteenth-century children were primarily workers in the household economy, after the American Revolution their responsibility was to gain an education. The rising standard of living permitted children to spend substantial amounts of time in school, allowing a culture of childhood and adolescence to begin to flourish. Although in early America the years between eight and eighteen were an ambiguous period between infancy and adulthood, shortly after the American Revolution these years took on a distinctive character similar to the present-day stage of adolescence.

See also Courtship; Education

Further Reading

Beales, Ross W. "In Search of the Historical Child: Miniature Adulthood and Youth in Colonial New England." *American Quarterly* 27 (1975): 379–398.

Demos, John. *A Little Commonwealth: Family Life in Plymouth Colony.* New York: Oxford University Press, 1970.

Earle, Alice Morse. *Child Life in Colonial Days.* New York: Macmillan, 1899.

Hiner, Ray. "Adolescence in Eighteenth Century America." *History of Childhood Quarterly* 3 (1975): 253–280.

Thompson, Roger. "Adolescent Culture in Colonial Massachusetts." *Journal of Family History* 9 (1984): 127–144.

Graham, Isabella Marshall

Philanthropist (1742–1814)

Although the tradition of charitable assistance to the poor dates to the earliest years of American settlement, Isabella Graham was one of the first people to structure charitable activities with long-range institutional planning in mind.

Isabella Marshall was born in Scotland into a well-to-do, middle-class family. At age twenty-three she married Dr. John Graham, with whom she was deeply in love. Dr. Graham was a physician to a British army regiment, and the family moved from post to post in several British territories throughout Canada. During the Grahams' eight-year marriage they lived in Quebec, Montreal, Fort Niagara, and finally on the Caribbean island of Antigua. Isabella had three children and was about to give birth to another when her husband was stricken with a tropical fever and died. Her emotional devastation was compounded by financial concerns. She had been left almost penniless except for a meager widow's pension that was inadequate to support her and her children.

Isabella returned to Scotland, hoping to find shelter with her parents. Upon arrival she found that her mother was dead and her father was also in severe financial need. Needing to support both her father and her children, Isabella opened a small school for local children in her hometown of Paisley. Her school was successful, but funds were still insufficient. She spent several years on the edge of poverty, often experiencing hunger because potatoes were all she was able to afford. Isabella had a strong aptitude for teaching, and she became convinced she could run a more substantial school in Edinburgh. The Edinburgh boarding school for young ladies was better funded and allowed Isabella to sponsor charitable drives for the city's poor. She founded the "Penny Society," a mutual-aid organization in which poor people paid a penny a week in exchange for financial assistance should one of them fall ill.

In 1789 Isabella decided to return to America with her family. A small bequest from a wealthy benefactor gave her the funds needed to sponsor the move. Once again she supported the family through teaching. Her daughters all married wealthy New York merchants and were able to provide a financial respite for Isabella. She soon retired from teaching and moved in with her daughter Joanna and her husband, Divie Bethune.

Isabella Graham (1742–1814) was one of the first people to structure charitable activities with long-range institutional planning in mind. (Library of Congress)

Freed from the necessity of working, Isabella was able to turn her attention to her true ambition, charitable works. After working with a variety of small-scale projects, Isabella was concerned that merely providing direct cash assistance to the poor would only serve to make them dependent and would not help them rise out of poverty. In 1797 Isabella and her friend Elizabeth Seton founded the institution they hoped would be a solution to this problem, which they named The Society for the Relief of Poor Widows with Small Children. Isabella had personal experience with the difficulties facing women who had lost their breadwinner but whose young children prevented them from obtaining employment. Isabella's exceptional education and her father's ability to mind the children had allowed her to earn a meager living through teaching. Other widows were less fortunate, and

without assistance, their only options were street begging, prostitution, or the public almshouse. Almshouses were unacceptable to most mothers, because they took their children from the mothers and placed them in custody or service elsewhere.

A small group of middle- and upper-class women were eager to lend their talents and their funding to the cause. A shop was opened that took in laundry and sewing projects. The work was distributed to needy widows. In order to be eligible for assistance, the widow needed to have at least two children under the age of ten, be of good moral character, and have no other source of income. A charity school was established for the needy children, and teachers were hired from among the society's poor widows. In its first year the society provided assistance to ninety-eight widows and 223 children. Isabella's connections with wealthy New York families proved to be a valuable asset, because the organization was not able to generate enough income from laundry and sewing to remain in operation.

Although The Society for the Relief of Poor Widows with Small Children was a noble experiment, its lesson was that the wages earned from menial sewing and laundry work would never be enough to make a widow with children self-sufficient. In 1802 the society succeeded in obtaining a state charter, which resulted in public funding to supplement their income. As Isabella grew older she passed leadership of the society to her daughter Joanna, but continued to be active in philanthropic causes. She visited inmates at the Lunatic Asylum and women incarcerated in prison. In her final year she established a school for adult factory workers that provided instruction on Sundays.

See also Benevolent Societies; Poverty; Seton, Elizabeth Ann Bayley

Further Reading

Becker, Dorothy G. "Isabella Graham and Joanna Bethune: Trailblazers of Organized Women's Benevolence." *Social Services Review* 61 (1987): 319–336.

Russell, Thaddeus. "Isabella Graham." In *American National Biography*, ed. John A. Garraty. New York: Oxford University Press, 1999.

Great Awakening

The Great Awakening was a series of religious revivals that swept through the American colonies. Beginning in New England, the Great Awakening stood in marked contrast to the formalism of Calvinist practice and grim representations of doomsday used to frighten congregants into moral behavior. A handful of ministers, including William Tennent, John Wesley, and George Whitefield, began to preach in a more hopeful, charismatic manner. This preaching appealed to the heart, rather than the head. Listeners became entranced with the idea that they could awaken a spiritual regeneration within themselves.

The Great Awakening had a democratizing effect on its adherents, who believed the most valuable quality a person could possess was spiritual conversion. The significance of a person's social class, race, and gender diminished in the face of spiritual enlightenment. Although the spiritual revivals appealed to people from a wide cross section of society, it was especially meaningful for women and African Americans. In the eyes of their fellow revivalists, they were not subordinate people, but individuals worthy of respect based on their spiritual condition.

Prior to the Great Awakening, women's activities for their church were limited to attendance at Sunday services, maintaining a pious demeanor, and catechizing their children. In the fervor of the Great Awakening, gender lines were blurred. Religious authority was believed to stem from grace, rather than formal theological training. For a short time, a few women were able to step outside traditional boundaries and preach, exhort the unconverted, and proselytize.

First Great Awakening (1720s through the 1750s)

Reverend William Tennent, a Scots-Irish immigrant, was the first preacher to be identified with the Great Awakening. He believed in the importance of conversion for salvation. Prior to Tennent, most preachers in the middle and northern colonies taught that salvation was entirely dependent on the whim of God, and no pious actions a person performed could "earn" salvation. Now people were being told they could save themselves by submitting to God and being open to the conversion experience. The Log College (later renamed Princeton) was established to train preachers who respected the value of the evangelical experience.

The Great Awakening was simmering in the 1730s, but ignited in 1739–1740 with the arrival of English minister, George Whitefield. Whitefield traveled throughout the colonies, preaching to vast crowds in open fields because no church was large enough to house the masses that came to hear him speak. Even the famous skeptic Benjamin Franklin was impressed with Whitefield's message. In his *Autobiography and Other Writings,* Franklin remarked how he attended one of Whitefield's revival meetings, knowing that Whitefield was seeking donations to continue his mission. Franklin wrote, "I silently resolved he should get nothing from me. I had in my pocket a handful of copper money, three or four silver dollars, and five pistols in gold. As he proceeded I began to soften and concluded to give the coppers. Another stroke of his oratory made me ashamed of that, and determined me to give the silver; and he finished so admirably, that I emptied my pocket wholly into the collector's dish, gold and all" (1961, 118).

Prior to Whitefield, most colonists had been indifferent to religion. During Whitefield's tour and in the years following, Franklin claimed one could not walk through the town without seeing preachers on street corners and hear religious songs coming from private residences.

One of the expectations of the newly converted was to share their salvation experience with others. Women were permitted to speak at meetings and counsel others who were in the process of salvation. Although women rarely led meetings or spoke from the pulpit, the experience of these saved women was respected and valued by fellow congregants. Some Baptist churches permitted women and African Americans to participate in business meetings and vote on matters of church governance.

These highly unorthodox practices did not pass without condemnation. Many churches split in response to the Great Awakening. "New Lights" embraced the changes, while "Old Lights" followed traditional practices and disapproved of the emotionalism of the revivals. Charles Chauncy, the most prominent critic of the New Lights, commented on the unorthodox preaching by women and African Americans: "Indeed young persons, sometimes lads, or rather boys: Nay, women and girls, yea Negroes, have taken upon them to do the business of preachers" (Labaree 1944, 339).

Although women's participation in the Great Awakening was unorthodox, it did not mark a revolutionary experience for the entire gender. For those who experienced salvation, the Great Awakening was of considerable spiritual importance, but this did not translate into the economic, social, or political changes in the status of women. Some scholars have claimed the first Great Awakening sparked a "feminization" of religion, because its emotionalism is associated with a female preference for spirituality, in contrast with the rationalism of traditional Protestant religion. Although the colonists themselves did not make this distinction along gender lines, later historians of the nineteenth century clearly associated the style with women.

Second Great Awakening (1790s through the 1830s)

A second great wave of revivals swept the nation in the decades following the American Revolution. There was no longer state support for any specific denomination, and churches needed to compete for members. A democratizing spirit had entered the country. No longer was church hierarchy to be obeyed without question, and there was a renewal of looking inward for spiritual rebirth. Rather than rejecting religion, many turned to it during this time of uncertainty for comfort. The excesses of anticlericalism in France caused people to rally to their churches, concerned that the same godless rage could take root in America.

America in the late eighteenth century was a time of tremendous change for women. Much of the home-based manufacture they depended on for income, such as spinning and weaving, was moving to factories. Women either had to leave home for low-paying work in the factories, or find some other means of income. The sex ratio was out of balance, with many men having lost their lives in the war or migrated West in search of greater opportunity. For the first time, large numbers of women were unable to find husbands. This coincided with a shift away from the concept of marriage as an economic alliance and toward the idea that marriage was the culmination of romantic love. Women having difficulty finding a mate were facing a dual disappointment. Some scholars speculate that women sought out religion as a refuge in this time of ambiguity. Church involvement was an acceptable outlet for women. It was one of the few places outside the home they could turn to for meaningful involvement in their communities. Although the first Great Awakening attracted about the same percentage of male and female converts, the Second Great Awakening had almost twice as many female participants.

One new feature of this revival movement was the camp meeting. As the revivals spread to the sparsely populated West, the arrival of itinerant preachers resulted in camp meetings that stretched over several days as settlers traveled for fellowship with like-minded people. Camp meetings took place in forest clearings. Revivalists stayed in tents or their wagons. A raised platform was surrounded by benches, with an isle dividing the audience. Men sat on one side, with women on the other. People spent their daytime hours singing hymns, preparing food, or in small-group fellowship. The major work of the revival took place under the glow of campfires after the sun set. Fervent preaching went on late into the night. "Mourners' benches" were in the front rows, where those who were not yet fully converted sat. "Exhorters" moved among this group, praying with them and supporting them on their way to conversion. The most famous camp meeting took place in 1801 in Cane Ridge, Kentucky. Upwards of four thousand people attended the meeting, coming from all races, classes, and genders. Stretching over nine days, the meeting only broke when they ran out of provisions.

Women played important roles in camp revivals. They were welcome to offer public testimonials of their conversion experience, and often worked as exhorters among the unconverted. Women preached in these meetings as well, especially in Methodist, African Methodist, and Freewill Baptist communities. Female preaching was by no means universally accepted even among the New Lights, but the more marginal denominations deliberately flaunted tradition and emphasized their nonconformity by allowing women and African Americans to preach. Most of the names of women engaged in public preaching have been lost to history. These women proved to be too controversial for more conservative future evangelicals to memorialize, but not daring enough for feminists to remember.

Women's experiences in the Great Awakening remained primarily on the personal level. Many found deep fulfillment and were able to have meaningful participation with others in an avenue outside their traditional place in the home. Women rarely had leadership positions, but the opportunity for them to participate in the groundswell of religious enthusiasm made the Great Awakening a significant event in American women's history.

Further Reading

Brekus, Catherine A. *Strangers and Pilgrims: Female Preaching in America, 1740–1845.* Chapel Hill: University of North Carolina Press, 1998.

Cott, Nancy F. "Young Women in the Second Great Awakening in New England." *Feminist Studies* 3 (1975): 15–29.

Labaree, Leonard. "The Conservative Attitude toward the Great Awakening." *William and Mary Quarterly* 3 (1) (1944): 331–352.

Lindley, Susan Hill. *You Have Stept Out of Your Place: A History of Women and Religion in America.* Louisville, KY: Westminster John Knox Press, 1996.

Stoll, Mark. "The Transformation of American Religion, 1776–1838." In *Encyclopedia of the North American Colonies*, ed. Jacob Ernest Cooke. New York: Charles Scribner's Sons, 1993.

Gynecological Issues

Many of the milestone markers of a woman's life are accompanied by significant physiological changes. The transition from girl to woman is accompanied by the onset of menstruation. Childbirth and nursing occurs with regularity throughout a woman's adult years. Finally, menopause transitions a woman from youth into old age. Each of these changes is accompanied by significant hormonal fluctuations that alter a woman's body and temperament. The women of early America would have experienced all these physical signposts, though they might not have understood the biological underpinnings that provoked the changes in their bodies and moods.

Physicians had only the vaguest understanding of women's reproductive anatomy, but they credited it with having an enormous amount of control over a woman's persona. Recognizing the pain and mood swings that regularly descended upon women each month, some speculated that the uterus had a controlling influence on a woman's personality, her bodily diseases, and her character. Men were considered stronger, healthier, and more intelligent than women. Women's shortfalls in these areas were attributed to the pull of her reproductive anatomy.

Menstruation

Young women of the eighteenth century would have had their first menstrual period around age seventeen. This is considerably later than what occurs in contemporary times, and scientists are currently searching for explanations to account for this difference. On the whole, women of colonial America were healthy and well nourished, so nutritional deficiency cannot account for the age discrepancy of menstrual onset. The younger age for the onset of menstruation appears to be a recent phenomenon in First World countries, causing speculation that hormonal supplement in the meat supply or other medicinal factors might account for the change.

Colonial Americans valued large families and women who were able to bear a large number of healthy babies. For this reason, menstruation was viewed as a necessary inconvenience, but not a shameful state, as it was seen in some other cultures. Medical texts recommended menstruating women avoid cold food or things that might sour the stomach, such as milk, fish, or fruit. The most common words for menstruation were *terms* and *courses*. Medical theory held that the purpose of menstruation was to rid the female body of impurities. Dating to ancient times, it was believed men sweated out their impurities, but the colder nature of women prevented this means of detoxification. They believed impurities were collected in women's blood, which was periodically and painfully expelled through menstruation.

A 1785 medical text by William Buchan correctly attributed many menstrual difficulties and anemia to a lack of iron. He recommended that iron shavings be infused in wine for several weeks. After filtering the wine, the patient should drink two small glasses of the iron-enriched wine per day until she recovered. Such a prescription was a primitive, but nevertheless effective, means of getting iron supplementation. Other recommendations to expedite a sluggish menstrual flow, such as sitting over steaming water or drinking hot beverages, met with less success. Cinnamon was commonly believed to be a remedy for easing excessive flow.

Amenorrhea, the absence of menstruation, was either a sign of pregnancy or a symptom of disease. Diagnosing pregnancy for a certainty could not be done until quickening—the first movement of the fetus—occurred, sometime in the third to fifth month. If a woman did not believe she was pregnant, a number of remedies were available to coax a period. "Footbaths" was a euphemism for vaginal douching, which was believed to stimulate the uterus. Bleeding the patient, or drinking red-tinted herbal remedies, was also thought to induce uterine contractions. Exercises such as horseback riding or jumping rope were thought to be healthy remedies for amenorrhea.

Intestinal worms caused abdominal bloating and discomfort and were often inaccurately blamed for blocked periods. Strong herbs used to kill the parasites were believed to clear the way for the resumption of menstruation. Juniper berries in particular were known to produce vaginal hemorrhaging, and medical texts strongly warned doctors not to prescribe them to pregnant women. Pennyroyal, rosemary, and feverfew also stimulated menstrual activity. They could be taken orally or via vaginal douche. Such remedies were published in almanacs, recipe books, or simply passed by word of mouth.

There is little documentation for how women handled the hygienic aspects of menstruation. It might be assumed that they used homemade pads from scraps of fabric, but this might not have been the case. Some folkloric anecdotes about health proclaimed that anything that impeded menstrual flow was dangerous and unhealthy. Because menstrual blood was believed to be loaded with impurities, using anything to block its flow was considered unhealthy. At various points throughout history, women simply bled into their clothing and rinsed them out daily. Very little written record or actual artifacts survive to indicate how colonial American women handled this problem. Washable cloth pads from the nineteenth century survive, and the first commercially produced disposable pads became available in the 1890s.

Women of colonial America would have had far fewer periods throughout their life than contemporary women. They began menstruating much later in life, and they spent an average of four to six years of their adult life pregnant. They breastfed each of their children for about one year, which also reduced the number of their menstrual periods.

Infertility

Both social and economic life in early America depended on a large, bustling household. Women who were unable to have children faced many problems, including failure to provide their husband with an heir, labor shortages in their household, economic insecurity in their old age, and the inability to share in the loving parent-child bond. In a society that highly prized a large family, a woman who was unable to bear children would have almost certainly felt a profound sense of failure. Approximately one in twelve women in early America were not able to conceive or carry a child to term.

The Puritans of colonial New England often considered childlessness to be the judgment of God. This view did not necessarily imply that barren women were immoral or unworthy. Biblical stories such as those about Abraham and Sarah and Rachel and Jacob testify to the anguish suffered by good women who simply were not blessed with a child. Most people of early America believed that inability to conceive was either the will of God or a physical shortcoming of the woman. Barren women were objects of pity, because women were unable to take their rightful place in their family and in society until they proved their value by bearing a child.

It would have been difficult for a barren woman to relate with other women in her community. Women took pride in large families, provided extensive assistance when a neighbor gave birth, and shared advice for rearing children. Women who had never borne a child would not have been a part of this sisterhood.

Infertile women were protected by the law. Although a woman could divorce a man for impotence, men could not leave their wives for infertility. It was acknowledged that sex served dual purposes of procreation and sexual companionship. A barren woman was capable and obligated to provide sex, and this protected her from possible divorce. Divorce was exceedingly hard to obtain in early America, but impotence in a man or the refusal of a woman to accept sex were grounds for divorce. If a period of several years passed and a couple did not conceive a child, it was viewed as the will of God that they should not be blessed, and a divorce action would not be heard by the courts.

Medical science was of little help to barren women. It was widely known that certain types of venereal disease could render a woman barren, but they could do nothing to reverse this damage. Other causes of infertility were a mystery to colonial scientists. Some medical texts speculated infertility was a result of high living, an excitable temperament, or indolence. Barren women were advised to take exercise, a diet of milk and vegetables, a cold bath, or a wide range of spurious-sounding potions. Other doctors attributed infertility to menstrual irregularities. Women who failed to have regular periods were advised to take hot baths to provoke the flow, while those who suffered from excessive flow were to be bled.

Early Americans often held with the common medical fallacy that conception would only occur if a woman experienced orgasm during intercourse. Medical texts acknowledged that women who despised their husbands were far less likely to conceive and recommended courting, companionship, and anything else that would kindle affection between the pair.

Menopause

Although the age for menopause varied wildly, most colonial women ceased menstruating around age fifty. There was little association between menopause and loss of youth or social worth. Because colonial women often bore children as long as they were physically able, a menopausal women might be tending toddlers and continuing to lead an active life. If anything, some women expressed relief at the physical end to childbearing. Means of coping with menopausal symptoms are almost completely absent in early medical texts, indicating that women either did not suffer excessively, or more likely, were reluctant to discuss such intimate matters with a physician.

Menopause has always been a benchmark in a woman's life cycle, and as such, the manner in which it is treated by society can signal that culture's attitudes toward aging women. Older women in early America were respected and revered. There was no association between menopause and the onset of elderly decline. Women who survived to this golden age were often looked up to by the entire community as "grandmother."

Diarist Elizabeth Drinker noted, "I have often thought that women who live to get over that time of child bearing, if other things are favorable to them, experience more comfort and satisfaction than at any other period in their lives" (Drinker 1994, 175).

Venereal Disease

Syphilis was the most dangerous of venereal diseases and was first noted among English colonists in 1646. Contemporary observers widely believed syphilis to be a disease given to Europeans by Native Americans, because the disease was unknown in Europe prior to the discovery of America. Skeletal remains of pre-Colombian Indians suggest evidence of the disease, and medical historian Alfred Crosby has suggested syphilis might be what America gave Europe in exchange for smallpox.

Dr. Buchan's Thoughts on Venereal Disease (1785)

William Buchan was a Scottish doctor whose popular book *Domestic Medicine* appeared in more than one hundred separate editions. The book was notable for its humane and sensible advice, often recommending practical regimens of diet, exercise, and cautious use of drugs. Here he laments the stigmatization that prevented many victims of venereal disease from seeking treatment:

Though the venereal disease is generally the fruit of unlawful embraces, yet it may be communicated to the innocent as well as the guilty. Infants, nurses, midwives, and married women whose husbands lead dissolute lives, are often affected with it, and frequently lose their lives by not being aware of their danger in due time. The unhappy condition of such persons will certainly plead our excuse, if any excuse be necessary, for endeavoring to point out the symptoms and cure of this too common disease. . . . It is particularly unfortunate for the unhappy persons who contract this disease, that it lies under a sort of disgrace. This renders disguise necessary, and makes the patient either conceal his disorder altogether, or apply to those who promise a sudden and secret cure; but who in fact only remove the symptoms for a time, while they fix the disease deeper in habit. By this means, a slight infection, which might have been easily removed, is often converted into an obstinate, and sometimes incurable malady.

Source: Buchan, William. *Domestic Medicine, 1785.* http://www.americanrevolution.org/medicine.html (accessed June 2004).

Venereal diseases tended to infect only the marginal fringes of society until the mid-nineteenth century, when it began creeping into mainstream society. Prior to this it was a disease of soldiers, sailors, prostitutes, and those who came into contact with them. "Respectable women" would be infected only if their husbands brought the disease to them. The majority of cases were contracted through intercourse, although an infected woman could pass the disease to her baby during childbirth. Wet nurses and midwives could also contract the disease in the course of their work. The disease seemed to manifest itself in waves, especially in times of war when large influxes of soldiers congregated in urban areas. Syphilis and gonorrhea were the most common forms of venereal disease, although medical records indicate the presence of others.

There was tremendous shame associated with contracting a venereal disease. Women were acutely embarrassed to seek a physician's treatment, and early medical texts advise doctors to withhold moral censure. Women were more likely to consult a midwife or other female healer for treatment. These untrained healers had little understanding of the distinctions among venereal infections and tended to provide the same treatment for all infections. This was unfortunate, because some treatments provided by physicians, though painful and dangerous, were occasionally successful.

Gonorrhea in women was characterized with painful urination, itching, and a white discharge. The accepted method of treatment was to avoid all spicy food, alcohol, and vigorous exercise. Patients were advised to soak the affected areas in warm milk or linseed tea. The most dramatic treatment was injecting a mixture of white vitriol (now known as zinc sulfate) into the urethra. Three to four daily injections were performed until the symptoms eased.

Syphilis was the most dreaded of venereal diseases. If untreated it could lead to insanity, disfiguration, and death. There are four stages of the disease: primary, secondary, latent, and tertiary. It was crucial for treatment to begin in either the primary or the secondary stage, or else it was impossible for colonial medicine to halt the course of the disease. Patients suffered chancre-like sores, headaches, swollen lymph nodes, and weight loss. In the latent stage the symptoms disappear for months or even years at a time. About half of the patients who progressed to this stage coped with these symptoms the rest of their lives without it ever progressing into the deadly, tertiary stage. At the final stage syphilis was no longer contagious, but lesions spread to the skin, bone, and vital organs. Ugly and painful tumors could occur on the skin or in the eyes or mouth. Internally, the disease could settle in either the heart or the brain, resulting in devastating physical and personality changes.

The most effective treatment for syphilis was oral and topical application of mercury. Rubbing mercury directly into the sores had been a common treatment for a variety of skin lesions since the Middle Ages. Although dangerous, for serious illnesses such as leprosy and syphilis, resorting to mercury was better than allowing the disease to go untreated. Mercury was mixed with an equal amount of hog's lard and rubbed over the thighs and genitals. Doctors also administered mercury internally. By the colonial era mercury was available in pill form, although most doctors preferred to mix it into a solution and have patients drink the concoction. This provoked the "salivation stage," during which the body's reaction to the mercury caused patients to begin excessively salivating, which was painful, awkward, and lasted at least four to six weeks. Patients needed to stay in bed throughout this period. Side effects included damage to the teeth and gums, severe diarrhea, and extreme bad breath.

Symptoms of the mercury cure were well known, and some patients might have resisted treatment because symptoms would disclose the nature of their illness to family members and neighbors. It was difficult to explain an absence of six weeks to curious neighbors and business associates, and any who visited the sickbed would know immediately that the patient was being treated for a venereal disease. There is evidence that people were so ashamed of seeking the mercury cure that some doctors advertised the confidentiality of their treatment. One study of English newspapers reveals that women were reluctant to seek treatment from male doctors. These doctors trained their wives to administer the treatment to women whose embarrassment would not allow them to seek treatment from a man.

Doctors did not administer mercury to menstruating women or to those in their final stage of pregnancy. Women of strong constitution who were in their early stage of pregnancy were advised to begin mercury treatments immediately, for there was a possibility that the treatment might spare the child from contracting the disease. Otherwise the infant would be born afflicted and would need to undergo mercury treatment after it had been born. Venereal disease and its caustic remedies could render a woman sterile or cause birth defects.

See also Abortion; Breastfeeding; Childbirth

Further Reading

Barbre, Joy Webster. "From Goodwives to Menoboomers: Reinventing Menopause in American History." Dissertation. University of Minnesota, 1994.

Buchan, William. *Domestic Medicine, 1785.* Available at http://www.americanrevolution. org/medicine.html (accessed 15 June 2004).

Drinker, Elizabeth, and Elaine Crane Forman, ed. *The Diary of Elizabeth Drinker: The Life Cycle of an Eighteenth Century Woman.* Boston: Northeastern University Press, 1994.

Klepp, Susan E. "Colds, Worms, and Hysteria: Menstrual Regulation in Eighteenth Century America." In *Regulating Menstruation: Beliefs, Practices, Interpretations,* eds. Etienne Van de Walle and Elisha P. Renne. Chicago: University of Chicago Press, 2001.

May, Elaine Tyler. *Barren in the Promised Land: Childless Americans and the Pursuit of Happiness.* Cambridge, MA: Harvard University Press, 1995.

Siena, Kevin P. "The Foul Disease and Privacy: The Effects of Venereal Disease and Patient Demand on the Medical Marketplace in Early Modern London." *Bulletin of the History of Medicine* 75 (2001): 199–224.

Hemings, Sally
Slave and probable mistress of Thomas Jefferson (1773–1835)

Sally Hemings is most commonly known as the mulatto woman who might have shared a thirty-year intimate relationship with Thomas Jefferson. DNA testing has found a genetic link between the Jefferson family and Hemings's descendants, and other historians have advanced circumstantial evidence that indicates Thomas Jefferson was the father of Sally's children. Conclusive proof has yet to emerge, but Sally Hemings is worthy of study in her own right.

Sally's mother, Betty, was a half-white slave who belonged to John Wayles. It is likely that Wayles was also Sally's father, making her only one-quarter African descent, but nevertheless a slave. Upon John Wayles's death, Sally was inherited by his daughter Martha Wayles Jefferson, Thomas Jefferson's wife. Sally grew up at Monticello, Jefferson's Virginia plantation. During the American Revolution, she and her mother were briefly captured by British soldiers, who tried to sell the slaves. Small girls during a time of war were of little economic value, and soon both Sally and her mother were returned to Monticello. In the hierarchy of slave occupations, the optimal position was to be a trusted household servant. Sally's mother served in such a position, and it appears that Sally inherited this prime position after her mother's death.

As a young woman Sally became a companion and maid to Jefferson's daughter Maria. Her role became more important after the death of Martha Jefferson in 1782. Despite her young age, Sally accompanied Maria to Paris in 1787 when Sally was fourteen and Maria nine. Abigail Adams, who encountered the pair during a stopover in England, remarked that Sally seemed to be a good-natured girl who was quite fond of Maria. Upon arrival in Paris, Sally began receiving wages, because slavery was illegal in France. It appears she spent most of her time in a convent where both of Jefferson's daughters were receiving an education. Sally acquired a good deal of polish while in France. Jefferson's account books reveal that he paid to have her vaccinated against smallpox and purchased fine clothing for her. She accompanied her young charges on social outings and might have learned some of the French language. It is unknown if Sally ever learned to read or write.

After returning from Paris, Sally worked at Monticello as a household servant. She did light chores, such as mending, spinning, and cleaning. Household servants were spared the backbreaking work in the fields, but this close association with the family presented its own challenges. Household slaves received better food and working conditions, but were on round-the-clock call. They had less privacy and limited ability to establish meaningful relationships with the majority of slaves who worked in the fields. They were also more prone to sexual exploitation. The nature of the sexual relationships between masters and slaves varied widely. Some relationships were outright rape, some the result of coercion, and others were the result of mutual consent. The father of Sally's children was clearly a white man, but the nature of that relationship remains a mystery.

It is rumored that Sally had a child named Tom Woodson shortly after returning from France in 1789. This child, said to be fathered by Jefferson, was moved from Monticello as an infant and was raised on another plantation. Tom Woodson thereafter vanishes from Monticello history, but he eventually attained his freedom, married a free black woman, and before he died in 1879 claimed Thomas Jefferson as his father. It is unclear if his mother was actually Sally Hemings or another slave at Monticello.

In 1795 Sally gave birth to a child named Harriet, who died in infancy. This was the first child that can be positively attributed to Sally. Other children followed: Beverly (1798), unnamed daughter who died in infancy (1799), Harriet (1801), Madison (1805), and Eston (1808). No father was ever named in plantation records, although it is certain the father of these children was white, making them seven-eighths white, but still slaves according to Virginia law.

Rumors that the father of Sally's children was Thomas Jefferson began circulating in 1802 by James Callender, a former supporter of Jefferson who became embittered when he was passed over for a government position. Callender published the following in the Richmond *Recorder* (1 September 1802), "It is well known that the man whom it delighteth the people to honor, keeps, and for many years past has kept, as his concubine, one of his own slaves. Her name is SALLY. . . . The African Venus is said to officiate as housekeeper at Monticello."

Over the coming years, Jefferson's political rivals kept the story of the liaison alive, finding it useful to tarnish the reputation of the leader of the anti-Federalist party. In keeping with his policy of ignoring attacks on his private life, Jefferson refused to either acknowledge or deny the rumor. Members of his immediate family stoutly denied the rumor, and none of the numerous visitors to Monticello noticed Jefferson show any preferential treatment toward Sally Hemings.

Since neither Jefferson nor Sally Hemings were known to have made any comment concerning the father of her children, historians have looked to the behavior and events that surrounded the life of Sally Hemings for clues. Thomas Jefferson eventually freed all of Sally Hemings's children, although she remained a slave as long as he lived. Sally is believed to have been released from slavery by Jefferson's daughter Martha a few years after Jefferson's death. Sally's youngest child, Eston, claimed Jefferson to have been his father, and he changed his name to Eston Hemings Jefferson in 1852. The conception of all six of her children coincided with times Jefferson was in residence at Monticello, and Sally never conceived a child when Jefferson was away from Monticello on many of his extended travels.

In 1998 the results of DNA testing established a definitive link to the descendants of Thomas Jefferson and Sally Hemings. Unfortunately, these test results still cannot establish conclusive proof that it was Thomas Jefferson who fathered the children. Eighteenth-century rumors also credited Jefferson's brother and two nephews with having fathered Hemings's children. DNA tests have excluded the descendants of Tom Woodson, the child rumored to have been Sally Hemings's child conceived in Paris, from having a link to the Jefferson family. It is possible these tests proved false because the family line was broken through adoption or illegitimacy. Historians are attempting to locate other descendants of Thomas Woodson. If a Jefferson-Woodson link can be established, this would be the only conclusive proof that it was Thomas Jefferson, and not one of his male relatives, who fathered the children. If Thomas Woodson was indeed Sally Hemings's child, he was conceived in Paris where no other Jeffersons had access to her. Short of such a discovery, it is unlikely that conclusive proof will ever emerge, but most historians now consider it highly probable that Jefferson was indeed the father of Sally Hemings's children.

After Jefferson's death in 1826 Sally remained at Monticello. It might seem odd that Jefferson neglected to free her in his will, but it is possible he thought it was the best course for Sally. Martha Jefferson, who inherited the bulk of Jefferson's estate, was known to be a kind mistress. At age fifty-three, Sally was becoming too old to earn a living on her own, and Jefferson might have thought it was best for Sally to remain in the home where she had lived most of her life. How long Sally remained at Monticello is unclear, but she eventually attained free status. In 1833 she appeared on a census list of "Free Negroes and Mulattos," and was living with her son Madison in Charlottesville, just a few miles from Monticello. Nothing is known about the rest of her life. Her children Harriet, Beverly, and Eston lived as members of white society as adults, but Madison Hemings lived among the free African American community.

Further Reading

Ellis, Joseph J. "Jefferson: Post-DNA." *William and Mary Quarterly* 57 (2000): 125–138.

Gordon-Reed, Annette. *Thomas Jefferson and Sally Hemings: An American Controversy.* Charlottesville: University of Virginia Press, 1997.

Graham, Pearl M. "Thomas Jefferson and Sally Hemings." *Journal of Negro History* 46 (1961): 89–103.

Neiman, Fraser D. "Coincidence or Causal Connection: Relationship between Jefferson's Visits to Monticello and Sally Hemings's Conceptions." *William and Mary Quarterly* 57 (2000): 198–210.

Ward, Harry M. "Sally Hemings." In *Women in World History*, ed. Anne Commire. Waterford, CT: Yorkin Publications, 2000.

Hobbies and Games

Early Americans, especially the settlers of Puritan New England, were mildly suspicious of leisure activities. Although it was acknowledged that a person could not labor during all the waking hours, it was hoped that periods of rest would be filled with wholesome activities such as reading or meaningful interactions with family members. Even the games of childhood often had an educational or developmental goal. Skill-enhancing tasks, such as fishing, riding, or quilting, straddled the areas of recreation and preparation for adult responsibilities.

Toys were generally limited to makeshift materials, such as dolls made of cornhusks or rags. During the long months of winter, fathers might whittle spinning tops for their children's amusement. Since most families lived on farms, it is likely they had some animals that could entertain children. Although "pets" as we know them were rare, a household cat for catching mice or a hunting dog was likely to be found on most farms. Children of large families could always rely on each other as playmates. Spontaneous games were among the primary means for young children to entertain themselves. Blindman's bluff, jumping rope, see-saw, and hopscotch were among common games that required minimal equipment. Possibly the most popular game for children was hoop and stick, in which hoops from barrels could be used in a variety of games. Children used the sticks to guide the hoop while running beside it or tossed it among each other from stick to stick.

As girls grew older the nature of their games changed. Highly physical games such as tag or blindman's bluff were discouraged in favor of feminine pastimes. Embroidery was common among all classes, whereas playing an instrument or dabbling in artwork was limited to the well-to-do. Card playing was another activity that women participated in, but it was loaded with the potential for condemnation. Puritans frowned on playing cards, because it was considered a waste of time and often associated with gambling. Upper-class women of the Chesapeake Bay area had no such restrictions, and card playing, even gambling, became quite common among elite women.

Much of an adult woman's leisure time would have been dictated by the season. Very often her "hobbies" had utilitarian purposes. Most gardening was to supply food for the table, but women took time to plant flowering plants and herbs. It is evident that women took great pride in their gardens, and some even marketed particularly successful strains of plants. All types of needlework were common pastimes during the long, closed-in days of winter. With most outdoor farmwork at an end for the season, women had little else to occupy themselves with inside the home. Needlework took on extravagant forms of embellishment, as can be seen from elaborate quilts and embroidered textiles.

During high summer, days were long and travel was easy. Visiting neighbors was the most common

Hoop & Stick was one of the most common games in colonial America. Children used a stick to balance a rolling hoop as they raced alongside. Hoops could be tossed from stick to stick, twirled, or used to skip through. (Colonial Williamsburg Collection)

form of recreation for adult women during temperate weather. Many women were isolated on rural homesteads, and the opportunity to gather for a cornhusking, quilting bee, or barn dance was a major event. Planting and harvest festivals were eagerly awaited by women whose lives were dominated by toil on lonely farmsteads. For those who lived in towns, visiting taverns was an acceptable activity for women in early America.

See also Gambling; Quilting; Sports and Leisure

Further Reading

Altherr, Thomas, ed. *Sports and Games in North America: A Documentary History.* Gulf Breeze, FL: Academic International Press, 1997.

Struna, Nancy. "The Recreational Experiences of Early American Women." In *Women and Sport: Interdisciplinary Perspectives*, eds. D. Margaret Costa and Sharon R. Guthrie. Champaign, IL: Human Kinetics Press, 1994.

Holidays and Festivals

Most of the holidays celebrated in early America were inherited from the Christian traditions of Europe. Holidays specific to America, such as Thanksgiving and the Fourth of July, took decades to become entrenched in the national consciousness. Other holidays, such as Pinkster, were curious mixtures of European tradition modified by conditions found in the New World.

Christmas

Festivities surrounding the celebration of religious holidays were shunned by the Puritans. In England, the celebration of Christmas had devolved into occasions for drunkenness, sporting, card playing, throwing dice, and uninhibited revelry. The Puritans who immigrated to America deliberately put a stop to all festive celebrations surrounding Christmas. There were no gift giving, feasting, or special

A highly romanticized interpretation of the first Thanksgiving, 1621 / J. L. G. Ferris. (Library of Congress)

decorations. Most did not even attend special worship services. Some Puritans observed the day by laying down their tools and taking it as a day of rest. Puritan authorities were wary of backsliding into the revelry common in England and encouraged their people to treat Christmas like any other day. Shop owners were discouraged from closing their business for fear of promoting idleness. In Massachusetts, a five-shilling fine was imposed on families who celebrated Christmas. The fine was not burdensome, but enough to discourage the trend.

In contrast, Christmas in the rest of the colonies was eagerly celebrated. Virginia was settled by descendents of the Cavaliers whose Christmas revels had so offended Puritan sensibilities in England. In Virginia, the Christmas holiday was a forty-day season, beginning with Christmas Day and lasting through the end of January with the Feast of the Purification of the Virgin Mary. Throughout the season, Christmas was celebrated with parties, dances, visiting, and gift giving. A woman would have decorated her home with garlands of holly and ivy. Mistletoe was hung in homes and public shops, and its associated custom of hugging and kissing was practiced.

Singing and dancing were common among the Protestant celebrations of Christmas. Many carols still popular today, such as "Joy to the World," "God Rest Ye Merry Gentlemen," and "The First Noel" were all popular in colonial America. Friends and families gathered to sing hymns and share spiced rum and eggnog. Much of the burdens for the heavy baking and brewing would have fallen to women, but because December was a season of light farmwork, it was not an unduly troublesome chore.

Thanksgiving

The custom of setting a day aside for the giving of thanks had a long tradition in Europe. Such days were periodically set aside throughout the year, to mark a good harvest, the winning of a battle, or to commemorate the birthday of an important person. They were rarely fixed on the calendar for regular celebration, but were observed whenever the fancy took a local governor or magistrate.

The first Thanksgiving in America was called by Governor William Bradford in 1621, when he invited local Indians to join the Pilgrim settlers for a three-day feast at Plymouth. Some ninety Indians joined thirty Pilgrims. The burden for food preparation fell to the four Englishwomen, assisted by a single servant and a few girls. Deer and turkey were roasted over open spits. Another thanksgiving was called on February 22, 1630, in Boston, to celebrate the arrival of ships carrying desperately needed provisions. From this time onward, thanksgivings were called every few years. Most of these were for general appreciation of God's providence, but sometimes they were called to celebrate a victory over the Indians, the birth of a new royal child, the eradication of pirates from the coastal waters, or the abatement of an epidemic.

Because these periodic thanksgivings were not tied to any specific season, the menu varied depending on region and time of year. Celebration of a general Thanksgiving in November did not become a regularly scheduled event until the mid-nineteenth century. Like the original Thanksgiving of 1621, it was set at a time of year that coincided with the autumn harvest.

Patriotic Celebrations

One of the earliest patriotic celebrations was the King's Birthday, which was observed by taking the day off work, ringing bells, setting bonfires, dancing, and drinking. In larger villages, parades, athletic competitions, horse racing, and cockfighting might have been scheduled as part of the festivities. The other popular holiday was November 5, Guy

Fawkes Day, which commemorated the foiling of a Catholic conspiracy to assassinate King James and his parliament in 1605. The day was observed in America with patriotic speeches, bonfires, and parading effigies of Guy Fawkes, the Pope, and the Devil through the streets. The effigies were typically burned at the end of the day. By the mid-eighteenth century, Guy Fawkes Day took on a more political character, with effigies of other controversial English aristocrats added to the fiery celebration. The political overtones of Guy Fawkes celebrations became fuel for Revolutionary fire.

Following 1776, the King's Birthday was no longer celebrated, except quietly among loyalist communities. After the Revolution, the Fourth of July came to be celebrated in the same fashion as royal anniversaries, with guns, bells, bonfires, and parades. Because the Fourth of July rarely involved elaborate feasting, it would have been one of the few relaxing holidays for women. Patriotic celebrations usually occurred outdoors. They were rambunctious and free of typical social restrictions, which would have been a refreshing change of pace for women.

Pinkster

Pinkster was a celebration that blended Dutch custom with African American tradition. *Pinkster* was the Dutch name for Pentecost, traditionally celebrated seven weeks after Easter. It commemorated the descent of the Holy Spirit onto the apostles, believed to have occurred fifty days after Easter Sunday. Because of the early spring season, it was often combined with a celebration of the renewal of life. It was brought to New York by Dutch settlers, and was a time for visiting neighbors, drinking, game playing, and dancing. Children dyed eggs and ate gingerbread.

The Dutch settlers allowed their slaves to participate in Pinkster celebrations. It initially was merely a day during which they were reprieved from work, but it evolved into one of the most important holidays for the slaves of New York. Many of these slaves lived isolated existences on rural homesteads, and an important component of Pinkster was visiting family. The Dutch owners usually allowed their slaves a few days' leave to reunite with loved ones in nearby towns. Many traveled to New York City and Albany, which had significant slave populations by the mid-eighteenth century. The large, Pinkster gatherings of African Americans inspired festivals where the slaves sold berries, herbs, baskets, and other items of home manufacture. In turn they used their earnings to fund their celebrations. Women had the opportunity to buy and sell goods, visit distant family members, and possibly visit husbands who lived on neighboring homesteads.

For African Americans, Pinkster meant a time of uninhibited celebration, dance, and music. Observers report that the style of dancing resembled that of the African tribes in the Congo. Drums and songs of African origin were sung. Over time these celebrations became large and ominous to the white population of New York. In 1811, Pinkster celebrations were outlawed in Albany on the grounds that they were contrary to the tenets of the Dutch Reformed Church. Pinkster ceremonies continued in some small pockets, but not in the overt manner of the past.

Masculine Gatherings

There were a number of celebratory occasions that were highly masculine in character, although women were doubtlessly involved in supporting roles. Training Days, later known as Muster Days, were considered vital for the survival of the community. Because of the absence of a standing army, all men of the community were expected to render military aid in times of emergencies. Early communities held training days weekly or monthly, and they were serious business. Little celebration or revelry occurred, and women and children rarely attended such events.

After settlements became established, training days diminished to three times per year, and they became more festive in character. Hundreds of men gathered in the nearest large town for military exercises, and their wives and children usually accompanied them to watch the spectacle of the event and partake in the celebration afterward. Training commenced at seven o'clock in the morning, meaning rural families began streaming toward town in the dark hours of the early morning. The

day began with military drills and shooting practice, but after a few hours a carnival-like atmosphere turned the event into impromptu festivals. Women brought gingerbread, sweets, and eggnog. Vendors came out to sell other beverages and trinkets. Younger children held footraces and card games, while women socialized and became reacquainted with distant neighbors they might not have seen since the last training day. Toward the end of daylight hours, a huge sham battle was conducted, more an opportunity to exercise local pride than to serve any real military value. Following training day, many communities held dances at local barns, where there was more drinking and revelry.

Election Day was another holiday where women were excluded from playing formal roles, but were often in attendance as spectators. Elections were usually conducted at the county courthouse, and candidates eagerly courted voters by offering free liquor and refreshments. "Election cake" was a rum-soaked spice cake that was liberally offered to all in attendance. Peddlers and vendors sold their wares, and many women took advantage of Election Day to sell herbs, baskets, thread, and other items they had made at home. Women were excluded from the voting process, but the day was highly anticipated as a reprieve from domestic chores and a celebratory social event.

See also Sports and Leisure

Further Reading

Earle, Alice Morse. *Customs and Fashions in Old New England.* New York: Charles Scribner's Sons, 1911.

Mook, H. Telfer. "Training Day in New England." *New England Quarterly* 11 (1938): 675–697.

Myers, Robert J. *Celebrations: The Complete Book of American Holidays.* New York: Doubleday, 1972.

Nissenbaum, Stephen. *The Battle for Christmas.* New York: Vintage Books, 1996.

Household Responsibilities

The domestic chores of rural and town women were dramatically different. Town women had ready access to processed goods, such as cloth,

The Benefits of a Wife

Although wives received no wages for their household labor, historian Jeanne Boydston estimates that the value of a woman's contribution to the household was worth twice the cost of her maintenance. The economic advantages were not lost on the author of an advice column to young men in the *Baltimore Weekly Magazine* (20 December 1800):

"Get married: a wife is cheaper than a housekeeper, her industry will assist you many ways, and your children will soon share and lighten your labor."

Source: Boydston, Jeanne. *Home and Work: Housework, Wages, and the Ideology of Labor in the Early Republic.* New York: Oxford University Press, 1990.

bread, soap, and perhaps most importantly, servants. Even families of modest means could afford to hire a teenage girl to help with chores. Spared the intensive work necessary for subsistence survival, town women were able to take greater care in providing for the comfort of their families. The daily lives of rural women were consumed with meeting basic needs, leaving little time or energy to pursue leisure activities or indulge in artful displays of domesticity.

Rural Responsibilities

Although most people who lived in seventeenth-century Europe probably resided within the sound of a church bell, those who traveled to America were confronted with a vast and isolated wilderness. As the first generations of immigrants carved out farms, they could not rely on purchased goods from local merchants or craftsmen. These settlers needed to establish a high level of self-sufficiency for all their household supplies and sustenance. The New World was land rich, but labor poor. Many of the early immigrants were able to stake out a claim of land, but could look no further than their own family members for assistance in turning a few acres of wilderness into a farm. Land needed to be cleared for homesteads, pasture, and planting. A settler could typically clear no more than an acre or two per year. Women and children assisted in clearing land, building fences, planting and tending crops, fishing, and gathering whatever foodstuffs could be gleaned from the wild.

The most common crop for farming was corn, because this versatile crop could be used for food, the stalks served as winter fodder for cattle, and the husks were used to stuff mattresses. It was the women's responsibility to grind corn into meal. This was done by hand, because water mills were rare and expensive to use. The diet of corn needed to be supplemented with produce from a kitchen garden, and this was usually the sole responsibility of the women in the family. Parsnips, onions, peas, cabbage, and carrots were all staples of early American settlers.

Food preparation consumed the majority of a rural woman's working day. For those who owned a cow, milking, making cheese, and churning butter were regular tasks. Because early Americans lacked means of refrigeration, meat and vegetables needed to be preserved in order to sustain the family through the winter. Infusing a food with salt suppresses unhealthy levels of microbial activity. Vegetables were pickled by soaking them in heavy salt solutions, and a similar technique was used for curing meat. Meat cured in this fashion was unpalatable, but smoking it helped disguise the flavor. People of the seventeenth and eighteenth centuries were suspicious of drinking water and preferred beer, wine, ale, or cider. The gathering of fruits and grains as well as the process of fermentation were other tasks undertaken by the farmer's wife.

Other household responsibilities included making candles, soap, and clothing. Very few women would have been able to produce cloth, because it required a heavy investment in a spinning wheel and loom. Most women knew how to use a spinning wheel to produce thread and yarn, but very few households possessed a loom necessary for making cloth. Fabric was one of the few items that rural women would have purchased from merchants or bartered from a weaver. The purchase of a manufactured good like cloth was an expensive luxury, and cloth was used literally until it was threadbare. Clothes were altered and mended by women to extend their life. A well-made article of clothing could see up to thirty years of use before it was too threadbare for further mending. When an article of clothing could no longer be repaired, it was cut into pieces and the usable sections were sewn into quilts or used as rags.

Washing clothes and linen consumed an enormous amount of time. Entire days were set aside for laundry, because the collection and heating of water was a time-consuming and arduous task. Fifty gallons, or four hundred pounds of water, was necessary to fill the washing and rinsing kettles. Clothes were boiled until clean, then pounded with a wooden mallet until dirt stains were lifted. They were then rinsed in another kettle of fresh water, and finally wrung out to dry. Water was hauled away when the washing was completed. The physical discomfort of hauling water, wringing clothes, stoking fires, and ongoing exposure to lye and soaps, made laundry a grueling chore.

All of these immensely time-consuming and physically difficult tasks were fitted around a rural housewife's primary responsibility of raising children. Because it was common for a woman to have as many as eight children, it was a necessity for older children to help with chores and supervise young children.

Rural women rarely lived so far away from their neighbors that trade was impossible. Given the enormous amount of work required to maintain complete self-sufficiency, informal networks of trade and exchange developed within farming communities. Items such as soap and candles might have been traded for cheese and butter from a housewife fortunate enough to have a cow. Especially in New England, where compact settlement patterns were established around the community church, neighbors were able to visit regularly, exchange goods, and work on communal projects. The middle and southern colonies tended to be more widely scattered settlements, reducing the opportunities for barter.

The diet of rural families was plain and lacking in variety. The primary source of protein would have been hogs, because they were the easiest livestock to raise. Although other livestock required clearing, fencing, and maintaining a pasture, hogs were

Fire Safety

Fire was an ever-present danger in colonial America, where kitchens featured enormous, walk-in fireplaces and most homes were built of wood. In the earliest years of settlement, even chimneys were made of wood and lined with mud and clay in a meager attempt to prevent chimney fires. Sparks could ignite either the chimney or the roof. Roof fires were the least damaging sort of fire, because they either burned themselves out or could be extinguished before igniting the body of the home. Far more dangerous were fires caused by sparks that spilled from the fireplace into the room. Women kept several pails of water on hand for daily household chores, but these were used to put out fires in an emergency. A bucket of sand was also kept close in case of a grease fire.

All families kept at least one fire bucket in the home. These were buckets made of leather, lined with pitch, and kept filled with water. If a structure caught on fire, the entire community assembled with their fire buckets in order to extinguish the flames. Fire buckets could be tossed on a roof fire and fall to the ground without cracking. Some communities passed laws in an attempt to mitigate fire hazards, including banning of shingle roofs or requiring that chimneys be made of brick or stone. Many communities had laws that required one fire bucket for every two fireplaces in a home.

Source: Taylor, Dale. *Guide to Everyday Life in Colonial America.* Cincinnati, OH: Writer's Digest, 1997.

allowed to forage in the woods and required no tending. Meals were served on basic, serviceable bowls and plates. Farm families did not have the variety of drinking glasses, serving pieces, and specialized cooking equipment that town dwellers often possessed. Houses were small, with only the minimum amount of furnishings.

Town Responsibilities

The major difference between rural and town women was in the amount of time they spent producing goods. Women living in a farming environment were expected to plant, raise, harvest, and produce their own basic supplies. Women of the town could buy flour that had already been ground, meat that had already been butchered, and cheese that had already been made. Much of a town woman's day was spent in the marketplace, usually walking to diverse shops or tradesmen. These trips to the marketplace needed to be undertaken several times per week, because milk, butter, and vegetables were perishable. After obtaining these foodstuffs, a town woman spent as much time in cooking and preparation as her rural sisters. We know from the lack of butter churns, cheese presses, candle molds, and spinning wheels among the estates of town dwellers that most of these women must have purchased these items rather than make them at home.

Although a town woman's chores were considerable, her ability to purchase processed goods and household supplies freed several hours per day. The surplus time was filled with greater attention to cleaning and care for clothing than rural women were able to give. Contemporary observers noted that women living in town typically spent several days per week cleaning. An entire day would be set aside for laundry, followed by a day of pressing and mending clothing. Clothes were laundered with greater regularity in town, because rural women rarely had the necessary time for frequent washing.

Raising children was a primary responsibility of women, whether they lived in rural or town settings. Most children were educated at home. Boys might be apprenticed to a tradesman or their father, and mothers instructed girls in the domestic arts of cookery, sewing, and household maintenance.

Wives of urban tradesmen often participated in running the family business. Women were known to be active participants making ale, tanning leather, operating a printing press, or preparing tavern fare. The businesses were usually based in the home, making it easy for the wife to help with production, selling, or bookkeeping. We know from the large percentage of widows who assumed administration of their deceased husbands' business that these women must have been active participants in the family trade. Thus, the hours of drudgery a town woman was spared by the ability to purchased man-

ufactured goods were often filled with skilled production as part of a family business.

Labor was more readily available in towns. Newspaper advertisements of the time make it clear that the services of working women or free blacks could be rented by the day, week, or month. For those who could afford it, such servants might have helped with laundry, cooking, or sewing. The arduous nature of laundry made it the most common task town women hired out.

Social and domestic expectations of town women differed from those of rural women. Rural women expended their full energies on producing the basic necessities, leaving little time for luxuries or variety in food and clothing. Urban women had access to processed food and were expected to prepare more interesting, varied, and complex meals. Cookbooks reveal meals that required numerous ingredients and had several courses—a far cry from the simple one-pot meals that were standard fare among rural households. Social visits occurred with regularity and were inevitably accompanied by tea and refreshments.

Urban households spent a greater percentage of their disposable income on social equipment, such as tea sets, china dinnerware, tablecloths, gaming tables, and a variety of drinking glasses. Many could afford to decorate their houses with pictures, clocks, and looking glasses. This emphasis on entertaining brought a new set of responsibilities to a housewife. Homes needed to be clean, spacious, and comfortable. Entertaining neighbors and business associates meant being able to serve appetizing meals. Presentation of the home assumed greater importance. Floors were adorned with rugs, tables covered with linen, and windows hung with draperies. All of these items needed to be cleaned and maintained. Showpiece items made of pewter, brass, and silver required more care than serviceable earthenware.

In middle-class and wealthy urban households, the eighteenth century witnessed an explosion in social display. Teatime became an elaborate ritual, and dinners became multicourse affairs. Such meals were served on distinctive table settings with china, glassware, and silver place settings. Elaborate food preparation for meals attempted to rival the opulent banquets of the English aristocracy. Although a woman presiding over such a gathering would most certainly have had the assistance of hired labor, she would have been expected to oversee the purchase of supplies and food preparation and host the affair.

The differences between life in urban and rural households can be studied from their household inventories. An urban woman ate her dinner from a ceramic plate, by the flickering candlelight. Most of the items on her plate would have been purchased at the local marketplace. She would be sitting on a chair at a table that was used exclusively for dining.

Her rural cousin would have eaten off of a wooden or pottery bowl, the same bowl she ate all her meals from. Her light source would be the kitchen fireplace. She would be sitting at a bench beside the family worktable, which served a variety of functions. Her meal would be simple, most likely a simmered pork stew from a hog she had raised herself.

Each lifestyle had its own set of chores. Rural households were largely self-sufficient, requiring a woman to perform manual labor and assume responsibility for all aspects of household production. Urban women needed less time for providing basic necessities, but spent more time on domestic display and cleanliness.

See also Cooking; Diet; Domestic Labor

Further Reading

Berkin, Carol. *First Generations: Women in Colonial America.* New York: Hill and Wang, 1996.

Hawke, David Freeman. *Everyday Life in Early America.* New York: Harper and Row, 1988.

Spruill, Julia Cherry. *Women's Life and Work in the Southern Colonies.* Chapel Hill: University of North Carolina Press, 1938.

Ulrich, Laurel Thatcher. *Good Wives: Images and Reality in the Lives of Women in Northern New England, 1650–1750.* New York: Knopf, 1980.

Walsh, Lorena S. "Urban Amenities and Rural Sufficiency: Living Standards and Consumer Behavior in the Colonial Chesapeake, 1643–1777." *Journal of Economic History* 43 (1983): 109–117.

Housing

The earliest settlers in America lived in crude, primitive conditions until they had the time and resources to construct housing similar to what they had known in Europe. When a ship full of immigrants arrived in uncharted territory, they initially stayed aboard the ship until a safe site had been located. Some might have continued to live aboard the ship for weeks, while others moved ashore and lived in tents.

The earliest structures made were wigwams, modeled after shelters constructed by Indians. The frame was made of flexible sapling branches that were bent and lashed together to form a dome. Straw, bark, and mud were intermingled to form the sides of the structure. A stone fireplace anchored one end of the structure, and a door was on the opposite side. Although a wigwam could provide warmth and shelter during a mild rain, heavier rains soaked through the structure. Letters and diaries of newly arrived immigrants speak of the dismay they experienced upon seeing the wigwams, which were more primitive than even the poorest housing in London.

As soon as possible, the settlers began constructing more permanent housing. Many immigrants were people of means, but labor was scare in the colonies, and the need for houses was urgent. Small and crude homes were constructed as quickly as possible. After settlers were able to construct a more substantial house, the initial shelters were often kept to serve as outbuildings. One-room houses were the most common among first-generation settlers. Usually averaging 18 by 20 feet, they typically had less than 400 square feet of living space. Although some of the earliest frame homes had wooden chimneys, many communities outlawed them because of the risk of fire, and stone quickly became the norm for chimneys. Dirt floors were covered with straw until plank floors could be installed. There were usually one or two windows for light. Only the wealthiest families were able to bring diamond-paned glass with them from England. The rest used oiled parchment, which allowed a surprising amount of light into the interior.

Log cabins were rarely used by colonists in early settlements; instead they preferred to split timber into boards for traditional clapboard and frame houses. Log cabins did not appear in any substantial way until Scandinavian and Scots-Irish settlers introduced them in the eighteenth century.

The furnishings of a one-room house, although scanty, would have filled the interior. A few chests and barrels would have been all most settlers had. These items doubled as seating, work surfaces, and storage. Almost no one had beds that were raised off the floor. Family members would have slept on a pallet on the floor in front of the embers of the fireplace. In the morning the pallets would be rolled up and pushed aside. The addition of a lean-to was the most economical way to add more space. A family with resources would have added a floor, window, and interior pass-through to the added room, making it suitable as a small bedroom. Otherwise it was suitable only for additional storage space.

The concept of a yard or a lawn was unknown to settlers. Cleared land was valuable real estate and could not be squandered for ornamental purposes. The area immediately outside the home was used for grazing chickens and hogs, raising root vegetables, and the disposal of trash. If the area was free of shade trees, crops such as corn might have been planted right up to the foundations of the house.

Homes

Wealthier immigrants were able to bring servants with them, and these people constructed more substantial homes. When a house had two or more rooms, the character of life inside the home took on a distinctly different atmosphere. Cooking and mealtime could be confined in one area, allowing the other room to serve as a more social, homelike setting. The kitchen became more spacious. Fireplaces increased in size and were often large enough for an adult to stand inside. Two or three small fires could be burning in the fireplace at any given time, one boiling water, another cooking stew, and so on. Such kitchens would have had room for a dining table. With a table large enough for a family to gather around, meals became more relaxed and sociable. The front room often doubled as a place of business. If the man of the house were a tradesman, the front room would be where he received customers and contracted business.

By the late seventeenth century, glass was becoming more common in homes. Small, diamond-shaped panes set into lead frames was the most practical form of window, because this glass was less likely to break during long ocean voyages. Glass was heavily taxed as it left England, meaning that most windows were small. Even in early America there was concern with fashion, and by the early eighteenth century diamond-paned windows were considered old-fashioned. Small, rectangular panes in casement windows were preferred by most who could afford them.

Most homes were unpainted, causing foreign visitors to complain that the towns had a dingy, unfinished appearance. When settlers were able to afford house paint, they usually selected a dark red color, as red ochre pigment was abundant in the colonies.

Wood was the primary building material used throughout the colonies, although brick was a sought after commodity. The expense of brick limited its use to foundations, cellar floors, and chimney stacks. As labor shortages eased in the eighteenth century, brick production increased, and it became affordable to build an entire house of brick.

Average farmers built their homes near lesser creeks. The average home of the eighteenth century would have had two rooms on the ground floor, with either a loft or second story. It was made of unpainted timber and a wood shingle roof. There were likely at least two outbuildings: a privy, and some sort of shelter for animals.

By the end of the seventeenth century, the dire labor problems of earlier generations had eased. Although one-room homes continued to be the norm in southern states, New England homes had expanded to two stories with stone fireplaces and slate roofs. There were some regional variations in homes. In northern areas fireplaces were in the center of the house, with a large, dominating chimney rising from the middle of the roof. Often with back-to-back fireplaces, this allowed for heat distribution throughout the home. In southern regions the concern was to minimize the heat, so fireplaces

A spacious Massachusetts farm house. (Library of Congress)

were either on the side of the house, or for the wealthy, kitchens were in a separate structure.

The earliest settlers attempted to reproduce the styles of homes they came from in Europe, although they quickly abandoned this practice. Labor shortages, different available building materials, and climatic considerations caused distinctive regional differences to emerge. Settlers in the North built steeped roofs to allow snow to slide off. Such roofs had the added benefit of allowing for the construction of a loft, where children could sleep or additional supplies could be stored. In the South, separate outbuildings were used for cooking, storage, and food preservation.

One thing lacking in most colonial homes, even those of the very wealthy, was privacy. Most homes had only a few, multipurpose rooms. People worked and slept in the same communal room. People who were born and raised in such congested environ-

ments would never have developed the sense of privacy taken for granted in later centuries. Floor plans from seventeenth- and eighteenth-century homes rarely had hallways. This meant that rooms opened into each other, and people were constantly moving through one room to get to another. People could have no expectation of privacy in a room through which traffic regularly passed. It was not until the second half of the late eighteenth century that hallways became standard features in homes. The expense of this addition meant it was a luxury for the well-to-do. Likewise, the average girl growing up could not expect to have her own bedroom until she married. Even then, she was likely to share it with her small children for a number of years.

Plantations and Estates
Over time the stratification of wealth made itself apparent in the grand homes of the wealthy planters

and merchants. Families of means built their plantations along desirable riverfronts, which were used as the primary means of transportation and irrigation. Georgian architectural design became the mark of wealth and distinction. Inspired by neoclassical design, these homes favored simplicity, symmetry, and size. The door was always centered on the front of the house, flanked by equal numbers of large windows on either side. The size of such houses permitted the addition of numerous bedrooms, unheard of in the simpler homes. The children of the family would no longer sleep on the floor of the main parlor, but might have use of a room exclusively designated as a sleeping room. As such, they were more likely to have bedroom furniture with a bed raised off the ground. For the first time, the idea that the occupants in a sleeping room should be segregated by gender was a possibility.

A distinctive feature of Georgian-style homes was the addition of a central hallway, which divided the first-floor rooms and contained a staircase leading to the upper stories. The addition of the hallways on each floor provided added privacy and consciousness of individual spaces. Although open floor plans were not immediately abandoned in other architectural styles, hallways were gradually incorporated into new home construction. By the end of the colonial period, many families were able to live in homes with far greater privacy than the earlier settlers.

Interiors

The addition of plank flooring marked an important transition in the habitability of a home. Plank floors were infinitely more desirable because of the comfort of avoiding the grime, mud, and unhealthy conditions caused by straw-covered dirt floors. Perhaps equally important was that a plank floor allowed for the construction of a cellar beneath the home. In an environment where the preservation of food throughout the long winter months was vital, the cool, climatic condition of a cellar was ideal.

Poor homes would have no special coverings for the interior walls. Those who could afford to do so covered their walls with plaster, both for insulation and the pleasing appearance. Some used wainscoting—carefully trimmed lumber panels—to line their interior walls, but this was too costly for most settlers. An interesting rebuke survives from Governor Winthrop in 1632, toward a Massachusetts settler "for bestowing so much cost on wainscoting his house and otherwise adorning it" that other settlers felt poor by comparison (Dow 1935, 19).

Over time the frontier character of the settlement gave way to small luxuries in homes. Plaster and wainscoting added both insulation and visual appeal to homes. Puritan communities usually left their walls white, in accord with their views on unpretentious simplicity. Others preferred to paint their homes. By the eighteenth century interior walls were usually painted a variety of colors, many of which would seem garish to modern eyes. A 1753 newspaper advertisement from one wealthy merchant selling his home described it as "handsomely painted throughout; one of the rooms is painted in green, another blue, one cedar and one marble, the other four of a lead color, the garrets are handsomely plastered" (Dow 1935, 24).

Although most homes had little in the way of furniture or decoration, the interior appearance would have appeared cluttered by modern-day standards. There were no closets, and storage space was limited. Typical kitchens would have been packed with barrels of preserved food, pots and cooking equipment dangling from hooks, and hanging strings of dried apples, herbs, and smoked meat stretched across the ceiling. Practical implements such as washtubs and butter churns would consume floor space. Other rooms in the house served multiple functions. The main room was used for sleeping children, and their bedding would be rolled aside during the day. Here is where women would have done their sewing, taught their children, and performed numerous other household chores. In addition to a few chairs or trunks, there might be a spinning wheel, loom, or storage barrels.

Further Reading

Carr, Lois Green, and Lorena S. Walsh. "The Standard of Living in the Colonial Chesapeake." *William and Mary Quarterly* 45 (1988): 135–159.

Chappell, Edward A. "Housing a Nation: The Transformation of Living Standards in Early America." In *Of Consuming Interests: The Styles of Life in the Eighteenth Century*, ed. Cary Carson et al. Charlottesville: University Press of Virginia, 1994.

Dow, George Francis. *Everyday Life in the Massachusetts Bay Colony.* New York: Benjamin Blom, 1935.

Fischer, David Hackett. *Albion's Seed: Four British Folkways in America.* New York: Oxford University Press, 1989.

Herman, Bernard L. "Home and Hearth." In *Encyclopedia of the North American Colonies*, ed. Jacob Ernest Cooke. New York: Charles Scribner's Sons, 1993.

Isaac, Rhys. *The Transformation of Virginia, 1740–1790.* Chapel Hill: University of North Carolina Press, 1982.

Hutchinson, Anne Marbury
Religious agitator (c. 1591–1643)

Anne Hutchinson was among the first generation of English Puritans to immigrate to America in order to worship without interference from the hostile authorities of the Church of England. These early settlers were seeking freedom to practice their own brand of Protestantism, but had no ideological commitment to religious freedom for those who differed from their point of view. When Anne Hutchinson began to stray from the ideological positions of the Puritan fathers, she learned that dissent was not to be tolerated in the new American colonies.

These earliest settlers believed they were seeking God's kingdom in the wilderness. They needed unity of purpose if they were to survive in this strange and dangerous land. Anne represented much of what they feared. She was a charismatic, intelligent woman, determined to advance controversial religious views. For a people who had fled a country that had endured more than a century of turbulent, religiously motivated violence, Anne Hutchinson was a potential menace to their society.

Born and raised in England, Anne made an advantageous marriage to William Hutchinson, a well-to-do merchant with whom she eventually had fourteen children. She and her husband were devout followers of the Puritan preacher John Cotton. When Cotton was forced to emigrate in order to avoid arrest for heresy, the Hutchinsons decided to follow him to America in 1634 and became one of the founding families of the Massachusetts Bay Colony. Anne's husband was elected to serve as deputy to the General Court and selectman for Boston, in which he had authority over local problems such as public works and the allocation of land. Furthermore, the new governor of the colony, Sir Henry Vane, was a man who shared the Hutchinson's religious convictions, leading to even greater political and social entrée into the Boston power structure. Governor Vane was to become one of Anne Hutchinson's most enthusiastic supporters, and while he was in power her religious activities thrived.

Anne's early years in America were happy. Having come from a family of small gentry origins, she was near the top of the social hierarchy in America. Her skills as a midwife and nurse made her a valuable asset to the community. Having delivered the babies of many women in the community and been a nurse to the seriously ill, she had the trust and respect of most settlers. Her marriage to William Hutchinson was extremely happy and described by one biographer as "one of history's all time great romances" (Williams 1981, 40). In 1636, Anne gave birth to her fifteenth child at age forty-four.

With the blessings of the town leaders, Anne held weekly prayer meetings in her home. Conversation at the meetings frequently strayed into commentary on sermons and scripture. Anne began offering her own opinions and interpretations to the group, which swelled to more than eighty persons at the height of her popularity. A woman of keen intellect and forceful convictions, Anne developed a particularly radical interpretation of scripture. Like her fellow Puritans, Anne believed that an individual was completely at the mercy of God for salvation. Anne and her critics both believed that good works and acts of charity were signs that a person had been called to Christ, but could not be used to "earn" redemption. Anne differed from other Puritans in believing that the very essence of the Holy Spirit was received into the soul of the saved. She rejected the idea that a people could participate in their own salvation through good works and believed that Christians were free from the moral code of the Old

Illustration depicting the trial of Anne Hutchinson, who defended herself at her 1637 trial. Undated woodcut. (Bettmann/CORBIS)

Testament and would do better to heed the inner light and guidance of the Holy Spirit. This radical doctrine freed the individual from obedience to man-made rules and hierarchy of the church. This philosophy was at the heart of the antinomianism, a doctrine reviled by many Protestants.

Anne had a special attraction for women of the colony. Most of the followers who gathered at her house were women, and the antinomian philosophy put men and women on an equal plane before God. The authority of the minister was downplayed, while the role of the individual was elevated. Some women traveled from nearby towns to partake in the meetings at Anne's house. As tensions between Anne and the ministers intensified, Anne was known to walk out of congregation in the middle of sermons. In shows of solidarity, other women often followed her out.

Most of the Puritan leaders saw Anne's ideas and her personal charisma as a threat that needed to be extinguished. Leaders of the Massachusetts Bay Colony blended church and state authority, and a challenge to the church was a challenge to the state. Heretical opinions were therefore a threat to every level of society, and could not be tolerated. The security of the colony required that Anne either be silenced or excised before her radical opinions could take root. In 1637 the governor of Massachusetts, Anne's erstwhile supporter Henry Vane, resigned his position and returned to England. With Anne's protector no longer in America, the way was cleared for the Puritan ministers to begin silencing this radical element in their midst.

The ministers believed there was only one version of religious truth, and it was the function of the state to protect this truth. Much of Puritan philosophy rested on the position that God had created a contract with his chosen people. If his ministers failed to punish heresy, the entire community would suffer God's vengeance. Anne clearly represented a voice of dissension.

In November 1637 Anne was brought to trial for heresy and "traducing the ministers and their ministry." She defended herself ably at trial and attempted to persuade the ministers of the validity of her preaching. After she set out her positions, seven ministers testified to the error of Anne's reasoning. The court recessed for the day, and Anne was ordered to "consider" the wisdom of the ministers. The following day Anne continued to parry and spar with the ministers, relying heavily on scripture to justify her positions. Although she conducted most of her defense with brilliant acuity, in an incautious moment she told the ministers "God will ruin you and your posterity, and this whole State." When questioned how she knew this, Anne replied "By an immediate revelation." By claiming she had divine insight into the future, Anne slipped into clearcut heresy, and the judges used this as evidence that she must be "banished from out of our jurisdiction as being a woman not fit for our society" (Battis 1962, 208).

With the onset of winter, authorities showed a small measure of mercy by allowing Anne to remain in the colony until spring. Their clemency did not extend to permitting Anne to continue her ministry or remain a member of their church. Formal excommunication hearings were held in March 1638. After the presiding reverend declared her a "leper" and not fit to be a member of the congregation, Anne left the church. As she walked down the isle, she was joined by Mary Dyer, who joined hands with her and walked out of the building. Mary Dyer would later have her own standoff with Boston ministers.

With the coming of spring, Anne was forced to leave Boston. She and her family traveled for six days by foot and canoe through Indian territory. They were forced to spend the nights in simple shelters dug into the ground for warmth. Eventually they arrived in Aquidneck, Rhode Island. The primitive cabin they lived in bore little resemblance to the grand home she had in Boston, and the Massachusetts ministers continued to harass her by sending delegations to ensure she did not continue her ministry. Anne's husband, whom she described as her best friend and devoted partner, died in 1642. At that time she elected to move farther away from her adversaries by relocating to the Dutch colony on Long Island. The following year the colony was attacked by Indians. Anne and her five youngest children were killed in the massacre. The ministers of Boston proclaimed the massacre a sign of God's vengeance, even going so far as to claim that her children had been killed to stop the spread of poisoned seeds.

Only one of the children living with Anne at the time of the assault survived the massacre. Ten-year-old Susanna was taken captive, and after four years she was ransomed back to relatives. By then a young woman, Susanna expressed reluctance to return to white civilization, although she did return and eventually married. Four of Anne's older children who were no longer living with their mother at the time of the attack also survived.

The Boston ministers did their best to excise Anne and her philosophy from their community, but she had a lingering influence on the women of the colony. In the coming years a number of Anne's followers continued to be censured for "obstinate persisting" in religious errors. Among the women to be prosecuted were Judith Smith in 1638, Katherine Finch later that same year, and Phillipa Hammond in 1639. Mrs. Hammond was excommunicated for claiming, among other things, that Mrs. Hutchinson had been unjustly censured by both the church and the community. In coming generations, Hutchinson's memory faded and Puritan women would become ever more passive. Seventeenth-century Puritans valued order and obedience to the church, and the Hutchinson controversy epitomized the danger schisms could bring to their City upon a Hill. Anne's reputation was steadily rehabilitated in the nineteenth century, when independent and strong-minded women were no longer aberrations. In 1922 a statue of Anne Hutchinson was placed in front of the Massachusetts State House.

Many historians have sought to imbue Anne Hutchinson with a fledgling spirit of feminist revolt. This is difficult on a number of fronts. Anne left no writings, and her views are relayed to us through the court records written by her persecutors. The entirety of their charges are focused on religious dissent. It appears that Anne's gender was of little concern to her judges. A man representing such factious rebellion would have suffered the same fate, as can be witnessed by the case of Roger Williams. A number of Anne's followers who voiced support for her after exile were mostly women. Whether their support was based on theological convictions or a sense of solidarity with an unjustly maligned sister will probably never be known.

See also Dyer, Mary; Puritan Women

Further Reading

Barker-Benfield, Ben. "Anne Hutchinson and the Puritan Attitude toward Women." *Feminist Studies* 1 (1972): 65–96.

Battis, Emery. *Saints and Sectaries: Anne Hutchinson and the Antinomian Controversy in the Massachusetts Bay Colony.* Chapel Hill: University of North Carolina Press, 1962.

Beaudin, Donna. "Anne Hutchinson." In *Women in World History: A Biographical Encyclopedia,* ed. Anne Commire. Detroit, MI: Gale, 2000.

Koehler, Lyle. "The Case of the American Jezebels: Anne Hutchinson and Female Agitation during the Years of Antinomian Turmoil, 1636–1640." *William and Mary Quarterly* 31 (1974): 55–78.

Williams, Selma R. *Divine Rebel: The Life of Anne Marbury Hutchinson.* New York: Holt, Rinehart and Winston, 1981.

Withington, Anne Fairfax. "The Political Trial of Anne Hutchinson." *New England Quarterly* 51 (1978): 226–240.

Hygiene

Standards of personal care and hygiene were different for women in early America owing to the lack of plumbing, understanding of medical implications, and standards of personal cleanliness. Although it is true that full body bathing was almost unheard of in colonial America, it would be wrong to conclude that typical people reeked of foul odors. Nor did all women lose their teeth or go years without washing their hair. For people who are accustomed to daily bathing, hygienic standards of the seventeenth and eighteenth centuries would be appalling, but in fact they were little different than what people practiced around the world throughout most of history.

Bathing

Bathing for women in early America would have been done primarily by using a piece of cloth and a basin of water. Sponging off would usually be done in the bedchamber, or wherever a woman could find some privacy. Because it required little effort to arrange for a bowl of water, this sort of bathing could be done as often as a woman saw fit, whether it was daily, weekly, or even longer. Soap was generally reserved for cleaning laundry, although some would have made use of it on skin. Soap did not gain widespread acceptance for cleaning bodies until the mid-nineteenth century.

Swimming, although rarely intended for hygienic purposes, did have the effect of cleaning a person. People swam primarily as a means of cooling down, so southern women were more likely to take a dip than their northern counterparts. Sea bathing was touted for its invigorating effect and was considered excellent for the health.

Wooden tubs were common in colonial households, but were used primarily for laundry or storage. Such tubs could be used to bathe a child or possibly provide a cramped and uncomfortable bath for an adult. Tubs specifically made for bathing did not make their appearance in America until the end of the eighteenth century. They were usually made of copper or some other type of metal. In most cases, full-body bathing in tubs occurred in the kitchen, for this is where the facilities for heating water would have been. It was also usually the warmest room in the house.

In the late eighteenth century some wealthier households also began to piece together makeshift showers in outdoor areas near the house. Tin water reservoirs were erected on a tall platform. The user would pull a cord, and water would fall down through a pipe and a colander. When women made use of such showers they wore thin cotton gowns in an attempt to preserve a semblance of modesty. In 1798 the Drinker family of Philadelphia installed such a shower. Mr. Drinker and the children enjoyed using it, although it took Mrs. Drinker more than a year before she was willing to venture a try. "I bore it better than I expected," she noted in her diary, "not having been wet all over at once, for twenty-eight years past" (Drinker 1994, 211). The previous occasion for Elizabeth Drinker's having been "wet all over" was during a 1771 trip to the spa at Bristol Springs. Taking the spa waters was a social and therapeutic activity, rather than an issue of cleanliness.

Medical literature offered conflicting advice on the issue of hygiene. Some doctors believed the oils of the skin served an important health function and stripping them away through soap and scrubbing would open a person to disease. Others argued the opposite, claiming many ailments could be traced to unhygienic bodies and dirty clothes. Such doctors recommended not only frequent sponging of the body, but regular changes of clothing and bed linens. By the mid-eighteenth century the danger of poor hygiene was clearly understood. General Washington insisted that his troops bathe and be supplied with clean clothes whenever possible.

Most women of early America would have had complete baths only as infants. Bathtubs were not common household features until the advent of piped in running water, which began appearing in cities such as Boston and Philadelphia in the mid-nineteenth century. This coincided with the rise of public baths, where less-wealthy individuals could partake of the new trend. Bathing houses, which were open to women, charged different fees, depending on whether the individual selected freshwater, saltwater, or warm-water baths.

There is little mention in colonial literature about how or how often women washed their hair. Extremely common chores such as dressing or visiting the outhouse are not mentioned in letters and diaries, but we are certain women did them regularly! Hair washing appears to have been equally unworthy of mention, as we know virtually nothing about how often or where it was performed. Very few colonial women wore wigs, and keeping clean hair was important. Contemporary beauty manuals indicate that unclean hair and teeth were slovenly signs of bad manners and poor health. Regular and vigorous brushing of hair was recognized as a means of keeping it clean and shiny. How often they truly washed their hair is unknown, and probably varied depending on personal preference.

Dental Care

The most common means of cleaning teeth was by rubbing them with a cloth dipped in a little salt and water. Apothecaries sometimes sold tooth powders made of brimstone, baking soda, gunpowder, or other abrasive substances. Various home remedies were used to cure bad breath, including chewing cloves or cinnamon, or drinking a concoction of rosemary and white wine.

Toothaches affected most adults at some point in their lives. Although few suffered George Washington's fate of losing all their teeth, it was common to have at least a few teeth pulled. Herbal remedies were usually tried first, because the problem could be merely a temporary infection. Swollen gums were soothed by pressing a toasted fig or bags of very hot chamomile leaves against the affected area. Some doctors prescribed lozenges containing small amounts of opium. These remedies provided fleeting relief, but if the pain persisted more than a few days, the pulling of a tooth was necessary. Identification of the proper tooth was determined by tapping all the teeth in the afflicted area with a piece of metal, because only the infected tooth would respond with serious pain. An attempt to numb the area by rubbing cinnamon on the gums was only mildly effective. Heavy use of liquor or laudanum was usually the only real pain remedy.

How many women lost their teeth is not known. Advertisements for tooth pulling and dentures were common in colonial newspapers. Dentures were created from wood, ivory, or metal, but were a costly item available only to the well-to-do. Most men and women who lost a tooth most likely could not afford to replace it with an artificial tooth. It was common after the pulling of a tooth to try to reimplant the original tooth in the hope that whatever infection or damage that caused the loss would be remedied by the removal, cleaning, and reinsertion of the tooth. Such procedures were sometimes successful, but diaries often reveal that these reimplanted teeth needed to be removed later.

Shaving

There is no evidence that women in colonial America shaved their legs or underarms, but neither is there conclusive evidence they did not. References to razors and shaving are almost completely absent from the historical record of colonial America, but we know from portraits that most men were clean-shaven despite the absence of references to shaving in letters, diaries, or inventories.

Western art has typically portrayed beautiful women as smooth skinned. In Europe and the Middle East there is some indication that courtesans, artists' models, and other women who were in the business of pleasing men shaved their body hair. It is difficult to believe that women in America did not attempt to emulate what appeared to be the norm for feminine beauty.

Arguing against the supposition that women shaved are the clothing styles of seventeenth- and eighteenth-century America. Legs and arms were not bared to the public until the twentieth century lifted hemlines and did away with sleeves.

Shaving was performed by use of a straight blade throughout the colonial period. When safety razors were introduced by Gillette in 1903 there was no assumption in their advertising that they were a strictly male implement. Within the decade the company was marketing a lady's razor, indicating they believed there was a market for women who shaved. Named "Milady Decollette," this feminine razor was introduced at a time when women were still covered from head to toe by voluminous skirts. The fact that a woman's skin was not on display to the public does not mean we can assume they did not care about smooth skin. Whether women of early centuries shaved has yet to be determined.

Bathrooms

For most of history, the disposal of human waste has been associated with the outdoors. Indoor water closets were unknown until the end of the colonial period. Although chamber pots may have been used when illness, climate, or time of day made visiting an outhouse impossible, such pots were always emptied outdoors as soon as possible.

Outhouses were known by a variety of names: privies, the convenience, the necessary house, or simply the necessary. They were usually simply a hole dug into the ground that was covered by an open-seated chair. The privy was usually in the backyard of the house, near enough to be convenient during poor weather, but far enough away so odor was not intrusive. People living in towns or on wealthier farms would have built a wooden structure around the privy, but these were by no means universal. People of early America did not have the same sense of privacy we have today. They shared beds with extended family members, changed in common rooms, and apparently had little qualms about maintaining privacy for bodily functions. Basic modesty could be preserved at all times by the voluminous skirts worn by women and long shirts used by men.

One reason some neglected to build a structure around their privy was the fact that many people chose to move privies for issues of cleanliness. Dirt and lime was tossed down privies to keep odors at bay, but eventually some elected to simply cover the hole over and dig a new hole a few yards away. Any sort of permanent structure made moving a privy too difficult, and the owners were required to per- form the far more odious task of emptying the privy. Elizabeth Drinker noted this chore in a 1779 diary entry, claiming they chose to do the task on a cold night in March, hoping the chill would keep the smell down.

Some communities passed rules regarding the disposal of waste. Boston passed a series of city restrictions in 1652 that regulated the construction of privies and their distance from wells and streets. They modified the rule in 1701 to forbid privies within forty feet of streets, wells, or shops, unless the privy were six feet deep and adequately enclosed. In an effort to discourage people from relieving themselves in the streets, New York created a "necessary house for the use of the public" directly across from the City Hall. They also made it a misdemeanor to empty chamber pots on the city streets.

Visiting an outdoor privy was no doubt uncomfortable and unpleasant. We know that people, especially women, deferred visits to the privy during the overnight hours or bad weather. Doctors warned their patients of the dangers associated with reluctance to make regular use of the privy. Engineer James C. Bayles noted the reluctance of people to make use of outdoor facilities in his efforts to promote the construction of indoor water closets: "It is not an uncommon thing for women in the country to allow themselves to become so constipated that days and sometimes weeks will pass between stools. . . . A visit to an outdoor privy in a cold storm or when the ground is covered with snow and the air frosty is attended with a physical shock which even strong men dread" (Strasser 2000, 96).

Indoor water closets began to appear in Philadelphia and New York in the late 1790s. Water from cisterns was used to flush out a marble trough, and carry the waste away through a series of pipes. There was a great deal of skepticism in the adoption of indoor water closets. They were expensive to build, but certainly not outside the reach of a well-to-do home. There was a sense that indoor water closets were not proper for a number of reasons. They were noisy, might not always clear away waste as easily as a chamber pot could be carried outside, and pandered to the unwillingness to be inconvenienced. Lack of piped water made the adoption of water closets rare until late in the nineteenth century.

Further Reading:

Bushman, Richard L., and Claudia L. Bushman. "The Early History of Cleanliness in America." *Journal of American History* 74 (1988): 1213–1238.

Carnes-McNaughton, Linda, and Terry Harper. "The Parity of Privies: Summary Research on Privies in North Carolina." *Historical Archaeology* 34 (2000): 97–110.

Drinker, Elizabeth, and Elaine Crane Forman, ed. *The Diary of Elizabeth Drinker: The Life Cycle of an Eighteenth Century Woman.* Boston: Northeastern University Press, 1994.

Olmert, Michael. "Necessary and Sufficient." *Journal of the Colonial Williamsburg Foundation* (Autumn 2002): 33–38.

Retallack, G. Bruce. "Razors, Shaving and Gender Construction: An Inquiry into the Material Culture of Shaving." *Material History Review* 49 (1999): 4–19.

Strasser, Susan. *Never Done: A History of American Housework.* New York: First Owl, 2000.

Incest

See Rape

Indentured Servitude and Convict Labor

Early America was rich in natural resources, but poor in a supply of labor. Europe had precisely the opposite problem, with enclosure of farmlands and swelling populations creating widespread endemic poverty. With chronic poverty came push factors for migration and an increase in criminal activity for many who chose to remain.

Indentured servitude and the export of convict laborers were two different processes; however, these people's lives were remarkably similar. Upon arrival in America, both groups were stripped of their liberty for a term of service. The only difference was that indentured servants chose their own fate, whereas convicts had it forced upon them.

Indentured Servants

For immigrants who wished to go to America but lacked the necessary £4–5 for passage, indentured servitude was often their only solution. Ship captains paid the cost of transportation, and in return the passenger agreed to work for a fixed period of years in America.

The indenture was a printed document that left blank spaces to be filled in with the name, age, and agreed on period of years to be served. Although most indentured servants were male, captains eager to fill spaces in their ships would take women when

necessary. In the earliest years of the seventeenth century, only one in six indentured servants was a woman, although by the late eighteenth century women represented one-third to one-half of incoming indentured servants. Most servants over the age of twenty agreed to work for eight years. Those between sixteen and twenty years of age were usually required to work between six and eight years, and those under age sixteen were bound into service until they reached twenty-one.

Women coming to America as indentured servants were usually orphaned girls with few family connections to fall back on in England. They were typically between fifteen and twenty-four years of age, and were required to be single. For most women who chose indentured servitude, it was likely a last resort. Embarking on a dangerous and uncertain voyage that forced a woman to abandon whatever home or family she had must have been a frightening prospect. Most of these women could have little idea of what to expect in America. They were likely to be illiterate and would know little about America except what they had heard from gossip and secondhand accounts. Indentured servants had no choice about whom their indenture was sold to and no choice in the nature of the work they would be bound to perform. Her indenture could be sold to another master without her consent. Living conditions in America were spartan for everyone and especially so for servants. Homes lacked privacy, and the servants were usually required to sleep in the kitchen or another communal room.

A Plea for Help from an Indentured Servant

Conditions for some indentured servants were miserable, as attested to by the chastened letter from Elizabeth Sprigs, a disobedient young woman who was forced into indentured servitude in America by her angry father. She sent the following letter home to England, pleading for mercy:

> Maryland, September 22, 1756
> Honored Father
> My being forever banished from your sight, will I hope pardon the boldness I now take of troubling you. . . . Oh Dear Father, believe what I am going to relate the words of truth and sincerity, and balance my former bad conduct to my sufferings here, and then I am sure you'll pity your distressed daughter. What we English people suffer here is beyond the probability of you in England to conceive, let it suffice that I, one of the unhappy number, am toiling almost day and night. . . . and then tied up and whipped to that degree that you'd not serve an animal, scarce anything but Indian corn and salt to eat and that even begrudged. Many Negroes are better used, almost naked no shoes nor stockings to wear, and the comfort after slaving during Master's pleasure, what rest we can get is to wrap ourselves up in a blanket and lye upon the ground. This is the deplorable condition your poor Betty endures, and now I beg if you have any bowels of compassion left show it by sending me some relief. Clothing is the principal thing wanting, which if you should condescend to, may be easily sent to me by any of the ships bound to Baltimore Town Patapsco Maryland, and give me leave to conclude in Duty to you and Uncles and Aunts, and Respect to all Friends.
> Your undutifull and disobedient child,
> Elizabeth Sprigs

Source: Calder, Isabel, ed. *Colonial Captives, Marches, and Journeys.* Port Washington, NY: Kennikat Press, 1935.

Most female indentured servants were assigned domestic duties. Food preparation was an ever-present and enormously time-consuming task. Farm animals needed to be slaughtered, plucked, cooked, and preserved. Produce needed to be planted, tended, harvested, and prepared. Other domestic tasks such as churning butter, making soap and candles, mending clothing, and washing clothes were typical chores for a domestic servant. In the early years of the seventeenth century most female indentured servants worked in agricultural labor. In the South, manual laborers were so scarce in the early years that every able-bodied person helped with tobacco cultivation at some point in the year.

A number of unique pressures applied to a female indentured servant. She usually had no protector or family structure for support, which made her especially vulnerable to sexual advances. In a land where the sex ratio could be skewed as badly as six men to every woman, these women were likely to be subjected to relentless sexual pressure. Because they were not permitted to marry until their indenture was completed, the women had to resist courtship from desirable suitors and be strong enough to fend off unwelcome harassment. Should a woman become pregnant during her indenture, not only did she suffer the social shame associated with being an unwed mother, but her pregnant state was considered theft from her master. She would be obliged to indemnify her master for the loss of services when she was unable to perform heavy labor and for her reduced productivity during the year she nursed the child. A woman who bore a child typically had one to two years added to the end of her indenture to compensate her master. The courts of early America were realistic enough to know that in many cases the master himself was responsible for his servant's pregnant state. Most colonies had laws that forbade a man from tacking on additional time to his servant's indenture if he was found to be responsible for fathering the child. Records show that as many as one-fifth of all female indentured servants became pregnant during their years in service.

Indentured servants left few letters or diaries to attest to their experiences, but we know from court records that many complained of overwork and scanty provisions. Some historians have speculated that because indentures lasted a mere four to eight years, masters had no interest in the long-term health or well-being of their indentured servants. As such, they were unwilling to invest in adequate food, clothing, and shelter for their temporary workers. Runaway servants were common. Although an

Girl at a Fountain by William Morris Hunt. Women coming to America as indentured servants were usually orphaned girls with few family connections to fall back on in England. They were typically between fifteen and twenty-four years of age, and were required to be single. (Francis G. Mayer/CORBIS)

indentured servant stood a better chance of being able to blend into a new community than a slave whose skin color made her immediately suspect, penalties for attempted escape were harsh. The servant had to reimburse her master ten days for every day of service missed plus the cost of apprehending her. He was also free to impose a whipping of twenty to thirty-nine lashes. The grueling physical aspect of indentured servitude is attested to by studies that indicate that as many as one-quarter of indentured servants died before their terms were completed.

Upon completing a term of indenture, women were to be provided with "freedom dues," which varied depending on where she lived. Most women could count on being provided with fifteen bushels of corn and forty shillings in either money or goods. In Maryland servants were also entitled to new clothing and shoes. During the seventeenth century most former indentured servants would have been able to immediately find husbands.

Because former indentured servants tended to marry later than those without contractual obligations, these women had far fewer children than other women. An indentured servant lost up to eight of her childbearing years while she was in service. Such women might have only been able to produce two or three children who survived infancy, compared with the six to eight common among other early American women. Many of the settlers of Maryland and Virginia arrived as indentured servants. The toll of disease, high infant mortality, and late age at marriage meant these colonies were unable to reproduce their own populations through natural increase until well into the eighteenth century. These colonies needed to depend on heavy immigration and fresh batches of indentured servants to meet their labor needs.

The drastic shortage of white women might have helped some indentured women escape serving their full terms. Should a settler be willing to pay for the remaining balance of her indenture, a woman might be released from service to become lawfully married. Although this might have proven to be a romantic boon for some women, others chose it as the lesser of two evils.

Convict Labor

The experiences of women who were transported to the colonies as convict laborers were remarkably similar to those of indentured servants. In 1718 Parliament passed the Transportation Act, which permitted the large-scale deportation of criminals from England. Twenty percent of the convicts shipped to America were women. Throughout the eighteenth century the reliance on convict labor grew, and indentured servitude waned. Slaves and convicts were cheaper than indentured servants, and, as the sex ratio evened out and the population became better able to sustain itself, there was less demand for expensive indentured labor.

Between 1700 and 1775, convicts represented 25 percent of all immigrants from Britain. Their term was seven years for noncapital offenses and fourteen years for capital crimes. Most of the women convicts were desperately poor, unskilled, and had committed crimes out of economic necessity. Probably the greatest difference between female convicts and indentured servants was the humiliating treatment endured by the convicts. They were auctioned off in the marketplace in the same manner as a cow or bushel of tobacco. There was also a severe social stigma attached to being a convict that did not impinge on indentured servants. Following their term, many convicts chose to return to England rather than settle in America. The practice of sending convicts to America abruptly ceased with the outbreak of the American Revolution.

See also Household Responsibilities

Further Reading

Morgan, Kenneth. *Slavery and Servitude in Colonial North America: A Short History.* New York: New York University Press, 2000.

Salinger, Sharon V. "Send No More Women: Female Servants in Eighteenth-Century Philadelphia." *Pennsylvania Magazine of History and Biography* 107 (1983): 29–48.

Smith, Abbot Emerson. *Colonists in Bondage: White Servitude and Convict Labor in America, 1607–1776.* Chapel Hill: University of North Carolina Press, 1947.

Indian Captivity

One of the consequences of violent race relations between settlers and Indians was the taking of captives. Throughout the colonial period, thousands of white settlers, the majority of whom were women and children, were taken into captivity. The experience of these captives varied widely. Some were tortured or murdered in acts of revenge, and others were treated kindly. Some remained captive only a few weeks; others were held for years, decades, or the remainder of their lives. In all cases, the women captives would have been traumatized by the violent events preceding their capture. Indian raids usually focused on small, poorly defended outlying farms. Because Indians were rarely interested in taking grown men captive, in all likelihood these women witnessed the deaths of husbands, brothers, or sons.

The Indians took whites as captives for four reasons: to use as slaves, to sell to other Indians, to acquire ransom, or to adopt the captive into their tribe. Indians of northern New England were usually interested in ransoming their captives back to their families. The women who were intended for ransoming were harshly treated, forced to perform menial chores, malnourished, and often beaten and abused. Hampered by language difficulties, they would have had no way of knowing they were not going to be put to death. Negotiations for ransom could have taken weeks or months. The demanded sums were often far greater than members of a farming community, who rarely possessed liquid assets, could pay. Time and again ransom money was collected from donations or public funds. In many cases communities had been so badly devastated by Indian attacks that the survivors were in no position to take the time and resources necessary to locate kidnapped relatives.

Negotiation for ransom could take years, or collapse in the face of continued warfare. In the intervening years the captives would be used as slaves. Retaliatory raids were usually launched against the Indians, which further endangered the survival of the captives and increased the likelihood that the captives would be harshly treated. Captives were

The Extraordinary Adventures of Penelope Stout

Penelope Van Princis Stout (b. 1622) experienced the best and the worst of Indian captivity. In the 1640s she emigrated from Holland to New Amsterdam with her husband. Their ship was blown off course and wrecked against the coast of New Jersey. All passengers were able to scramble ashore, but Penelope's husband was too injured to travel. The other passengers set off on foot after promising to send help back to Penelope, who remained near the shoreline with her husband. Only a few hours later, hostile Indians found and attacked the stranded pair. They killed her husband, then beat and partially scalped Penelope. Knowing that her best chance for survival was to feign death, Penelope remained motionless until the Indians left. She dragged herself to a hollowed tree, where she remained for several days until discovered by a friendly Indian. This unnamed Indian took pity on Penelope, who was suffering from a fractured skull and terrible wounds to her scalp. He brought her to his village, where she was gradually nursed back to health. The Indian took Penelope by canoe to New Amsterdam, where she was taken in by sympathetic settlers. She soon married Richard Stout, with whom she ultimately had ten children. Folklore claims that the friendly Indian continued to visit Penelope in her new village and even warned her of an impending Indian attack in 1664. Because of the warning, the settlers were able to present a show of strength at the moment of attack, convincing the Indians to negotiate rather than attack. It is said that she died in 1732, thus living to the improbable age of 110. At the time of her death she was the matriarch of a family of 502 descendants.

Source: Waldrup, Carole Chandler. *Colonial Women: 23 Europeans Who Helped Build a Nation.* Jefferson, NC: McFarland, 1999.

forced to work for their own support, as well as to compensate the Indians for the wounds inflicted on them by the colonists. Women were set to raising crops, tending cattle, curing meat, preparing skins, and hauling water. They would have been forced to learn new ways of cooking, such as preparing boiled hominy for cakes that would be baked in an open fire. The preparation of animal skins for use in clothing or shelter would also have been new to most white women. Following the attack on the community of Martin's Hundred in 1622, many of the women were held as slaves for more than five years. Upon return, some of the women were so broken in body and spirit that they either died or returned to England.

Throughout the seventeenth and eighteenth centuries, Indians suffered heavy losses from war and disease. Indians of the middle and southern colonies were often motivated by a desire to replace dead family members with captives from the white community. Children were the most sought after captives, because the younger the child, the greater the likelihood they would accept assimilation into Indian society. Women were also considered far more likely to accept acculturation than were men.

Captives who were intended for adoption were usually forced to run through a gauntlet—a line of villagers armed with switches and clubs. This ritualized beating, though rarely fatal, was so severe as to cause many to lose consciousness. The gauntlet was an opportunity for the Indians to assuage their grief by inflicting revenge on one of the settlers. After this beating, it was as though the captive had the whiteness beaten out of her and was then ready to become a member of the community. At this point she would be stripped of her European clothes and dressed in Indian garb. A great celebration would take place, and the confused captive would be told she was now a sister or daughter of a particular family. Jewelry, feathers, face painting, and Indian hairstyles completed this physical transformation. The adopted captive was entitled to all of the deceased relative's clothing, titles, and sometimes even the same name.

Sexual abuse was almost never an issue for female captives. Although Europeans often viewed rape as an extension of war, such was not the case among Indians. As part of ritual purification before and during warfare, Indian warriors abstained from sex, making rape highly uncommon. Women who were adopted into Indian families were protected by incest taboos and the security offered by their new clan.

The Adventures of Mary Draper Ingles

Mary Ingles and her husband lived on the edge of the frontier in western Virginia. In July 1755, their tiny community was attacked by Shawnee Indians, and Mary, her two young sons, and her sister-in-law were captured. The husbands of both women were harvesting fields and escaped the attack. Mary and her family endured a grueling, 500-mile march into western Ohio. When they finally settled into an encampment near Cincinnati they encountered one other captive, "the old Dutch woman," whose name has not been recorded.

Mary's youngest child died soon after their capture, and her older boy, four-year-old Thomas, was adopted into a distant Indian village. Mary's sister-in-law was also sent to another village. Mary and the old Dutch woman were sent on a hunting party into southern Indiana when they conceived a plan of escape. They slipped away under cover of darkness, and began their journey homeward, staying close to the banks of the Ohio River as their only means of finding their way home. The exhausting journey lasted almost two months. The women were so starved for food the old Dutch woman lost her sanity and twice attacked Mary. After the second attack, Mary crossed the river to prevent further assaults. After a journey of almost 800 miles she reached her home. She was half-starved, missing several teeth, and almost naked, but Mary had survived.

Mary's sister-in-law was ransomed after six years, and her son Thomas returned to their home at age seventeen. Alexander Thom's novel, *Follow the River*, recounts Mary Draper Ingles's remarkable story.

Source: Jennings, Gary. "An Indian Captivity." *American Heritage* 19, no. 5 (1968): 64–71.

Although numerous women fought their captors or succeeded in escaping, a remarkably high number were successfully assimilated into Indian society. Given the brutal nature of their capture and the inherited cultural suspicion of Indians, the question of why so many women became willing captives is one that has fascinated historians for centuries.

Even Benjamin Franklin noted with bewilderment how English captives who had been repatriated frequently tried to return to their Indian families. Unless carefully watched, they seized "the first good opportunity of escaping again into the Woods, from whence there is no reclaiming them" (Benjamin Franklin to Peter Collinson, 9 May 1753).

A number of theories have been put forward to explain this phenomenon. As many as 20 percent of the women were either pregnant or nursing an infant at the time of their capture. Such a woman would probably have been more cooperative with her captors in hopes of protecting her child. Captivity removed some women from undesirable circumstances. Abigail Willey of New Hampshire had made numerous complaints against her husband for insane jealousy and recurring cruelty. Following her 1689 capture, she successfully resisted attempts to secure her return.

The most frequently cited explanation for why women chose to remain living with Indians was because they had married and given birth to Indian children. Such women almost never willingly returned to white society. Knowing that the stigma of having been intimate with an Indian male was high and that their children were unlikely to be accepted with open arms, such women usually chose to remain with their adopted families. Mary Jemison was the most famous woman of the colonial period who chose to remain living with her new family among the Seneca Indians.

Some women resisted repatriation to white society because their original families were scattered or dead. Having found a replacement family, they were content to remain in the relative security of their Indian home. Because these women did not return to white society, we have no written record to explain their decisions. The best we can do is examine the numerous writings left by women who did return for clues as to what was so appealing about Indian society. Although some women, including Hannah Duston and Mary Rowlandson, spoke of horrific experiences, others had come to respect the Indian way of life. They wrote of the strong sense of community and egalitarian family structure. Standards of living were more primitive than those for white families, but daily life among the Indians was not consumed by the endless chores that characterized the workload of a typical farmer's wife. Also absent was the rigid morality that was highly restrictive for women in early America. Women who were raised to believe God was harsh and punitive might have found the less restrictive world of Indian spirituality a more welcoming environment. These women brought skills to their new environments that would have made them valuable to the community. Knitting, sewing, and the ability to serve as translators would all have been highly valued. Perhaps having a position of importance in Indian society was more appealing than a life of drudgery in white society.

In some rare early cases, white settlers took captives from the Indians. Most of these captives were female or children. Very early Indian captives were intended for slavery, although this almost never occurred. Within a few years the women were able to escape back to their families. Attempts made to convert Indian children to Christianity were met with lukewarm success. These children tended to be socially isolated and were usually treated as servants or dependents. Such children rarely embraced white society and often chose to return to their Indian families when given the opportunity.

See also Duston, Hannah Emerson; Jemison, Mary; Rowlandson, Mary

Further Reading
Axtell, James. *The Invasion Within: The Contest of Cultures in Colonial North America.* New York: Oxford University Press, 1986.

———. "White Indians of Colonial America." In *Colonial America: Essays in Politics and Social Development,* eds. Stanley N. Katz and John M. Murrin. New York: Knopf, 1983.

Fausz, J. Frederick. "The Missing Women of Martin's Hundred." *American History* 33 (1998): 56–62.

Fickes, Michael L. "They Could Not Endure that Yoke: The Captivity of Pequot Women and Children after the War of 1637." *New England Quarterly* 73 (2000): 58–81.

McDaid, Jennifer Davis. "Living on a Frontier Part: Virginia Women among the Indians, 1622–1794." *Virginia Cavalcade* 42 (1993): 100–111.

Namias, June. *White Captives: Gender and Ethnicity on the American Frontier.* Chapel Hill: University of North Carolina Press, 1993.

Indian Women

The diversity of cultures among Native Americans makes generalizations about how Indian women lived a daunting task. It has been estimated that at the time of European contact with the Americas, more than two thousand languages flourished among the Indians, representing greater linguistic diversity than anywhere else in the world. For the purposes of this essay, the Indian cultures of the eastern seaboard will be studied. The Algonquian and Iroquois cultures were dominant in this region. Several distinctive tribes considered themselves culturally aligned with the Iroquois, including the Mohawks, Oneidas, Tuscaroras, Onondagas, Cayugas, and Senecas. Among the more notable Algonquian tribes were the Pequot, Wampanoag, Narraganset, Nipmuck, and Powhatan.

There was no unitary view of women's proper place within native society. Each Indian culture had its own set of traditions and beliefs, but some broad generalizations of the major life issues can be offered for the eastern seaboard Indians.

The Life Cycle

Young children would have had a close bond with their mothers. Indian women breastfed their children for several years, and the contraceptive effect of this practice spaced children far enough apart so that a child had her mother's primary attention for the first few years of life. Indian women often strapped their babies to their backs and brought them to work in the fields or to gather berries. When women engaged in more physical activities, such as gathering firewood or constructing tepees, they left their small children in the care of older women.

Young Indian girls spent their days with light chores, such as learning to grind corn or prepare skins to be used for clothing. They had little formal education and learned subsistence skills primarily through following their mother's example.

Menstruation marked an important turning point in a girl's life. She abruptly left childhood behind as soon as she began her period, and rites of passage into womanhood were observed with solemnity. Most Indian cultures viewed menstruation as a powerful, but potentially contaminating, event. Blood represented both life and death, and a menstruating woman was believed to possess heightened spiritual powers, which could be used for good or evil. Even the glance of a menstruating woman might be enough to bring bad luck. In order to protect women from being blamed for random tragedies, menstruating women were isolated in a hut for a few days. During their first period, girls were given almost no food or water, nor were they allowed to bathe. Upon the completion of her period, she would be ritually bathed and given a new set of adult clothing. Henceforth, her community regarded her as a woman.

Most women isolated themselves during menstruation, although customs varied from tribe to tribe. Some had special "moon houses" where women retreated during their period. In some tribes menstruating women were allowed to remain in their home, but other members of the family did not join them. Close contacts, especially sexual relations, were off-limits to a menstruating woman.

Indian women became sexually active at a young age. Premarital sex was condoned in almost all Indian cultures, and there was no shame associated with the loss of virginity. One of the few sexual taboos was a public display of affection. Sexuality was condoned, but not to be flaunted. Kissing was unknown among Indian cultures until the arrival of Europeans.

When a young man wished to marry a girl, he usually sent an intermediary to ask the consent of the girl's parents. Girls were almost never forced into marriages they found distasteful. If the match was approved, the marriage was celebrated with feasting and an exchange of gifts. In most societies, the new couple moved in with the bride's parents for at least a year. In some tribes, notably the Micmac Indians of the northeast, the couple abstained from sex for the first year of marriage in order to cement their friendship.

Native American women at a menstrual lodge. (Library of Congress)

Indians did not view marriage as necessarily permanent or monogamous. Men often took more than one wife. Should a man die, it was considered proper for his brother to marry the widow. Tribal chiefs often took numerous wives to solidify family alliances. If a couple proved unhappy with one another, divorce was a simple matter. A woman usually set her husband's belongings outside the home as a clear indication he was no longer welcome. Indian women were not dependent on their husbands for economic support. Women provided the bulk of agricultural produce, and the communal nature of their society meant she had no trouble acquiring the other necessities of life through barter.

Motherhood was a central feature of life for Indian women. The period of pregnancy, like menstruation, was believed to endow a woman with heightened spiritual power. Each tribe had different customs for childbirth. Special huts were set aside for laboring women. Some were expected to give birth entirely alone, although the assistance of midwives, sisters, or shamans was common among most tribes. What was almost universal among Native Americans was the expectation of stoicism on the part of laboring mothers. Women were not supposed to cry out during labor, and they viewed childbirth as a test of courage. This stoicism was considered so odd by Europeans, they believed Indian women felt no pain during childbirth. This mistaken assumption gave rise to harmful conclusions. Some concluded that Indians were so far outside the realm of civilization they were spared the biblical charge that women should suffer great pain in childbirth. Others equated Indians with animals, which also appeared to feel little pain during childbirth.

Indian child-rearing customs were considered lenient by European observers. Children were allowed to play and had few responsibilities, and obedience did not rank high in the qualities valued by Indian families. Despite the permissive nature of child rearing, Indian women took great pride in the children, because the admirable qualities of their children were a reflection on their skills as a mother. As with Catholic and Quaker families of the era, guilt was the primary technique used to shame a child into proper behavior. Conversely, praise was used lavishly to encourage brave, adventurous, or stoic behaviors.

Death customs varied greatly, but most Indians believed in some form of afterlife. The possessions of the dead were divided among their friends, rather than passing them on to the children. During the mourning period, women dressed slovenly and did not groom their hair. The closer the relative, and the higher the rank of the deceased, the longer a woman was expected to mourn. Among Algonquians, a woman was to mourn her husband for one to two years, then marry her deceased husband's brother or another man selected by her in-laws.

Matrilineal Family Organization

One of the Indian customs most curious to Europeans was the matrilineal family line among many Native American tribes, particularly noticeable among the Iroquois. When a man married, he joined his wife's family. If they divorced, his children remained with the mother.

Matrilineal societies tend to allow women greater power in the tribal decision making. Among the Iroquois, councils of senior women were known as *ohwachiras,* and they had the authority to appoint the men who would represent the village at tribal councils. The senior women usually attended important tribal meetings. Although they rarely spoke, they consulted with their male representatives prior to meetings and had the power to remove them if the women were dissatisfied with their representation.

Agriculture played a major role in provisioning the village with their food supply. Although men supplemented the diet with their hunting, the agricultural produce grown by women typically accounted for 75 percent of the calories consumed by Indians. Women had authority over how the produce was distributed among villagers. Some have speculated they could use this power to thwart warring expeditions that met with their disapproval, because if the women withheld provisions, it amounted to a veto of the campaign. Should a war take place, women had the power of life, death, or slavery over the prisoners of war.

Although it cannot be asserted that women were dominant in any Native American culture, they were not as subordinate as European women, whose entire legal and economic status was dependent on their husbands. Most Indian women were capable of supporting themselves. There were no legal or social prohibitions against divorce, and Indian women did not depend on men for economic or emotional support. Indian marriages seemed to have been motivated primarily by companionship and could be easily dissolved when this need was no longer being fulfilled.

Matrilineal organizations began unraveling after prolonged contact with European cultures. Indians were anxious to trade their furs for European goods such as iron tools, guns, needles, kettles, and fishing nets. Women's activities were diverted away from agriculture and redirected to the preparation of animal skins for trade. Many tribes abandoned self-sufficiency altogether in the quest to produce the more highly valued furs. With their role as primary food provider undermined, women's authority within the village began to erode.

Spirituality

Religious tradition varied tremendously among the ethnic groups. Some Indian societies had highly complex cosmologies explaining creation and afterlife, while others relied on a more generalized spirituality defined primarily by respect for nature. Most relied on ritualized ceremonies in which women figured prominently.

Beliefs in creation of the earth usually featured a woman. The Iroquois tell of a woman who fell from the sky, after mating either with the Sky or Moon god. This Earth Mother gave birth to a daughter, who then bore twin children, representing good and evil. From the Earth Mother's body then sprang the holy triad of corn, beans, and squash. The Earth Mother was equated with the Moon, because lunar calculations are used in the planting and cultivation of crops. Furthermore, women's mysterious monthly cycles appeared to be timed to the passages of the moon.

Among the eastern Indian tribes, in which agriculture figured prominently, women's participation in spiritual rituals was paramount. Women bore primary responsibility for tending and harvesting crops, and an annual calendar of religious ceremonies marked each stage of the plant cycle. Just after corn shoots first appeared, Iroquois women celebrated a corn sprouting ceremony, in which the spirits were entertained so they would continue to bless the crop.

Indians of both sexes read great significance into visions and dreams, believed to have been sent by spiritual forces to guide people in their life choices. The visions were rarely straightforward and usually needed interpretation. Highly spiritual people were more likely to receive and interpret visions correctly. Women who were menstruating were believed to have sensitized spiritual insight, which could be developed during a vision quest. All vision quests required a person to fast and be in isolation for one to four days. Vision quests were undertaken for a number of reasons, including the need to mark the onset of puberty, to prepare for becoming a shaman, or to seek spiritual guidance.

Following the arrival of Europeans, some Indian women were attracted to Christianity. The first Europeans encountered by eastern seaboard Indians were trappers or explorers who had little interest in missionary activities. Even in the absence of proselytizing, Indians were impressed with the strange tools, healing medicines, and inexplicable power of these travelers. Many attributed the apparent supremacy of the Europeans to a more powerful God. When missionaries began moving into Indian communities, they had a curious, if not always receptive, audience. Women and young adolescents tended to be the most receptive to missionaries, possibly because they remained in the villages while men were often gone on extended hunting trips.

Indians who accepted Christianity did so with varying degrees of enthusiasm. Some merely grafted aspects of Christianity onto their existing religious traditions, whereas others, such as Kateri Tekakwitha, ardently embraced the full spectrum of Christian teaching. Indians who eagerly accepted Christianity were viewed with suspicion by their fellow villagers and were often encouraged to leave the tribe for a new community of "praying Indians." A handful of these towns were established throughout the colonial period. The Christian Indians in these villages were caught between two worlds, not wholly trusted by the Europeans and despised by Indians who viewed them as traitors.

Recreation

The distinction between work and play was blurred for Indian women. They lived in an intensely cooperative society, and most of their days would have been spent in the company of other women. Their chores, whether it was tending fields, making baskets, or preparing hides, would have been performed alongside other women. A great deal of socializing would have interspersed the chores throughout the day. Sometimes a chore such as pottery or basket making could be elevated into an artistic recreation by embellishing the product with carefully planned details. Sporting contests were sometimes held between tribes for recreation, but were also used to resolve disputes in a peaceful manner.

Sporting events were more common for Indian women than for European women. Indian girls engaged in physical tests of strength and dexterity, such as footraces and ball games. They usually competed only with other girls, because boys had their own sets of games and rituals. All forms of ball games were highly popular. Kick ball, dodgeball, juggling, and volleyball (without the net) were all commonly played by girls.

Intertribal athletic contests were held in which the men competed in games such as lacrosse. Although women did not participate in male sports, they were spectators and facilitators.

At the end of the day, singing and dancing were common. Both men and women participated in the dance, though the dancers did not touch one another. Religious ceremonies often involved dances that could last for hours.

See also Colonization, Effect on Indian Women; Indian Women and Leadership; Indian Women and Work

Further Reading

Axtell, James, ed. *The Indian Peoples of Eastern America: A Documentary History of the Sexes.* New York: Oxford University Press, 1981.

Berkin, Carol. *First Generations: Women in Colonial America.* New York: Hill and Wang, 1996.

Brown, Judith K. "Economic Organization and the Position of Women among the Iroquois." *Ethnohistory* 17 (Autumn 1970): 151–167.

Nash, Gary B. *Red, White, and Black: The Peoples of Early America.* Englewood Cliffs, NJ: Prentice-Hall, 1974.

Ruether, Rosemary Radford, and Rosemary Skinner Keller, eds. *Women and Religion in America: The Colonial and Revolutionary Periods.* San Francisco: Harper and Row, 1983.

Indian Women and Leadership

The role of women in American Indian society is often either glamorized or belittled. Some paint a picture of wonderfully enlightened tribes where women were revered for their contributions and active participants in the tribal decision-making process. There is some evidence to support this, including the matrilineal kinship patterns among many Indians of the northeast. Other characterizations of Indian women are grim, appearing to be little more than drudges for Indian men and victims of European aggression. The truth is far more complex than either stereotypical image. The status of women varied dramatically across Indian cultures and changed as the circumstance of each Indian village evolved through time.

Indians had many levels of political organization. At the most basic level was the clan, a group of closely related families. They were often organized in a matrilineal pattern, with the children joining the clan of the mother. It is on the clan level that women had most influence, making the primary decisions about food production and religious ceremonies. The next level was the village, which was the basic political and territorial unit of Indian society. Villages contained several extended family clans and usually had a few hundred members. They were presided over by a sachem and a chief. Chiefs made decisions about warfare and diplomacy, and sachems were responsible for most of the internal issues, such as the distribution of land and collection of tribute. Tribes were a collection of villages that shared ethnic and familial bonds. Within this hierarchy, women had substantial power only in the lower levels, but some exceptional women rose to positions of power on the village and tribal levels.

Sachems

Sachems ruled over Indian villages, making most of the decisions that affected internal affairs. Sachems were traditionally men, but on occasion a woman became a sachem. Most female sachems inherited the office from a deceased husband or brother, but this was clearly an exception to the norm. Women who became sachems needed to be strong public orators, intelligent, and trusted to be wise and fair leaders.

When the English arrived in Jamestown in 1607, they heard rumors of "the Queen of Appamatuck," who ruled one of the Powhatan villages. In New England, the early English settlers dealt with the Massachusetts queen, who was struggling to maintain an alliance among several Indian villages. The Indians had been decimated by an outbreak of bubonic plague that had run its course shortly before the arrival of the English. There are fleeting references to numerous other female sachems dating to the first half of the seventeenth century, but we know almost nothing of these women, or how they coped with the onslaught of European settlement.

A few female sachems made a more lasting mark through close association with the English. Awashonks was sachem of the Saconnet band of Indians, part of the Wampanoag confederacy living near Rhode Island. She ruled at a time when tensions between the English and Indians were about to boil over into King Philip's War, one of the most violent periods of warfare in seventeenth-century America. In 1671 she agreed to a nonaggression pact with the English and loaned some of her warriors to fight against Metacom, also known as King Philip. In exchange, her people were spared the massacre of Indians that followed the routing of Metacom.

Weetamoo is the other famous sachem involved in King Philip's War. She succeeded her father as sachem of the Pocasset village of the Wampanoag confederacy. As such, she had influence over 300 warriors, whom she used in support of Metacom and his quest to oust the English from further encroachment into Indian territory. Weetamoo is remembered primarily because of the accounts of her recorded by Indian captive Mary Rowlandson, who characterized her as a "severe and proud dame." Weetamoo was considered very beautiful, and Rowlandson records the sachem took care to neatly arrange her hair and wear an impressive array of jewelry and beadwork each day. Near the end of the war, Weetamoo and her surviving band of warriors were on the run. What ultimately happened to them is uncertain, but it is believed that Weetamoo drowned in 1676 during the final weeks of the war.

It is possible there were more female sachems than were noted in the records. Ethnohistorians have tended to consider all Indian leaders male unless otherwise noted. It is difficult to determine gender from the names English colonists transcribed centuries ago, and it is possible that some of these leaders were female.

See also Colonization, Effect on Indian Women; Ward, Nancy

Further Reading

Berkin, Carol. *First Generations: Women in Colonial America.* New York: Hill and Wang, 1996.

Grumet, Robert Steven. "Sunksquaws, Shamans, and Tradeswomen: Middle Atlantic Coastal Algonkian Women During the 17th and 18th Centuries." In *Women and Colonization: Anthropological Perspectives,* eds. Mona Etienne and Eleanor Leacock. New York: Praeger, 1980.

Indian Women and Work

Indian women had a full range of varied work responsibilities. The primary duty of women living among the eastern seaboard and woodland tribes was the cultivation of crops, usually corn, beans, and squash. So central were these three crops to Native American diet, they were referred to as the three sisters.

Agriculture and Food Preparation

Without iron tools or draft animals, Native American agricultural practices were markedly different than those on European farms. A woman used a stick to create a hole, into which she dropped and covered a seed. Hoes were made of deer scapula fastened to long wooden handles. Women carefully nurtured the crops throughout the season, clearing away weeds and pulling off pests. Many women would have had a baby strapped on their backs as they performed these chores. Each field contained a mix of plants, with beans growing up the tall corn stalks and the squash growing close to the ground. The plants provided complementary nutrients to the soil, allowing a high-yield crop from a small patch of cleared land. The women staggered their planting cycle across several small, acre-wide fields, so that the workload would be evenly spaced throughout the summer.

Harvesting and preparation of the crops were also female responsibilities. Corn was ground into a meal using stone pestles against large wooden mortars. Nuts such as acorns, hickory nuts, chestnuts, and walnuts were ground into flour, mixed with water, and baked over fires to make flat breads.

Women walked the nearby woods to gather berries, edible greens, firewood, nuts, and water. This sort of foraging was done daily, and depending on the amount of firewood and water retrieved, could be a physically demanding task. *Tuckahoe* was a word for a variety of tuber or fungi plants from which a starchy paste could be made. Common sources for tuckahoe were arrow arum, sweet flag, and wild calla. Most of these plants grew in marshes, and the roots could be as deep as twelve to eighteen inches in the mud. Retrieving such roots without the aid of iron tools was a highly physical task. Two or three adults usually surrounded the plant, whose leaves floated in the marsh water, and worked the roots free by digging their feet into the mud. The roots would be cooked in a pit beneath a slow fire for at least a day. After they were dried, the roots were reduced to flour through use of mortar and pestle. The result was a bland, unappetizing flour, the taste of which had to be disguised by other foods. Tuckahoe was a labor-intensive crop, but was essential to survival in years of drought when the corn crop failed.

Textiles and Manufactured Goods

Women were responsible for the production of most of the manufactured goods found in an Indian village, including leather, pottery, and baskets. Women also assisted in the construction of tepees and huts. The creation of baskets was a labor-intensive activity. Women gathered and prepared the reeds that would be used to weave into baskets and mats. These reeds were usually gathered in marshes and transported home via canoe. Because of the biodegradable nature and heavy use of these items, baskets and mats had to be replaced frequently.

Obtaining clay for pottery also took place at the water's edge. The clay was kneaded with sand or crushed shells to serve as a tempering agent, which was necessary if the pot was to withstand changes in temperature. Women made pots by pinching a small ball of clay into a dish shape and placing it into a hole in the ground. Coils of additional clay were layered onto the initial dish, shaping it taller. The coils were slowly layered, so as not to cause the pot to slump under the weight. The pot was finished by smoothing the surface free of the coil lines. The work was a slow and careful process. A large pot could take a woman two days to build. The finished product was fired in a shallow pit, rendering it suitable for cooking.

The primary responsibility for the preparation of leather fell to women. The tanning process took several days and involved stretching the hide on a wooden frame, repeatedly scraping it free of tissue and hair, soaking, and restretching. After preparing the leather women might sew it into clothing, blankets, or sacks.

Gender and Labor

Europeans considered the distinctive gender division of labor among Native Americans strange and contemptible. It appeared that Indian women were little more than overworked drudges, responsible for all aspects of agriculture, food preparation, and domestic chores. Indian men appeared to have few or no responsibilities aside from bringing home an occasional deer, which the women carefully butchered, cooked, tanned the hide, made needles from the bones, and stitched clothing from the leather. The immensely disproportionate workload appeared contemptible to European settlers, who believed women ought to be sheltered from demanding physical labor.

Indian women performed more physically demanding labor than European women, but the workload was equitably divided between Indian men and women. The misperception that Indian men were pathologically lazy can be attributed to the distorted impression formed by Europeans visitors to Indian camps during the summer months. Most contact between the settlers and Indians occurred in the summer, because it was the season both cultures had the time and favorable weather conditions to trade. Settlers inevitably saw Indian women in the full swing of agricultural chores, preparing food, mending tents and clothing, and caring for children. Indian men appeared to be playing games, smoking, or idly making arrows. Although the pace of work in the summer quickened for women, it was one of the few times men were not far from home hunting or trading. This was their opportunity to replenish their supply of bows, arrows, and spears. They engaged in sporting activities to keep fit. They trained their sons in physical games, so they would be prepared to become hunters and warriors. Autumn, winter, and spring were devoted to the physically demanding hunting activities, performed out of sight of European observers.

Europeans formed an impression of Indian women as overworked, subservient drudges. The Algonquian word *squaw* was a general term for an Indian woman. It was adopted by Europeans, but over time took on the derogatory overtones of a passive and slave-like Indian woman.

In fact, Indian women had a great deal of freedom within their society. A woman was able to leave a marriage with ease if she felt mistreated. Her ability to supply herself with food and material goods meant she was not dependent upon the good graces of any man who attempted to take advantage of her labor. Almost all of the work performed by Indian women was done in the company of other women. Contemporary observers often commented on the cheerful demeanor of Indian women, who gossiped and laughed throughout their chores.

Further Reading

Berkin, Carol. *First Generations: Women in Colonial America.* New York: Hill and Wang, 1996.

Brown, Judith K. "Economic Organization and the Position of Women among the Iroquois." *Ethnohistory* 17 (Autumn 1970): 151–167.

Roundtree, Helen C. "Powhatan Indian Women: The People Captain John Smith Barely Saw." *Ethnohistory* 45 (1988): 1–29.

Infanticide

Single women who gave birth to an illegitimate child in early America faced appalling consequences. Such women were often publicly shamed through whippings or time in the stocks. Living in small communities where there was little place to hide from a checkered past, the woman's reputation was ruined for life. Her odds of marriage dropped, and unless she had the support of a well-to-do and sympathetic family, she was likely to face a life of extreme poverty and isolation.

Although rates of premarital sex were not as high as they are in contemporary society, early Americans had little means for controlling pregnancy. There was no reliable form of contraception other than breastfeeding, which was obviously not an option for young, single women. Methods of abortion were primitive and generally ineffective, leaving unmarried pregnant women with few choices but to carry the baby to term. Paralyzed with fear and unwilling to face the bleak repercussions of bearing a bastard, some women hid their pregnancies as long as possible. Although many women's pregnancies were discovered and means for supporting the child were found, some were successful in carrying and delivering their children in secret. At this point they had only three options. Some fell upon the mercy of their employer, parents, or lover in looking for assistance. Some abandoned the infant in a place where it was likely to be discovered and cared for. Others concealed the birth through infanticide, usually by abandoning the child in the woods or drowning it.

When the body of a dead newborn was found, it was almost impossible to determine if it had been born dead, died of natural means, or had been killed through violence or neglect. A 1624 English law resolved this problem by declaring that any woman who concealed a birth shall be assumed to have given birth to a live child unless she could conclusively prove otherwise. The law assumed that women who hid their pregnancies and gave birth in private were anxious to hide their sin from the community and were likely to have hostile intentions toward the infant. Women who concealed the birth of a child who subsequently died were to be sentenced to death. Most American colonies adopted the English law, and several women were hanged after the bodies of their newborn infants had been discovered.

Most women charged with infanticide were poor, single women. Many of them were indentured servants, who knew they would have one to three years added to their term of service if they gave birth to a child. Free women who were employed knew they were likely to lose their job, as a nursing mother was unlikely to keep apace with a normal workload. Few people wanted to be associated with a woman of dissolute character, and mistresses were likely to dismiss any servant girl who was guilty of fornication. Most women would have seen firsthand how unmarried mothers became social outcasts in their communities and knew their likelihood of ever marrying would plummet if they had a child. Pregnant single women could even be driven out of town as an undesirable. This was especially likely to happen if the town officials believed she lacked means of supporting herself and there was no family to either take her in or defend her. The severe social pressures that discouraged single motherhood might have been exacerbated by hormonal depressions and mood swings.

In the rare instances that a well-to-do defendant was charged with killing her newborn, juries were more likely to accept her version of events. Anne Tayloe was a wealthy planter's widow in 1714 when rumors began circulating she had given birth to a child, killed it, and buried it in her yard. There was strong evidence of her guilt, including the body of the child and eyewitness testimony from a servant and a slave who had seen Anne burying an object in the yard. Tayloe flatly denied having been pregnant, and she was ultimately released despite the strong evidence against her. Despite her legal good fortune, Tayloe's reputation never recovered, and she was subsequently brought to court for immoral behavior.

Infanticide was a woman's crime. Men were rarely charged, even when the paternity of the infant was known. In some cases an accused woman claimed the father of the child participated in the concealment or murder of the infant. In 1786, the murdered bodies of twin babies were discovered in the Pennsylvania woods. Twenty-seven-year-old tavern maid Elizabeth Wilson was quickly identified as the mother, but pointed to the infants' father as the murderer. Wilson claimed he had stomped the children to death when she threatened to take him to court for child support. Wilson was hanged, but her lover was never apprehended or brought to trial. Many people were uncomfortable for sentencing Wilson to death when it appeared she was prepared to raise the children. There was sympathy for a woman who might have feared her lover's brutality could turn against her if she reported him.

In part because of the Elizabeth Wilson case, there was a shift in the attitudes toward concealed births in the late 1780s. Concealing a birth was viewed as a lack of judgment that should be punished in jail, not on the gallows. The burden of proof shifted, and the state had to prove the child had been born alive, rather than the mother proving it was born dead. A woman could help her case if she could prove she intended to care for the child, usually by having infant clothes and bedding prepared prior to delivery of the child. Following the American Revolution the role of mothers became romanticized, and it was difficult for juries to believe a woman would choose to harm her own child. Juries became more willing to accept a woman's story, so long as she expressed remorse and love for her infant.

Judging from the number and detail of information relating to abandoned or killed infants, it appears that people were fascinated with this topic. Babies found in wells, ponds, or abandoned in the woods were noted in local newspapers. If the mother had not yet been determined, the articles provided enough details of the infant's location and approximate date of birth in hopes of soliciting people with information. The confessions of young women after their convictions were often printed and distributed in town as a means of warning others of the folly young girls could be led into. Other stories focused on abandoned babies. It is clear some of these infants were cared for, wrapped carefully in clothing and left on doorsteps where they were sure to be found soon. One baby found in 1807 Philadelphia was "sewed up in a double blanket with a straw pillow under its head and a sugar teat in its mouth." (Smith 1999, 178).

The case of slave women who killed their children must be treated separately. There are a handful of cases in which slave women killed their children in the face of despair over their condition. In 1787 Spanish Florida, the slave woman Juana was informed she was to be sold to a new owner in Cuba, but her two children (five-year-old Juan and two-year-old Isabel) would remain in Florida. Juana drowned her children rather than see them be raised alone in a harsh environment, then attempted to flee. She was apprehended and found guilty of murder. Despite the horror of her crime, she was not sentenced to execution in accordance with homicide law, but rather received a severe flogging and sale to a new master. There was clearly a recognition that Juana acted not from attempt to cover her own illicit behavior, but rather out of despair.

See also Crime and Punishment; Fornication; Mothers, Single

Further Reading

Gilje, Paul A. "Infant Abandonment in Early Nineteenth Century New York City: Three Cases." *Signs* 8 (1983): 580–590.

Harris, Sharon M. "Feminist Theories and Early American Studies." *Early American Literature* 34 (1999): 86–93.

Hoffer, Peter C., and N. E. H. Hull. *Murdering Mothers: Infanticide in England and New England, 1558–1803.* New York: New York University Press, 1981.

Hull, N. E. H. *Female Felons: Women and Serious Crime in Colonial Massachusetts.* Urbana: University of Illinois Press, 1987.

Smith, Merril D. "Unnatural Mothers: Infanticide, Motherhood, and Class in the Mid-Atlantic, 1730–1830." In *Over the Threshold: Intimate Violence in Early America,* eds. Christine Daniels and Michael V. Kennedy. New York: Routledge, 1999.

Infertility

See Gynecological Issues

Inheritance

See Wills and Inheritance

Insanity

See Mental Illness

Interracial Marriage

From the outset of the European colonization of America, there was close contact between Europeans, Native Americans, and Africans. Because the overwhelming majority of people coming from Europe and Africa were male, the skewed sex ratio created pressure to form unions with Indian women. Such a pattern was exceptionally strong in Latin America, where almost no Spanish women immigrated to the colonies. There was far less interracial mixing in North America, but it occurred with regularity until the sex ratio came into balance in the eighteenth century. The exception to this pattern was in the New England colonies, where Puritans encouraged immigration in family groups. A normal sex ratio, as well as a reluctance to intermingle with non-Christians, resulted in little sexual mingling among Europeans and Indians or African slaves. New England settlers were able to transplant their traditions to America with ease, unlike people in settlements in the middle and southern colonies. There, the unbalanced sex ratio, lack of family structure, and frontier conditions created an environment in which European men were willing to shed restrictive social norms.

One notable feature of interracial marriage and sex in North America was that it did not result in widespread acculturation and assimilation, as it did in Latin America. This might be because the sex ratio in the British colonies came into balance relatively quickly, which never occurred in the Spanish colonies.

White/Indian

During the earliest phases of settlement, both French and English authorities endorsed marriage between white men and Indian women. Recognizing the opportunity to improve relations with the Indians, the French government even offered dowries to settlers who married Indian women. French fur traders were especially eager to take Indian wives. Usually traveling alone deep into the American wilderness, these traders benefited from healthy relations with the Indians, for both ensuring basic survival and securing access to hunting

Marriage of Pocahontas to John Rolfe, Virginia Colony. Hand-colored halftone of painting by Henry Breuckner. (North Wind / North Wind Picture Archives)

grounds. The need for human companionship also played a role. Living a solitary existence in the wilderness doubtlessly made a liaison with an Indian woman a welcome solution to a man's loneliness. Indian women likewise benefited from affiliation with a European. When a European trader married into an Indian community, he increased the prestige of the tribe. Access to trade and friendly relations with European settlements benefited the entire tribe. Consequently, the woman married to the trader assumed increased authority and prestige within her tribe. The fur traders' wives rarely joined European communities. The extent of their acculturation to European ways was usually limited to learning a smattering of French or English, possible religious conversion, and some interaction at Jesuit missions. They served as cultural mediators between Indian and European communities, but these women clearly retained their native identity, language, dress, and customs.

Perhaps the most famous Indian-white marriage was that between Pocahontas and John Rolfe in 1614. Although it is likely that both partners had affection for one another, it was clearly a marriage motivated by political expediency. Requiring the permission of both the deputy governor of Virginia and the Indian king Powhatan, both sides wished to see an expansion of trade and a reduction in conflict between the settlers and Indians. During Pocahontas's lifetime these objectives were achieved, although they did not long survive her death.

The primary motivations for interracial mixing between Indians and English colonists were sex, military alliance, and trade. All of these objectives could be accomplished without marriage. Indian communities did not condemn women for premarital sexual relations, and alliances could be cemented without the formal bonds of marriage. In almost all cases it was European men who entered into relations with Indian women. Children born to such unions almost always remained within the Indian culture. Such children were fully embraced by Indians, but were tainted in the eyes of Europeans.

Few white women entered relationships with Indian men. The major exception was when women were captured and adopted into Indian communities. If a girl was captured while an adolescent or younger, there was a good chance that she would elect to remain with her new family, even when offered the opportunity to return to European civilization. Speculation for this curious phenomenon is rampant. Mary Jemison, taken captive in 1758, stated that by the time she was offered the opportunity to return she had a number of Indian children she did not believe would be warmly embraced by the English colonists. Other women reported they had formed loving ties to their new families and husbands. Some historians speculate that women might have found Indian culture, free of European restrictions, a more meaningful and untroubled way of life.

One of the few cases in which a white woman freely chose to marry an Indian occurred in 1740, when Molly Barber, the daughter of well-to-do Connecticut parents, eloped with James Chaugham, a Narraganset Indian. The couple fled to the rural area of Barkhamsted, where they created a small, mixed-race community known as "the Lighthouse." Stagecoach drivers dubbed the community the Lighthouse because the cracks in the inhabitant's cabin walls emitted firelight, guiding coaches along their way. For over a century, families of blacks, Indians, and whites found refuge at the Lighthouse.

After the sex ratio came into a healthy balance in the eighteenth century, unions with Indian women were stigmatized. Still envious of the excellent relations between the French and the Indians, American authorities made a few halfhearted attempts to encourage English-Indian marriages. In 1784 Patrick Henry proposed a bill that would offer tax relief, free education, and a financial bonus to white men who married Indian women. This and similar bills were defeated, but they document the government's attempt to encourage marriage along such lines. Despite the wishes of the government, society was growing increasingly suspicious of interracial mingling, and both North Carolina and Virginia ultimately passed legislation outlawing Indian-European marriage.

White/Black

Relations between Africans and Europeans were complex in early America. Most Africans were slaves imported into the southern colonies, where the unbalanced sex ratio resulted in sexual liaisons between slave owners and black women. Even after the sex ratio among Europeans came into balance, sexual contact between white men and black women continued unabated. Such liaisons rarely resulted in marriage, and little attempt was made to regulate these relationships.

During the earliest period of colonization, Africans brought to the colonies did not remain enslaved for the duration of their lives. Like white indentured servants, these Africans eventually earned their freedom after a predetermined number of years. The small community of free blacks occasionally chose to intermarry with whites, usually fellow indentured servants. Complications with such marriages arose after slavery became a lifelong condition. When a white woman chose to marry a black slave, the status of the children and the wife were ambiguous. In 1661, Maryland passed a law clearly intended to wipe out such ambiguities and discourage interracial marriage. Any white woman who married a slave was to become enslaved for the duration of her husband's life. Any children born to the marriage would be permanently enslaved. This law backfired when it became apparent that white masters were coercing their female indentured servants to marry slaves, so they might gain economic advantage by acquiring an additional slave, plus future child slaves. The law was modified in 1681 so that if a master consented to the union, the woman and her children would retain their free status.

Although there were social stigmas associated with black-white marriages, the flurry of laws prohibiting interracial marriage make it clear that such unions were occurring with enough frequency to call for legal constraint. Marriage between blacks and whites was outlawed in Virginia (1691), Massachusetts (1705), and Maryland (1715). Delaware, Pennsylvania, North Carolina, South Carolina, and Georgia all passed legislation that gradually prohibited interracial marriage in the eighteenth century.

Despite the infrequency of marriages between blacks and whites, the fact that there were numerous mulatto children indicated that sexual relations between the races had not ceased. Further laws were passed to punish interracial sexual activity. Any white woman who bore a mulatto child was fined, and in many cases the child would be bound out into a life of servitude until he or she reached the age of thirty. Although treated more leniently, white men who fathered children of black slaves were also occasionally fined, and the children of such unions clearly remained slaves their entire lives. Curiously, the laws against interracial sex punished only the white partner. This was possibly an acknowledgment that slaves often had little choice in the relationship.

The greatest condemnation for interracial alliances was directed toward white women who willingly had relations with a black man. There was overwhelming concern with preserving the whiteness of the European race. White women who produced mulatto children were clearly a threat, whereas black women who did likewise were not viewed as endangering white racial purity.

Rules in the French colonies provided more protection for black women. The *Code Noir*, first passed in 1685, required that a man who fathered a child with a willing black woman should be punished with a fine of 2,000 pounds of sugar. If he was not married to another, he was required to marry the woman, and she and her children would be set free. A revision of the *Code Noir* in 1724 outlawed interracial marriages, although acceptance of biracial relationships remained far greater in French colonies than in British areas. Frenchmen often openly took black or mulatto mistresses and housed them in separate quarters. Such relationships were not condoned, but were tolerated.

Indian/Black

There was substantial intermingling between Indians and blacks in early America. Slaves who escaped often fled to the wilderness where they found refuge within Indian tribes. Such escaped slaves were almost always black men, because women were far more reluctant to flee and leave children and family behind.

Sex ratios in eighteenth-century Indian communities tended to be badly skewed, with an overabundance of women. Colonial wars took such a heavy toll on the male Indian population that some Indian communities had 50 percent more women than men. Because there was a preference for importing male slaves from Africa, the sex ratio in the black population was the inverse of the Indian imbalance. There were mutual advantages for Indian women who married black men. In most Indian communities, women performed all the agricultural work, food preparation, and other chores. Slave men had no such tradition, and their willingness to undertake manual labor might have been welcome among Indian women. There is evidence that some Indian women even purchased black male slaves before setting them free and marrying them.

There were many advantages for black men who married into an Indian community. Usually landless and penniless, they gained access to land and other resources. Indians were usually willing to fully accept newcomers regardless of their race. Former slaves therefore found a welcoming refuge from an otherwise predominantly hostile world. Although most mixed marriages involved black men and Indian women, there are a handful of known cases of black women who married Indian men.

Black-Indian marriages increased as white settlements expanded. As whites gradually appropriated Indian land, dispossessed Indians often migrated to towns and port cities where they found employment. They were generally compelled to live in segregated areas, where they shared the same taverns, jobs, and neighborhoods as members of the free black community.

In the northern colonies there were no cultural or legal impediments to interracial marriage between blacks and Indians. Conversely, settlers in southern colonies were deeply suspicious of fraternization between blacks and Indians. Acutely conscious of their numerical weakness, whites feared that if Indians joined forces with blacks they would have the power to overwhelm white settlers. Various methods were deliberately employed to foment hostility between slaves and Indians. Black men were rewarded for taking part in Indian wars. Indians were rewarded with substantial bounties for the return of runaway slaves. Despite these efforts, a large number of slaves succeeded in escaping and living productive lives in Indian communities.

See also Fur Traders' Wives; Pocahontas

Further Reading

Clinton, Catherine, and Michele Gillespie, eds. *The Devil's Lane: Sex and Race in the Early South.* New York: Oxford University Press, 1997.

Feder, Kenneth L. "Legend of the Barkhamsted Lighthouse." *Archaeology* 47 (July/August 1994): 46–49.

Kaplan, Sidney. "Historical Efforts to Encourage White-Indian Intermarriage in the United States and Canada." *International Social Sciences Review* 65 (1990): 126–132.

Mandell, Daniel R. "Shifting Boundaries of Race and Ethnicity: Indian-Black Intermarriage in Southern New England, 1760–1880." *Journal of American History* 85 (1998): 466–501.

Nash, Gary B. *Red, White, and Black: The Peoples of Early America.* Englewood Cliffs, NJ: Prentice-Hall, 1974.

Smits, David D. "Abominable Mixture: Toward the Repudiation of Anglo-Indian Intermarriage in Seventeenth Century Virginia." *Virginia Magazine of History and Biography* 95 (1987): 157–192.

Sollers, Werner, ed. *Interracialism: Black White Intermarriage in American History, Literature, and Law.* New York: Oxford University Press, 2000.

Islamic Women

Islam had spread into West Africa from the eleventh through the seventeenth centuries. This was the same region from which much of the slave trade operated, and it is certain that thousands of African slaves brought their Islamic traditions with them to America. Between 1760 and 1790 it is known that many of the Africans sent to America were heavily drawn from Islamic regions of Africa. Although it is impossible to know exact numbers, historians have estimated at least 30,000 African Muslims were sent to America as slaves, and many of these people were women.

Evidence of Muslim tradition and practices among slaves is scanty. White masters occasionally noted the strange customs of newly arrived slaves, but rarely did they associate these with Islam. All first-generation African slaves brought a myriad of foreign customs with them, and general ignorance of the Islamic faith among Americans meant they rarely noted particular slaves as being Muslim. The handful of Islamic slaves who did achieve prominence and recorded their stories were all male. Examining the experience of these men, and knowing the tenets of African Islam, it is possible to surmise what some of the daily life of Islamic female slaves would have been like.

The five "Pillars of Faith" include rules of prayer, charity, fasting, pilgrimage, and belief in only one God. Dietary restrictions prohibit the consumption of alcohol and pork. It is known that some Islamic slaves refused to eat pork, a staple of the American slave diet, and their primary source of protein. If a woman refused to eat pork, she would have suffered from greater malnutrition from what was already an insufficient and bland diet. She would have also tried to pray at hours of the day that would have appeared odd to her owners and fellow slaves. There are records of Islamic slaves being taunted for these unusual rituals, and some stole into the woods to pray in private. Muslim women from West Africa wore strings of beads around their waists, which were used in their prayer rituals. Muslim women would also have worn some sort of scarf or veil over their heads.

The practice of polygamy was widespread in Africa, but was rarely possible in America. The majority of slaves transported from Africa were male, setting up fierce competition for the companionship of a few female slaves. Among subsequent generations of American-born slaves, women were less inclined to submit to the foreign practice of polygamy. Muslim slaves were always a minority on any plantation, and a polygamous tradition was at odds with the Christian teaching embraced by other slaves. Though it was not unheard of for male slaves to have more than one wife, most Islamic women would not have been involved in a polygamous marriage.

The majority of Islamic slaves were clustered in the coastal areas of Georgia and the Carolinas. It is not coincidental that these regions cultivated rice and indigo, both of which had been grown for centuries in West Africa. Slaves from western Africa were considered especially desirable because of their knowledge of growing problematic crops. According to historian Allan D. Austin, Muslim slaves were also considered more desirable than other Africans because they were perceived to be "more intelligent, more reasonable, more physically attractive, more dignified people" (Austin 1984, 29). Muslim slaves were often given more responsibility, including supervising the planting of crops, working in the house, and transporting goods off the plantation.

Possibly the chief impact Islam would have had on a female slave was the sense of isolation it created between her and other slaves. Muslim slaves were often described as holding themselves aloof from the rest of the slave population. In Africa, Muslims were associated with more sophisticated societies and a higher socioeconomic status than other Africans. A sense of cultural superiority was clearly evident among some Muslim slaves, who usually cooperated with fellow slaves, but kept their distance during periods of recreation. It is known that some Muslim slaves referred to themselves as "Moors," and considered "Negro" slaves to be of a lower class.

This ethnocentric sentiment worked against the perpetuation of Islam as a significant force within slave communities. They were not inclined to proselytize among non-Muslim slaves and were therefore dependent on sustaining their faith among subsequent generations of their offspring. Without religious texts, mosques, and the ability to adequately educate their children, the collective memory of their Islamic roots began to fade. Because Muslims were always a minority within their communities, many had no choice but to marry non-Muslims. It is known that subsequent generations of slaves often shunned traditions that smacked too much of Africa, so there might have been peer pressure among younger slaves to conform to Christian worship.

Never very large, the numbers of Islamic women tapered off in nineteenth-century America. Names such as Fatima, Yaruba, Hestuh, Khadeeja, and Aisha had once been popular among slaves with Islamic roots, but these tapered off in favor of more Anglicized names. The importation of slaves from West Africa began to dwindle. It was not until the twentieth century that Islam returned as a force among African Americans.

Further Reading

Alford, Terry. "Islam." In *Dictionary of Afro-American Slavery*, eds. Randall M. Miller and John David Smith. New York: Greenwood Press, 1988.

Austin, Allan D. *African Muslims in Antebellum America: A Sourcebook*. New York: Garland, 1984.

Gomez, Michael A. "Muslims in Early America." *Journal of Southern History* 60 (1994): 671–710.

J

Jemison, Mary
*Indian captive who remained with her
Seneca family (c. 1743–1833)*

Mary Jemison was born aboard the *William and Mary* to Scots-Irish parents who were immigrating to the New World. Her memories of a childhood growing up on a farm near Gettysburg, Pennsylvania, were happy. Her family was prosperous, and she received a basic education in reading and religion. She recalled that her parents feared the Indians, because they lived on the outer edges of settled territory, and the local Indian tribes felt they had been cheated of their land. In 1758 tensions boiled over, and a raiding party attacked the Jemison farm, taking the entire family captive save for two brothers who managed to escape. Fearing detection, the band of Indians retreated at a brisk pace, forcing the family to travel 175 miles in six days. Their captivity was brutal, punctuated with physical abuse and deprivation. At one point Mary was given a pair of moccasins. Her mother correctly interpreted this as a sign the Indians meant to adopt Mary. She implored Mary to remember her name, her prayers, and her language. Shortly thereafter, Mary was separated from her family, who were executed. Mary later saw the Indians drying and preserving the scalps of her mother, father, sister, and two brothers.

Mary was approximately fourteen years old at the time of her abduction. She was given into the care of two Seneca women, who communicated to her that she was to become their sister. According to Seneca custom, Mary was stripped of her European clothing, ceremoniously bathed, and then dressed in the Indian style. She was brought to a wigwam, where a number of Indians assembled and began lamenting a dead brother. The mourning ceremony gradually evolved into one of celebration, as Mary was welcomed as a new sister, renamed Dehgewamis.

Over the next few years Mary wrestled with her desire to return to white culture and her growing respect and camaraderie with her new Indian family. Trying to maintain a link with her past, she faithfully repeated her prayers and spoke English to herself. Memories of her lost family kept her lonely and gloomy. Alarmed by Mary's somber demeanor, her Seneca sisters persuaded her to marry the brave Sheninjee. Although at first reluctant, Mary married, and grew to love her husband, whom she characterized as tender and generous. She bore him two children, one of whom died in infancy.

Mary eventually moved with her tribe to land near Geneseo, New York. After being widowed, she remarried another Indian many years her senior, to whom she bore six children. Following Indian custom, the children took their names from the maternal line. Thus Mary's children carried the English names of John, Nancy, Betsy, Polly, Jane, Thomas, and Jesse Jamison. During the American Revolution the Seneca tribe sided with the British, and her village was destroyed during one of the retaliatory raids. Her family resettled nearby, but their land and economic power were in swift decline.

Following the war, Mary refused an offer of repatriation. Even after twenty-five years among the

Statue of Mary Jemison, by H. K. Bush-Brown, in Letchworth Park, Genesee County, near Portage, New York. (Library of Congress)

Indians, Mary did indeed contemplate returning. Her son Thomas, who had always shown an affinity for white culture, expressed a desire to go, and promised to accompany his mother should she wish to return. The tribal elders, knowing Thomas to be a strong warrior with great potential as a leader, refused to let him leave. Unwilling to be parted from Thomas, Mary elected to remain. She further noted that with seven half-Indian children, she was skeptical of the welcome she and her children would receive among the white community.

By virtue of a tribal grant, Mary came into possession of a large tract of land in New York. She lived in a log cabin on this land for the remainder of her days. Like other Indian women, she planted and cultivated her own crops, tended livestock, hauled water, and ground her corn. Although she lived among the Indians, she clearly maintained

some ties with her European roots. Her clothing was a mix of Indian and European dress. She chose to live in a log cabin rather than an Indian-style wigwam. Although she was fluent in the Seneca tongue, when she spoke English, it was with a Scottish brogue. Just before her death she reconverted to Christianity. Her sons Thomas and Jesse showed strong affinity for European culture and wished to live among them. Mary's son John had no such inclination, and the hostility among the brothers, mixed with alcohol, became deadly. John killed both his brothers during separate incidents of drunken rages, and he was himself subsequently murdered in a brawl.

Mary's story was committed to print by Dr. James E. Seaver, who interviewed her over a period of three days when Mary was in her eighties. *A Narrative of the Life of Mrs. Mary Jemison* became one of the best-selling books of its day.

See also Indian Captivity

Further Reading

McLamore, Richard V. "Mary Jemison." In *American Women Prose Writers, 1820–1870*, eds. Katharine Rodier and Amy E. Hudock. Detroit, MI: Gale, 2001.

Seaver, James E. *A Narrative of the Life of Mrs. Mary Jemison.* New York: Corinth Books, 1961.

Wyss, Hilary E. "Captivity and Conversion." *American Indian Quarterly* 23 (1999): 63–82.

Jewish Women

The first Jews to come to North America settled in the Dutch colony of New York, sometime in the early 1650s. The earliest Jewish immigrants were almost entirely male, usually employed in the establishment of outposts for international trading networks. The first Jewish women arrived in 1653, when six women arrived on the ship *St. Catherine.* These women were among a group of Jews who had first tried to establish a settlement in Dutch Brazil, but fled when the Portuguese attacked the territory. Throughout the Dutch colonial period, Jewish settlements in America remained extremely small. Few of the merchants intended to establish perma-

Touro Synagogue, founded 1763 in Newport, RI. (Library of Congress)

nent residences, and the number of wives and children were always small.

In 1684 the first permanent Jewish congregation, Shearith Israel, was founded in New York. It was a Sephardic congregation, as were most of the early Jewish immigrants. Sephardic Jews originated in Spain or Portugal and had established extensive trade networks in South America and the Caribbean. Ashkenazic Jews did not arrive in great numbers until the nineteenth century, when immigration from Germany and Eastern Europe increased.

It is known by the late seventeenth century that Jewish women had established themselves in New York, raising families and participating at the synagogue. According to Jewish custom, these women would have sat apart from the congregation in an upstairs gallery during services. Women did their best to maintain Jewish customs, keeping kosher,

honoring the Sabbath, and observing Jewish holidays. Nevertheless, it was difficult to sustain the full range of Jewish life within such tiny communities. It appears that few Jews were fluent in Hebrew. There were only a few shohets (kosher butchers) or people who knew how to perform a circumcision. There were no ordained rabbis in the colonies until 1840. Jewish communities were tiny, often with fewer than a dozen families per synagogue. Throughout the colonial period the Jewish population was rarely more than 1 percent in any town.

Most Jewish women in the colonies married around age twenty-three. The small Jewish population made finding a husband difficult, and a number of women chose to remain spinsters rather than marry outside their faith. Arranged marriages were common. There were a handful of widely scattered Jewish communities in New York, Pennsylvania,

Georgia, South Carolina, and Jamaica. Parents arranged for their daughters to marry Jewish men in these distant communities. Although it was hard for the women of these close-knit communities to part, arranged marriages conferred economic advantages, because they cemented far-flung trading networks.

Some women did marry gentiles, although marriage outside the faith was more common for Jewish men than women. There was often pressure from parents not to marry Christians, as can be witnessed by the experience of Abigail Franks (1688–1746) and her children. The Franks family was the most prominent Jewish family in New York. Although Abigail mingled with elite society, had numerous close Christian friends, and appears to have had a cosmopolitan attitude toward society, she was bitterly disappointed when two of her children married Christians. When her oldest daughter, Phila, eloped with the scion of New York's most prominent family, Oliver de Lancey, Abigail disowned Phila and never spoke to her again. Like most Jewish women who married Christians, Phila chose to raise Christian children.

Jews maintained a unique position in colonial society. Although there might have been some small-scale anti-Semitism, it was rarely overt, and almost no official laws barring voting, property ownership, or freedom of worship were in effect during the colonial period. Sephardic Jews, who made up the majority of the colonial Jewish population, have historically been more integrated into local culture than Ashkenazic Jews. They sent their children to local schools, socialized with non-Jews, and almost always learned the local language. Aside from the establishment of a few synagogues, there is no evidence that colonists created Jewish communal organizations to cultivate an exclusive sense of solidarity.

Many Jewish wives were intimately involved in the operation of their family business. Most Jewish families were involved in international trade or banking. Men frequently traveled, and their wives operated the family business during their absence. Jewish women were accustomed to handling correspondence and clerical duties. Many Jewish men named their wives as executors of their estate.

Sorrow and Opportunity for a Jewish Woman in Virginia

Rebecca Samuel immigrated to Virginia in the 1780s with her watchmaker husband, Hyman. After settling in the small town of Petersburg, the Samuels were thrilled with the abundance of economic opportunities, which allowed Hyman to expand his trade into silver and goldsmithing. Guild restrictions prevented such entrepreneurial activities in their home in Germany. She wrote to her parents that she considered Virginia "the greatest province in the whole of America. And America is the greatest section of the world."

Rebecca claimed to have experienced no prejudice from her Christian neighbors. Indeed, she was welcomed by the people of Petersburg, and her husband's shop thrived with more business than they could handle. Despite her feeling of ease in America, Rebecca suffered from a void of Jewish culture. She longed for the Jewish holidays and the ability to celebrate the Sabbath in the manner she learned in Germany. There was no Jewish quarter in Petersburg, no synagogue, and no network of other Jewish women to whom she could turn for support.

Like thousands of other Jewish immigrants who lived scattered across early America, Rebecca Samuel felt her minority status. She did not suffer from overt discrimination, but keenly felt a longing for the rich Jewish culture she left behind in Germany.

Source: Diner, Hasia R., and Beryl Lieff Benderly. *Her Works Praise Her: A History of Jewish Women in America from Colonial Times to the Present.* New York: Basic Books, 2002.

Given that these estates were often large and complex, the appointment of a wife to undertake this task was a testament of faith in her abilities. The literacy rate among Jewish women appears to have been higher than the average for women of colonial America.

Emigration from Germany gathered momentum following the American Revolution, bringing more Ashkenazic Jews to America. There was some tension between the newer immigrants and the Sephardic Jews. The Ashkenazic Jews of the German states were more richly immersed in their culture and more likely to create ethnic enclaves. Despite the cultural differences between these two groups of Jewish settlers, the influx of German immigrants made it possible for more Jewish women to marry within their faith.

Further Reading

Diner, Hasia R., and Beryl Lieff Benderly. *Her Works Praise Her: A History of Jewish Women in America from Colonial Times to the Present.* New York: Basic Books, 2002.

Hershkowitz, Leo. "Judaism." In *Encyclopedia of the North American Colonies,* ed. Jacob Ernest Cooke. New York: Charles Scribner's Sons, 1993.

Hyman, Paula E., and Deborah Dash Moore. *Jewish Women in America: An Historical Encyclopedia.* New York: Routledge, 1998.

Marcus, Jacob R. *The American Jewish Woman, 1654–1980.* New York: KTAV Publishing House, 1981.

———. *The American Jewish Woman: A Documentary History.* New York: KTAV Publishing House, 1981.

K

Key, Elizabeth
Plaintiff in antislavery suit (fl. 1650s)

We know of Elizabeth Key's existence only from a few court documents in Northumberland County, Virginia. These fragmentary records are all that is left to document an extraordinary lawsuit that freed Elizabeth Key from slavery, but ironically forced a change in the legal system that condemned thousands of others to a lifetime of slavery.

Elizabeth was born in the early1630s to a native African slave woman and her white master. Thomas Key acknowledged that Elizabeth was his daughter, but she spent her childhood as a slave on Key's farm in rural Virginia. For reasons that are not clear, Key bound Elizabeth out as a servant to a neighbor, Humphrey Higginson, for a period of nine years. Before her nine-year term of service was completed, Thomas Key was dead, Higginson had returned to England, and ownership of Elizabeth had been passed to Colonel John Mottrom. The promise of a mere nine years of service appeared to be forgotten, as Elizabeth served a total of nineteen years before Colonel Mottrom died.

Following Colonel Mottrom's death, Elizabeth attempted to sue for her freedom. By the mid-seventeenth century, laws regarding slavery in the American colonies had yet to be solidified. It was unclear if a Christian could be enslaved, if African slaves were entitled to freedom after a fixed number of years (as was the case with indentured servants), or how a mixed racial heritage might influence a slave's status. Elizabeth had three solid reasons under which she might gain freedom. She had been baptized, and many in Virginia were uncomfortable with enslaving a fellow Christian. Her term of nine years of service had long since been completed, and there was no indication that her father, Thomas Key, intended to keep her in service after the term of nine years. Her best shot at freedom was her paternity. According to English common law, a child inherited his or her status from the father, and Elizabeth's father had been a free man.

Elizabeth's attorney was William Greensted. He argued that Elizabeth was entitled to liberty because her father had been a free man. The court agreed, and in 1655 Elizabeth was declared a free woman. The case was appealed, but subsequent rulings ultimately agreed that Elizabeth was entitled to the status she inherited from her father, based on English common law.

An unintended consequence of the ruling was that the law in the colonies was changed. Sexual exploitation of female slaves was rampant, and if the Key ruling were allowed to set a precedent, the children of these liaisons would be born into freedom. In 1662 the law of Virginia was altered so that all children born in the colonies would inherit the legal status of the *mother,* rather than the father.

The last mention of Elizabeth Key in the historical record is a note mentioning her marriage to her attorney, William Greensted, in 1659.

Further Reading

Ashcraft-Eason, Lillian. "Freedom among African Women Servants and Slaves in the Seventeenth Century British Colonies." In *Women and Freedom in Early America*, ed. Larry D. Eldridge. New York: New York University Press, 1997.

Billings, Warren M. "The Cases of Fernando and Elizabeth Key: A Note on the Status of Blacks in Seventeenth-Century Virginia." *William and Mary Quarterly* 30 (1973): 467–474.

Knight, Sarah Kemble

Travel writer, shopkeeper, teacher (1666–1727)

During her life, Sarah Kemble Knight was in no way a famous or extraordinary person. It was not until her journal was discovered and published a century after her death that she came to public attention. The forty-page document provides a fascinating window into the life of a colonial businesswoman.

Sarah Kemble was born into a middle-class family, received a solid education, and assisted her father in keeping his shop on Moon Street in Boston. She married Richard Knight, a tavern keeper and bricklayer, and had one daughter. In addition to assisting in her father's shop and raising her child, Sarah also conducted a writing school. One of her early biographers claimed that the young Benjamin Franklin was once her pupil, although there is little other documentation for this claim. After the deaths of both her father and husband, Sarah took over management of her father's business, took in boarders, and ran a stationery shop in the ground floor of her house. Sarah had a firm understanding of the law, which she could have attained during her employment as a copier of legal documents. In 1704 she was called upon by a relative to help settle the estate of her cousin Caleb in New York. Sarah embarked on a journey from Boston to New York and kept a journal to document her adventures during the five-month trip.

Travel during this period was difficult. Roads were narrow, rutted, and lacked any signage. It was essential to enlist a series of local guides to assist travelers unfamiliar with the roads. Traveling alone, Sarah relied on people she met at local taverns to either point her in the right direction or accompany her on a portion of the journey. She reimbursed such people with a few coins or the purchase of a meal. On occasion she waited for the local post riders and traveled with them from one village to the next. Sarah's journal also recounts the number of rivers and streams she needed to cross via ferry, canoe, narrow bridges, or fording.

Never intended for publication, Sarah's journal records her reflections on the variety of people she encountered, the difficulties of travel, and the conditions typically found in rural America during the early eighteenth century. Although usually humorous and good-natured, her frank journal vividly portrays people she considers to be country bumpkins, cantankerous innkeepers, slovenly tavern wenches, and backwoods inhabitants. She records events such as entering a tavern where dull-witted patrons could not tear their lips off their pewter tankards long enough to provide her directions. She speaks of bedding down in lumpy, cornhusk beds and eating wretchedly prepared food she could not identify. The poverty she describes in the backcountry stands in stark contrast to the sophistication she found in Boston and New York. Here she admires the pleasant, tidy brick homes of New York and the variety of manufactured goods for purchase. She speaks of the genteel manners of the inhabitants, a refreshing change from the crude backwoods environment she had traveled through.

Sarah's writing, with its humor, colorful portraiture of local inhabitants, and mock-heroic qualities of the narrator, has been compared with that of Mark Twain. Her journal remained in private hands until coming to the attention of Theodore Dwight Jr. in 1825, who edited and published the document. Titled *The Journals of Madam Knight*, its keen insight into the manners and customs of the early eighteenth century made the document of interest to historians and humorists alike.

Sarah died in 1727 a wealthy woman with an estate valued at £1,800. Her writing provides us with a glimpse at how an industrious and intelligent woman could become financially successful in early eighteenth-century America.

Further Reading

Andrews, William L. *Journeys in New Worlds: Early American Women's Narratives.* Madison: University of Wisconsin Press, 1990.

Dietrich, Deborah. "Sarah Kemble Knight." In *American Women Prose Writers to 1820,* ed. Carla Mulford. Detroit, MI: Gale, 1999.

Martin, Wendy, ed. *Colonial American Travel Narratives.* New York: Penguin, 1994.

Stephens, Robert O. "The Odyssey of Sarah Kemble Knight." *CLA Journal* 7 (1964): 247–255.

Thorpe, Peter. "Sarah Kemble Knight and the Picaresque Tradition." In *American Women Humorists,* ed Linda A. Morris. New York: Garland, 1994.

L

Lee, Ann

Spiritual visionary and founder of the Shakers (1736–1784)

Mother Ann Lee was born into a working-class family in Manchester, England. She had no schooling and from an early age worked in a mill preparing cotton for the looms. Despite her parents' traditional Anglican beliefs, Ann was attracted to a radical sect of Quakers led by Jane and James Wardley. This sect engaged in dancing, shouting, and speaking in tongues. Ann had little inclination to marry, but after sustained pressure from her parents, she reluctantly married Abraham Standerin in 1762. Standerin was a blacksmith who worked for Ann's father, and like Ann, he was illiterate. The couple had four children, but they all died at very young ages.

All of the deliveries were difficult, and Ann almost died giving birth to her last child. She became obsessed with seeking an explanation for her children's tragic deaths and her unhappy marriage. She concluded that relations with the opposite sex were at the root of her troubles and were contrary to the ways of Christ. Ann returned to the Wardleys for spiritual comfort and gradually assumed spiritual leadership of the tiny religious group. Ann took her crusade to the streets, shouting exhortations at bystanders and disrupting services at local churches. Ann was arrested and imprisoned for disturbing the peace, destroying property, and assault. She eventually spent time in Bedlam, the notorious English insane asylum. Her visions intensified while she was confined, convincing her she was the female successor to Jesus Christ.

After her release from Bedlam, Ann's rowdy evangelization activities continued, but a vision told her to carry her mission to America. Mother Ann left England with eight followers in 1774, and immigrated to New York. There the tiny group disbanded in order to seek employment. It is likely Ann worked as a domestic servant for several years before her followers reunited and established a community at Niskayuna, near Albany. Ann was a committed pacifist, and the group's refusal to support the Revolutionary War caused suspicion among their neighbors. Ann was suspected of being a front for the British and was briefly imprisoned. Upon her release she garnered sympathy from other charismatic religious followers.

Independent religious revival groups flourished in New England, and Ann's group began attracting substantial followers for the first time. Celibacy and the public confession of sin were the cardinal principles of the group. Emulating the primitive church, Ann insisted that all things be held in common. She stressed neatness, economy, and charity toward the poor. Under her guidance, women enjoyed equal rights and responsibilities with men. Ann's followers expressed themselves through unrestrained dancing, chanting, and foot stamping. Her insistence on egalitarian order, communal lifestyle, and rejection of marriage attracted many converts, but also roused the suspicion of traditionalists.

Shaker Center Family Ann Lee Cottage, Mount Lebanon, Columbia County, NY. (Library of Congress)

Mother Ann Lee's beliefs bordered on heresy for the generally conservative people of the eighteenth century. When questions arose about a woman's ability to lead a church, Ann replied that she was acting in place of her absent husband, Jesus Christ. Her wild dancing was condemned as erotic displays. Her pacifism during a time of war appealed to some, but further stoked the fires of suspicion among many. She claimed to have the ability to speak in tongues and commune with the dead.

Ann died in 1784, following a deep depression caused by the death of her brother and most devoted follower, William Lee. She claimed that she wished to join him in death, and shortly before she passed, she claimed to have seen William coming toward her on a gold chariot. Ann was illiterate and never committed any of her philosophy to print. Twenty-five years after her death, her followers set about interviewing the people who had known her, in an effort to record her life. *The Testi-*

monies were completed in 1816. Only twenty copies were printed and circulated to the leaders of Shaker communities. The book, commonly called "the Mother's sayings," was closely guarded, as they reveal a woman who was prone to bouts of weepiness, fluctuating moods, erratic behavior, and possibly alcoholism.

Despite the mystery that surrounded Ann Lee, the success of her charismatic religious movement is without question. The Shakers' rigid adherence to celibacy meant they could not sustain the group without a constant influx of converts. Within a few decades of Ann's death, the Shakers had more than six thousand followers and were developing a unique style of artwork, architecture, and furniture that reflected Ann's philosophy of simplicity without adornment. Ann believed that skillful workmanship was in itself an act of prayer. An enormous amount of care and attention to detail went into the crafting and construction of Shaker products. They believed form must follow function, and each item should be carefully crafted to suit its intended purpose, but nothing else. All superfluous decoration, such as scrolls, inlays, and molding, were eliminated. Shaker furniture and products have a distinctive severe appearance and have had a lasting influence on America design.

Further Reading

Humez, Jean M. "Ye Are My Epistles: The Construction of Ann Lee Imagery in Early Shaker Sacred Literature." *Journal of Feminist Studies in Religion* 8 (1992): 83–103.

Stein, Stephen J. "Ann Lee." In *American National Biography,* ed. John A. Garraty. New York: Oxford University Press, 1999.

———. *The Shaker Experience in America: A History of the United Society of Believers.* New Haven, CT: Yale University Press, 1992.

Legal Status of Women

Most of the American colonies inherited English common law, a system of justice derived from tradition and custom rather than statutory law enacted by legislatures. English common law evolved from centuries of judicial decisions. The most important common-law principle relating to women was *coverture,* a doctrine that sublimated a woman's legal identity under that of her husband. A married woman could not buy, sell, earn, or possess property in her own name. She had no authority over how family money was spent, she could not enter into contracts, nor could she sue or be sued. Any legal action she wished to take needed to be brought to the court's attention via her husband's authorization. Naturally, this presented a problem if a woman had a legal dispute with her husband, such as in the case of divorce, child custody, or control over her premarital assets.

English law had a unique remedy for people, especially women, who did not believe common law addressed their needs. Equity law was a system aimed at addressing the inflexible nature of common law. A person who felt an injustice had been done in a common-law court could appeal to a chancery court, which was governed by equity law, rather than common law. The judge at the chancery level was free to base his decisions on the spirit of the law, rather than on what was dictated by common law. Chancery courts used no juries. Although the judges paid heed to common-law tradition and precedent, it was a court where judges could use their instinct, or their whim, to render decisions. Many colonial settlers were highly distrustful of chancery courts, because such courts were often tools for the king's imperial dictates. Aside from the potential for arbitrary and tyrannical abuse, chancery courts offered women a place to take their grievances.

An example of how a chancery court could serve a woman can be seen in the establishment of separation contracts between feuding spouses. Divorces were difficult to obtain in colonial America, and many feuding couples opted to create a legal document outlining terms of a legal separation and financial support. Because the law of coverture virtually erased a wife's ability to have an independent legal identity, common law refused to recognize the validity of any legal document created between spouses. In such a case, the couple could appeal to a chancery court, where the judge had the freedom to rule according to principles of reason and justice. Chancery courts also allowed for prenuptial agree-ments to be created and honored and for trusts and inheritances to be granted to married women without interference from their husbands.

Despite the protection afforded women by chancery courts, they had little effect on ordinary women's lives. Most colonial women lacked the sophistication and financial assets to bring a case before chancery courts. In some cases, the suit needed to be heard in a lower court before the chancery court could hear it. In other colonies, there might be only one chancery court located in the colony's capital city, an obvious barrier to a woman living in a remote area.

Suspicion of chancery courts ran high, especially as the eighteenth century witnessed the stirrings of political rebellion in the colonies. Each colony developed its own rules regarding the extent that equity rulings could encroach on common-law tradition. Eventually, New England and the middle colonies eliminated separate chancery courts, opting instead to incorporate aspects of equity law into their common-law courts.

The law of coverture did not apply to women who were single or widows. Lacking husbands, these women retained their legal identities and had all the rights and privileges that men had, except for the right to vote and hold public office.

Dutch Colonies

Women in the Dutch colonies of New Netherlands had an unusually high level of legal autonomy. Holland's legal system was an amalgamation of Roman law and local Germanic customs. Called Roman-Dutch law, it was transplanted to the colonies in New Netherlands, where it afforded women greater legal autonomy than anywhere else in America. Dutch women preparing to marry had a right to select either a *manus* marriage or an *usus* marriage. A *manus* marriage meant a woman was subject to her husband, and her legal identity was sublimated under his authority. A woman who selected an *usus* marriage had substantial legal independence from her husband. She retained rights to all her premarital property, she could initiate and litigate contracts, establish and run a business, and retain her maiden name. A woman could renounce *manus* status after marriage and assume the legal responsibilities associated with an *usus* marriage if she chose.

Inheritance custom was generally blind to gender. Whereas primogeniture was often the law of the land in English societies, sons and daughters tended to inherit equal amounts of property in Dutch colonies. Furthermore, many parents made provisions in their wills for their daughters to receive the same amount of education as their sons.

A combination of legal freedom and enterprising Dutch merchant tradition afforded women the opportunity to participate in business to a high extent. Seventeenth-century records tell of Dutch women working as shopkeepers, brewers, shippers, fur traders, and tavern owners. It is possible that the women of New Netherlands did not participate in business at a markedly higher rate than women in the Anglo-American colonies, where wives of businessmen were often active participants in a business in all but name. Because Dutch women were entitled to an independent legal status, they left traceable records to document their involvement in the business world. Women whose legal identity was subsumed under that of their husbands were unlikely to leave such clear evidence, but might have been participating in such business activities at an equally high rate.

In 1664 the British took control of New Netherlands, renaming it New York. Property rights of Dutch settlers, including businesses owned by Dutch women, were respected. There was little dramatic change in Dutch women's status in the years immediately following British conquest, but as the decades passed, the colony became more English in character. Fewer women were business owners, and the option of an *usus* marriage dissolved.

Under Dutch law, divorces could be obtained through appeal to civil magistrates. Dissolving a marriage usually meant that important business and family connections would be severed, and both clergymen and the courts encouraged couples to resolve marital difficulties. If this proved impossible, Dutch law allowed for a divorce. It appears that after English authorities assumed control over New York, English governors typically respected Dutch tradition and continued to grant divorces under similar circumstances.

Enslaved Women

Each colony established a series of "slave codes," which provided for the policing of slaves, the rights of slaves, the conduct of whites in dealing with slaves, and the rules for the manumission of slaves. Slaves were deprived of most basic human liberties the white population took for granted, but they were provided with a slim margin of protection by the law. Although there were variations among the colonies, the rules outlined below were generally applicable in all the southern colonies.

One of the first major legal cases regarding the laws of slavery was the decision to make slavery heritable through the mother. The common-law tradition of England granted children the legal status of their father, but this was unacceptable in the American South, where a high percentage of slave women bore the children of free white men. In 1655 Elizabeth Key successfully sued in a Virginia court for her freedom because she had a white father. Following this case, the law was changed to prevent children of enslaved women from becoming free based on their paternity.

Enslaved women were highly vulnerable to sexual exploitation from their owners, and the slave codes did nothing to protect them from such abuses. There were numerous antimiscegenation laws on the books throughout the colonies, but the laws were largely ignored unless a white person attempted to marry a black. Such a marriage would present a host of problems for the colonies, which were reluctant to recognize a black person's right to share the spousal benefits from marriage to a white. The mere sexual exploitation of slaves, even when it resulted in mulatto children, was ignored. Although sexual exploitation of slaves was considered immoral among the white population, it was widespread and considered in poor taste to acknowledge the problem.

The isolation of women on plantations gave them virtually no ability to seek social or legal recourse for sexual harassment. Slave women could not physically defend themselves, because striking a white person was against the law, and punishment could be brutal. The first time a slave struck a white person, she was to be punished with a whipping. Second or third offenses could result in the death penalty.

One of the most important factors in determining the emotional well-being of a slave was her ability to form a stable family. No slave had the legal ability to enter a contract, making a binding marriage impossible. Slaves had ceremonial weddings, but they could be terminated if one partner was sold. Likewise, a woman could not be assured of her right to raise her own children. Because the children were the legal property of her master, he had the freedom to sell or relocate those children as he saw fit.

Protections for slaves were pitifully few and were often designed to benefit the local government. It was forbidden for owners to free their slaves unless the slave was able-bodied and capable of attaining self-sufficiency. Before this rule was established, cruel masters would free a slave when they were too old to work, and thus became a burden on the state. Masters were required to provide sufficient food, shelter, and clothing for a slave, although the standard of what was "sufficient" was sadly meager and subjective. South Carolina and Georgia insisted that slaves be allowed a day of rest on Sunday, but the working time for the other six days could be up to sixteen hours.

Most rules in the slave codes were designed to restrict the liberty of slaves. Above all, it was important for slave owners to prevent anything that gave a slave the opportunity to escape or incite a rebellion. Slaves could not travel to neighboring plantations without a pass. Curfews required they be home before nightfall, and no one was to sell liquor to a slave. Limitations were placed on the number of slaves who could gather during off-work hours. Most colonies forbade slaves the ability to learn to write, although reading was acceptable in most areas. Reading and writing were taught as separate skills in colonial America, and many women were able to read without ever acquiring the subsequent skill of writing. Some masters even encouraged Christian slaves to learn to read the Bible, because doing so was believed to make them passive. Con-

version to Christianity had no legal bearing on a slave's status, despite the claims of Quakers and other antislavery advocates that it was a sin to enslave a Christian.

Colonies assumed that all blacks were slaves unless they could prove their free status. Many women, especially those of mixed blood, attempted to pass for white after making a bid for freedom. Sumptuary laws that prohibited slaves from wearing elegant clothing were attempts to prevent women from acquiring the clothing that might aid in their escape.

Punishment for escape was severe and became more debilitating for each subsequent attempt. The South Carolina punishment for escaped slaves was typical: Forty lashes was given at the first attempt, the second attempt resulted in branding the left cheek with an *R,* signifying a runaway slave. The third attempt was forty lashes and the right ear cut off, the fourth attempt was branding on the right cheek and severing the other ear. At the fifth attempt the owner had the option of cutting off a foot or putting the slave to death.

There were a few limited laws that protected slaves from abuse from whites. The killing or maiming of a slave was a punishable offense in most colonies, but it was often limited to a fine. A few colonies made killing a slave a death-penalty offense, but there were loopholes, which protected an owner if he killed a slave during "moderate correction." The slave codes provided for the use of corporal punishment on disobedient slaves, giving owners tacit permission to use any form of torture short of death.

Slaves could not testify against a white person in court, effectively closing the courts to them as a means of redress. Only two colonies, Georgia and South Carolina, permitted a slave to bring suit to question the legality of their enslavement.

See also Coverture; Divorce; *Feme Sole;* Wills and Inheritance

Further Reading

Berkin, Carol. *First Generations: Women in Colonial America.* New York: Hill and Wang, 1996.

Biemer, Linda Briggs. *Women and Property in Colonial New York: The Transition from Dutch to English Law, 1643–1727.* Ann Arbor, MI: UMI Research Press, 1983.

Gunderson, Joan. "Married Women's Legal Status in Eighteenth Century New York and Virginia." *William and Mary Quarterly,* 3d ser. 39 (1982): 111–134.

Katz, Stanley N. "The Politics of Law in Colonial America: Controversies over Chancery Courts and Equity Law in the Eighteenth Century." In *Colonial America: Essays in Politics and Social Development,* 2nd ed., ed. Stanley Katz. Boston: Little, Brown, 1976.

Salmon, Marylynn. "Equality or Submersion? Feme Covert Status in Early Pennsylvania." In *Women of America: A History,* eds. Carol Berkin and Mary Beth Norton. Boston: Houghton Mifflin, 1979.

———. *Women and the Law of Property in Early America.* Chapel Hill: University of North Carolina Press, 1986.

Spindel, Donna J. "Women's Civil Actions in the North Carolina Higher Courts, 1670–1730." *North Carolina Historical Review* 71 (1994): 151–173.

Wiecek, William M. "The Statutory Law of Slavery and Race in the Thirteen Mainland Colonies of British America." *William and Mary Quarterly* 34 (1977): 258–280.

Leisler's Rebellion

See Civil Disobedience

Lesbians

Although women have engaged in homosexual behavior as far back as can be recorded by history, they were not categorized as a distinct class, lesbians, until the late nineteenth century. Early American laws frequently cited homosexuality as a profoundly serious crime, but the laws, biblical scripture, and early sermons seem to imply that only men engaged in homosexuality. Sermons of the time were abundantly concerned with unrestrained female sexuality, but never alluded to the possibility of lesbianism. In 1636 the Plymouth Colony enacted the first antisodomy law that gave the death penalty for convictions of sodomy or buggery. No mention was made of gender, but the absence of such language probably implied it was intended to apply only to men. That same year John Cotton proposed a law for Massachusetts Bay that specifically enunciated that sexual relations between two men or two women would be a capital offense. The law was not enacted, possibly because Puritans did not conceive of women who had relations with other women as being sodomites, merely sinners.

There is barely any record of women engaging in homosexual acts. Although Puritans were highly sensitized to the dangers of male homosexuality, they were not inclined to scrutinize the behavior of women who formed intimate friendships. Only two fleeting references to prosecution of women for homoerotic behavior survive. Elizabeth Johnson, a servant living in the Massachusetts Bay Colony in 1642, was sentenced to a fine and severe whipping for "unseemly practices betwixt her and another maid." In 1649 Sara Norman and Mary Hammon were convicted of "lewd behavior each with the other upon a bed" (Shurtleff 1855, 137).

Zealous concern for rooting out and punishing homosexuals declined in the eighteenth century. Never much of a concern to legal authorities, prosecution of women for homosexuality appears to have been nonexistent in the eighteenth and early nineteenth centuries. Despite lack of legal interest, it is certain that lesbian affairs occurred. The artist Mary Ann Willson (fl. 1810s) appears to have lived with her lover, Miss Brundage, in rural New York for decades. Miss Brundage farmed the land, while Mary Willson sold her vibrant, playful folk paintings to the locals. Their story inspired Isabel Miller's 1972 novel, *Patience and Sarah.*

Sexuality in Native American communities was more fluid than in Anglo-America. In rare instances, some Indian women chose to adopt the clothing and lifestyle of men. Known as "manly hearted women," they married female wives and took male names.

See also Manly Hearted Women

Further Reading

Shurtleff, Nathaniel B. *Records of the Colony of New Plymouth, Vol. 1.* Boston: William White, 1855.

Mary Ann Willson's 1815 folk painting, *Mermaid*. Mary Ann Willson appears to have lived with her lover, Miss Brundage, in rural New York for decades. Miss Brundage farmed the land, while Mary Willson sold her vibrant, playful folk paintings to the locals. (New York State Historical Association)

Taylor, Verta, and Leila Rupp. "Lesbianism." In *The Readers Companion to U.S. Women's History.* New York: Houghton Mifflin, 1998.

Thompson, Roger. "Attitudes toward Homosexuality in the Seventeenth Century New England Colonies." *Journal of American Studies* 23 (1989): 27–40.

Literacy

See Education

Literature

Books in early America were few and precious. Household inventories derived from wills reveal that fewer than half of colonial families possessed any books at all. By the late eighteenth century, lending libraries became established in a handful of larger American cities, but the ability to borrow books was limited by memberships that only the well-to-do could afford.

Reading scripture was considered an important part of a family's spiritual well-being, and as such, many women would have had access to a Bible or Book of Psalms. Practical manuals were the next most common type of book to be found in most households.

Household and Medical Manuals

The earliest female settlers to America felt a pressing need for practical advice on managing a household and providing basic medical care. Because so much of this information was traditionally passed from mother to daughter, these women were often cut off from the customary source for learning housewifery skills. Most of them were unprepared for life in crude frontier conditions, where candles, cheese, cured meat, and medicinal remedies were rare. Such resources could be purchased in England, but in the colonies they needed to be made. The need for household manuals was quickly realized and supplied with imported texts from England.

The English-Housewife (1615) by Gervase Markham was the first-known housewifery book to arrive in the American colonies, having been specifically requested by Virginia settlers in 1620. The book contained information on preparing all sorts of meals, as well as a variety of medical remedies. Markham's advice on growing flax, spinning thread, dying fabric, making cheese and butter, and brewing beer would have been especially important to these early settlers. Trade for such items was the norm in England, so few of the first settlers had experience with the wide array of skills they would need in their new environment. Other books for maintaining a household were soon imported and eagerly purchased by women who had few alternate resources for learning what they needed to know.

The most popular household manual in colonial America was *The Compleat Housewife* (1727) by Eliza Smith. Containing more than five hundred recipes and two hundred remedies for common ailments, this was the most comprehensive volume available. Tips on washing clothes, killing insects, cooking in a brick oven or over a fire, and growing vegetables were also included. Other titles popular on colonial women's bookshelves included *The Art of Cookery* (1774) by Hannah Glasse, *House-Keeper's Pocket-Book* (1755) by Sarah Harrison, and *The Frugal Housewife, or Complete Woman Cook* (1792) by Susannah Carter.

Though not as common as cookbooks, medical books were also used by women. John Tennent's *Every Man His Own Doctor* (1734) was directed toward a lay reader. Despite the title being geared toward a male audience, we know that this book was popular among women and was widely available throughout the colonies. English woman Mary Morris apparently took issue with the gender bias in the title. She published a remarkably similar volume called *Every One Their Own Physician*, which also became popular among the women on both sides of the Atlantic. Near the end of the eighteenth century, physicians increasingly dominated the medical profession, taking the place of folk healers, midwives, and reliance on medical manuals. The later colonial period witnessed a drop in the number of medical texts geared to the layperson, as women turned to professionals for medical advice.

Women also relied on almanacs for advice on issues as wide-ranging as diagnosing diseases, planting crops, astrology, and delivering a child. Almanacs typically contained a variety of folklore, practical advice, and gossipy news.

Conduct Books

Written with young adults in mind, conduct books provided advice and training in the morals, decorum, and virtues considered important in colonial society. Such books were highly conservative and reflected an idealized interpretation of the social identity and role of the colonial woman. Although these books often touched on etiquette and housewifery, their main purpose was to teach young minds to internalize the principles important to colonial society. By molding the attitudes and expectations to the traditional standards of submissive femininity, conduct books sought to turn young women into obedient daughters and biddable wives.

Typical conduct books for young women provided insight on the importance of domesticity, the

An engraving by Louis Truchy based on Joseph Highmore's paintings of scenes from *Pamela, Or Virtue Rewarded* by Samuel Richardson. (Historical Picture Archive/CORBIS)

love of home, courtship, and duties toward husbands and children. Running throughout these books is an ever-present theme of the importance of humility, submission, and modesty. The books frequently contained examples of the dire consequences in store for women foolish enough to flout the rules of conduct.

The most popular conduct book in early America was the anonymously published *The Ladies' Calling* (1673). Later determined to have been penned by Englishman Richard Allestree, the book began by defining the virtues a woman should strive toward, such as modesty, meekness, compassion, and spirituality. Allestree seeks to convince the female reader that because she is inferior to men, she should be

meek. Because her province is in the home, she has time for private religious devotion. Because she is not burdened with a man's responsibilities, she has the liberty to show compassion and be affable. A woman's chief responsibility, Allestree condescendingly states, is a little easy work within her own home and "the oversight of a few children." As such she ought to have time to pursue pious reflection and care for her husband. The rest of the book outlines a woman's responsibilities at various stages of life, as a young girl, as a wife, and as a widow. Young ladies were not to attempt to select their own husbands, but should obey their parents' guidance in such matters. Wives were told to obey their husbands, and Allestree suggested it might be easier to reconcile themselves to such by always casting the most favorable interpretation on any doubtful action their spouse might take. If her husband was to stray into adultery, she should not rail at him; she had a better chance of reclaiming him through gentle appeals. Should this fail, she should patiently accept the situation and interpret it as God's punishment for some sin she must have committed in her past. Her duties to her husband did not cease with his death, because she was to honor his memory and vindicate him from damaging rumors. Although Allestree acknowledged that the Bible permits a widow to remarry, he advises against it. The widow of a good husband should not grasp after good fortune a second time, and the widow of a bad husband should be cautious of the institution.

Allestree warned women against "mischievous curiosity" and the reading of novels. Despite its joyless nature, *The Ladies' Calling* met with such critical acclaim that portions of the text were heavily plagiarized and copied in other writers' conduct books.

The first women's conduct book written in America was Cotton Mather's *Ornaments for the Daughters of Zion* (1692). Like Allestree, he structures his work around the duties of the virgin, the wife, and the widow. He implores women to learn all the various aspects of housewifery. Rather than stress the gloomy inferiority of women, Mather sets out an impressive array of pursuits for them to master, such as cooking, sewing, medical arts, and the intellectual stamina necessary to instruct their children in reading, writing, and arithmetic. She might pursue music and languages if she has time left in her day. Although Mather clearly outlines a subservient role for women in relation to men, he shows a healthy respect for their abilities and contributions to their families.

The conduct books of the eighteenth century were still rooted in conservative interpretation of women's role as compliant and subservient, but seem less dour than their predecessors. Dr. James Fordyce's *Sermons to Young Women* (1766) was the most popular conduct book of its time. By the eighteenth century, novels had become far more widespread, and Fordyce knew the heroines featured in such books had enormous appeal, but bore little resemblance to the grim and humorless women extolled in earlier conduct books. In order to interest his audience, Fordyce pays special heed to women's emotions and desires. He offers practical advice for attracting a desirable husband and seeking personal happiness. He recognizes a double standard in society when he writes,

> The world, I know not how, overlooks in our sex a thousand irregularities, which it never forgives in yours; so that the honor and peace of a family are, in this view, much more dependant on the conduct of daughters than of sons; and one young lady going astray shall subject her relations to such discredit and distress as the united good conduct of all her brothers and sisters. (17)

Rivaling Fordyce's *Sermons* for popularity was Dr. John Gregory's *A Father's Legacy to his Daughters* (1774). Written to his motherless daughters when Dr. Gregory's own health was in swift decline, the book sought to provide instruction on a range of practical topics, such as how to attract a decent husband, how to avoid mistakes in judgment, the perils of gossip, and how to protect oneself against betrayal. Perhaps given that the primary audience was the author's own daughters, the book lacked the disdain for women seen in earlier conduct books. He even recommends life as a spinster, if the only alternative was "becoming the slaves of fools or tyrant's caprice" (31). Despite the more respectful tone, Dr. Gregory makes it plain that in order to appeal to a man, women should mask their intelligence and strive to appear delicate and modestly reserved.

Although conduct books of the colonial era instruct women on the ideals of womanhood, it is difficult to know to what extent they mirrored reality. Premarital pregnancy rates in colonial America were often as high as 30 percent, standing in direct contrast to the ideal demur virgin described by conduct books. Sermons of the era characterize young adults as coarse and falling away from Puritan ideals, another sign that conduct books reflected what conservative writers hoped girls would aspire to, rather than the actual behavior of young women. As such, the attitudes and etiquette outlined in conduct books should not be interpreted as a reflection of actual colonial life.

Fiction and Leisure Reading

Reading fiction played an important role in many women's lives. In an era in which travel was difficult and the majority of women lived in isolated or provincial towns, escaping into the pages of a novel proved an exciting and broadening experience. As a genre, fictionalized romance and adventure stories began to gain popularity in the mid-eighteenth century. Fielding's *Tom Jones*, Rousseau's *Nouvelle Heloise,* and Richardson's *Pamela* all featured heroines who tested the bounds of acceptable conduct for ladies.

The reading of novels was almost universally frowned upon by social commentators. Scores of conduct books and sermons from the pulpit condemned such reading as a waste of time at best and a dangerous temptation at worst. The adventures of dashing heroines seemed to be tacitly condoned by their authors, creating an enthralling and perilous moral climate. Future Congressman William Gaston warned his young sister about the hazard of novels: "under those stories, which are thought to be entertaining, lies a venomous poison . . . setting aside religion, they never fail to inspire those who read them, with romantic ideas, to give them a disgust for all serious employments" (Kerber 1980, 240). Women were thought to be vulnerable to the temptations so vividly and enticingly portrayed. Exposure to romantic novels was liable to affect women's behavior and conduct. Novels celebrated passion, and even though most heroines who dared to be seduced by dissolute lovers usually came to a bad end, it was believed the novel could sway the impressionable minds of young ladies. Social commentators believed girls were naturally ruled by emotion and impulse, and if they were exposed to exciting literature they might be awakened, inflamed, and led astray.

Samuel Richardson's *Pamela* (1740) was the most talked about, celebrated, and condemned novel of the eighteenth century. Its melodramatic plot set the tone for the romantic novel throughout the next century. The lovely but impoverished Pamela becomes a servant in the household of the dashing and attractive Mr. B., whose persistent efforts to seduce her have failed. In frustration, Mr. B. resorts to kidnapping and imprisoning Pamela in his country estate, where he again attempts seduction, rape, and deception in order to lure Pamela to his bed. All his efforts are frustrated by the heroic Pamela, who finds herself falling in love with her captor. The sentiment is ultimately returned, and Pamela marries Mr. B.

Although Pamela never succumbed to temptation until after she is respectfully married, the melodramatic plot featuring a sweet girl as the subject of relentless male lust was heady reading. Respectable women such as Abigail Adams expressed guilty pleasure at reading the exploits of *Pamela* and other such novels. Escaping into a novel proved irresistibly attractive to women despite the widespread condemnation of the practice. Time and again novels featured young women who struggle to balance preservation of their virtue, while finding happiness in love and marriage. Novels allowed women to experience the vicarious thrill of the dangers of the world without leaving the safety of their homes.

Travel literature was also popular leisure reading. It captured the drama and pathos of a novel, without the stigma associated with scandalous novels. The most popular travel book among colonial American women was George Anson's *Voyage around the World* (1744). Complete with naval battles, shipwrecks, bouts of scurvy, and captured Spanish galleons, Anson's vivid travel narrative captured the imagination of women who lived a comparatively confined life.

Although travel books educated the reader about geography and world affairs, they were still tainted by the association with pleasure and adventure. Reading religious or conduct books could be perceived as moral instruction, and therefore a legitimate activity to occupy a woman's time. Reading for pleasure implied a woman might be neglecting other duties, such as child care or work associated with the household. Sometimes women might skirt this disapproval by reading aloud. One woman would read aloud while her family members continued sewing or doing other household chores. Thus they were able to indulge in adventure stories without the stress of neglecting more "worthy" chores.

Captivity literature was another genre of book that sold amazingly well in colonial America. Most accounts of settlers who had been taken captive by Indians were written by the actual captives, although some were highly fictionalized accounts that cannot be independently verified. Tales such as the harrowing experience of Mary Rowlandson became best-sellers in colonial America. Captivity narratives delivered adventure and heroism, but did not carry the taint associated with novels.

Newspapers and Magazines

Both men and women were eager for news of the world. In 1765 there were twenty-five newspapers being published in various colonial cities. Ten years later that number had grown to thirty-nine, and by 1800 there were at least 150 regularly produced newspapers, mostly concentrated in eastern seaboard cities and towns. Most of these newspapers simply reprinted news articles that had appeared in other papers, and the stories were out of date by several months. Even early Americans loved gossip, and aside from a few dated news stories, the papers carried reports of nearby murders, fires, and trials.

Magazines found an audience among women who might not have been able to invest the time in reading novels or travel literature, which often ran three hundred to five hundred pages in length. *The Lady's Magazine* could claim both educational and entertainment value. Containing articles on child rearing, manners, and the dangers of social ambition, it had a moralistic tone that shielded it from conservative criticism. Each issue contained a biographical sketch of a woman of historical importance and excerpts from notable books of the day. The text was liberally highlighted with more entertaining topics such as fashion, recipes for cosmetics, and embroidery patterns. Although printed in England, copies of *The Lady's Magazine* were shipped to America where they were eagerly purchased.

Further Reading

Clark, Charles E. "The Colonial Press." In *Encyclopedia of the North American Colonies,* ed. Jacob Ernest Cooke. New York: Charles Scribner's Sons, 1993.

Hall, David D. "Books and Reading in Eighteenth Century America." In *Of Consuming Interests: The Style of Life in the Eighteenth Century,* ed. Cary Carson et al. Charlottesville: University Press of Virginia, 1994.

Hayes, Kevin J. *A Colonial Woman's Bookshelf.* Knoxville: University of Tennessee Press, 1996.

Kerber, Linda K. *Women of the Republic: Intellect and Ideology in Revolutionary America.* Chapel Hill: University of North Carolina Press, 1980.

Kerrison, Catherine. "By the Book: Eliza Ambler Brent Carrington and Conduct Literature in Late Eighteenth Century Virginia." *Virginia Magazine of History and Biography* 105 (1997): 27–52.

Newton, Sarah E. *Learning to Behave: A Guide to American Conduct Books before 1900.* Westport, CT: Greenwood Press, 1994.

Loyalist Women and the American Revolution

All women living in the colonies during the American Revolution were affected by chaos and deprivation caused by the war, but loyalist women lived under some unique circumstances. They were usually in the minority in their communities, which subjected them to intimidation and occasionally violent harassment. Their property was often subject to confiscation, and many of them left the country following the war.

Loyalists came from all classes, races, and religions, but the majority shared some defining characteristics. Loyalists tended to be socially conservative, wealthy, and Anglican. They were better-educated and more likely to be well-traveled than their patriot counterparts. Most recent immigrants were loyalists, as were merchants and those who made their living through commerce. Although estimates of loyalty are difficult to ascertain, approximately 15 percent of the population preferred loyalty to England over independence or neutrality.

Women generally shared their husband's political stance on the independence question, although it is clear from letters and diaries that some women disapproved of their husband's position. Regardless of their personal view of the war, women were usually bound by law to share the fate chosen by their husband. Most states were prepared to confiscate land and property of loyalists following the outbreak of the war. Even if the property had been a woman's premarital asset, the laws of coverture gave her husband legal control over the property.

Determining who was a loyalist was not always an easy task for patriots. All states eventually passed loyalty oaths in order to identify "traitors." Free men over the age of sixteen were required to swear their allegiance to the new nation. Those who refused to do so were subject to disarmament, heavy bonds to discourage them from aiding the British, and possibly imprisonment. If it was believed a loyalist was rendering aid to the British, land and property could be confiscated. Some women vigorously fought these actions. Grace Galloway was the wife of a prominent loyalist, who had inherited a vast fortune prior to her marriage. Although she shared her husband's loyalist sympathies, she objected to the confiscation of her property. A well-educated and well-connected woman, she appealed to the courts for redress. Preliminary rulings indicated that although her husband's property would be permanently confiscated, her premarital portion of the estate would revert to her only upon her husband's death. Grace Galloway was brusquely turned out of her Philadelphia mansion and forced to rely on the charity of friends. She died before the conclusion of the war and never had a chance to regain her property.

Except for a few areas under British occupation, most loyalists were a distrusted minority. Diaries of loyalist women recount the harassment they endured, including having their windows broken, stones thrown at their homes, and anonymous letters threatening harm left on their doorsteps. Many shopkeepers and artisans would not do business with known loyalists. Even patriots who were not hostile to loyalists were reluctant to do commerce or socialize with them for fear of bringing retaliation from their less-forgiving neighbors. Friend-

ships between patriot and loyalist women also suffered. Some loyalist women wrote of childhood friends with whom they were no longer on speaking terms.

Many loyalist women were left without male protection during the war. Some men joined the English army, and others fled the state when it became apparent their loyalist ties would result in their arrest and imprisonment. Their wives did the best they could to keep shops open or their crops planted, but such chores were especially challenging. Not only were they deprived of their husbands' assistance, but their shops and farms were more likely to be plundered by patriots seeking provisions or revenge. The stress of harassment, the loss of friendships, and the frequent absence of husbands made the life of a loyalist woman especially difficult. One woman wrote how her twelve-year-old daughter suffered "nervous fits" from being exposed to harassing mobs. Heckling crowds often harassed loyalist homes under cover of darkness, and many women reported persistent insomnia. Throughout the letters and diaries written by loyalist women during the war, they express feelings of anger, depression, anxiety, and loneliness. Although the physical deprivation and fear for their soldier husbands was no different from those of patriot women, the sense of isolation and loneliness was distinctly different.

Following the war, most states passed laws regarding how and to what extent loyalist property should be confiscated. Much of the initial legislation was highly punitive, taking everything that could be identified with a loyalist family. After a few years, attitudes began to soften, especially toward loyalist widows. It was assumed these women were merely following the leads of their husbands, and although their property might be confiscated, the law was willing to allow women to retain certain possessions, such as household furniture, utensils, linen, apparel, and ironically, slaves. Many widows of loyalists were able to retain their rights to a portion of a confiscated estate. According to common law, widows were entitled to one-third of their husband's estate. Widows appealed to the new state governments, pleading that they and their children should not be punished for their late husbands' actions. They often disavowed loyalist sympathies. John Mitchel's widow even suggested that he had been insane, and Florence Cook claimed her husband James had failed to join the patriots through ignorance of public affairs. In most cases, the legislatures granted the widows one-third of the confiscated estate. In cases where the widow had been an outspoken supporter of the king, it was not unusual for her to receive nothing.

Following the war, a large percentage of the overtly loyalist families chose to emigrate. It is estimated that more than 80,000 loyalists left the United States. Those from New England usually went to Canada, and wealthy southern planters often fled to the West Indies or Bermuda, seeking to re-create the large-scale plantations they had operated before the war. Approximately 7,000 loyalists went to England. Many of these emigrants had never set foot in England before, and felt pangs of homesickness for the country where they were no longer welcome. Among the loyalist refugees were several thousand African Americans, most of whom had been persuaded to throw their lot in with the English in exchange for freedom.

Living conditions for the refugees varied drastically. Their flight from America was rushed, and they had to leave most of their possessions behind. The English government promised to make restitution to the loyalists, and loyalist claims submitted to the Crown reveal interesting details about the property losses and sacrifices of the refugees. More than four hundred of the petitions were submitted by women, most of them widows who had lost their husbands to wartime service. The petitions describe their homes, material possessions, livestock, and other investment of value. The claims submitted by loyalist men were reimbursed by the English government at 39 percent of their value, whereas loyalist women received 34 percent of the value of the claims they submitted. The discrepancy might be accounted for by the fact that loyalist men were usually veterans and thus considered to be more worthy of reimbursement. Also, women were deemed less likely to be the sole support of a family, although many of these women were widows and too old to remarry.

All refugees were expected to find employment or other means for supporting themselves. Employment opportunities for women in England were always scarce, but more so for a foreign woman with no connections, few skills, and with children to care for. Most women were only able to find work as domestic servants, a sharp decline compared to what most of them had had in America. Petitions from some women report grinding poverty. One woman was at last able to find employment by taking in sewing, but after long months of living on little but tea, had to spend most of her money on doctor's bills. Many women reported having to pawn even their own clothing in order to buy food for their children.

The situation for the estimated 50,000 loyalist refugees who fled to Canada were also dire. Although the grinding poverty of London was daunting for refugees, at least there were poorhouses and some opportunity for employment in the urban environment. Canada had no such opportunity, and most loyalists were settled in the isolated and untamed wilderness of Nova Scotia. Sarah Tilley described the aching loneliness she felt as she watched the departure of the ship that had delivered her to Nova Scotia: "I climbed to the top of Chipman's Hill and watched the sails in the distance, and such a feeling of loneliness came over me that though I had not shed a tear through all the war, I sat down on the damp moss with my baby on my lap and cried bitterly" (Berkin 1996, 193).

During the first winter the refugees to Nova Scotia pitched tents in the shelter of the woods, trying to provide protection against the snow by covering the tents with spruce bows. Hastily constructed barracks were erected, but some women and children were forced to live for years in the crowded barracks before they could be relocated to a homestead of their own. One factor that weighed in the refugees' favor was the quality and diversity of their population. As a group, loyalists were well educated, with a healthy cross section of tradesmen, skilled laborers, and professionals. These hardworking people were determined to re-create a civilized society in Canada.

Some loyalists, especially the less-prominent or less-wealthy loyalists, elected to remain in the United States. Although many were shunned or had property confiscated, by the 1790s most who had elected to remain were reintegrated into society.

See also African American Women and the American Revolution

Further Reading

Berkin, Carol. *First Generations: Women in Colonial America.* New York: Hill and Wang, 1996.

Coker, Kathy Roe. "The Calamities of War: Loyalism and Women in South Carolina." In *Southern Women: Histories and Identities,* ed. Virginia Bernhard. Columbia: University of Missouri Press, 1992.

Evans, Elizabeth. *Weathering the Storm: Women of the American Revolution.* New York: Charles Scribner's Sons, 1975.

Norton, Mary Beth. "Eighteenth-Century American Women in Peace and War: The Case of the Loyalists." *William and Mary Quarterly* 33 (1976): 386–409.

———. *Liberty's Daughters: The Revolutionary Experience of American Women, 1750–1800.* Boston: Little, Brown and Co., 1980.

Potter-MacKinnon, Janice. *While the Women only Wept: Loyalist Refugee Women.* Buffalo, NY: McGill-Queen's University Press, 1993.

M

Manly Hearted Women

Native American women who
adopted masculine gender roles

Many Native American tribes allowed for great flexibility in their gender roles, condoned aspects of homosexuality, and permitted cross-dressing. Perhaps the most famous of the gender variations was the *berdache,* an Indian man who chose to dress and act like a woman. Although there were numerous instances of *berdaches,* there was a comparatively small segment of Indian women who elected to live highly masculine lifestyles.

Traditions for such women varied widely across tribes. In most instances they adopted masculine clothing, hairstyles, and names. They almost always undertook masculine work responsibilities, including hunting, trapping, tribal leadership, and warfare. They ate, talked, sat, and carried themselves as men. Manly hearted women made no attempt to "pass" as males. Their family and tribal members were well aware of their biological gender, but were willing to treat them as masculine members of the tribe. Most manly hearted women rejected female qualities altogether, rather than assuming characteristics of both sexes.

In some instances the manly hearted women took female wives. The nature of this relationship varied from tribe to tribe and from couple to couple. It is apparent that many such couples had a sexual component to their relationship, but others probably lived platonically. Manly hearted women who had a sexual element in their marriage were considered lesbians by their tribe. The "wife" in such partnerships was always a traditional female. Manly hearted women did not marry another cross-gendered woman. The "wife" was not considered to be a lesbian or cross-gendered person. Should the union end in divorce, such women usually reverted to traditional, heterosexual unions, with no homosexual stigma attached to them.

Raising children was often a component of these relationships. Divorce was common in Indian communities, and many of the wives would have children from prior relationships. Adoption of orphans or captives of war was another common means for the couple to become parents.

Girls who assumed cross-gendered status usually displayed a preference for the male role in childhood. They rejected traditional female games, dolls, and friends in order to pursue life among the boys. If the girl's parents condoned her choice, she would be raised from childhood to learn masculine skills such as hunting, fishing, raiding, and warfare.

Puberty would have been an important stage, after which it would be difficult to revert to a female role. Most Indian tribes condoned sexual experimentation during puberty, and it is possible these women would have had sexual experiences with men. If she found it pleasing, it was not too late to learn essential female skills, such as basket weaving, making clothes, child rearing, and food preparation. She would then be capable of becoming a traditional wife. Should she never learn these tasks, it is unlikely she could abandon her masculine gender.

After reaching adulthood, there is little evidence that manly hearted women ever elected to switch back to the female gender. On rare occasions parents who had only daughters might select a child to be raised as a cross-gendered person. This was most common in the northern areas of Canada, where harsh climactic conditions caused families to live much of the year in isolation, and they depended on masculine hunting activities for survival.

Not all of the manly hearted women adopted the full range of masculine gender roles. "Warrior women" challenged traditional gender roles by engaging in battles, but had no intention of renouncing their gender status. These were women who accompanied their husbands to war. Some did not fight, but merely spurred their husbands on and provided aid during a battle. Others took up arms after their husbands had fallen in battle. The interpretation of dreams was an important element in Native American raiding, and some women used their visions as justification to take up arms and lead men into battle.

Warrior women and manly hearted women were distinctly different. Although both engaged in warfare, manly hearted women did so not out of any fierce desire to achieve fame in warfare, but merely as one aspect of their gender switch. Warrior women had no interest in switching genders, but they had intense desire to partake in battle for its own sake.

Manly hearted women were rare in the plains and on the eastern seaboard. They were most common among western and northern tribes of Canada. Europeans coming into contact with *berdaches* and manly hearted women were confused by these gender-bending individuals. Such people would not have been tolerated among European society, but there was no shame tied to cross-gendered existence among Native Americans during the early centuries of European settlement. This changed after contact with European traders and missionaries. Cross-gendered people became increasingly rare and the subject of ridicule. By the mid-nineteenth century, the custom of raising girls as manly hearted women had died out.

See Also Lesbians

Further Reading

Blackwood, Evelyn. "Sexuality and Gender in Certain Native American Tribes: The Case of Cross-Gender Females." *Signs* 10, no.11 (1984): 27–42.

Jacobs, Sue-Ellen, ed. *Two-Spirit People: Native American Gender Identity, Sexuality, and Spirituality.* Urbana: University of Illinois Press, 1997.

Lang, Sabine. *Men as Women, Women as Men: Changing Gender in Native American Cultures.* Austin: University of Texas Press, 1998.

Mariners' Wives

The sea played a huge role on the economy of early America, especially in the New England colonies. Fishing was second only to farming in terms of the number of men it employed. Aside from the men employed by fishing, other men took to the sea on merchant vessels sailing to Europe, the Caribbean, or the Indies in search of trade. Although women did not directly participate in maritime work during the colonial period, the absence of their husbands and fathers on extended voyages created a unique subculture of women who had little or no male presence in their daily lives. These women needed to find means of economic and social support during absences that could last up to a year.

The lives of shore fishermen and men who worked on whalers were markedly different, as were the conditions created for their families. Shore fishermen might leave home for only a few weeks until the hull of their ship was full. Whalers left for much longer periods of time. The best whaling grounds in the eighteenth century were off the coasts of Greenland, Africa, and the Azores. Whales were slaughtered at sea, and their oil harvested and stored in casks. Whalers were under instruction not to return home until the hull of their ship was full. By the end of the eighteenth century, it was common for whalers to be at sea for almost a year.

Most mariners' wives lived in harbor towns, typically the place where population and development were the densest of the colonies. This allowed women not only the opportunity for employment, but also access to a social support system. By the eighteenth century, many of these harbor towns had more women than men, a highly unusual occurrence in early America. Because a large percentage of men were literally out to sea, women were expected to perform traditionally male tasks. They carted hay, operated shops, assisted with the delivery of the post, ran inns and taverns, and were even known to help with the repair of roads and bridges.

The wives of sailors and fishermen had special responsibilities for the support of their families. Although they were usually supplied with a generous sum of money before their husbands left for sea, the uncertainty of the duration of the voyage left many women in a precarious position. Most turned to some form of employment to supplement their income. They took in boarders, taught day school, preserved food, sold cheese, took in laundry, carded wool, made twine, or assisted at shops, inns, and taverns. Some of the work might have been seasonal. During heavy agricultural seasons women might have assisted for a few weeks in the fields. When the apples were ripe, some women brewed cider. Many mariners' wives found work in support of the maritime industry, such as making nets, rope, and barrels.

Employment came in addition to normal activities expected of any colonial woman. Her primary role was to raise her children, which entailed a heavy round of cooking, washing, teaching, and minding the youngsters. In the absence of a husband, they undertook household chores usually associated with men. They whitewashed their homes, tended to the livestock, shot wild game, and did almost any other chore associated with masculine labor.

In towns with large maritime employment, the community often had a network of support mechanisms. Neighbors looked after children if a mother had a few hours of weekly employment outside the home. Shop owners routinely extended credit to mariners' wives. One sailor's wife noted in her diary that a neighbor regularly chopped wood for her. "I told him if my husband lived to return it would be made up to him . . . he said he would not take anything for it," and he enjoyed the satisfaction in providing her with a service (Norling 2000, 34).

Sometimes women fell into times of extreme economic need. They could turn to the church for funds to tide them over, although they were more likely to turn to the ship's owner, pleading an advance on their husbands' wages. Extended family members provided what assistance they could, but because working at sea often ran in families, there might have been no man in the extended family to turn to.

The emotional toll taken on women at home was high. Diaries of mariners' wives complain more of loneliness than economic need. Lydia Almy poured into her diary the solitude she felt on being separated from her husband, Christopher: "I ought not to complain or think my lot was hard. . . . I have everything to make me comfortable and happy and want for nothing of this world's good except for the company of my dear husband" (Norling 2000, 77–78). Even the prattling of Lydia's three-year-old son caused her lonesomeness, such as when the boy asked her to make extra johnnycakes, because perhaps his daddy would come home that day. There is evidence that sailors' wives leaned heavily on one another for company. They visited regularly, shared meals, attended church together, and held quilting bees. During times of need they would look after one another's children or loan whatever material goods might be needed.

Communication with absent husbands was scanty and uncertain. Illiteracy was sometimes a problem, although a sailor could usually find someone willing to pen a few lines. Letters were dropped off at ports where the ships reprovisioned, then were sent out with the next ship bound for the home colony. It was not uncommon for letters to arrive six to eight months after being written. The letters men wrote home often brought news of other men on the ship. They sometimes bid their wives to tell other women of the town their husbands were fine, or their son was eating well. This served several functions. Letters were known to go astray, so by providing news of other sailors on the ship, townswomen could keep informed, even if their own husband had failed to write or his letter was lost. It also reinforced the social network of women at home. They traded news as soon as they heard it, leaning on one another for support and comfort. Women had very little chance to write letters in reply, because the destinations of the whaling ships were always uncertain.

Because there was no fixed date for a ship to return, a woman might watch a year stretch into two, with no knowledge as to the safety of her husband. Whaling was a dangerous occupation, and it was common for returning ships to have lost crew members during the voyage. On rare occasions, an entire ship might go down at sea, causing years of anxiety for family members, who scanned the horizon waiting for the ship's return. Wives in such a position were neither married women nor widows. They were not free to remarry, nor could they transact business without their husbands' consent. Negotiations such as selling a piece of property or leasing a home had no legal standing without a husband's signature. A woman who believed her husband to be lost at sea could appeal to a court to grant her legal autonomy in order to transact business in her own name. Remarriage was also difficult. In some colonies, a woman had to wait seven years before her missing husband could be declared formally dead.

A Husband Lost at Sea (1670)

When a ship failed to return to port, sailors' wives were left in a precarious state, neither widowed nor single. The following is the successful petition to a Connecticut court to dissolve such a marriage:

> In answer to the petition of Hanna Huitt of Stonington, she having declared that she hath not heard from her late husband Thomas Huitt for the space of eight years and better, and the neighbors also testifying that the said Huitt hath so long been absent and that they have not heard of him or of the vessel or company he went with since their departure, The Court having considered the premises, declare that she the said Hanna Huitt is at liberty to marry if she see cause.

Source: Colonial Connecticut Records, 1636–1776, vol. 2. Hartford, CT: Brown & Parsons, 1850, p. 129.

The unique culture of mariners' wives became even more pronounced in the nineteenth century, when whaling voyages lengthened to two and three years.

Further Reading

Crane, Elaine Forman. *Ebb Tide in New England: Women, Seaports, and Social Change, 1630–1800.* Boston: Northeastern University Press, 1998.

Norling, Lisa. *Captain Ahab Had a Wife: New England Women and the Whalefishery, 1720–1870.* Chapel Hill: University of North Carolina Press, 2000.

Marriage

The institution of marriage underwent a dramatic transformation between the seventeenth and nineteenth centuries. At the forefront of concerns for early settlers was survival. Families had very few surplus goods. Land was plentiful, but cleared land suitable for farming was scarce. Housing was rudimentary, the food supply uncertain, and mortality was high. As families struggled to scratch out an existence in unfamiliar territory, a marriage based on love was a luxury few could afford or even expect.

Seventeenth-century families depended on communal support to withstand periods of drought, Indian attacks, or illness. Families turned to the community for help when a mother needed a few weeks to recover after giving birth, a father was out of commission because of a broken leg, or an ox died during plowing. Community ties were strengthened by intermarriage, and families sought to create alliances with other families of good character and sound resources. Communities were small, and single men far outnumbered available women. With a limited marriage pool, single people could not afford the luxury of seeking out a romantic soul mate. Although parents hoped their daughter would marry a man she would be friendly with, love was not a prerequisite for marriage, nor did girls grow up expecting it.

By the eighteenth century, communities had grown in size and the sex ratio had come into balance. With families no longer living on the edge of

A Mother's Concern

By the late eighteenth century, young adults were beginning to choose their marriage partners based on romantic attachment. The following letter from Ann Randolph captures the concerns raised when very young people made such an important decision. Her concerns were well founded, because her sixteen-year-old daughter, Judith, married her nineteen-year-old cousin, which ultimately proved to be a disastrously unhappy marriage.

Dear Sir,

    . . . It has ever been my wish to keep my Daughters single 'till they were old enough to form a proper judgement of Mankind; well knowing that a woman's happiness depends entirely on the Husband she is united to; it is a step that requires more deliberation than girls generally take, or even Mothers seem to think necessary. The risk, though always great, is doubled when they marry very young. It is impossible for them to know each other's disposition; for at sixteen and nineteen we think everybody perfect that we take a fancy to. . . . they are apt to be sorry when the delirium of love is over and reason is allowed to re-ascend her throne, and if they are not so happy as to find in each other a similarity of temper and good qualities enough to excite esteem and friendship, they must be wretched without remedy. . . .

    I have given Judy Richard's letters, but have desired her not to answer them before she has her Father's leave. With good wishes for your self and family, I am dear sir your Affectionate Humble Servant,

    Ann Randolph

Source: "Randolph and Tucker Letters." *Virginia Magazine of History and Biography* 42 (1934): 49–50.

survival, the economic demands placed on marriage eased. Parents still had heavy influence over the final selection of a spouse, but young women were beginning to consider companionship and love to be among the important factors to consider in a potential match. Now that survival was no longer at the forefront of concern, compatibility was more important than economic alliances. Following the American Revolution, romantic love became the primary component in marriage, and too much consideration of the economic aspects of the alliance was considered in poor taste.

Most people did not marry until they were financially capable of maintaining a separate household. In America, this tended to delay marriage until a couple was in their early twenties. Most husbands were three to four years older than their brides, although high rates of mortality often drastically skewed this figure. If a widowed man remarried a young woman, he might be ten to fifteen years her senior.

The timing of most weddings was dependent on the agricultural season. Marriage rates slumped during the work-intensive summer and the weeks of Lent and Advent. November was by far the most popular month for weddings, with January and February being the next preference. Many brides in colonial America came to the altar pregnant, and these weddings took place as expediently as possible.

Betrothal and Wedding Ceremonies

Throughout most of the early American period, a young man would need to gain permission of a woman's father or guardian before courting her. Fathers discouraged all but potential husbands. A young woman could not be seen with more than a few sweethearts before her reputation began to be tarnished. Young women were not considered to be worldly enough to decide on their own marriage partners. It was the responsibility of her parents to evaluate a suitor for his financial wherewithal, character, and prospects. Once the young man had the approval of a girl's parents, he was free to propose marriage to her.

Young women almost always had veto power over a proposed marriage. Although they might not have been free to choose their own suitors, few parents ever forced their daughters to marry against their will. Love was not a prerequisite, but a companionate marriage was valued. If a young woman expressed revulsion for the suitor, town ministers and judges usually supported her decision and would not marry the couple.

Once a proposal had been accepted, banns had to be read at the town church on at least three separate occasions. Banns were a public announcement of the betrothal and were intended to put the community on notice of the marriage so that any who saw an impediment to the match might come forward. Impediments included a prior marriage still in force or a blood relationship. The Anglican Church, which dominated the southern colonies, had extensive rules regarding marriage and consanguinity (blood relationships). For example, a man could not marry his deceased brother's widow, uncle's widow, or almost any other in-law who was once married to a family member. Curiously, the custom did not prohibit the marriage of first cousins, which was common in some parts of the South.

The primary motivation for the publication of banns was the attempt to ensure that neither of the parties had been previously married. Because divorces were almost impossible to obtain, unhappy couples often abandoned their spouses and began living separate lives. Publishing banns, both locally and in nearby towns, was an attempt to prevent bigamous unions.

Breaking an engagement was serious business, and men could be sued in court for breach of promise. A spurned woman's reputation was seriously damaged. It was assumed that betrothed couples engaged in some sexual dalliance, if not outright intercourse. The would-be bride was left with questionable virginity and speculation as to what made her so undesirable that a man would call off an engagement. Newspapers carried stories announcing the verdicts in breach-of-promise suits, such as when Elizabeth Leatherdale won £25 and Rebecca Roods was awarded £100, both in 1773. Other women took out newspaper advertisements, warning women to beware of particular men and not to marry them until they consulted with the spurned woman.

The trappings of a wedding ceremony differed owing to religious, economic, and regional variations. New England Puritans considered marriage to be a civil contract, rather than a sacred union. In keeping with Puritan custom to simplify and strip embellishment from ceremonies, weddings were brief and without excessive celebration. On the Sunday prior to the wedding, the bride had the option to choose the text on which the minister's sermon would be based. This was the extent of the church's involvement in the marriage. The actual ceremony took place at the home of the bride and was conducted by a judge. Documents were signed, but no rings or holy vows were exchanged. The bride wore her best gown, but it was not tailor-made for her wedding.

Following a Puritan wedding ceremony, a meal was served and toasts to the couple were offered. The standard wedding drink was a spiced hard cider called sack-posset. Because few families were equipped to serve large numbers of people, most guests would have brought their own mugs, spoons, and forks. Gifts were expected from close relatives only. Linen and pewter were the most common wedding gifts. Over time Puritan weddings lost their austerity, and celebration of the union became more festive. By the late eighteenth century, dancing and music were common in after-wedding celebrations.

Weddings in the middle and southern colonies were generally more religious in nature. They usually took place in the home, but were always presided over by a minister. These weddings were considered a sacred rite. Vows were exchanged, biblical passages were read, and attendees prayed for the new couple. The ceremony was followed by elaborate feasting, dancing, and drinking. Gifts were widely exchanged among all parties, including customary gifts from the groom to the guests.

Special wedding dresses were often made for these more festive, elaborate ceremonies. There was no special color for a wedding dress, merely the best fabric the family could afford. Silk and brocade were the most desirable. By the early nineteenth century, wedding veils were sometimes used, but they did not become a standard part of wedding attire until far later in the century.

Financial and Legal Aspects of Marriage

Parents had a tremendous amount of influence over the pairing of marriage partners. Early Americans did not marry until they were financially capable of maintaining a household. It was almost impossible for a young man to accumulate enough capital to do so without parental assistance. It was customary for fathers to give their adult sons portions of land or enough money to become established on another piece of land. Marriage would have to wait until the father was willing to do so.

Women usually brought "movable goods" into the marriage. Fathers provided their daughters with dowries of farm animals, tools, or possibly slaves. Rarely did a father give a daughter land, unless he had no sons. The negotiations for the transfer of goods usually took place between the two fathers of the prospective marriage partners. Both fathers were expected to provide the union with something of value. The following exchange written by Mr. Thomas Walker is typical of wealthy Virginia planters:

> Dear Sir: My son, John Walker, having informed me of his intention to pay his addresses to your daughter Elizabeth. . . . it may not be amiss to inform you what I feel myself able to afford for their support, in case of a union. My affairs are in an uncertain state, but I will promise one thousand pounds, to be paid in 1766, and the further sum of two thousand pounds I promise to give him; but the uncertainty of my present affairs prevents my fixing on a time of payment. The above sums are all to be in money or lands and other effects, at the option of my son, John Walker. (Spruill 1938, 146)

The future father-in-law answered with an equally businesslike letter, promising five hundred pounds worth of goods, when his affairs were able to afford the cost. Middling and poor families obviously had no such formal arrangements, but something was almost always provided from both parents, even if it were only a calf or some farm tools. In poor families, the couple might live with one of the parents until they could afford their own farm, but this was usually for only a brief period and not common.

When a woman married, she lost her independent legal status. In the eyes of the law, she was one with her husband, but her husband was granted all decision-making authority. A woman could not have control over property or goods, decide how resources were to be allocated, or enter into legal agreements without the consent of her husband.

Wealthy fathers who had concerns about protecting their daughters' financial assets might insist on a prenuptial trust, which put financial resources beyond reach of the husband. Wealthy widows also were able to put premarital assets into separate estates for the use of their children. In almost all cases involving separate trusts, the document was not binding under law unless the prospective husband agreed in writing to the creation of the separate trust.

The Nature of Colonial Marriage

It is apparent that romantic love was not viewed as a prerequisite for marriage during most of the colonial period. Girls were advised to look for common sense and economic potential when evaluating a marriage prospect. Love was considered to be a fickle emotion, liable to skew a girl's judgment. It was hoped that love would come *after* marriage, but its absence prior to marriage was generally not an impediment.

Because marriage was viewed primarily as a force of economic and social stability, it has been common to conclude that colonial marriages were loveless. One historian even suggested that the death of a wife was less troublesome for a farmer than the death of a cow. This perception of cold, businesslike marriages is reinforced by surviving documents. Court records for divorce and spousal battery survive, as do advertisements in newspapers where angry husbands disavow their wives and refuse to pay any debts she accumulates. Happy marriages did not leave such traces in the historical record. The few surviving journals kept by colonial men make nonchalant references to their wives and family life, such as when Matthew Paxton wrote in 1755: "My wife was delivered about 8 in the morning of a Son, and sold a cow to William Macmeal of New Boston" (Ulrich 2003, 170). Colonial diaries made scant comments about loved ones, but this cannot be interpreted as a dismissive attitude toward one's spouse. Diaries were practical documents that recorded daily purchases, home consumption, and labor on the farm.

One of the few areas where affection can be documented was in letters. These are scarce, not only

A colonial wedding, the marriage of Dr. Francis Le Baron and Mary Wilder, Plymouth, 1695. As with many colonial marriages, the Le Baron wedding took place in the home. (Library of Congress)

because of the rarity of literate couples, but also because of the fact that few couples saw the need to write letters to one another. In an age when people rarely traveled outside of their own town, there was little need for written letters. Nevertheless, some touching letters survive, such as when Theodorick Bland, a soldier serving in New Jersey, wrote to his wife in the winter of 1777: "My dear, when you are writing, write of nothing but yourself . . . tell me of your going to bed, of your rising, of the hour you breakfast, dine, sup, visit, tell me of anything, but leave me not in doubt about your health. . . . Heaven never means to separate two who love so well, so soon" (Morgan 1952, 50).

Jeremias Van Cortlandt wrote to his parents that the best thing he could hope in his life was to spend it with his wife, Maria, at his side. No matter the practical considerations that gave rise to these marriages, it is clear that the partners loved one another.

Although mutual respect characterized most colonial marriages, in all but the most extraordinary partnerships, the role of wife was submissive and subordinate to the husband. Men and women were considered spiritual equals in the eyes of God, and a husband was therefore required to treat his wife with respect, but this did not preclude a sense of intellectual inequality. A man was to be master of his home, and most colonial women accepted this without question. Legal and social tradition also cast the colonial wife in the role of helpmeet. Her purpose was to raise her husband's children, tend her husband's house, and be a source of comfort and affection for the family. The secondary position of women in marriage did not prohibit happy and satisfying marriages. Abigail Adams, whose marriage to John Adams has been cited as a model of domestic harmony, wrote, "a well ordered home is my chief delight, and the affectionate domestic wife with the relative duties which accompany that character my highest ambition" (Abigail Adams to John Adams, 20 June 1783). Such casual acceptance of a subordinate role may seem odd to contemporary women, but very few colonial women ever questioned this status.

The expectations for a wife were simple and clear-cut. She was responsible for the smooth operations on the domestic front and sexual fidelity. Sex was viewed as an important and healthy activity in a marriage. Fidelity was expected of both partners, but a double standard allowed men to stray without serious consequences. Adultery was a more serious offense for a woman, because she could impose an illegitimate heir on her husband through her promiscuity. In return for her faithful service, a wife could expect her husband to provide her with all the necessities needed to maintain her home and support herself and children. If he refused to provide such, the "doctrine of necessities" allowed a wife to obtain necessary goods from the local shopkeeper. The items would be charged to her husband's line of credit, for which he would be obligated to pay.

Common-Law Marriages

Divorce was almost impossible to obtain throughout most of the colonial period. Many unhappy couples simply agreed to separate, often moving on to a new community to start afresh. Although reading banns was an attempt to prevent such persons from entering into a bigamous marriage, many couples who knew this to be a problem simply bypassed the marriage ceremony altogether. One such couple was Deborah and Benjamin Franklin. Deborah had been married to John Rogers, who she later discovered to have abandoned his first wife. After a few months of a tempestuous union, Rogers fled to the West Indies, leaving Deborah neither a wife nor a single woman. With her legal standing in limbo, she and Benjamin Franklin elected to simply live together as man and wife. Their unconventional marriage was common knowledge, causing whispers behind Deborah's back, but she was not snubbed outright.

Couples living within a common-law marriage did not advertise their state. The couple might move to a new town, where most villagers would accept their marital status at face value. Were it to be known the couple was "living in sin," they might endure a certain amount of social ostracism. The higher the status of the couple, the more damaging such a revelation would have been.

Common-law marriages had little standing in a court of law until the late seventeenth century. Should a former spouse emerge and demand access to property or children, there was little the common-law spouse could do to prevent such actions. The first official recognition of quasi legitimacy of common-law marriage was in 1809, when Mrs. William Reed succeeded in gaining a pension from her late common-law husband's employer. The New York Supreme Court ruled that because the couple held themselves out to be married, their families accepted them as such, and both parties supported each other as spouses, Mrs. Reed should be entitled to be considered Mr. Reed's widow. Mrs. Reed's saving grace was that her first husband had died a few years prior to Mr. Reed's demise. Had the first marriage still been in force, it is not likely the court would have been willing to grant her common-law marriage any standing.

Despite the reluctant willingness of courts to grant legal protection to common-law marriages in limited circumstances, the social stigma attached to women who were known to be living without benefit of marriage was high. The ideal woman was to be modest, submissive, and devout. A woman living in a common-law marriage was unlikely to be any of the three, casting doubt on her character and barring her from many social venues.

Elopement

There were rigid prohibitions against elopement. Such marriages occurred only when parental disapproval was so strong that the couple knew there was little chance parents would offer a financial settlement. The eloping couple usually hoped that after the marriage was accomplished, disapproving parents would relent and grant a settlement. In the interest of preventing elopements, many colonies passed laws against secret courtships. The Plymouth Colony's statute was typical: "If any shall make motion of marriage to any man's daughter . . . not having first obtained leave and consent of the parents or masters so to so, [he] shall be punished wither by fine or corporal punishment or both"

(*Records of the Colony of New Plymouth,* vol. 11, 29). Virginia and Maryland had statutes on the books that fined ministers who performed marriage ceremonies without publication of banns or a license.

Despite the attempts to legally prevent elopements, fortune-hunting suitors were often willing to run the risk. Twelve-year-old Elizabeth Charleton, from one of the wealthiest families in Virginia, was persuaded to elope with John Severne in 1662. In 1688 Archibald Burnett was sent to prison for marrying eleven-year-old Sarah Vanhart, an heiress from Maryland. Some colonies passed laws that blocked fortune hunters from inheriting property. In such cases, the daughter could only come into possession of an inheritance after her husband had died. If she died first, the inheritance would go to her children.

Wife Selling

Folklore tells of the odd custom of wife selling as an alternative means of ending an unhappy marriage in early modern England and America. According to the legend, both husband and wife agreed to terminate the union by placing the wife up for auction at the town center. The wife was led to town with a rope about her neck, much like a cow going to auction. The husband paid the toll necessary to auction goods at the marketplace and then accepted bids from onlookers. The highest bidder was often conveniently the wife's lover, and all parties were pleased with the outcome. The new "husband" was given the toll ticket as proof of new ownership, and the deal was sealed with a mug of beer.

The most famous instance of wife selling is the fictional account in Thomas Hardy's *The Mayor of Casterbridge.* Rumors of purported wife sales occurred in eighteenth- and nineteenth-century England and America. These events took place in small, rural towns among poor, uneducated people. Newspapers reporting an occurrence of a wife sale were usually short on details, and always expressed shock and distaste at the prospect of such crass dealings. Whether wife sales were real events or mere folkloric rumor can probably never be known. The nature of a wife sale meant there were no recorded documents, and little beyond vague, secondhand

stories in newspapers to document their occurrence. Given that the newspapers described wife selling to be an ancient custom practiced by rural people, it would be foolish for any historian to claim that such an event *never* happened, though simple abandonment seems to be a much more commonly resorted to technique for ending a marriage.

See also Courtship; Divorce; Interracial Marriage; Motherhood; Sex and Sexuality; Widowhood.

Further Reading

Eberhardt, Lynne A. "Passion and Propriety: Tidewater Marriages in the Colonial Chesapeake." *Maryland Historical Magazine* 93 (Fall 1998): 325–347.

Dubler, Ariela R. "Governing through Contract: Common Law Marriage in the Nineteenth Century." *Yale Law Journal* 107 (1998): 1885–1920.

Fischer, David Hackett. *Albion's Seed: Four British Folkways in America.* New York: Oxford University Press, 1989.

Ktorides, Irene. "Marriage Customs in Colonial New England." *Historical Journal of Western Massachusetts* 2, no. 2 (1973): 5–21.

Morgan, Edmund S. *Virginians at Home: Family Life in the Eighteenth Century.* Charlottesville, VA: Dominion Books, 1952.

Salmon, Marylynn. "Marriage." In *Encyclopedia of the North American Colonies,* ed. Jacob Ernest Cooke. New York: Charles Scribner's Sons, 1993.

Semonche, John E. "Common-Law Marriage in North Carolina: A Study in Legal History." *American Journal of Legal History* 9 (1965): 320–349.

Spruill, Julia Cherry. *Women's Life and Work in the Southern Colonies.* Chapel Hill: University of North Carolina Press, 1938.

Ulrich, Laurel Thatcher. "Women's Travail, Men's Labor: Birth Stories from 18th Century New England Diaries." In *Women's Work in New England,* ed. Peter Benes. Boston: Boston University Press, 2003.

Marriage and Family among Enslaved Women

One of the few psychological refuges a slave woman had was in the comfort of her family life. Marriage usually occurred for black women in their late teens or early twenties. On average their husbands were four years older than they were and were often slaves of the same master.

Finding a satisfactory mate could be a difficult challenge. If a slave lived on a small plantation, there might not have been any man of appropriate age, with whom marriage was not precluded by a blood relationship. By 1711 only 28 percent of slaves lived on plantations with twenty or more slaves. The rest lived on scattered farms with only a handful of slaves. For such people, marriage with a slave from a neighboring farm was the only alternative to a single life. During the pre-Revolutionary era, only about one-quarter of slave women were living with a husband. The rest were either single or married to a man who lived elsewhere. Although both masters and slave women would prefer marriage to someone who lived on the same property, lack of available partners often prompted them to look outside their plantation. Husbands who lived at neighboring plantations were usually granted passes to visit their wives on weekends.

Norms governing sexual conduct in the slave quarters did not mirror those of white society. There was little prohibition on premarital sex, and it was not uncommon for a girl to have a child before wedlock. Sexual freedom came to an end upon marriage, after which any infidelity was strongly condemned. In Africa, marriages tended to be a social contract rather than a religious rite. As such, marriages could be dissolved when they were no longer beneficial for the parties involved. A small degree of this fluid concept of marriage was transported across the ocean. If a slave marriage proved unsatisfactory to either or both of the people involved, they were free to declare themselves no longer married.

Most slave weddings took place during the comparatively idle months of December and January. Sometimes the master or a white minister performed the ceremony, but black preachers seemed to be the preference. Slave marriage had no legal standing, and the phrase "Till death do you part," could not be a part of the ceremony. Certain elements of African tradition, such as jumping over the broomstick, were often incorporated into the ceremonies. The broom represented the birth of a new

---

A Woman "Steals" Her Husband

Many African American women were unable to live with their husbands, either because they lived on separate plantations or one of them was free. The following advertisement for an escaped slave tells of such a marriage:

> Run away from the Subscriber, in York County, in August last, a Negro Man Slave who calls himself Stepney Blue, upwards of six feet high, of a tawny complexion, a black spot on his forehead, and has lost some of his fore teeth. He was the property of Mrs. Sarah Mingham, whom I have since married; and, as I have been informed, has forged a pass with his mistress's name to it, giving him leave to hire himself. He went away with a free Negro woman named Esther Roberts, who I am told is his wife, and I make no doubt but he has (or will get) a Pass, in order to pass as a Free Man. Since he went off, he has been seen in Gloucester County. Any person who will take up the said Slave, and secure him so that I get him again, shall have 20 shillings if taken within 20 miles of this place.
>   Nathan Yancey

Source: Virginia Gazette, 29 September 1744.

---

household, and jumping across it at the conclusion of the ceremony symbolized a leap into married life.

The ability to live together depended on the availability of housing. Many newly married couples continued to live in their respective parent's cabins until the birth of their first child. Quality of slave quarters varied dramatically, but most would have had straw bedding, barrels for seating, and a grindstone for beating corn into meal. Each hut or cabin usually contained an extended family, or possibly two small families. One-room cabins often had a loft where children slept, and two-room cabins were not unusual. Most had hard dirt floors. They had few windows or doors, and cabins were invariably hot in the summer and cold during the winter. It was in this setting that slaves cooked their meals, played in the yard, raised a small garden, smoked, sang, and socialized.

Most slave women bore their first child between the ages of sixteen and twenty-three. The average spacing between children was two to three years, indicating they breastfed their children for an extended period of time, possibly as a means of birth control.

The greatest fear of any slave woman was that her husband or children would be sold away from her. Almost all slave children were permitted to remain with their mothers until age five, as infants and toddlers were of little economic value and not likely to be sold. There were social prohibitions against selling children under twelve years of age, although callous masters had no qualms about doing so. Male slaves carried a higher value and were more likely to be sold. Daughters were more likely to be raised by their mothers to adulthood, but as many as 60 percent of male slaves were sold before they reached manhood. There were practical reasons a master was reluctant to break apart a slave family through selling off husbands or children. Family was vitally important to slaves, and they could retaliate against a master by sabotage, arson, work slowdowns, or running away.

Most women were never sold from the place they were born, and they benefited from a network of extended kin: mothers, grandmothers, aunts, cousins, and nieces. This network was important for the rearing of children. Because most able-bodied adults performed hard labor during daylight hours, small children were looked after by grandmothers or older children. Some women would have been able to bring infants to work with them, but as the children became toddlers, it became necessary for them to be supervised by someone other than their working mother.

Slave marriages varied greatly in terms of affection, support, and endurance. One of the primary motivations behind slave escapes was an attempt to reunite families, a testament to the bonds of love. Conditions of slavery imposed extraordinary stresses on the family. Men were helpless witnesses to their wives' and daughters' sexual degradation by white men. Women knew their sons or husbands could be sold away from them. They might witness the humiliating effects of beatings on their family members. These extraordinary circumstances might have caused some partners to emotionally withdraw from a relationship. In other cases, destructive patterns that can strike any group also plagued slave families. Alcoholism, domestic violence, jealousy, and depression could all be found in the slave quarters.

In the event a wife was separated from her husband by the sale of one or both parties, some women remained loyal to their husband for years. They may have tried to visit, send letters, or attempt to be sold to the same master. Most of these women never saw their husbands again. Slave marriages had no legal standing, and they were free to remarry whenever they chose, but the memory of a forcibly sundered marriage would likely remain forever.

Women played a uniquely central position in slave families. Less than one-half of slave children were raised in families with two parents. The other children had fathers who lived on neighboring plantations, had been sold, or died. Mothers became the primary teacher, parent, and disciplinarian in her child's life. The "black matriarchy" cited in sociological debates might have its origins in this family structure.

The effect of slavery on the black family has been a matter of intense scholarly interest. Stanley M. Elkins and E. Franklin Frazier lead a group of academics who claim that sexual exploitation, separation, miscegenation, and restrictive legal codes combined to corrode the stability of the black family. Other historians such as Herbert Gutman, Robert Abzug, and John Blassingame contend that strong black families emerged despite the damaging effects of slavery.

The sense of solidarity fostered in the slave quarters cannot be underestimated. Extended families lived together and helped raise the children. A sense of communal fellowship was kindled through sharing the same burdens and anxieties. In the hours after sundown and on Sundays they relaxed and celebrated together. Many of the spirituals sung in slave quarters portrayed a sense of worthiness and belief that slaves would ultimately prevail over the earthly struggles of life.

Further Reading

Genovese, Eugene D. *Roll, Jordan, Roll: The World the Slaves Made*. New York: Pantheon Books, 1972.

Gutman, Herbert G. *The Black Family in Slavery and Freedom, 1750–1925.* New York: Pantheon Books, 1976.

Kulikoff, Allan. "The Origins of Afro-American Society in Tidewater Maryland and Virginia, 1700–1790. *William and Mary Quarterly,* 3d ser. 35 (1978): 226–259.

Nash, Gary B. *Red, White, and Black: The Peoples of Early North America.* Englewood Cliffs, NJ: Prentice-Hall, 1974.

Norton, Mary Beth, et al. "The Afro-American Family in the Age of Revolution." In *Slavery and Freedom in the Age of the American Revolution,* eds. Ira Berlin and Ronald Hoffman. Charlottesville: University Press of Virginia, 1983.

Steckel, Richard H. "Slave Marriage and the Family." *Journal of Family History* 5 (1980): 406–421.

Stevenson, Brenda E. "Slavery." In *Black Women in America: An Historical Encyclopedia,* ed. Darlene Clark Hine. Brooklyn, NY: Carlson Publishing, 1993.

McCauley, Mary Hays

See Molly Pitcher Legend

McCrea, Jane

Casualty of the American Revolution, folk heroine (c. 1752–1777)

Little is known about the life of Jane McCrea, but the circumstances surrounding her death were a catalyst around which Americans found renewed strength in their battle with England. The only witnesses to her death were those responsible for her killing, and it remains unclear if the incident was a result of friendly fire or intentional murder. What is certain is that American rebels seized on the event and quickly spread the word that an innocent young woman was brutally murdered and scalped by savage Indian allies of the British.

Jane McCrea was an odd candidate for a Revolutionary martyr, because it is likely she had loyalist sympathies. She was born in New Jersey, but after her parents' death she resided in the home of her brother, John, in rural New York. John McCrea was a colonel who enlisted in the patriot cause, but Jane was enamored of a young British officer named David Jones. If Jane had political leanings of her

Murder of Miss Jane McCrea A.D. *1777.* (Library of Congress)

own, they are not remembered by history. All that is known for certain was that in July 1777 she planned a rendezvous with Jones at the home of a friend, Sarah McNeil.

Jane McCrea's liaison coincided with the launch of a major British campaign to sever New York from the rest of the New England colonies. British general John Burgoyne moved a force of 8,000 British troops south along the Hudson River. He took Fort Ticonderoga in early July and then moved south toward Fort Edward. Burgoyne summoned various Indian allies to converge along the Hudson River for a major battle at Saratoga. It is believed that a small band of these Indians descended on Sarah McNeil's home, taking both Mrs. McNeil and Jane McCrea captive. By the time the Indians arrived at the British camp, one of them was bearing the scalp of Jane McCrea.

Jane McCrea's death created a volatile and highly charged propaganda incident. It was generally believed the Indians killed and scalped her for no apparent reason, although it has also been suggested that the Indians were attacked by a small party of American militia who were in pursuit of the Indians. According to this version, Jane was caught in the cross fire, and the Indians subsequently scalped an already dead woman.

General Burgoyne was appalled by the presentation of McCrea's scalp, but was reluctant to punish the Indians on the eve of a critical battle. Facing a mass desertion of his Indian allies if he proceeded with a trial, Burgoyne settled for a harsh reprimand of the handful of Indians responsible.

The death of Jane McCrea inflamed the American troops, despite the fact that she had been killed on the way to meet her British sweetheart. The British were characterized as vicious invaders who were incapable of controlling their brutal Indian allies. In the absence of facts, stories about Jane's horrific death circulated. Some say she was hacked to death by axes, others that she was sexually molested before being scalped. The name of Jane McCrea became a rallying cry for the American troops, much the way *"Remember the Alamo"* would unite future soldiers.

The Americans won the Battle of Saratoga, but the propaganda value of Jane's death did not end with the decisive victory. Within a year, a poem describing the death of the innocent young maiden at the hands of "cruel savages" kept Jane's story alive. Paul Revere called Jane "the American Joan of Arc." Long after the war she was memorialized in plays, novels, and paintings.

Advances in forensic science have renewed interest in the circumstances of Jane's death. She was initially buried near the scene of her death in 1777. She was exhumed in 1821 and 1852, at which time her bones were examined. Nineteenth-century medical examiners believed they found evidence of gunshot wounds, but could find no trauma to the skull. She was once again exhumed in 2003, but experts were disappointed by the lack of the skull, which appears to have been lost.

Further Reading

Carola, Chris. "18th Century Victims' Bones Studied." *Columbian,* 14 April 2003, D3.

Kosterm, John. "Jane McCrea, Remembered as a Victim of American Indian Brutality, May Have Died under Different Circumstances." *Military History* (June 2000): 12–16.

Namias, June. *White Captives: Gender and Ethnicity on the American Frontier.* Chapel Hill: University of North Carolina Press, 1993.

Medical Care

Women were the primary providers of medical care in colonial America. When a wound needed stitching, a sprain needed a poultice, or a feverish child needed bedside tending, there was usually a wife, mother, or daughter there to provide the needed services. If a woman was not confident in her abilities to tend a sickness or injury, she usually turned to a network of female healers who could step in. Physicians who had received formal medical training at a college were scarce and expensive in early America. Women resorted to physicians for only a handful of procedures, including tooth pulling, the setting of bones, bloodletting, and the administration of strong drugs.

The nature of disease was misunderstood in early America. Physicians and patients alike believed most illness related to imbalances in the humors. This philosophy derived from the ancient Greek belief that good health requires equilibrium of the four bodily fluids, or humors: yellow bile, black bile, blood, and phlegm. Because most physicians attempted to cure illness by manipulating the humors, their success rate in curing patients was low. Modern pathology did not emerge until the nineteenth century, and the treatments provided by early American physicians were not markedly more effective than the folkloric and herbal remedies offered by female healers.

The most notable contribution made by female healers was their service as midwives. Pregnancy and childbirth were the domain of women healers dating to ancient times, and mothers in labor had a clear preference for treatment by female midwives. The wives of ministers were also highly notable healers. Perhaps as an extension of a minister's job to tend to his flock, a minister's wife visited the poor, tended the sick, and brought medicines to those who could not afford them. Ministers' wives were known to exchange letters with trained physicians, from whom they solicited advice and medicines. This arrangement was beneficial to both the physician and the healer. Physicians were often unable or unwilling to travel to remote locations for the treatment of the poor. Changing dirty linens, bathing patients, and tending to the sickbed were not tasks relished by physicians, but ministers' wives were willing to do these tasks.

Aside from the specialized services offered by professional midwives and ministers' wives, the average colonial housewife would have been prepared to offer basic medical services. Most of her knowledge would have been folk wisdom passed from mother to daughter. Books such as *The Compleat Housewife: Or Accomplished Woman's Companion* (1742) contained sections on homemade remedies and courses of treatment for injuries. Copies of such books would be passed down through generations, heavily annotated with information about homemade tonics and ointments. Other women compiled journals filled with their remedies, which were likewise passed from mother to daughter. Many women grew their own herbs in their kitchen gardens. Because these were generally the same herbs relied on by physicians, women typically offered more convenient and cheaper access to herbal remedies.

The most time-consuming aspect of tending to an ill person was "watching," a chore inevitably performed by women. Patients were not to be left alone. A woman usually sat with the patient, watching for changes in symptoms, bringing food and drink, or helping the ill person change positions. The moral support from having a trusted nurse nearby might have been as comforting as any of the somewhat dubious remedies prescribed in colonial medical books.

Some ambitious women were so proud of their homegrown remedies they attempted to market them. Colonial newspapers abound with advertisements for miraculous tonics, powders, and teas.

Eighteenth-Century Cough Medicine

The remedies used by early Americans were often based on trial and error. They had access to a few powerful drugs and often used them in a seemingly casual manner. This remedy from an eighteenth-century guidebook uses both laudanum and opium for treating a cough.

Remedy for a Consumptive Cough
Syrup of white and red poppies of each, three ounces
Barley, cinnamon water, and red poppy water, of each two ounces
Tincture of saffron, one ounce
Liquid laudanum, forty drops
Spirit of Sulfur as much as will make it acid
Take three or four spoonfuls of it every night going to bed; increase or diminish the dose, according as you find it agrees with you.

Source: Smith, Elizabeth. *The Compleat Housewife.* London: Buckland, 1766.

Mary Bannister advertised her "Drops of Spirit of Venice" and launched a public argument in 1721, when another woman sold a product under the same name. Some of the remedies were sheer quackery, such as Mary Johnson's cures for cancer and Mary Adams's cures for blindness. Others remedies proved effective, such as Sarah Murray's tonic of tar water for scaled skin disorders such as psoriasis.

By the late eighteenth century the practice of medicine was shifting toward professional doctors. As university-trained physicians became more available in America, women were gradually excluded from the public practice of medicine. Although wives and mothers surely continued to provide the majority of medical services for their family members, the growing number of physicians discouraged reliance on midwives and other female healers. Treatment for colds and scrapes could be handled by mothers, but more serious illnesses were to be referred to a doctor. Improved medical instruments, the sanctioning of medical research using human cadavers, and increasingly sophisticated medical education improved the success of trained physicians. Formal medical training was not available to women, and folk healers and midwives were slowly driven out of a field that had offered a healthy supplement to their income.

See also Childbirth; Midwives

Further Reading

Estes, J. Worth. "Medical Practice: Colonial Medicine." In *Encyclopedia of the North American Colonies,* ed. Jacob Ernest Cooke. New York: Charles Scribner's Sons, 1993.

Tannenbaum, Rebecca J. *The Healer's Calling: Women and Medicine in Early New England.* Ithaca, NY: Cornell University Press, 2002.

———. "What Is to Be Done for These Fevers: Elizabeth Davenport's Medical Practice in New Haven Colony." *New England Quarterly* 70 (1997): 265–284.

Ulrich, Laurel Thatcher. *A Midwife's Tale: The Life of Martha Ballard, Based on her Diary, 1785–1812.* New York: Vintage Books, 1990.

Watson, Patricia A. "The Hidden Ones: Women and Healing in Colonial New England." *Dublin Seminar for New England Folklife, Annual Proceedings* 15 (1990): 25–33.

Menopause

See Gynecological Issues

Menstruation

See Gynecological Issues

Mental Illness

People of the seventeenth and eighteenth centuries did not converse easily about psychological distress. Unless depression was linked to an obvious cause, such as the death of a child, it was viewed as a mental and moral failing. Religion played an important role in the lives of most women, and prolonged grief could be viewed as mistrust in the divine underpinnings of the world. It was customary for people to hide unhappiness behind a facade of well-being.

Women in early America suffered from the same range of mental illnesses that afflict contemporary women, although they often attributed psychological problems to different causes. There was little understanding of severe depression and insanity as different phenomena. It was falsely believed that if depression was not promptly cured, it could worsen into insanity.

Depression

The word *depression* was rarely used. Women with symptoms consistent with depression were said to be suffering from grief, melancholia, or nervous disorders. Treatments for these conditions were often listed in medical texts. Noting that grief is often brought on by the death of a child or sudden misfortune, women were advised to engage in exercise, visit with friends, or take a trip. Distracting the mind from present troubles seemed to be the goal of such actions.

When depression could not be attributed to an obvious cause, patients were considered to be suffering from a nervous condition. Doctors grasped at a variety of explanations to explain such fragile dispositions. Noticing that nervous tempers sometimes ran in families, they acknowledged there might have been a hereditary character to the illness. In cases where there was no such family trait, the drinking of too much tea or alcohol was sometimes blamed. Cold baths were recommended to strengthen the nervous system. Sometimes stronger drugs were used. Tinctures of opium mixed with cinnamon were known to ease symptoms, but surely never brought a cure.

Letters and diaries reveal that women suffered from clinical depression, sometimes to the point of suicide. Martha Laurens Ramsay (1759–1811) compiled a remarkable journal chronicling her yearlong battle with severe depression. Martha came from a wealthy and prominent family. Her marriage to David Ramsay was a love match, and they produced several children in rapid succession. One child died in infancy, and financial troubles soon beset the couple. She managed these difficulties with little complaint for several years, but in 1795 she was plunged into what she described as a dark and dismal night of trial. She searched in vain for an explanation for her uncharacteristic gloominess and concluded she was suffering from spiritual failing. She believed her grief was the result of falling away from the love of Jesus. For months she wrestled with her affliction, "I can no longer say the skies are darkening, for they are so darkened I can see no light" (Gillespie 1991, 86). She wrote in an obsessive manner, reiterating her feelings of worthlessness and sense of failure. Although she sought comfort from scripture and the writings of spiritualists, she never confided her grief to her husband, and she didn't seek medical attention. It is likely Martha's troubles might have been caused by a combination of several pregnancies, calcium depletion, or postpartum depression. Her gloom began to lift in early 1796 when she wrote that the melancholy "under which I have groaned for near eleven months" had begun to lessen (Gillespie 1991, 90). Her husband did not discover the depth of her depression until after her death sixteen years later when he learned of the existence of her diary.

Other women coped with depression quite differently. Faith Huntington (1742–1775) had always been known to her family as a woman of intensely nervous and sensitive disposition. She made a successful marriage to Jedediah Huntington, with whom she had one son. Her husband's rising political and military career often took him from home, and Faith appears to have been unable to care properly for her son. Her husband's parents took custody of the child, while Faith did her best to maintain her mental health in the face of mounting political tumult surrounding the outbreak of the American rebellion against England. Unlike Martha Ramsay, Faith sought help from a physician, who assured her he had successfully treated such cases of nervous melancholy in the past. It is not known which medicines Dr. Sprague prescribed for Faith, but common treatments included tea made from Peruvian bark, black masterwort, and even tincture of opium. There appears to have been enough initial improvement in Faith's condition for her husband to feel confident to return to his regiment, where he was serving as colonel. When she learned her husband would not be returning to her for Thanksgiving, it appears Faith had a profound relapse, and she hanged herself in the early morning hours of 24 November 1775. An obituary

appearing in the *Connecticut Gazette* described her mental condition with striking clarity. It acknowledged her sensitivity, the tragic nature of her death, and a life that had always consisted of "intervals of calm tranquility and composure, but frequent turns of great and surprising pain and distortion. The grand temper and seducer of mankind . . . overcame her to put an end to her life" (Brandwein 1985, 28).

Mental illnesses have confounded medical scientists for centuries, and colonial doctors had little hope of providing serious clinical treatments. It was known that women were prone to weepiness following childbirth, but the standard advice was to let time heal this complaint. Intensely religious women often experienced spiritual melancholy, prompted by their feelings of unworthiness and inability to live up to the impossibly high standards extolled by Puritan ministers. In such cases, more spiritual study and sublimation were recommended.

One form of depression seemed to be exclusive to women. "Languishing" was a profound sense of hopelessness, in which women expressed no interest in their surroundings, rarely ate, and had no ability to make decisions. Although some men clearly suffered from depression, there are no records to suggest men suffered the degree of immobilization that characterized languishing. Historian Lyle Koehler has suggested that languishing was an extension of women's dependent role in society. Depressive people who feel they have little control over their fate can slip into extreme social withdrawal and find themselves unable to exert themselves physically or make even the simplest decisions.

Depression among slaves falls into a different category. These women were confronted with devastating personal trauma that created the circumstances for depression in otherwise healthy individuals. Suicide was most common among first-generation slaves. Ship captains kept close watch on newly captured Africans, knowing many of them would attempt suicide if given the opportunity. There was no shame associated with suicide in most African religions, like there was in Christianity. Many Africans believed their soul would return to their homeland after death. Others were profoundly depressed because of separation from family members, the trauma of close confinement, strange food, and physical illness. Uncertainty about the future caused many African slaves to commit suicide upon arrival in America.

Women who were born into slavery were less likely to suffer from depression and also less likely to attempt suicide than male slaves. Slave suicide was usually associated with severe physical punishment, foiled escape attempts, and unsuccessful rebellions. The overwhelming majority of slaves who were involved in such events were male. Also, once a woman bore children she was less likely to abandon them through suicide. There is no doubt that slave women experienced depression, but there are few written records to document the experiences of these women.

Insanity

In some cases, women who were perfectly normal were labeled as mentally ill because they did not conform to societal norms. Anne Hutchinson was accused of mental instability for her fierce commitment to her own brand of religious interpretation. Women who suffered from epilepsy might also be considered to be suffering from fits of insanity. Cotton Mather's third wife has long been considered to have been insane, until historian Virginia Bernhard pointed out that the evidence for her insanity rests entirely on Mather's diary. The diary reveals that after a year of marriage, Lydia no longer adored her husband unconditionally. She had fits of vociferous temper, resented the time he spent on his writing, and was willing to "make scenes." Given that there were periods of months when Mather considered Lydia a delightful companion, it is possible that she had a bipolar disorder or did indeed suffer from a more serious mental imbalance. It is also possible that she was merely a temperamental person in an era when women were expected to be docile and devoted.

Despite the possibility for women to be inaccurately labeled insane, there is no doubt that some were indeed insane. Such individuals were said to be "out of their wits," "deluded," or "crazy-brained." People who were truly insane were rarely

able to care for themselves, and town records reveal attempts to provide care for such people. When possible, family members were required to care for the afflicted, often putting their own family in danger by sheltering a person who could become violent. The psychological and financial stress of such care could last for years. John Heydon and his wife appealed for financial aid to the General Court of Massachusetts seven times, seeking assistance for coping with their severely disturbed son. In 1645, the husband of Goodwife Lampson placed her in the care of the town, claiming he was no longer capable of bearing the burden.

When no family members were able to step in, the town usually provided community funds to look after the person. These arrangements did not always work smoothly. In 1699 Susanna Brown was supplied with a stipend to look after Charles Cullins, a man who did not appear to be in his right senses. After several disturbances, she attempted to return him to the care of the court, which refused to take the man back into custody.

Only in the most extreme cases were the mentally ill incarcerated or physically restrained. The expense of long-term care was too great a burden for a town to sustain. Little is known about how women like Susanna Brown, who were unhappily dealing with housing a mentally ill person, would have coped. It is known that in the case of violent individuals, some were shackled or locked in strong rooms.

Although doctors were willing to try to cure people suffering from mere melancholia, few even attempted a cure for insanity. Beyond bleeding, purging, and induced vomiting, medical science offered little hope. Ministers advised family members to pray and fast on behalf of their loved one. Insanity was often believed to be the work of witchcraft, and ministers might be called to try to rid the afflicted of devilish enchantment.

Colonial courts were surprisingly sympathetic to insane defendants. Recognizing that insane defendants lacked moral culpability for a crime, judges dismissed charges for small offenses such as theft. Even arson could be forgiven, provided no one was killed as a result of the crime. If the actions of an

A Seventeenth-Century Mental Breakdown

A woman of whom we know tantalizingly little was Ann Yale Hopkins (c. 1615–1698). By all accounts she was a curious and intelligent woman. She was born in England, where she married Edward Hopkins. The couple immigrated to Connecticut in 1637, at a time when the colony was a crude, fledgling settlement. On a 120-acre farm they built a home, a barn, and a warehouse. Edward rose quickly in Puritan society and became the second governor of the colony in 1640. Ann showed signs of increasing mental difficulty. She had no children, and thus the traditional maternal role for Puritan women was closed to her. Ann had always enjoyed reading and even attempted to write a book. This sort of prolonged mental activity by women was looked on with disfavor. It was believed that women were mentally weaker than men and exhaustion of the brain could lead to insanity.

The governor of Massachusetts, John Winthrop, wrote in his journal that it was Ann's excessive thinking and reading that provoked her breakdown. If she had "attended her household affairs, and such things as belong to women, and not gone out of her way and calling to meddle in such things as are proper for men, whose minds are stronger, etc., she had kept her wits, and might have improved them usefully and honorably in the place God had set her."

Ann Hopkins suffered a severe mental breakdown and was later described as being completely insane. Only fleeting references to her illness survive, and it is impossible to know if the breakdown was caused by the crude and dangerous conditions under which the first generation of Puritan immigrants lived, or a physiological disorder. It is believed that her mental illness played a role in her husband's decision to return to England in the early 1650s. Ann lived into her eighties and never fully recovered her mental health.

Source: Koehler, Lyle. *A Search for Power: The Weaker Sex in Seventeenth Century New England.* Urbana: University of Illinois Press, 1980.

insane person resulted in homicide, courts usually had little mercy. There are a handful of cases where women who were believed to be insane were executed for murder. In 1690, Mercy Brown, a woman known for her "distracted condition," was hanged for killing her son with an axe. Dorothy Talbie had a long history of attempted suicide and violent assaults on her family members. When she succeeded in killing one of her children in 1636 she was executed. In 1642, Ann Hett tried to drown her three-year-old daughter by flinging her into a pond. When the child scrambled out and returned to her mother, Ann threw the girl out farther into the water. The child was saved from drowning by a passerby, who, in so doing, also saved Ann from an almost certain appointment with the hangman. When Ann was asked to explain her actions, all she could say was that she hoped to spare the child from misery.

It appears that gender played a role in how mental illness was recognized. In seventeenth-century New England around 80 percent of the documented cases of insanity were women, but in the middle colonies the overwhelming majority of people labeled insane were men. It is possible that the different cultures of the region affected how they perceived mental illness. As a whole, mentally disturbed women were more likely to be considered depressed or bewitched rather than insane.

Further Reading

Bernhard, Virginia. "Cotton Mather's Most Unhappy Wife: Reflections on the Uses of Historical Evidence." *New England Quarterly* 60 (1987): 341–362.

Brandwein, Ann. "An Eighteenth-Century Depression: The Sad Conclusion of Faith Trumbull Huntington." *Connecticut History* 26 (1985): 19–32.

Eldridge, Larry D. "Crazy Brained: Mental Illness in Colonial America." *Bulletin of the History of Medicine* 70 (1996): 361–386.

Gillespie, Joanna Bowen. "1795: Martha Laurens Ramsay's Dark Night of the Soul." *William and Mary Quarterly* 48 (1991): 68–92.

Koehler, Lyle. *A Search for Power: The Weaker Sex in Seventeenth-Century New England.* Urbana: University of Illinois Press, 1980.

Pierson, William D. "White Cannibals, Black Martyrs: Fear, Depression, and Religious Faith as Causes of Suicide among New Slaves." *Journal of Negro History* 62 (1977): 147–159.

Rubin, Julius H. *Religious Melancholy and Protestant Experience in America.* New York: Oxford University Press, 1994.

Merchants

See Shopkeepers and Merchants

Merry, Anne Brunton
Actress (1769–1808)

Anne Brunton, like most other actresses of the day, was born into an acting family. Her father was an actor in the Theatre Royal in Norwich, England, but the family occasionally traveled to London to perform at the more prestigious Covent Garden. Anne had been taught to memorize Shakespeare as a child and made her debut on the stage at age sixteen. Her popularity made her a regular at Covent Garden, but she elected to tour during the summer months with various traveling performers.

When she was twenty-two Anne met Robert Merry, an aristocratic gentleman with a taste for the fine arts and loose living. Robert Merry wrote poetry, mingled with high society, and held politically controversial views. When Anne and Robert married, the union was unpopular for both parties. Robert's aristocratic family was appalled by his marriage to an actress, a profession considered only one step above prostitution. Out of respect for his family, Robert persuaded Anne to temporarily retire from public performance. Anne's alliance with the dangerously liberal Merry was also unpopular. Merry had recently begun voicing support for the detested French Revolution, making him persona non grata among high society. His gambling and expensive tastes made it essential for Anne to begin earning a living, and the couple eagerly embraced the opportunity to immigrate to America where Anne could perform without fear of judgment from Robert's family or earning an unsavory reputation.

Anne Merry soon became the leading actress at the Chestnut Theater in Philadelphia. Her acting

Mrs. Merry (Anne Brunton), as Alzira in a play. (Library of Congress)

style was distinctively different than those of other leading actresses of the day, who emphasized dramatic gestures and soaring vocal exclamations. Anne's style was subtler and less stylized. Rather than exciting the passions of the spectators, she elicited more reflective and thoughtful responses from her audience. She became the first "star" of the American stage.

In 1798 Robert Merry died of an apparent stroke. A few years later Anne married her manager, Thomas Wignell. Anne and Thomas had already enjoyed a long friendship and business partnership, but their marriage lasted only seven weeks. Thomas died of an infection, leaving a pregnant Anne to assume management of the acting company on her own. Thomas and Anne's daughter, Elizabeth, was Anne's only child to survive infancy.

Anne's final marriage, to actor William Warren, occurred in 1806. The pair enjoyed a successful acting career and toured frequently. When Anne became pregnant at age thirty-nine, her doctor advised her to remain at home. Anne elected to follow her husband on tour to Virginia, where she died after giving birth to a stillborn child.

See also Theater

Further Reading

Cramb, John Adam. "Merry, Robert." In *Dictionary of National Biography,* eds. Leslie Stephen and Sidney Lee. London: Oxford University Press, 1921.

Gagey, Edmund. "Anne Brunton Merry." In *Notable American Women, 1607–1950,* ed. Edward T. James. Cambridge, MA: Belknap Press of Harvard University, 1971.

McGovern, Catherine B. "Anne Brunton Merry." In *Notable Women in the American Theatre: A Biographical Dictionary,* ed. Alice M. Robinson et al. New York: Greenwood, 1989.

Methodist Women

Methodism was brought to America by itinerant Irish preachers in the mid- to late eighteenth century. The preachers appealed to a wide swath of the population that had felt neglected by the formality of the Church of England and the rigidity of Puritanism. Methodism was characterized by simplicity of worship, a personal relationship with God, and concern for the underprivileged. The preachers had little formal education. Rather than relying on college-educated ministers, the Methodists used ardent working-class men whose passion for salvation was inspirational. The populist style of their preaching appealed to women, minorities, the young, and the poor.

Converts to Methodism were intensely passionate about their newfound religion. It spoke to women on a deeply personal level, and many women joined Methodist congregations while still young and single. The decision to become a Methodist was often disruptive to families among whom only a few members converted. Methodism demanded a single-mindedness considered unseemly among women.

The most highly prized virtues in an eighteenth-century woman were modesty, thrift, and devotion to family. Methodist women were encouraged to make their newfound religious passion the primary focus of their lives. They were not shy in advancing their radical social and religious views. Many of the young converts were disinterested in marriage and starting a family. Much of the Methodist doctrine carried an implication of social leveling, a dangerous concept in a world of strict gender and racial roles. Methodists believed obedience to one's parents and husband was a virtue, but if this obedience created a conflict with God, a woman was advised to obey God. If disapproving family members interfered with a woman's devotions, she should distance herself from her family.

Women were particularly active in nurturing the fledgling Methodist congregations. The wives of many well-to-do merchants found Methodism appealing, possibly because they were seeking an outlet for genuine social concerns. Often acting independently of their husbands, these women sponsored the travels of itinerant preachers and the building of Methodist congregations. In New York City, a group of Methodists, including thirty-six women, constructed a chapel from the benefits of a subscription in 1768. Prudence and Harry Gough, who had been converted to Methodism by their slaves, created a center for the rapidly growing religious movement at their home, Perry Hall. The Goughs set their slaves free and allowed Perry Hall to be used as a lodging for traveling preachers and occasional Methodist meetings.

Early Methodist communities were sustained by itinerant preachers, who rarely stayed in one place for more than a few nights. Sweeping through towns with their fiery rhetoric and impassioned messages, they represented an exciting version of spirituality for people who remained unmoved by traditional ministers. Itinerant preachers were almost always men in early America, a departure from British Methodism where women were encouraged to preach. Women who married Methodist preachers faced unique challenges. Preachers were encouraged to travel far and wide seeking converts, leaving their wives at home, sometimes for months on end.

This situation caused these women to depend on the charity of friends and family for support.

American women sustained the movement by providing lodgings and meals to the itinerant preachers. Women made up the majority of most early Methodist congregations, assuming roles in organization, fund-raising, and support activities. Black women were particularly active in Methodism, often amounting to between 10 and 30 percent of Methodist congregations in New York and Baltimore.

Further Reading

Andrews, Dee E. *The Methodists and Revolutionary America, 1760–1800: The Shaping of an Evangelical Culture.* Princeton, NJ: Princeton University Press, 2000.

Ruether, Rosemary Radford, and Rosemary Skinner Keller. *Women and Religion in America: The Colonial and Revolutionary Periods.* San Francisco: Harper and Row, 1983.

Midwives

The care of pregnant women was the province of female midwives in the early centuries of America. Their primary responsibility was the delivery of the child, although they might be consulted during pregnancy if irregularities arose. Most midwives had no formal training, although it was not unheard of for a woman to apprentice herself with a male physician to learn basic skills. Books were available, such as Nicholas Culpeper's *Directory for Midwives* (1653), the anonymously written *Compleat Midwife's Practice* (1656), and Jane Sharp's *The Midwives Book* (1671). Aside from such basic resources, a midwife would have been trained through observation, folk knowledge, and her own experience of giving birth.

In the course of a normal childbirth, the midwife did very little other than let nature take its course. She provided comfort with soothing words, administered liquor or wine to the mother, and tied the child's umbilical cord. In difficult cases she would attempt to turn a child that was in danger of a breach birth. Maternal mortality rates were surprisingly low in colonial America, with only about one in two hundred births resulting in a maternal death.

Aside from assisting in childbirths, midwives were called on by the state for the examination of female prisoners who pleaded pregnancy to avoid imprisonment or execution. They were also called to testify in cases regarding illegitimate children. Folklore claimed that a woman would not lie about the identity of the child's father while she was in the midst of labor pains. In cases where mothers refused to reveal the identity of the father, midwives were asked to attempt to learn the truth during labor so the town might compel the father to provide financial support for the child. Midwives were also asked to estimate dates of conception. In many communities it was a crime to conceive a child before wedlock. If a woman delivered a child less than nine months after her marriage, midwives were asked to inspect the infant and determine if it was a full-term child. In cases of abandoned infants, a midwife would be used to examine an accused mother to determine if she had recently given birth.

There was little regulation of the midwife profession in early America. Only New York and Virginia required civil licensing for midwives. The 1716 ordinance in New York required that a midwife take an oath that she shall be willing to help any woman in labor, that she not attempt to conceal the true identity of the father, not collude in the concealment of a child, and that she not participate in any activity that would result in a miscarriage or death of the infant.

The role of midwife was a respectable profession in colonial society. Some midwives delivered between two and three thousand babies over the course of their career. Having been a participant in the central event of so many people's lives, the town midwife was greatly respected and sometimes even revered. Midwives would have mixed with a large cross section of society, ranging from the desperately poor to the wealthiest women in town. Many New England towns provided free housing to a midwife provided she was willing to assist in deliveries regardless of the time of day or remoteness of location. In the Dutch colony of New Netherlands, midwives were called "Zieckentroosters," and received pay from the town payroll. Most midwives in English colonies were paid by the family of the patient. A typical fee ranged from five to ten shillings, which was usually paid in goods. Midwife Martha Ballard's diary reveals she was paid in items such as store credit, a baby pig, candles, cheese, wool, a looking glass, coffee, and a pair of flat irons. Sometimes the midwife would be paid on the day of delivery, although more often than not she had to collect the payment when the family was able to pay the fee.

A midwife's fee per delivery was roughly equal to what a skilled workingman could earn in a single day. What she could earn depended on the size of the town and the number of midwives competing for the town's business. A typical midwife could expect to deliver one to two children per week, meaning that it was unlikely she could support herself on her earnings, but it would provide a healthy supplement to a family's income.

Midwives often had to travel great distances at inconvenient hours to reach their patients. They were forced to travel through winter blizzards, summer storms, floods, and the darkness of night. If the expectant mother lived far outside of town, a midwife might try to estimate the time of arrival and board with the family until the birth. Following the birth, the midwife was usually accompanied home by the father. Tending the new mother and infant in the weeks immediately following birth was the responsibility of neighborhood women.

Prior to the mid-eighteenth century, midwives had virtually exclusive claim to the child delivery business in America. Physicians and midwives had roughly the same success rate in the delivery of healthy children. Modesty prevented many women from being intimately examined by male physicians, giving a clear preference to female midwives. If a physician was called in to assist in a prolonged birth, it was usually a last resort to save the life of the mother. Physicians had access to medical instruments for the extraction of a child, but use of these tools required the death and dismemberment of the child.

In the mid-eighteenth century, male physicians began to participate more in the deliveries of infants. Medical research had led to improved developments of medical instruments. Forceps could now be used as a lifesaving device. Midwives almost never owned forceps, possibly because of the expense of the tools, or because the manufacturers would not sell the instruments to anyone who wasn't a physician. Although midwives were generally credited with having more experience with childbirth, physicians had a reputation for having greater knowledge. By the 1760s, some wealthier families began to turn to physicians in lieu of midwives, although poor and middling classes continued to use midwives. The preference for midwives persisted for more than a century for a combination of reasons, which included female modesty, the association of doctors with grisly and ill-fated deliveries, and the higher fee charged by doctors ($12 to $15).

The character of the childbirth experience differed when it was presided over by a physician. Women traditionally had a number of female companions and relatives with them in the birthing room, but these women were banished by doctors who found their conversation distracting. Lingering prudery prevented physicians from carefully examining the patient, and deliveries occurred with the physician blindly feeling beneath sheets that were modestly draped over the mother to be. Despite the professional competition existing between midwives and physicians in the late eighteenth century, they usually cooperated with each other. Sometimes both a doctor and a midwife would be called to assist in a birth, perhaps because the summoning family could not be certain who would be available, so both would be asked to come. In such cases, whoever arrived first was usually charged with seeing the birth through.

See also Childbirth; Medical Care

Further Reading

Leavitt, Judith Walzer. *Brought to Bed: Childbearing in America, 1750–1950.* New York: Oxford University Press, 1986.

Scholten, Catherine M. *Childbearing in American Society: 1650–1850.* New York: New York University Press, 1985.

———. "On the Importance of the Obstetrick Art: Changing Customs of Childbirth in America,

1760 to 1825." *William and Mary Quarterly* 34 (1977): 426–445.

Ulrich, Laurel Thatcher. *A Midwife's Tale: The Life of Martha Ballard, Based on Her Diary, 1785–1812.* New York: Vintage Books, 1991.

Wertz, Richard W., and Dorothy C. Wertz. *Lying-In: A History of Childbirth in America.* New York: Schocken Books, 1979.

Military Service and the American Revolution

The American Revolution was fought over eight years and swept across much of the physical territory of the colonies. It was inevitable that women would become involved in military operations, either by choice or circumstance. Some women followed the army as laundresses, tailors, cooks, or nurses. Others took daring positions on the battlefield, assisting with watering down cannons or aiding wounded soldiers. No women were openly allowed to fight in combat positions, although a few women picked up rifles or fired cannons in the heat of battle. Military service was not compatible with the traditional female stereotypes of the eighteenth century, but it was impossible to isolate women from the ravages of warfare. Although some women became refugees in the face of an approaching army, others rushed toward the scene of combat of their own free will.

Most of the women following the army were there in a nonofficial capacity, making it impossible to know how many women were actually present alongside the British or American forces. It has been estimated that at least 20,000 women lived among the American army camps between 1775 and 1783. Among the British, it has been estimated that as many as one in eight people traveling with the army were women. These army encampments looked more like primitive villages, rather than exclusively male military bases. Rules as to where the women slept varied. Some regiments insisted on separate tents, although records indicate that it was not unusual for large tents to contain men, women, and even children.

Most of the women traveling with armies received a half-ration of food, but no pay. Each regiment had a few paying positions for women, and these were highly coveted. The reasons women followed the army were many. Some were refugees who no longer had a home, but most were women who refused to be separated from their husbands. In some cases the choice was financial. Army wages were meager, irregularly distributed, and not intended to subsidize a soldier's dependent family. Some women who could not afford to maintain a home in the absence of their husbands chose to follow them. Other women, especially the officers' wives, had the financial resources to stay home, but chose to spend part or all of the year in the field with their husbands.

Women in the army were considered a necessary annoyance to General Washington. In 1777 he complained in a letter that they slowed the advance of the army: "the multitude of women in particular, especially those who are pregnant or have children, are a clog upon every movement" (Ward 1999, 119). Despite Washington's frustration, the services of women were necessary, and no thought was given to forbidding their presence. The women of the army were subject to the same rules of military discipline that applied to men. When Mary Johnson plotted to desert from the encampment at Valley Forge, a military court sentenced her to 100 lashes and dismissal from the army.

The women who followed the army can be classed in two categories. Those who supplied military services on behalf of the army are addressed here. Those who had no military role but provided informal services directly to the soldiers, such as cooking, mending, and laundry chores, are addressed in the entry entitled Camp Followers and Women of the Army.

Medical Service

The provision of medical care seemed a natural service for women, because it was believed women had a natural ability to nurture and tend to the sick. Women employed as nurses were expected to be sober, industrious, and healthy. No medical training was necessary. They changed bandages and helped soldiers bathe and eat. Better-educated nurses also assisted with writing letters home. Perhaps the greatest difficulty for these women was the psychological challenge of working in an area where men routinely died. Most of the nurses had husbands who were also combat soldiers, and tending battlefield injuries of fellow soldiers was a demanding ordeal.

Most women serving as nurses traveled with the armies and staffed regimental hospitals. These were small medical units that traveled with the troops from place to place and provided emergency care for battlefield injuries. Because they were staffed by doctors and women who traveled with the troops, regimental hospitals were considered friendlier and more concerned for the well-being of the soldiers. Soldiers who needed lengthy recovery time were transferred to a general hospital. Large schools and churches were converted to general hospitals for the duration of the war. Though larger and better supplied than field hospitals, general hospitals had a poor reputation. Hospitals in the eighteenth century were associated with pest houses, asylums, and death. People only entered hospitals in life-threatening situations, because the likelihood of contracting a disease in these cramped, unsanitary buildings was high. The women who served as nurses in the general hospitals were usually from the local community and did not travel with the troops. Women also tended to men on hospital ships and the "sick in town," referring to wounded soldiers who were quartered in private houses when hospital space was scarce.

Work in the army hospitals was a frustrating experience. Supplies, food, and warm clothing were in notoriously short supply. Sometimes patients were literally naked, as they could not be refitted with new clothing after their blood-soaked uniforms were cut off of them. In 1777 the Continental Army ordered that one matron and ten female nurses be supplied for every one hundred wounded men. These women received a food ration and pay equivalent to that of an army sergeant.

Women who served in field hospitals worked in a dangerous profession. Smallpox, dysentery, and yellow fever haunted the hospital wards. The shortages of provisions gave rise to scurvy and jaundice. The risk of dying from communicable disease was enormous, and many nurses sickened and died in the cramped, unsanitary environment.

Battlefield Service

The most common job for women in battle was artillery support, usually as part of crews servicing cannons. The prominence of the fictitious Molly Pitcher has given the impression that she was the only woman to serve in this capacity. It is now believed that thousands of women served in such a role. Cannon barrels were swabbed out with water-drenched rags after each firing in order to extinguish sparks and remove gunpowder residue. To fire a cannon without doing so could result in a disastrous explosion. Swabbing the cannon was usually performed by a member of the gun crew, which numbered at least three men per cannon. Support personnel, often women, moved throughout the battlefield bringing buckets of water to keep the cannons clean and quench the thirst of the soldiers. Documentation exists that at least a few of these water-carrying women replaced fallen soldiers among the cannon crews. Having seen the operation of the cannons at close view, it is likely they needed little instruction in how to perform the needed tasks.

In a few extremely rare cases, women donned men's clothing and passed as soldiers during the war. Deborah Sampson was one such woman, whose 5-foot 8-inch frame allowed her to serve more than a year without detection. The British army required a medical exam for new recruits, but there were no physical exams required for American soldiers, making passing as a man easier in America. We know frustratingly little about the women who chose to wear men's clothing and shoulder a rifle. Sally St. Clair followed her lover into battle and was not discovered to be a woman until she met her death at the Battle of Savannah. Samuel Gay rose to the rank of corporal, but a brief note in Record Group 93 at the National Archives records the swift end to her career, "Discharged, being a woman dressed in men's clothes, August 1777."

Betty Zane and the Rescue of Fort Henry

The frontier outpost Fort Henry was built to defend the western lands of Virginia during the Revolutionary War. In September 1782 a band of 300 Indians and a handful of loyalist troops descended upon the fort. Having advance word of the attack, settlers living near Fort Henry had taken refuge behind the palisade walls. Sixty women and children joined the forty men holding the fort. Colonel Ebenezer Zane and a band of sharpshooters took refuge in Zane's cabin, located about sixty yards southwest of the fort.

On the first day of the battle, the Indians tried twice to storm the fort and capture Colonel Zane's cabin, but were driven back. By the second day, gunpowder in the fort was running dangerously low. Betty Zane, the sixteen-year-old sister of Colonel Zane, knew there was more gunpowder at her brother's cabin. The commander of the fort was unwilling to order any man to undertake the desperate trip to the cabin and asked for a volunteer. Although a few men offered to make the trip, Betty Zane argued that every man was required to defend the fort and her loss would not be noticed. She also had the element of surprise on her side, because the attackers might not know what to make of her dash to the cabin. Around noon on 12 September 1782, Betty Zane slipped out of the fort and raced toward the cabin. The attackers, amazed at her audacity, did not fire on the girl. When she emerged from the cabin a few minutes later with a small keg of gunpowder cradled in her apron, a hail of bullets was fired in her direction. The teenager managed to dodge the bullets in her fifteen-second dash back to the fort. With their supplies replenished, Fort Henry's defenders were able to last out a third and final day of siege. The enemy withdrew, and Betty Zane's heroic dash was immediately credited with having saved the fort from certain capture.

Source: Hintzen, William. "Betty Zane, Lydia Bodd, and Molly Scott: The Gunpowder Exploits at Fort Henry." *West Virginia History* 55 (1996): 95–109.

Margaret Corbin made no effort to disguise her gender. Dressed in men's clothing, she served beside her soldier husband for several years before losing part of an arm in battle. Sometimes identified as the source of the Molly Pitcher legend, Margaret Corbin was accepted by fellow soldiers and received a pension for her service following the war. Anna Maria Lane was another woman who dressed in men's clothing and fought alongside her husband. She was severely wounded at the Battle of Germantown in 1777. Her gender might have been discovered at the army hospital, but she was allowed to continue in the army, and served until the end of the war.

How many women passed as male soldiers? It is known that at least 400 women passed as male soldiers during the American Civil War, and it is likely that the Revolution had a similar share of such soldiers. Boys as young as twelve enlisted during the Revolution, although the army was not supposed to take boys so young. In desperate times, if officers were willing to overlook such boys, might they not also overlook a woman who was capable and willing to serve?

Military Duty on the Home Front

Many women did not travel with the army, but were forced into military roles while on the home front. The militia consisted of civilian men who assembled and fought when needed. In emergencies, towns gathered their able-bodied men into militia units, leaving their families in vulnerable positions at home. The story of Prudence Wright (1739–1823) and her guard embody the spirit of women who were forced to defend their homes. Immediately following the Battles of Lexington and Concord, militia units throughout Massachusetts headed for Boston. Rumors of spies and British troop movements were rampant, and Prudence Wright assembled the women of Pepperell, Massachusetts, to defend the town. She recruited between thirty and forty women, armed with a few muskets and pitchforks, to protect the town in the absence of their men.

Some women acted alone. Sybil Ludington (1761–1839) was the daughter of the local militia leader. An exhausted messenger arrived at her doorstep the evening of 26 April 1777 to report that the nearby town of Danbury, Connecticut, was under siege and in desperate need of troops. Sixteen-year-old Sybil made a dangerous, forty-mile ride on dark paths and horse trails to warn local militia members of the assault. Lydia Darragh (1729–1789) also learned of a planned British assault in 1777 and was able to slip out of occupied Philadelphia to warn American officers of the attack.

See also Camp Followers and Women of the Army; Molly Pitcher Legend; Sampson, Deborah

Further Reading

DePauw, Linda Grant. "Women in Combat: The Revolutionary War Experience." *Armed Forces and Society* 7, no. 2 (1981): 209–226.

Gillet, Mary C. *The Army Medical Department, 1775–1818.* Washington, DC: Center of Military History; U.S. Army, 1981.

Hagist, Don N. "The Women of the British Army during the American Revolution." *Minerva* 13, no. 2 (1995): 29–85.

Sarnecky, Mary T. "Nursing in the American Army from the Revolution to the Spanish-American War." *Nursing History Review* 5 (1997): 49–69.

Treadway, Sandra Gioia. "Anna Maria Lane: An Uncommon Soldier of the American Revolution." *Virginia Cavalcade* 37 (Winter 1988): 134–143.

Ward, Harry M. *The War for Independence and the Transformation of American Society.* London: UCL Press, 1999.

Milliners and Seamstresses

There was a wide range of terms for people who made a living through sewing. Tailors were people who made men's clothing, and mantua makers specialized in women's gowns. A woman who sold occasional piecework that she produced in her own home was a seamstress, and a person who owned a shop where she sold her sewing was a milliner. By the late 1800s the term *milliner* referred to a person who specialized only in making hats, but during the colonial era it had no exact parameters. Milliners might make hosiery, dresses, gloves, or bonnets. Unlike other occupations, millinery work was wide open to women, and it was common to see millinery shops owned by women.

A typical woman in an early American household sewed only basic clothing for her family. Under-clothing, skirts, stockings, and bed linens required little specialized knowledge or time commitment. More complicated clothing such as jackets and fine dresses were often purchased from seamstresses and handed down for generations of use. Clothing was repeatedly altered and repaired so that a shirt might see thirty years of use before becoming too threadbare for further wear. Because households produced most of their basic goods, millinery shops tended to cater to people wealthy enough to purchase clothing that reflected current fashions.

Milliners were in the business of selling goods that allowed their customers to appear fashionably dressed and adorned. As such, their shops usually carried goods beyond mere clothing. Jewelry, cosmetics, ribbons, fans, hats, and hosiery were commonly sold in a millinery shop. A milliner was skilled with a needle and produced much of her own inventory, but also imported a number of goods. These women needed to understand accounts, import regulations, and have contacts in the merchant world for the selection of wares. Some well-to-do milliners even traveled to London to learn the latest fashions and select their own goods.

Most milliners had an apprentice, either a young family member or a person who was willing to work for modest wages in exchange for learning the trade. Their shops were usually on a main street in town, and they often lived above or behind the shop. Because they were usually in the business of importing goods, there was no reason to limit their business to apparel. It was not uncommon to see milliners advertise clocks, imported china, shoes, perfume, tea, or liquor.

Milliners could supplement their income by offering cleaning, mending, and ironing services. Delicate lace and silk could not be boiled clean in the typical way of colonial laundry practices. Sarah Brown placed an advertisement notifying the public that they could have "all sorts of silks, quilted coats and gowns, silk stockings, gloves, and camlet cloaks scoured, dyed, and dressed; burdets and tabbies watered; men's clothes dry and wet scoured, linen and cotton dyed blue, green or yellow. Likewise, mildew or stains taken out of pieces of silks or stuffs, or worsteds that are damaged at sea; all sorts of worsteds scoured and pressed; all which works will be performed in the most speedy, and after the most reasonable manner" (*Pennsylvania Gazette*, 2 May 1751).

A woman who did not wish to devote herself to full-time employment as a milliner might take in occasional work as a seamstress. Much of the colonial economy depended on the barter of goods and services. A woman skilled in needlework might offer to make a coat for a neighbor in exchange for a few coins or services she needed.

Some women also worked for wages from a local milliner. "Piecework" was when a worker was paid per item produced, usually in her own home and sometimes using her own materials. Piecework was highly favorable to the employers, as they did not need to set aside space or regular wages for a full-time employee. It was less profitable for the woman performing the work. Wages were usually very low. A study of pieceworkers in early nineteenth-century Baltimore found that a woman needed to sew seven shirts in order to earn what a man earned in a single day. Given that pieceworkers usually had a whole range of household and child-rearing responsibilities to interrupt her work, the benefits she gained through piecework were small. It was also irregular and seasonal in nature, so a family could not depend on piecework for anything other than supplemental income.

See also Quilting; Sewing; Textile Industry

Further Reading

Crews, Edward R. "Millinery Shop: 18th Century Department Store." *Colonial Williamsburg* (Winter 1997–1998): 63–67.

Dexter, Elisabeth Anthony. *Colonial Women of Affairs: Women in Business and the Professions in America before 1776.* Boston: Houghton Mifflin, 1931.

Spruill, Julia Cherry. *Women's Life and Work in the Southern Colonies.* Chapel Hill: University of North Carolina Press, 1938.

Molly Pitcher Legend

The name "Molly Pitcher" was a generic reference to women who provided artillery support during the Revolution. Thousands of women lived among the army as camp followers and performed odd jobs such as mending, cooking, and nursing. Most camp followers were married to soldiers and stayed behind the lines during battle. Some courageous women stayed at the front, resupplying troops with ammunition, reloading guns, and serving on cannon teams. Each cannon needed at least three people to load, clean, and fire. Cannons needed to be kept cool and clean, lest remnants of smoldering gunpowder ignite while the cannon crew was reloading. Large amounts of water were needed to swab out the barrel of the cannon and relieve the thirst of the crew. No single woman can be credited with being the original Molly Pitcher, although two well-documented cases of female cannoneers are usually associated with the legend.

Margaret Corbin (1751–1800)

Margaret Corbin lived most of her life in hardscrabble conditions, having been orphaned at the age of five when her father was killed by Indians and her mother taken captive, never to be heard from again. She married as a teenager and followed her husband, John, into the army at the outset of the American Revolution.

In November 1776 Margaret and her husband were defending Fort Washington along the banks of the Hudson River. The British frigate *Pearl* made its was up the river, firing on the fort at the same time Hessian troops assaulted the American position from below the ridge. Unable to lower their cannons to defend against the advancing Hessians, the American troops came under heavy fire. John Corbin was mortally wounded, and Margaret took his place swabbing and loading the cannon. She took three grapeshot wounds in her arm, almost severing it from her body. Totally disabled, she was taken prisoner after the fort fell to the British. Perhaps because of her gender, she was given over to the American hospital at Philadelphia, where she partially recovered.

Margaret never regained the use of her arm, but was willing to continue in service. She became part of the Corp of Invalids, composed of disabled vet-

Molly Pitcher. Molly McCauley loading cannon at Battle of Monmouth, 1778. (Library of Congress)

erans who could no longer fight but were able to perform guard duty and instruct new soldiers. Margaret was transferred to the fort at West Point, where she served for the duration of the war. In 1779 she was awarded with a lifetime annuity of one-half monthly pay in recognition of her service.

In her later years Margaret suffered lingering pain from her injuries and bitterness from not receiving the full pay of a soldier. She had always been a hard drinker, which worsened her already cantankerous temper. She was called "Captain Molly" by the locals, but "Dirty Kate" behind her back. The command at West Point sympathized with Margaret, knowing she was unable to care for herself, and tried to find families who would take her in. In 1786 an officer wrote: "I am at a loss what

to do with Captain Molly. She is such an offensive person that people are unwilling to take her in charge" (Ward 1999, 684).

Margaret Corbin remained in the West Point area for the rest of her life. She was able to receive rations from the fort, but probably had little comfort in her final years. She is the only soldier of the Revolutionary War buried at the Military Academy at West Point.

Mary Ludwig Hayes McCauley (c. 1754–1832)

Mary Ludwig was working as a domestic servant when she married John Hayes, a barber. When he enlisted in the army at the beginning of the Revolution, she chose to continue working as a servant in Carlisle, Pennsylvania. After a few years, she decided to join her husband in the army as a camp follower. She was at his side during the Battle of Monmouth, where the temperatures soared to almost 100 degrees. She brought water to the thirsty troops, and when her husband collapsed from heat exhaustion, she took his place at the cannon. A private, Joseph Plumb Martin, later published his memoirs of the war. He recorded an incident at the Battle of Monmouth, which probably referred to Mary Hayes. He noted that a woman was helping her husband load a cannon when: "a cannon shot from the enemy passed directly between her legs without doing any other damage than carrying away all the lower part of her petticoat. Looking at it with apparent unconcern, she observed that it was lucky it did not pass a little higher, for in that case it might have carried away something else, and continued her occupation" (Teipe 1999, 120).

Both Mary Hays and her husband survived the war and returned to Carlisle, Pennsylvania. After her husband died, she married John McCauley, also a Revolutionary War veteran. Mary was never a person of comfortable financial means. She worked most of her life as a cleaning woman and received no pensions from the government until 1822, when she was awarded a modest annual annuity of $40.

Although Mary had a reputation for swearing like a trooper and chewing tobacco, she was well liked by those around her. Described as a tough, muscular woman of homely appearance, a neighbor recalled her as a bighearted woman who would do a kind act for anyone.

See also Camp Followers and Women of the Army; Military Service and the American Revolution

Further Reading

Landis, John B. *A Short History of Molly Pitcher: The Heroine of the Battle of Monmouth.* Carlisle: Cornman Printing, 1905.

Teipe, Emily J. "Will the Real Molly Pitcher Please Stand Up?" *Prologue: Quarterly of the National Archives and Records Administration* 31 (1999): 118–126.

Ward, Harry M. "Two Mollies." In *Women in World History,* ed. Anne Commire. Waterford, CT: Yorkin Publications, 1999.

Moody, Lady Deborah Dunch
Founder of an early Manhattan colony (1586–1659)

Deborah Dunch was born into a prosperous English family, but after confronting religious persecution in London she chose to travel to the wilds of America where she established the first colonial enterprise to be led by a woman.

Deborah came to adulthood during a time when Queen Elizabeth valued religious compromise and conformity. The Dunch family was steeped in Puritan fervor and found the queen's lukewarm religious compromises troublesome, but tolerable. In 1606 Deborah married Henry Moody, and his knighthood a few months later elevated her to the status of "Lady." She bore one child, Henry, who survived into adulthood. After her husband's death in 1629, Deborah traveled to London, where her religious fervor intensified. The Puritan Revolution was more than a decade away, but radical elements were beginning to ferment and gather momentum. In an effort to quell dissent, the court had ruled that gentry could only reside in London for short stretches of time. This order, in addition to her growing dissatisfaction with the religious policies in England, prompted Lady Deborah to sail for America in 1639.

Lady Deborah initially settled in Massachusetts, where she purchased a large farm of nine hundred acres called Swampscott. She lived in a comfortable farmhouse that was built of rock and had glass windows. She joined the Salem church, but did not find the religious kinship she had thought she would find among other Puritan immigrants. Although Lady Deborah's wealth and title bought her entrée into the Puritan community at Salem, it could not buy her acceptance. Her radical religious beliefs smacked of the antinomian controversy that had recently caused the banishment of Anne Hutchinson. Unlike Hutchinson, Lady Deborah chose not to challenge the Puritan authorities and simply gathered what belongings, cattle, and followers she could, and went in search of a new beginning. She eventually received permission from Dutch authorities to establish a colony in a section of Long Island, in the area that later became known as

Brooklyn. The land grant consisted of 7,000 acres, which she named Gravesend.

Although Gravesend was as yet untouched by European settlers, local Indians made use of the land. In the interest of keeping peace, Lady Deborah paid the Indians for the land and began establishing her colony. Tensions between the Indians and the colonists were strained during the initial years of settlement. In 1643 the band of Indians that had murdered Anne Hutchinson and her family descended upon Gravesend. With forty men to defend the fledgling settlement, they were able to fend off the attack, but Lady Deborah was discouraged. Although her home had survived the assault, many of the other dwellings were ruined and the band of colonists sought refuge in a nearby Dutch settlement. Lady Deborah considered returning to the relative security of Massachusetts, where she still owned property. When the deputy governor of Massachusetts got wind of Lady Deborah's desire to return, he wrote to Governor John Winthrop and characterized her as a "dangerous woman" who should not be permitted to return. Lady Deborah ultimately decided to remain in Gravesend, where she knew she and her followers would be permitted to quietly pursue their unique religious doctrines.

By 1646 the Gravesend Colony was beginning to establish permanent roots. Twenty-three individuals had been granted parcels of land for the establishment of a home. Unlike other English communities where the quality and size of lots were distributed according to wealth and status, all of Lady Deborah's lots were assigned on an egalitarian basis. A wood palisade wall was built around the community, and farms were established to support the economy when the local harbors proved too shallow for large ships and fishing vessels. The original street grid established by Lady Deborah is still in existence and has been in continuous use for more than three hundred years.

The one thing strangely lacking in Gravesend was a church. Dutch authorities were willing to permit Lady Deborah to seek sanctuary in their land, but they loathed the spectacle of religious zealots flocking to New Netherlands. One of the conditions Lady Deborah agreed to in exchange for her land grant was that she would neither build a church nor hire a minister. Lady Deborah agreed to the restriction, and small religious gatherings were held quietly in private homes.

Lady Deborah died in 1659, and her son Henry traveled to Gravesend to help administer the estate. Henry later served as an ambassador to Virginia from New Netherlands, where he died in 1661. He died without heirs, and the baronetcy thereby became extinct.

In her final years it is likely that Lady Deborah privately converted to the Quaker faith. Gravesend was known to be a religious refuge for Quakers fleeing persecution in Massachusetts, and basic tenets of the Quaker faith were in accord with Lady Deborah's beliefs. Unlike other religious radicals of the age, Lady Deborah was willing to keep her views private. Some historians have attributed her greater success in establishing her colony to her willingness to compromise and practice her faith in an unobtrusive manner. Gravesend flourished after her death, and the small community of free thinkers eventually became part of the city of New York.

Further Reading
Biemer, Linda Briggs. *Women and Property in Colonial New York: The Transition from Dutch to English Law, 1643–1727.* Ann Arbor, MI: UMI Research Press, 1979.

Cooper, Victor H. *A Dangerous Woman: New York's First Lady Liberty.* Bowie, MD: Heritage, 1995.

Koppelman, Lucille L. "Lady Deborah Moody and Gravesend, 1643–1659." *Halve Maen* 67 (1994): 38–43.

Moravian Women

The Moravians were an offshoot of the fifteenth-century Hussite movement in Eastern Europe, where various periods of persecution prevented the group from becoming established beyond a few small enclaves. Despite their small numbers, the Moravians had some wealthy patrons, and the first small groups of Moravians began immigrating to America in search of religious freedom in 1735. The establishment of enduring communities occurred with the arrival of Count Nicolas von Zinzendorf

A view of Bethlehem, the great Moravian settlement in the province of Pennsylvania. Painted and engraved by Paul Sandby. (Library of Congress)

and his daughter, Benigna. They developed planned communities in Pennsylvania with biblical names: Bethlehem, Nazareth, and Emmaus. The other region for Moravian development was in North Carolina, where Salem became the focus of Moravian life.

The most distinctive feature of these early Moravian settlements was their communal lifestyle. They rejected private property and the concept of autonomous households. Married couples raised their children during the child's infancy, but around age two children were moved to a nursery during the day. Around age twelve children left the home altogether and took up residence in a "choir." The choirs had nothing to do with music, but were rather groups of people who lived together according to gender and age. Count Zinzendorf believed that spiritual growth progressed according to age and similar life conditions. Grouping people together

along age and gender lines in a communal setting would allow for the creation of strong support, camaraderie, and limit the temptations presented by the larger world.

Young adolescent girls lived in the Little Girls' Choir. Around age nineteen they moved to the Single Sisters' Choir, whereas the young men moved to the Single Brethren Choir. Members of a choir worked, studied, prayed, slept, and ate together. Teaching the young people in the choir was a communal responsibility of the adults. Parents no longer had supervisory powers over their own children. Discipline, training, and even matters of courtship were decided by town elders, rather than parents.

Young women and men had little opportunity to mingle. Marriage was not a romantic affair between individuals, but was rather a matter of community concern. Marriages were arranged by town elders, based on the suitability of the partners and the likelihood the couple would become a productive, harmonious team. Although either party could refuse a proposed match, they had little say in initiating their own romantic partnerships. After marriage, couples rarely created their own household, but rather continued the communal ideal by moving to a Married Brothers' Choir and Married Sisters' Choir. The husband would have been trained in a profession chosen for him by elders. A person's time, skills, and labor were all to be directed by the church. All the land, buildings, and tools were owned by the community. In exchange, everyone was guaranteed a home, all the necessities for daily living, and the fellowship of other like-minded people.

A by-product of the gender segregation was a great deal of leadership opportunities for women. Moravian teaching did not assume that women were entitled to equality, but because too much interaction between the sexes created unnecessary temptations, women were recruited into teaching, ministering, and administrative responsibilities within the female choirs. Women were invited to be members of most councils that decided matters of faith or the town economy. They were ordained as deaconesses, eldresses, and for a brief time, even as ministers. Diaries of these female leaders indicate they enjoyed their roles and were even reluctant to marry, because it meant leaving the Single Sisters' Choir where they had established leadership. Once in the Married Sisters' Choir, they would need to find new roles as junior members.

Aside from the unusual communal living arrangements, one of the striking characteristics of Moravian communities was the amount of emphasis placed on female education. Schooling was segregated by gender, but girls received roughly the same educational training as boys. The Bethlehem Female Seminary, a Moravian school for girls, was established in 1749. The excellent reputation of the school spread, and people from outside the Moravian community wished to send their daughters to the school. It became one of the most prestigious boarding schools for young women in the eighteenth and nineteenth centuries. Its emphasis was on academic subjects, rather than the ornamental arts, such as sewing and music, which predomi-

nated at other female boarding schools. The Bethlehem Female Seminary ultimately integrated with the Moravian men's college in 1954, when it was renamed Moravian College.

By the 1760s, the unusual communal experiment of Moravian age and gender segregation was beginning to dissipate. Subsequent generations of Moravians were less willing to embrace the odd living arrangements. The children of the original immigrants had no say in the creation of this rigid lifestyle, and acceptance of it was difficult for parents to pass down to their children. The Moravians were not an isolationist sect. They did business with outsiders and knew how the rest of society organized their towns. Pressures to cast aside Count Zinzendorf's utopian plan gathered momentum, and the choirs for married people were the first to be abolished. Young adults continued to live in choirs for several more generations, but after marriage they were allowed to form their own households.

Economic self-interest was likewise hard to repress. Moravians did business with neighboring communities where hard work was rewarded in a land of plenty. The insistence on communal property and fixed prices began to wear thin on well-educated and ambitious Moravians. So, too, did the restrictions on romantic alliances. In the 1780s and 1790s a number of Moravian couples began to elope rather than submit to arranged marriages. Following the American Revolution, with its emphasis on personal freedom, the restrictions within Moravian communities were no longer functional. The rules that had previously worked well to discipline family life, sexual attraction, and economic well-being were now viewed as oppressive. Rather than continue to lose their brightest and most ambitious members, the Moravian communities gradually abandoned the communal lifestyle, although their churches still flourish today.

Further Reading

Faull, Katharine. *Moravian Women's Memoirs: Their Related Lives, 1750–1820.* Syracuse, NY: Syracuse University Press, 1997.

Smaby, Beverly. "Female Piety among Eighteenth Century Moravians." *Pennsylvania History* 64 (1997): 151–167.

———. "Forming the Single Sisters' Choir in Bethlehem." *Transactions of the Moravian Historical Society* 28 (1994): 1–14.

Sommer, Elisabeth. "A Different Kind of Freedom? Order and Discipline among the Moravian Brethren in Germany and Salem, North Carolina, 1771–1801." *Church History* 63 (1994): 221–234.

Motherhood

People of colonial America celebrated motherhood as the culmination of a woman's purpose in society. Religious traditions, from the Puritans of New England to the Episcopalians of the mid-Atlantic, all believed it was in accordance with God's will for a woman to be fruitful, multiply, and rear God-fearing children. Despite the central role motherhood commanded for most women, the experience of mothers in early America was quite different from that of present-day mothers. Caring for a large number of children in addition to performing extensive duties of running a household meant women did not have the time to develop an intimate and deeply attentive relationship with a few children. Rather, they provided general supervision for a large number of children, receiving much help in child rearing from extended family and neighbors.

Puritan tradition held that children were born with a large degree of natural depravity. This view of childhood had ramifications for how women raised their children. Religious instruction from an early age was vital. Children's will must be tamed and molded into an obedient and respectful attitude toward God and parents. Threats of Hell were dangled before disobedient children, and corporal punishment was common. Authoritarian styles of parenting were recommended. Despite the strict and apparently loveless tone of religious sermons aimed at breaking the will of the child, surviving letters and diaries make it apparent that Puritan women loved their children. Then, as now, parents tended to be more tolerant toward their children than advice literature would condone. Most child-rearing manuals of the eighteenth century were directed toward men, and in the few cases where they mention mothers, they typically suggest mothers are too lenient with children, lending credibility

to the likelihood that severe Puritanical advice was not consistently practiced by mothers.

In the eighteenth century, philosophers such as John Locke and Jean-Jacques Rousseau rejected the notion that children were inherently bad. They taught that children were born as blank slates and needed affectionate nurturing in order to grow into healthy and moral adults. These teachings were enormously influential, giving an acceptable alternative to mothers who balked at the harsh discipline of Puritanical teaching. By the end of the colonial period the view of children's inherent wickedness had been almost completely rejected, with profound implications for childhood discipline, education, and religious training.

Infancy

Large families were welcomed by early Americans, owing both to religious approval of large families and the economic buffer provided by numerous children. Most women lacked the medical knowledge or the will to control their own fertility. Because women generally married between the ages of eighteen and twenty-two and would not reach menopause until their forties, it was quite common for a woman to have a twenty-year span dominated by pregnancy and lactation.

Managing a Large Family

"When I had but one child my hands were tied, but now I am tied hand and foot. How I shall get along when I have got half dozen or ten children I can't devise." Esther Burr, writing in her journal shortly after she gave birth to her second child in 1756.

Like most colonial women with large families, it was impossible for Esther to care for her children in addition to the large amount of cooking, cleaning, and sewing required of colonial women. Even the poorest of families relied on family or neighborhood girls to help look after young children, and Esther soon came to depend on hired help with household chores and caring for youngsters.

Source: Fisher, Josephine. "The Journal of Esther Burr." *New England Quarterly* 3 (1930): 297–315.

There is some evidence that women were reluctant to immediately bond with their newborn children. The first few months of life were always the most precarious, and as many as 10 percent of children died before their first year. When infants died or were injured, letters, diaries, and sermons almost unanimously imply that it was the will of God, and no actions on the part of the parent could have prevented the tragedy. It has been suggested that women might have psychologically braced themselves by delaying the naming of a child until it was a few months old, and referring to an infant as "it" rather than he or she. Although both practices clearly occurred, it is difficult from this distance to interpret what such actions symbolized.

Women usually breastfed their infants for one year, which provided some form of birth control. During this year the child would be constantly near, whether sleeping in a cradle while the mother worked indoors, or strapped to her back as she moved about the fields. The child would be weaned somewhere between nine and twelve months of age. Many New England mothers practiced the curious custom of leaving home for a few days while weaning occurred.

An infant greatly increased the amount of laundry needing attention. When possible, women held infants over a chamber pot. Most often they had to rely on "clouts" or small swatches of fabric that were wrapped around the baby's bottom and secured with a "belly band." Laundry was a tedious and physically burdensome chore, in some households done only once per month. In households with infants, laundry could not have been neglected. At a minimum, clouts were regularly rinsed out.

Rearing Toddlers

Ninety percent of the families in early America were connected to agricultural production. As such, a woman did not have the luxury of devoting her time exclusively to her children. Although her work allowed her to stay near to the home, a woman's day was filled with planting, harvesting, washing, tending to livestock, preparing meals from scratch, preserving food, and making clothing, candles, and soap. Care of the children was worked in around the other chores that were necessary for daily survival.

Mothers regularly resorted to corporal punishment to prevent curious toddlers from burning themselves or wandering into danger. A typical home would have been a hazardous place for a child. Large open fires, cauldrons of boiling water, unattended candles, open wells, farmyard animals, all manner of sharp tools, and countless other potential hazards loomed throughout the colonial home. Spanking, spraying the child's face with water, and even dunking children in water were all methods used to make sure children learned quickly which areas were off-limits.

The rearing of children was a cooperative venture in early America. Extended family members, friends, and servants all assisted in the supervision of very young children. It was not possible for a farmer's wife to provide close supervision of young children in addition to her other responsibilities. If there were no older siblings to perform this task, it is likely the family would either have a hired servant or a neighboring youngster to assist in looking after the children. Colonial families tended to be very large, and neighboring adolescent girls who did not have enough chores in their household to keep them fully employed were frequently sent to assist in other households. This was a mutually beneficial arrangement for all parties, because it provided the youngster with the opportunity to bond with another family, earn a few coins, and possibly learn valuable skills not available at home. A woman assumed a parental duty toward any young girl she accepted into her home as a servant. She was to provide guidance and supervision for the girl in addition to instruction in housekeeping chores.

Young Children

As soon as a child was old enough to pluck feathers or wash dishes they were assigned household tasks. By the age of five, most children knew how to keep occupied with chores. Some of these children were entrusted with tasks that would likely horrify the modern parent. At age eight John Adams was given a gun and told to hunt birds. Children were routinely assigned the tedious chore of turning the spit

Mrs. Elizabeth Freake and Baby Mary by Unknown American Painter, late seventeenth century. Many women were reluctant to immediately bond with their newborns as the first few months of life were always the most precarious. As many as 10 percent of children died before their first year. (Burstein Collection/CORBIS)

to keep meat roasting, requiring them to stand for several hours near a large, open fire. Children would have participated in the butchering of animals, and performing heavy manual labor was deemed a virtue.

Teaching children to read usually fell to the mother. Most women were able to read, if not write, and both boys and girls typically received rudimentary instruction at their mother's knee. Many mothers sent their children to "dame schools," in which a neighborhood woman took in children aged three to seven for a few hours each day. In addition to its educational value, the dame schools undoubtedly provided mothers with a much-needed reprieve from supervising children.

As her children grew older, a mother would be able to turn some of the basic supervision of toddlers and infants over to them.

Older Children

As children reached their teenage years, a sharp division in their rearing occurred along gender lines. Boys either went to school or performed heavy manual labor in the fields. A lucky few might be apprenticed to learn a skilled trade, which meant the boy would leave home to live and work in another household. For the majority who remained at home, fathers became the dominant parent for boys, whereas mothers continued to be the primary parent for girls. Girls rarely went to any sort of formal school, but if they did it was in the evenings or summers when the boys were not in attendance. Girls were trained for household responsibilities, and these tasks were to be learned at home from their mother. Girls would have been helping in domestic chores since childhood, but as they became adolescents their responsibilities would increase. They might assume full-time responsibility for caring for younger children, as well as for ever-increasing domestic chores.

Girls married and became mothers at a young age, often before twenty. As such, it was important for them to gain as much insight from their mothers as possible. Since most girls did not marry outside of the town in which they were born, it would have been a comfort for them to have their mother nearby to help them set up their own household and care for newborn babies. It appears that mothers developed a companionate relationship with their daughters, whereas fathers tended to assume the role of supervisor and instructor with their sons.

The Republican Mother

Following the American Revolution, motherhood assumed a heightened sense of importance. The war had a highly politicizing effect on women as well as society. This new society wanted to throw off the shackles of dissipation and corruption they believed was embodied in the English system. In order to do so, children had to be reared to value work, opportunity, and civic virtue. It would be the duty of mothers to rear such citizens. Although the objective of republican motherhood was to raise a class of politicized sons, as a by-product, women and girls were expected to attain a certain base level of knowledge and political awareness. This emphasis on rearing children from the cradle to value civic virtue and republican ideals required women to be educated. Formal schools were established exclusively for the education of women.

Although the concept of republican motherhood made no allowances for women's direct participation in government, it elevated mothers' roles as important contributors to society. It preserved traditional notions of gender, but gave women and mothers credit for helping to shape the minds and future of the nation.

The Evolving Nature of Motherhood

The enormously demanding tasks associated with running a farm in the seventeenth and eighteenth centuries made it impossible for any but the wealthiest women to devote substantial amounts of undivided time and attention to their children. Mothers relied on a network of extended kin, dame schools, and older children to assist them with rearing their broods. Except during times of medical crisis, children were rarely the exclusive focus of the mother's attention.

A number of factors led to a shift in the nature of motherhood in the eighteenth century. The Industrial Revolution provided greater availability of material goods, making it possible for women to purchase manufactured items such as cheese, candles, and clothing. With more free time, a woman was able to redirect her attention toward her children. Furthermore, families tended to become more isolated and private in the 1800s. No longer dependent on community support for survival in a hostile environment, families began to turn inward. The network of dame schools and informal arrangements to assist in the rearing of children gradually faded. Finally, the fire and brimstone rhetoric of child-rearing manuals eased. Whereas once the children were taught to fear Hell, obey their parents, and be dutiful workers, a shift in child-rearing advice now advocated a more loving, child-centered environment. Children were no longer morally depraved beings who needed their wills broken, but were considered the future of American civilization. They were to be nurtured and taught to become productive members

of society. Mothers were to have the primary role in shaping the next generation.

See also Breastfeeding; Childbirth; Mothers, Single

Further Reading

Dye, Nancy Schrom, and Daniel Blake Smith. "Mother Love and Infant Death, 1750–1920." *Journal of American History* 73 (1986): 329–353.

Gunderson, Joan R. *To Be Useful to the World: Women in Revolutionary America, 1740–1790.* New York: Twayne Publishers, 1996.

Kerber, Linda K. *Women of the Republic: Intellect and Ideology in Revolutionary America.* Chapel Hill: University of North Carolina Press, 1980.

Ulrich, Laurel Thatcher. *Good Wives: Image and Reality in the Lives of Women in Northern New England, 1650–1750.* New York: Random House, 1980.

Mothers, Single

Hester Prynne and her infamous scarlet letter personified the shame and humiliation that accompanied an out-of-wedlock birth in Puritan New England. Bearing a child outside the bonds of wedlock was not merely shameful, it was a crime. Women were prosecuted for fornication, as were the fathers, if they could be identified.

Around 40 percent of premarital pregnancies occurred among young, female servants, living outside of their family's protection. Such women were frequent targets of sexual pressure from their employers, usually older men who would have been in a position of trust or power. In other cases, these girls were sought after by young men their own age. Living outside of the supervision of family, the girls were easier to seduce.

Despite the high occurrence of premarital pregnancy among the servant class, 60 percent of out-of-wedlock pregnancies occurred among girls of the middling or upper classes who lived at home. The reasons these women conceived children out of wedlock were as numerous in early America as they are today. Some were hoping to snare a reluctant suitor into marriage; others were indulging in an affair with a married man. Others were the victims of rape. Sometimes the pregnancies were the result of sheer spontaneous passion. Young sweethearts, lusty widows, and naive servant girls are all represented in court fornication records.

Most premarital conception occurred in April and September, which was in sharp contrast to married couples, for whom conception occurred at a steady rate throughout the year. Illicit unions were difficult to accomplish during winter months when people lived in crowded, indoor conditions. During spring and autumn it was easier to find a secluded place in a barn or field. September was the highest month for illegitimate conception, which corresponds to the one time of year women were likely to join men in the fields during harvest.

The pressure for a woman to name the father of her child was enormous. Ultimately, around two-thirds of pregnant women married the father of their child. The remaining one-third usually did not marry because the father was already married. In a few cases, one or both parties simply refused to commit to wedlock.

In some cases women refused to name the father. This usually occurred when the mother knew there was no chance of marriage, and she wished to spare him social shame. In such cases, midwives were charged with trying to coax the name of the father from the woman during childbirth. Folklore held that a woman in the midst of labor pains would not lie about the identity of the father, nor would she prove as willing to protect a man who was responsible for her pitiful condition.

Childbirth in early America was usually a bonding event for women. As many as a dozen of the local women would attend the birth, bringing food, supervising the laboring woman's other children, or merely comforting her with anecdotal stories. This ritual gathering would have had a different character if the mother was single and had yet to name the father. In most cases the laboring mother would be a young girl giving birth to her first child. Her attendants would be older, disapproving women, intent on discovering the name of the father. Records indicate that many women did indeed name the father in the midst of childbirth.

Naming the Father

Midwives were often charged with learning the name of the father of an illegitimate baby. It was believed that no woman would lie about such an important matter in the midst of life-threatening childbirth. In 1686, a midwife and three neighborhood women gathered to attend the labor of Elizabeth Emerson of Salem, Massachusetts. Elizabeth was a single woman of twenty-one when she delivered her daughter, and the town wished to know the identity of the father.

In the midst of her labor, Elizabeth obediently supplied the name of twenty-four-year-old Timothy Swan. All four women who attended the birth submitted documents to the court verifying that Elizabeth had been repeatedly questioned and maintained that Swan was the father. At the time of delivery, Elizabeth and Swan loathed one another. Elizabeth claimed he had raped her, although there are no records of Swan ever being charged with that crime. Following the birth of the child, Timothy Swan was ordered by the court to pay ten shillings per week for the support of the child. Two years later, Elizabeth's family brought Swan to court for failure to pay anything beyond lumber, molasses, and comparable sundries.

Source: Fitzpatrick, Ellen. "Childbirth and Unwed Mothers in 17th Century New England." *Signs* 8 (1983): 744–749.

The word of the mother regarding paternity was usually accepted at face value, but if the reputed father strenuously objected, the matter had to be determined by the court. Officials knew it was in the mother's interest to name a wealthy man. In 1724, Bathsheba Lyston accused a wealthy neighbor of fathering her child. At trail, witnesses testified Bathsheba had bragged, "I will let any young man get me with child and then . . . I can lay it to who I please because a woman has that liberty granted to them" (Ulrich 1991, 150). Neighbors, midwives, ministers, and family members would be called to testify as to the moral character of both the mother and the supposed father. Unless there was overwhelming evidence to prove the man's innocence, he was usually charged with supporting the child.

Such was the case with Bathsheba Lyston. Despite her suspicious comments, the reputed father was unable to prove his innocence and was fined for the child's support.

A single mother who had no family to support her was in an especially precarious situation. Although she might receive minimal support from the father of the child, it would be inadequate to house and feed her and her child. Only the largest towns, such as Philadelphia, had almshouses. They were an undesirable place for single mothers, because in them, children were usually separated from their mothers and could be bound out to a life of service without the mother's consent. Few families would have been willing to hire a domestic servant with a child in tow. Single mothers often attempted to work from home, taking in laundry or serving as a wet nurse. Such forms of employment were too meager to provide self-sufficiency, and she would have had to rely on the kindness of family or charities.

There was a great deal of regional variation in prebridal pregnancy rates and societal reaction to such women. Variations in religious tradition and family structure made the experience of single mothers drastically different in New England than it was in the Chesapeake Bay area.

Single Mothers in New England

Comparatively few cases of premarital pregnancy occurred in New England, where strict Puritan morality reigned and family ties were strong. The sex ratio of males to females was usually balanced in New England, and mortality rates were low. As a result, girls were likely to grow up in families with both parents, active adult supervision, and less pressure from single men. Virginity was highly prized and expected of all young brides. Those who strayed from the path were held up to public shame and lingering social repercussions. Although premarital pregnancy was rare, it did occur. Young girls would have grown up witnessing the consequences of lax moral behavior. Couples prosecuted for fornication were punished with whipping, time in the stocks, and monetary fines. They were forbidden entrance into religious services until they had read humiliat-

ing penances before the congregation. The reputation of the woman never fully recovered, even if she married the father of her child.

The motivation for this severe reaction was to punish those who had strayed from Puritan ideals. Puritans had fled England in order to create a godly society guided by spiritual principles. Women were to embody the standards of feminine purity and modesty. They were entrusted with the rearing of children and provision of spiritual sustenance to the family. Women who strayed from that ideal were considered filthy, dissolute, and untrustworthy. They represented a cancer staining the concept of the City Upon the Hill. If such behavior were not severely punished, it threatened to spread and weaken the strength of the kingdom of God.

A hasty marriage of a pregnant bride could not stave off condemnation. Any couple whose child was born within eight months of their wedding was prosecuted for fornication. Although the couple had done the proper thing by marrying, they had still violated the doctrines of their religion by indulging in premarital sex, and needed to be punished. They were temporarily excommunicated and prosecuted for fornication. They were required to pay a substantial fine and make a humiliating appeal for forgiveness to their assembled congregation before they could be readmitted to this fundamental organization. A woman in such circumstances could be accepted back into society, but she would be forever tainted. The shame of the act would be attributed to her. Although lust in a man was considered normal, women were expected to restrain these base instincts. If a woman indulged in premarital sex, it was a sign that she was possessed of a licentious nature and could not control her sexual appetite. It was considered humiliating for a man to be wed to such a woman.

Marriage of pregnant women usually occurred when they were four to eight months along. This indicates there might have been reluctance on the part of the father to wed. Those who were in a committed relationship could have married within a month of discovering the pregnancy. A longer delay could indicate a court session was necessary to determine paternity or persuade a groom to the altar.

Approximately one-third of single mothers did not marry the father of their baby. If the father was already married or one of the parties balked at matrimony, such women found themselves in a dire situation. Financial maintenance of the child was temporarily provided by the father, but the mother was often relegated to the status of friendless outcast. After delivery of the child, the mother would usually be punished by a public whipping of between ten and thirty lashes.

The mother would be allowed to care for the child until it had been weaned, but the town had custody of a child born out of wedlock. After the child was no longer a toddler, the town had the right to bind him or her out as an indentured servant until the age of eighteen. Puritans believed that allowing the single mother to raise the child would reward her unsavory behavior and cause a child to be raised in a polluted atmosphere. The court records of Susanah Durbin's case illustrate how rending this experience could be. When town authorities arrived to take her child into custody, they stripped him of his clothes and turned him over naked to his new environment. Even allowing the child to wear clothing provided by his mother might taint him. Susanah was subsequently brought to court for attempting to see the child after it had been placed in a new home.

If the woman's family was willing to support her and the child, it might be permitted. The father's responsibility for paying support usually ended when the child neared the age of six. The social shaming that accompanied single mothers must have been effective, for very few of them were ever prosecuted for becoming pregnant a second time.

The lingering shame of having a child out of wedlock can be witnessed by how few of these women subsequently married. In a society in which 95 percent of women married, less than 30 percent of the women who bore bastards ever married anyone other than the father of the child. Because social life in Puritan society revolved entirely around family and church, women who were excluded from these institutions led a lonely and isolated life. Records indicate the single mothers who were able to marry almost always came from families of means, who could provide financial incentives for marriage.

Single Mothers in the Chesapeake Bay Area

The situation was drastically different in the Chesapeake Bay area, where there were as many as six men to every woman. Many of the women in Maryland and Virginia had arrived as indentured servants. With no parental protection, these women were vulnerable to the sexual pressure that would have surrounded almost any single female in a male-dominated world. One-third of the women who immigrated to the Chesapeake Bay area were pregnant when they married, whereas one in five brides who had been born in the Chesapeake Bay area were pregnant. Although both statistics are high, it demonstrates the greater vulnerability of immigrant women who rarely had extensive family to serve as a protective safeguard.

Indentured servants were particularly likely to become pregnant. They usually had no family and might have been subject to pressure from their employers. Because bearing a child represented a financial burden, one to two years would be added to a servant's indenture to compensate her employer. This law was set aside in instances when the employer was proven to be the father.

Settlement patterns in the Chesapeake Bay area were far more disperse than they were in New England. There was less community pressure for conformity, more opportunity to find a secluded trysting place, and a wildly unbalanced sex ratio that made women targets of sexual attention.

Most settlers in the southern colonies did not share the rigid moral code that governed New England. Although fornication was still a crime, the reasons were based on practical issues rather than on moral condemnation. Illegitimate children needed financial support and were liable to become public burdens. Fornication trials in the Chesapeake Bay area were primarily to identify the father, force him to financially support the child, and ensure the infant did not become a burden to the community. If a couple decided to marry prior to the birth of the child, there was usually no court action taken, and little lingering shame attached to the bride.

The unbalanced sex ratio made it easier for single mothers to find husbands in the Chesapeake Bay area. Few women immigrated to this region, and many who did died from malaria, yellow fever, or in childbirth. Men who were desperate for a wife were usually willing to overlook a woman's lack of virginity.

The Children of Single Mothers

The taint of bastardy clung to illegitimate children. Conditions were especially harsh in New England, where such children were not entitled to any form of inheritance from their biological parents. Most of these children would have been bound out to service. Upon their eighteenth birthday they would be provided with a suit of clothes and sent on their way.

Inheritance laws were less harsh in the Chesapeake Bay area, where bastards were entitled to a portion of their father's estate. Although there was a stigma associated with illegitimacy, it did not stain the child's reputation as much as it did the mother's. Some illegitimate children attained high status in the colonies, including Alexander Hamilton and William Franklin, son of Benjamin Franklin, who became the royal governor of New Jersey. Despite their success, even these men were occasionally taunted with the circumstances of their parentage.

See also Children, Custody of; Fornication

Further Reading

Fitzpatrick, Ellen. "Childbirth and an Unwed Mother in Seventeenth Century New England." *Signs* 8 (1983): 744–749.

Hambleton, Else K. "The World Fill'd with a Generation of Bastards: Pregnant Brides and Unwed Mothers in Seventeenth Century Massachusetts." Dissertation. University of Massachusetts, 2000.

Mason, Mary Ann. *From Father's Property to Children's Rights: The History of Child Custody in the United States.* New York: Columbia University Press, 1994.

Ulrich, Laurel Thatcher. *A Midwife's Tale: The Life of Martha Ballard, Based on Her Diary, 1785–1812.* New York: Vintage Books, 1991.

Mumbet

See Freeman, Elizabeth

Murray, Judith Sargent Stevens
Writer (1751–1820)

Judith Murray's voluminous writings can be credited with helping to define the role of American women and shaping the way they should be educated in the nineteenth century. Her father was a wealthy merchant, and Judith grew up in a financially privileged environment. After being raised in a home where she was envious of the fine education provided to only her brother, Judith railed against the sense of inadequacy she felt because of her inferior educational opportunities.

At age eighteen Judith married John Stevens, a sea captain and merchant. The marriage was childless and appears to have been a disappointment to Judith. The couple struggled with finances throughout much of their marriage, causing Judith intense psychological anxiety. Her helplessness in the face of the family's mounting debts convinced her that women should be educated not only to be fit wives and mothers, but to provide them with the tools of economic self-sufficiency. In 1786 the family finances had sunk to such a state that her husband fled to the West Indies in order to avoid being sent to a debtors' prison. He died before he could repair his finances, leaving Judith to pay off the creditors. Although she was eventually able to do so, the experience gave her a lasting fear of financial insolvency.

In 1774 Judith had met and become intrigued by the Universalist minister John Murray. She cast aside her strict Congregationalist upbringing to embrace this optimistic doctrine, which stressed the beauty of human spirituality and God's benevolence toward mankind. Two years after she was widowed, Judith married John Murray and moved to Boston, where they established the first Universalist congregation in the city. Once again Judith was plagued by financial uncertainty, and she tried supplementing the family income through writing. Throughout her adulthood Judith had written poems and essays, but most of these had been privately circulated only among friends and family. She occasionally published under a pseudonym beginning in 1782, but by the 1790s she was turning out numerous poems and essays for publication under the pen name Constantia. In 1790 she published "On the Equality of the Sexes" in the *Massachusetts Magazine*. The provocative essay argued that women possessed essentially the same degree of reason, imagination, and intelligence as did men, but had been deprived of the education necessary to apply these talents toward worthy goals.

Many of Judith Murray's writings relate to education and the role of women. She is often credited with setting the stage for what is now called "Republican Motherhood," which stressed the importance of educated mothers. Well-educated women were most likely to be capable of raising children to become productive citizens in the new society. Although women had no formal role in the governance of the new republic, they were essential to instilling the virtues of honor and perseverance in their children. The survival of the republic depended on the quality of its citizens, and Judith Murray argued that it was women who were best positioned to convey these qualities to their children during their crucial, formative years. Her ideas were persuasive, and her writings were widely published in a number of journals throughout New England. It is ironic that as she succeeded in elevating the importance of motherhood, she helped create a cult of domesticity that kept women within the ever-narrowing realm of the home in the nineteenth century.

In 1798 Murray published a collection of her essays in the three-volume collection called *The Gleaner*, named after a male character she created, Mr. Virgillius, who was free to wander through the city, talking and observing various aspects of urban life. The fact that she chose to tell her stories through the male viewpoint of Mr. Virgillius speaks to Murray's belief that the thoughts of a man had a credibility that the average reader was unwilling to extend to a woman. She also delved into the world of the theater, writing two comedies, *The Medium* (1795) and *The Traveler Returned* (1796). Neither play was successful, and Murray blamed their failure on the unpopularity of her husband's Universalist religion.

Judith Murray was able to earn a modest living from her writing, but John Murray's health declined after a series of strokes. After his death in 1815 she moved to Mississippi to live with her daughter, who had married a wealthy planter.

See also Education

Further Reading

Harris, Sharon M. *Selected Writings of Judith Sargent Murray.* New York: Oxford University Press, 1995.

Skemp, Sheila. "Judith Sargent Murray." In *Dictionary of American Literary Biography: American Women Prose Writers to 1820,* ed. Carla Mulford. Detroit, MI: Gale, 1999.

Wilcox, Kirsten. "The Scribblings of a Plain Man and the Temerity of a Woman: Gender and Genre in Judith Sargent Murray's *The Gleaner.*" *Early American Literature* 30 (1995): 121–144.

Musgrove, Mary

Native American translator and negotiator (c. 1700–1763)

Also known as Coosaponakeesa, Mary Musgrove was the daughter of a Creek Indian woman and a white fur-trading father. The Indian society into which she had been born was markedly different than the embattled and hostile Indians of the northeast. The Indians of the southeast had experienced centuries of contact with the Spanish and had already suffered through the cataclysmic experience of disease. By the time of Mary's birth, the worst of epidemic diseases had subsided and the Creek Indians had adapted their culture to trade and negotiate with white settlers. Mary thus grew up in a climate that welcomed mutually beneficial trade.

Mary lived among the Indians until she was seven, at which point her father brought her to live in South Carolina. There she learned the English language and was given training in the Christian religion. After spending almost ten years among the white settlers, Mary moved back to Indian country west of the Savannah River. There her language skills brought her into contact with representatives of the white government who had been sent to negotiate with the Indians. She soon married John Musgrove, the son of one of the negotiators. The couple spent several years moving between white and Indian culture, but eventually settled in Indian country where they established a trading post in 1732. At the crossroads of trade between backcountry hunters and white settlers, this trading post put the Musgroves in a pivotal position between the cultures.

In 1733 James Oglethorpe arrived to found the colony of Georgia. Mary's language skills and her key position of trust among the Creek Indians made her an ideal translator for Oglethorpe. The two established a healthy bond of trust, and Mary accompanied Oglethorpe on his diplomatic missions throughout Indian country as he secured deals with various Indian leaders. Historians have claimed it was because of Mary's influence that the English were able to establish friendly relations with the Indians in the Georgia colony. At Oglethorpe's request, the Musgroves established the Mount Venture trading post on the bank of the Altamaha River near the Spanish settlements. She was asked to pass on any gossip or suspicious activities of Spaniards in the area. Her husband, John, died shortly thereafter, and Mary promptly married his indentured servant, Jacob Matthews.

Mary's assistance would prove crucial to the struggling colony in 1739, when war between England and Spain was waged in the borderlands between Georgia and Florida. Known as the War of Jenkins' Ear (1739–1743), this European dispute was fought between English and Spanish colonists, with each side recruiting bands of Indians friendly to their cause. During one of the sessions that Mary was translating, Oglethorpe was surprised when some Creek Indians suggested that she be awarded three hundred acres of prime coastal territory in exchange for her loyal service. Although Oglethorpe had no legal right to grant such a request, he felt obligated to agree. The Indians had ceded enor-

mous tracts of lands to the English and were preparing to render additional military assistance. Should Oglethorpe have begrudged his loyal interpreter such gesture of goodwill, the delicate negotiations would have been threatened.

Mary continued to render service to Oglethorpe until he left the colony in 1743. Upon his departure he gave her a large diamond ring and £200. She continued to provide various services for the English Crown, working as a mediator between the English and Indians, who were beginning to be tempted by offers from both the French and Spanish.

Mary's second husband died in 1742, and in 1744 she married an unscrupulous opportunist, the Reverend Thomas Bosomworth. He skillfully engineered a series of ambitious cattle-trading ventures and succeeded in convincing the Creeks to grant Mary additional coastal islands for her use. Mary then proceeded to assert her right to the three hundred acres she claimed Oglethorpe had promised her. The colonists denied the legitimacy of the land grant despite Mary's repeated appeals. In the summer of 1749 Mary and the Reverend Bosomworth brought several dozen Creek warriors to Savannah to help persuade the colonists to grant Mary's land claims. By now her demands were escalating to include large cash payments. Accounts of that tense month have varied, some claiming Mary to have been a drunken savage, while others claimed that she was merely a woman demanding legitimate payment for her valuable services. The Indians may have vandalized the town, and colonists report having been "terrorized" in their homes until the Indians left after a month.

With their claims still unsatisfied, Mary and her husband went to England in 1754 to seek a settlement. In 1759 Mary came to an agreement with the English government for a settlement of £2,100 and title to St. Catherine's Island. She and her husband built a large manor house on the island. Mary died in 1763 and is buried on the island. Her only children, from her first marriage, all died in infancy.

Mary is a woman of mixed reputation. Numerous rumors that Mary was an Indian princess were encouraged by Mary and her third husband, but were apparently without foundation. Although she is celebrated for her association with James Oglethorpe, she is vilified for what appears to have been extortion attempts. Some claim that her association with Oglethorpe, although it resulted in good relations between the settlers and the Creeks during her lifetime, was ultimately an act of betrayal for the Indians of Georgia. Like many Indian women who served as "cultural brokers," Mary was considered highly successful during her own lifetime, but subsequent generations have reinterpreted her actions using contemporary standards of ethnic allegiance that show her in a less heroic light.

Further Reading

Baine, Rodney M. "Myths of Mary Musgrove." *Georgia Historical Quarterly* 76 (Summer 1992): 428–435.

Coulter, E. Merton. "Mary Musgrove, Queen of the Creeks: A Chapter of Early Georgia Troubles." *Georgia Historical Quarterly* 11 (March 1927): 1–30.

Gillespie, Michele. "The Sexual Politics of Race and Gender: Mary Musgrove and the Georgia Trustees." In *The Devil's Lane: Sex and Race in the Early South*, eds. Catherine Clinton and Michele Gillespie. New York: Oxford University Press, 1997.

Music

Music did not play an important role in the lives of most early American women until the basic necessities of survival had been established and communities became wealthy enough to support luxuries such as musical instruments. Contrary to popular myth, Puritans had no aversion to music, and the most likely exposure to music most women experienced was in church, where the singing of hymns was common.

As an elite class became established in the American colonies, emulation of European aristocratic manners was highly valued. The ability to play musical instruments became a sign of social status by the mid-eighteenth century. Women were discouraged from playing wind instruments, as the contortion of facial muscles was considered unfeminine. The harpsichord and the English guitar were the most common instruments a cultured lady learned to play. The English guitar was a ten-stringed version of a Renaissance cittern, carved into a teardrop shape. A few women played harps, but these were not common in America until the close of the eighteenth century.

The ability to play an instrument required an investment not only in the instrument, but in private lessons as well. Itinerant music teachers traveled throughout the South giving lessons, while larger cities were able to support a small class of teachers. Most music teachers were male, but a few advertisements from colonial newspapers indicate that at least some women earned a living through music. In the 1770s Mrs. Neill of Williamsburg advertised guitar lessons, charging one guinea for eight lessons. Ann Winsor of South Carolina offered harpsichord lessons and might also have worked as a church organist.

The playing of musical instruments was not without its critics. In his famous essay "Thoughts on Female Education," Benjamin Rush stated that true proficiency in a musical instrument requires years of daily practice. He believed those hours would have been better spent enriching a woman's mind by reading the classics.

Although playing musical instruments was a luxury for most white colonists, it played a more important role in the daily life of slave women. African musical traditions were passed down through generations of slaves. Songs were closely associated with daily events, whether it was working in the fields, relaxing in the evenings, worship, or celebrating with family. Their vocal music often took the form of a call-and-response pattern and could be sung in rounds. The most common instruments among slaves were homemade drums or sometimes a fiddle. The singing was punctuated with hand clapping and foot stamping. Music was a powerful means of self-expression among the enslaved population and eventually developed into a uniquely American form of music.

Further Reading

Hitchcock, H. Wiley, and Stanley Sadie, eds. *The New Grove Dictionary of American Music.* London: Macmillan, 1986.

Hoover, Cynthia Adams. "Music and Theater in the Lives of Eighteenth-Century Americans." In *Of Consuming Interests: The Style of Life in the Eighteenth Century,* ed. Cary Carson. Charlottesville: University Press of Virginia, 1994.

Keller, Katie Van Winkle. "Music and Dance." In *Encyclopedia of the North American Colonies,* ed. Jacob Ernest Cooke. New York: Charles Scribner's Sons, 1993.

N

Native American Women

See Colonization, Effect on Indian Women; Indian Women; Indian Women and Leadership; Indian Women and Work; Interracial Marriage

Nuns

See Convents

Nurse, Rebecca

Early settler, victim of the Salem witch trials (1621–1692)

With the exception of the tragically bizarre events that occurred the final year of her life, Rebecca Nurse's experience in early America was a classic example of a Puritan woman whose hard work helped to create a level of prosperity unlikely to be earned in England. In her twenties Rebecca immigrated to Massachusetts during the earliest years of the Puritan settlement. She married Francis Nurse, a woodworker and farmer. Rebecca was a hard-working Puritan goodwife. She tended her garden, spun flax into thread, and raised a large brood of children. The family fortune prospered, allowing them to purchase a large farm near Salem in 1678. They raised their eight children to emulate their devout religious traditions, and the entire family enjoyed community respect and financial success.

The first stirrings of trouble began in the winter of 1691, when young girls complained of torments inflicted on them by witches. Most of the townspeople initially accused of practicing witchcraft were outcasts. They included beggars, loose women, or contentious people who argued with neighbors. Belief in witches was widespread in seventeenth-century America, and the charges were taken seriously. As the accused were put on trial, most of the townspeople were forced to choose sides. Few were willing to come forward as character witnesses for the accused, but many attended the hearings where the dramatic hysterics displayed by the young girls held the community transfixed.

Rebecca Nurse did not attend the hearings. She was in her seventies, and her health was rapidly failing. When asked her opinion on the topic that was consuming public interest, she voiced guarded skepticism. Rebecca did not completely reject the truth of the charges, but proclaimed some of the accused to be innocent. As sometimes happened to people who doubted the veracity of the girls' accusations, suspicion soon turned to Mrs. Nurse. In March 1692, Ann Putnam claimed to have been tormented by the apparition of Rebecca Nurse, and less than two weeks later the elderly Mrs. Nurse was arrested.

The arrest and trial of Rebecca Nurse marked a turning point in the witchcraft trials. She was widely known and respected within the community. Unlike most of the others accused of witchcraft, Rebecca Nurse had a spotless reputation in the community and was the matriarch of a large and prosperous

The house of Rebecca Nurse, who was accused of witchcraft in the Salem trials. (Lee Snider/CORBIS)

family. Also unlike other accused witches, Rebecca Nurse had a large group of supporters who were willing to publicly proclaim their belief in her innocence. Forty members of the community signed a petition attesting to Rebecca Nurse's good character.

Rebecca Nurse was found not guilty at her trial. Upon the reading of the verdict, four of her young accusers went into hysterics. Taken aback by the display, the judge ordered the jurors to reconsider their verdict. The jurors proceeded to ask questions of Mrs. Nurse. Partially deaf, ill, and distracted by the ongoing commotion in the courtroom, Mrs. Nurse did not have ready answers for the questions put to her. After another round of deliberations, the jury returned a guilty verdict. Despite the appeals of her family, Rebecca Nurse was hanged along with four other accused witches. Her body was placed in a common grave, but family members later retrieved her body under cover of night and

reburied her on the family farm. Two monuments were later erected on the property, one to memorialize Rebecca Nurse, another with the names of the forty people brave enough to sign the petition in her favor. In 1712, the Nurse family succeeded in having her excommunication from the church overturned.

It has been suggested that the trial and hanging of Rebecca Nurse marked the beginning of the end of the witchcraft trials. The conviction of the accused depended almost entirely on "spectral evidence," or the testimony of a victim who claimed to be able to see invisible events. The acceptance of spectral evidence allowed anyone with imagination to launch damaging accusations that could not be refuted. It was easier to believe hideous accusations when they were lodged against outcasts, than it was when people of sterling character were accused. The accusations against Rebecca Nurse pushed skeptical observers off the fence, and spectral evidence was banned from the trails. The Salem trials ground to a halt shortly thereafter.

See also Salem Witch Trials; Tituba; Witchcraft

Further Reading

Norton, Mary Beth. *In the Devil's Snare: The Salem Witchcraft Crisis of 1692.* New York: Alfred A. Knopf, 2002.

Perry, Marilyn Elizabeth. "Rebecca Nurse." In *American National Biography,* ed. John A. Garraty. New York: Oxford University Press, 1999.

Nursing

See Medical Care; Midwives; Military Service and the American Revolution

O

Orphaned Girls

Life could be difficult and dangerous for orphaned girls in early America. There was little recognition of childhood as a distinctive stage of emotional or intellectual development. Although most parents would have instinctively reared their children in a secure and loving atmosphere, children who lost both parents had to depend on guardians who might have had no interest in providing a nurturing environment. The fragile life span in the colonial era meant that it was not unusual for a child to lose one or both parents before reaching the age of majority. Mortality rates in the Chesapeake region were exceptionally high. Seventy-five percent of children lost one parent before they reached the age of twenty-one. A third of children lost both their parents before that time.

There were no public institutions for the care of orphaned children throughout most of the colonial period. It was not feasible for a town to house and provide for children if they could be placed in homes where their labor could contribute toward their maintenance. "Orphans' Court" was the name for special court days that were set aside when judges would assign indentures and review the estates that were in trust for orphans who were under the supervision of guardians. Toward the end of the colonial period, Quaker and other charitable societies were established to soften the cold, bureaucratic system that cared for orphans. The orphans in larger cities of the middle colonies and northeast benefited from such enlightened institu-tions, but rural and southern children still faced dire circumstances.

If an orphaned child was fortunate, she would have brothers or sisters who were old enough to take custody of her. Older siblings raised about half of the orphans of colonial America. If there were no older siblings to take the child in, aunts, uncles, or good friends were usually named as guardians. The guardian administered any inheritance the child received. Boys usually inherited property and farms, whereas girls received movable goods and livestock.

Such was not the case for many impoverished orphaned children, who either lacked family or whose family members were too poor to take in another child. In such cases the town or local parish took charge of the child. The most common out-come was for a girl to be bound out as an inden-tured servant. Children as young as six years old were considered suitable for employment, and town officials routinely bound out indigent orphans. The following entry from court records was typical in the case of an impoverished orphan:

April 15, 1701. Sarah, the daughter of John Allen, deceased, is bound to Thomas Bentley until she arrives at the age of eighteen years—the said Bentley obliging himself to instruct her in the rudiments of the Christian religion, to learn or cause her to read perfectly, and at the expiration of the said term to provide and give her a decent suit of apparel, and ordered that indentures be drawn accordingly. (Tyler 1897, 222)

This entry typifies the requirements a guardian owed his indentured servant. Beyond teaching her to read, allowing her to attend church services, and providing her with clothing, the guardian was not required to provide any of the emotional support expected in a family setting. Most guardians who signed indentures were doing so to gain an economic asset, not a family member. Girls were expected to be productive members of the household, usually assisting with domestic chores and occasional field labor. They would have looked to a guardian as an employer rather than a parental figure.

At age fourteen, orphans who were dissatisfied with their situation could appeal to a court for a new guardian. If a girl married she could also be released from her indenture. Courts and guardians generally refused to allow orphaned girls younger than fourteen to marry, unless the girl was pregnant.

Statistics reveal that orphaned girls were far more likely to conceive a child before wedlock than girls from intact families. Historians speculate that girls who had no protector or close family ties were far more susceptible to seduction. Part of this could be accounted for by lack of parental discipline, although it could also be a result of a lonely girl's longing for affection wherever it could be found. This is consistent with other studies, which show indentured girls who traveled to the New World alone were almost twice as likely to conceive a child out of wedlock as girls who lived with their family.

Orphan asylums began to be founded in the early 1800s, but did not become widespread until the 1830s. They were initially established by charitable religious associations in the nation's larger cities. As cities grew, immigration increased, and the labor problems of the New World eased. The demand for the labor of very young indentured children evaporated. Orphan asylums began caring for young children, although it was still common to indenture children out for service around age fourteen. This would remain the common practice for dealing with orphaned children until the Civil War.

Adoption was not a legal option until the mid-nineteenth century. There were slight distinctions between adopted children and those who were under the care of a guardian. Adopted children were entitled to inheritance rights and a permanent status within a family. Guardianship had no such benefits. Children could be reassigned to other guardians, and at the age of majority be emancipated with nothing more than a set of "decent apparel." Given that most orphaned children were taken in by family members, it is hoped they were raised in a nurturing environment. Children who were indentured out were not likely to be so fortunate.

See also Children, Custody of; Stepfamilies

Further Reading

Hacsi, Timothy A. *Second Home: Orphan Asylums and Poor Families in America.* Cambridge, MA: Harvard University Press, 1997.

Rutman, Darrett B., and Anita Rutman. "Now-Wives and Sons-in-Law: Parental Death in a Seventeenth Century Virginia County." In *The Chesapeake in the Seventeenth Century: Essays on Anglo-American Society and Politics,* eds. Thad W. Tate and David L. Ammerman. Chapel Hill: University of North Carolina Press, 1979.

Tyler, Lyon G. "Education in Colonial Virginia: Part I, Poor Children and Orphans." *William and Mary Quarterly* 5 (1897): 219–223.

P

Philipse, Margaret Hardenbrook
Merchant trader (fl. 1659–1690)

The adventures and fortunes of Margaret Hardenbrook Philipse serve as a personification of the power and status to which a woman in the Dutch colonies could aspire. Margaret emigrated from Elderfield, Germany, to the Dutch colony of New Amsterdam (present-day New York) in 1659. She worked as an agent for her Dutch cousin's shipping business. Margaret arranged for the sale of pins, cooking oil, and vinegar in exchange for furs, which she shipped back to her cousin in Amsterdam. She represented her cousin in courts to collect debts and oversee the colonial end of his business. In 1659 she married wealthy merchant Pieter Rudolphus DeVries, although she continued to conduct business under her maiden name. She gave birth to a daughter shortly after her marriage, but her husband died in 1661.

Two years later Margaret married a former carpenter, Frederick Philipse. She entered into an *usus* marriage contract, a unique form of marriage permitted under Dutch law that allowed a woman to preserve her legal identity and the ability to conduct business in her own name. Margaret was a self-directed businesswoman who was legally free to operate a business, buy property, and initiate contracts. Margaret signed a prenuptial contract with Frederick that ensured the preservation of her former husband's vast wealth for her daughter.

The fortunes of the Philipse family blossomed. Frederick and Margaret purchased several properties and expanded their various trading ventures. They owned at least two ships and had a flourishing transAtlantic trade. Margaret made numerous voyages to Europe, usually serving as the ship's supercargo, meaning she was responsible for the purchase and sale of the goods.

In 1664 the Dutch colony of New Amsterdam became a possession of England. Although the 1664 Articles of Capitulation assured the Dutch inhabitants that their property rights and freedom of religion would be respected, the colony was now to be governed by English law. The change in administration was profound. No longer a legally independent woman, Margaret's marital status was now defined by English law as *feme covert,* meaning her legal identity was subsumed under her husband. Although Margaret continued to carry on her business affairs, she could no longer act as legal agent or purchase goods under her own authority. The substantial profits generated by their vast business empire were now the sole property of her husband. There is no evidence to suggest that Frederick took advantage of this change in his wife's legal status. To the contrary, her continued activities as a merchant trader indicate their personal and professional lives continued to flourish.

We know little of Margaret's personal life, but the insights of two missionaries who traveled with her on one of her voyages to Europe give a somewhat unflattering insight into her personality. They complained about her parsimonious attitude and recounted an incident in which she demanded the entire crew spend more than an hour in search of a lost mop, which the missionaries believed had been lost overboard. They claimed she suffered from shameless avarice and excessive covetousness. Whether this is an accurate characterization of Margaret, or merely the opinions of men who were unaccustomed to seeing a woman operating in a traditionally male profession, is impossible to determine more than three hundred years later.

Although Margaret continued her trading activities following the English conquest of New Netherlands, the new administration was clearly less accepting of women in the professions. In the last decade of Dutch rule, there were forty-six women identified as traders. By 1700 there was not a single woman so identified. Margaret retired from business in 1680, one of the wealthiest women in New York.

See also Dutch Settlement, Women's Life and Culture in

Further Reading

Berkin, Carol. *First Generations: Women in Colonial America.* New York: Hill and Wang, 1996.

Biemer, Linda Briggs. *Women and Property in Colonial New York: The Transition from Dutch to English Law, 1643–1727.* Ann Arbor, MI: UMI Research Press, 1979.

Garraty, John A., and Mark C. Carnes, eds. *American National Biography.* New York: Oxford University Press, 1999.

Gunderson, Joan. "Married Women's Legal Status in Eighteenth Century New York and Virginia." *William and Mary Quarterly*, 3d ser. 39 (1982): 111–134.

Jordan, Jean P. "Women Merchants in Colonial New York." *New York History* 58 (1977): 412–439.

Pilgrim Women

Women living in the small handful of Pilgrim villages had different experiences from women of the much larger Puritan communities. Although the Pilgrims and the Puritans are often considered synonymous in the minds of present-day people, they were markedly different groups during the seventeenth century.

The primary difference between the Pilgrims and Puritans was their attitude toward established religion. Both groups disapproved of the Church of England, which they believed retained the corruption of the Catholic Church. They believed that religious authority should be grounded in scripture. When the Church of England elected to place ultimate authority in the English monarch, both Puritans and Pilgrims were convinced the Church of England was destined for the same corruption that was brought to the Catholics by way of a papacy. Where the Puritans and the Pilgrims parted ways was in their solution to the problem. The Puritans believed the Church of England could be "purified" and made clean through reform. The Pilgrims were unwilling to wait and wanted a complete separation from the Church of England. They referred to themselves as separatists. The term *Pilgrim* did not become regularly associated with this group until the late eighteenth century.

The laws of England left no room for religious separatists, and the Pilgrims needed to build their community in a foreign land. The first group of about 125 Pilgrims immigrated to Holland in 1608. They remained there for twelve years, but problems of unemployment and the likelihood of war with Spain made them uneasy in their new home. Most importantly, they saw their children becoming more Dutch than English, and wished to find a land where they could enjoy religious liberty, economic advancement, and an English culture. They believed they could find all three in the fledgling colonies in America. A group of 102 Pilgrims boarded the *Mayflower* and landed off the shores of New England on 11 November 1620. Among their number were nineteen adult women and several adolescent girls.

The women lived aboard ship during the first few months until shelters could be built in the colony they named Plymouth. The first winter was brutal, and most of these initial female settlers died within the year. More women arrived in the coming years, but the sex ratio was skewed, with men far outnumbering women in Plymouth. Over the next few decades, more ships arrived, bringing new settlers, and the sex ratio was eventually brought into bal-

What Happened to the Women of the *Mayflower?*

The *Mayflower* set sail for America in 1620 with nineteen adult women on board. All the women survived the crossing, even the three who were in their last trimester of pregnancy. Upon arrival off the rugged coast of Massachusetts, the women remained aboard ship for several months while the men scouted for a suitable site and constructed the initial shelters. The first woman to die was Dorothy Bradford, who fell overboard and drowned in the frigid harbor while living aboard the *Mayflower.* A number of the other women sickened in the cramped and enclosed quarters of the ship. Pneumonia and colds spread easily under such conditions, and before the winter was over, thirteen of the nineteen women had perished.

By the time of the first Thanksgiving, a year after arriving in Plymouth, only four women were still alive. They were Eleanor Billington, Elizabeth Hopkins, Mary Brewster, and Susanna White Winslow. These four surviving women had immigrated first to Holland to escape persecution in England, then into the dangerous wilds of America in search of freedom. The curious names Mary Brewster chose for her children might indicate the drama and anxieties they had shared: Patience, Fear, Love, and Wrestling.

After the brutal conditions of the first year, survival rates dramatically improved, and all four surviving women lived long enough to become well established in the New World.

Source: Deetz, James, and Patricia Scott Deetz. *The Times of Their Lives: Life, Love, and Death in Plymouth Colony.* New York: W. H. Freeman, 2000.

unable to afford servants. Their wives had a larger responsibility to perform the entire range of household chores. As such, their workday was filled with merely providing the rudiments for survival, with little surplus time or money to acquire amenities.

Typical homes in Pilgrim villages were very small, usually containing two rooms and a loft. The furniture in these homes was almost all made locally, because furniture does not appear in the provision lists of ships that arrived from England. The earliest homes had small windows, covered with oiled parchment that made them translucent and allowed light to penetrate. Families were large, and privacy was minimal. Contrary to family life in England, where several generations might live under one roof, most Pilgrim couples immediately established their own home upon marriage.

The rights of married women were severely circumscribed, and they had no voice in town government. The settlers based this arrangement on biblical precedent, which shows women to be the "weaker vessel," whose proper place was to be subordinate to men. Male-dominated social structures were the norm in the seventeenth century, but there is evidence that the frontier environment of early Pilgrim communities offered women more legal rights than was common in Europe. Husbands were required to obtain their wives' consent before they could sell land or homes. Court records indicate that Pilgrim women entered into a number of contracts, which was highly unusual in the seventeenth century. The law in Pilgrim communities also required mothers to give consent for the indenturing of their children, unheard of in most Anglo-American communities where the father had complete authority over such decisions.

Pilgrim communities lacked the hierarchy of Puritan communities, where the wives of ministers and "gentlemen" had more status than the blacksmith's wife, who in turn had more status than the poor farmer's wife. The structure of Pilgrim government was more democratic. Those who were elected to power served to represent the concerns of the governed. In Puritan communities, those elected into power considered themselves divinely

ance. As Plymouth reached capacity, new communities needed to be established. Between 1636 and 1687, twenty small Pilgrim villages were established.

The daily life of women living in Pilgrim communities differed from that of their Puritan counterparts. Their villages were tiny in comparison to the burgeoning Puritan towns. As a group, Pilgrims were poorer and not as well educated as the Puritans. Most Pilgrim men were yeomen laborers who were

Public worship at Plymouth by the Pilgrims. Although both the Puritans and Pilgrims disapproved of the Church of England, the Pilgrims wanted a complete separation from the Church of England. (Bettmann/CORBIS)

appointed, and believed they were to rule based on their own best judgment. This subtle distinction manifested itself in a more authoritarian form of community in Puritan towns.

Although both Pilgrims and Puritans came to America motivated primarily on religious grounds, the nature of their devotion to a godly community differed. Puritan towns had a high percentage of ministers, lawyers, and other well-educated professionals. Their leaders relied on the advice of ministers and depended on scripture for guidance in community affairs. Religion pervaded society in Puritan communities, which translated into more traditional roles and higher expectations for female subservience. There was a much greater separation of church and state among the Pilgrims. Punishment

for moral failings, such as adultery or blasphemy, were not as harsh or freely given among the Pilgrims. Unlike the Massachusetts Bay Colony, where Puritans tried and executed a number of women as witches, no one was ever executed for witchcraft in the Plymouth Colony. As a whole, accusations of witchcraft were markedly lower in Pilgrim communities than among the Puritans.

Over time the distinction between Pilgrim and Puritan communities blurred, then disappeared. This was due largely to the fewer numbers of Pilgrims. By the 1640s there were only around 2,500 Pilgrims in New England, but the ranks of the Puritans had swelled to more than 20,000. Their communities depended on each other for defense and trade. Settlers moved among the communities and intermarried. Pilgrims gradually integrated among the Puritans, until the distinctions between their cultures were no longer evident.

See also Puritan Women

Further Reading

Deetz, James, and Patricia Scott Deetz. *The Times of Their Lives: Life, Love, and Death in Plymouth Colony.* New York: W. H. Freeman, 2000.

Demos, John. *A Little Commonwealth: Family Life in Plymouth Colony.* New York: Oxford University Press, 1970.

Pinckney, Eliza Lucas
Plantation manager who perfected the cultivation of indigo (c. 1722–1793)

Eliza Lucas was born in the West Indies, where her father, George Lucas, served as lieutenant governor of the island of Antigua. She was well educated and well traveled, having attended school in England. She was encouraged by her father to read from a wide range of classical writers. In 1738 the family moved to South Carolina, where Eliza's father had inherited the Wappoo Plantation, six miles upriver from Charleston. Within a year of moving to South Carolina, George Lucas was forced to return to the West Indies because of the brewing war between England and Spain. Known as the War of Jenkins' Ear, the maritime conflict would stretch over several years and wreak havoc on the economies of both Europe and America.

Seventeen-year-old Eliza Lucas was entrusted with management of the six-hundred-acre plantation. Like most other plantations at this time, Wappoo's staple crop was rice. The bulky nature of rice made it prohibitively expensive to ship to England during wartime, and George Lucas advised his daughter to seek out other potential crops. He shipped her numerous seeds from the Indies to experiment with, including hemp, flax, and indigo. Indigo would have been especially lucrative, because England's traditional suppliers of indigo in the West Indies had abandoned the crop in favor of sugar, which was easier to cultivate. Compact, easy

to ship, and expensive, indigo would be an excellent alternative to the bulky and less-valuable rice.

To grow, the indigo plant required a hot and humid climate. It was an easy crop to grow, but the process of turning it into dye was problematic. Eliza Lucas spent several years in failed attempts to process the plant into dye. The chemical process required the leaves of the plant to be soaked in open-air, water-filled tanks. It was essential for the temperature to be maintained at a hot, even level if fermentation was to occur. Next, a violent stirring of the tanks produced an oxidation process. Too little or too much stirring could ruin the batch. While the solution settled, particles of dye sunk to the bottom of the tank. The tanks were drained, and the mud-like residue was strained, dried, and cut into cakes. If cold air interfered with the process, it would ruin the crop. Adding lime to the solution could mitigate the damaging effects of cold air, but determining the proper quantities of lime was difficult.

Throughout Eliza's years of experimenting with the indigo plant, she consulted with neighboring planters and two experts on indigo cultivation from the West Indies. She freely shared indigo seeds with a number of planters, hoping that someone would develop the proper technique to permit indigo to flourish in the South Carolina climate. Eliza's first three years experimenting with indigo were failures, but through modifying the amount of lime used in the processing, her fourth year resulted in a viable product. She shared the technique with other planters, and indigo rapidly became the colony's primary cash crop.

The contributions that Eliza's indigo made to the colonial economy of South Carolina were remarkable. The French recognized the burgeoning threat of Carolina indigo and made it a capital offense for anyone to export indigo seeds from the French West Indies into Carolina. The warnings did little good, because Eliza and her neighbors freely shared their seed with one another. Eliza's first crop of indigo in 1744 yielded just a few pounds of dye. By 1747 the colony produced 135,000 pounds for export, and in the coming years it was possible for the colony to produce almost a million pounds per year. The

American Revolution interrupted the ability to export indigo to Europe. After the war, the crop faded in popularity, because cotton emerged as the South's leading export.

One of the neighbors with whom Eliza had shared seeds was Charles Pinckney, a lawyer nearly twenty years her senior. Eliza was friendly with both Pinckney and his wife, with whom she exchanged books and planting advice. Pinckney had served as a mentor to Eliza when she had assumed control of her plantation while still only a teenaged girl. When Pinckney's wife died, Eliza married the childless widower. They had four children, three of whom grew to adulthood. Her letters indicate that Eliza dedicated herself to motherhood with as much enthusiasm as she had to her indigo. When her first child was merely a few months old, she wrote to a friend in England requesting a new toy for her son "to teach him according to Mr. Locke's method, which I have carefully studied, to play himself into learning" (Berkin 1996, 133).

Eliza's extensive notebooks and letters give us a window into the world of a wealthy, colonial plantation mistress. She typically rose at five o'clock and read for two hours. She then toured the plantation fields to ensure that the day's work was commencing in a proper manner. She returned home for breakfast, then spent a few hours in music or the study of language. Her afternoon was spent instructing her younger siblings and her children in lessons. Her evenings were spent with more reading or needlework. At least one day per week she set all amusements aside and devoted herself entirely to plantation business. Eliza had a strong entrepreneurial instinct. She maintained a correspondence with an agent in London for the marketing of her plantation's commodities. She maintained an excellent library and became something of a legal authority among the locals, to whom she gave assistance in drawing up wills and pursuing debts.

Despite the difference in their ages, Charles and Eliza's marriage was extremely happy. She wrote that during the fourteen years of her marriage, she was "the happiest mortal on earth" (Ravenel 1896, 175). Her affectionate letters to Charles reveal a loving marriage, in which both partners depended on one another in the running of their business and for social support. Although she was widowed when she was only thirty-six, Eliza never remarried. Following Charles's death she was so deeply depressed it took her almost a month to write her children at school in England to inform them of their father's passing. Eventually the necessity for her to resume her business concerns brought her back into regular life. Charles had owned seven plantations throughout South Carolina, all of which Eliza assumed control of following her husband's death.

Aside from her role in making indigo a viable crop for South Carolina, Eliza Lucas Pinckney's other contributions to America were her two sons, Charles and Thomas. Both sons served in the American Revolution. Charles Pinckney Jr. was an aide to General Washington during the war, represented South Carolina at the Constitutional Convention, and was the Federalist candidate for president in 1804 and 1808. Thomas Pinckney was governor of South Carolina and minister to Great Britain. Both sons shared Eliza's interest in botany and initiated their own experiments in innovative planting on their own plantations.

In 1793 Eliza Pinckney was diagnosed with a fast-growing cancer. She traveled to Philadelphia to seek treatment. She died shortly after arrival and was buried in St. Peter's Church in Philadelphia. President Washington, at his own request, served as one of her pallbearers.

Further Reading

Bassett, Sam S. "Eliza Lucas Pinckney: Portrait of an Eighteenth Century American." *South Carolina Historical Magazine* 72 (1971): 207–219.

Berkin, Carol. *First Generations: Women in Colonial America.* New York: Hill and Wang, 1996.

Coon, David L. "Eliza Pinckney and the Reintroduction of Indigo Culture in South Carolina." *Journal of Southern History* 42 (1976): 61–76.

Ravenel, Harriot Horry. *Eliza Pinckney.* New York: Charles Scribner's Sons, 1896.

Williams, Frances Leigh. *Plantation Patriot: A Biography of Eliza Lucas Pinckney.* New York: Harcourt, Brace and World, 1967.

Pitcher, Molly

See Molly Pitcher Legend

Plantation Mistresses

The role of a plantation mistress was too dissimilar from that of a farmer's wife to be a useful comparison. Because plantation labor was overwhelmingly delegated to a slave population, the planter and his wife were rarely burdened with physical labor. Plantations were larger and more self-sufficient than northern farms. Located in rural and isolated regions, plantations usually supported populations of between fifteen and fifty individuals. The higher number of workers and the inconvenience of travel made self-sufficiency important. Most plantations featured a main dwelling house for the owner's family, although the stereotypical grand mansions with imposing columns were limited to only the wealthiest plantations. Most plantation homes were modest, two-story homes with a wraparound gallery. A series of outbuildings were needed for local production and to house slaves. Most plantations would have had a separate kitchen, stables, smokehouse, poultry barn, and warehouse. Slave huts were crude buildings with dirt floors and homemade furniture.

Southern women were famous for their hospitality. Their barbeques, formal dinners, and balls were largely motivated by the lonely isolation that pervaded much of their daily existence. The plantation mistress was often the only white woman living within several miles. It was common for wealthy southern women to move great distances upon their marriage, and these women felt keenly the absence of sisters, relatives, and other friends. When Anne Nicholas married and moved to her husband's plantation, Bremo Recess, in 1807, she wrote to a friend that she felt "absolutely as far removed from every thing like intercourse from my species, as if I was in a solitary tomb" (Kierner 1998, 177). The solitude weighted so heavily on some newly wedded brides that they made extended visits home until the cares of motherhood made travel difficult and mitigated their sense of isolation.

Work on a Plantation

The primary responsibility of the plantation mistress was ensuring that adequate provisions had been made for food, clothing, and household supplies for the entire plantation. How much of the work she personally engaged in was heavily influenced by the size of the slave population. Typical plantations ranged from ten to forty slaves, although some had several hundred. Slaves performed the majority of the manual labor, but the plantation mistress took part in the supervision of work and some skilled labor.

Providing the annual food supply for an entire plantation was an imposing task. Large plantations, such as Nomini Hall in Virginia, annually consumed 27,000 pounds of pork, 550 bushels of wheat, and 150 gallons of brandy. It was usually the responsibility of the housewife to keep track of the number of pigs, cows, and chickens. She made arrangements for the slaughter, salting, and smoking of meat. She needed to designate how much milk would be churned into butter or processed into cheese. Many plantation mistresses personally tended the chicken coop, as it was not a physically difficult chore but was important to the running of the plantation. Alcohol was an important commodity throughout the colonial period, and some of it was distilled on the plantation. Beer and cider were commonly brewed on typical plantations, and brandy was made, the type depending on the locally produced fruit.

Most of the supplies used on the plantation were produced on-site. Domestic manuals include instructions for the making of soap, candles, paint, medicines, and furniture wax. The grueling process of soap making was usually relegated to slaves, but the mistress of the house made the candles. The planter's wife was also usually responsible for most medical care on the plantation, for both her own family and the slaves.

Sewing consumed an immense amount of the plantation mistress's time. The clothing for slaves would be made from cloth produced on the plantation, and it is likely she would assist in sewing the garments. Plantation families tended to buy imported

A Plantation Mistress Managing on Her Own

It is believed that Affra Harleson fled her wealthy English home in 1670 to elope with John Coming, the first mate on a ship bound for America. The pair was married by the time the ship arrived in the rugged Carolina colony. The ambitious couple bought land and established themselves as planters. John Coming eventually became a ship's captain, leaving his wife to manage their flourishing plantation on her own during his extended absences.

There is some evidence that Affra had difficulty in her semisolitary role as plantation manager. She brought criminal charges against her indentured servants because they would not recognize her authority. She wrote to her sister in England of the plight of living alone and with no family to turn to for aid. When her husband died in 1694, he left Affra the entire estate. Although Affra's easiest course would have been to cash out her considerable estate and return to a comfortable life in England, she knew this was not what John Coming would have wished. Of her husband, she wrote, "In my heart, I think he was the best in the world." She honored her husband's desire to establish a colonial dynasty and succeeded in convincing her nephews to immigrate to America in order to inherit the estate after her death, which occurred in 1698.

Source: Anzilotti, Cara. "Autonomy of the Female Planter in Colonial South Carolina." *Journal of Southern History* 63 (1997): 239–268.

fabric for their own clothing needs. Wealthy southerners were famous for their fine dressing, and homespun would not suffice for such splendid displays. Women purchased bolts of imported silk, damask, calico, and lace. They typically sewed the garments themselves, although they might turn to a dressmaker to make clothing for special occasions. Embroidery was also considered a high art among genteel ladies. They embellished clothing, draperies, handkerchiefs, seat covers, and bedding with delicate stitches. Such dainty and artistic endeavors were perfectly in keeping with the ornamental role many families believed a refined gentlewoman should bring to a household.

There was clearly no single model for a plantation mistress. Whether by choice or from necessity, many plantation mistresses took an active role in agricultural labor. Some contemporary observers witnessed such women up to their elbows in brine while preparing freshly slaughtered beef. Letters written by plantation mistresses make mention of exhaustion following a day in the garden or dairy. Many women of the planter class had their days heavily scheduled with domestic activities, but others relied on housekeepers to shoulder the majority of household supervision. Housekeepers were sometimes slaves, but more often they were white women who were hired for their domestic managerial skills. If the plantation overseer was married, his wife was often expected to supervise the dairy or poultry barn. It is apparent that some southern women had enormous time for leisure, as efficient housekeepers supervised the majority of the work.

Hospitality

Southerners were famous for their hospitality, and it was expected that a plantation mistress would be a gracious and accomplished hostess. "Visiting" was a recreational event in the South. Living on isolated plantations, often with little activity to fill the day, southerners enjoyed traveling by horseback to nearby plantations where they stayed anywhere from a few hours to a few days. Travelers were likewise encouraged to stay at plantations, even if they had no prior acquaintance with the host. A Swiss traveler in 1702 wrote, "It is possible to travel through the whole country without money, except when ferrying across a river. . . . Even if one is willing to pay, they do not accept anything, but they are rather angry, asking whether one did not know the custom of the country. At first we were too modest to go into the houses to ask for food and lodging, which the people often recognized, and they admonished us not to be bashful, as this was the custom of rich and poor" (Morgan 1952, 83).

Hospitality also took the form of large-scale celebrations. During mild weather it was common to hold grand picnics. Initially each family brought their own food, but over time it became customary for the host to provide elaborate feasts for visitors.

Events such as baptisms, engagements, an interesting visitor, or the King's Birthday were all occasions for celebration. Distant family members might gather from throughout the colony, causing the event to spill over into several days of celebration. The plantation mistress would need advance planning for such an event. The appropriate number of pigs would need to be slaughtered, and bedding prepared. Southerners were enormously fond of sweets, and an endless round of baking would be required to prepare pies and cakes in advance of the arrival of guests.

Historian David Hackett Fischer reports, "Virginians dined; New Englanders merely ate" (Fischer 1989, 352). Southern dining was considered an art form, and expectations for formal dining were high. The main meal of the day was dinner, served between two and four in the afternoon, and was an elaborate affair with multiple courses. Both men and women were expected to dress formally for dinner. Silver, china, and glassware were important indicators of status, and the southern dining table and sideboard displayed an impressive array of such items. Well-to-do northern families were content with stoneware, but southerners often spent above their means to have complete sets of silver on the sideboard.

Social and Sexual Dimensions of Slavery on Plantations

The existence of chattel slavery forced white Christian southerners to form elaborate justifications for their peculiar institution. The planter class claimed slavery was a mutually beneficial arrangement. The slaves were exposed to the civilizing influences of Christianity and Western culture. In exchange, a stable labor force was established for the first time in the colonial South. Southern women averted their eyes when decidedly unchristian behavior was directed at their slaves. Sexual exploitation, brutal punishments, and substandard living conditions were all rampant in plantation society.

Growing up in an isolated environment, it was natural for the children of the white masters and black slaves to play together. Such play by very young children was considered harmless by most

southerners, but as the children became aware of their respective positions, white children sometimes cruelly exalted in their newfound power. One early advice manual by Virginia Cary warned mothers against allowing their children to play with slave children, for if they began indulging in pernicious cruelty at too early an age, they might become the worst sort of lawless individual as they come of age. Others believed that nurturing childhood friendships would have the opposite effect, and the white child would grow up to be more respectful of the slaves he or she would eventually inherit. All children were expected to shed such biracial friendships as they grew older. White parents worried their children would acquire crude manners or speech patterns from associating with slaves. The successful implementation of slavery depended on a level of fear and submission that was impossible to maintain in an atmosphere of mutual respect.

White girls often developed curious relationships with female slaves. A slave girl of similar age was often paired with a white girl to be a companion and servant. The slave might have even slept in the same room as her mistress. When the mistress married, the young slave woman usually accompanied the bride to her new home, and might have become a nanny to the children born to her mistress. The dynamics of this relationship varied wildly, depending on the character of the individuals involved. Some level of friendship might have existed, although the dramatically unequal positions doubtless underscored these lifelong unions.

The matter was complicated on some plantations when the slave children were clearly of mixed race. Sexual exploitation of slaves was rampant. Although such relationships were considered unseemly by polite society, so long as the man was discreet, the offense was ignored. The isolation of plantation life made discretion a simple matter. The mistress might have been fully aware of her husband or son's indiscretions upon the arrival of a light-skinned baby, but to acknowledge the fact would be humiliating on several levels. For a man to prefer spending time with a slave in lieu of his wife was an insult to the wife's sense of womanly pride. Women of conscience would have disapproved of the sexual exploitation committed by their loved ones against people for whom she had responsibility. Knowing that her children's enslaved playmates were blood relatives must have caused an unnerving moral dilemma.

How the wife of a philandering planter reacted to such a situation must be left to speculation. Most women opted for dignified silence, although others might have taken their anger out on the slave women. There are occasional references to white women brutally beating female slaves. In 1705, Catherine Hedman took a hoe to a neighboring plantation, where she beat a female slave so badly the woman nearly died. Lucy Parke Byrd, wife of the notorious philanderer William Byrd, was known to beat several female slaves. She was particularly vengeful toward a slave named Jenny, who she beat on several occasions. On one incident, William Byrd had to restrain his wife from branding Jenny with a hot iron. Although the cause of these women's anger is not specified, such vicious actions were most likely to have been prompted by jealous rages.

Sexual exploitation of slaves produced several victims. Although some planter-slave liaisons stretched across decades and might have involved mutual affection, the element of coercion inherent in such a relationship gave slave women little choice but to concede to their masters' demands. If she had a husband or children, they were no doubt aware of and traumatized by their inability to stop the abuse. If the enslaved woman found the sexual advances repugnant, she had few options. Her isolation on the plantation made it impossible to appeal to authorities. Appealing to the plantation mistress had its own set of dangers, as indicated by the examples above. For her part, the plantation mistress might have been deeply troubled by such liaisons. Few southern women ever initiated divorce proceedings based on their husband's infidelity, and aside from such action, there was little recourse she could take. Most chose to avert their eyes and pay no special attention to the light-skinned offspring of their slaves.

See also Elite Women; Slavery

Further Reading

Brown, Kathleen M. *Good Wives, Nasty Wenches, and Anxious Patriarchs: Gender, Race, and Power in Colonial Virginia.* Chapel Hill: University of North Carolina Press, 1996.

Clinton, Catherine. "Caught in the Web of the Big House: Women and Slavery." In *The Web of Southern Social Relations: Women, Family and Education,* ed. Walter J. Fraser et al. Athens: University of Georgia Press, 1985.

———. *The Plantation Mistress: Woman's World in the Old South.* New York: Pantheon Books, 1982.

Fischer, David Hackett. *Albion's Seed: Four British Folkways in America.* New York: Oxford University Press, 1989.

Kierner, Cynthia A. *Beyond the Household: Women's Place in the Early South, 1700–1835.* Ithaca, NY: Cornell University Press, 1998.

Morgan, Edmund. *Virginians at Home: Family Life in the Eighteenth Century.* Charlottesville, VA: Dominion Books, 1952.

Spruill, Julia Cherry. *Women's Life and Work in the Southern Colonies.* Chapel Hill: University of North Carolina Press, 1938.

Pocahontas

Mediator between early European settlers and local Native Americans (c. 1596–1617)

When the English settlers began their initial settlement efforts at Jamestown in May 1607, the Native American population of tidewater Virginia already had reason to fear and resent Europeans. Sporadic visits in the previous decades by Spanish and English explorers had resulted in the kidnapping and enslavement of Indian boys. An atmosphere of mistrust was already in place when 107 white Englishmen landed on the shores of Virginia.

A young Indian girl was one of few who had no such reservations about the settlers. Immediately curious and intrigued by the white men, Pocahontas paid frequent visits to the settlement, where she watched in awe as they built a church and a fort. Pocahontas was an advantageous friend, because her father was the most powerful Indian chief in coastal Virginia. She became a familiar visitor and showed a willingness to learn English. Captain John

Pocahontas leaning over Captain John Smith's head, to prevent Powhatan's warriors from clubbing him to death. (Library of Congress)

Smith gave the Indian girl, whom he estimated to be ten or eleven years of age, a few trinkets in exchange for teaching him some of the Indian language.

Most of the Native Americans were hostile to the Englishmen and refused to trade. Settlers on foraging expeditions were occasionally attacked by local Indians, further discouraging their efforts to hunt and fish. Conditions worsened throughout the summer of 1607. The settlers were suffering from malaria, fevers, and possibly salt poisoning from drinking tainted water. Their provisions were dwindling and could not be replenished owing to hostilities with the Indian population. As a frequent visitor to Jamestown, Pocahontas was no doubt aware of the difficulties facing the colonists. She succeeded in convincing her father to supply the settlers with some corn and also directed Captain Smith toward

the handful of sympathetic Indians who would be willing to trade.

It is unknown what prompted Pocahontas's friendly attitude toward the settlers. John Smith noted that she had a carefree disposition and natural curiosity, so perhaps it was this inquisitiveness into these strange settlers that piqued her interest. The settlers were friendly to her and gave her trinkets and jewelry. It is also possible that Pocahontas's father, the chief, Powhatan, subtly encouraged his daughter's role as emissary to ease the tense relations between the two groups.

The most famous incident involving Pocahontas was her "rescue" of Captain John Smith, after Smith had been captured during a scouting expedition in December 1607. Smith wandered too far into Indian territory and was taken captive following a violent confrontation. He was taken to Powhatan's village where he was welcomed and offered a feast. After the feast he was forced to lie on a large boulder, and Indians with clubs stood over him as though they were about to club him to death. Pocahontas intervened, stretching her body over Smith's and begging the execution to be stopped. Powhatan conceded, offered to adopt Smith as a son, and Smith was released.

It is likely that this event was a ritualized ceremony in which Smith was never in real danger, and Pocahontas's intervention could have been staged. Whatever the truth, Smith chose to record the event in a highly dramatic fashion and credited Pocahontas with saving his life. Over the next few years Pocahontas continued to act as a mediating force between the Indians and the European settlers. She brought food to the settlers and helped negotiate the release of Indian prisoners captured by the colonists. She might have even warned Smith of a planned attack by the Indians in 1609. Despite the undoubted mediating effects of Pocahontas's friendship with the colonists, by 1610 relations between the colonists and the Indians had worsened. Pocahontas may have married an Indian named Kocoum, and her visits to the colonists ceased.

Pocahontas disappeared from the historical record until 1613, when she was captured by Captain Samuel Argall. She had been lured onto Argall's ship after hearing that the English wished to meet with her. Upon realizing she was a captive, she was initially described as being extremely pensive and angry. Argall's plan was to use Pocahontas as a hostage to force her father to sue for peace. Powhatan refused all demands, and Pocahontas was taken to Jamestown, where she was treated as a royal prisoner. She was eventually given over to the care of Reverend Alexander Whitaker, who began instructing Pocahontas in Christianity. Pocahontas soon adapted well to her circumstances, embracing her religious teaching, further developing her English skills, and apparently glad to be living among the English. She was eventually baptized as "Lady Rebecca."

At some point during her captivity, Pocahontas became acquainted with the Englishman John Rolfe, and the two expressed a desire to marry. It is unknown what Rolfe and Pocahontas's feelings were for one another, although it is certain that both parties realized the political expediency of the marriage. Rolfe wrote that he desired the marriage for "the good of the plantation, the honor of our country, for the glory of God, and mine own salvation." The two of them were married on 5 April 1614, and tensions between the English and the Indians immediately eased. Chief Powhatan gifted them with a stretch of land on the shore of the James River. They raised tobacco and named their home "Varina," after a strain of tobacco Rolfe had imported from Spain. Pocahontas gave birth to a son named Thomas.

In the spring of 1616, the impoverished colonists were hoping to persuade their backers in England to loan them more financial support. A fund-raising expedition was sent to England, with twelve Native Americans on board, including Pocahontas, her infant son, and her husband. Pocahontas was greeted in England with great fanfare and was presented to the king. She renewed her friendship with Captain John Smith and visited the ancestral Rolfe estate, Heacham Hall. Their tour of England lasted seven months, but Pocahontas contracted a respiratory disease while in England. Shortly after embarking on the ship to return to Virginia, it became apparent she would not survive the voyage home. The ship returned to England, and Pocahontas died at Gravesend on 21 March 1617.

Although only twenty-two at the time of her death, Pocahontas has been credited with proving that peaceful Anglo-Indian relations were possible. Her son, Thomas, was raised in England, although he returned to Virginia as a young man of twenty, where he assumed ownership of the land that had been granted to his parents. By that time the relations between the Indians and the English settlers had deteriorated so badly that contact between the races was forbidden. Thomas petitioned the Virginia General Assembly for permission to visit with his Indian relatives, and this was granted. Although he lived the rest of his life among the English, Thomas appears to have shared his mother's ability to live peaceably among either race.

Further Reading

Barbour, Philip L. *Pocahontas and Her World.* Boston: Houghton Mifflin, 1970.

Mossiker, Frances. *Pocahontas: The Life and the Legend.* New York: Knopf, 1976.

Tilton, Robert S. *Pocahontas: The Evolution of an American Narrative.* New York: Cambridge University Press, 1994.

Political Wives

A typical woman in early America had little public role beyond the confines of her own household. Women who did attract attention, such as those who operated a business or were outspoken advocates of a cause, were often looked on with suspicion. Women married to important leaders were the exception. The wives of governors, military figures, or presidents had duties beyond those of an ordinary wife and mother. These responsibilities varied depending on geography and time period, but all involved a public display of hospitality. Depending on the nature of her husband's commitments, she might be left alone at her home for long stretches of time. There she provided a contact between her husband and local constituents.

Margaret Winthrop (c. 1591–1647) can be considered the model political wife of seventeenth-century America. In 1618 she married John Winthrop, who was then a justice of the peace in England. Over the next few years her husband rose through the ranks of Puritan leaders in England, leaving his wife alone in their manor house while he pursued business in London. Margaret administered her husband's estate during his lengthy absences, all the while raising her children and being stepmother to John's children from a previous marriage. Her numerous letters to John document her consistently supportive but submissive role, bowing to his judgment even when he began formulating a plan to immigrate to the wilds of America. Once in America, John became the first governor of the Massachusetts Bay Colony, and Margaret became the embodiment of a good New England housewife. Margaret assumed a prominent position among the town's women, consistently supporting her husband through the early trials of the colony.

There is some evidence in her private letters to John that she disapproved of his hard-line approach to the Anne Hutchinson controversy, but she remained silent of any misgivings in public. In these early years of Puritan New England, the role of a politician's wife was to be a caring mother and supportive wife, but not an active participant in the administration of the colony.

Over time, some political wives became more engaged in the public role of their position, as can be seen in the lives of Frances Berkeley (1634–c. 1695) and Hannah Penn (1671–1726). Frances Berkeley became the most powerful political wife during the colonial period. She had an aptitude for creating political alliances and, as the wife of Virginia's governor, played an active role in solidifying the support of Virginia's elite planters. When a rebellion threatened to overthrow her husband, Frances traveled to England where she succeeded in gathering an army of one thousand soldiers to quell the rebellion. Even after the death of her husband, Frances remained a unifying force among the Virginia gentry, which caused the new lieutenant governor to bitterly complain about her continuing influence. Hannah Penn had a softer approach to her role as the wife of the proprietor of Pennsylvania. Although she only lived in America between 1699 and 1701, she made an impression by serving as a gracious hostess to official visitors and other leading members of Pennsylvania society. After her return to England, her husband became disabled, and she acted as an intermediary between her husband and his associates in Philadelphia. Her work in these matters was smoothed by the healthy rapport she had established with these leaders in her role as a hostess.

After the American Revolution, a more formal culture of political influence was established in New York, Philadelphia, and Washington, D.C. Whereas women of early centuries were often left at home alone when their husbands traveled to colonial legislatures, the culture of the early national period was for wives to accompany their husbands to the capital. Congressman Thomas Hubbard described the few congressmen who did not bring their wives as dysfunctional, like a single side of a pair of scissors. A wife helped provide a crucial element of networking, with the "social call" becoming her chief responsibility. A call was a brief, ritualized visit that rarely lasted more than half an hour. Although the ostensible purpose of the call was a social visit, in actuality it provided a way for important families to establish connections, exchange information, and plan social gatherings. It was an essential tool for a new congressman to be brought into the loop through his wife's round of calls.

The wives of politicians often came to the capital without children and lived in small townhouses, where their domestic responsibilities were few. With little to keep them occupied, social calls consumed a large part of their time. It was not uncommon for a woman to have fifty to sixty calls in a single week. Calling was governed by an unwritten set of rules. A newcomer to the capital was expected to call on established families to introduce herself. If she met with approval, her call would be returned, and her family would be invited to other teas and dinners. A woman who did not pass muster did not have her calls returned, and establishing connections within society became much more difficult for her husband.

At the top of the Washington hierarchy was the president's wife. Much of the protocol that would define the role of first lady was established by Martha Washington. She saw her role was putting a welcoming face on her husband's administration by hosting evening dinners and receptions. Dolly Madison was famous for her ability to cultivate goodwill by making continual visits to congressmen's wives. She established friendships with them and gathered their recipes, which she served at White House functions to flatter the women. At the same time, she highlighted regionally diverse menus.

Upper-class women exercised influence over politics through the salon culture. These informal social gatherings occurred in the homes of the intellectual and political leaders in society. The salon was dominated by the hostess. She controlled access to her gatherings and could shape topics of conversation. Although European salons emphasized intellect and education, the salons of the early American republic were consumed with the politi-

cal culture of the new nation. Open participation of women in the political life of the country was severely constricted by the lack of the vote. Although an occasional voice was heard seeking extension of the vote to "the ladies," women appeared remarkably content to abstain from the formal political process.

As factions between competing political interests emerged, the salon offered a civilized space where ideas could be discussed. Famous political hostesses such as Anne Willing Bingham and Abigail Adams had time to converse with leading politicians and had a form of access closed even to most men in early America. Salon culture was a phenomenon limited to a tiny segment of wealthy, educated women. Most women lacked the access to important political figures or the knowledge of how to exercise such informal power, but the wives of politicians could generally gain entrée into salons.

See also Berkeley, Lady Frances Culpeper; Elite Women; Washington, Martha Dandridge Custis.

Further Reading

Allgor, Catherine. *Parlor Politics: In Which the Ladies of Washington Help Build a City and a Government.* Charlottesville: University Press of Virginia, 2000.

Branson, Susan. *These Fiery Frenchified Dames: Women and Political Culture in Early National Philadelphia.* Philadelphia: University of Pennsylvania Press, 2001.

Kierner, Cynthia A. *Beyond the Household: Women's Place in the Early South, 1700–1835.* Ithaca, NY: Cornell University Press, 1998.

Portraiture

Studying the images of women in early American portraits is a tempting, but frustrating, means of learning more about their lives. A number of factors make the study of portraits a highly unreliable source for generalizations regarding dress, attitudes, or even physical appearance. Limited to a tiny fraction of society, portraits reflected wealthy, upper-class individuals. The background and clothing reflected in the paintings were more likely to derive from the artist's imagination, than from the sitter's actual possessions. Furthermore, the highly stylized painting styles popular in the eighteenth century tended to render all subjects similar in facial expression, appearance, and posture. Despite the limitations of using portraits to learn more about early American women, attitudes about the feminine ideal can be gleaned from studying their portraits.

Portrait painting was almost nonexistent in seventeenth-century America. A few European painters came to the colonies for a year or two, but returned home after supplying portraits to the handful of families who could afford them. Most paintings displayed in early America were "public portraits" of powerful individuals, intended to honor the sitter by presenting their power in a grand setting. Kings, governors, military leaders, and an occasional religious leader were thus immortalized by painters in Europe, and the portraits were sent to be displayed in far-flung American colonies. Women were rarely portrayed, unless they were a queen or an allegorical figure. By the early eighteenth century, the custom of portrait painting was extending to wealthy individuals to be used to adorn their private homes, or to preserve their likeness for loved ones or future generations. By the 1740s, enough wealthy families had become established in America to begin supporting a class of itinerant portrait painters.

The itinerant nature of portrait painters' lifestyle influenced their final product. They often resided with a wealthy family throughout the harsh winter months, painting portraits of family members to earn their board. The rest of their time would be spent creating an inventory of stock canvases, painting the setting and body of a generic sitter, but leaving the head area empty. As the artists toured the country during warmer seasons, they could quickly fill in the head of a sitter onto a canvas that was close to completion. A few personal items, such as a favorite pet or book might be added as well, but the final product often did not reflect the sitter's actual clothing or home. Several women who posed for John Singleton Copley (1738–1815) wore the same splendid blue silk gown.

Although most eighteenth-century portraits were highly stylized, there is a difference in the

Young Girl with Strawberries by an American artist, ca. eighteenth century. Stiff portraits of children were a reflection of practical matters. Only a tiny fraction of eighteenth-century paintings contained children, and inexperienced artists portrayed them as miniature adults, with mature clothing, posture, and props. This portrait is a classic example. (Geoffrey Clements/CORBIS)

way male and female sitters were portrayed. Male sitters were more realistically portrayed, with flaws or physical quirks apparent. They were often posed with objects that reflected their profession or interests, such as a globe, ledger, or hunting rifle. Women were more idealized, with flaws rarely in evidence. They were posed with objects commonly associated with femininity, such as a basket of fruit to imply fertility, or pink carnations, associated with marriage. Other symbolic emblems common in women's portraits included a bird in a cage (chastity), roses (joy), squirrels (diligence), and trailing vines (love). In the absence of these stock props, their smooth, white hands were gracefully posed empty, implying leisure and wealth. Men were to be portrayed as accomplished individuals, whereas women were lovely accessories.

Both male and female portraits suffered from over-idealization in the eighteenth century. Most portraits reflect the ideals of their day, including overly large, almond-shaped eyes, full mouth, and perfectly smooth, white skin. Jonathan Richardson, in his *Essay on the Theory of Painting* (1715), expressed the typical portrait painter's position when he suggested that ladies should have their flaws overlooked while their beauty was to be embellished. Men were to be made to look masculine and brave, even in the absence of such features. The gestures, poses, and props used in portraits were all geared to convey gentility and elegance. Originality was not valued in portraiture, and most paintings reflect traditional, safe poses. This resulted in a uniformity of poses and expressions, rendering the portraits bland to modern-day observers.

Perhaps most unusual to modern-day observers is the manner in which children were portrayed. Children appeared as miniature adults, with mature clothing, posture, and props. The rigid poses show no signs of playfulness or spontaneity. With solemn expressions and wooden postures, children appeared to be merely adults in the making. These portraits have occasionally been misinterpreted to imply that children were in fact treated as miniature adults in early America, but such was not the case. Stiff portraits of children were a reflection of practical matters. Only a tiny fraction of eighteenth-century paintings contained children, and most artists had little experience capturing the unique features of childhood. Posing for portraits was time-consuming and tedious even for adult sitters, and it was difficult to have children maintain a naturalistic pose. Given the difficulty of painting a child crawling on the floor or curled in a mother's arms, the artists relied on safe, stock poses that attempted to give a measure of dignity to children. By 1770 paintings of children began to soften. Toys began to be included, and once again there was a gender distinction in the props. Boys were portrayed with pony whips, drums, balls, and hoops. Girls were almost always shown holding a doll or a flower.

The cost of an oil painting put it outside the reach of most Americans, but portraits became available to the masses with the popularity of silhouette portraits. In the 1780s a number of devices for the mechanical tracing of profiles were invented. The popularity of profile machines was fueled by the new trend in physiognomy, the belief that physical characteristics could reveal character traits. Such profiles could be created in a few minutes and were easily affordable by most Americans.

The late eighteenth century witnessed growing realism in American portrait painting. The stiff formality of portraits that tried to emulate aristocratic portraiture gave way to frank, egalitarian portraits. Postures were relaxed, and faces were no longer molded into the formulaic expression so common in earlier portraits. The women who sat for Charles Willson Peale and John Singleton Copley have character and expressions that were absent from most earlier portraits. Artistic conventions by the end of the colonial period no longer conveyed idealized, aristocratic pretensions, but celebrated the individuality of the sitter.

Further Reading

Calvert, Karin. "Children in American Family Portraiture, 1670–1810." *William and Mary Quarterly* 39 (1982): 87–113.

Craven, Wayne. *Colonial American Portraiture: The Economic, Religious, Social, Cultural, Philosophical, Scientific, and Aesthetic Foundations.* Cambridge: Cambridge University Press, 1986.

Fleischer, Roland E. "Emblems and Colonial American Painting." *American Art Journal* 20 (1988): 2–35.

Prosser, Deborah I. "The Rising Prospect or the Lovely Face: Conventions of Gender in Colonial American Portraiture." *Dublin Seminar for New England Folklife* 19 (1994): 181–200.

Saunders, Richard H., and Ellen G. Miles. *American Colonial Portraits, 1700–1776.* Washington, DC: Smithsonian Institution Press, 1987.

Poverty

Colonists in the New World did not suffer from the grinding level of poverty that plagued Europe, where overpopulation led to high unemployment. Densely crowded European cities suffered from lack of adequate food, shelter, and employment. The economic blight was exacerbated by the gradual enclosure of agricultural land, driving increasing numbers of rural poor to the cities. By contrast, America had a shortage of labor, an abundance of resources, and seemingly limitless opportunity for the young and able-bodied.

Despite the opportunities, the people of early America often lived on the edge of subsistence. A poor harvest, a debilitating epidemic, a broken limb, or the death of a breadwinner could push a woman into poverty. Mortality rates were high, and a woman with two small children and a hardworking husband could quickly find herself a widow with an outbreak of malaria or an Indian attack. If she were young she might remarry, but if she did not succeed in finding a husband, her situation could be difficult. Without labor to operate the farm, she had no means of income. Her children would likely be bound out to serve as apprentices until they were eighteen. She would receive a small supplement of food and firewood from the town, but would be expected to begin supporting herself through domestic work or remarriage.

The American colonies relied heavily on the Elizabethan Poor Law of 1601 to guide their policies regarding aid and care of the destitute. This law assumed that a community had a responsibility toward the poor until they could become self-sufficient. Poor relief was organized at the local level—individual towns had sole responsibility for the welfare of their impoverished residents. Family members were held accountable for the well-being of their kin, and they were the first place to which town authorities turned for support. If a cousin, parent, or adult child had the financial wherewithal to take the poor person into their homes, the town council insisted on it. Only the poor who had no family would become the charge of the town. In the earliest decades of settlement this usually meant the poor person would be lodged with a family, with the town supplying a small fee to the host family. The children of poor women were likely to be apprenticed to a local employer. If the poor person

had a home, the town might supply food, firewood, or other provisions until the need passed.

Colonial town councils drew a distinction between the deserving poor and the undeserving poor. Deserving poor were people who had fallen on hard times through no fault or idleness of their own. Among the deserving poor were widows, single mothers, the elderly, or women who were married to men either incarcerated or at sea. Such women were likely to be treated kindly until their situation could be remedied. The undeserving poor received little sympathy. They included the mothers of illegitimate children and able-bodied people who refused to work. Early America had a severe labor shortage, and a poor person who would not work was likely to be sold to the lowest bidder in a "pauper auction." The pauper would then be required to provide labor to the individual in exchange for basic maintenance.

There was a noticeable shift in the attitude toward the destitute in the eighteenth century. Immigration increased, labor shortages eased, and towns became more crowded. Town officials were less likely to be acquainted with a person who appealed for assistance. There was greater suspicion that their poverty was a result of their moral failings, rather than circumstance. Poor laws took on a punitive characteristic. Whereas once a person would receive assistance in the form of goods delivered to their home, now they were more likely to be bound out to service, or incarcerated in a workhouse. In an effort to save money, town councils experimented with workhouses where the poor would be required to provide labor in exchange for shelter and provisions. Conditions in poorhouses were deliberately uncomfortable in an effort to discourage the undeserving poor from reliance on state aid. Women were always separated from their children, who were either housed in a separate section or bound out be apprentices.

Towns were only required to provide poor relief to their own residents. This encompassed people who owned property within the town, had been born there, or who were married to a resident. A woman who moved to a town to become a servant could live there several years, but if a downturn in the economy or debilitating illness struck her, she was not entitled to poor relief in that community. She needed to return to the town of her birth to receive such aid. Poor people could be driven out of town if it appeared they were on the verge of requiring economic assistance.

The refusal of towns to provide assistance to non-residents was especially important for women about to give birth. An unmarried pregnant woman was likely to become a public charge. Town councils could "warn her out" by requiring her to leave town with two weeks' notice. A divorced or abandoned woman lost residence in the town once she was no longer living with her husband. If she was not a resident of the town in her own right, the poor law required her to seek assistance from her town of residence when she married. One elderly widow was driven from town after living there thirty years with her husband. When it became apparent she was about to become a public charge after his death, she was required to return to the town where she had had residence as a single woman. Other reasons women were warned out of town included conflict with neighbors, ill health, and lost employment.

Women who had been warned out of town were free to move from town to town at will. Few towns tolerated such itinerant poor people, and if their presence were discovered they were vulnerable to another driving out. Although most transient poor women were widows, single mothers, or in ill health, some fell into the "undeserving poor" category. Disorderly women, alcoholics, prostitutes, and mentally unstable persons were among the people who hardened the attitudes of town officials toward poor people. Towns wanted to segregate such people from society. They were unwelcome in the homes of people who were willing to house the deserving poor for a small fee, and institutionalization became the norm by the 1820s. These bleak almshouses were intended to provide moral reform, a cost-effective means of supporting the destitute, and the protection of society from undesirable elements.

Some towns required their paupers to wear badges of the letter *P* on their left shoulder, plus the name of the town. New York, Pennsylvania, and Rhode Island all required individuals accepting poor relief to wear such badges. Other colonies deprived paupers of their civil rights and could sell their labor at auction or bind their children out to service. Begging was illegal in most colonies, and women who were caught soliciting alms could be imprisoned. Women made up the majority of the truly destitute poor, as they were rarely able to find employment that provided wages adequate to support themselves and dependent children.

Despite the rise of poverty in the eighteenth century, most poor women were not forced into almshouses for subsistence. Able-bodied women could almost always find employment. They took in washing, stitched shirts for piece rates, or could work as a servant. Such employment was not steady, and the woman needed to be prepared to seek out another position as soon as the work ran out. Many widows were able to remarry. If a poor woman was married to a man capable of work, their lives might be sparse, but she was almost always able to provide care for her children and keep a roof over their heads.

See also Benevolent Societies

Further Reading

Cray, Robert E. *Paupers and Poor Relief in New York City and Its Rural Environs, 1700–1830.* Philadelphia, PA: Temple University Press, 1988.

Herndon, Ruth Wallis. *Unwelcome Americans: Living on the Margin in Early New England.* Philadelphia: University of Pennsylvania Press, 2001.

———. "Women of No Particular Home: Town Leaders and Female Transients in Rhode Island, 1750–1800." In *Women and Freedom in Early America,* ed. Larry D. Eldridge. New York: New York University Press, 1997.

Jernegan, Marcus Wilson. *Laboring and Dependent Classes in Colonial America, 1607–1783.* New York: Frederick Ungar Publishing, 1960.

Rockman, Seth. "Women's Labor, Gender Ideology, and Working-Class Households in Early Republic Baltimore." *Pennsylvania History* 66, supplement (1999): 174–200.

Trattner, Walter I. *From Poor Law to Welfare State: A History of Social Welfare in America.* New York: The Free Press, 1974.

Printers and the Printing Trade

The first printing presses in the American colonies were housed in small shops and were typically operated as a family business. Lacking skilled labor and a large supply of type, most of the initial presses could only produce short works of a religious or governmental nature. The first American press was established by Elizabeth Glover in 1639. The press had belonged to her husband, the Reverend Joseph Glover, who had died during the Atlantic crossing.

Elizabeth Glover was to be the first of many women who would inherit a printing press. High mortality rates often left control of printing presses to widows and daughters. These women frequently sold their interest in the presses, but many chose to become professional printers. Printing, publishing, and writing were among the few occupations in which a woman was able to apply and derive a profit from her education. The primary responsibility of any colonial wife was to see to the welfare of her family. As such, involvement in her husband's business was common among colonial women. In the event of an untimely death, the wife might have had no choice but to step in and assume responsibility for the family trade. Often, the tools of the family trade were the only real inheritance a widow received. Thus, many colonial women became printers, including Dinah Nuthead, Elizabeth Timothy, Cornelia Bradford, Anna Catherine Zenger, Margaret Draper, Clementina Rind, and Anne Catherine Greene. Such women typically assumed responsibility for the business until a son became old enough to operate the printing press.

Literacy rates among colonial women varied widely, but could be as high as 50 percent. It was not unusual for educated wives to assist their husbands in the daily operation of their printing presses. The work consisted of loading a line of metal type into compositing sticks, then screwing the composed type into frames that were inked, covered with a sheet of paper, and pressed between a vise to produce a sheet of printed text. Other tasks involved proofreading, editing, and bookbinding.

One of the most prominent colonial printers was Ann Franklin, the wife of Benjamin Franklin's older brother, James. Founder of the *New England Courant,* James Franklin used his paper to criticize both the church and government. He was frequently in legal trouble and imprisoned, during which time his wife, Ann, is believed to have assumed responsibility for his press. When James died a premature death in 1735, Ann was ready to emerge as a printer in her own right. She became the official printer for the colony of Rhode Island, meaning that she was granted the commission for printing all official government documents from the colony. She brought her two daughters into the business with her, until she handed control of the press to her son in 1762. Benjamin Franklin also played a pivotal role in the sponsorship of Elizabeth Timothy. Franklin had a frustrating relationship with Timothy's husband, Lewis, with whom he shared ownership of a printing press in South Carolina. Upon Lewis's death, ownership and operation passed to Elizabeth, who immediately corrected her husband's errant accountancy and frustrating business practices. Elizabeth Timothy continued to operate the press and served as the first female editor of a newspaper, the *South Carolina Gazette.* In due time she was able to purchase the entire share of the printing business from Franklin and establish herself as a noteworthy businesswoman. Franklin wrote about her in his autobiography with glowing terms, concluding his passage by noting: "I mention this affair chiefly for the sake of recommending that branch of education for our young females, as likely to be of more use to them than music or dancing, by preserving them from the losses by imposition of crafty men, and enabling them to continue, perhaps, a profitable mercantile house" (Hudak 1978, 2).

Mary Katherine Goddard came into the printing business by working with her brother, who established presses and newspapers in Providence, Philadelphia, and Baltimore. While her brother busied himself with his far-flung operations, Mary Katherine took over primary responsibility of the Baltimore printing press and its newspaper, the *Maryland Journal.* She also printed the first official copy of the Declaration of Independence in 1777.

Another notable printer was Catherine Zenger, whose husband, Peter, was the center of the landmark 1735 trial, which established the principle of freedom of the press in British North America. During her husband's ten-month imprisonment, Catherine Zenger continued to keep his press in operation. Following his death in 1746 she assumed responsibility for the press until her stepson, John Zenger, was old enough to take charge.

Although the overwhelming majority of printers in early America were male, the regularity with which women were able to inherit and operate printing presses demonstrates the active role these women played in the daily operation of their husbands' trade. For every widow who inherited and operated a printing press, we must assume that there were at least as many wives anonymously working beside their husbands, but who never assumed direct control of the press. Working in the printing trade would have permitted these women active contact with a wide spectrum of society. Printers contracted with writers to produce sermons, almanacs, and literature. Printers would have done business with government officials, who regularly needed laws, ballots, and legal forms printed. The production of a newspaper naturally necessitated contact with politicians, leaders of society, and other news makers. People from all walks of society purchased items through the shops that printers typically operated to sell their materials.

Because of the nature of printing, which required literacy and resulted in a printed end product, we know a great deal about the material produced by women printers. Women printers helped mass-produce sermons, popular novels, political broadsides, educational materials, and government forms. Printing was one of the few forms of employment in which a colonial woman could gain social prominence and make use of her intellectual skills.

See also Bradford, Cornelia Smith; Franklin, Ann Smith; Timothy, Elizabeth.

Further Reading

Barlow, Marjorie Dana. *Notes on Woman Printers in Colonial America and the United States, 1639–1975.* New York: The Hroswitha Club, 1976.

Demeter, Richard L. *Primer, Presses and Composing Sticks: Women Printers of the Colonial Period.* Hicksville, NY: Exposition Press, 1979.

Hudak, Leona M. *Early American Women Printers and Publishers, 1639–1820.* Metuchen, NJ: Scarecrow Press, 1978.

Oldham, Ellen M. "Early Women Printers of America." *Boston Public Library Quarterly* 10 (January 1958): 6–26; (April 1958): 78–91; (July 1958): 141–153.

Oswald, John Clyde. *Printing in the Americas.* Port Washington, NY: Kennikat Press, 1937.

Prostitution

"The world's oldest profession" existed in early America, but was not considered a serious social problem until the mid-nineteenth century when increasing urbanization made the existence of red-light districts common in most large mercantile centers. Prior to this, women who traded sex for money usually did so as discretely as possible, and rarely congregated in groups large enough to attract attention.

The character of prostitution in early America was usually casual and temporary. Women seldom earned their living solely through prostitution. Social prohibitions and the lack of enough customers made it impossible to support a class of prostitutes in small-town environments, but this did not stop women from dabbling in prostitution on an occasional and casual level. Some women resorted to trading sex when their husbands were away from home for extended periods, such as at sea or in the military. A single woman who earned a meager living through piecework or domestic service might supplement her low wages by casual prostitution. They did not loiter on street corners in search of business, but usually had a few regular customers. The shame of exchanging sex for money was mitigated by asking for a pair of new shoes, a bag of cornmeal, or a bolt of cloth instead of coins.

Women who operated taverns and boardinghouses were sometimes accused of running a *disorderly house,* a term synonymous with *brothel* in the eighteenth century. Taverns usually had rooms that could be rented for short-term accommodations. If a single woman or a widow operated the tavern, she could easily become the subject of unjust accusations by rival tavern owners who wished to damage her reputation or cause her to lose her license. A number of serving girls who worked in taverns could have easily dallied in prostitution, with or without the tavern keeper's consent. Not all the charges of running a disorderly house were unfounded. Hannah Dilley let rooms in her boardinghouse to women she knew were prostitutes and even funneled customers to them, until Boston authorities put a stop to her operations in 1753. "Madam Juniper," a free woman of color in Newport, Rhode Island, was more discreet, and her brothel operated without interference.

We know little about the women who chose to engage in casual prostitution, because the covert nature of this activity was unlikely to be documented through letters or diaries. If no one complained to authorities, little evidence survived. On occasion, a woman was prosecuted for "fornication" if she had the misfortune to become pregnant with no husband to claim paternity. When it became apparent that a tavern was actually little more than a brothel, citizens did their best to close it down. The license to operate a tavern could be revoked. If this was unsuccessful, violence sometimes occurred. "Whorehouse riots" occurred in Boston in 1734 and 1737 and in New York City in 1753, 1793, and 1799. The buildings were ransacked and sometimes torched. The women working in them were fined, whipped, or driven from the city.

As larger towns turned into small cities, the ability of women to earn their living solely through prostitution increased. New York, Boston, Philadelphia, and Charleston were the first cities where the necessary conditions to support a class of full-time prostitutes were established. The city needed to be large enough for people to live in an environment of anonymity, where people were unlikely to know or care how women in a certain part of town earned their living. There needed to be a large population of unattached men to supply these women with enough business to support themselves. Seaports with their regular influx of sailors were the first areas where red-light districts took hold. Prostitutes were called a number of colorful terms, including *molls, whores, doxies, bawds,* and *nightwalkers.*

For the women, prostitution was a dangerous, but lucrative, profession. A prostitute could earn more in a day than a woman sewing shirts for piecework could earn in a week. Women who were full-time prostitutes lived a very different lifestyle than a woman who merely supplemented her income with occasional prostitution. The full-time prostitute needed to be walking the streets, establishing contact with as many men as possible, most of whom were total strangers. Whereas a casual prostitute was likely to have a family and practice her trade secretly, a full-time prostitute probably had no family support. The nature of her business made it impossible for her to hide how she earned a living. She most likely lived in a rented room. If she fell ill or needed help, there were few people to whom she could turn for aid. On a daily basis she exposed herself to the possibility of venereal disease, pregnancy, and strange men who were often intoxicated with liquor.

Following the American Revolution, fornication and other laws regulating moral behavior were removed from the statutes. Prostitution was not a criminal act in most states, and prostitutes living in red-light districts felt no need to conceal their activities. We know little of early nineteenth-century women's motivations for becoming prostitutes, but a study conducted in the 1850s is the closest we can come to a formal analysis about the cause of prostitution. In 1855, physician William Sanger was commissioned by the city of New York to interview more than 2,000 prostitutes in search of an explanation. To his surprise, severe poverty could only be credited as the primary motivator in about one-quarter of the cases. The women motivated by hardship had been abandoned by husbands, widowed, or orphaned at a young age, and some had children to support. Ultimately, Sanger found that most prostitutes chose their life because of a variety of reasons not directly related to poverty. Among the common reasons cited were the following: It was an easier life than working in a shop or factory; they were alcoholics, and the life allowed them easy access to liquor; they were runaways who preferred life on the streets to life at home; and they were influenced by other prostitutes who persuaded them it was an easy way of life.

Women who became prostitutes in early America were living on the fringe of society. The traditional housewife in early America was burdened with heavy rounds of repetitive household chores, but she enjoyed security and an extended network of family and community friends. Prostitutes had fewer responsibilities, but were exposed to more danger and lacked the social support available to most other women. When she was too old to earn a living as a prostitute, her life would have been especially bleak. With no skills, no family, and not the sort of "deserving poor" who could rely on charity, the ultimate fate of most prostitutes was unenviable.

Further Reading

D'Emilio, John, and Estelle B. Freedman. *Intimate Matters: A History of Sexuality in America.* Chicago: University of Chicago Press, 1988.

Gill, Harold. "Disorderly Houses, the Blue Bell, and Certain Hints of Harlotry." *Colonial Williamsburg* (Autumn 2001): 27–31.

Stansell, Christine. *City of Women: Sex and Class in New York, 1789–1860.* Urbana: University of Illinois, 1982.

Thompson, Roger. "Sexual Morals and Behavior." In *Encyclopedia of North American Colonies*, ed. Jacob Ernest Cooke. New York: Charles Scribner's Sons, 1993.

Puritan Women

The social and religious movement known as Puritanism developed in England, late in the reign of Queen Elizabeth I. The Protestant queen had done her best to meld disparate forces of Catholicism and Protestantism into a unified religious policy. Her compromises resulted in an uneasy truce between these warring factions. Some of the more radical elements within Protestantism were opposed to any form of compromise with "corrupt" Catholics. They believed the moral laxity, privileges, and luxury of the Catholic hierarchy had been grafted onto the Protestant clergy. Conservative reformers mourned the loss of the simplicity and honest virtue reflected in the New Testament, and longed for a purification of the church. These early Puritans wanted to reform the Church of England, not break from it. After several generations of strife and repression, some of the early Puritans decided to leave England and seek a new home in the wilderness of America. Hoping to carve out a perfect society in the pure and unspoiled New World, they set out in family groups, determined to create a model Christian society in the form of a City on a Hill for all the world to see.

First-Generation Puritans

Between 1630 and 1640 a large number of English Puritans set out for the uncertain shores of the New World. The first generation of Puritan women to immigrate to America endured grueling emotional strains and physical labor. They toiled in the fields, cut firewood, skinned animals, and ground grain. They lived in huts for years while more substantial structures were slowly erected. The contributions made by women were essential to the survival of these early communities, and they earned a corresponding respect, if not equality, within Puritan society.

As a group, Puritans were wealthier and better educated than other Anglo-American settlers in the New World. Most men had either a skill or profession that was capable of supporting a family. The majority of settlers constructed their homes in small villages clustered around a few main streets. Almost all the early Puritan immigrants had come from urban areas in England, and village life suited them. Puritan towns all shared a few basic features. At the heart of the village was a town commons and meeting house, a school, a few streets, and some enclosed fields. Many families owned plots of farmland outside the walls of the village. The Massachusetts Bay Colony passed a law in 1635 that forbade the construction of homesteads more than one-half mile from the meeting house. This was a reflection of the Puritan belief in the value of community. Members of the village relied on one another for defense, skilled labor, and moral support. A few brave yeomen established farmsteads as remotely as possible in the countryside, but these loners were looked upon with suspicion.

The women living in Puritan villages relied on one another for companionship as well as basic housekeeping needs. Contrary to the popular myth of American self-sufficiency, almost no settler was capable of producing all their household needs. Most Puritan goodwives specialized in a skill, whether it was bread baking, weaving, candle dipping, cheese making, or midwifery. They bartered their wares with one another, which provided these town dwellers with a greater variety of goods than was available to settlers who lived in remote areas.

Sundays were set aside as a day of complete rest. No manual labor was to be performed on the Sabbath. All members of the community were required to attend church services, which typically began at nine o'clock. After breaking for lunch, services would resume for two more hours in the afternoon. The Puritan style of preaching was vigorous, passionate, and highly dramatic. Sermons dwelled on the nature of sin, the fires of damnation, and the joys of salvation.

Although contemporary observers might object to their only day of rest being spent on a hard church pew, from the standpoint of a seventeenth-century Puritan woman, this was unlikely to be the case. The Sabbath was the only day free of manual labor and endless household chores. In a world without television, radios, or widely available reading material, the opportunity to listen to a charismatic preacher perform for a few hours might have been a welcome relief from the monotony of daily toil.

Later Generations

The first generation of settlers shared an intense commitment to a godly kingdom in the New World, for which they endured hardship and gambled their lives. They were willing to undertake the sacrifices necessary in order to conform to the standards of behavior expected of Puritans. Subsequent generations did not automatically inherit this level of commitment. Many of the tensions so famously recounted by authors such as Nathaniel Hawthorne reflect the anxiety of traditional Puritans as they witnessed the worldly concerns of the younger generation overriding the spiritual ideals of the early settlers.

Puritan woman, standing in snow, holding holly in her apron. A typical Puritan woman would have worn well-fitting clothes, in dark shades of red, green, and brown. Her head was normally covered with a cap or bonnet. Brightly colored ribbons were commonly used on sleeves, although women who used too many ribbons were reproved. (Library of Congress)

Those who lived in the major commercial centers, such as Salem and Boston, were more likely to drift away from strict Puritan ideals. Ambitious merchants eager to capitalize on the opportunities of these thriving communities established themselves in such towns, even if they did not share Puritan beliefs. Church membership declined, and prosecutions for moral failings such as fornication and slander increased. The smaller and more isolated the town, the more likely it was to retain traditional Puritan values.

In the 1670s and 1680s, a series of fires, droughts, epidemics, and Indian attacks were viewed as God's punishment for the moral decline of Puritan communities. The text of sermons became inundated with fire and brimstone in an attempt to shock the community back into conformity.

Life in Puritan Villages

Deeply ingrained in Puritanism was a desire to return to the wholesome simplicity of the primitive Christian Church. Their meetinghouses were plain and unadorned, as were their clothing and hairstyles. Complex theological explanations were pushed aside in favor of plain speaking and literal interpretation of the Bible. Sin was to be harshly and publicly punished. If a congregant sinned, it was a sin against the family and the community. As such, his or her penance must be similarly public. Records from a 1654 Essex County church reveal that members were required to make public apologies, such as when Mistress Elizabeth Julett was ordered to appear before her congregation with a note reading "A slanderer of Mr. Zerobabel Endecott" pinned on her person. Others were ordered to appear wearing sackcloth and ashes and appeal on bended knees before the community for forgiveness.

Although the present-day impression of Puritan women generally portrays them dressed in stark black dresses with plain white collars, this is far from accurate. Puritans enjoyed fine clothing and considered it a reward for hard work. Women who could afford to do so indulged themselves with lace, expensive silks, and embroidery. Their reputation for dour clothing stems from the contrast they presented with the more lavish cavalier style of England, where women wore tight corsets that exaggerated their bustlines. Both cavalier men and women wore cosmetics and high heels and curled their long hair. Such adornment was abhorrent to Puritans, who considered this a mark of effeminacy and corruption. Puritan clothing appeared plain in comparison with the sumptuous and provocative clothing of the cavaliers, but few Puritan women dressed in the drab manner in which they are commonly portrayed today. A typical Puritan woman would have worn well-fitting clothes, in dark shades of red, green, and brown. Her head was normally covered with a cap or bonnet. Brightly colored ribbons were commonly used on sleeves, although women who used too many ribbons were reproved. Many of their garments would have been nicely embroidered, as such was a common pastime during the long months of winter.

At the heart of a Puritan woman's world was the family. It was through the family that God formed a covenant with his children. The family represented a complex web of relationships and mutual obligations for women: daughter to parent, mother to child, wife to husband. Women were viewed as naturally subordinate to men. The ideal woman was modest, obedient, and gentle. Through her efforts children would be raised to love and respect God. A husband would be provided with the assistance he needed to create a comfortable home. Despite their subordinate role in Puritan society, women outnumbered men as members of the church. They were generally regarded as sources of virtue and moral stature within the home. It was through the pious work of the women in the home that men's coarser natures were tamed.

John Winthrop, the leading political figure in early Massachusetts, characterized the ideal Puritan wife as follows: "A true wife accounts her subjection her honor and freedom and would not think her condition safe and free but in her subjection to her husband's authority. Such is the liberty of the church under the authority of Christ, her king and husband; his yoke is so easy and sweet to her as a bride's ornaments" (Saxton 1994, 29).

Despite the high level of submission expected of Puritan wives, marriages were not regarded as a sacred state. The Anglican Church believed that no marriage could ever be "put asunder," but Puritans believed that a healthy marriage was so important to the spiritual well-being of the family that divorce was acceptable in cases of extreme incompatibility. Marriage was not a religious rite but a civil contract and could thus be dissolved when necessary. The laws in Puritan societies gave women other legal protections not common elsewhere. Wives could not be physically beaten or verbally abused by their husbands. Husbands were forbidden to command their wives to do anything contrary to the law of God. Courts also granted married women the right to own property in their own name and enter into contracts. Puritan girls were given a better education than other girls in the American colonies, and the ability to read was highly valued among the Puritans. Possibly because of their educations, Puritan wives were entrusted with more financial and legal responsibilities than was common elsewhere in the colonies.

Puritans had a great respect for order and conformity. Their entire purpose in abandoning England had been so they might establish their own godly kingdom on earth. Although they were fleeing religious persecution, this never translated into a commitment to freedom of religion. They merely wanted the ability to practice, and enforce, religion according to their own design. Any who chose to emigrate or join a Puritan community was expected to respect the Puritan way of life.

The word *Puritan* has acquired a negative connotation in contemporary society, and some of this antagonism is warranted. The Puritans could be intolerant, sexist, and backward. Women like Anne Hutchinson and Mary Dyer were drummed out of the community when their views became unpopular. And yet the Puritan movement was a force of immense energy, charismatic enough to convert huge segments of the population wherever it spread. The Puritans' appeal was based on their compassion for the poor, desire to serve God, and intolerance of corruption. Although they viewed women as subordinate to men, the Puritans carved out a place of respect for women in the family unit and in church membership.

See also Pilgrim Women

Further Reading

Dunn, Mary Maples. "Saints and Sisters: Congregational and Quaker Women in the Early Colonial Period." *American Quarterly* 30 (1978): 582–601.

Fischer, David Hackett. *Albion's Seed: Four British Folkways in America.* New York: Oxford University Press, 1989.

Koehler, Lyle. *The Search for Power: The "Weaker Sex" in Seventeenth Century New England.* Urbana: University of Illinois Press, 1980.

Saxton, Martha. "Bearing the Burden: Puritan Wives." *History Today* 44, no. 10 (1994): 28–33.

Ulrich, Laurel Thatcher. *Good Wives: Images and Reality in the Lives of Women in Northern New England, 1650–1750.* New York: Vintage Books, 1991.

Q

Quaker Women

The Society of Friends was founded by George Fox in the 1650s, and the early members were religious radicals who had become disillusioned with the course of the Puritan Revolution in England. Among their tenets was the commitment to the equality of all people, without regard to class or gender. This allowed women to develop and flourish to an extent not seen in other Protestant denominations. Members of the Society of Friends were typically called Quakers, based on the passionate preaching that caused trembling and exuberant gestures by their ministers.

Like other radical religious groups of the seventeenth century, Quakers believed in spiritual rebirth, direct inspiration from God, and the ability of laypeople to assume leadership roles. One of the major differences was in their view of women. Puritans based their perception of women on the Old Testament interpretation of sex roles, which placed women in a subordinate position to men. As women were prone to moral weakness, Puritans believed they were in need of spiritual guidance from male leaders. Quakers rejected this philosophy, claiming the process of rebirth meant Christ could dwell within any person. There was nothing inherent in women that hindered their ability to experience rebirth. Any person, regardless of race, class, or gender, in whom the divine light dwelled, was to be accorded full respect and dignity.

Although the family was a vitally important unit in Quaker life, women who chose to remain single were fully accepted within the community. Although most Protestant denominations saw marriage and motherhood as the only appropriate calling for women, Quakers saw the ministry and social service as an equally acceptable choice. Compared with other colonial women, a much higher percentage of Quaker women never married, and those who did marry typically made this commitment at an older age.

The lay ministry, evangelization, and charitable work were all options open to Quaker women. The Quaker meetinghouse was arranged so that men sat on one side, and women on the other. Meetings were for quiet reflection, with members speaking only when the spirit moved them. In addition to the sessions for worship, Quakers had regular but separate business meetings for men and women. The women's meetings were formed to assist in management, church governance, and control of membership. They made arrangements to look after the poor, counsel younger members about marriage and motherhood, enforce discipline, and oversee the process of marriages. The women's group investigated couples wishing to marry, to ensure that there were no prior commitments, that the applicants were in good standing, and that the couple was compatible. More than 50 percent of the women's meetings were devoted to the business of marriage.

In theory the men's and women's meetings were to have equal weight, although it is apparent from early records that the women's group often deferred to the men's group for final decision making.

Society of Friends Meetinghouse, Berkshire County, MA. Quaker worship centered around reflective meditation and had little institutional hierarchy. Their meetinghouses reflected simplicity of design, lack of a focal point, and emphasis on symmetry. (Library of Congress)

Some historians have suggested that the women's meetings were created to give women the illusion of power, but they were blocked from real decision-making authority. Whatever the truth, the generations of women who took an active role in these meetings gained administrative and leadership experience far beyond that available to women in other Protestant denominations.

Quaker women founded and operated many of the first charitable institutions in the colonies. Most of these charities were related to poor relief, but others were schools for the illiterate. In 1795

Quaker women created the Society for the Free Instruction of African Females, which taught evening reading classes to adult African American women. Other societies were formed for the instruction in a trade such as sewing or weaving. These charitable institutions required substantial financial support, and their administrators became able fundraisers. They solicited politicians and merchants for donations, organized charity subscriptions, and appealed to wealthy donors for legacies in wills. As they accumulated funds they increased their earning power by lending excess funds at a rate of interest.

Quaker Missionaries

Quaker women, sometimes called "Friends," have a long tradition of participating in missionary activities. The following newspaper story relates an interesting encounter of a Quaker woman, who traveled throughout the American colonies on her missionary work.

On Sunday last, Mrs. Rachel Wilson, an eminent preacher among the Quakers, embarked for Philadelphia; but the ship waiting off Gravesend for a wind, she went on shore and preached, by permission, in the Town Hall. During the discourse an old woman, who was very abusive, fell off a stool and broke her leg; when, notwithstanding her insolence, the Friends immediately collected seven guineas for her relief.

Source: Virginia Gazette, 3 November 1768.

In this aspect these women operated in a professional sphere of society not common among colonial women.

Quaker women eagerly embraced missionary work. Usually moving in pairs, Quaker women were known to travel in various parts of Europe, the American colonies, and the Caribbean. This missionary work occasionally landed them in trouble, especially in Puritan-dominated New England. The Puritans viewed the Quakers as a corrupting sect that was attempting to infect and destroy their religiously pure society. In the 1650s Quaker missionaries descended upon Massachusetts, which retaliated by passing laws outlawing the preaching of Quaker doctrine. Whipping, mutilations, and sentences of banishment were all resorted to, although these proved ineffective in dissuading the missionaries. In 1659 several Quakers were condemned to death, including Mary Dyer.

Mary Dyer's execution was a vivid reminder that the Puritan settlers of New England had not come to America to practice religious freedom, merely to worship according to their own system of belief. The Quakers were truly committed to the principle of religious freedom for all, including denominations that differed markedly from their own doctrines. In

1682 William Penn founded Pennsylvania as a haven for Quakers, as well as for other settlers fleeing religious persecution. Although the colony was founded as a holy experiment, Penn's commitment to religious freedom meant that he had no religious requirements of people who chose to settle there. Quakers assumed an early leadership role, but they soon became a minority in the colony. Despite the rigorous pressure asserted by the women's meetings to ensure that Quaker girls married only Quaker men, intermarriage soon began to have a dwindling effect on the Quaker population. Other forms of political pressure also caused members to leave the sect. Quakers' commitment to pacifism, even in the face of hostile Indian wars and the American Revolution, made them unpopular and isolated.

The Quakers remained a small but influential group throughout the colonial period. Perhaps their greatest contribution would come in later centuries, when women raised in the Quaker tradition played a disproportionate role in abolition, social justice, and women's rights. It is estimated that 40 percent of the female abolitionists and 15 percent of the suffragists were Quakers. Given that Quakers never accounted for more than 2 percent of the population, it is clear that the contributions they made to American society is remarkable.

See also Dyer, Mary

Further Reading

Bacon, Margaret Hope. *Mothers of Feminism: The Story of Quaker Women in America.* San Francisco: Harper and Row, 1986.

Dunn, Mary Maples. "Saints and Sisters: Congregational and Quaker Women in the Early Colonial Period." *American Quarterly* 30 (1978): 582–601.

———. "Women of Light." In *Women of America: A History,* eds. Carol Ruth Berkin and Mary Beth Norton. Boston: Houghton Mifflin, 1979.

Haviland, Margaret Morris. "Beyond Women's Sphere: Young Quaker Women and the Veil of Charity in Philadelphia, 1790–1810." *William and Mary Quarterly* 51 (1994): 419–446.

Larson, Rebecca. *Daughters of Light: Quaker Women Preaching and Prophesying in the Colonies and Abroad, 1700–1775.* New York: Alfred A. Knopf, 1999.

Quilting

The motivations behind labor-intensive quilting were economy, warmth, and necessity. By joining two layers of fabric, a cloth could be made warmer and stronger than before. By adding a layer of filler, it became warmer still. Many of the earliest settlers who arrived in New England lacked clothing warm enough to withstand the chilly Atlantic winds that buffeted their coastal communities. Their homes were cold and drafty, and lining their walls and beds with quilts was the most economical way to create a comfortable environment. Although current connotation of the word *quilt* implies large bed coverings, the women of early America used quilting techniques on vests, petticoats, bonnets, and jackets. The filler used to add warmth to the garment ranged from cotton batting to old blankets, wool, rags, and even newspaper.

The necessity for salvaging old material was heightened with the passage of the Navigation Act of 1660. The English economy depended on local wool and linen production, and the Crown was determined to halt any activity in the colonies that threatened this industry. Protectionist laws forbade American creation of any substantial textile industry. Markups on fabric imported from England ranged from 100 to 300 percent. The expense of new fabric encouraged women to salvage old material by piecing scraps into patchwork quilts.

Intricate quilting stitches were a practical necessity in order to prevent the filler from slipping within the outer layers. Many of the early quilts of the seventeenth century reflect utilitarian construction, with large pieces sewn together without concern for pattern or color. As leisure time increased, women began pouring more time and design principles into their sewing. Quilting became an art form. With hundreds of tiny stitches per foot of fabric, the technique was clearly well in excess of what was required in order to secure the filling.

The time-consuming nature of quilting made it ideal for cooperative work. Quilting bees were a female equivalent to male barn raisings or a logrolling. The frontier environment of early America made people willing to lend communal support for large-scale projects. When all the women of a community gathered together to work on a single quilt, what might take a lone woman months to complete could be done in the space of two or three days. Beyond the utilitarian function of the end product, the event provided an important avenue of social bonding and community building. Most women in early America lived in sparsely settled rural communities, and quilting bees were the primary form of social interaction for many of them. Much of their week was spent in physically demanding farm labor, with no communication with other adult women. A quilting bee allowed them physical respite and an opportunity to trade advice, news, and gossip. Heavy workloads on the farm during summer and autumn precluded quilting bees, but during winter and early spring a woman might attend as many as thirty quilting bees. Despite the highly social nature of the event, its practical function allowed women to indulge in quilting bees with a minimum amount of guilt.

The woman who was to receive the quilt after a quilting bee put in a considerable amount of work prior to the event. It was her responsibility to cut and stitch together the top layer of the quilt. The most labor-intensive part of the project, the actual assembly of the top, filler, and bottom lining with thousands of tiny stitches, would take place during the quilting party. All the furniture in the room would be pushed to the side, and the women gathered around a large quilting frame. Consisting of four pine poles lashed together to form a rectangle and braced atop two sawhorses, quilting frames were part of the inventory of most colonial households, even the poorest. After the quilting bee, the frame could be easily disassembled and stored away.

Not all women participated in the quilting. Some might be assigned to food preparation, because meals were served throughout the day, and many quilting parties concluded with a dance or celebration. Young girls kept needles threaded or supervised toddlers. Many women would have brought children with them, and the youngsters would play beneath the quilt frame.

Quilting bees were called for a number of special occasions. An upcoming wedding called for the assembly of a bridal quilt. Such quilts were usually

Colonial quilting bee. Most women in early America lived in sparsely settled rural communities, and quilting bees were the primary form of social interaction for many of them. (Library of Congress)

made of white pieces of fabric and stitched with hearts, a pattern reserved for bridal quilts. Most young women would receive two to three quilts prior to marriage. "Freedom quilts" were made for young men when they came of age. "Album quilts" were made for departing friends or community leaders. Such quilts were embellished with elaborate floral, animal, patriotic, or fraternal motifs. Other quilts were made for church raffles or to sponsor a charity event.

Following a quilting bee, the hostess usually presided over a celebration. Dancing and games were played. It was a tradition to place a cat in the center of the newly constructed quilt. The unmarried boys and girls at the celebration lifted the quilt, tossed the cat into the air, and whomever the cat landed closest to was said to be the next to be married. Following the quilting bee there was a little finishing

work that was done by the new quilt owner. Threads needed to be cut and tied. A border was stitched along the edges to preserve the quilt's shape and durability.

Quilting is often associated with the image of working-class women struggling to salvage scraps of rags in order to construct a new blanket. Although this was doubtlessly true of many quilters, the art form reached into the upper classes, where women used silk, velvet, satin, and damask fabric in their quilts. Clearly these women were not quilting from economic necessity. Whether it was done for artistic expression, the social opportunities of quilting bees, or merely pride in domestic economy, quilting was an activity enjoyed by women regardless of social station.

The social importance of the quilting bee can be measured by its longevity. Even after industrialization provided large supplies of inexpensive blankets, the quilting bee endured. Some historians have speculated that the quilting bee served as a force of social and political consciousness-raising. As colonists wrestled with the upheavals associated with the impending American Revolution, the long hours women spent gathered in a circle would have provided them with an opportunity to discuss the implications of the war. Such discussions can have a politicizing effect on people. In later generations, quilting circles discussed abolition, states' rights, temperance, and suffrage.

See also Sewing; Textile Industry

Further Reading

Bassett, Lynne Zacek. "A Dull Business Alone: Cooperative Quilting in New England, 1750–1850." *Annual Proceedings of the Dublin Seminar for New England Folklife* 24 (1999): 27–42.

Finley, Ruth. *Old Patchwork Quilts and the Women Who Made Them.* New York: Charles T. Branford, 1929.

Mulholland, Joan. "Patchwork: The Evolution of a Woman's Genre." *Journal of American Culture* 19 (1996): 57–69.

Orlofsky, Patsy, and Myron Orlofsky. *Quilts in America.* New York: McGraw-Hill, 1974.

Robertson, Elizabeth Wells. *American Quilts.* New York: Studio Publications, 1948.

R

Rape

The typical victim of rape in early America was unmarried, knew her attacker, and was unlikely to report the crime. Most of the population lived in small towns where strangers were rare. In the majority of cases, the judge and jury would have known both the defendant and the accuser. Women had much to lose and little to gain by bringing a rape charge, because the rules of evidence tended to favor the defendant, and rape convictions were rare. Virginity was prized, and a rape trial inevitably called the woman's integrity into question.

Rape was defined as the forcible carnal knowledge of a woman against her will. The age of consent was ten years old, and it was impossible for a man to rape his own wife. The American colonies inherited the legal tradition set by Lord Matthew Hale in his *History of the Pleas of the Crown*, where he stated: "The husband cannot be guilty of a rape committed by himself upon his lawful wife, for by their mutual matrimonial consent and contract the wife hath given herself in this kind unto her husband, which she cannot retract."

Conviction for rape brought a mandatory death sentence throughout most of the seventeenth and eighteenth centuries. The stark finality of hanging a man, when there was a possibility the sexual act was consensual, made many juries reluctant to convict except in the most convincing cases. Although it was extremely difficult to win a rape conviction in early America, judges and juries tended to believe that some sort of misconduct had occurred and were often willing to punish defendants for a lesser crime. With the exception of pregnant women who might be seeking to avoid a fornication conviction, people tended to believe that no woman would willingly undergo the public humiliation of a rape trial unless some sort of transgression had occurred.

To obtain a rape conviction, the woman had to prove she had resisted, made an attempt to cry out, and have two witnesses to testify they had heard or seen signs of a struggle. Judges were often willing to be satisfied with the testimony of one witness if there was additional evidence, such as physical injuries. Midwives were sometimes called to examine women for damage to hymens or other vaginal tearing. A woman's claim of rape was simply not strong enough to condemn a man to death in the absence of physical injuries and testimony from eyewitnesses.

Despite the rarity of cases that had the mandatory eyewitnesses, a handful of cases went to trial. The woman needed to convince an all-male jury that she resisted and was in no way responsible for enticing her attacker. If a woman had been willing to socialize alone with the defendant, the jury would almost certainly fail to convict the defendant of rape, as shown by the cases of Mary Hawthorne and Elizabeth Bissell. Mary Hawthorne brought rape charges against Moses Hudson in 1698, but because she had asked him for some tobacco and smoked with him prior to the assault, her claim was not found credible to the jury. Elizabeth Bissell had a similar experience in 1736. She had been walking from her home to a fair in town when her neighbor,

John Green, offered her a ride on horseback. Elizabeth accepted the ride, but when Green veered off into the woods she became suspicious and slipped off the horse. She claimed Green chased her down, raped her, and threatened her with further harm if she dared report the crime. She was so badly injured from her attempted flight and assault that she could barely walk and appeared "crippled" to her family. After confiding what had happened, Elizabeth's sister convinced her to bring charges. Green defended himself at trial by declaring Elizabeth had attempted to seduce him on earlier occasions. Green was a man of high stature in his community, and the acknowledgment by Elizabeth that she had accepted a ride from him was enough to cast doubt on her integrity.

Juries considered a woman's age, reputation, and the reputation of her accused attacker when weighing the credibility of a rape charge. The testimony of an unmarried woman was less credible than that of a married woman. The lower the socioeconomic status of the woman, the less weight her charges carried, especially if she accused a man from a higher class. Servant women, although they made up only 10 percent of the population, accounted for almost one-third of the rape charges. They were in an especially difficult position, because they were usually single, of low status, and often living in a vulnerable position. The 1669 case of Susanna Reade illustrates the plight of such women. She had fended off three attempted rapes by her employer, Ephraim Herrick, before finally reporting him to a committee from Herrick's church. Herrick retaliated by bringing slander charges against Reade. At Reade's slander trial a number of other women testified in her defense regarding Herrick's long history of unwelcome sexual advances. The testimony of these women, mostly from the servant class, was not enough to outweigh the testimony from Herrick's well-to-do family. Reade was found guilty of slander.

Although many aspects of rape trials favored the defendant, there was one technique that was of enormous benefit to the victims. Many colonies allowed defendants to be repeatedly tried for the same incident. Although numerous men were acquitted of the capital crime of rape, judges who doubted the absolute innocence of the defendant were often willing to retry him on attempted rape charges. Such was the 1791 case with Stephen Burroughs, who was accused of the attempted rape of a fourteen-year-old girl. The jury found him not guilty, but the judge ordered him retried for lewd and lascivious conduct. There was plenty of supporting evidence that he had engaged in highly sexual conduct with the girl, and the second jury was willing to find him guilty of the charge. He was later tried and found not guilty of the rape of a twelve-year-old girl. Once again he was retried for lewd conduct with the girl and found to be guilty as charged. Both girls, being over the age of ten, were capable of consent. The fact that neither girl was charged with lewd conduct indicates the juries did not believe they were willing participants. Juries were hesitant to convict a man for a potentially capital offense, but did not want to see accused rapists go entirely unpunished.

A large complicating factor in rape cases occurred when a woman claimed the rape resulted in a pregnancy. It was commonly believed that a woman could only conceive if she had climaxed during intercourse. No man could be accused of raping a woman who had participated in the incident. Further complicating matters was the mistaken belief that a virgin could not get pregnant. A single woman claiming her pregnancy was the result of a rape was automatically assumed to have had prior sexual experience, thus damaging her reputation and ability to lodge a credible rape charge. Many colonies insisted that rape be immediately reported. Women who elected to come forward only after they knew themselves to be pregnant were therefore usually believed to be covering the sin of fornication, rather than reporting a forcible rape.

Aside from the difficulty of winning a rape prosecution, women had many reasons for failing to report a sexual assault. Virginity was highly prized, and even if the woman succeeded in convincing an all-male jury she was the unwilling victim of assault, her reputation was still tarnished. Records indicate that only about 30 percent of unmarried rape victims in seventeenth-century New England subsequently married. In a society with a 98 percent rate of marriage, this statistic speaks volumes about the lingering damage a rape could do to a woman's public standing.

The small-town nature of early America made it difficult for a jury to convict a neighbor of a hanging offense. If an accused rapist were nonwhite or an outsider in the community, the chances he would be brought up on rape charges were much higher than if he were a local white man. In eighteenth-century Connecticut, two-thirds of the men put on trial for rape and all of the men sentenced to hang were either nonwhite, foreigners, or transients.

Incest was prohibited in early America by laws preventing marriage between blood relations, but it was only treated as a rape if the victim was under the age of ten. Females over the age of consent were considered willing participants and liable to punishment. The 1703 case of Hannah Rood illustrates there was little understanding of the damaging psychological effects of incest. While a young adolescent, Hannah's stepfather began forcibly and repeatedly raping her with her mother's knowledge and consent. Hannah became so depressed she would wander the town seeking someone to confide in: "I went to one house and to another and to a third thinking to declare my grief to them, but when I came there, they being strangers to me I had not the power to speak but did sit down and cry, as my neighbors have often taken notice of" (Dayton 1995, 278). Although both Hannah's mother and stepfather were tried and found guilty of incest, Hannah was tried and punished as well for failing to promptly report the assaults. She was sentenced to a severe public whipping. Her parents received a harsher punishment: severe whipping, an hour in the gallows, and the requirement to wear a capital *I* of at least two inches embroidered on their clothing for the rest of their lives. The lifetime wearing of an *I* was the common punishment for those found guilty of incest.

Shortly after the American Revolution it was recognized that the mandatory death penalty for rapists might have been discouraging juries from convicting guilty men of this crime. Many states repealed the death penalty for rape, although it remained an option in some states until the twentieth century, when it was repealed by *Coker v. Georgia* (1977).

See also Fornication; Sex and Sexuality

Further Reading

Dayton, Cornelia Hughes. *Women before the Bar: Gender, Law, and Society in Connecticut, 1639–1789.* Chapel Hill: University of North Carolina Press, 1995.

Hambleton, Else K. "The World Fill'd with a Generation of Bastards: Pregnant Brides and Unwed Mothers in Seventeenth Century Massachusetts." Dissertation. University of Massachusetts, 2000.

Koehler, Lyle. *A Search for Power: The "Weaker" Sex in Seventeenth Century New England.* Urbana: University of Illinois Press, 1980.

Lindemann, Barbara S. "To Ravish and Carnally Know: Rape in Eighteenth Century Massachusetts." *Signs* 10 (1984): 63–82.

Religion

Religion played a central role in early American social and spiritual life. Some women were more spiritual than others, but virtually no one in early America considered herself to be an atheist. Many people expressed uncertainty about spiritual matters, but the belief that there was some sort of divine underpinning to the world was common throughout all cultures in the American colonial period. For most women, religion was a source of real comfort in an uncertain world. The prospect of premature death in childbirth was something all women faced. Other concerns included fear of Indian attack, the loss of a child in infancy, or the profound sense of loss after moving thousands of miles from family and home. Religion was a place to turn for comfort and insight in uncertain times.

The extent to which religion guided behavior and custom varied widely. People who lived within easy walking distance of a church were more likely to attend weekly meetings, whereas others in rural areas might live for months without seeing a preacher. The Puritans of New England came to America with the intent to establish a godly community in which religion would provide a strong influence over work, recreation, and family life. The

Singing Colonist Procession Going to Church. The extent to which religion guided behavior and custom varied widely. People who lived within easy walking distance of a church were more likely to attend weekly meetings. (Bettmann/CORBIS)

settlers of Virginia were primarily seeking economic opportunity, and overt attention to religious matters was usually displayed only on Sundays. African women brought an entirely different type of spirituality to the New World, which was adapted to the new conditions and religious traditions found in America. Although some Native American women freely embraced Christianity, others held fast to their traditional religious beliefs.

Europeans who came to America were accustomed to heavy state control of religion, and most colonists were prepared to submit to some form of government intervention in their church. The idea that colonists were seeking "religious freedom" was seldom true. Most Puritans, Catholics, and other religious dissidents were seeking a place where they could establish their own religious society, but were rarely interested in extending freedom for other denominations to do likewise within the borders of their colonies. A few notable exceptions of true religious toleration were Roger Williams in Rhode Island and William Penn in Pennsylvania. In other colonies, people were expected to conform to the established church, although rigidity of the rules varied tremendously. In Virginia, the Anglican Church required the inhabitants to be church members, pay taxes, and attend services, but enforcement of these rules were lax. Massachusetts and Connecticut had strong Puritan churches, and punitive measures were enforced to ensure its citizens abided by their rules. The middle colonies of Pennsylvania, New York, and New Jersey had much more religious diversity.

See also African American Women and Religion; Anglican Women; Catholic Women; Great Awakening; Indian Women; Islamic Women; Jewish Women; Methodist Women; Moravian Women; Pilgrim Women; Puritan Women; Quaker Women

Reputation

A woman's reputation was immensely important in early American society. Seventeenth- and eighteenth-century conceptions of womanhood were usually reduced to the simplistic dichotomy of virtuous or vicious. Women who were obedient wives and devoted mothers were virtuous. Women who engaged the world outside their domestic environment risked public censure. If a woman pursued personal pleasure, whether in the form employment, excessive socializing outside the home, flirting, or a sexual liaison, she was liable to lose her reputation. Anytime a woman spent too much time outside the home, she risked being accused of neglecting her domestic responsibilities.

In the early years of colonization, a woman enhanced her reputation by being a productive member of the household. The stereotypical "goodwife" was expected to provide valuable assistance on the family farm. A goodwife was constantly engaged in tasks that would benefit her family. She was to be a diligent housekeeper, caring mother, and productive member of the household. Even during times of rest she should be engaged in some activity that would enrich the home, such as reading the Bible or stitching garments while she chatted with friends. Idleness was contemptible. It was believed that people were led into temptation when they did not have enough to occupy their time.

In colonial America, the notion of virtue was not as strongly tied to sexual chastity as it would be in the nineteenth century. Hard work, devotion to family, and frugality were as highly prized as premarital abstinence. The reputation of a woman who strayed into premarital sex was badly damaged, but she could be forgiven if she married her partner. The reputation of a woman who committed adultery was generally destroyed forever.

By the late eighteenth century, upper-class women no longer needed to engage in endless toil to keep their households operating. A redefinition of respectability was needed. Elite women were expected to elevate the standards within their homes by providing elegant and exotic meals, finely embroidered clothing, and ornamental domestic arts such as music and paintings. Especially in the southern colonies, with their more relaxed attitude toward recreation, women could indulge in dancing, socializing, or other forms of leisure without risking their reputations. The new standard of genteel womanhood allowed no lowering of standards in regard to sexual chastity. Modesty, piety, and cheerfulness continued to be the most celebrated attributes of an upper-class woman's reputation.

Sexual indiscretions loomed as the fastest and most likely way a woman could lose her good reputation. Although chastity was valued, as many as one-third of the brides in colonial America were pregnant on their wedding day. Unwed pregnancy was a damaging event, but a woman's reputation could be restored if she married the father and proceeded to live as a proper and virtuous goodwife thereafter. If marriage was not possible, such as in cases where the father was already married, a woman's prospects for acceptance back into the community were grim. She had violated the social order not only through sexual indulgence, but also in corrupting the sanctity of another family. Such a woman needed to be shunned, for without such sanctions her example might corrupt other members of the community.

The Most Scandalous Woman of Eighteenth-Century America

Nancy Randolph was from a prominent Virginia family and lived with her sister and brother-in-law, Richard Randolph. In September 1792, Randolph slaves reported finding the body of a newborn child buried in a woodpile. In the weeks before the discovery, Nancy had gained weight and suffered from depression. Most ominously, she had been violently ill one evening, during which time she was attended only by her brother-in-law. Nancy and Richard were assumed to be the parents of the dead child. Murder charges were brought against the pair. Brilliantly defended by the aging Patrick Henry at trial, both parties were exonerated, but Nancy's reputation was forever ruined.

For the next fifteen years Nancy drifted between the homes of relatives where she was barely tolerated. She was the target of baseless rumors, such as that she had liaisons with slaves, prostituted herself, and even poisoned her brother-in-law, who died a few years after the 1792 scandal. Eventually the entire Randolph family turned away from Nancy, and she desperately sought employment in New England. There she became housekeeper to Gouverneur Morris, an elderly bachelor and one of the wealthiest men in America. They married on Christmas Day in 1809 when Nancy was thirty-five. It was a love match and the two were devoted to one another until Morris died in 1816. Despite her remarkable change of fortune, Nancy Randolph Morris was haunted by her reputation for the rest of her life. Relatives still snubbed her, and strangers pointed her out on the street. She became resigned to her situation and lived a reclusive life on Morris's grand estate.

Source: Crawford, Alan Pell. *Unwise Passions: A True Story of a Remarkable Woman and the First Great Scandal of Eighteenth Century America.* New York: Simon and Schuster, 2000.

A woman's reputation could not be shielded by wealth or family connections. Oftentimes, scandal within a high-ranking family had stronger reverberations than for those of lower circumstances. The greater a woman's position in society, the harsher the shame of an indiscretion. In 1782 Rachel Warrenton, a young woman from a prominent Virginia family, gave birth to a child fathered by the Viscount Rochambeau. The viscount refused to acknowledge the child or his responsibilities and soon sailed to his home in France, leaving his unmarried lover to face the shame of scandal alone. Rachel was abandoned and disinherited by her family. Ridiculed by the townspeople and even members of her own family, she eventually married a laborer and lived the rest of her life in poverty. Although Rachel Warrenton's offense left an indelible stain on her reputation, the shame and harsh retaliation did not extend to her son, who was held blameless and supported by sympathetic relatives and ultimately had a successful career in the navy.

Historian Laurel Thatcher Ulrich concisely explained the unique importance of reputation to colonial women: "For a woman, sexual reputation was everything; for a man, it was part of a larger pattern of responsibility" (Ulrich 1991, 98). Men had a variety of skills and public responsibilities that made them valuable members of a community, but women were largely defined by their ability to be good wives and mothers. If the role of respectable wife and mother was closed to her, a woman had very little upon which to build respectability.

Once damaged, a woman's reputation was difficult to restore. Most Americans lived in small towns where gossip spread quickly. Women who had been wrongfully slandered were known to turn to the courts for redress. Slander was the most common reason for women to file lawsuits during the colonial period, and many women succeeded in gaining a public apology and financial compensation for the damage done to their reputations. If there was truth to the rumor, a woman generally carried a lingering stain on her reputation. Women who were correctly accused of theft, slander, drunkenness, or abuse of a child were generally scorned. If they expressed penitence and mended their ways they could be forgiven, but the shame of their behavior was not forgotten.

Reputation tended to be less important in urban areas. By the end of the eighteenth century cities had developed to such a size that anonymity was possible. Women whose reputations had been destroyed in their hometown could find a new home where neighbors were accustomed to seeing new faces and rarely asked for extensive personal histories.

See also Slander

Further Reading

Brown, Kathleen M. *Good Wives, Nasty Wenches, and Anxious Patriarchs: Gender, Race and Power in Colonial Virginia.* Chapel Hill: University of North Carolina Press, 1996.

Gunderson, Joan R. *To Be Useful to the World: Women in Revolutionary America, 1740–1790.* New York: Twayne Publishers, 1996.

Saxton, Martha. *Being Good: Women's Moral Values in Early America.* New York: Hill and Wang, 2003.

Ulrich, Laurel Thatcher. *Good Wives: Images and Reality in the Lives of Women in Northern New England, 1650–1750.* New York: Vintage Books, 1991.

Roanoke, the Lost Colony of

See *Dare, Virginia*

Ross, Betsy Griscom

Seamstress (1752–1836)

Betsy Ross was commissioned to sew flags during the American Revolution, but it is doubtful she can be credited with designing and producing the first flag of the Revolution.

Born and raised in Philadelphia, Elizabeth Griscom grew up in a pacifist Quaker family. She received a basic education, after which she was apprenticed to upholsterer William Webster. There she met fellow apprentice John Ross, with whom she eloped in 1773. Ross was an Episcopalian, and the marriage caused Betsy to be expelled from her church. By 1775 John Ross had opened his own upholstery shop, supported the patriot cause, and had joined the local militia. In January 1776 he was killed as the result of a gunpowder explosion.

Legend claims George Washington visited the young widow in June 1776. Accompanied by war financier Robert Morris and George Ross, her deceased husband's uncle and member of the Continental Congress, the trio supposedly commissioned Betsy to produce the first American flag. The committee suggested a layout of stars and stripes, which Betsy concurred with, except she suggested arranging the stars in a circle rather than in awkward rows. Thus, she accepted the commission and proceeded to produce American flags.

This story was not publicly circulated until the 1870s, when Betsy Ross's grandson, William Canby, read a paper before the Pennsylvania Historical Society. As the nation approached its first centennial, the public displayed a renewed interest in patriotic history and was hungry for such a story. Betsy Ross was one of the few female heroines who could be identified with the war, and her story was uncritically accepted. Aside from family oral history, there is little evidence to document her involvement in the creation of the first American flag. George Washington was in New York during the time her grandson claims he visited her in Philadelphia. It is now believed that the Bennington Flag, with nine stripes and thirteen stars encircling the number *76*, was the first design used by the American army. Betsy Ross might not have sewn the first American flag, but minutes of the Pennsylvania State Navy Board record payment to Elizabeth Ross for making "ship's colors" in May 1777.

Except for the legend of her participation in making the first American flag, Betsy Ross would have faded from memory. She lived a life like many other American women during a time of war, and her personal sacrifices were substantial. She was widowed twice as a result of the war. In 1777 she married seaman Joseph Ashburn, with whom she had two children. He was captured by the British in 1781 and died the following year while still confined in a British prison.

In 1783 Betsy married John Claypoole, a childhood friend and a privateer who had been imprisoned alongside Betsy's second husband. He survived the war, and Betsy agreed to marry him on the

Betsy Ross sewing an American flag. Betsy Ross was commissioned to sew flags during the American Revolution, but it is doubtful she can be credited with designing and producing the first flag of the Revolution. Betsy Ross lived a life like many other American women during a time of war, and her personal sacrifices were substantial. (Bettmann/CORBIS)

condition that he quit privateering. The couple had five daughters and lived happily until Claypoole's death in 1817. Betsy continued to work as a seamstress until she retired in the late 1820s.

Further Reading

Kashatus, William C. "Seamstress for a Revolution." *American History* 37 (2002): 20–26.

Preble, George H. *Origin and History of the American Flag*. Philadelphia: N.L. Brown, 1917.

Wulf, Karin A. "Betsy Ross." In *American National Biography*, ed. John A. Garraty. New York: Oxford University Press, 1999.

Rowlandson, Mary
Indian captive and author (c. 1637–1711)

Mary Rowlandson was the most famous Indian captive of the seventeenth century and author of the earliest full-length account of such an ordeal. Mary's family immigrated to America shortly after she was born. She was raised in Salem, Massachusetts, but eventually moved to the frontier town of Lancaster. She married the village's first minister, Joseph Rowlandson, in 1656. Like other women of this generation in Massachusetts, Mary's life consisted of raising her children, performing household

We took up our packs and along we went, but a
wearisome day I had of it. As we went along I saw an
Englishman stripped naked and lying dead on the
ground, but knew not who it was. Then we came to
another Indian town, where we stayed all night. In
this town there were four English children, captives,
and one of them my own sister's. I went to see how
she did, and she was well, considering her captive
condition. I would have tarried that night with her,
but they that owned her would not suffer it. Then I
went to another wigwam, where they were boiling
corn and peas, which was a lovely sight to see, but I
could not get a taste thereof. Then I went to another
wigwam, where there were two English children; the
squaw was boiling horses' feet. Then she cut me off a
little piece, and gave one of the English children a
piece also. Being very hungry, I had quickly ate up
mine . . . and savory it was to my taste. Thus the Lord
made pleasant and refreshing, which another time
would have been an abomination. Then I went home
to my mistress's wigwam, and they told me I dis-
graced my master with begging, and if I did so any
more they would knock me in the head. I told them
they had as good knock me in the head as starve me
to death.

Source: Lincoln, Charles H. *Narratives of the Indian
Wars, 1675–1699.* New York: Charles Scribner's Sons,
1913.

be attacked, one of which was the tiny village where
Mary Rowlandson lived.

On the morning of 10 February 1676, Indians
began attacking and burning homesteads of Lancaster. Three dozen villagers sought refuge at
Mary's house, but their resistance failed in the face
of concerted onslaught by the Indians. The house
was burned to the ground, and a number of the villagers, including Mary's sister, were killed in the
fighting. Mary and three of her children were taken
captive. Thus began a three-month ordeal for Mary,
who was suffering from a gunshot wound. It is estimated that she traveled about 150 miles during her
captivity, much of it on foot. Her six-year-old
daughter, Sarah, died in Mary's arms after going for
a week without food. Mary eventually recovered
from her wound and was assigned as a slave to the
household of the squaw-sachem, Weetamoo. Conditions were terrible, with little food and frequent
physical abuse. The Indians were fleeing colonial
pursuers, and the frequent displacement added to
the physical stress of Mary's ordeal.

The Indians were aware of Mary's prominent
position within white society, and negotiations were
begun for her ransom. Mary's husband had survived
the attack on Lancaster, and he eventually raised
£20 for ransom, roughly equivalent to a year's
income. Mary was returned to her husband, and
her two surviving children were successfully ransomed later that year. Throughout her ordeal,
Mary's strong Christian beliefs never wavered. She
believed that the Indian triumph over the settlers
was a result of the failure of the Puritans to uphold
their covenant with God, and she believed that she
was destined to survive in order to renew the commitment of her people to the Lord. She believed
that the Indians' ability to wage war on the Puritans
was a result of God's intervention. She passionately
believed that the trials of war were God's warning to
the Puritans to mend their ways and renew their
covenant with the Lord.

In 1682 Mary published an account of her ordeal,
titled *Narrative of the Captivity and Restoration of
Mrs. Mary Rowlandson.* This was to be the first and
most famous of the Indian captive books. These

chores, and playing a key role in the spiritual activities of her Puritan community.

In 1675 Mary's situation became far more precarious with the outbreak of hostilities between
white settlers and the Indians. Decades of white
encroachment onto Indian hunting grounds had
long been a source of frustration for the Indians. By
the 1670s the Wampanoag Indian, Metacom, better
known to the whites as King Philip, began to form
alliances with other Indian tribes to resist the land-
hungry settlers. Eventually known as "King Philip's
War," this would prove to be the bloodiest period of
colonial American history. More than half of the
ninety Puritan settlements of New England would

Mary Rowlandson, in canoe, being held captive by Indians. Mary Rowlandson was the most famous Indian captive of the seventeenth century and author of the earliest full-length account of such an ordeal. (Library of Congress)

captivity narratives were enormously popular in both Europe and America, and some historians refer to Mary's book as "America's first best-seller."

It had long been believed that Mary died shortly after her book was published, because she appeared to have vanished from the historical record. This was disproved in 1983, when it was discovered that after being widowed, Mary had remarried, assumed her new husband's name, and moved to Connecticut. We now know that she lived until her seventy-third year.

See also Indian Captivity

Further Reading

Davis, Margaret H. "Mary Rowlandson's Self-Fashioning as Puritan Goodwife." *Early American Literature* 27 (1992): 49–60.

Faery, Rebecca Blevins. "Mary Rowlandson (1637–1711)." *Legacy* 12 (1995): 121–132.

Greene, David L. "New Light on Mary Rowlandson." *Early American Literature* 20 (1985): 24–38.

Leach, David Edward. "The 'Whens' of Mary Rowlandson's Captivity." *New England Quarterly* 34 (1961): 352–363.

VanDerBeets, Richard, ed. *Held Captive by Indians: Selected Narratives, 1642–1836.* Knoxville: University of Tennessee Press, 1973.

Rowson, Susanna Haswell

Novelist, playwright, and teacher (1762–1824)

Susanna Haswell was born in Portsmouth, England. Her mother died in childbirth, and her father, a lieutenant in the Royal Navy, left for America just weeks after her birth. After he found a new bride in Massachusetts, he retrieved his four-year-old daughter and brought her to Boston. Susanna came of age surrounded by some of the most prominent families in the Boston area. The famous patriot and scholar James Otis took an interest in the curious child and provided her with instruction in the classics.

Susanna's idyllic time in Massachusetts came to an end when she was sixteen, when the simmering of political rebellion made life uncomfortable for those who remained loyal to the king. Her father worked as an agent of the hated revenue-collection service. His loyalty to the king resulted in the confiscation of his property and the confinement of the entire family as prisoners of war. In 1778 they were permitted to return to England as part of a prisoner exchange.

With the family finances destroyed, Susanna immediately began looking for work. She soon found employment as a governess for the children of the Duchess of Devonshire. In this capacity she was able to travel throughout Europe and witness the private lives of the aristocracy, which she later incorporated into her fiction. By the mid-1780s she was no longer working for the duchess, but had taken an interest in the stage. She wrote songs for Vauxhall Gardens and began writing her first novel, called *Victoria*. She played the harpsichord, guitar, and could improvise a song.

In 1787, Susanna met and impulsively married William Rowson, a man too fond of drink and women to make a good husband. William Rowson was a trumpeter and part-time actor who dabbled in business when he could not find work in the theater. His business sense was poor, and he repeatedly failed through trusting unworthy business partners or neglecting his work in favor of the bottle. Susanna quickly realized her marriage was a mistake, but was determined to make the best of it. She followed her husband into the theater as a performer and playwright. When one of his affairs resulted in an illegitimate child, Susanna raised the boy as her own. It is safe to assume that the recurring theme in Susanna's fiction of innocent women being led astray by charming scoundrels can be attributed in part to William Rowson.

Neither Susanna nor William were exceptional performers, and they were forced to take work where they could find it. In 1793, they agreed to travel to America with Thomas Wignell's fledgling acting company. Over the next few years Susanna earned a modest living from the theater, acting in 126 different productions. Despite her success as a performer, she never really enjoyed being on stage, and preferred to write.

It was writing that made Susanna famous. In 1791 she published *Charlotte Temple*, her signature novel. Charlotte was a charming but naive young lady who allowed herself to be seduced by a dashing officer. She follows him to America, believing his promise of marriage, only to find he has been lured away by a wealthy heiress. Charlotte is betrayed again and again, until she finds herself wandering through a snowstorm, pregnant and abandoned. She delivers the child just before dying in a tender reunion with her distraught father.

Although *Charlotte Temple* seems maudlin and overly sentimental to contemporary readers, it was a pioneering novel in the creation of the sentimental genre novel. Readers, especially women, readily identified with the tragic heroine. American audiences responded to the American setting, the blatant disapproval of snobbish ambitions, and the celebration of middle-class virtue. Although the novel was a sensation, the book business brought meager returns, and Susanna's finances were as precarious as ever.

Susanna Rowson's other major work was *Slaves of Algiers* (1794), a farcical musical drama. The plot centers around the true story of Barbary pirates who terrorized American merchant shipping. They captured American ships and enslaved the crew, demanding Congress pay an outrageous ransom for the return of the captives. Into this national drama, Susanna created a fictional group of American women among the captives, who successfully execute a daring escape. She wrote a number of other plays that were also staged, including *The Volunteers* (1794), *The Female Patriot* (1795), and *Americans in England* (1796).

Susanna left the theater for good in 1797 when she established a school for young women in Boston. The school was so successful she moved it several times in order to accommodate additional students.

The school flourished, and Susanna genuinely enjoyed providing instruction for women. She taught until her retirement in 1822. Although Susanna had stopped writing for the stage, throughout her teaching career she continued to publish poems, novels, and textbooks. She contributed numerous articles to magazines such as the *Monthly Anthology* and the *New England Galaxy.* For a short time she was the editor of the *Boston Weekly.* Although Susanna was born into a loyalist family, she strongly identified with the American ideals of democracy, self-reliance, and personal freedom. Her writings portrayed women who were as intellectually capable as men.

See also Theater

Further Reading

Kritzer, Amelia Howe. "Playing with Republican Motherhood: Self-Representation in Plays by Susanna Haswell Rowson and Judith Sargent Murray." *Early American Literature* 31 (1996): 150–166.

Parker, Patricia. "Susanna Rowson." In *American National Biography,* ed. John A. Garraty. New York: Oxford University Press, 1999.

Robinson, Alice McDonnell. "Susanna Rowson." In *Notable Women of the American Theatre,* ed. Alice M. Robinson et al. New York: Greenwood Press, 1989.

Turner, Mary M. *Forgotten Leading Ladies of the American Theatre.* Jefferson, NC: McFarland, 1990.

S

Sacagawea

Interpreter and guide for the Lewis and Clark expedition (c. 1786–1812?)

Sacagawea was born into a Shoshone tribe, in what is now present-day Idaho. As a young girl she was captured by a group of rival Indians, the Hidatsa, and forced into slavery. The Hidatsa traveled alongside the Missouri River trading furs. Sacagawea learned their language and the skills necessary to assist in the fur trade. She was eventually sold to Toussaint Charbonneau, a French Canadian fur trader, and became one of his several Indian wives. Fur traders scouted hundreds of miles in search of game and trading posts. As the wife of a fur trader, Sacagawea was expected to help prepare skins and assist with transporting them to trading posts.

Sacagawea gave birth to a child, Jean Baptiste, and the family spent time at Fort Mandan in North Dakota to rest and wait out the worst of the winter. It was while at Fort Mandan that the pair encountered Meriwether Lewis and William Clark, who were in the midst of their cross-country expedition. In April 1805 Charbonneau agreed to accompany the expedition, because he and Sacagawea had valuable language skills that would be useful in negotiating with various tribes of Indians. Charbonneau spoke French and Hidatsa, and Sacagawea spoke Hidatsa and Shoshone. Lewis and Clark communicated to the pair through a French-speaking American officer. The round of multiple translations was convoluted, but appeared to function well.

Sacagawea was the only woman to accompany the group of thirty-three permanent members on their trek to the West Coast. She carried her infant son throughout the physically grueling journey, during which she also gathered edible plants, berries, and roots. Sacagawea and her baby brought an unexpected benefit for the expedition. Their presence sent a clear message to Indians that the expedition was a peaceful one, because war parties never traveled with women or children. Although Sacagawea did not speak English, she gained the healthy respect of William Clark, who nicknamed her "Janey" and took her son under his wing.

In August of 1805 another unexpected turn of events proved beneficial to the group when they came into contact with a large group of Shoshone Indians. Although the Indians initially appeared skeptical of the expedition, this evaporated when Sacagawea recognized their leader, Cameahwait, to be her long-lost brother. There was an emotional reunion, and Cameahwait supplied the band with a number of sturdy ponies that were desperately needed by the expedition to complete their journey across the Continental Divide.

The Lewis and Clark expedition reached their goal in November 1805 when they located the point at which the Columbia River emptied into the Pacific. Near present-day Astoria, Oregon, they built Fort Clatsop, where they spent the winter. Some members of the expedition had not yet seen the ocean, and when the group heard rumors that a

Sacagawea Monument in City Park, Portland, Oregon. Statue by Alice Cooper. (Library of Congress)

whale had washed ashore, Sacagawea was adamant that she be allowed to accompany the group to see the whale. Clark wrote in his journal: "The Indian woman was very [importunate] to be permitted to go, and was therefore indulged; she observed that she had traveled a long way to see the great waters, and that now that monstrous fish was also to be seen, she thought it very hard she could not be permitted to see either" (Clark 1983, 54).

On the return journey home Sacagawea was able to provide some insight into trails and landmarks she remembered from her childhood. In August 1806 the expedition once again reached Fort Mandan, where Sacagawea and her husband left the expedition. Six years later Sacagawea gave birth to a daughter named Lisette, but little else is known of her subsequent life. It is believed that Sacagawea died at Fort Manuel after a lingering illness. This is based on some notes made by English fur traders. One note in April 1812 mentioned that Sacagawea was very ill and wanted to return to her people. Seven months later, John Luttig, the head clerk at the trading post noted, "This evening the wife of Charbonneau, a Snake squaw, died of a putrid fever. She was a good and the best woman in the fort, aged about 25 years, she left a fine infant girl" (McBeth 1999, 172).

William Clark legally adopted Sacagawea's two children and provided an education for Jean Baptiste in St. Louis. When he was around eighteen, Jean Baptiste was sent to Europe with a German prince. Little is known of Lisette's fate, and it is believed she died in childhood.

Some controversy surrounds the date of Sacagawea's death. Shoshone tradition claims she left Charbonneau after Lisette's death and returned to her own people. Because Charbonneau had more than one wife, it was possible the reference in John Luttig's journal was to another wife. According to Shoshone tradition, Sacagawea lived to be ninety-eight and died on the Wind River Reservation in Wyoming.

See also Fur Traders' Wives

Further Reading

Anderson, Irving W. "Probing the Riddle of the Bird Woman." *Montana* 23, no.4 (1973): 2–17.
Clark, Ella E., and Margaret Evans. *Sacagawea of the Lewis and Clark Expidition.* Berkeley: University of California Press, 1983.
Howard, Harold P. *Sacagawea.* Norman: University of Oklahoma Press, 1971.
Kidwell, Clara Sue. "Indian Women as Cultural Mediators." *Ethnohistory* 39 (Spring 1992): 97–107.
McBeth, Sally. "Sacagawea." In *American National Biography,* ed. John A. Garraty. New York: Oxford University Press, 1999.

Salem Witch Trials (1691–1692)

The events that occurred in Salem, Massachusetts, during the witch hysteria unnerved the residents at the time and has baffled historians ever since. When a group of adolescent girls began charging their neighbors with unspeakable crimes, the only explanation the town elders could summon was witchcraft. Three hundred years later, the explanations have included mass hysteria, misogyny, economic jealousy, psychological need for attention, and even hallucinogenic confusion caused from eating fungus on bad rye.

Whatever the explanation, trouble began brewing in the household of the Reverend Samuel Parris in 1691. The household was a small one, with only the reverend, his ailing wife, his nine-year-old daughter, Betty, and a twelve-year-old niece, Abigail. There were two household slaves from Barbados, John Indian and his wife, Tituba. Tituba fascinated the children with her stories of magic, spells, and voodoo charms. The Parris kitchen soon became a gathering place for other girls of the village, willing to allow Tituba to forecast their future sweethearts by floating an egg white in a glass of water.

Betty Parris was the first to show signs of abnormality. She was overcome by spells in which she was so rapt in some secret occupation that she could not be roused from her trancelike state. During these spells she sat motionless and with her eyes fixed in a deathlike stare. When she was finally awakened from this state, she was agitated and incoherent. Recent scholars have speculated that Betty might have been suffering from epilepsy, asthma, or child abuse. Her relatives were bewildered and became more alarmed when these same symptoms began to manifest in Abigail, whose behavior was more bizarre than that of her young cousin. Abigail crawled on all fours, snarled, barked, and sometimes fell into convulsions. Although Reverend Parris attempted to keep this disturbing behavior private, news of the peculiar behavior soon became public. An explanation had to be found. Physicians were baffled and could find no explanation other than that an evil force was afflicting them. Ministers came to pray for the children, and soon the entire town knew of the troubles in the Parris house. Soon other girls in the town started showing similar symptoms. Eventually nine girls, ranging from twelve to nineteen years of age, would become principle accusers

in the trials. As their symptoms increased, so did the urgency to find an explanation.

Suspecting that some foul sorcery was afoot, the girls were pressed to name their tormentors. Initially, the girls remained mute, refusing to answer the question. When the girls did not produce a name, names were suggested. On 29 February, the girls named three women as being responsible for their misery. Dozens more would be accused in the coming months. Most of the initial women accused of witchcraft were in some way outcasts. Sarah Good

---

An Apology from an Accuser

The only extensive account we have from one of the accusers is that of Ann Putnam, who fully recanted and apologized for her role in the witchcraft hysteria. In 1706, the twenty-six-year-old Putnam stood before her congregation while a pastor read her confession to the assembly:

I desire to be humbled before God for that sad and humbling providence that befell my father's family in the year about ninety-two; that I, then being in my childhood, should by such a providence of God, be made an instrument for the accusing of several persons of a grievous crime, whereby their lives were taken away from them, whom, now I have just grounds and good reason to believe they were innocent persons; and that it was a great delusion of Satan that deceived me in that sad time whereby I justly fear I have been instrumental, with others, though ignorantly and unwittingly, to bring upon myself and this land the guilt of innocent blood. . . . I did it not out of any anger, malice, or ill will to any person, for I had no such thing against any one of them; but what I did was ignorantly, being deluded by Satan. And particularly as I was a chief instrument of accusing Goodwife Nurse and her two sisters, I desire to lie in the dust and to be humbled for it, in that I was a cause with others of so sad a calamity to them and their families. I desire to lie in the dust and earnestly beg forgiveness of God, and from all those unto whom I have given just cause of sorrow and offense whose relations were taken away or accused.

Source: Rosenthal, Bernard. *Salem Story: Reading the Witch Trials of 1692.* Cambridge: Cambridge University Press, 1993, pp. 36–37.

Illustration, *There is a Flock of Yellow Birds around Her Head*, depicting the accusation of a bedeviled girl during the Salem witch trials. Engraving by Howard Pyle. (Bettmann/CORBIS)

was a penniless, pipe-smoking beggar known to snap at those who refused to grant her alms. Bridget Bishop wore scarlet clothing, kept a tavern, drank, and played games with passing travelers. Sarah Osborne was widely suspected of having lived in sin with her foreman for years before she finally married him. The majority of the accused were poor women over the age of forty. In the coming year, more than 185 people would be charged with witchcraft.

The accused witches were jailed pending a trail. Despite their imprisonment, the tormenting of the girls continued. Formal investigations were com-

menced. During the inquisitions the girls wailed, howled, and claimed to be physically tormented by the "shapes" of the witches, invisible to all but the girls. Strangely, after the sessions were over the girls resumed normalcy, their color good, and spirits high.

The behavior of the girls became ever more outlandish and dangerous. Abigail Williams would flap her arms like a bird, throw burning logs out of the fireplace, and writhe in pain whenever one of the accused witches glanced her way. When the truthfulness of the girls was called into question, the hysterics intensified, discouraging further skepticism.

At trial, three principal forms of evidence were used against the accused. Spectral evidence was the most damning. Spectral evidence was testimony by a victim who claimed the ability to see invisible events in which the "witch" engaged in supernatural behavior. Because spectral evidence was invisible, it could not be refuted by onlookers unable to see the behaviors. Other evidence of witchcraft was the inspection of the body for "witch's teats," flaps of skin, birthmarks, or other imperfections that were cited as places for Satan to suckle. The third factor in many prosecutions involved the confession of a supposed witch. Confessions became unusually common when it appeared that those who vigorously claimed innocence were condemned to the gallows, while those who confessed to the charges were granted a reprieve. These confessing witches were required to name other accomplices, thereby widening the circle of the accused and lending credibility to the stories of the adolescent girls.

By May 1692, almost 200 people were imprisoned in Salem under charges of witchcraft. Eventually, nineteen people were executed, fourteen of them women. Another four people died in prison while awaiting trial, and one man was pressed to death during an attempt to extract a confession. Many have speculated that the predominance of females among the accused witches was a result of the Puritans' curious attitudes toward women. Although Puritans revered women as wives, mothers, and models of Christian humility, those who strayed from this virtuous stereotype were looked at with suspicion and hostility. The accused witches tended to be women who broke the Puritan mold. They had brought legal action against family members to fight for inheritances, they smoked pipes, had affairs, were childless or otherwise troublesome to the traditional Puritan image of saintly womanhood. The few men who were accused of witchcraft were most often the husbands or sons of "witches."

The momentum was taken out of the witchcraft movement when the charges began to spread to the neighboring town of Andover. An Andover man concerned over his wife's inexplicable illness suspected witchcraft as the cause. He invited a number of Salem's young girls to come to Andover to see if they could identify the witches who tormented his wife. They did. They accused numerous people, respectable and outcast alike, as being witches. The citizens of Andover were not as credulous as the people of Salem. One outraged man accused of sorcery in Andover tried a novel tactic. He swore out a warrant for the arrest of his accusers based on defamation of character. Although no action was taken on the legal charges, the threat of legal action had an oddly humbling effect on the girls. The wind was taken out of their sails, and they no longer appeared anxious to seek out witches in Andover.

The gathering suspicion in Andover and other towns led to petitions to the governor to intervene. Governor Phips and a number of Puritan ministers were concerned that spectral evidence was being misused. After deliberation among the ministers and correspondence with legal counsel in England, it was decided that the admission of spectral evidence would no longer be allowed. With the removal of the testimony of the young girls, the majority of evidence against the witches immediately evaporated. Most of the imprisoned defendants were released. Although still firm in his belief in witchcraft, Puritan leader Increase Mather became so distraught over the course of events at Salem, he wrote "It were better that ten suspected witches should escape than one innocent person should be condemned" (Konig 1992, 11).

Four years after the trials, one of the judges, twelve jurors, and a number of accusers publicly repented the errors they had committed during the

hysteria of 1691–1692. On 13 January 1697 a day of fast was proclaimed in Massachusetts in repentance for the wrongdoings of the community. Public confessions were read in which the jurors proclaimed their deep sorrow for the role they had in believing the delusions of darkness, which caused them to condemn innocent people to death.

The fate of the girls after the hysteria of the trials remains unclear. Tradition claims that many of them "went bad," while others married and began a traditional family life. The Parris family left Salem in 1696 after the town decided on a new minister. It is believed that Abigail Williams, the leader of the young girls, died within a few years of the trials.

See also Nurse, Rebecca; Superstition and Belief in Magic; Tituba; Witchcraft

Further Reading

Boyer, Paul, and Stephen Nissenbaum. *Salem Possessed: The Social Origins of Witchcraft.* Cambridge, MA: Harvard University Press, 1974.

Karlsen, Carol F. *The Devil in the Shape of a Woman: Witchcraft in Colonial New England.* New York: Norton, 1998.

Konig, David Thomas. "Witchcraft and the Law." In *Historic U.S. Court Cases, 1690–1990,* ed. John W. Johnson. New York: Garland, 1992.

Rosenthal, Bernard. *Salem Story: Reading the Witch Trials of 1692.* New York: Cambridge University Press, 1993.

Starkey, Marion L. *The Devil in Massachusetts: A Modern Inquiry into the Salem Witch Trials.* New York: Alfred A. Knopf, 1949.

Watson, Bruce. "Salem's Dark Hour: Did the Devil Make Them Do It?" *Smithsonian* 23 (1992): 116–130.

Sampson, Deborah
Cross-dressing soldier during the American Revolution (1760–1827)

Deborah Sampson admitted late in life that she had an uncanny desire for travel and adventure. Her life began in a conventional manner, having been born into a rural farming family in Plympton, Massachusetts. Her father died when she was young, and the family sank into severe poverty. As was the custom for very poor children who had been orphaned; Deborah was bound out to become a servant in a neighboring farm. She was treated well at the prosperous farm of Jeremiah Thomas, learning to spin, sew, and care for animals.

Deborah stayed with the Thomas family even after her indenture ended in 1778, but the drudgery of life on a farm seemed too mundane for Deborah, who was tempted to see the world by joining the army. She could have joined as a camp follower, performing laundry and chores like thousands of other women during the American Revolution. She might have rejected becoming a camp follower because the overwhelming majority of women who followed the army were married to soldiers, and becoming a camp follower was an unsafe prospect for a single woman. Furthermore, camp followers were rarely paid wages beyond a half-ration of food. Deborah Sampson wanted to join as a full-fledged soldier.

Deborah was a tall woman (five feet eight inches) and had a muscular build. In 1782 she made her first attempt to join the army by binding her breasts with a strip of cloth, tying her hair back, and dressing in boy's clothing. She successfully enrolled under the name Timothy Thayer and pocketed the substantial bounty the army was awarding men who agreed to enlist for a three-year term. That evening Deborah went to a tavern where she became drunk and boisterous, but she never reported to duty the next morning. An elderly woman from the neighborhood had recognized Deborah when she enlisted and reported her to authorities. Deborah was forced to return the money she had not already consumed in drink, and her reputation in her small town was ruined.

In May 1782 Deborah traveled to Uxbridge, Massachusetts, where she once again disguised herself as a young man and successfully enrolled in the Fourth Massachusetts Regiment under the assumed name of Robert Shurtlieff. This time her disguise would not be discovered for years. Her family suspected that Deborah had absconded to the army and made a few attempts to locate her. Seeking to allay her mother's fears, Deborah wrote a letter home, saying she had "found agreeable work" among a "large but well-regulated family" (Ward 1999, 744).

Over the coming months Deborah partook in a series of raids, battles, and sieges. She went on campaigns to hunt down raiding parties of Tories. She fought against Indians in western New York. She lived in tents with men, using the latrine and bathing under cover of darkness. She wore a tight vest to bind her breasts throughout her service in the military. In one skirmish she took a bullet in the thigh and had to be treated at a hospital. A French doctor cut away her pant leg and treated the wound, but her secret remained safe.

In 1783 her regiment was sent to Philadelphia to help suppress a group of American soldiers who were threatening to mutiny. She was assigned to be an orderly for Major General John Patterson, who was in charge of court-martial proceedings. Shortly after arriving in Philadelphia, Deborah became infected with a debilitating fever and was hospitalized. She drifted in and out of consciousness. During one of her lucid moments, she recalled overhearing fellow soldiers discussing who would inherit her clothing after she died. At the worst of her illness, Deborah was examined by Dr. Barnabas Binney, who discovered her secret while feeling for a heartbeat. The doctor did not immediately reveal her secret, but ordered her to be transferred to his home where she was cared for in private.

Deborah maintained her male disguise while recovering and was eventually sent home to West Point at the close of the war, still dressed as a man. With her she carried a sealed letter from Dr. Binney addressed to her commanding officer, Major General Patterson. The letter revealed Deborah's sex, which was met with disbelief by the officers until Deborah verified its truth. They accepted the situation with good humor and provided Deborah with a private apartment and clothes of either sex. She generally preferred to continue wearing men's clothing, claiming she suffered less harassment from the soldiers when she was so dressed.

In October 1783 Deborah was granted an honorable discharge from the army. She headed to a small town in Massachusetts, where she took work on her uncle's farm. Initially, she continued to live as a man, using the name Ephraim Sampson, although her uncle certainly knew the truth. In 1784 she began living as a woman again and married Benjamin Gannett the following year. They moved into a two-story farmhouse, where they raised three children.

The Gannetts always suffered from poverty. Deborah later claimed her war injuries prevented her from fully helping on the farm. In 1797 she became acquainted with Herman Mann, who set upon a plan to capitalize on Deborah's unusual story. He helped her write her memoirs and wrote a prepared speech for her to deliver at public gatherings. The memoirs were highly exaggerated, which Deborah later acknowledged and wished to correct. Her speaking engagements were popular and earned her a decent living. She began the lecture dressed in female clothing and explained her motives for wishing to serve in the military. She then changed into uniform and performed the "manual of arms" with a regulation musket. She lectured throughout New England and is believed to have been the first paid female lecturer in America.

Despite her speaking tour, Deborah died in poverty at the age of sixty-six. Her husband appealed for a widower's pension, claiming that Deborah's war wounds had contributed to her death. By the time the pension was granted, Benjamin had died. The generous pension award was divided equally among Deborah's three children.

See also Military Service and the American Revolution

Further Reading

Brookey, Robert Alan. "Keeping a Good Woman Down: Normalizing Deborah Sampson Gannett." *Communication Studies* 49 (1998): 73–85.

Evans, Elizabeth. *Weathering the Storm: Women of the American Revolution.* New York: Charles Scribner's Sons, 1975.

Ward, Harry M. "Deborah Sampson." In *Women in World History,* ed. Anne Commire. Waterford, CT: Yorkin, 1999.

Scarlet Letters

See Adultery

Schuyler, Catherine Van Rensselaer
Patriotic leader during the American Revolution (1734–1803)

Catherine Schuyler's claim to fame is based on an event so clouded by time we may never know if it actually occurred or if it was a mere folk legend.

Married to an American general and one of the wealthiest women in New York, Catherine presided over a number of large estates. During her husband's long periods of service in the American Revolution, Catherine continued to run her estates as best she could, despite frequent shortages of food, labor, and occasional vandalism. She spent much of her time divided between her estates in Albany and Saratoga.

During the British march toward Saratoga, Catherine was living in Albany when she heard news of the advancing troops. She set out for Saratoga, determined to save as many of her possessions in the Saratoga house as possible. As she neared Saratoga, she encountered fleeing civilians who warned her against attempting to reach her estate. Catherine replied that a general's wife must not show fear and proceeded to her home. She successfully salvaged many of her belongings from the home, but realized the British would soon overrun the land. Tradition claims that Catherine deliberately set fire to her fields of wheat to prevent it from being harvested by the British.

This incident was immortalized in the 1852 painting by Emanuel Leutze, but might never have occurred. There was no contemporary account of the event, and it was first told in 1846 by Catherine's youngest daughter. The story of the fearless woman sacrificing her own property in the American cause appealed to the romantic sense of nineteenth-century idealism.

Whether this event actually happened does not diminish the role Catherine played as a courageous symbol of fortitude for the American cause. By the time British troops arrived at her doorstep, the house was ordered burned by General Burgoyne, claiming it was a military necessity, because the house was blocking the line of artillery fire and needed to be brought down. Burgoyne claimed the estate was in

Mrs. Schuyler sets her fields on fire on the approach of the British. (Corbis)

good condition when he set it to flames, thus undermining the tale of Catherine's burning of the wheat, but others in Burgoyne's company claimed to have seen a swath of charred fields. From a distance of more than 200 years, it is unlikely that we will ever be able to determine whether Catherine's actions were a mere apocryphal tale or were based on the actions of a brave and determined woman.

In one of the ironies of war, after Burgoyne was captured in October 1777, he was forced to accept the hospitality of the Schuylers in their home at Albany. Both Catherine and General Schuyler accepted Burgoyne into their home with graciousness. When Burgoyne expressed regret over the burning of the Saratoga home, General Schuyler replied that he would have done the same had their positions been reversed.

Following the war General Schuyler was elected to Congress. Catherine followed him to Philadelphia, where she served as a political hostess. Eight of the Schuyler's fifteen children survived to adulthood. Their daughter Elizabeth became the wife of Alexander Hamilton.

Further Reading

Garraty, John A., and Mark C. Carnes, eds. *American National Biography.* New York: Oxford University Press, 1999.

Humphreys, Mary Gay. *Catherine Schuyler.* New York: Scribner, 1897.

James, Edward T., ed. *Notable American Women, 1607–1950: A Biographical Dictionary.* Cambridge, MA: Belknap Press of Harvard University, 1971.

Science and Technology, Women in

Women played a participatory role in the study and experimentation of scientific matters during a time when there were few professionals who earned a living from its study and practice. The healing effects of herbs, observations on weather, techniques for growing plants, and methods for the delivery of children were all within a woman's normal sphere of interest. Women have traditionally been considered healers and nurturers, so interest in medicine was consistent with the expectations of society. Likewise, because so many women in early America depended on agriculture for their families' livelihood, experiments with the plant world were also common. In the eighteenth century, medicine and scientific inquiry came under the influence of a growing body of professional practitioners. The establishment of scientific societies and formal college degree programs became standard means of acceptance in the scientific community. Denied access to these organizations, women became marginalized in the practical applications of science. Although women still participated in science, they were considered amateurs, whereas the stature of male doctors and scientists became more respectable and professional.

Women held a monopoly on midwifery until the early nineteenth century, when competition from physicians began encroaching into their business. Women handled other aspects of traditional healing, which depended on a mixture of folklore, trial and error, and intuition. Because so much nursing was carried out by housewives and mothers, it was a natural extension for women with healing skills to earn a supplemental income from their services. Town records reveal that women were often paid to provide nursing services at poorhouses. Parishes occasionally paid women to house and nurse impoverished individuals. During times of war and epidemics, demand for such nurses skyrocketed.

A more scientific approach to science was taken by women who studied agriculture and botany. Often the daughters or wives of scientists, these women studied, cataloged, and created artistic renderings of plants native to the Americas. The most notable colonial female botanist was Eliza Pinckney (c. 1722–1793), whose experiments with rice and indigo fueled the economy of the Carolinas for decades. Martha Daniell Logan (1702–1779) experimented with growing various strains of plants. She sold seeds to neighbors, corresponded with other noted horticulturalists, and published *A Gardener's Calendar*, which served as a standard reference work for gardening in South Carolina for the last portion of the eighteenth century.

Jane Colden (1724–1766) made extensive studies of plant life in the lower Hudson Valley. She compiled a catalog of more than 300 species of plants and developed a technique for making ink impressions of leaves. With her father's assistance, she participated in a lively correspondence with a renowned circle of international scholars. Jane's father, Cadwallader Colden, was one of the most famous botanists of his day. He was aware of the difficulties facing women who wished to pursue science, notably, their lack of training in Latin, the universal language for scientific communication in colonial times. Latin was rarely part of any woman's education, which compromised their ability to pursue formal training. Women such as Jane Colden were therefore dependent on the tutelage of a male teacher, as well as on their assistance in publicizing their findings. Much of Jane's communication with European scientists took place with her father's assistance.

Sybilla Righton Masters (d. 1720) combined her interest in botany with engineering. Her invention for a corn-grinding mill was awarded a patent in 1715, making her the first female to earn a patent in the Americas. Because British law prohibited women from applying for a patent under their own names, Sybilla's patent was submitted under the name of her husband, Thomas Masters. The patent was for a new way of cleaning and curing Indian corn, which used hammers instead of the traditional wheel to grind hominy. In 1716 Thomas Masters applied for another patent for one of Sybilla's inventions, this one for an innovative method of weaving straw and palmetto leaves. Because straw hats and bonnets ultimately became such an important commodity for the American economy,

Sybilla's inventions were substantial contributions to the establishment of these American products.

We know of only a handful of colonial women scientists by name. These women were from wealthy families, whose fathers or husbands were willing to communicate the women's findings to the wider scientific community. Only women from wealthy families, such as Jane Colden, had time to pursue matters of purely academic interest. As science became an increasingly prestigious field of study in the eighteenth century, it became more difficult for women to be active participants. Whereas midwives, herbalists, and nurses had been welcome in the healing arts, they were marginalized by academic circles in which women were not welcome.

Despite the fact that only a handful of early American women are remembered for their scientific contributions, there were doubtlessly thousands of women whose experiments with new plants, crops, and herbs added to the knowledge of the New World. Techniques for plant grafting, crop rotations, and seed exchanges among farmers' wives helped agriculture flourish. Experiments with herbal remedies were anonymously folded into American folklore and medicinal arts. Although such women's names are not recorded in scientific biographies, their contributions were genuine and notable.

See also Midwives; Pinkney, Eliza Lucas

Further Reading

Ogilvie, Marilyn, and Joy Harvey, eds. *The Biographical Dictionary of Women in Science: Pioneering Lives from Ancient Times to the Mid-Twentieth Century.* New York: Routledge, 2000.

Schiebinger, Londa. *The Mind Has No Sex? Women in the Origins of Modern Science.* Cambridge, MA: Harvard University Press, 1989.

Wilson, Joan Hoff. "Dancing Dogs of the Colonial Period: Women Scientists." *Early American Literature* 7 (1973): 225–235.

Self-Sufficiency

The goal of most immigrants coming to America was not wealth, but the ability to achieve self-sufficiency. The majority of immigrants had been tenants or wage-laborers in Europe, never owning land or tools of production. As such, the possibility of being driven from their homes by enclosure laws was a constant threat. Although the earliest settlers might have been lured by visions of gold inspired by Spanish conquistadors, these dreams were quickly replaced with the reality of scraping out an existence on the hardscrabble New England coast or steaming Chesapeake lowlands.

The dream of America was embodied by an agrarian ideal of self-sufficiency far removed from the poverty, vice, corruption, and powerlessness associated with European cities. Ideally, a self-sufficient family would be capable of supplying their own food and material needs. Grain was to be planted, harvested, and milled by the farmer. The housewife baked it into bread or brewed it into beer. Meat was likewise raised, slaughtered, and butchered on the farm. Wool was gathered from sheep, linen produced from a few acres of flax plants, and the family thus had the raw materials necessary to clothe itself. Items such as candles, soap, cheese, cider, shoes, furniture, and bricks could be made by clever settlers.

In practice, pure self-sufficiency almost never happened. Although most women could make woolen thread, few possessed the looms necessary to convert it into cloth. Most settlers had at least one cow, but it took several cows to produce the quantity of milk necessary for cheese making. Household inventories reveal that only a minority of households possessed candle molds or equipment for cheese making.

Farm labor was dictated by gender divisions. Men produced raw goods such as grain and livestock. Women transformed the goods into a finished product. Although they generated and consumed most of their dietary needs, the barter economy was essential to survival. Each family likely sold some surplus goods, be it candles, wool, grain, or services. A shoemaker likely did not have extensive crops, so he would trade his services for grain or meat. A midwife would be paid in cheese or a bolt of cloth.

The items bartered or sold for supplemental income were usually generated by female labor. Women spun thread and made cheese, candles,

Interior of a colonial kitchen. The dream of America was embodied by an agrarian ideal of self-sufficiency far removed from the poverty, vice, corruption, and powerlessness associated with European cities. Ideally, a self-sufficient family would be capable of supplying their own food and material needs. (Bettmann/CORBIS)

bread, and cider for sale. Women also bartered their services such as nursing, midwifery, or domestic help. It was through bartering these goods and services that women were able to acquire items for their family they were not likely to produce for themselves.

It appears that although *communities* might have been self-sufficient, individual families rarely were. Pure self-sufficiency required large landholdings, expensive equipment, and a huge range of skills. It was much easier for a farmer to buy a handful of nails from a local blacksmith than learn the skill and invest in the equipment for himself. Only by drawing on the resources of the entire community could incidentals such as nails, shoes, and soap be supplied. Even with the combined labor of a town, some items needed to be imported from abroad.

Tea, coffee, rum, cotton, paper, and salt were among the most common imports from England. With the exception of salt, none of these items was essential to survival, but most settlers could afford to indulge in these quality-of-life goods. More expensive imports, such as mirrors, silver, wine, ceramics, window glass, and silk, were reserved for the well-to-do. It is estimated that the average colonist spent approximately one-quarter of their annual income on imported goods.

Self-sufficiency evolved into a patriotic ideal in the eighteenth century. As tension with England mounted, women boycotted imported goods. Recipe books were modified to replace imported brandy, wheat, and sugar with local ingredients such as cider, rye, and maple syrup. Americans had a sense of moral superiority based on their ability to work their own land, which they contrasted with English peasants, who slaved for lazy and effete aristocratic masters.

The market economy gathered momentum in the eighteenth century. As cities developed and population increased, more goods were manufactured for local consumption. As the economy developed beyond mere subsistence agriculture, market specialization and profits increased. The price of manufactured goods became affordable, and families were no longer bound to the backbreaking labor associated with subsistence agriculture. Although most greeted the influx of market goods with a sigh of relief, a sense of nostalgia for self-sufficiency almost immediately made itself heard. A famous letter from a farmer, which appeared in a Philadelphia magazine in 1787, echoed this nostalgia. The farmer wistfully recounted how he used to manufacture almost everything he needed on his farm, earning $150 a year, and only spending $10 on nails and salt. His wife was a thrifty helpmeet, working to make cloth, dip candles, and bake bread. Alas, his wife eventually fell victim to the lure of consumer goods. Soon she wanted only store-bought cloth and pewter spoons. Whereas they used to eat a simple but hearty meal of home-grown grain, now his wife wanted tea served in delicate china cups. The family savings dwindled away, and the farmer closes his letter by vowing "no one thing to eat, drink, or wear shall come into my house which is not raised on my farm or in my parish, or in the country except salt and iron-work, for repairing my buildings and tools—no tea, sugar, coffee, or rum. The tea-kettle shall be sold" (Shammas 1982, 248).

In all likelihood, the anonymous, letter-writing farmer never existed at all, and was merely the fabrication of a writer expressing dismay over the decline of agrarian self-sufficiency. Most of the advantages associated with consumer goods benefited female concerns. Dining off a ceramic plate instead of a wooden trencher, wearing cotton instead of woolens, and having a glass window instead of oiled paper all clearly improved the quality of domestic life. Consumerism was thought to benefit women more than men, partially because

the home was considered the female domain, but also because they were freed from the drudgery of subsistence labor. Although women's labor was freed from domestic production, new demands on their time were created by raising standards of cleanliness and meal preparation.

Aspects of self-sufficiency continued to be practiced in rural farmsteads throughout the nineteenth century, more from necessity, rather than nostalgic longing. Those who lived in towns eagerly embraced the rising standards of living afforded by the market economy.

See also Household Responsibilities; Shopping

Further Reading

Hobbes Pruitt, Betty. "Self-Sufficiency and the Agricultural Economy of Eighteenth Century Massachusetts." *William and Mary Quarterly* 41 (1984): 333–364.

Kulikoff, Allan. *From British Peasants to Colonial American Farmer.* Chapel Hill: University of North Carolina Press, 2000.

Ridley, Glynis. "The First American Cookbook." *Eighteenth Century Life* 23 (1999): 114–123.

Shammas, Carole. "How Self-Sufficient Was Early America?" *Journal of Interdisciplinary History* 13 (1982): 247–272.

Witkowski, Terrence H. "The Early Development of Purchasing Roles in the American Household, 1750–1850." *Journal of Macromarketing* 19 (1999): 104–114.

Seton, Elizabeth Ann Bayley

Founder of first American order of Catholic women and canonized saint (1774–1821)

Elizabeth was the second of three daughters born to Dr. Richard Bayley, a compassionate physician committed to public health. She grew up in a privileged environment in New York City, where she received an adequate education, undertook a busy social calendar, and led a life of easy leisure. At age nineteen she married William Seton, a young merchant on Wall Street. It was a love match, and the couple's first years of marriage were idyllic, save for the concern over William's health. Shortly after their marriage it became apparent he had consumption, a condition that was usually fatal.

Despite her husband's gradual decline, Elizabeth gave birth to three daughters and two sons. She engaged in activities typical of prosperous ladies, such as hosting afternoon teas and attending balls and theatrical shows. Perhaps as a balance to her affluent life, Elizabeth took a sincere interest in charitable works. Her father's occupation as New York's first health commissioner exposed her to the plight of the poor and the sick. She witnessed malnourished Irish immigrants disembarking at the port of Staten Island and sensed frustration with her inability to change their dilemma. In 1797 she joined forces with Isabella Marshall Graham to establish one of the first organized charities for the relief of the poor.

Nearing the end of the 1790s Elizabeth Seton began to experience the gnawing fear of poverty herself. Her husband's business suffered a series of downturns and went into bankruptcy in 1800. Her father died of yellow fever, contracted during his duties as a quarantine officer. Her husband's health became so critical she was advised to take him to the Mediterranean in an attempt to save his life by exposure to a new climate. Elizabeth sold most of her remaining household goods to fund the voyage, but William died less than two months after arriving in Italy.

In a state of profound spiritual depression, Elizabeth was cared for by the Filicchi family, associates of her husband's business. She attended Catholic mass and was counseled by members of the Catholic clergy. By the time she returned to New York, she was ready to convert to Catholicism, but faced severe pressure from family, friends, and her Episcopal minister to refrain from conversion. Catholics were considered by many in high society to be poor, uneducated, and unenlightened. Lingering prejudice against Catholicism was alive and well among the elite society in which Elizabeth lived, and pressure against conversion was strong. In addition to her spiritual uncertainty, Elizabeth was confronted with earning a living to support herself and her five children. She accepted charity from her in-laws and established a boardinghouse for boys who were attending private school in New York. She formally converted to Catholicism in 1805.

Elizabeth was barely able to make ends meet, but her relationship with her husband's sisters grew closer as they too became attracted to Catholicism. When Cecilia Seton converted to Catholicism, much of Elizabeth's financial support from her in-laws evaporated. In 1808 she accepted a position teaching in a Catholic girls school in Baltimore. The following year she began working toward a long-cherished dream, the establishment of a convent for a charitable order of nuns. Her sisters-in-law, Cecilia and Harriet Seton, joined the order along with four other young women. Called the Sisters of Charity, the order began in a small farmhouse in Emmitsburg, Maryland. On formal occasions they wore black habits with white bonnets, but for daily work they dressed in ordinary clothing of the day. They established St. Joseph's School for the education of Catholic girls. Some of the wealthiest families in Maryland were Catholic, and many sent their daughters to be educated at Elizabeth's private school. Using the generous tuition payments, Elizabeth was able to fund charitable work, including free schooling for poor girls, nursing for the sick, and relief for the hungry.

The Sisters of Charity flourished. Within a few years they were able to build a more substantial home for the order, and additional communities were founded in Philadelphia (1814) and New York (1817). Despite her professional success, Elizabeth's personal life continued to be marred by tragedy. The consumptive disease that killed her husband had spread to many members of her family. Elizabeth's three daughters were being raised at the convent, and two daughters died of the disease while they were teenagers. Both of Elizabeth's sisters-in-law died of the disease, and by her forties, Elizabeth herself was suffering from consumption. Elizabeth did not let her health impede her charitable work. She vowed to a sister, "I will be wild Betsy to the last." She died at age forty-six. Her daughter Catherine became a Sister of Mercy and carried out charitable works until she died at age ninety-one. Elizabeth's son William was a disappointment to her. He had a reputation for living a self-centered life; he had squandered much of the money his mother saved for him. Despite her disappointment in

William, Elizabeth would have been pleased to know that his son Robert Seton would one day become an archbishop. Seton Hall College was named in her honor in 1856.

Efforts to seek canonization for Mother Elizabeth Seton began in the 1880s. In 1963 she was beatified, and in 1975 she became the first American saint of the Catholic Church. Her order of the Sisters of Charity has expanded to include more than 11,000 women.

See also Catholic Women; Convents; Graham, Isabella Marshall

Further Reading

Dirvin, Joseph I. *Mrs. Seton: Foundress of the American Sisters of Charity.* New York: Farrar, Straus and Giroux, 1975.

Spalding, Thomas. "Elizabeth Ann Bayley Seton." In *American National Biography,* ed. John A. Garraty. New York: Oxford University Press, 1999.

Randolph, B. "St. Elizabeth Ann Seton." In *The Catholic Encyclopedia,* ed. Charles G. Herbermann. New York: R. Appleton, 1912.

Sewing

Among a colonial woman's primary duties was the sewing of clothing, bedding, and linens. Although some households had the ability to spin thread, weave linen, or make wool, most women did not possess all the tools or the skill to manufacture cloth. Household inventories reveal that only about half of colonial households possessed spinning wheels, which were used for making thread or yarn. Fewer than one in ten households owned a loom, used for making linen or other cloth.

Most households lacked the tools to produce their own fabric, but the ability to sew would have been almost universal among women. Purchasing fabric was common, but purchasing ready-to-wear clothing was a luxury reserved for the very wealthy. Girls would have been taught to knit when they were around five or six years old. Stitching hems would have followed a few years later. Although all women would have been trained in basic sewing, knitting, and simple construction, some never developed their skills beyond these basic needs. It was desirable, though not essential, for a young woman to learn "marking," the ability to stitch initials and numbers on items. Fancy needlework and embroidery was reserved for women who had enough leisure hours to embellish designs on their work.

The value of a woman's sewing is difficult to appreciate from today's perspective. Household inventories reveal that aside from the land and the house, the next most valuable possessions owned by colonists would have been bedding and clothing. Around 60 percent of eighteenth-century Massachusetts's inventories listed bedding as the most valuable item within the home, followed by clothing, then by furniture. The ability to produce and repair textiles was essential to a typical household.

Knitting

Knitting was usually the first sewing task learned by young girls. The tools for knitting were cheap, and the technique was easy to learn. By the age of five they could hold knitting needles and begin looping yarn to make simple towels or mittens. Colonists used flax, wool, or silk yarn to knit.

The most ubiquitous items produced by knitting needles were stockings and socks. Throughout most of the colonial period men's stockings were a highly visible part of their apparel. These were usually made of white linen. Women, by contrast, had their legs covered, but often enjoyed wearing brightly colored stockings. The names of the owner were usually stitched in near the top of the stocking, and they were often numbered as well, making their pairing easier.

Commercial knitting machines became available in America in the 1770s, but they did little to slow home production. Knitting was an easy task, and it allowed a woman physical respite from her other chores. Because it could be done while socializing, women often gathered to knit as a group.

Plain Work

Around age eight a girl would learn to stitch, putting in hems, adding darts, or making simple garments such as a nightshirt. If she had younger brothers or sisters, she would likely be in charge of altering their clothing as they grew. Toddlers all wore dresses, regardless of their sex. It made sense to have garments that could be used for all children, and it was easier to keep letting a hem down as the child grew.

Clothes were a valuable asset, and they were mended until they were too threadbare to take another repair. It appears that a well-made shirt might have seen thirty years of service before it was no longer salvageable. Girls would have been responsible for mending tears, adding patches, and altering hems to accommodate the current owner.

More sophisticated work, such as creating shirts and overskirts, would have been the province of an older woman. A typical housewife would have been capable of creating the basic clothing for her family, although tailored coats or fancy wear might be purchased from either a tailor or a woman of greater skill.

Fancywork

Adding embellishment to fabric was a desirable skill for women who had the leisure to do so. Embroidery was a luxury many women never had the time to learn or practice. Around the age of fifteen, a girl who was to learn fancywork would be instructed by either her mother or possibly a paid tutor. Her work would be displayed on a sampler, a small piece of fabric on which the girl practiced her skills. Most samplers were made with silk thread on heavy linen fabric. Marking stockings and linens with the owner's name was common, so the first thing a girl learning fancy stitching would need to learn was how to stitch the letters of the alphabet. After displaying the alphabet, girls learned to embroider design elements such as flowers, vines, or birds.

Homes in seventeenth- and early eighteenth-century America rarely had separate bedchambers. The master bed was usually in the parlor where all could see it, so embroidery of bed hangings and coverlets was a primary means of decorating a home. Bed hangings from this era reveal lush, twisting vines, flowering blooms, and small animals.

Beaded handbags and purses were also fashionable items on which women enjoyed displaying their needlework. Almost any design was suitable

Early American sampler. Most samplers were made with silk thread on heavy linen fabric. (Francis G. Mayer/CORBIS)

for these bags, including landscape scenes, patriotic designs, or bouquets of flowers. Embroidery also adorned dresses, bonnets, and collars. "Canvaswork," or what is now called needlepoint, was used to embellish upholstered seat cushions or create wall tapestries.

A distinctive form of needlework was mourning art, also called memorial art. Designed to commemorate a loved one, memorial art depicted images of the deceased, gravestones, weeping willows, angels, and downcast mourners. Some women might even use locks of hair from the deceased to sew into the fabric. Especially after the death of George Washington in 1799, public displays of bereavement became acceptable. Mourning art was a popular means of not only memorializing a loved one, but also displaying a woman's artistic talent.

See also Milliners and Seamstresses; Quilting; Textile Industry

Further Reading

Earle, Alice Morse. *Home Life in Colonial Days.* New York: Grosset and Dunlap, 1898.

Harbeson, Georgiana Brown. *American Needlework: The History of Decorative Stitchery and Embroidery from the Late Sixteenth Century to the Twentieth Century.* New York: Coward-McCann, 1938.

Swan, Susan Burrows. *A Winterhur Guide to American Needlework.* New York: Crown Publishers, 1976.

Sex and Sexuality

When assessing colonial attitudes toward sex, it is important to draw the distinction between marital and extramarital activity. Prohibitions against sex outside of marriage were deep-seated among all classes of Anglo-American colonists, giving the misleading impression colonists had universally austere attitudes toward sexuality. On the contrary; sex within marriage was considered a vital and healthy activity.

Although young people were discouraged from engaging in any aspect of sexual experimentation, they were not sheltered from its existence. Most colonists lived on farms, where they could hardly be shielded from the rudiments of procreation. Colonial homes, many possessing only two or three rooms, could not afford privacy. During the winter months, it was common for family members to sleep in the same room before the heat of the single fireplace. Many children slept alongside their parents until their adolescent years, and no doubt understood the meanings behind muffled sounds at night.

Sex was considered a major component of a healthy marriage throughout colonial America. Much of early modern Europe was still heavily influenced by Catholic doctrine that regarded marital sexuality as less than the ideal of clerical celibacy. Even the Puritans of New England, long considered the embodiment of repressive sexuality, considered regular and satisfying sex to be essential for nurturing affection in a marriage. Both partners were expected to experience pleasure during intercourse. Should one partner be unable or unwilling to perform sex, the other partner was permitted to sue for divorce.

Most women in early America remained virgins until they were betrothed. Although they were supposed to delay sex until marriage, it appears that many couples began having sex after they became engaged. Premarital pregnancy rates ranged between 5 and 30 percent for much of the colonial period. Most of these premarital births were less than eight weeks shy of the nine-month mark, indicating that conception had occurred after the announcement of an engagement, but before marriage.

Colonial Americans believed in many misconceptions about the nature of sex and reproduction. It was commonly believed that sperm was generated in the spinal cord, and women could conceive a child only if they reached orgasm. It was believed that sex during menstruation could produce monsters and venereal diseases could be treated by having relations with a virgin. Regular orgasm was generally considered beneficial to good health, but overindulgence could lead to weakness and a shortened life span.

Religious and social commentators both asserted that the ultimate goal of sex was to conceive a child. Acts that were contrary to this, such as masturbation, oral sex, and the use of contraception, were discouraged. Despite the procreative goal of sex, there was no prohibition on sex after menopause, when conception was clearly no longer an issue. Older couples were advised that sex was essential to the health and intimacy of their marriage. Likewise, pregnant women continued to engage in sex, although medical texts warned them to cease as their time drew near.

Despite the healthy attitude toward sex within marriage, ministers warned couples about allowing their affection for one another to compete with their love of God. Cotton Mather warned that a couple must not become so enchanted with their spouse that they lose sight of their duty to God. Marriage was to bring people nearer to God, rather than distract them from God. On days of fasting, sex was to be put aside, as were food and drink.

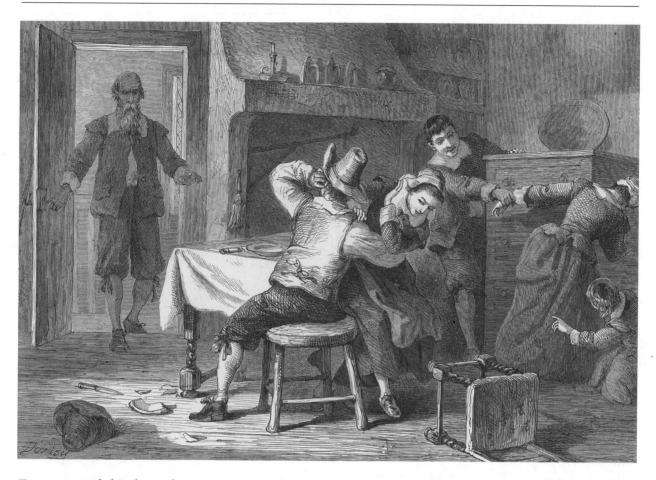

Engraving entitled *Stolen Frolic in a Puritan Farmhouse,* depicting a man entering upon two "frolicking" young couples. Undated illustration. (Bettmann/CORBIS)

Native Americans and Sexuality

Sexual mores among Native Americans varied widely. European settlers who came into contact with various tribes universally perceived them as more sexually promiscuous than Christian cultures. Premarital sex was common in most tribes, and some condoned polygamy and cross-dressing. Girls as young as thirteen were often sexually active. Few Native Americans associated nudity with sexual promiscuity. Public displays of affection were considered in poor taste, and kissing was unknown among Native Americans until the arrival of Europeans.

No generalizations about Native American sexuality can be universally applied. Although most tribes condoned premarital sex, some were more restrictive than Europeans. Groups such as the Micmac of the northeast abstained from sexual relations for the first year of marriage, so that the couple could foster their platonic relationship. If they proved incompatible, the union could be dissolved before the arrival of children.

Europeans might have used their disdain for perceived promiscuity among the Indians as justification for their right of conquest. In the absence of formal regulations for sexual restraint and establishment of stable families, the Indians lacked the fundamental bedrock to create a godly civilization. Europeans could take comfort in the idea they would show Indians the proper way to establish a civilization, to which they could either conform, or yield.

See also Adultery; Birth Control; Fornication; Manly Hearted Women; Rape

Further Reading

D'Emilio, John, and Estelle B. Freedman. *Intimate Matters: A History of Sexuality in America.* Chicago: University of Chicago Press, 1988.

Godbeer, Richard. *Sexual Revolution in Early America.* Baltimore, MD: Johns Hopkins University Press, 2002.

Morgan, Edmund S. "The Puritans and Sex." *New England Quarterly* 15 (1942): 591–607.

Smith, Merril D., ed. *Sex and Sexuality in Early America.* New York: New York University Press, 1998.

Thompson, Roger. "Sexual Mores and Behavior." In *Encyclopedia of the North American Colonies*, ed. Jacob Ernest Cooke. New York: Charles Scribner's Sons, 1993.

Sex Ratio

A sex ratio is the number of males to females in a given population. Under normal conditions the number will be roughly equal, with an average of 106 males born for every 100 females. As a group ages these numbers come into balance, because males typically experience a higher mortality rate throughout their lives.

The experience of the earliest European settlers to America was in no way normal. Travel to the American wilderness was a dangerous and uncertain adventure, and far more men than women chose to hazard the journey. Ship records indicate that among the immigrants to Virginia in 1609, there were 873 men and 222 women. Using the traditional sex ratio measure for listing the number of men per 100 women, this indicates the sex ratio of Virginia was 393.2. This unbalanced ratio in the southern colonies would continue throughout much of the seventeenth century. Passenger records from the twenty ships arriving in Virginia in 1634–1635 reveal 1,636 men, and only 271 women. The 603.7 sex ratio created a climate in which normal family relations could not be established in these initial decades of settlement.

The motivation of many of the men who immigrated to Virginia was the quest for wealth. Traveling without the burden of a wife and children, these men set about seeking gold, planting cash crops, or staking claim to land. Early records by officials of

	Free White Population of the United States, 1790		
State	Males	Females	Sex Ratio
Kentucky	32,211	28,922	111.4
Vermont	44,710	40,362	110.8
South Carolina	73,298	66,880	109.6
South West Territory	16,548	15,365	107.7
Delaware	23,926	22,384	106.9
New York	161,742	152,486	106.1
Maryland	107,254	101,395	105.8
Virginia	227,051	215,046	105.6
Pennsylvania	218,226	206,623	105.6
Georgia	27,147	25,739	105.5
Maine	49,314	46,935	105.1
North Carolina	147,453	140,857	104.7
New Jersey	86,667	83,287	104.1
New Hampshire	70,930	70,179	101.1
Connecticut	115,011	117,547	97.8
Rhode Island	31,818	32,652	97.4
Massachusetts	182,942	190,582	96.0
United States	1,616,248	1,557,242	103.8

Source: Moller, Herbert. "Sex Composition and Correlated Culture Patterns of Colonial America." *William and Mary Quarterly*, 3d ser., no. 2 (1945): 128.

the Virginia Company reveal a frustration that these settlers were failing to establish homes or procure the necessities of life. Letters by the officers of the company indicate an awareness that their settlements will not flourish until "families be planted." The settlers were rootless and often traveled from place to place rather than investing the time to establish homesteads and self-sufficient farms. Various techniques were tried to lure more women across the Atlantic. It was difficult to persuade "suitable" young single women to make the journey, although records show a handful of ships that contained single women specifically intended for marriage to the settlers. The man who married one of these "Virginia brides" was required to reimburse the company with 120 pounds of the best tobacco leaf. By all accounts the few women who were

Wives of the settlers at Jamestown. To address the unbalanced sex ratio in Virginia, records show that a handful of ships contained single women specifically intended for marriage to the settlers. (Bettmann/CORBIS)

brought over for such ventures were quickly married to eager settlers. Such measures were never able to supply more than a handful of brides in each community, and eventually the company turned to the more successful technique of promising substantial land grants to people who immigrated in complete family groups.

The rate of reproduction in the colonies was high, but so was the rate of mortality. It was not until the end of the last quarter of the seventeenth century that the people of Virginia and Maryland were able to stabilize their population through natural means, rather than depending on the continued influx of immigrants. The sex ratio became less lopsided in subsequent generations, although it did not perfectly balance out. Immigrants and indentured servants continued to be predominantly male, and when these were added to the mix of those

born in the colonies, the sex ratio remained skewed until the end of the eighteenth century.

The sex ratio was of a markedly different character in the New England colonies. Most of the immigrants to New England were Puritans, who tended to travel in family groups. Men outnumbered women two to one in the first twenty years of settlement in New England. Although an unnaturally high ratio, their ratio was only 200 compared with 603 in Virginia. The character of the early settlements in New England stood in sharp contrast to those in the southern colonies. The New England families immediately set about constructing houses and farms and established viable forms of government, education, and tolerable relations with the native population. The greater stability of these settlements has typically been attributed to the more balanced sex ratio.

Taken as a whole, the European settlers had a strong majority of males in their population. The lopsided sex ratio caused some men to look to the native or slave populations for sexual companionship. Especially in the French colonies where European women were almost nonexistent, it was perfectly acceptable for a man to form alliances with Indian women. Sometimes called *left-handed marriages,* signifying their temporary nature, these unions often resulted in children who could serve as interpreters and mediators. Although European-Indian marriages were common among the French, there were no recorded intermarriages between Indians and New Englanders. This can partly be attributed to the more balanced sex ratio, and partly to the rigid cultural and religious rules of Puritan society that forbade such relations.

Among the southern states, the tremendous surplus of men and the abundance of African slaves resulted in large-scale mixing of the races. Although prohibitive legislation forbade sexual relations between Europeans and Africans, the laws were rarely enforced. Rules against miscegenation were far harsher in the North, once again owing largely to the balanced sex ratio, which made fraternization between the races unnecessary. In areas where the sex ratio was dominantly male, records indicate greater restlessness, higher mobility, fewer social establishments such as churches and schools, and increased violence. The relatively balanced sex ratio found in Puritan New England resulted in a society with far greater social stability.

One of the side effects of the scarcity of women was the rapidity with which they married. Young women could find partners with no need of a dowry to entice a groom, unlike in Europe, where a woman without a dowry would be at a serious disadvantage. Adam Smith observed that a poor widow with several small children would have little chance of finding a marriage partner in Europe, but would be snapped up quickly in the colonies. The subsequent marriage and remarriages had profound implications on the children of these unions.

Some historians have speculated that the scarcity of women elevated them to a status far higher than that of their European sisters. Women had their choice of suitors, and the value of a women's contributions to a household were keenly felt by those who had to wait years for a wife. Ironically, women were far more able to seek a divorce in America than in Europe. Although domestic squabbles certainly must have happened with similar frequency in both continents, American women sought and obtained divorces at a substantially higher rate. Women filed the majority of divorces in America during its earliest centuries.

By 1790 the sex ratio for New England was beginning to tilt, with a slight majority of women. As soon as land was no longer abundant in New England young men began migrating west, usually alone, in search of cheap land. The toll taken on the male population from war and migration led to a small but noticeable surplus of women in the New England states.

See also Interracial Marriage; Stepfamilies

Further Reading

Carr, Lois Green, and Lorena S. Walsh. "The Planter's Wife: The Experience of White Women in Seventeenth-Century Maryland." *William and Mary Quarterly,* 3d ser. 34 (1977): 542–571.

Moller, Herbert. "Sex Composition and Correlated Culture Patterns of Colonial America." *William and Mary Quarterly,* 3d ser. 2 (1945): 113–153.

Tate, Thad W., and David L. Ammerman, eds. *The Chesapeake in the Seventeenth Century: Essays on Anglo-American Society and Politics.* Chapel Hill: University of North Carolina Press, 1979.

Shippen, Peggy

See Arnold, Margaret Shippen

Shopkeepers and Merchants

The eighteenth century witnessed a dramatic increase in the use of consumer goods in America. Although the earliest settlers scratched out a living from the land, purchasing only the barest necessities, subsequent generations had access to a wide variety of imported goods and luxury items available at retail shops. Although most shopkeepers and merchants were men, their wives were usually intimately involved in the running of retail shops. If the shop sold goods produced by the owner, such as shoes, barrels, or ceramics, the wife would have the primary shop-tending duties while the husband manufactured the goods. If the shop sold a variety of goods, wives still played active roles keeping accounts and waiting on customers.

Women were the sole proprietors of a number of shops in colonial America. Although estimates of how many shops were owned and operated by women vary, as many as 10 percent of New York shops and 25 percent of Philadelphia shops were run by women acting on their own. Most of these women were the widows of shopkeepers, although some were single daughters who took over the family business when they came of age.

There was a marked distinction between shopkeepers and merchants. Shopkeepers sold goods directly to the consumer and lived a comfortable middle-class life. Merchants imported and exported goods in bulk, selling their wares to shopkeepers. They were usually members of the upper class, but because they did business on such large scales, their potential for loss was much greater. The majority of merchants were men, but a few women, especially in New York, were notable merchants in their own right.

One of the few areas of commonality between shopkeepers and merchants was in the area of credit. Almost all transactions in colonial America revolved around the extension or collection of credit. Gold and silver coins were too scarce to be relied on for payment. Most goods and services were bartered. Farmers paid for consumer goods with a wagon of tobacco or a side of beef. A blacksmith might offer his services in exchange for meat and cheese. Because it was rarely possible to exchange goods of exact value, records were kept to account for the differences in the value of the goods traded. A woman would need to be literate not only in bookkeeping, but in the nature of barter and estimating the value of respective goods. The success of this barter economy depended on mutual trust. The reputation of shopkeepers and merchants for integrity in their bookkeeping affected people's willingness to do business with them. Likewise, mer-

chants and shopkeepers made it their business to know the creditworthiness of their clientele.

Shopkeepers

Many shopkeepers operated out of their own homes. If it was a small operation, they might use the front room of their home for business. Larger establishments might consume the entire ground floor of a building in the town center, with the family living in quarters above the shop.

Most women shopkeepers dealt in dry goods, textiles, and domestic merchandise. Imported foodstuffs such as coffee, sugar, spices, chocolate, and liquor were the most common items stocked in women's shops. They rounded out their inventory with a variety of items, depending on what the latest ship arriving in port carried. Advertisements from women's shops list goods such as china, glassware, paper, ribbons, pins and needles, fans, calico, and silk. Records indicate that women shopkeepers rarely specialized in farming tools, guns, hardware, or other items associated with the male world.

Women had a variety of options for supplying their stores with goods. Most would have purchased imported goods wholesale from a merchant. Because so many shopkeepers would have bartered with customers, their stores no doubt contained plenty of locally produced goods, such as candles, soap, cheese, gloves, and so on. Other options for stocking their stores included attending public auctions, or buying at vendue. Vendues were the sale of large lots of damaged or out-of-season goods. Because the lots sold at public vendues were sometimes far too large for a small shopkeeper to purchase, there is evidence that shopkeepers often formed partnerships to purchase lots that would be divided between them. Mary Coates, a Philadelphia shopkeeper in the 1760s, made twenty-one such joint purchases at vendue, almost always with other female shopkeepers.

Shopkeepers were members of a small but growing middle class. They generally enjoyed a comfortable standard of living, but with so much of their wealth tied up in the store's inventory, many lacked an economic safety net. On occasion, the need to call in debts arose, such as seen in this 1773 newspaper advertisement: "All persons indebted to Mrs. Hannah Lee of Marblehead upon Bond, are desired to come and make speedy payment; and if not convenient to pay the money, to come and bring surety and change bonds into negotiable notes of hand, on Monday and Tuesday, the 22nd and 23rd, and those neglecting will be sued in the December Court" (*Essex County Gazette,* 9 November 1773).

There is evidence that shopping became a social pastime for women in eighteenth-century America. Well-to-do women who could afford to indulge in a diversion joined with other local ladies and visited shops. Diaries suggest they might spend several hours walking from one shop to the next, rarely purchasing more then a few items. This female socializing was far more likely to occur in shops operated by women, which tended to sell items that appealed to women.

Merchants

The life of a merchant was markedly different from that of a shopkeeper. They would have stored their goods in a warehouse, rather than a shop. They not only imported goods, they exported raw materials, such as lumber, fur, and tobacco, to England. Merchants commissioned ships and sloops to travel up navigable rivers, stopping at planters' wharves to collect the goods to be shipped to England. Once arriving in England, the goods would be sold by an English "factor," or agent. The agent would in turn arrange for resupplying the ship with goods specified by the American merchant. It was not unheard of for merchants to travel with their cargo, as Margaret Philipse was known to do. Most merchants, especially female merchants, made heavy use of their agent. The success of their business depended on the number and extent of trade associates on both sides of the Atlantic.

Most merchants were members of the upper class. Although a few sought to emulate the English gentry by building large manor estates in the country, most needed to remain in the urban centers of Philadelphia, New York, and Charlestown in order to keep their business operating. These merchants opted for the classic, square brick house in the most fashionable part of town. The spacious, five-window-wide home became closely associated with these well-to-do merchants.

Most women merchants were the widows of successful merchants who chose to continue their husbands' business. The complexity of the work would have made it unlikely any of these women could have taught themselves the trade after their husbands' death, so it is reasonable to assume they had been active in the family business throughout their marriage.

One of the most famous and wealthy female merchants was Mary Provoost Alexander (1693–1760). Although she came of age after the Dutch had fallen from power in New York, it was still a society that respected the ability of women to function in business. Mary and her first husband were joint partners in a vast international trading company. She also operated a shop where some of the goods were sold directly to consumers, whereas the remainder of the goods were sold wholesale to other shopkeepers. After her first husband died, Mary married a wealthy lawyer, James Alexander. Although Alexander assisted his wife by sometimes collecting payment for his services in goods that were sold in her shop, Mary ran the mercantile business. Despite raising eight children, Mary clearly embraced her career as a merchant. Her husband claimed that a day after giving birth to a daughter, she was back at work in her store, selling more than £30 worth of goods.

Although few women attained the wealth or prestige of Margaret Philipse or Mary Alexander, there were dozens of female merchants who operated on a smaller scale. Most shipped fur and rum to England, in exchange for manufactured goods such as silk, books, tea, spices, and glassware. It is difficult to determine how many female merchants were in business in eighteenth-century America. Because so many records were burned during the American Revolution, the most reliable source we have is newspaper advertisements of merchants offering goods for wholesale purchase. Many of the known female merchants, such as Mary Alexander, never placed advertisements, so it is difficult to speculate on how many other women have left no trace in the historical record.

One interesting snapshot of female mercantile activity can be gleaned from the nonimportation controversy of 1770. When Parliament elected to keep duties on imported tea, there was pressure on merchants to cease all trade with England until the tax was lifted. A poll of New York merchants was taken, among which were sixteen women. Fourteen of the women, or 87 percent, voted to continue imports. Among male merchants, 63 percent wished to continue English imports. Although this figure might indicate women were less patriotic than the male merchants, it is more likely an indicator that female merchants were less wealthy than their male counterparts. Because the women had smaller inventories, a boycott could have put them out of business. Only one of the sixteen women on the nonimportation poll, Anne Hammersley, ever appeared in newspaper advertisements. This revealing poll indicates there were far more female merchants in business than can be documented by traditional means.

See also Philipse, Margaret Hardenbrook; Shopping

Further Reading

Bruchey, Stuart. "The Colonial Merchant." In *Encyclopedia of the North American Colonies*, ed. Jacob Ernest Cooke. New York: Charles Scribner's Sons, 1993.

Cleary, Patricia. "She Will Be in the Shop: Women's Sphere of Trade in Eighteenth-Century Philadelphia and New York." *Pennsylvania Magazine of History and Biography* 119 (1995): 181–202.

Dexter, Elisabeth Anthony. *Colonial Women of Affairs: Women in Business and the Professions in America before 1776.* Boston: Houghton Mifflin, 1931.

Jordan, Jean P. "Women Merchants in Colonial New York." *New York History* 58 (1977): 412–439.

Spruill, Julia Cherry. *Women's Life and Work in the Southern Colonies.* Chapel Hill: University of North Carolina Press, 1938.

Shopping

Even in the earliest days of settlement, virtually no households were entirely self-sufficient. Goods needed to be acquired, either through sale, trade, or barter. By the late eighteenth century, towns had developed to such a size that they could support shops, but women from earlier times rarely had access to such luxuries. Trading goods and services among neighbors was the most common means of exchange for the early generations of American settlers.

Peddlers were among the most highly anticipated visitors to rural communities. Traveling with a wagon full of goods, peddlers sold items not likely to be produced on the farm. Cheap, town-produced goods were the staples of the peddlers' business. Pins, needles, buttons, scissors, shoes, books, spices, and all manner of trinkets were offered for sale or trade. Some peddlers specialized in a particular product, such as only books or tinware, but most carried anything that was portable and of value.

For women living on isolated farms, the peddlers' trinkets were only a minor part of his attraction. Peddlers roamed throughout the local area, and they brought news and gossip to women who might go weeks without visiting with people outside their immediate families. An engaging personality has always been an important component in salesmanship, and peddlers were famous for chatting up housewives as they tempted them with displays of their merchandise. By the nineteenth century, peddlers were sometimes considered tricksters, but they were generally well regarded in colonial times.

Somewhat lower on the socioeconomic scale was the huckster. Hucksters made their living in towns by selling fruit, vegetables, fish, or other foodstuffs on street corners. They usually purchased the items at a local market, then walked them into a residential area, where busy housewives could purchase with greater ease. Hucksters were often women, and huckstering was one of the few forms of employment available to women who had no skills. They brought convenience to the housewife, whose child care and domestic responsibilities might have made it impossible for her to leave the home long enough to walk into town.

For women who were fortunate enough to have a servant or older daughter to mind the children, visiting shops was often a welcome break in their day. It is apparent from some diaries that women enjoyed walking from shop to shop and visiting with tradespeople and fellow shoppers. Elizabeth Drinker's diary entries from 1759 and 1760 record several shopping expeditions that resulted in no purchases, but many social exchanges. There is some evidence from account books that women were more likely to purchase goods at a store operated by a female shopkeeper. Although shopping was clearly a necessary part of a woman's housekeeping responsibilities, it was one that served an important social outlet for women.

See also Self-Sufficiency

Further Reading

Cleary, Patricia. "She Will Be in the Shop: Women's Sphere of Trade in Eighteenth-Century Philadelphia and New York." *Pennsylvania Magazine of History and Biography* 119 (1995): 181–202.

McCain, Diana Ross. "Yankee Peddlers." *Early American Life* (August 1989): 6–15.

Single Women

The stigma attached to single women in colonial America can be witnessed by the derogatory terms used to describe them: spinsters, old maids, and thornbacks. Never married women were a tiny percentage of the population, with only 2 to 5 percent of women falling into the "old maid" category. Single women were scarce in the middle and southern colonies, where in the early decades of settlement the men outnumbered women six to one. Single women were more prevalent in New England, where the sex ratio was either balanced or had a surplus of women. By the end of the eighteenth century, scarce land in New England encouraged the migration of young, landless men to less-settled regions in the West, leaving a surplus of women behind.

The reasons women remained single were complex. The oldest or youngest daughter of a large family might have been assigned a caretaker role, either supervising a large brood of young children or caring for elderly parents. When their services as

a caretaker were no longer needed, they might have been too old to be considered marriageable. In other cases the labor of a daughter might have been considered essential for the household economy, and marriage was therefore discouraged. Contemporary letters and diaries reveal that many young women feared pregnancy and childbirth and might have shunned marriage in order to avoid the risks. Likewise, a small percentage of women might have found the prospect of sexual relations distasteful. In other cases a woman might have considered herself unmarriageable, either because she lacked social graces or was simply unable to attract a beau. In cases of women living in remote rural communities, it is possible there would have been no eligible men who were not related by blood.

The majority of women who remained single would initially have lived in the family home with their parents. It was rare, though not unheard of, for the parents to leave the family home to a single daughter in their will. More commonly the family home would pass to married siblings, with the provision that a room in the house be provided for the single daughter. As the woman grew older, she might alternate living among several of her siblings' households. Her services as a caregiver would have been welcome. Because daily operation of a colonial household required an immense amount of work, having an unpaid assistant in the household to help supervise children and perform chores would have been a beneficial arrangement for all parties. As the children grew older, they were no longer in need of supervision and were able to participate in chores. Most single women would find their roles increasingly marginalized as they grew older.

Diaries of single women reveal their insecurities as they became dependent on the goodwill of siblings, nieces, and nephews for shelter. The greatest fear was that they would fall ill in their old age, and no family member would be willing or able to provide shelter for an invalid. The diary of Rebecca Dickinson, a single woman living in Hatfield, Massachusetts, reflects such anxieties as she tended her own elderly mother: "What shall I do or where shall I go, with whom shall I live when I am old and helpless?" (Miller 1998, 349). After her mother's death

Rebecca lived alone in her weather-beaten saltbox house. In other places her diary displays heartrending loneliness, so severe she resisted visiting with family members because it made her isolation more keenly felt when she returned to her lonely house with no other companions. Another evening she wrote: "Yesterday was at Sister Billings. Came back to this house about half after seven and found it dark and lonesome here. I walked the room and cried myself sick" (Miller 1998, 361).

Some women were able to find paid employment outside the home. Domestic labor was the most readily available, but also the least desirable because of the low wages it paid. Other options included working as a seamstress, teaching, or working in a shop. Toward the end of the eighteenth and early nineteenth centuries, millwork became available. This was the most desirable, because the wages in New England textile mills were high until managerial reforms of the 1850s drastically reduced them. Women could expect to be paid no more than half what a man earned for a similar job, making a woman's ability to support herself unlikely. Despite the availability of paid work outside the home, few women would have been able to maintain an independent living, and most would have been dependent on siblings or other family members for board.

Most spinsters in colonial America were regarded with either pity or contempt. A distinction was drawn between honorable and contemptible old maids. Women who rejected the notion of marriage or foolishly disregarded legitimate marriage proposals were disdained for their willingness to break with feminine ideals. Marriage and motherhood was the culmination of a woman's role in society, and for a woman to squander her opportunities in this area was deplorable.

Alternatively, if a woman had become a spinster through selfless or tragic means, she was a subject of sympathy. If a woman cared for aged parents to the point that she bypassed a marriageable age, this was considered a pitiful, but honorable, condition. Likewise, if her single state was because of an ill-fated romance, in which her lover died or was torn from her, a spinster could at least lay claim to having once been a desirable and feminine woman. In

1786 William Haley wrote *Philosophical, Historical and Moral Essay on Old Maids,* in which he advised unmarried women to have an acceptable justification for her state. She should make sure it is known she was unmarried not because she has elected a cold and irrational aversion to marriage, but because she was the victim of circumstance, such as devotion to a dead lover or her need to nurture an elderly parent.

One area in which single women had greater power than their married sisters was in their legal status. Single women had the same property rights and degree of legal identity as men, with the sole exception that these women could not vote. They could buy and sell property, sue and be sued, manage estates, and enter into contracts. Married women lost these privileges, as their legal identity was subsumed under that of their husband. Some women opened small businesses of their own. Women were known to operate dry goods shops, greengroceries, taverns, inns, and millinery shops. Other women could sell services such as teaching or midwifery. The moment a woman married, the income she derived from these ventures would become the property of her husband. A single woman in one of these professions, whether she was a widow or never married, would have to consider the impact of losing her ability to conduct business in her own name after marriage.

Prior to the American Revolution, women who were single were assumed to have been unwilling spinsters. It was rarely suggested that women were old maids by choice, but rather, they were victims of circumstance. After the Revolution, some women began to tentatively assert that there was honor in the status of old maid. During the years of struggle with England there was great articulation of personal freedom and liberty. This was not lost on women who saw their legal identity and privileges obliterated by marriage. The ideals of personal autonomy and equality of persons had been factors driving a national struggle with England, but these same principles could be applied on the personal level as well. The percentage of never married women began steadily climbing after the American Revolution, in a manner that far surpassed the skewed sex ratios. In

1794, *The Massachusetts Magazine* published an anonymous poem by a lady who had been questioned why she chose to remain single:

No ties shall perplex, no fetters shall bind
That innocent freedom that dwells in my mind.
At liberty's spring such droughts I've imbibed,
That I hate all the doctrines by wedlock prescrib'd.
[R]ound freedom's fair standard I've rallied and
     paid,
A Vow of Allegiance to die an old maid. (Norton
     1980, 242)

See also Coverture

Further Reading

Chambers-Schiller, Virginia Lee. *Liberty, A Better Husband: Single Women in America: The Generations of 1780–1840.* New Haven, CT: Yale University Press, 1984.

Miller, Marla R. "'My Part Alone': The World of Rebecca Dickinson, 1787–1802." *New England Quarterly* 71 (1998): 341–377.

Norton, Mary Beth. *Liberty's Daughters: The Revolutionary Experience of American Women, 1750–1800.* Boston: Little, Brown and Co., 1980.

Slander

The insult of slander seems an antiquated and fussy complaint, but it was deadly serious business to the people of early America. Almost all business in early America depended on a handshake. There was very little currency for the first century of settlement, and most goods were bartered or purchased on credit. A farmer promised to pay a blacksmith when his crop was harvested. The blacksmith paid the midwife by shoeing her horse the next time she was in need of his services. A woman spent weeks tending to the children of a neighbor who had just given birth, knowing that neighbor would return the favor in her time of need. This system only worked if people trusted their neighbors to deal honestly. If a person could not be counted on to fulfill his or her end of the bargain, they became dangerously isolated from the social and economic system upon which survival depended. Slander was an attack on a person's trustworthiness, and therefore, livelihood.

Mistress Page's Slander Suit

Phebe Page was a single woman of unquestionably bad reputation when she brought a slander suit against the town deacon in 1650, accusing John Fleming and his wife of falsely asserting that Phebe was pregnant. In order to prove the slander false, Phebe submitted to an examination by skilled midwives, who confirmed she was not with child.

In their defense, the Flemings produced sixteen witnesses to testify to Phebe's flagrant misconduct with a variety of neighborhood men. Ten witnesses testified they had seen Phebe and John Poole in compromising positions in fields or on the highway. Others testified Phebe had been willing to exchange kisses with "old Knap" for five shillings. Even Phebe's own father testified she was guilty of notorious conduct. In light of the damaging testimony, Phebe withdrew her petition. She was charged with the defendants' court costs and forced to pay a bond of £10 to ensure future good conduct.

Phebe Page knew she was not pregnant and wanted to preserve her reputation from that most damaging accusation. In this she was successful, despite the embarrassment of having her behavior discussed in a public hearing. Her poor reputation was a hindrance to her ability to find a husband. Phebe remained single until she was a middle-aged woman, when she married an elderly, twice-widowed man.

Source: Thompson, Roger. "Holy Watchfulness and Communal Conformism: The Functions of Defamation in Early New England Communities." *New England Quarterly* 56 (1983): 504–522.

Women were vulnerable to the effects of slander on another front. A woman's position in the community depended on her reputation as a virtuous, modest, and dutiful woman. Rumors that she engaged in extramarital sex destroyed her standing in the community. If she were unmarried, it jeopardized her ability to find a husband. It would take a highly unusual man to overlook a sexual indiscretion. Even if he were a freethinking man who could accept a nonvirgin as a bride, his standing in the community would suffer through his association

The ducking stool was designed to publicly humiliate those who indulged in gossip. (Bettmann/CORBIS)

with an unsavory wife. Many women turned to the courts to quash gossip and restore their reputations.

Slander was a legally actionable offense, and it was the most common reason women were involved in court proceedings. Roughly half of the slander cases brought before the courts involved a woman, either as a target of the slander (plaintiff) or the cause of the gossip (defendant). Gender played an important role in the type and circumstances surrounding slander. Men were most likely to sue over allegations of theft or fraud. Most suits initiated by women occurred because of allegations of sexual misconduct or witchcraft. Although most men were slandered by fellow men, a woman was as likely to be slandered by another woman as a man. The slander suits involving men were usually the result of face-to-face confrontations, whereas those involving women were the result of behind-the-back gossip.

Men often sued on behalf of slander directed toward their wives or daughters. Allegations that a wife or daughter was promiscuous reflected badly on the ability of a man to keep control over his household. High-ranking men, such as judges or governors, were particularly likely to sue, because if they could not control their women, how could they be trusted with the administration of a community?

Slander cases were common occurrences in the seventeenth century, but by the late eighteenth century they were in sharp decline. As a general rule, the smaller the community, the more likely the county court was to be hearing slander cases. Gossip was more prevalent and damaging in small towns. Some anthropologists have noted that gossip is one of the few forms of entertainment in isolated villages. In communities where everyone is well known to one another, a damaged reputation severely limited choices for an outcast. Larger towns offered anonymity to people whose reputations were less than sterling. Gossip was not as rampant or as damaging in urban areas, resulting in far fewer lawsuits.

If the plaintiff was successful in her slander suit, the punishment for the defendant (the spreader of the gossip) was usually a fine and a public apology. Many plaintiffs angrily refused to accept the fine, claiming the point of their lawsuit was the restoration of their good name. Women who were found guilty of spreading a slander were often unable to pay anything more than the most modest of fines and were whipped instead.

The motivation for women to initiate slander is fascinating. In cases where a woman genuinely believed herself to have been cheated, she would have considered her speech to be a beneficial service to her neighbors. Looking through court records of slander cases several centuries after the event, it is rarely possible to determine if women who accused others of theft or fraud were justified in their actions, did so as the result of a misunderstanding, or were motivated by malice.

The most common allegation was of sexual misconduct, where motivation is more clear-cut in the historical record. When men accused a woman of promiscuity, it was usually the result of bragging or revenge for a frustrated sexual proposition. When they broadly proclaimed a woman to be a whore or a bawd, they often later admitted to have been turned down by the woman after a sexual proposition. In cases where they testified to having been intimate with a woman, a man enhanced his own reputation at the expense of the woman's, whether the event actually occurred or was fabricated.

In cases where women gossiped about the sexual promiscuity of other women, the motivations were different. Their talk was motivated by a desire to punish women they believed to be disreputable. They sought to uphold community standards by stigmatizing one who dared step outside the bounds of respectable behavior. Although men on the losing end of a sex slander case often admitted their slander was a fabrication, women rarely did so. Even though the information they reported was some-

times second- or third-hand accounts of misconduct, they typically insisted the plaintiff was indeed guilty of promiscuity.

The Ducking Stool

Along with the stockade and pillory, the ducking stool stands as a symbol of humiliating public punishments used in colonial days. The ducking stool is unique in that it was to be used almost exclusively on women. They took various forms, but all ducking stools were designed to plunge a woman into water several times as a punishment for gossip or being a "scold." A chair or bench was suspended over a pond, and the woman was dunked as often as the sentence dictated, to "cool her immoderate heat."

Gossip was not a crime, but it could border on slander when uncontrolled. Women were warned against gossiping, as it was unladylike and unneighborly. Likewise, a scolding woman was considered undesirable. The ideal woman was meek and obedient. Women who ordered their husbands about, made heavy demands, or were quarrelsome, were labeled scolds. The ducking stool was considered a suitable punishment for any woman who talked too much, whether her offense was gossip or scolding.

The ducking stool is one of those folkloric punishments that might loom larger in the imagination than it ever did in life. It does not appear to have been used in New England, although several references to ducking women appear in Virginia records. One town that lacked a ducking stool sentenced a "scolding queen" to be ducked three times off the side of a ship lying in the James River. In 1708 the Common Council of Philadelphia recommended the construction of a ducking stool, but it was apparently never done, because they were still complaining about the lack of one in 1718.

See also Crime and Punishment

Further Reading

Dayton, Cornelia Hughes. *Women before the Bar: Gender, Law and Society in Connecticut, 1639–1789.* Chapel Hill: University of North Carolina Press, 1995.
Earle, Alice Morse. *Curious Punishments of Bygone Days.* Chicago: H. S. Stone, 1896.

Fischer, Kirsten. "False, Feigned, and Scandalous Words: Sexual Slander and Racial Ideology among Whites in Colonial North Carolina." In *The Devil's Lane: Sex and Race in the Early South*, ed. Catherine Clinton. New York: Oxford University Press, 1997.

Norton, Mary Beth. "Gender and Defamation in Seventeenth Century Maryland." *William and Mary Quarterly* 44 (1987): 3–39.

Thompson, Roger. "Holy Watchfulness and Communal Conformism: The Functions of Defamation in Early New England Communities." *New England Quarterly* 56 (1983): 504–522.

Slavery

It is difficult to write a general article on the lives of female slaves, because their experiences differed so radically, depending on geographic location, nature of their work, family situation, and sympathy of their owner. The lives of women who had been captured in Africa were markedly different than those who were born in America. The ability to create and sustain a stable family is often cited as the most important factor in determining a slave's emotional well-being. The other factor that played a major role in the nature of her life depended on if she lived in a rural or urban environment.

Enslaved Women in Rural Environments

The majority of slaves in the American colonies worked in rural farming environments. Large plantations began developing throughout the eighteenth century. Rice and tobacco farming were both enormously labor intensive, and large communities of slaves were established to make these plantations operate.

The day began before dawn with the overseer blowing a horn. Women were involved in almost all aspects of field labor, from planting, growing, and harvesting crops to preparing them for market. Slaves usually worked six days per week, laboring in the fields during the day and mending tools, weaving cloth, or other household chores in the evening. Rice and tobacco were the primary cash crops in the southern colonies, although wheat and corn were also grown for consumption. Cotton did not

---

Slave Women's Life on George Washington's Plantation

With the exception of a handful of women who worked indoors and provided domestic service, most slave women who lived on large, rural plantations performed strenuous manual labor. An excerpt from George Washington's journal testifies to this fact:

> Friday, January 4, 1788:
> Ride to all the plantations.
> At Muddy Hole, the men were getting rails and the women making fences.
> At Dogue Run, the men were cutting coal-wood and the women hoeing swamp as yesterday.
> At French's the men were cutting and mauling fence stakes and the women leveling old ditches and grubbing.
> At the Ferry, the men were getting stakes, making racks, etc. and the women thinning trees in the swamp.

Source: Berkin, Carol, and Leslie Horowitz, eds. *Women's Voices, Women's Lives: Documents in Early American History.* Boston: Northeastern University Press, 1998.

---

become a widespread crop until the end of the colonial period.

Rice was the most labor-intensive crop. Most plantations that grew rice needed between thirty-five and seventy-five slaves. Rice had been cultivated in Africa as far back as the first century A.D., and African women had long traditions of raising and winnowing the crop. Fields were planted with seedlings in early spring, and throughout the summer the fields were manually flooded, drained, and weeded. Cutting the rice stalks was a woman's job, as was cleaning and whitening the rice using a mortar and pestle. Winnowing was performed through the use of wide, flat baskets called fanners. The slave women weaved these baskets, using traditional African techniques, intertwining marsh grass into cords wrapped with strands of saw palmetto reeds. After the rice had been pounded by mortar and pestle, it was transferred to the fanner basket, where it was repeatedly tossed in the air, allowing the husk to be blown away.

Tobacco farming was the other crop that dominated the lives of a significant portion of American slaves. Slave women began nurturing tobacco seedlings in the late winter. By spring the plants were ready to be transferred to the fields. This backbreaking work was the task of both men and women. Individual slaves were assigned specific rows, so the overseer could monitor the quantity and quality of their work. Each seedling needed to have a mound of soil carefully built around it. Throughout the growing season the plants needed to have new shoots trimmed to control their growth. Because tobacco was highly susceptible to infestation by worms, such pests needed to be manually plucked off. Women working in the fields would hike their dresses up so their skirts would not damage the plant's leaves. Harvesting the tobacco was the most labor-intensive part of the job, with both men and women toiling all day and even building bonfires to work into the night.

The diet of rural slaves was limited, consisting almost entirely of ground cornmeal and a small amount of pork. Many slaves were able to augment their diets by tending to small garden plots allowed for personal use. Slave women were known to grow potatoes, pumpkins, peanuts, melons, and peas. Sometimes they consumed this produce, although most were permitted to sell it in the open market. A thriving internal economy developed on many of the larger plantations, where slaves were able to put their limited free time to use cultivating a wide variety of goods and produce for sale. Slave women marketed their goods to other slaves, traveling peddlers, and their own plantation master or mistress.

Fieldwork consumed a female slave's days from late winter through late autumn. The remaining months would be spent repairing fences, making clothing, and improving irrigation systems. Although most women were put to work in the fields, some were assigned to domestic work inside the master's home. This work was not as physically demanding as fieldwork, and the physical environment was vastly more comfortable than the sweltering fields. These domestic workers cleaned house, cooked and served meals, cared for children, and assisted in the production of clothing. Many of them would have lived in either the house or the kitchen.

Although the physical environment of a domestic slave was more comfortable than that of a fieldworker, it brought a unique set of stresses. Living in close proximity to their master and on call twenty-four hours a day, these women did not have the psychological respite from work that the field slaves did. Because they lived in or near the house, they were not able to return to their families at the end of the day. Plantation masters and mistresses had a different set of standards for their household slaves. Domestic slaves were expected to assimilate into the Anglo lifestyle to a far greater extent than their counterparts who worked in the field. Their English needed to be good, their dress had to be more in accord with European norms, and their behavior needed to conform to Christian, European standards. This process of acculturation created a sense of alienation between the house slaves and the field slaves.

Enslaved Women in Urban Environments

The nature of work, family patterns, and acculturation for enslaved women in urban environments were markedly different than what was experienced in rural life. There were few large units of slave workers in towns. Approximately one-third of urban slaves were the only slave of a particular master. Another third were one of two, and the final third were part of a small group of slaves. These slaves lived and worked side by side with whites. They became more familiar with the language, religion, and culture of the dominant white population. African culture was far less a part of these slaves' lives, and acculturation to white social norms took place in a few years, rather than a few generations, as happened on large rural plantations.

It was not uncommon for urban slaves to perform skilled labor, although men did most of the skilled work. We have records of slave blacksmiths, dockworkers, tanners, and shipbuilders. Slave women would have worked primarily in domestic service, usually cleaning and laundering. Food preparation was far less burdensome in towns, where cheese,

The Old Plantation. This circa 1790s watercolor view shows African American slaves dancing and playing music before a backdrop of plantation buildings. (Abby Aldrich Rockefeller Folk Art Museum, Colonial Williamsburg Foundation, Williamsburg, VA)

bread, meat, and other staples were purchased rather than produced. Though cooking still made up part of a typical slave woman's day, most of her time would have been spent washing, ironing, tending the fires, shopping for supplies, and supervising children. Some urban slave women would have worked in commercial establishments. Government buildings needed cleaning, taverns needed cooks, and shops needed clerks.

Slaves living in a town were likely to be hired out during slow periods. A middle-class family that could not afford a slave might rent one to help once a week for laundry work. Such an arrangement was a double-edged sword for the slave. It meant that she was unable to take advantage of slow periods at home because she was rented out to perform hard

labor elsewhere. But it expanded her world by allowing her freedom of travel, the opportunity to have contact with another part of town, and possibly mix with other black slaves or free servants. On occasion the slave might be permitted to keep a small percentage of her earnings. Historian Loren Schweninger recounts the story of Sally, a slave woman in Nashville, Tennessee, who generated such lucrative fees from hiring out that her master permitted her to set up a shop where she took in laundry and sold homemade soap. She was able to save enough from these activities to purchase the freedom of her son, although Sally herself died a slave.

Life in an urban environment expanded opportunities for trade and commerce, in which many slave women were allowed to participate. All towns had marketplaces in which goods were traded or sold. During a slave woman's few hours of free time she might be permitted to grow vegetables in a small plot of land, spin some cloth, or piece together items of clothing. Usually in exchange for a cut in the profits, slave owners permitted these women to sell the items at the marketplace. They might have peddled their goods through the streets, though many had stalls or even worked in retail shops. In some towns, such as Charleston, black women traders outnumbered white traders. Over time the Charleston marketplace evolved into a lively place for black women to meet, trade, and socialize.

Although the physical conditions of work in towns was not as backbreaking as in agricultural work, the life of an urban slave woman would have been a lonely one. Finding a mate would have been difficult, because slaveholdings were too small for her to find a husband within her same household. Should she marry a slave from a neighboring household, it was unlikely she would ever be able to cohabit with her husband. If she were fortunate, her master would not mind if she bore children. Although slave children were an economic boon to a southern plantation owner, in a small, urban household they were a burden. A woman who bore a child risked having the infant sold south, where it could easily be folded into plantation society. Some urban colonists would sell a pregnant slave, rather than undertake the inconvenience and expense of having their servant raise an infant under their roof.

The family life of urban slaves was more tenuous than that of those who lived on large plantations. Families were more likely to be broken up through sale or death of the owner. If a slave family grew too large, there was rarely enough work to fully occupy the children. If they were fortunate, the master arranged to hire these children out for day labor. More likely, the children would have been sold. Although a slave woman on a southern plantation might spend her entire life in one place, it was not uncommon for an urban slave to have three or more owners over the course of her life. Each transfer represented a break with surroundings and possibly family members.

Despite the loneliness and lack of community experienced by slaves in urban environments, they had far greater opportunity for establishing independence, and possibly obtaining their freedom. Especially in the North, where hostile racial attitudes were not so firmly entrenched, manumission of slaves was not an extraordinary event. Slave women often had the opportunity to earn an independent income and thereby save toward purchasing their freedom. Northern slave owners were more likely to have conflicted attitudes regarding the moral justification for owning slaves, which often translated into manumission upon the owner's death. There were a number of abolition societies that were ready to render aid to slaves who were working toward their freedom or had recently been freed. Finally, it was easier for a slave to escape in an environment where they had permission to move freely about a town.

Dress and Appearance

Newly arrived slaves from Africa were quickly stripped of their clothing and dressed in garb that conformed to European standards of modesty. Surprisingly, most of this clothing was not alien to African women. European penetration into West Africa had resulted in the trade of European fabric and clothing styles, which by the seventeenth century had become status symbols among well-to-do Africans. Slaves were given cast-off clothing, generally very drab and loose fitting. As they spent more time in America, they were likely to acquire other, more colorful pieces of clothing. Masters occasionally rewarded slaves with such items. Slaves also had the opportunity to earn a few coins from selling produce and could purchase some fabric on their own.

Until slaves reached puberty, they wore androgynous clothing, usually a long shirt or smock. It was a mark of impending adulthood when girls began wearing dresses and boys donned trousers and a shirt. It was at this time they would receive their first pair of shoes.

Women who were house slaves were better dressed than their agricultural sisters. House slaves generally wore calico dresses or perhaps a fitted blouse and skirt. Despite a 1735 law passed by the South Carolina legislature that prohibited slaves from wearing the cast-off clothing of their masters, this regulation was widely ignored by both slaves and whites. Other colonies passed similar laws, believing well-dressed slaves had either stolen the clothing, were preparing to escape and "pass" as whites, or were simply masquerading above their station. There was particular concern about well-dressed female slaves. A beautiful slave wearing fine clothes caused suspicious minds to speculate she had illicit intimacy with the master or his son, neither of which would have been a comforting thought for the mistress of the house.

Choice of dress differed on workdays and on Sunday. Serviceable, homespun clothing would have been worn most days. Kerchiefs tied around the head were common for both male and female slaves. It was on Sunday that slave women were allowed to dress themselves however colorfully their imagination and resources would allow. They often combined clothing in a manner odd to European eyes. The more color and patterns that could be added to an outfit, the grander it appeared to a slave.

Slaves brought from Africa their love of vivid patterns and contrasting colors. Slave women were often responsible for the production and manufacture of fabric on a plantation. Drawing on a rich knowledge of botanical plants, slave women knew how to dye fabric in a way that made slave clothing distinctive and unique. Sometimes they merely dyed threads that were used to embellish plain cloth or create deliberate clashes in colors, patterns, and stripes.

The spinning, dyeing, and embellishment of fabric would have been done on the slaves' own time. After the day's end, during inclement weather, or on Sunday, slave women often gathered in circles and fashioned clothing designed to reflect their personalities and culture.

Hair was also an important means of self-expression for black women. Grooming and dressing hair were important social rituals in Africa, and this was one tradition that was easy to transport to the New World. Elaborate hairstyles could denote class, gender, age, and status. Black hair could be cut, shaved, wrapped, teased, or braided into striking designs. The most elaborate hairstyles were reserved for Sunday. Early in the week women would braid their hair with long threads, then wrap their heads with kerchiefs to preserve the braiding. On Sunday or holidays the kerchief and braids would be removed, and the hair brushed out into a smooth, lightly curled style.

Throughout most of the eighteenth century, slave women seemed to have preferred long hair, but by the 1790s the fashion had shifted to short hair. They typically wore bandannas wrapped around their hair. It served many purposes, from helping to set a hairstyle to keeping the hair clean and providing protection from the sun. Some masters resorted to cropping hair as a means of punishing slave women. This punishment is a sign of the value a woman placed on her hair, and the pride she took in her personal appearance.

Recreation

No slave had abundant time for recreation, and women had far less than men. After sundown and on Sundays men could relax, smoke, and indulge in games. Women used the time to teach children, cook meals, and mend clothing. Some of the women's chores bordered on recreation. Women enjoyed embroidering elaborate patterns on clothing, and this could be done in a social setting. Likewise, spending relaxing time with their children was not considered a chore.

Records indicate that young slave girls often participated in footraces. Slaves were permitted to attend county fairs, where they both watched and participated in races. The fairs also provided an important social and economic outlet for slaves. Women could barter items they had made, such as handmade baskets, embroidered cloth, or perhaps vegetables they had grown in their own garden plot. If there were no slave men of courting age on their property, this might be a chance for young women to meet eligible men from other farms.

Music played an important part of recreation. Drums were always a central part of African musical tradition, but were outlawed by owners because of their association with rebellion. In lieu of drumming, slaves clapped their hands, stamped their feet, and beat their thighs to create a rhythm. Other African-style instruments, such as banjos and rattles, were used to create music. Songs during the colonial period were distinctly different from the songs of sorrow that would characterize nineteenth-century African American music. Colonial slaves tended to borrow more heavily from African tradition, which were satires that ridiculed improper behavior. Most melodies were based on improvisational lyrics and could be heard in the work fields and around cooking fires in the evenings.

As slaves converted to Christianity, they eagerly embraced hymns and spirituals. White ministers noted that black attendance at services was markedly higher in churches that permitted singing. The African American spirituals were a distinctive blend of call-and-response style, punctuated with foot stamping and hand clapping. The exuberant spirituals eventually evolved into what has been considered the first truly American musical form of expression.

See also African American Women and the American Revolution; African American Women, Free; First-Generation Immigrants; Freeman, Elizabeth; Islamic Women; Marriage and Family among Enslaved Women

Further Reading

Berkin, Carol. *First Generations: Women in Colonial America.* New York: Hill and Wang, 1996.

Berlin, Ira. "The Slave Trade and the Development of Afro-American Society in English Mainland North America, 1619–1775." *Southern Studies* 20 (1981): 335–349.

Gould, L. Virginia. "Urban Slavery–Urban Freedom: The Manumission of Jacqueline Lemelle." In *More Than Chattel: Black Women and Slavery in the Americas,* eds. David Barry Gaspar and Darlene Clark Hine. Bloomington: Indiana University Press, 1996.

Monaghan, E. Jennifer. "Reading for the Enslaved, Writing for the Free: Reflections on Liberty and Literacy." *Proceedings of the American Antiquarian Society* 108 (1998): 309–341.

Olwell, Robert. "Loose, Idle and Disorderly: Slave Women in the Eighteenth Century Charleston Marketplace." In *More Than Chattel: Black Women and Slavery in the Americas,* eds. David Barry Gaspar and Darlene Clark Hine. Bloomington: Indiana University Press, 1996.

Pierson, William D. "African American Culture." In *Encyclopedia of the North American Colonies,* ed. Jacob Ernest Cooke. New York: Charles Scribner's Sons, 1993.

Sanders, Eulanda Annette. "African American Slave Appearance: Cultural Analysis of Slave Women's Narratives." Dissertation. University of Nebraska, 1997.

Sobel, Mechal. *The World They Made Together: Black and White Values in Eighteenth Century Virginia.* Princeton, NJ: Princeton University Press, 1987.

Schweninger, Loren. "A Slave Family in the Antebellum South." *Journal of Negro History* 60 (1975): 29–44.

White, Shane, and Graham White. "Slave Clothing and African American Culture in the Eighteenth and Nineteenth Centuries." *Past and Present* 148 (1995): 149–186.

———. "Slave Hair and African American Culture in the Eighteenth and Nineteenth Centuries." *Journal of Southern History* 61 (1995): 45–76.

Society of Friends
See Quaker Women

Spanish Colonies, Women in

Life for women of the Spanish colonies that later became part of the United States (Florida, California, Texas, and other southwestern states) was markedly different from those of women in English, Dutch, and French colonies. The most prominent difference was the scarcity of European women. The nature of Spanish colonization, in which large contingents of troops were sent to conquer and hold territory, placed little value on the establishment of families. In the absence of European women, Spanish men turned to Indian women for sexual companionship, though rarely marriage. From the outset of Spanish colonization, there was a large set of mixed-race children, which eventually led to a racially based class system. "Pure-blooded" Spaniards occupied the top level of the hierarchy. Although the actual standard of living for most of these full-blooded Spanish women was not markedly superior to that of women with a mixed-race background, they claimed higher status on the social scale.

Spanish women had two options in colonial America: They could marry or serve the church. Spanish convents were contemplative, meaning the nuns' primary purpose was to pray and serve as spiritual examples of holiness. These nuns did not play active roles in education, medical care, or evangelization. The unpopular decree, the *vida comun*, insisted that nuns simplify their life by renouncing public intellectual pursuits and all worldly goods. This created tensions among many nuns who had come from Spain, where wealthy women had traditionally entered convents with servants and plenty of material goods. Some women worked for the Spanish missions while not actually becoming nuns. These women kept the churches functioning through cooking, cleaning, raising crops, sewing altar cloths, and even repairing the adobe wall on church structures.

Most Spanish women married and became wives and mothers. Life in the Spanish colonies was highly patriarchal, and women were expected to display deference and obedience to their husbands. Because Spanish settlements were sparsely populated with few educational or market institutions, women had great responsibilities within their family. In addition to cooking and domestic chores, they were responsible for teaching and socializing their children. Many Spanish women were illiterate, meaning the education of their families would have been rudimentary at best. The wealthiest families sent their sons back to Spain for formal education, but there was little incentive to provide girls with a quality education.

Unlike English colonies, where families subsisted on agriculture or hunting, most Spanish colonists relied on ranching. Sheep, goats, pigs, and chickens were all raised by Spanish settlers. Slaughter of animals usually occurred during winter to avoid spoilage. What could not be quickly consumed was dried in the sun to make jerky. Small-scale agriculture raised corn, squash, and beans.

Records indicate that life for women in Spanish colonies was spartan. The typical family would have had a small collection of rustic furniture, with little more than a small table, some straight-backed chairs or benches, and a wooden cupboard in the kitchen. Wealth was measured by the number of animals a family owned. Security was always a concern, and most homes were adobe structures built in a fortresslike floor plan, with a courtyard in the center. Doors and windows opened into the courtyard, whereas the outside of the home was heavily protected with sturdy walls and fences. Timber and furniture was scarce, so the home would have had built-in features such as niches and shelving set into the adobe walls. Most decorative features would have been religious in nature, with images of saints and a small altar around which the family prayed.

In the strict, patriarchal world of Spanish America, women occupied a curious position of subordination and reverence. Although they were expected to be docile and obedient to their husbands, they were revered by their children. High value was placed on chastity, and any form of sexuality outside of marriage could destroy a woman's reputation. A single woman might recover from such a scandal, because the scarcity of Spanish women worked in her favor. Far worse was a married woman who committed adultery. If she was childless, she might be cast out from her family.

Despite the patriarchal nature of society, Spanish women enjoyed many legal rights unavailable to Anglo-American women. They were allowed to appear in court and bring lawsuits in their own name. They were permitted to own land in their own name, which was the most important generator of income in the southwest. Spanish daughters generally inherited property on an equal basis with their brothers. These girls were traditionally awarded a substantial dowry upon marriage, which accounted for the majority of their inheritance. Husbands could invest and administer the goods his wife brought into the marriage, but this property clearly remained *her* property. The husband was legally obligated to return the full value of the dowry to the wife's heirs upon her death, or back to the wife should the marriage be terminated. A Spanish widow was entitled to half the estate upon her husband's death, compared with merely one-third of the estate that Anglo-American widows received.

Widowhood was problematic for Spanish women. Hasty remarriages were discouraged, because they were associated with lustful women who lacked respect for their deceased husbands. If a woman had sons old enough to assist her in the operation of the family ranch, she might never remarry. Extended families were the norm in Spanish America, and a widow could rely on the assistance of nearby family members.

Further Reading

Gonzalez, Deena. "Gender Relations: Spanish." In *Encyclopedia of the North American Colonies,* ed. Jacob Ernest Cooke. New York: Charles Scribner's Sons, 1993.

Gutierrez, Ramon. *When Jesus Came, the Corn Mothers Went Away: Marriage, Sexuality, and Power in New Mexico: 1500–1846.* Stanford, CA: Stanford University Press, 1991.

Lamadrid, Enrique R. "Home and Hearth: Spanish." In *Encyclopedia of the North American Colonies,* ed. Jacob Ernest Cooke. New York: Charles Scribner's Sons, 1993.

Rosen, Deborah A. "Women and Property across Colonial America: A Comparison of Legal Systems in New Mexico and New York." *William and Mary Quarterly* 60 (2003): 355–381.

Spies and the American Revolution

Both the British and the patriots used spies during the American Revolution, and many of these spies were women. We know very little about the history of women spies, because the nature of spying is covert. They left few written records, and their existence was known about by only a handful of people. In order to be a successful spy, a person had to be the sort who did not crave public attention or tribute. Information on spying is scanty, but can be pieced together from a few well-known cases.

Most spies were engaged in gathering intelligence about the strengths and plans of the opposing side. General Washington turned to civilians who were living in or near areas occupied by the British to gather information regarding the number of vessels in the harbor, the number of troops stationed in

a city, and what sort of fortifications had been built. The kidnapping of important officers for ransom or trade was rampant on both sides, and the whereabouts of officers' quarters was valuable intelligence. Civilians were ideally placed to gather this sort of information. The difficulty was in communicating the information to the other side without arousing suspicion. Few spies dared to commit information to paper, so word of mouth was the preferred means of communication. Civilians were not free to travel through enemy-occupied territory, so creative means for transmitting information needed to be devised. Women tended to arouse less suspicion than men when asking for a pass to travel and were therefore often included as parts of spy rings.

The Culper spy ring, based in New York City, was one of the most successful and famous groups of patriot spies. New York City was under the control of the British for much of the war. So strong was the British grip on the city that loyalists throughout the nation fled to New York, and American prisoners of war were kept either in the city or on one of the infamous prison ships docked in the harbor. The Culper spy ring was headed by Robert Townsend, a journalist and owner of a dry goods store. His position as a journalist allowed him entrée into a variety of social functions throughout the city, where he gossiped with society hostesses and junior officers. His gregarious and lighthearted demeanor opened doors. His work as a merchant allowed him access to people moving in and out of the city. When he learned information of importance, he passed messages, written in code, to a merchant who had been given permission to transport goods in and out of the city. Anna Strong was a member of the Culper spy ring. Her home was located across the bay from the city. She hung a black petticoat on her wash line when Caleb Brewster, a local fisherman, was nearby and prepared to carry messages. She used a series of handkerchiefs to signal to the spies exactly where in the bay Brewster's boat could be found.

Other spies for the American side included Lydia Darragh (1729–1789) and Sarah Bradlee Fulton. Lydia Darragh was a "fighting Quaker," someone who supported the war, despite the pacifist philosophy of her religion. A number of British troops had

The Mystery of Agent 355

The Culper spy ring made heavy use of coded numbers in their messages, revealing the existence of an intriguing woman known only as Agent 355. So thin is the historical documentation of Agent 355 that her very existence has been questioned. Tradition claims that 355 was a New York society lady who was able to supply Robert Townsend, her lover and a leader of the spy ring, with valuable information. In October 1780 she was captured by the British, possibly based on information provided by Benedict Arnold. She was held on the prison ship *Jersey*, notorious for its brutally foul living conditions. There she gave birth to Townsend's son and later died in the cramped and filthy environment. The child, named Robert Townsend Jr., was taken off the ship and raised by his father.

The only firm evidence of Agent 355's existence is a single line in a coded message written by one of the Culper leaders, which read: "I intend to visit 727 before long and think by the assistance of 355, a lady of my acquaintance, shall be able to out wit them all." 727 was the code for New York, but it is unclear if 355 was a reference to a specific woman or merely a code for women in general. All other evidence of Agent 355's tragic story is purely speculative. Robert Townsend became a lifelong bachelor, but raised an illegitimate son. Robert Townsend Jr., the child supposedly born to Agent 355, grew to be a prominent member of New York society and sponsored a memorial to the patriots who had died aboard the infamous prison ships.

Skepticism about the truth of this story is raised by the age of Robert Townsend Jr., who was probably born too late to correspond with Agent 355's October 1780 capture. Some New York genealogists believe his mother to have been Mary Banvard, Townsend's housekeeper.

The truth surrounding Agent 355 will probably never be known. The nature of spying is to leave no traces, and if she existed, Agent 355 was successful in this objective.

Sources: Dewan, George. "The Mystery of Agent 355: Unraveling the Case of the Patriot Spy Who Never Was." *Newsday*, 22 January 1998, A19.

Miller, Nathan. *Spying for America: The Hidden History of U.S. Intelligence.* New York: Dell, 1989.

been quartered in her Philadelphia home in late 1777. Mrs. Darragh occasionally eavesdropped on the soldiers' conversations, and late one night, she learned of plans to launch a surprise attack on Washington's camp at Whitemarsh. The next day Mrs. Darragh obtained permission to leave the city in order to purchase flour. Outside the city, she changed her course and walked thirteen miles in order to deliver the message to the American troops. As a result, the Americans were well prepared for the raid launched by the British, who retreated after a few days.

Sarah Bradlee Fulton also carried dispatches through enemy lines, but is perhaps best known as the "Mother of the Boston Tea Party." On the night of the famous protest, members of the Sons of Liberty gathered at Fulton's house to be made up to look like Indians. Following the event, participants returned to Fulton's house to celebrate. Anne Trotter Bailey and Emily Geiger have also gone down in history as women who carried messages across British lines on behalf of the patriots.

The wife of British general Thomas Gage was suspected of spying for the patriots. Born in America, Margaret Kemble Gage was known to have strong sympathy for the patriot cause. It is believed she might have passed information about British plans to the rebels just before the Battle of Lexington. Shortly after this battle, Mrs. Gage was sent to England for the duration of the war.

The British had their share of female spies. Ann Bates was a loyalist teacher in Philadelphia. In 1778 she began posing as a peddler, following the American troops to sell utensils and other goods to the needy soldiers. All the while, she was counting troops and taking inventory of their weapons and supplies. This information was passed back to the British whenever she could arrange it.

Spying carried risks, even for women. Lorenda Holmes of New York spied for the British by carrying letters across lines. After she was captured by patriots, she was stripped naked and exposed on the public streets. She later recounted that during the event, she endured no broken bones, but only "shame and horror of the mind" (Norton 1976, 398). A few months later she was caught assisting

Patriotic American woman serving tea to gather information from a British officer, American Revolution. (North Wind / North Wind Picture Archives)

fleeing loyalists to safety behind British lines. An American officer held her foot to burning coals as punishment.

The most infamous of spies was Mrs. Benjamin Arnold. Although her husband's reputation bore the brunt of American anger, Peggy Shippen Arnold is widely believed to have been an active participant in her husband's schemes. Although born in America, Peggy had strong loyalist sympathies and introduced her husband to prominent members of the British command. It is not clear what role she played in convincing her husband to switch loyalties, but the British government was grateful for her assistance. Following the war, the queen awarded her with a generous pension, even though her unpopular husband was never warmly received by either side.

Most women who spied, carried letters, or slipped disinformation to the opposing side have not been remembered by history. One of the key hallmarks of a successful spy is the ability to leave no traces. We know that women spied, but we do not know many names.

The motivation for these women was the same thing that motivated their husbands to pick up a musket and fight. Most did so out of love of country, although others might have had more practical motivations. Lydia Darragh made her thirteen-mile journey because her son was stationed with the regiment slated to be attacked within the week. Lorenda Holmes continued to spy for the British, even after having been terrorized and humiliated by the patriots. These women did not gain monetary benefit, merely the satisfaction of working toward a cause they believed in.

See also Arnold, Margaret Shippen; Wright, Patience Lovell

Further Reading

DePauw, Linda Grant. *Founding Mothers: Women of the Revolutionary Era.* Boston: Houghton Mifflin, 1973.

Norton, Mary Beth. "Eighteenth Century Women in Peace and War: The Case of the Loyalists." *William and Mary Quarterly* 33 (1976): 386–409.

Randall, Willard Sterne. "Mrs. Benedict Arnold." *MHQ: The Quarterly Journal of Military History* 4, no. 2 (1992): 80–89.

Samuelson, Nancy B. "Revolutionary War Women and the Second Oldest Profession." *Minerva* 7, no. 2 (1989): 16–25.

Spy Letters of the American Revolution: From the Collections of the Clements Library. University of Michigan Clements Library. http://www.si.umich.edu/spies/ (accessed 31 May 2003).

Spooner, Bathsheba
Murderer (c. 1746–1778)

Although there was no doubt as to the guilt of Bathsheba Spooner, her controversial death sentence raised serious questions regarding the execution of women in Massachusetts.

Bathsheba Spooner was the privileged daughter of Brigadier General Timothy Ruggles. She was profoundly unhappy in her marriage to Joshua Spooner, a man to whom she confessed "an utter aversion." In March 1777, Bathsheba took an ailing continental soldier into her home. Probably suffering from influenza, Ezra Ross was nursed back to health by Bathsheba. He rejoined the army, but visited the Spooner house on two more occasions in the coming year. At some point the two embarked on a romantic relationship, and Bathsheba became pregnant. Knowing she could not pass the child off as belonging to her husband, Joshua, she panicked and began plotting his murder. She enlisted the aid of her lover and two additional soldiers, promising them money and alcohol in exchange for the murder.

On the night of 1 March 1778, Joshua Spooner was beaten to death and dumped headfirst down his own well. All three soldiers were apprehended the following day, confessed to the crime, and named Bathsheba as the instigator. The four conspirators were tried, found guilty, and sentenced to hang.

Bathsheba Spooner begged for a delay of execution until her child could be born. Condemned women who were known to be pregnant were always permitted to carry a child to term, both in England and America. Spooner was examined by a panel of twelve women, all of whom signed a statement declaring she was not pregnant. Spooner appealed their finding, asserting that she knew herself to be approximately four months pregnant. She wrote in a letter to the Council of Massachusetts that her child was "innocent of the faults of her who bears it, and has, I beg leave to say, a right to the existence which God has begun to give it" (Navas 1996, 117).

A second physical examination of Bathsheba took place less than three weeks later, at which several of the examining matrons switched their opinions, claiming they believed the condemned to be quick with child. Two of the examiners were adamant in their conviction that Bathsheba was not with child, and authorities chose to proceed with the execution.

The insistence upon a speedy hanging for Bathsheba raises questions as to the motives of the authorities. Bathsheba's father was the notorious Brigadier General Timothy Ruggles, whose powerful loyalist support for the British made his name anathema in Massachusetts. It is possible that the intolerance shown to Bathsheba was prompted in part owing to political vengeance. The legal validity of her execution was further tarnished by the council member who authorized the final warrant for execution, John Avery Jr., the murder victim's stepbrother. The failure of Avery to recuse himself from this case added another layer of unseemly bias to the execution.

Although Bathsheba never formally confessed to the crime, on the scaffold she acknowledged that she "died justly." Following the execution an autopsy was performed per Bathsheba's request. The perfectly formed five-month-old male fetus proved the state had caused the death of a child in their haste to carry out the execution of a notoriously unpopular woman. Bathsheba roused the wrath of her community for her adultery, the murder of her husband, and stubborn loyalist sympathies. They retaliated against her by refusing to allow her a few additional weeks to prove the existence of her pregnancy. The horror of executing a pregnant woman so upset the community that the execution of females was called into question. Although there were two additional women executed in Massachusetts before female execution was outlawed, never again would a woman claiming pregnancy be summarily executed in the American colonies.

See also Crime and Punishment

Further Reading

Navas, Deborah. *Murdered by His Wife.* Amherst: University of Massachusetts Press, 1999.
———. "New Light on the Bathsheba Spooner Execution." *Proceedings of the Massachusetts Historical Society* 108 (1996): 115–122.

Sports and Leisure

The pursuit of sporting activities has always served several functions. It is a healthy outlet for competitive impulses, an inexpensive recreational activity, and provides physical exercise. The women of early America, although they engaged in some small-scale sporting activities, had limited interest in the pursuit of sports. Daily life on a farm already had a high element of physical exertion for a typical woman. Hauling water, preparing meals, tending the vegetable gardens, and caring for farmyard animals left little need for women to seek additional physical release through sports.

Men led even more strenuous lives, but still sought out sports as a channel for competitive tendencies. Determining who could throw an axe farther, run a faster footrace, or win tests of strength and dexterity have always been important components of male bonding and competition. A desire to display physical prowess was contrary to the feminine ideal in early America. Although there were no misconceptions that women were delicate flowers to be preserved from manual labor, it was considered unseemly for a woman to make a display of her physical competence. Modesty was among the highest of virtues for women throughout the colonies, and the competitive aspect of sports did not flourish among adult women.

Sport and work sometimes intersected, as with recreational fishing. There is evidence that fishing was acceptable activity for women, but hunting was not. Women's perceived lack of physical strength and dexterity with firearms put hunting off limits to most women. Gardening was another activity some women used as a physical and creative outlet, rather than being a sheer economic necessity.

Girls were permitted to indulge in some competitive sports. Footraces were popular among girls in European settlements, Native American villages, and among the daughters of slaves. The farther south and the poorer the girl, the more likely she was to compete in sports. The Puritan reserve of New Englanders tended to discourage participation in sports and games as soon as a girl left childhood.

Another barrier to be overcome before sports could be an acceptable activity for women was the deep suspicion of leisure in early America. Time and labor were the most valuable commodities in the early settlements. Daylight hours not used for productive labor should be directed toward the education of children, religious activities, or an endeavor to make the home more pleasant. Settlers acknowledged that the sheer exhaustion caused by the enormous burdens of work needed to be punctuated with periods of rest. Even the most devout Puritans condoned periods of daily rest, considered necessary if labor was to be performed efficiently. Sporting was not considered "rest." Puritans believed sport aroused competitive passions, drained physical strength from the body, and took parents away from their responsibilities. Sport for adults was therefore a luxury to be indulged in only occasionally. Sports for youngsters were considered a normal part of childhood, but women were expected to set aside such games when they came into adulthood.

Many ordinary chores performed by women could be done in a manner that suggested recreation. Fishing and clamming could be done by groups of women who congregated specifically for the activity. Early American women engaged in

Women seated at spinning wheels and reels in an eighteenth-century drawing room. Women could enjoy sporting activities that encouraged cooperative activities rather than individual competition. One of the few competitive activities indulged in by women was spinning contests. (Christel Gerstenberg/CORBIS)

spinning matches to see who could produce more yarn in a given period of time. Community gatherings, such as Muster Days or Election Days, provided an opportunity for sports to gain an inroad into respectable society. Footraces were highly popular among the younger set. Impromptu ball games took place among the assembled townspeople. Communal events provided an easy rationalization for indulging in sport.

Middle- and upper-class women had other forms of physical recreation. They were less likely to be exhausted from manual labor, so their need for a physical outlet was greater than that of their working-class counterparts. Rules of decorum prevented unladylike sports like footraces, but boating and horseback riding were permissible. Dancing was also a highly popular diversion. Although all classes could engage in traditional folk dancing, well-to-do women were trained in formal dancing styles. Rather than attending the dance in a barn, as

the typical colonial women would have done, wealthy women danced in spacious private homes.

Sporting in the southern colonies was often stratified by class. Annual tournaments in which men competed in games of strength and skill were strictly limited to "gentlemen." Although women clearly were not permitted to compete, they participated as spectators. Horse racing was also wildly popular among the wealthy. Women enjoyed the social environment at these races, often partaking in the rampant gambling common among southern gentry. A notice in the 19 November 1736 *Virginia Gazette* announced a number of sporting events for the men and a beauty contest to determine "the handsomest maid."

Many of the sporting activities indulged in by women encouraged cooperative activities rather than individual competition. Dances, candle dippings, fishing parties, or berry picking were physical activities women engaged in that lacked the competitive angle so common among male sports. One of the few competitive activities indulged in by women was spinning contests. Women divided themselves into groups, either by neighborhood, extended families, or skills, and set about spinning as many skeins as possible within a limited period of time. Prizes were awarded to the winning group. Even in spinning contests, women usually competed as a team, rather than as individuals. Spinning contests faded in popularity after the mechanization of yarn production removed this chore from most women's realm of activities.

As living conditions improved in colonial America, the stigma associated with leisure sports diminished. Women who had access to a boat might paddle a canoe or sail a small sloop. Most families possessed at least one horse, and horseback riding was common among women. By the late eighteenth century, sidesaddles were in vogue among upper-class women. Walks in the countryside, fishing trips, and canoeing were acceptable activities for women. In northern areas, ice-skating and sleigh rides were common winter sports. In the South, it was not uncommon for a woman to go swimming. Always clothed in their shift or a nightshirt, women took advantage of swimming primarily to cool down during the sweltering summer heat.

Following the American Revolution, gender roles in society underwent rapid development. For men, the "cult of manliness" did away with the silk stockings, wigs, and elaborate ruffled shirts. Men now dressed more soberly and were expected to display masculine ideals of strength through vigorous sports, hunting, wrestling, and reckless horse racing. At the same time, the "cult of domesticity" created new expectations for women. In contrast to ruggedly male roles, the ideal woman was to be a model of reserve and delicacy. Although indulging in leisure activities was permissible for women, vigorous physical activity was frowned on. Upper-class women were not to engage in an impromptu afternoon swim or a rollicking harvest dance. Rather, any display of physical strength or stamina was associated with the laboring classes.

The cult of domesticity only embraced the uppermost tiers of society. Working-class women

could not afford the luxury of frailty. Sporting became more popular in the early national period. Ball fields were set aside specifically for sporting events. Sporting equipment, such as badminton rackets and baseball bats, became commercially available for the first time. Although most of this equipment was used by men, women in rural or working-class environments indulged in the growing American interest in sports.

Further Reading

Gerlach, Larry R. "Recreations." In *Encyclopedia of the North American Colonies,* ed. Jacob Ernest Cooke. New York: Charles Scribner's Sons, 1993.

Parks, Roberta J. "Embodied Selves: The Rise and Development of Concern for Physical Education, Active Games and Recreation for American Women, 1776–1865." *Journal of Sport History* 5 (1978): 5–41.

Struna, Nancy L. "Gender and Sporting Practice in Early America, 1750–1810." *Journal of Sport History* 18 (1991): 10–30.

———. *People of Prowess: Sport, Leisure, and Labor in Early Anglo-America.* Urbana: University of Illinois Press, 1996.

———. "The Recreational Experiences of Early American Women." In *Women and Sport: Interdisciplinary Perspectives,* eds. D. Margaret Costa and Sharon R. Guthrie. Champaign, IL: Human Kinetics Press, 1994.

———. "Sport and the Awareness of Leisure." In *Of Consuming Interests: The Style of Life in the Eighteenth Century,* eds. Cary Carson et al. Charlottesville: University Press of Virginia, 1994.

Stepfamilies

For a woman in colonial America, the pattern of early death and rapid remarriage meant that she rarely presided over a traditional nuclear family. Historians Darrett and Anita Rutman provide an excellent example of the complexities caused by colonial patterns of marriage and remarriage. They trace the story of Mary Keeble, who had at least four children with her first husband, George. Following his death she married Robert Beverley in 1666, with whom she had five more children. Mary died in 1678 at the age of forty-one, and her widower immediately married Katherine, herself a widow with a child. Robert and Katherine proceeded to produce four children. Following Robert's death, Katherine remarried and had additional children with a third husband. All of the children born into this household experienced the death of at least one parent and one stepparent. The children in the household were a combination of half- and stepsiblings.

A nuclear family, in which a husband and wife raised their own children to adulthood, was a rarity in early America. Early deaths and the necessity to quickly remarry resulted in complex family structures in which stepparents, stepchildren, and orphaned children lived under one roof. Studies of particular seventeenth-century communities reveal that almost 25 percent of children lost at least one parent before they reached their fifth birthday. Almost 75 percent had lost one or both parents by the time they reached twenty-one. Although it is impossible to analyze the psychological effects that death waged on families, children of early America would have been accustomed to an impermanent family structure. A consequence of this high rate of parental death was the need for extended families to participate in the raising and support of orphaned children.

Remaining a single parent was rarely an option in the seventeenth century. Daily household chores involved food preparation and preservation, butchering, gardening, cleaning, sewing, and tending to young children. Men needed wives for these activities, and women needed the economic earning power of a husband. Records show that a high percentage of widowed women remarried within a year of their husbands' deaths. The use of the terms *now-wives* and *now-husbands* that was common at the time, gives witness to the need to distinguish between the present spouse and one or more deceased spouses.

The blending of various family units together doubtlessly added a tremendous amount of stress into a marriage. Already traumatized by the loss of a parent, children were forced to adjust to additional pressures of stepsiblings and possibly relocating to a new home. Because most colonial homes

had only two or three rooms, living conditions were cramped, and privacy was almost nonexistent.

The prevalence of stepfamilies was dictated in part by geography. The healthier living conditions of New England meant that adults were far more likely to live into old age. Disease and the unhealthy effects of hot climates in the mid-Atlantic and southern colonies led to earlier mortality and a higher rate of remarriages. The average length of marriage in the Chesapeake was between nine and twelve years, whereas in the healthier New England colonies two-thirds of first marriages lasted for more than twenty years.

Colonial patterns of inheritance introduced a complication into stepfamilies. Widows were automatically entitled to one-third of their deceased husband's estate. Children who were old enough to understand the financial implications of remarriage might have tried to dissuade their fathers from remarrying, thus preserving his estate intact for his biological heirs. Furthermore, a new wife who was young enough to bear more children represented an additional threat to future inheritances. These financial considerations were not as callous as they might appear to modern eyes. Young adults were not free to marry until they could establish their own households. Because their labor was devoted to family businesses, it was almost impossible for them to achieve financial independence without the assistance of their parents. The smaller their inheritance was whittled down by remarriage and additional children, the more meager their life was likely to be.

The guardianship of children was not automatically assigned to a surviving biological parent. Studies of wills reveal that men typically assigned guardianship of their children to their wives, even though it was almost a certainty that these women would remarry and place their estates under the control of a stepfather. By the eighteenth century, evolving laws began to permit fathers to establish trusts and entailments to their estates, which would prohibit their widows and future husbands from endangering the inheritance of the children. Couples also wrote premarital contracts to clearly define how property would be passed on to children of previous marriages. In cases where both natural parents were dead, elder siblings were often assigned guardianship of minor children.

See also Orphaned Girls

Further Reading

Berkin, Carol. *First Generations: Women in Colonial America.* New York: Hill and Wang, 1996.

Main, Gloria L. *Peoples of a Spacious Land: Families and Cultures in Colonial New England.* Cambridge, MA: Harvard University Press, 2001.

Rutman, Darrett, and Anita Rutman. "Now Wives and Sons-in-Law: Parental Death in a Seventeenth-Century Virginia County." In *The Chesapeake in the Seventeenth Century: Essays on Anglo-American Society and Politics,* eds. Thad W. Tate and David L. Ammerman. Chapel Hill: University of North Carolina Press, 1979.

Walsh, Lorena S. "Till Death Do Part: Marriage and Family in Seventeenth-Century Maryland." In *The Chesapeake in the Seventeenth Century: Essays on Anglo-American Society and Politics,* eds. Thad W. Tate and David L. Ammerman. Chapel Hill: University of North Carolina Press, 1979.

Suffrage

Women rarely had the opportunity to vote in early America, but this made them little different from other disenfranchised people, including racial minorities, the poor, and recent immigrants. There were a few isolated instances of women who protested their disenfranchisement. In 1648, Margaret Brent requested the right to vote based on her status as a major landholder in Maryland. Her request was dismissed with little discussion.

Early America was governed primarily by English common law, which extended the vote only to men who possessed substantial property. Although there are no reliable statistics for what percentage of the population met the property qualifications in England, the number was roughly 10 percent of adult males. The colonies of early America tended to be slightly more egalitarian, but they retained their concern for limiting the vote to men of property. It was believed that poor people who were dependent on others for employment were not stakeholders in society, and their votes could be bought.

At the time of the American Revolution, each colony drafted its own state constitution. Most states included language that excluded women from the right to vote. Various exclusionary phrases were used. Pennsylvania, Maryland, Delaware, and North Carolina extended the vote to all *freemen.* Other terms used included *white male inhabitant* (Georgia), *free white man* (South Carolina), *male inhabitant* (New York), *male person* (Massachusetts), and simply *man* (Vermont). The only state that did not exclude women from the franchise was New Jersey, whose constitution extended the vote to adult inhabitants "worth £50."

Because New Jersey did not exclude women from voting, any single woman with at least £50 of property was entitled to vote. Married women, because they could own no property exclusive of their husbands, did not qualify to vote. It has been suggested that the ability of women to vote in New Jersey was the result of sloppy wording in the constitution, but there was no outcry against the female vote once it became apparent that women intended to exercise their right to participate in elections.

Between 1776 and 1807 single women of property took an active part in New Jersey elections. The liberal election law in New Jersey also extended the vote to any blacks or immigrants who could meet the property requirement. In the late 1780s when the two-party system began developing, both the Federalist and Republican Parties courted women voters in New Jersey, although there was no emergence of a "women's issues" platform. It has generally been assumed that women and blacks were attracted to the Federalist Party, whereas immigrants and less-wealthy people voted Republican.

In the years prior to the 1808 presidential election, New Jersey reformed its election law to exclude blacks, women, and immigrants. The amendment passed without controversy or outcry from women. Their disenfranchisement was justified as protecting women from the crude world of politics, and there is little to reflect that women complained of the action.

The case of New Jersey was an anomaly. Most women in the early republic never aspired to the vote. Disenfranchisement did not mean a disinterest in public life. Women took an active part in community affairs through church and charity involvement. During times of political unrest they took part in boycotts and petition campaigns. The most common belief about the proper role of women in the political sphere was in their role in raising intelligent, virtuous sons who would safeguard the republic. Not until the abolition movement of the mid-nineteenth century would a feminine consciousness emerge in which women drew a parallel between their disenfranchised and dependent status and that of the powerless and enslaved blacks.

See also Brent, Margaret; Feminism

Further Reading

Baker, Paula. "The Domestication of Politics: Women and American Political Society, 1780–1920." *American Historical Review* 89 (1984): 620–647.

Klinghoffer, Judith Apter, and Lois Elkins. "The Petticoat Electors: Women's Suffrage in New Jersey, 1776–1807." *Journal of the Early Republic* 12 (1992): 159–193.

Zagarri, Rosemarie. "Suffrage and Representation." In *A Companion to the American Revolution*, eds. Jack P. Greene and J. R. Pole. Malden, MA: Blackwell, 2000.

Sumptuary Laws

Clothing has always been an indicator of social position, and it was expected that people would dress in accord with their position in society. That people have often dressed above their station is evidenced by the passing of sumptuary laws, designed to regulate the grandeur of clothing allowed to particular social classes. Sumptuary laws existed in ancient Greece and Rome, feudal Japan, and Renaissance Europe. Although usually regulating manner of dress, they could extend to other displays of extravagance. Edward II of England passed laws against serving too much meat at a feast, and eleventh-century Japanese law regulated the materials houses were made out of as well as their size. A profusion of sumptuary laws regulating dress were passed during the Tudor and Stuart eras in England, and the settlers of America came from a long tradition that understood the rules of dressing in accord with status.

In 1634, the General Court of Massachusetts issued a sumptuary law that prohibited the purchase or wearing of clothing embroidered with gold thread or embellished with lace. The number of slashes on a sleeve was limited to two per sleeve, and there were to be no silver or gold hatbands or belts. Only individuals of great wealth were exempted from these laws, and even they were prohibited from wearing long wigs or excessively great sleeves, because these were considered a tasteless display of riches. Governor John Winthrop was known to rebuke colonists who embellished their homes with too many adornments, noting that such display made others feel badly by comparison, and thus interfered with a communal spirit of the new settlement.

The reasons why colonists believed it was necessary to create limits on how people dressed is an interesting issue for contemporary observers, who might misconstrue these laws as meddlesome interference in private decisions. To the settlers of early America, there was no such thing as private business. They lived in a strange and dangerous world, and the harmony of the community was paramount. Doubtless some thought it was arrogant for people of little means to ape their "betters" and welcomed a quick and easy means of identifying members of the genteel class. Another facet of the law was concern for the squandering of precious resources. A 1651 Massachusetts Bay Colony law explained the distaste for high fashion among the poor, claiming it a "dishonor of God, the scandal of their profession, the consumption of estates, and altogether unsuitable to their poverty" (Fischer 1989, 143). Authority's tender concern for the "consumption of estates" was not without justification. If a member of the community became too impoverished to meet his or her basic needs, the town was required to provide support for that person.

American colonial portrait of Elizabeth Paddy Wensley, seventeenth century. Modest dressing for seventeenth-century Puritan America allowed for formfitting and flattering clothing, as evidenced by portraits of stunningly attired, upper-class women. (Library of Congress)

Although Virginia and other southern colonies had limited sumptuary laws, New England regularly passed and attempted to enforce their legislation to a far greater extent than elsewhere in the colonies. Part of this might have been the rejection of the extravagant fashions popular in England, where men wore long wigs, high heels, and tight breeches. Women's faces were painted, and dramatically plunging necklines were flaunted. These ostentatious, gender-bending styles were part of what drove Puritans to flee Europe, and they sought to prevent such fashions from tainting the purified world they had traveled across the ocean to establish.

Particular styles and articles of clothing were often permitted only to the wealthy. New England proclaimed £200 to be the dividing line between the elite and the working classes. The overwhelming majority of women who were not among the elite were forbidden from wearing silk hoods, excessively wide sleeves, or plunging necklines. Flamboyant display of gold, silver buttons, ribbons, and lace was also forbidden. Hairstyles came under censure, too. In 1679, the Massachusetts General Court was prompted to express their offended sensibilities by writing: "Whereas there is manifest pride openly appearing among us by some women wearing borders of hair, and their cutting, curling, and immodest laying out of their hair," women were advised to choose more modest styles (Fischer 1989, 41). Although a number of women were asked to appear before court for immodest frizzing, curling, and display of hair, it seems none were ever punished for the offense.

In addition to concern for squandering money and engendering jealousy, sumptuary laws were intended to assist in the maintenance of virtue. A low-necked dress, dripping with expensive lace, was a sign of vanity, pride, and undue attention to material goods. Puritans did not summarily reject the concept of beauty. Indeed, they believed outward beauty often expressed inward virtue. Modest dressing for seventeenth-century Puritan America allowed for formfitting and flattering clothing, as evidenced by portraits of stunningly attired women. Clothing was considered immodest only when it displayed too much flesh, too much wealth, or anything that blurred gender lines.

It was easy enough for a woman to emulate a status to which she was not entitled. Perhaps she was a servant who was given a silk scarf by a sympathetic mistress or an overly ardent admirer. Some poorer women knew how to make lace and therefore could afford to make some for themselves or their daughters. Although there does not appear to have been widespread enforcement of sumptuary laws, an occasional woman was hauled in for reprimand. In 1676 the town authorities in Northampton, Connecticut, decided a number of the young women in their town were in violation of the sumptuary laws, and thirty-eight women were summoned to court to explain their attire, notably, the wearing of silk. Sixteen-year-old Hannah Lyman appeared in court wearing the offending silk hood! These girls were all fined, but when the same court attempted to prosecute another round of sumptuary violations six years later, the motion was quashed by town select-men who believed violation of dress codes was no longer a threat needing public condemnation. By the eighteenth century sumptuary laws were no longer enforced.

Further Reading

Earle, Alice Morse. *Two Centuries of Costume in America.* New York: Macmillan Company, 1903.

Fischer, David Hackett. *Albion's Seed: Four British Folkways in America.* New York: Oxford University Press, 1989.

Fischer, Gayle Veronica. "The Daughters of Zion Are Haughty: Clothing and Sexual Oppression in Puritan New England." *Journal of Unconventional History* 3 (1991): 27–50.

Trautman, Patricia A. "When Gentlemen Wore Lace: Sumptuary Legislation and Dress in Seventeenth Century New England." *Journal of Regional Cultures* 3, no. 2 (1983): 9–21.

Superstition and Belief in Magic

The people of seventeenth-century Europe and America believed there were supernatural powers that could impact their lives, for either good or evil. It was a world buffeted by pounding storms, the inexplicable failure of harvests, and epidemics that killed entire families, while leaving others un-harmed. In an attempt to understand the random forces of nature or circumstance, they turned to supernatural explanations. Many credited such powerful forces to God, but others sought for expla-nations closer to home. If a man's cow died for no apparent reason, he might recall the previous week when he had angry words with the old woman liv-ing on the outskirts of town. Perhaps she had some supernatural control over nature that caused the cow to die. Worse yet, if the old woman was in a pact with the Devil, she might be practicing witch-craft.

Belief in the supernatural was likely to take two different forms. Some believed that particular humans had the ability to manipulate the forces of nature through witchcraft or knowledge of ancient pagan customs. The belief in this type of magic was minor, sporadic, and confined mostly to the lower classes. Far more popular was the belief that certain individuals had the ability to forecast the future, either through reading the stars, the lines on the palm of a hand, or other techniques of divination. This sort of fortune-telling involved no ability to manipulate events; rather it simply provided advice as to the best day to sail, marry, harvest crops, or conceive children.

Although Christian ministers frowned on both forms of the occult, most people in early America viewed forecasting the future as a harmless source of diversion. Far more suspicion was directed at any-one who was believed to have the ability to manipu-late events, a person's health, or remote objects. Very few persons ever claimed to have any such power, and those who did were usually mentally ill or so badly marginalized in their society they resorted to claims of supernatural power for a feel-ing of importance. People likely to be charged with witchcraft were usually in already contentious rela-tions with neighbors. Hostile neighbors blamed their problems, such as harm to their animals or crops, on meddlesome witches.

A number of factors combined to make the belief in magic less prevalent in America than it was in Europe. Belief in the occult was more common among marginalized classes of people. Migration to America tended to involve people of means and ambition. Europe was heavily strewn with ancient sites associated with magic. Stone circles, sacred springs, and strange carvings in the ground could be found throughout the countryside. Despite cen-turies of Christian practice that had attempted to discount or ignore such archaic remnants of the pagan world, these ancient reminders kept memo-ries alive among the people who lived beside them. The newness of the American wilderness lacked these traditional sacred sites to help nourish and sustain belief in the supernatural over centuries.

Supernatural beliefs differed depending on region of the country. The people of New England were heavily influenced by Puritan culture and were especially prone to believing in providential magic: the idea that God smiled and bestowed blessings on

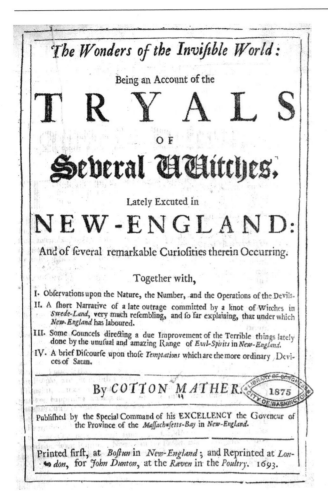

The Wonders of the Invisible World:

Being an Account of the

TRYALS

OF

Several Witches,

Lately Excuted in

NEW-ENGLAND:

And of several remarkable Curiosities therein Occurring.

Together with,

I. Observations upon the Nature, the Number, and the Operations of the Devils.

II. A short Narrative of a late outrage committed by a knot of Witches in *Swede-Land*, very much resembling, and so far explaining, that under which *New-England* has laboured.

III. Some Councels directing a due Improvement of the Terrible things lately done by the unusual and amazing Range of *Evil-Spirits* in *New-England*.

IV. A brief Discourse upon those *Temptations* which are the more ordinary Devices of Satan.

By COTTON MATHER.

1875

Published by the Special Command of his EXCELLENCY the Govencur of the Province of the *Massachusetts-Bay* in *New-England*.

Printed first, at *Boston* in *New-England*; and Reprinted at *London*, for *John Dunton*, at the *Raven* in the *Poultry*. 1693.

The most infamous association of New England Puritans with the supernatural was the witchcraft trials at Salem. Puritans believed in the existence of witches and credited their power to allegiance with the Devil. Shown here is the title page of Cotton Mather's *Book on Witchcraft*. (Burstein Collection/CORBIS)

those he favored, while sending tribulations to those who warranted correction. Puritans discounted the notion of direct communication with God and believed that spiritual communication was likely to take place through ambiguous signs that needed careful interpretation. Was the flash of a comet a portent of evil or a sign of God's delight? If a plant dropped its leaves out of season, a minister might be consulted to determine the cause of God's apparent displeasure. Very little in the Puritan world was attributed to simple accidents. If a child was scalded or a fire was spread by a sudden shift in the wind, God was likely trying to communicate a message.

The most infamous association of New England Puritans with the supernatural was the witchcraft trials at Salem. Puritans believed in the existence of witches and credited their power to allegiance with the Devil. The accused witches of Salem were charged with dabbling in "black magic," intended to harm or torment their neighbors. This type of witch-hunt was rare in early America. Allegations of witchcraft were sporadic and occurred in times of great social stress when scapegoats needed to be found. Despite the prominence of witch-hunts in the historical record, very few people claimed to possess paranormal powers, and fewer still believed them.

There was strong societal pressure among Puritans to reject all tampering with supernatural forces, but some superstition did take root. Only about one-third of adults were formal members of the church, and nonmembers appear to have been less rigid in their absolute rejection of the supernatural. "White magic" might consist of turning to a fortune-teller to find a lost item, get romantic advice, or to endow a charm with good luck. Large boulders used to mark property boundaries sometimes were inscribed with special symbols designed to keep evil at bay.

The people of the middle colonies were less suspicious of witchcraft and more willing to rely on astrology and fortune-telling than were the Puritans. Instead of reading nature as a means of determining God's message, the settlers of Virginia and the Carolinas were deeply interested in tracking the stars as a method of determining their own fate. Astrology was believed to contain the clues for advice on when to travel, whom to marry, and what to plant. Astrological advice was painstakingly reported in almanacs, the most prevalent literary genre of the era. In some colonies almanacs outsold the Bible. In addition to astrological information calculated for the locale in which they were sold, most almanacs listed numbers and days that would have special value in the coming year. Much of an almanac's success depended on the amount of astrological advice it contained. Some almanac printers complained bitterly about including what they believed to be superstitious nonsense, but found their volumes would not sell without such features.

Backcountry and frontier areas tended to abound in reliance on folkloric superstition. Among a handful of common early American superstitions: breaking a mirror portended the death of a family member; farmyard animals acquired the power of speech on Christmas Eve, although if any dared to witness such an event they would be punished; bad fortune was destined for a child born on the first three days of a new year; if a warm current of air was felt, witches were passing overhead; and it was bad luck to bathe on your wedding day.

Archaeological excavations have revealed traces of superstition among early settlers. In accord with English tradition, "witch bottles" were sometimes planted within the walls of a home or underneath the threshold during construction. The bottles were filled with nails, hair, urine, or pins, sealed with a stopper, and buried upside down. A witch bottle was supposed to prevent witches from entering the home, and dozens of early American homes have been found to contain them. Shoes were also believed to have the power to prevent witches from entering a home. The largest stash of shoes ever found was in the childhood home of John Adams in Quincy, Massachusetts. During a renovation of the home, thirty shoes were found hidden behind the chimney. It is impossible to know why the shoes were there, but it was clearly a deliberate decision to place them there.

A number of factors caused belief in the supernatural to swiftly decline in the early eighteenth century. Revulsion over the events at Salem caused peo-

ple to associate belief in witchcraft with backward, ill-educated people. The rise of Enlightenment philosophy and scientific experimentation demystified many of the natural forces that had given rise to supernatural explanations. Evangelical Christianity took root in many communities, which strongly discouraged continued indulgence in superstitious practices. There was a decline in the publication of astrological and other occult-related books. Belief in the supernatural had never been deeply ingrained in America, and it lost what little strength it had over common people in the eighteenth century, surviving only in isolated pockets.

See also Salem Witch Trials; Witchcraft

Further Reading

Bond, Edward L. "Source of Knowledge, Source of Power: The Supernatural World of English Virginia, 1607–1624." *Virginia Magazine of History and Biography* 108 (2000): 105–138.

Butler, Jon. "Magic, Astrology, and the Early American Religious Heritage, 1600–1760." *American Historical Review* 84 (1979): 317–346.

Crews, Ed. "A Shadowy Side of Early American History." *Colonial Williamsburg* (Summer 2001): 32–37.

Eisenstadt, Peter. "Almanacs and the Disenchantment of Early America." *Pennsylvania History* 65 (1998): 143–169.

Fischer, David Hackett. *Albion's Seed: Four British Folkways in America.* New York: Oxford University Press, 1989.

Godbeer, Richard. *The Devil's Dominion: Magic and Religion in Early New England.* New York: Cambridge University Press, 1992.

T

Tavern Keepers and Innkeepers

Keeping a tavern, boardinghouse, or inn was a viable means of earning a living for women in colonial America. Many of these women were the widows of tavern keepers and merely succeeded to their husbands' businesses. Others were widows who had large and comfortable houses and opened an inn or tavern as a means of supplementing their income. Serving meals and providing lodging could be seen as an extension of traditional female labor, and perhaps this accounts for why women were able to make inroads into this occupation. Taverns and inns usually doubled as the tavern keepers' private residence. Thus, the female tavern keeper usually had her children underfoot and juggled her household responsibilities while serving customers. Keeping a tavern in a larger town was one of the most profitable occupations a single woman could pursue.

Public houses varied widely in quality and services. Some establishments were little better than cramped, filthy shanties, whereas others were large, elegant buildings that provided entertainment and private lodgings. Small establishments in rural communities were known as "ordinaries." They served one meal at a fixed price and usually had a semiprivate room where travelers could find a place to sleep. Travelers' letters abound with tales of grim, backwoods establishments. In 1748, a young George Washington rented a bed in a rural ordinary, where "to my surprise, I found it to be nothing but a little straw matted together without sheets or anything else but one threadbare blanket with double its weight in vermin" (Sargent 1999, 9). Experienced travelers knew to bring their own sheets with them, because ordinaries could not be depended on to have an abundance of clean linen available.

Taverns were associated with towns. They served a variety of dishes and alcoholic beverages, but such fare represented only a tiny fraction of what a tavern had to offer. Taverns were important public spaces where merchants bought and sold cargoes, judges held sittings, planters sold their crops, postal riders exchanged letters, and political debates flourished. Taverns were central places for the dissemination of information. Notices of public meetings and new laws were posted there, and a copy of the latest broadside news sheet was usually available. Both men and women gathered in taverns to exchange news and gossip. People played cards, dice, and bet on cockfighting. Most taverns would have had a number of rooms for overnight lodging. Because taverns were usually located near ferries, courthouses, or well-traveled roads, they served an interesting cross section of local residents and people traveling to town on business. Tavern keepers were usually respectable members of the town community, and as such, women tavern keepers enjoyed a measure of prestige not usually open to them.

Although women were well prepared to handle the domestic duties associated with keeping a public house, it is likely most of them would have had servants or family members assisting in the business.

Eliza Harvey, Keeper of the Harvey Tavern

When Captain Thomas Harvey was captured by the French in 1697, his wife needed to find supplemental income. Her home was located close to the docks of Portsmouth, New Hampshire, making it an ideal location for the establishment of a tavern. After receiving a license from town authorities, she opened her home for business as a tavern. Eliza's husband died in a French prison before his release could be arranged, but her tavern met with better luck. The town used it as a central location for government business and committee meetings. In 1699 it was chosen as the town's postal center. Newspapers, new legislation, and notices of town meetings were all filtered through Eliza's tavern. As such, her tavern became a gathering place for people seeking news or the delivery of letters.

By 1706 the town was using a public room in her tavern to host General Assembly meetings. Soldiers used her rooms for lodging, and merchants, for transacting business. Eliza even hosted the colony's governor in 1706. When Eliza died, administration of the tavern passed to her daughter-in-law Ann. By then the Harvey Tavern was also used to provide food and shelter to the indigent, for housing of French prisoners of war after the 1745 siege at Louisbourg, and as a meeting place for various legislative and court functions. Both Eliza and Ann sent bills to the government for reimbursement after each event, providing a documentary history of the central role their tavern played in the administration of town business.

Source: Blaine, Marcia Schmidt. "Entertaining the Government: Female Tavern-Keepers and the New Hampshire Provincial Government." *Dublin Seminar for New England Folklife* 25 (2000): 191–201.

Food and supplies had to be purchased from local markets. The daily walk to the various markets consumed a considerable amount of time. Then food had to be prepared, linen laundered, horses stabled, firewood chopped, customers served, and dishes washed. Because taverns usually offered several dishes from which to choose, the amount of labor required in daily food preparation alone would have

been substantial. Meat was plentiful in early America, and typical tavern meals were based around pork, turkey, duck, or venison. Stews were the most popular meal, because they were easy to keep simmering throughout dining hours. Corn bread, chestnut stuffing, and sweet potatoes might accompany the meal.

Tavern keepers needed to obtain a license to sell liquor. Unlike other professions where women's contributions left few traces in the historical record, it is possible to track the number of women who operated taverns through their tavern licenses. In Boston, 30 to 40 percent of the tavern keepers were women, whereas about 20 percent of the Philadelphia taverns were owned by women. In addition to the women who were the sole applicants for the license, it is highly likely that most of the male tavern owners worked side by side with a wife who was an active participant in the business. The number of widows who successfully operated their former husband's taverns for the duration of their widowhood indicates they were already familiar with running the business.

Tavern keepers were required to keep certain standards. Anyone who was granted a tavern license needed to be of good character and capable of maintaining order in the establishment. Women tavern keepers had to safeguard their reputations. Tavern keepers, especially if they were female, were always vulnerable to charges of operating a "disorderly house." Any hint a tavern keeper might condone illicit sexual behavior in her establishment would cause her to lose her license.

The prices of drinks, meals, and lodging were usually fixed by the town government. The only means of competition was to operate a cleaner establishment, serve better meals, or provide a more pleasant environment. The success of women tavern keepers testifies to their ability to operate a competitive establishment. Tavern keepers needed to have a good head for business, because their jobs often required extending credit to customers for food, lodging, and even for their gambling debts.

Social life inside the tavern had curious gender customs. Women were welcomed in taverns as patrons, but their activities were constrained. They might eat, drink, and socialize with neighbors of both genders. Participation at the gambling tables was off-limits for women. Although some women indulged in private gambling, it was not to be condoned in public. Rougher activities, such as cock-fighting, also occurred behind taverns, another sphere where women were not welcome. Over time, the presence of women in taverns, both as tavern keepers and as patrons, became less acceptable. By the end of the eighteenth century, gender roles were relegating women to the domestic scene. Although many women still worked outside the home, highly visible activities, such as operating a boisterous tavern, carried an unseemly taint for a female tavern keeper.

During the years when tavern keeping was still a viable option for women, it was a unique opportunity to market domestic skills to an audience beyond a woman's own family. In comparison with the lonely isolation that characterized the life of a farmwife, the mistress of a tavern would have had a stimulating career in the midst of a community's intellectual, economic, and social crossroads.

Further Reading

Daniels, Bruce. "Another Type of Meetinghouse: Puritan Ordinaries and Provincial Taverns in Colonial New England." *New England Journal of History* 51 (1994): 14–28.

Lanning, Anne Digan. "Women Tavern-Keepers in the Connecticut River Valley, 1750–1810." *Dublin Seminar for New England Folklife* 25 (2000): 202–214.

Miles, Lion G. "Anna Bingham: From the Red Lion Inn to the Supreme Court." *New England Quarterly* 69 (1996): 287–299.

Sargent, Sarah E. "Elizabeth and Thomas Roper, Proprietors: Tavern Keeping in Colonial Virginia." *Virginia Cavalcade* 48 (1999): 4–13.

Thorp, Daniel B. "Taverns and Tavern Culture on the Southern Colonial Frontier: Rowan County, North Carolina, 1753–1776." *Journal of Southern History* 62 (1996): 661–688.

Teachers

Europeans of the early modern era considered teaching to be a male profession, and most settlers to America brought this assumption with them. When the Massachusetts Bay Colony passed its famous School Law of 1647, the mandatory schooling put such demands on towns that the profession was eventually opened up to women. The law required that all towns of at least fifty families provide a public school that taught reading and writing. Towns with more than one hundred families were also required to provide instruction in Latin. Schools that taught Latin were called grammar schools, and needed to be staffed by a schoolmaster fluent in the language. Such teachers were always men, and they were a considerable financial drain on their communities. The schools met for only nine months of the year, releasing the students during the summer months when their labor on the farm could not be spared. During the summer months, the schools were often opened to girls and staffed by a female teacher, whose salary requirements were less demanding than those of the Latin master.

In addition to formal grammar schools, early American communities made use of dame schools. The dame schools had a unique role in society, providing both day care for very young children and rudimentary reading instruction. Overworked mothers sent their children to the dame school for several hours each day, with the dame receiving a few coins in return. Such quasi employment was well within a woman's traditional function, because the schools were located in her home and she took a maternal interest in young children. Because the Massachusetts law of 1647 required small towns to provide literacy instruction to all children, those who could not afford a full-time teacher sometimes designated the dame school mistress as the town's teacher. Over time, some of these dame schools became more sophisticated. The pupils were older, and the school's mistress was respected as an important person in the town.

As settlements developed and homesteads were established farther from the town center, people living in the outlying areas preferred to send their children to smaller schools closer to home. Once again, the dame school seemed the logical place to turn. These informal schools became infused with

A Teacher Looks for Pupils

Mrs. Neill (who for a considerable time past has lived in Colonel Lewis's Family, Gloucester County) purposes to open a boarding school in Williamsburg for the reception of young ladies, on the same plan of the English schools, provided a sufficient number of scholars engage to enable her for such an undertaking. She will instruct them in reading, tambour, and other kinds of needlework, find them board and lodging, washing, [etc] for one guinea entrance and thirty pounds a year. The best Masters will attend to teach dancing and writing. She will also teach the guitar. Those who choose to learn any of those accomplishments are expected to pay for each separately . . . as nothing tends more to the improvement of a country than proper schools for education of both sexes, she humbly hopes her scheme will meet with encouragement, and those who choose to lend their children will please to let her know as soon as possible, that she may provide accordingly for their reception. . . . Direct for her at Col. Lewis's, Senior, in Gloucester, or at Mess. Dixon & Hunter in Williamsburg.

Mrs. Neill will take day scholars at one guinea entrance, and four guineas per year.

Mrs. Neill's endeavors must have been successful, because in July 1777 she placed another advertisement indicating her school had opened in Williamsburg.

Source: Virginia Gazette, 27 December 1776.

public money, fulfilling the law's requirement that children be provided with literacy instruction. Few of these rural settlers saw the need to send their children to town in order to receive Latin instruction. The local dame school seemed a much better option.

Women who chose to run a dame school were usually typical members of the community. They were either married or widowed, because possessing a home was a requirement. They needed to be literate and well respected. The money they earned was not enough to support themselves, so they were usually married to a man who made a decent living, or they had inherited a respectable sum.

By the eighteenth century, an elite class had developed to the point that there was a market for private instruction. Some women lived with wealthy families as private tutors. These women were usually of less secure financial position than were school dames. Most of these women were single and past the age where they were likely to find a husband. Often they were recent immigrants. The ability to speak French became important within elite circles, and women from England and France were more likely than native-born women to speak the language.

More adventurous women opened formal schools, usually specializing in ornamental educational refinements, such as needlepoint, painting, or dance. These women were likely to be the wife of a schoolmaster. Time and again advertisements in local newspapers told how the schoolmaster provided boys with instruction in mathematics, writing, and accounts, while his wife taught young ladies needlework and the like. Female schools almost never boasted of teaching academic subjects or domestic skills. Most girls grew up in households where they were already well trained in chores for running a household. Families who chose to send their older daughters to school were usually seeking to polish their social skills and give them the qualities deemed necessary for a high society wife. The mistress of such a school had only a small segment of society from which to draw her clientele. She was at the mercy of these families for her livelihood, always knowing that should a patron's family experience an economic downturn, a daughter's ornamental education would be an easy expense to trim.

There are many indications that aside from those who provided instruction in a dame school, women did not relish the profession of teaching. Many did so only during their widowhood and immediately quit upon remarriage. The tone apparent in the wording of teachers' paid advertisements reveal desperation. The women who worked as private tutors lived in isolated households where they had no family and were neither servants nor family.

Mistresses of dame schools seemed to derive greater satisfaction from their work. They rarely were in the dire financial circumstance that tutors or owners of a school were, simply because they were rarely the family breadwinner. Dame schoolmistresses were almost always women who enjoyed the respect and affection of the community.

See also Education

Further Reading

Dexter, Elizabeth Anthony. *Colonial Women of Affairs: Women in Business and the Professions in America before 1776.* Boston: Houghton Mifflin, 1931.

Perlmann, Loel, et al. "Literacy, Schooling, and Teaching among New England Women, 1730–1820." *History of Education Quarterly* 37 (1997): 117–139.

Spruill, Julia Cherry. *Women's Life and Work in the Southern Colonies.* Chapel Hill: University of North Carolina Press, 1938.

Tekakwitha, Kateri

Algonquin Catholic convert, first Native American the Catholic Church beatified (1656–1680)

Tekakwitha was born near the town of Auriesville, New York, in 1656. Like many of the Native American population, the tribe she lived with was ravaged by a smallpox epidemic in 1660. Both her parents died of the disease, and Tekakwitha was seriously disfigured. Her face was badly scarred, and her eyesight was permanently damaged. According to Indian custom, she was adopted by her paternal uncle, a member of the Mohawk tribe.

Tekakwitha came of age in a time when tensions between French colonists and Native Americans were high. Her village was in danger of being conquered by the French, and as a condition of peace, the French insisted that Jesuit missionaries be permitted to preach in their village. Eleven-year-old Tekakwitha was charged with seeing to the needs of the missionaries. She was very impressed with the three kindly missionaries, who found Tekakwitha an eager audience for their message.

As Tekakwitha grew older she remained intrigued by the Christian faith and increasingly dissatisfied with her life in the Mohawk village. She refused to marry the young man her family chose for her, and her religious inclinations prohibited her from working on the Sabbath. These odd choices, along with her disfigured face, made her the topic of ridicule and contempt. When another traveling priest visited her village in 1676, she asked to be baptized and was renamed Catherine. Following her conversion, and then her insistence to remain a virgin, the taunts and derision became so bad that Tekakwitha left her village. It took almost two months for her to travel the 200 miles to the Christian Indian mission of St. Francis Xavier, near Montreal.

Surrounded by like-minded Christians, Tekakwitha's religious fervor grew at an alarming rate. She subjected herself to severe physical mortifications, such as whipping herself, walking in ice, burning herself, and refusing to eat anything but corn. She had never been strong, and it was soon apparent that this rigorous physical ordeal was taking a toll on the young woman's health. The priests tried without success to discourage these self-imposed penances.

Tekakwitha was eager to spread Christianity to other Native Americans. Very much impressed with the Ursuline nuns at Montreal, Tekakwitha hoped to establish a similar community for Indian women. Permission to do so was refused by the Jesuits, who believed the idea was premature and were also concerned about Tekakwitha's failing health. On 17 April 1680 Tekakwitha died at the age of twenty-four, her body exhausted from her self-imposed penances. Tradition claims that immediately following her death the disfiguring smallpox scars vanished from her face.

In the decades following her death, Tekakwitha's grave became a pilgrimage site, and there were hundreds of claims of miraculous cures. Her spirituality made her an icon among other Native Americans who converted to Christianity. Throughout the twentieth century there were efforts to canonize Tekakwitha. The first step was taken in 1943 when she was declared Venerable, and in 1980 she was beatified by Pope John Paul II.

See also Colonization, Effect on Indian Women

Further Reading

Garraty, John A., and Mark C. Carnes, eds. *American National Biography.* New York: Oxford University Press, 1999.

Holmes, Paula Elizabeth. "The Narrative Repatriation of Blessed Kateri Tekakwitha." *Anthropologica* 43 (2001): 87–103.

Ruether, Rosemary Radford, and Rosemary Skinner Keller. *Women and Religion in America: The Colonial and Revolutionary Periods.* San Francisco: Harper and Row, 1983.

Walworth, Ellen H. *The Life and Times of Kateri Tekakwitha: The Lily of the Mohawks.* Buffalo, NY: B. Paul, 1891.

Textile Industry

Despite the common assumption that early Americans were completely self-sufficient and capable of producing their own food, clothing, and consumer goods, the average colonial woman would not have been able to produce all the cloth needed for her family. Although most women were capable of spinning yarn and thread, only a handful of households owned the looms necessary to turn thread into fabric.

Women participated in the textile industry as both producers and consumers. Most women owned spinning wheels and sold the yarn they spun to local weavers, who in turn sold the finished linen or wool fabric back to housewives. Although spinning yarn has always been a female task, using a loom was a trade dominated by men. In Europe, weavers created trade guilds to protect their profession. No such restrictive structures existed in America, and some women learned the craft of weaving. Only about 5 to 10 percent of households owned looms, many operated by the housewife.

Much of colonial labor was dictated by the seasons, but spinning and lace making could be done during the cold days of winter, when other farm labor ground to a halt. Spinning was an easy task to pick up and put down, making it ideally suited for women whose days were punctuated with child care, cooking, or assisting with farm labor. Yarn and thread were sold to weavers. Lace was marketed in town fairs by a woman who was designated the "lace merchant."

Spinning

Women spun wool into yarn and flax into linen thread. It was an easy skill to learn, and literally any family could afford a simple spindle, a mere stick with a weight on one end. Although not as efficient as a spinning wheel, the drop spindle could twist thread with the added momentum of the weight.

Before spinning could begin, the raw material needed to be prepared. Wool was washed, usually by soaking it overnight. Care was taken not to remove too much of the natural oils, because the oil aided in spinning. It was carefully squeezed dry, then "carded" by brushing the fleece between two flat wire brushes. The carding helped smooth out and straighten the fibers. The washed and combed wool was stored in a basket on the floor, and a single strand was plucked out, twisted, and pulled. This initial strand was tied to a spindle, which was mounted on a spinning wheel. The spinning wheel was cranked by a foot pedal called a treadle. This wheel kept the spindle twisting, thus pulling more yarn from the bundle of raw wool. The tension and the twisting worked in harmony to create stronger and finer yarn. The larger the wheel, the faster the spindle turned. Early spinning wheels were compact, but over time the wheel size expanded to as much as six feet in diameter. A small bowl of water was kept beside the wheel, and the spinner carefully wet the fibers as they twisted, helping create a tight, strong strand of yarn.

The process of making linen thread was similar, the only major difference being in the preparation of the raw material. The flax plant was harvested in the autumn, and the stalks of the plant were allowed to dry in the sun for a few days. The stalks were then combed to remove the seeds and debris. The most delicate part of the process, the retting, involved breaking the outer hull in order to extract the fibers within. It was these fibers that were spun into linen thread.

Examination of probate inventories reveals that spinning was a widespread occupation. Early in the eighteenth century, about half of American homes owned a spinning wheel. By the American Revolution almost 70 percent of homes had at least one spinning wheel. Ideally, women used the great wheel for spinning wool, and a smaller wheel for flax. The natural oils in wool made spinning flax dif-

This print shows an interior view of a room where a man and several women are engaged in beetling, scutching, and hackling flax. (Library of Congress)

ficult, so separate wheels were desirable if the family produced both types of thread.

Most colonial women knew how to knit, and they would have used their own yarn to knit stockings and mittens. Any remaining yarn was sold. Very few women had the ability to weave linen, and flax thread was almost always sold. Weavers needed an enormous amount of thread, and a single weaver might do business with a dozen spinners.

Weaving

It took eight to ten spinners to supply a full-time weaver with yarn and thread. Although men dominated the European weaving trade, such was not the case in America. Landownership was far more profitable and prestigious than weaving, and many male weavers abandoned their looms to work the soil upon arrival in America. Without a trade guild to discourage casual participation in weaving cloth, a number of women learned the skill. Cloth consumed a large portion of a household's income. A housewife who could weave fabric for home consumption was a highly valuable resource, especially if there was surplus to sell. Although less than 10 percent of colonial households owned looms, some women began to weave cloth as a means of supplementing their family's income.

Weaving was a difficult skill that required intensive training. When the profession was dominated by men, this training was accomplished through an apprenticeship system. Women appeared to have learned through observation and neighborly exchange of advice. *Warping* was the crucial, initial threading of the loom, which was so difficult that many part-time weavers never learned the skill. In such cases skilled weavers would initially warp the loom for the less-experienced weaver.

Most housewives, who were also responsible for cooking, cleaning, child care, and gardening, could not afford to spare substantial amounts of time for weaving. The majority of women who owned a loom engaged in only casual weaving, usually producing around 150 yards of cloth per year. This would require an average of 200 hours of labor per year, or around four weeks of full-time work. A handful of women kept their looms in heavy use, producing between 500 and 1,000 yards per year. Clearly, weaving was merely a supplemental means of income for most families, although a few highly skilled weavers made it a central part of the family economy.

By the mid-eighteenth century, American weavers had to compete with cheaper and finer cloth imported from factories in England. If a family already owned a loom, it is likely a housewife would have continued to produce fabric for home consumption, but it was no longer a highly profitable means of supplemental income.

Lace Making

Making lace dates as far back as the 1500s. Lace making was an extraordinarily labor-intensive art, and wearing lace was a luxury reserved for the rich. Ladies-in-waiting to queens were charged with creating exotic lace to adorn the royal wardrobe.

Women in early America could not afford to spend their time in the creation of such a labor-intensive item that had no practical value beyond decoration. Not until the mid-eighteenth century did a segment of society become wealthy enough to support the creation of a lace-making industry. The women who made lace were from the middling classes, and it was usually sold to the wealthy women for trimming dresses, bonnets, shawls, and bed hangings. Although a well-to-do woman could afford lace trim on her dress, the wealthiest women might make a display of an entire dress swathed in lace.

Lace workers used an oblong pillow, about ten inches in diameter. A strip of pasteboard was wrapped around the pillow, on which the lace pattern was traced. As many as 120 pins outlined the pattern. A corresponding number of bobbins—small wooden sticks that contained a spool of thread at the end—were attached to the pins, and the careful weaving of the lace commenced. Lace making was a tedious and exacting art. A diligent worker could produce a maximum of seven inches per day, and it sold for around eighteen shillings per yard.

Lace makers worked in their homes. Beyond the initial expense of bobbins, making lace required little capital outlay. It was a craft women and daughters produced to supplement the family income. Ipswich, Massachusetts, had an especially vibrant community of lace makers. Once a woman produced a substantial amount of lace, she turned it over to a female lace merchant, who took it to the market for sale. The lace merchants might sell lace locally, but they often traveled to neighboring communities to sell their wares.

Becoming skilled at lace production took many years. A girl would likely receive instruction either from her mother, or if she were a servant, the mistress of the family where she lived. Beginning with the simplest patterns, it would take months for the girl to master the skill. The ability to produce richly textured laces took years.

Lace making occurred primarily among town dwellers. Women who lived on farms spent most of their day producing subsistence items for their families. Town women had access to a greater variety of processed goods, such as candles, cheese, dairy, bread, and butchered meat. Because they were able to purchase such goods, they had more disposable time they could use for creating a marketable product such as lace.

The viability of the home lace-making trade came to an end in the 1820s, when imported lace-making machines from England put an end to handmade lace. The price of lace plummeted, closing off this means of supplemental income for women. Ironically, factory-made lace afforded the average woman the ability to wear lace for the first time.

See also Milliners and Seamstresses; Quilting; Sewing

Further Reading

Cottrell, Marta C. "The Laces of Ipswitch, Massachusetts: An American Industry, 1750–1840." *Annual Proceedings of the Dublin Seminar for New England Folklife* 22 (1997): 82–99.

Little, Frances. *Early American Textiles.* New York: The Century Co., 1931.

Morse, Alice Earle. *Home Life in Colonial Days.* New York: Grosset and Dunlap, 1898.

Ulrich, Laurel Thatcher. "Wheels, Looms, and the Gender Division of Labor in Eighteenth Century New England." *William and Mary Quarterly* 55 (1998): 3–38.

Theater

Theater was a luxury that could not be supported in the first century of European settlement in America. The majority of labor in the colonies was devoted to the production of the necessities of survival. Theater was a costly extravagance, requiring communities large and wealthy enough to support a population of actors whose only contributions to society were diversion and entertainment. It also required a substantial class of people who had leisure time to travel to the theater and spend a few idle hours in personal indulgence.

The first efforts to establish a theater occurred in Williamsburg, Virginia, which hosted a professional company of actors in 1716. New York and Charleston had occasional theatrical performances in the 1730s, but colonists were too ambivalent about indulging in theater to support these companies for long-term engagements. The actors soon returned to more profitable venues in London. The first substantial troupe of professional actors arrived in the colonies when Mr. and Mrs. William Hallam made their 1752 debut in Virginia. The Hallams traveled among the few large urban areas, finding eager audiences hungry for entertainment, but also provoking protest from a large segment of society that believed theater embodied vice, indolence, and corruption. Several decades passed before theatrical companies could become established without controversy.

Women participated in theater as playwrights, actresses, and spectators. Much of the controversy regarding theatrical entertainment was focused on the fragility of female virtue. The highly public nature of theatrical performance was at odds with the modesty and reserve expected of women. Actresses who flaunted themselves in public and traveled through the country with shiftless actors were not the sort of people conservative Americans wished to celebrate. Some believed that, even as spectators in the audience, women could be corrupted through exposure to plays with scandalous themes. Forces hostile to the theater were concerned with protecting domestic harmony and virtue. Women who took themselves out of the home, either as spectators or participants in the theater, were a threat to the stability of the home.

Moral Objections

Many of the original settlers of the colonies were Puritans, who had a long-standing aversion to attending theatrical performances. Most Puritans had no objection to the private reading of plays, for it was acknowledged that virtue usually triumphed over evil by the final act. Problems arose when the plays were performed in a public setting. The most popular themes of plays were revenge tragedies, in which cruelty, anger, and betrayal are vividly portrayed on the stage, sometimes invoking similar emotions in the audience. Despite their bad ends, villains were often portrayed by attractive actors and actresses, who imparted a sense of glamour and tragedy to these dangerous characters. The most famous female characters of the stage, Lady Mac-Beth, Helen of Troy, the Duchess of Malfi, and the tragic heroine Juliet, had nothing to offer by way of moral development for women in the audience. Exposure to such characters could merely provoke rebellion and a loosening of the moral foundation so highly valued by the Puritan settlers.

The raucous nature of audience behavior added another layer of unseemliness to theater. Smoking and drinking were common among the spectators. Prostitutes were known to ply their trade among the audience. Disrespectful conduct, such as shouting and throwing vegetables at performers, was considered normal behavior. It appeared that the theater attracted all the least-desirable elements of society and confined them in a small space. The resulting behavior was appalling, but predictable. Many communities passed laws attempting to outlaw all manner of public spectacle, including sporting events, animal fighting, maypoles, and theater.

Objection to the theater was not confined to rigidly conservative Puritans. Other critics focused their indignation on the sins of leisure, idleness, and the squandering of precious resources. Time was a valuable commodity to colonists. America was a land of splendid natural abundance, but it lacked labor to harness and exploit these God-given resources. Although it was acknowledged a person could not perform strenuous labor during all waking hours, periods of rest should be devoted to mental or familial enrichment. Parents should spend time with their children. Young women should read edifying passages from the Bible. Men should renew their bodies by quietly relaxing at home in the company of their family. Attending theatrical performances violated the principle of proper rejuvenation on a number of fronts. It was not possible to physically relax if one was traveling to town to attend a play. Instead of mental relaxation, a person was subjected to ribaldry from the audience and unwholesome excitement from the plays. Precious coin was wasted on the cost of admission, and vital hours that could have been spent in productive labor were lost.

Establishment of Professional Theater in the Colonies

The Hallam family began touring America as the first notable group of professional actors. They consisted of twelve adults, four of whom were women. Three Hallam children grew up with the troupe and eventually took to the stage as they came of age. Because there were no buildings suitable for staging plays, the group performed in makeshift spaces such as warehouses or in open-air fields.

Controversy surrounded the group wherever they performed. Some colonies passed laws that banned theatrical performances. The Pennsylvania Assembly passed a series of laws to ban theaters, but the laws were repeatedly struck down by the English Crown, which said Pennsylvania had no authority to restrict the rights of British citizens in the colony.

The Hallams knew suspicion of actors was high, and they behaved with scrupulous decorum. They cultivated an image of utmost respectability, performing plays with highly moralistic themes. Prior to their arrival in New York City, they advertised their company bore little resemblance to typical theatrical troupes. The company denied any association with the drunken carousing common in English theaters. Some cities demanded the actors perform an occasional play for the benefit of local charities as a condition for granting a license to act. After a few decades of blameless behavior, the theater became gradually accepted in most colonies.

The American Revolution had a detrimental effect on theater. Radical elements in the Continental Congress claimed their struggle could not be won without every form of extravagance or dissipation eliminated from society. Pressure for people to abstain from indulging in luxuries was high. Despite the decorous behavior of the Hallams and other fledgling acting companies, the decades of the 1760s and 1770s were too inhospitable for the actors to remain in America. The Hallam company withdrew to Jamaica for the duration of the Revolution. A few of the actresses chose to remain in the colonies, opening dancing schools to earn a living.

Following the Revolution, theater once again took root in the new country. The nation was now large enough to support leisure institutions such as theaters. Hostility to the theater came only from fringe groups and was not taken seriously by people who believed that individual choice should count for more than community purity. No longer concerned with placating Puritanical concerns about theatrical immorality, acting companies tended to revert back to what was the most marketable. Daring plays and liberal selling of alcohol increased attendance.

The loosening of decorum had important implications for the role of women in theater. As audiences became more raucous, respectable women withdrew from attendance. Men drank, smoked, and indulged in boisterous behavior. Some brought their wives or girlfriends, but respectable women would not have been able to attend such an unruly public event without a male escort. Fewer reputable women felt comfortable attending, and as they withdrew, prostitutes became more likely to mingle in the crowd. It was not until well into the nineteenth century that theater regained the measure of respectability that permitted women to attend in significant numbers.

Professional Women of the Theater

Most actresses were born into the profession. They usually grew up assisting in backstage aspects of production, before taking to the stage in their early teen years. In addition to a measure of composure and aptitude for performance, actresses needed to have an enormous capacity to memorize lines. In 1766, the Hallam company had forty-two plays in its repertoire. With only a few actresses in the company, it is likely each of them played roles in most of these plays. Little is known about what sort of salary these women received. Payment depended on the number of performances and the size of each part. The profit margin for theater companies in America was slight, and women would not have been able to accumulate any significant wealth from acting.

Actresses were commonly believed by eighteenth-century Americans to be unsavory women who were a potential source of corruption for any town that welcomed them. Because most acting troupes needed to travel, these rootless people were regarded with suspicion by provincial townspeople.

Attractive young actresses were assumed to dabble in prostitution. Even a married actress could be tainted by association with her husband, who was likely a "shiftless actor." If she was a mother, she could be accused of neglecting her children by failing to provide a stable environment.

Actresses tended to marry men associated with the theater. No matter how blameless their life, their profession gave them a taint that discouraged respectable men from associating with them. Even before marriage, many actresses used the title "Mrs." in order to carry an air of respectability and discourage unwelcome male attention. Doubtlessly, some actresses did grant sexual favors to men in exchange for monetary gain. Such alliances almost never resulted in marriage.

Some women chose to become involved in theater through playwriting. These playwrights were overwhelmingly of the privileged and educated class. On the whole, playwrights were considered more respectable than the actors who presented their plays. A handful of playwrights, such as Susanna Rowson, also dabbled in acting, but they were the exception.

A number of women saw their plays professionally produced on the stage. Their plays almost always had women in the central roles and revealed insights into daily American life as perceived by women. The themes often focused on the highly charged topics of the American Revolution, patriotism, and the moral character of the new nation. Mercy Otis Warren is typically remembered as the most significant American playwright of the 1770s. Her works helped articulate what she perceived to be the moral gulf between patriots and loyalists. Susanna Rowson helped inflame nationalist passions when she wrote *Slaves of Algiers* (1794) in protest of a series of attacks on American shipping vessels in the Mediterranean. Although women writers in other fields occasionally disguised their gender through the use of a male pseudonym or anonymous publication, female playwrights almost unanimously used their real names or a clearly female pseudonym.

Although Susanna Rowson and Mercy Otis Warren tower over other female playwrights in terms of enduring reputation, dozens of other women contributed plays to the American theater. Like the majority of men who wrote plays, most of these women faded into obscurity with the passage of time. Despite the lack of long-standing fame, the theater was a place where women could express their opinions and creativity.

See also Merry, Anne Brunton; Rowson, Susanna Haswell; Warren, Mercy Otis

Further Reading

Houchin, John H. "The Struggle for Virtue: Professional Theatre in 18th Century Philadelphia." *Theatre History Studies* 19 (1999): 167–188.

Kritzer, Amelia Howe. *Plays by Early American Women, 1775–1850.* Ann Arbor: University of Michigan Press, 1995.

Silverman, Kenneth. *A Cultural History of the American Revolution: Painting, Music, Literature, and the Theatre.* New York: T. Y. Crowell, 1976.

Wilmeth, Don B., and Christopher Bigsby, eds. *The Cambridge History of American Theatre: Volume One, Beginnings to 1870.* Cambridge, UK: Cambridge University Press, 1998.

Timothy, Elizabeth

Printer (?–1757)

Nothing of Elizabeth Timothy's early life is known, other than she was born in Holland. As a young adult she arrived in America with her husband, Louis Timothée, a French Huguenot, and their four small children, Peter, Louis, Charles, and Mary. After settling in Philadelphia in 1731, Louis placed an advertisement in young Benjamin Franklin's newspaper offering his services as a French teacher and translator. Franklin and Timothée apparently became friends, because they soon embarked on a plan to launch America's first German-language newspaper, the biweekly *Philadelphische Zeitung.* Timothée was the paper's editor and translator, and Franklin did the printing. The paper was unable to attract the necessary 300 subscribers and folded quickly. The partnership between Franklin and Timothée lasted much longer, with Franklin sponsoring the Timothée family's move to Charleston, South Carolina, where they were to establish and publish a newspaper. Under the agreement, Franklin supplied the printing press, type, and one-third of the funds, while Timothée provided the labor and two-thirds of the operating funds. Timothée proved an excellent printer, but a poor businessman, unable to keep accurate accounts of the business and exasperating Franklin with his slipshod manner. Weekly issues of the *South Carolina Gazette* soon appeared under the Anglicized name of Lewis Timothy.

Elizabeth's activities during these years were occupied with raising her family of now six children and assisting her husband in the operation of the press. Her training in operating the press served her well, because when Lewis was killed in an accident in 1738, the only substantial asset to Elizabeth's name was her skill and access to the printing press. She issued her first copy of the paper, on time, a mere five days after her husband's funeral. In it she appealed to her husband's readership to "continue their favors and good offices to his poor afflicted widow and six small children and another hourly is expected" (Hudak 1978, 133).

Elizabeth had a keen head for business, and Franklin praised her administration of the paper. Her success as a newspaper editor and printer were merely passable. English was Elizabeth's second language, and her paper often showed grammatical and spelling errors. She had at least one complaint of poor print quality from the House of Assembly, with whom she had a contract to produce legal forms. Despite her difficulties, Elizabeth continued to edit and publish the *South Carolina Gazette* until her son Peter came of age and took charge of the business.

After Peter assumed primary responsibility for the paper, Elizabeth opened a shop next to the print shop, where she sold books, stationery, and almanacs. It is clear that she was financially successful in her later life, because in her will she left her children three houses, eight slaves, land, furniture, and coin. The "poor afflicted widow" clearly possessed a keen sense for business.

The Timothy family published the *South Carolina Gazette* for a total of sixty-eight years. Peter Timothy controlled the paper for the majority of this time, but at his death, his widow, Ann Donovan Timothy (1727–1792), followed in her mother-in-law's footsteps and became a newspaper editor and printer.

See also Printers and the Printing Trade

Further Reading
Avery, Donald R. "Elizabeth Timothy." In *Biographical Dictionary of American Journalism.* New York: Greenwood Press, 1989.
Baker, Ira L. "Elizabeth Timothy: America's First Woman Editor." *Journalism Quarterly* 54 (1977): 280–285.
Hudak, Leona M. *Early American Women Printers and Publishers, 1639–1820.* Metuchen, NJ: Scarecrow Press, 1978.

Tituba

Principal witness at the Salem witch trials (fl. 1680–1700)

If not for a brief two-year period in which Salem, Massachusetts, descended into a frenzy of hysteria, the only trace of the slave woman Tituba left in the historical record would have been a bill of sale. Her role as a catalyst for the witch panic brought the glare of public attention for a brief period, but Tituba's early years and her life after the trials remain shrouded from view.

Tituba was a slave purchased by the Reverend Samuel Parris during a voyage to Jamaica. Her racial identity has been the subject of much speculation. Although her name suggests an African origin, the people of Salem referred to her as an Indian. It is most likely that she had been kidnapped from an Indian tribe in South America and transported as a slave to Barbados. There she was surrounded by the African-Caribbean culture, including voodoo. In 1680 she was brought to Massachusetts, where she became the center of the maelstrom that gripped Salem Village in 1692.

Tituba and her husband, John Indian, were both slaves in the household of Salem's minister, the Reverend Parris. One of her responsibilities was to tend to the two children in the household, the reverend's daughter, Elizabeth, and his orphaned niece, Abigail. The girls were later to recount how Tituba showed them how to float an egg white in a glass as a means of reading the future. Other neighborhood girls became intrigued, and soon a small group formed who eagerly listened to Tituba's stories and observed her tricks and spells. Although Tituba's tales were probably nothing more than harmless sport, the severe world of Puritan morality had no room for anything that carried the odor of witchcraft. During the same period that Tituba enchanted the girls with her fortune-telling, the girls began exhibiting strange behavior at home. They were secretive and prone to fits and convulsions and even periods of trances.

Although the behavior of the girls still baffles historians, most point to the guilt they might have experienced after dabbling with Tituba's charms and superstitions. Others speculate the youngest girl suffered from epilepsy and the older girls were envious of the attention such episodes garnered. When local ministers and doctors failed to find a medical explanation for the girls' behavior, the village elders credited supernatural forces. After extensive questioning, the girls finally named a few of Salem's outcasts as the source of their afflictions. Tituba was among those accused.

Those accused of witchcraft vehemently denied the charges, but after a beating by the Reverend Parris, Tituba confessed. Her confession was embellished with tales of red rats, talking cats, and a mysterious man clothed in black who made her sign her name in his book. She also claimed to have witnessed the other women accused of witchcraft consorting with the Devil. A number of theories for Tituba's confession have been suggested. Perhaps she did it out of fear or guilt for having dabbled in fortune-telling. Others say it might have been prompted by resentment over her status as a slave. Tituba's new position as an expert witness, with power to alarm and control the community, might have appealed to her. Most likely she saw it as a way to preserve her life, because as long as she continued to provide information she was not beaten or under eminent threat of execution. Indeed, a number of the accused witches without Tituba's status as a slave or a fortune-teller ultimately confessed to witchcraft when it became apparent that those who

Tituba telling tales to children in Salem, Massachusetts Bay Colony, 1690s. (North Wind/North Wind Picture Archives)

confessed were spared execution. After a three-day examination in which Tituba supplied numerous colorful details about the spirit world, Tituba was imprisoned and additional people were arrested and examined.

Tituba was forgotten as the trials expanded, the girls' fits became more dramatic, and the list of suspects grew. It would take fourteen months and the deaths of twenty-four people before the trials were called to a halt. Even then Tituba's problems were not over. She had been imprisoned during the entire length of the trial. According to custom, she could not be released until she had paid her jailer for the cost of her keep during this period. Along with other impoverished, accused witches, Tituba languished in jail long after she should have been freed. Her owner, the Reverend Parris, eventually sold Tituba to an unknown purchaser in order to pay her jail fees. She left Salem Village afterward. It is not known if she was ever reunited with her husband, or what her fate was after she was released from prison.

See also Salem Witch Trials; Superstition and Belief in Magic; Witchcraft

Further Reading

Breslaw, Elaine. *Tituba, Reluctant Witch of Salem: Devilish Indians and Puritan Fantasies.* New York: New York University Press, 1996.

Hoffer, Charles. *The Devil's Disciples: Makers of the Salem Witchcraft Trials.* Baltimore, MD: Johns Hopkins University Press, 1996.

Rosenthal, Bernard. "Tituba's Story." *New England Quarterly* 71 (1998): 190–203.

Tucker, Veta Smith. "Purloined Identity: The Racial Metamorphosis of Tituba of Salem Village." *Journal of Black Studies* 30 (2000): 624–634.

Tobacco

See Addictive Substances

Tourism and Leisure Travel

The custom of "the grand tour" had a long history among the elites of Europe. People of wealth took several months to visit the major European capitals and scenic cities with ancient Roman ruins. Imbibing culture, establishing ties with other people of influence, and visiting health spas throughout Europe were all considered an important component of being a member of the upper class.

Tourism of this sort was clearly not possible within the American colonies. The wealthiest few sent their young adults to Europe in order to gain exposure to a semblance of aristocratic culture. Travel within seventeenth-century America was hindered by the absence of reliable roads and lodgings, limited points of interest, and a culture that could not support a leisure class.

Organized tourism in America did not begin until the mid-eighteenth century. A period of prosperity was ushered in following the end of the French and Indian War in 1763. New money was invested in the construction of roads and bridges. This resulted in the establishment of roadside taverns that made travel more comfortable for women and even families. Reliable guidebooks and maps began to be published for the first time. The expanding economy made it possible for people of means to amass enough money for leisure travel.

The next hurdle in the establishment of tourism was overcoming the social condemnation of the concept of leisure. The famed "Protestant work ethic" was in full swing in early America. The colonists were on a mission to carve the wilderness into a haven where hardworking and upright people could prove their worth. Time was a valuable commodity. During lulls in work, women were to make constructive use of their free time. They could improve themselves by reading educational literature, providing tutelage to their children, or embellishing the domestic environment with ornamental needlework. The idea that time could be used for nothing other than relaxation seemed wasteful, self-indulgent, and even immoral.

The easiest way to overcome the negative connotations associated with leisure travel was to couch it in terms of improving health. It was long recognized that the steaming summers in southern climates gave rise to disease. Even when dangerous epidemics were not in evidence, the relentless humidity caused a sense of malaise widely believed to be unhealthy. Spending the hottest period of the summer in the North or the mountains became a tempting prospect for those who could afford the diversion. Seaside towns in New England also became popular destinations for southerners escaping the heat.

"Taking the waters" was considered a health benefit. In several places throughout the colonies, hot water heated deep in the earth's core seeped to the surface. As it rose to the surface, the hot water dissolved minerals in the earth, becoming saturated with magnesium, potassium, iron, and sodium. Warm mineral water was widely believed to cure any number of ailments, from arthritis to consumption. Some of these benefits were real, but others merely provided a placebo effect.

The mid-eighteenth century witnessed the first attempts to capitalize on health benefits associated with natural hot springs. Property owners who had hot springs on their land encouraged visitors by placing newspaper advertisements boasting of the healthful benefits of soaking in the warm mineral water. Modest fees were charged, but the real profit derived from selling lodging and meals to the visitors.

In order to preserve modesty, owners constructed wooden huts around the spring. Some hot springs had separate huts for men and women. Other proprietors chose to invest in a single larger and more comfortable enclosure and have alternating two-hour shifts for men and women. Visitors wore large, sacklike gowns while they soaked in the steaming waters. Women who were having difficulty becoming pregnant were advised to soak in the springs, because it was believed exposure to sulfur would enhance fertility.

Early visitors to the springs almost always came for relief of real physical disabilities, because the lack of amenities discouraged all but the most determined visitors. Road conditions were poor, accommodations rudimentary, and other entertainment nonexistent. One such visitor was George Washington. In 1769 he brought his stepdaughter Patsy to spend two months at Berkeley Springs, Virginia, in a vain attempt to cure her epilepsy. Conditions were lacking, and Washington arranged for the services of a carpenter and baker to provide them with provisions during their stay.

Following the American Revolution, another surge in the national infrastructure resulted in increased tourism. Better roads and a rapidly expanding middle class made tourism a viable industry for investment. The beginnings of modern-day resorts grew up around hot springs in Virginia, Pennsylvania, New York, and Massachusetts. The crude cabins in the woods were expanded to become more spacious. Adequate boardinghouses and homes for rent were built nearby. Various forms of entertainment became available. Concerts, pleasure boats for hire, and horse races were common diversions for those who needed a respite from the springs. Warm Springs was one of the more elegant resort spas in Virginia. In 1810 a hotel, complete with a large ballroom and dancing, made it the chosen destination for Virginia aristocracy.

Leisure travel was an expensive investment. To take full advantage of the health benefits, doctors advised their patients to have at least three weeks of exposure to the mineral waters. Because most needed a few days of travel time, tourists needed to have the financial wherewithal to be away from their business for at least a month. It was not uncommon for some southerners to spend the entire summer in the more pleasant environments at northern spas.

Local residents also took advantages of the mineral springs. "Day-trippers" were not as profitable for spa owners, but they greatly outnumbered long-term visitors and were therefore welcome. Day-trip visitors could only afford to soak for a few hours before beginning their return journey. Enterprising proprietors sold bottled mineral water to the day-trippers for home consumption, convincing them greater exposure to the waters was needed for true health.

Most women who visited spas would have been accompanied by their husbands or fathers, but not all. In 1771, Elizabeth Drinker spent six weeks at Bristol Springs, accompanied only by a maid and her young son. Her husband visited at least once, but even a woman so proper as Mrs. Drinker felt it was acceptable for a woman to travel unaccompanied. The total cost for her six-week visit was £88, about what an average working man earned in a year.

Early Americans justified leisure travel by claiming it was for health reasons, but by the late eighteenth century shifting attitudes about work and leisure made it acceptable to spend time in sheer recreation. Hot springs were still popular destinations, but people no longer felt the need to find medical justification for a visit. The desire to see new parts of the country, experience people beyond the immediate neighborhood, or simply try something new were all good reasons for a trip to a spa.

See also Travel

Further Reading

Berdan, Marshall S. "The Spa Life: Taking the Cure in Antebellum Bath County." *Virginia Cavalcade* 40 (1991): 110–119.

Bridenbaugh, Carl. "Baths and Watering Places of Colonial America." *William and Mary Quarterly*, 3d ser. 3 (1946): 151–181.

Carson, Barbara G. "Early American Tourists and the Commercialization of Leisure." In *Of Consuming Interests: The Style of Life in the Eighteenth Century*, eds. Cary Carson et al. Charlottesville: University Press of Virginia, 1994.

Travel

Most early Americans rarely traveled outside of the immediate area surrounding the village where they were born. The wilderness had few roads, and methods of transportation were generally uncomfortable. Straying too far away from established villages also presented potentially dangerous altercations with Native Americans. Extended families tended to settle near their original village, so there was rarely need to travel far in order to visit family. Transportation of goods to distant marketplaces usually did not involve women.

A handful of women married men who came from far-off colonies. These women likely undertook sporadic visits home. There is some evidence that first-generation settlers were more prone to relocate in search of better lands. These women may have accompanied their husbands in scouting out new homesteads.

Shipboard Passage to America

Seventeenth-century European immigrants to America were overwhelmingly male. For the early part of the century, male immigrants outnumbered women five to one. The reluctance of women to embrace immigration was understandable. No matter how meager their life in Europe, immigration to America was a dangerous and uncertain undertaking. The mere prospect of the shipboard voyage was enough to discourage many would-be travelers.

Typical transatlantic voyages lasted between eight and ten weeks. English immigrants gathered in ports such as Gravesend, Ipswich, or Portsmouth, where they almost always needed to wait a few weeks until the ship was provisioned and tidal conditions were right. This period of initial delay often tested the mettle of the immigrants. They might be waiting out this time on the vessel, where they had a taste of the cramped and uncomfortable conditions. They might also be exposed to seaside gossip about the dangers of travel, ferocity of the Indians, and deprivations in the American wilderness. Despite the annoyance of the delay, during this time many of the passengers began forming a sense of community among themselves. This sense of camaraderie would be strengthened during the voyage. Fellowship and a sense of solidarity flourish under adverse conditions in which a group of people are seeking a common goal. Decades after the voyage, some settlers spoke of the bonds of friendship that were forged while on the ship.

Conditions on the ships were cramped, unsanitary, and lacking in adequate food and provisions. Most immigrants had never been at sea before, and travel on the small vessels usually resulted in heavy amounts of seasickness. Because the duration of the voyage was uncertain, food and water had to be rationed with care. Fresh water inevitably tasted rancid because it was stored in casks, and beer and spirits were preferred over water. Most of the food had to be heavily salted or dried in order to survive the voyage. The shipboard diet consisted almost entirely of hard-baked biscuits, salted pork, and oatmeal.

Most dangerous was the spread of disease. Inadequate food, the rocking ship, and cramped surroundings all resulted in severe discomfort, but were rarely life-threatening conditions. Typhus, dysentery, and typhoid could sweep through a ship's population with devastating results. Surprisingly, travel in the first half of the sixteenth century was much healthier than in later centuries. Because ships contained relatively small numbers of immigrants, often fewer than one hundred, the ravages of contagious disease were not nearly as profound as they became when ships started transporting hundreds of immigrants per ship. Likewise, although passengers had great fear of shipwreck or becoming lost at sea, this rarely happened. Perhaps only once every five to seven years would an entire vessel be lost in such a manner.

Boredom was no doubt another factor of discomfort. Those emigrating for religious reasons spent many hours per day in prayer or religious study, but there was little else to occupy their time. Memoirs speak of the delight passengers took when the ship encountered unfamiliar wildlife, such as schools of porpoises or enormous seabirds. The normally somber Richard Mather commented on the fascination the passengers had when a porpoise was hauled aboard. Watching the butchering of the porpoise, Mather wrote "upon the deck in view of all our company was wonderful to us all, and marvelous merry sport, and delightful to our women and children" (Cressy 1984, 517).

After arriving in America, the memory of the arduous voyage tended to become engraved on the spirit of the settlers. It was a winnowing experience, in which the strong and adventurous risked so much to travel to the New World. The shipboard experience provided a time of bonding that prepared the settlers for lives in their new communities.

Waterways

Transportation by canoe, barge, or raft proved to be the quickest and most comfortable means of travel for much of the colonial period. Settlement patterns can be traced along rivers, not because of easy access to water for agricultural purposes, but because the river provided a means of transporting goods and crops to urban areas. Water transportation proved to be the only affordable means of getting heavy and bulky products such as corn and rice to market. Difficulties associated with water travel were presented by floods or low water levels, floating debris, rapids, or treacherous reefs. Water travel was also limited by the location of navigable rivers. Most rivers in eastern America run east–west, forcing those who needed to travel north–south to use more expensive ships on the ocean.

Transportation by water tended to be reserved for the wealthy. Less than one-quarter of the residents of the middle colonies owned a boat. Well-to-do ladies typically preferred to travel by boat rather than on the crude bridal paths used by horseback riders. Many ladies paddled their own canoes, and both boys and girls were taught to handle a boat from a young age.

Land Transportation

Walking was the most common form of transportation in early America. Women would have been accustomed to walking to neighboring farms, church services, and about the marketplace. Four miles per hour is a pace that can easily be maintained for several hours. Although travel by horse would have been faster, horses were not a universal possession in agricultural America. They were expensive to maintain and of limited use on a farm,

---

Colonial Roads

The poor state of roads in colonial America was partially responsible for the limited travel engaged in by American women. Road building was a slow and laborious process that required clearing trees, rocks, and stumps. The difficulty of grading roads to divert water was only partially successful. Attempts were made to divert roads from low-lying areas in order to avoid water damage, but no amount of grading or site selection could prevent a road from turning into muck during heavy rains. Over time, erosion etched gullies into the roads and brought tree roots to the surface. Pooled water was especially dangerous during winter, when icy road conditions hampered the footing of horses.

Roads were often so narrow, crooked, and rocky that travelers dismounted from their horses rather than risk a dangerous fall. Travel by carriage was even more uncomfortable, and when possible, most colonists preferred walking.

Source: Crews, Ed. "Colonial Roadways." *Journal of Colonial Williamsburg* 26 (Spring 2004): 56–61.

---

putting their purchase out of reach for poor families. If a farmer could only afford one draft animal, an ox was a more versatile and better choice.

The well-to-do could afford travel by horseback, although this had limitations. Few roads were built in the early years, and Indian hunting paths were relied on for travel through densely forested areas. Using carts proved difficult until more substantial roads could be built. Road building was a slow process and was carried out with varying degrees of efficiency throughout the colonies. Clearing stumps and boulders and leveling surfaces were all enormously labor intensive in a land that was habitually short of labor. Streams and rivers were abundant, requiring the construction of bridges and ferries. Despite the difficulties, the demands of agriculture, commerce, and public safety required the construction of roads.

Improved public roads joined most of the major urban centers by the late eighteenth century. There were two periods of heavy investment in the infrastructure of transportation in America. Following the French and Indian War in 1763 and after the conclusion of the American Revolution, money was heavily invested in building roads and bridges. Creation of reliable roads brought increased trade among villages, a better postal system, and even a fledgling tourism industry.

Middling and wealthy women were likely to have access to a horse for transportation. Use of the sidesaddle was considered the most elegant way for a lady to ride a horse in early America. Dating to late medieval times, it was considered more graceful and elegant for a woman to sit sideways in a saddle, thereby avoiding what was considered a crude straddling of the horse. Although a woman riding sidesaddle gave a more genteel appearance, she had far less control of a horse than someone using a traditional saddle. Sidesaddle riders could rarely travel at more than a walking pace. Additionally, the expense of a second saddle was not feasible for middling- or working-class families. Although sidesaddles were clearly the most genteel manner for a woman to ride, it was by no means unheard of for women to ride astride the horse.

Carriages came into use by the eighteenth century. These were the exclusive property of the wealthy, because most families could afford no more than carts or wagons, which could double for transportation when necessary. To own a vehicle that served as nothing more than covered transportation for humans was an extravagant expense. Public stagecoaches were available as early as 1730, connecting New York and Philadelphia in a five-day journey.

Travel in early America was slow and uncomfortable. Because most roads were not graded, they were muddy and full of ruts. There were awkward turns that lacked good visibility, owing to overgrown brush. Under the best circumstances, a rider on horseback could cover seven miles per hour. Passengers in wagons or carriages moved considerably slower, averaging twenty to thirty miles per day, depending on road conditions.

Exacerbating the difficulty of travel was the problem of finding one's way. Roads had no signage, and maps were inadequate. Most travelers depended on hiring local guides to show them the way from town to town. If the trip was timed correctly, a traveler might be lucky enough to travel alongside postal riders.

For those traveling long distances, lodging in a tavern or with a local cottager was necessary. The quality of such lodgings varied widely, with cornhusk beds or pallets on the floor being common. Few taverns or inns had more than one or two rooms available for sleeping. The rooms usually had a few large beds. Women travelers would share a bed with their female servants or friends, but it was common for the other beds in the room to be occupied by men. In 1783, Elizabeth House Trist recorded her discomfort of lodging in taverns because of sharing a room with strange men, sleeping in her clothes, the crying of babies, and filthy bedding. She was teased by a fellow female traveler as being "very insecure in herself that she was afraid to sleep in the room with a strange man" (Andrews 1990, 206). Most female travelers slept fully clothed, both for reasons of modesty and distaste for bedding down in dirty linen. Many rural taverns could do no better than offer travelers a corner in the kitchen or use of a common room where travelers of both sexes would sleep on the floor. Most desirable were inns and taverns in large towns on the eastern seaboard, where conditions were generally clean and comfortable, if not private.

Women and Travel

There were no prohibitions on women traveling alone in early America, although the danger and difficulty of travel discouraged many women from attempting a substantial journey alone. The journal of the indefatigable Sarah Kemble Knight traces this thirty-eight-year-old woman's solo journey from Boston to New York. The trip spanned a five-month period, with Mrs. Knight riding horses, fording streams, hiring guides, traveling in unsteady canoes, and boarding in public houses. Her writing details the difficulties facing any traveler, but also illustrates the fact that women were in no way barred from traveling alone.

The largest group of female travelers during the colonial period consisted of Quaker missionaries, who traveled in pairs. Once again, such women usually hired local guides to either escort them or point them in the correct direction. These traveling women provoked little commentary or condemnation for their travels without trusted male companions. Although suspicion of women traveling alone greatly increased during the Victorian era, women in colonial America were free to travel alone.

See also Knight, Sarah Kemble; Tavern Keepers and Innkeepers; Tourism and Leisure Travel

Further Reading

Andrews, William, ed. *Journeys in New Worlds: Early American Women's Narratives.* Madison: University of Wisconsin Press, 1990.

Cohen, Patricia Cline. "Safety and Danger: Women on American Public Transport, 1750–1850." In *Gendered Domains: Rethinking Public and Private in Women's History,* eds. Dorothy O. Helly and Susan M. Reverby. Ithaca, NY: Cornell University Press, 1992.

Cressy, David. "The Vast and Furious Ocean: The Passage to Puritan New England." *New England Quarterly* 57 (1984): 511–532.

Duffy, John. "The Passage to the Colonies." *Mississippi Valley Historical Review* 38 (1951): 21–38.

Dunbar, Seymour. *A History of Travel in America.* New York: Tudor, 1915.

Gragg, Larry D. "Transportation and Communication." In *Encyclopedia of the North American Colonies,* ed. Jacob Ernest Cooke. New York: Charles Scribner's Sons, 1993.

Imbarrato, Susan Clair. "Ordinary Travel: Tavern Life and Female Accommodation in Early America and the New Republic." *Women's Studies* 28 (1998): 29–57.

V

Van Rensselaer, Maria van Cortlandt
Administrator of the Rensselaerswyck estates (1645–1689)

Maria van Cortlandt was born into a Dutch merchant family in New Amsterdam. For almost ten years after her husband's death in 1678, she was the administrator of one of the largest independent estates in American history. The vast estate of Rensselaerswyck resembled a feudal kingdom in terms of size and administration. Stretching twenty-four by forty-eight miles, it encompassed most of what is present-day Albany County in New York. On this land, hundreds of people worked as farmers, hunters, and craftsmen, ceding a portion of the profits to the Van Rensselaer estate. The director, or "patroon," of these estates created the rules, established taxes, and provided protection for his tenants.

The semifeudal estate had been created in 1630, when the immense tract of land was awarded to Kiliaen Van Rensselaer, a diamond merchant and director of the Dutch West India Company. His duties in Amsterdam never permitted Kiliaen to come to America, and he appointed a series of relatives to administer the estate. Although daily control of the estate was handled in America, ownership of Rensselaerswyck always remained with family members in Amsterdam.

In 1662 Maria van Cortlandt married Jeremias Van Rensselaer, the current patroon of Rensselaerswyck. Although only seventeen years old, Maria already had an interest in business, learned from managing her father's brewery. Shortly after moving to Rensselaerswyck, Maria set up a brewery there as well. Her correspondence indicates that Maria had a far better head and more active interest in business than her husband. Jeremias had a negligent attitude toward business, but Maria had both the financial and managerial skills to make Rensselaerswyck run smoothly.

The legal status of Rensselaerswyck was complicated. Granted under a feudal Dutch system of government, by 1664 New Netherlands had become an English colony. Although terms of the surrender agreement between the Dutch and the new English government officials guaranteed Dutch property rights, it was unlikely that Rensselaerswyck, with its independent political status and its immeasurable wealth, would remain intact. The situation remained unsettled for a number of years, as Jeremias attempted to convince the new English officials to grant the Van Rensselaers a free and clear title to the estate.

Maria had six children and became lame during the difficult delivery of her last child. For the rest of her life she would need the aid of a cane and a crutch to walk. It is now believed that Maria was suffering from septic arthritis that was compounded by osteomyelitis of the femur. She was pregnant with her sixth child when her husband suddenly and unexpectedly died in 1674. Because Jeremias had not owned Rensselaerswyck and was merely acting as patroon for its true owners in Holland, it was not his to dispose of in his will. Furthermore, the title had never been officially granted to the Van Rensselaers by the new English government. The vast Rensselaerswyck estate was one of the richest prizes in America, and a number of well-connected relatives began circling around the estate, hoping to wrest full or partial control away from Maria.

Unwilling to entrust such a massive responsibility to a woman, the Rensselaerswyck directors living in Holland ordered her brother-in-law, Nicolaes Van Rensselaer, to serve as provisional director of the estate. Over the coming years, the official management of Rensselaerswyck shifted among a number of individuals, but their management was characterized by ineptitude, avarice, or extreme ill health. Several of these interim directors died, leaving Maria the only long-term person involved in the operation of the estate. Maria maintained residence at Rensselaerswyck as she raised her children to adulthood, and she played the most active role in overseeing the affairs of the estate. Her most serious challenge came when Robert Livingston, a shrewd and well-connected Englishman, married the widow of one of the interim directors. Livingston was determined to claim Rensselaerswyck as part of his wife's estate, and the question of ownership was once again the subject of a complex legal battle. Throughout the entire battle Maria continued to manage the estate, conduct trade with her European partners, and oversee the interest of her tenants. Her plan was to convince the owners back in Holland that her effective management of the estate warranted their faith in her. She traded in wheat—which she ground into flour in her own mills—lumber, and beaver skins. Under her management the estate was far more profitable than it had been under her husband's control.

Through her careful management of the property and negotiation of various legal claims against control of Rensselaerswyck, Maria was eventually able to secure title to the property for her eldest son, Kiliaen. She had already begun shifting responsibilities to him when she died of septic arthritis in 1689.

Maria's life was in no way representative of colonial women. The vast estate she managed was one of the largest ever to exist in America. Her refusal to remarry was also uncommon in a land where well-to-do widows often found new husbands within a year. Maria grew up under Dutch law, which permitted women far greater economic and legal autonomy than women would have under English rule. Perhaps her greatest similarity to other women of the era was her determination to hold on and preserve the inheritance for her children.

See also Legal Status of Women, Dutch Colonies

Further Reading
Biemer, Linda Briggs. *Women and Property in Colonial New York: The Transition form Dutch to English Law, 1643–1727.* Ann Arbor, MI: UMI Research Press, 1983.

Christoph, Peter. "Worthy, Virtuous Juffrow Maria van Rensselaer." *De Halve Maen* 70 (Summer 1997): 25–40.

Goodfriend, Joyce. "Maria van Cortlandt van Rensselaer." In *American Women Prose Writers to 1820,* ed. Carla Mulford. Detroit, MI: Gale Group, 1999.

Nissenson, Samuel G. *The Patroon's Domain.* New York: Columbia University Press, 1937.

Venereal Disease
See Gynecological Issues

W

Ward, Nancy
Indian leader and "Beloved Woman" of the Cherokees (c. 1738–1822)

Nancy Ward was named Nanye'hi at birth, and she became one of the most influential Cherokee women in early America. She was raised in eastern Tennessee, where her early life was like that of any other Cherokee girl. In her late teens she married Kingfisher, a Cherokee warrior with whom she had two children. The action that first brought her renown occurred when she accompanied Kingfisher to the 1755 Battle of Taliwa against the Creek Indians, long-standing enemies of the Cherokee. Nanye'hi took cover behind a log and helped Kingfisher reload his rifle. When he was killed beside her, she took up his rifle and rallied other warriors to help rout the Creek. The Cherokees won the battle, and Nanye'hi was given the title "Beloved Woman," a position of great honor reserved for heroic women.

In her capacity as Beloved Woman, Nanye'hi was allowed to sit with and vote as part of the General Council of Chiefs. It was believed that the Great Spirit used Beloved Women to communicate his message. Nanye'hi was given the authority to speak at council, even though her messages were not always heeded.

In the late 1750s Nanye'hi married a white trader named Bryant Ward and Anglicized her name to Nancy Ward. They had one child, Elizabeth, before Bryant returned to live in white society. The Wards had a curious relationship. Their marriage endured only a few years, but they remained friendly for the rest of their lives. Even after Bryant married a white woman, Nancy was known to spend extended periods of time visiting the couple in South Carolina. She maintained friendships within the white community in both Tennessee and South Carolina, which had important implications during the Revolutionary War.

The Cherokees, in tandem with most other Native American tribes, sided with the British during the Revolution. For reasons that remain unclear, Nancy sided with the patriots. In 1776 she passed information to John Sevier, a leader of the Tennessee militia, warning of an impending Cherokee-British attack. Sevier was able to head off the brunt of the attack, but Mrs. Lydia Bean was taken captive by the Cherokees. When Mrs. Bean refused to reveal conditions within the settlers' fort, she was tied to a stake and condemned to be burned alive. Nancy Ward, in her capacity of Beloved Woman, had been given power of life or death over prisoners of war. She arrived in camp just as the flames had been lit and rescued Mrs. Bean from the fire. In gratitude, Lydia Bean taught Nancy the art of making cheese and butter. Nancy later became the first Cherokee person to own a herd of cattle, and she profited greatly from this skill.

Over the years Nancy passed other messages to the patriots regarding British and Indian raids. Various theories have been proposed for her actions. Most likely, Nancy believed the patriots would be victorious and the Cherokee people would benefit from her alliance. Her intelligence work was not common knowledge, and if the patriots' cause failed, Nancy would not be punished. If the British won, the Cherokees would reap the rewards for their British alliance. When the tide turned in favor of the patriots, Colonel William Christian led a series of retaliatory raids against Cherokee villages. Out of respect for Nancy, her home village of Chote was left untouched.

Following the Revolution, Nancy retained her position of prestige within the Cherokee community. She was a spokeswoman for peace at a 1781 meeting between Cherokee and U.S. representatives. She presented the diplomats with a string of beads, which she called a "chain of friendship." Nancy eventually opened an inn alongside the Ocoee River and became a semilegendary figure during her own lifetime. She died in 1822, and witnesses at her death swore they saw a light rise from her body and flutter toward her ancestral home of Chote.

The Nancy Ward legend was memorialized in books, including Theodore Roosevelt's *The Winning of the West* (1891) and E. Sterling King's highly romantic novel *The Wild Rose of the Cherokee* (1895).

See also Indian Women and Leadership

Further Reading

Kidwell, Clara Sue. "Indian Women as Cultural Mediators." *Ethnohistory* 39 (1992): 97–107.

McClary, Ben Harris. "Nancy Ward: The Last Beloved Woman of the Cherokees." *Tennessee Historical Quarterly* 21 (1962): 352–364.

Perdue, Theda. "Nancy Ward." In *American National Biography*, ed. John A. Garraty. New York: Oxford University Press, 1999.

Tucker, Norma. "Nancy Ward: Ghighau of the Cherokees." *Georgia Historical Quarterly* 53 (1969): 192–200.

Warren, Mercy Otis

Poet, historian, political activist (1728–1814)

Mercy Otis Warren lived amidst the leaders and opinion shapers of the American Revolution. To a large extent, her own writing helped compel fence-sitters to take a stand during the turbulent years of revolution.

Mercy was born into a prosperous farming family in Barnstable, Massachusetts. Although she had no formal education, she was surrounded by highly intellectual friends and neighbors and had access to her father's excellent library. A college education for a woman was unheard of at the time, but as her brothers prepared for entrance into Harvard, Mercy read the same classical texts as though she herself were preparing to enter school. In 1754, the twenty-six-year-old Mercy married James Warren, a wealthy farmer and aspiring politician who shared her family's radical Whig political beliefs. The Warren marriage was a love match, as evidenced by the affectionate letters written throughout their fifty-four-year marriage.

Mercy and her husband were passionately interested in politics. They loathed the concept of a monarchy and a privileged class. They eagerly embraced revolutionary doctrines and were at the forefront of radical Boston political action. Mercy's eldest brother, James Otis, coined the famous phrase, "Taxation without representation is tyranny." Her neighbors were John and Abigail Adams. She counted Alexander Hamilton among her close personal friends. In this environment, it is not surprising that Mercy Otis drank deeply from the well of revolutionary propaganda. By the early 1770s, she had become one of the Revolution's most articulate public voices.

The Adulateur: A Tragedy As It Is Now Acted in Upper Servia (1773) was Mercy's first publication to skewer royalist policies. It was published anonymously in serial form in the radical newspaper the *Massachusetts Spy*. The publication was so popular she released it in an expanded version in pamphlet form. The piece was written in the form of a play, and the lead character, Rapatio, is a clear personification of Massachusetts's hated governor, Thomas Hutchinson. Rapatio is depicted as a corrupt force eager to bleed the colony white in order to enrich himself. The outraged patriots Brutus (modeled after Mercy's brother James) and Cassius (Sam Adams) urge their fellow citizens to "force a way to freedom." The play was wordy and clearly never intended for public performance, but as propaganda, it had value. A sequel, *The Defeat*, was published the following year, featuring many of the same characters.

Following the Boston Tea Party in December 1773, Mercy acted on John Adams's advice and memorialized the event in the poem "The Squabble of the Sea Nymphs." Other political poems followed, such as one appearing in the *Royal American Magazine*, in which she castigated ladies who refused to forgo imported luxuries. Mercy's criticism of loyalist women grew harsher in her 1779 play, *The Motley Assembly.* Characters such as Mrs. Flourish and Miss Turncoat flirt with British officers, exposing themselves as provincial Anglophiles who are easily dazzled by fancy uniforms and effeminate manners.

The fervor of revolution gave Mercy Warren entrée into the highest political circles of the patriots' cause. Following the successful conclusion of the war, her radical beliefs were no longer as popular. Mercy and her husband were accused of supporting Shays Rebellion (1786–1787), an uprising in Massachusetts when rural farmers complained of high taxes. More serious was the Warrens' opposition to the ratification of the Constitution. Mercy and her husband believed government should remain as small and local as possible, and the proposed Constitution smacked too much of an all-powerful distant government that had little concern for the common man. The long friendship between the Warrens and the Adamses cracked under the pressure of political differences. Whereas John and Abigail Adams were revolted by the excesses of the French Revolution, the Warrens believed it was an expression of true democracy.

The conclusion of the American Revolution gave Mercy an opportunity for a new style of writing. She immediately embarked on writing a history of both the war and the creation of the new government. Although the work was not published until 1805, the three-volume *History of the Rise, Progress, and Termination of the American Revolution* was a remarkable work because of the insight Mercy provides into the leading figures of the patriotic cause, many of whom she counted as personal friends. The book

Portrait of Mercy Otis Warren (1728–1814), historian, poet, and political satirist. Screened illustration after a painting by John Singleton Copley. (Bettmann/CORBIS)

furthered her rift with John Adams, who had recently completed his term as president. Mercy makes it clear she disapproved of Adams's Federalist tendencies, believing him to have lost faith in genuine democracy. She wrote that she was reluctant to criticize her old friend, but felt it was her moral obligation to alert the public to the danger of encroaching federalism.

James Warren died in 1808, leaving Mercy an eighty-year-old widow. Remarkably, it was not too late for her to repair her friendship with the Adamses. James had been the most zealous in his condemnation of John Adams, and without him, Mercy was able to extend the hand of reconciliation and friendship.

Not all of Mercy Warren's writings were political. Some of her poems were deeply personal reflections on her family and religion. Aspects of Puritanical guilt sometimes underlay her writing. She struggled to maintain her faith in God and feared that she placed her love of her husband and children before her devotion to God.

A notable writer, opinion maker, and mother, Mercy Warren's life was remarkably full, but marred with tragedy. Prior to the Revolution, her adored brother, James, had been savagely beaten for his political views and never fully recovered. His head injuries resulted in prolonged periods of insanity, through which Mercy nursed him until his death in 1783. Three of her five sons died in early adulthood, and her son James suffered severe physical and emotional problems. Her writing on the history of the Revolution was repeatedly delayed as she wrestled with bouts of blindness and sank into depression following the death of her sons—Winslow in 1791 and George in 1800.

See also Political Wives

Further Reading

Cohen, Lester H. "Explaining the Revolution: Ideology and Ethics in Mercy Otis Warren's Historical Theory." *William and Mary Quarterly* 37 (1980): 200–218.

Hayes, Edmund M. "The Private Poems of Mercy Otis Warren." *New England Quarterly* 54 (1981): 199–224.

Richards, Jeffrey H. *Mercy Otis Warren.* New York: Twayne, 1995.

Robinson, Alice McDonnell. "Mercy Otis Warren." In *Notable Women of the American Theatre,* ed. Alice M. Robinson. New York: Greenwood Press, 1989.

Shuffelton, Frank. "Mercy Otis Warren." In *American Colonial Writers, 1735–1781,* ed. Emory Elliott. Detroit, MI: Gale Research, 1984.

Warrior Women

See Manly Hearted Women

Washington, Martha Dandridge Custis
First Lady (1731–1802)

The conventional image of Martha Washington is one of a frumpy woman who was a pleasant, though bland, counterpart to George Washington. Although Martha pales in comparison to her outspoken successor, Abigail Adams, she played a large role in shaping the public presentation and character of the nation's first administration. George Washington was highly revered at the time he ascended to the presidency, and the temptation to emulate the imperialistic formality set by the English royal court ran strong among his supporters. Other segments of society abhorred the notion of an executive office and resented the creation of a presidency. Martha Washington maintained an astute balancing act, careful to preserve the dignity of the newly established office, but insisting on periods of informality that would have been unheard of in the English court.

Martha Dandridge came from a family of moderate means. The Dandridges lived on a comfortable Virginia farm, but were not members of elite society. Like most young southern women, Martha received only a rudimentary education. Social gatherings were important among Virginia's farming families, and at them, Martha was able to mingle with some of the wealthiest members of society. When she was eighteen, Martha married Daniel Parker Custis, twenty years her senior and heir to the largest fortune in the area. They had four children, but only two, Patsy and John, survived past infancy.

Martha was widowed by her twenty-seventh birthday and found herself a very wealthy woman. A year later she was being courted by George Washington, then a colonel of respectable means, if not great wealth. Historians have often cited Martha's immense fortune as the initial attraction for Washington. At the time he began courting Martha, Washington was deeply infatuated with Sally Fairfax, a married woman. The nature of Martha and George's relationship is obscured because Martha burned almost all of the couple's correspondence before she died. Both Martha and George were reserved people, and forthright displays of affection were out of character for them. Despite the lack of written evidence documenting a passionate marriage, Martha went to great lengths to spend time with her husband during the Revolution. She spent most winters at her husband's camp, including the

Martha Washington played a large role in shaping the public presentation and character of the nation's first administration. She insisted on periods of informality that would have been unheard of in the English court. (Library of Congress)

infamous winter at Valley Forge. Both before and after the war the couple seemed to cherish the few years they were able to live in peaceful solitude at Mount Vernon.

Martha Washington is best remembered for her role in defining the position of first lady of the United States. The nation's first executive mansion was located in New York City. Upon her arrived in New York, she was greeted by well-wishers as "Lady Washington." In accord with centuries of English tradition, many people instinctively used this title as a show of respect for a high-ranking woman. Some members of the Federalist Party believed all wives of men serving in Washington's administration should be awarded the title of *lady*. Martha never

used the title for herself or others, but she never renounced it either.

The first months of the Washington presidency witnessed a constant stream of visitors to the executive mansion, some of them curious women eager to meet Mrs. Washington, others who wished to shake George Washington's hand. Reluctant to discourage these democratic exchanges, but recognizing the situation could not continue, the Washingtons announced that well-wishers with no official business could call between two and three o'clock twice a week, and Martha would host a Friday evening reception each week for any who wished to come. During these receptions she remained seated beside Abigail Adams, the wife of the vice president. Despite Martha's efforts to maintain a welcoming environment, those critical of the executive branch criticized her for her "queenly" demeanor by remaining seated, as though on a throne.

In letters to family members, Martha revealed that during her years as first lady, she felt akin to being in a prison. "I have not had one half hour to myself since the day of my arrival," she wrote to a niece (Truman 1995, 19). Following Washington's retirement in 1797 she returned to Mount Vernon, where she claimed she was happiest living a life of quiet domesticity.

See also Political Wives

Further Reading

Bryan, Helen. *Martha Washington: First Lady of Liberty.* New York: Wiley, 2002.
Crompton, Samuel Willard. "Martha Washington." In *American National Biography*, ed. John A. Garraty. New York: Oxford University Press, 1999.
Thane, Elswyth. *Washington's Lady.* New York: Meredith Press, 1960.
Truman, Margaret. *First Ladies.* New York: Ballantine Books, 1995.

Wheatley, Phillis
Poet (c. 1754–1784)

Later to become known as the "Negro poet," Phillis Wheatley was born in Gambia, Africa, and brought to Boston as a slave in 1761. After the horrors of life

Phillis Wheatley, servant to Mr. John Wheatley, of Boston. Despite the extraordinary privileges she had in the Wheatley household, Phillis was still a second-class citizen in colonial society. In 1770 Phillis's elegy "On the Death of Rev. George Whitfield" was published in the *Newport Mercury*, and brought Phillis her first public recognition. (Library of Congress)

aboard a slave ship, which she later described as miserable and excruciating, Phillis was purchased by wealthy Bostonians John and Susanna Wheatley. Mrs. Wheatley had intended to train Phillis as a maid, but after realizing the girl's intelligent and gentle nature, she decided that Phillis should have an education. Although when she arrived in Boston she couldn't speak one word of English, within sixteen months Phillis had mastered the language.

Phillis's position in the Wheatley household was an odd and ambiguous one. Her chores were light, she was given her own bedroom, and she took meals with the family. She was provided with candles in the evening so she could read and study. The Wheatleys' twin children, Mary and Nathaniel, were her companions. After mastering English, Phillis learned Latin and embarked upon a classical education. Despite the extraordinary privileges, Phillis was still a slave. She could not mix with whites on an equal basis and was discouraged from mingling with other slaves.

Phillis began writing poetry in the late 1760s. All of her poems celebrate learning, virtues, and redemption through Christ. Although by contemporary standards her poetry is stiff and lacking emotion, it is consistent with the classical style of poetry popular during her era. The Wheatleys were delighted with their child prodigy and introduced her to high society. In 1770 Phillis's elegy "On the Death of Rev. George Whitfield" was published in the *Newport Mercury*, and brought Phillis her first public recognition. Her exotic background and intelligent nature made her a celebrity in the drawing rooms of Boston society. She conversed with leading intellectuals about literature, theology, and topical issues of the day. At some point in the early 1770s Phillis was manumitted, meaning that she was no longer a slave. This change in her legal status had little practical effect, because she continued to live with the Wheatleys in her capacity as a quasi family member.

When she was twenty, Phillis's health began to fail. A doctor advised that sea air would be beneficial, and Phillis was sent to London in the company of Nathaniel Wheatley. It was while she was in England that Phillis's first collection of poems was published in 1773, in a book titled *Poems on Various Subjects, Religious and Moral*. Perhaps to dispel any doubts as to the authenticity of Phillis's authorship of the poems, the book was issued with a foreword signed by eighteen prominent Massachusetts men, including John Hancock and the governor of the colony.

Phillis's travels in England would be the high point in her life. She was presented to the mayor of London, who gifted her with a copy of *Paradise Lost*. The Earl of Dartmouth provided her with funds to purchase books. She visited with Benjamin Franklin and was granted patronage by the Countess of Huntingdon. Phillis was dazzled by her experiences in England. She wrote to a friend in Rhode Island, "The friends I found there among the nobility and Gentry, their benevolent conduct towards me, the unexpected and merited civility and complaisance with which I was treated by all, fills me with astonishment, I can scarcely realize it" (Williams 1986, 250). There was talk of presenting Phillis to the king, but before this could occur, Phillis received word that Mrs. Wheatley was gravely ill.

By the time Phillis returned to Boston, Mrs. Wheatley had died. This marked the point at which Phillis's life took a rapid decline. Mr. Wheatley soon died as well, and the Wheatley children were no longer in Boston. In 1778 Phillis married a free black man named John Peters, who has been described by a contemporary as a man who "kept a shop, wore a wig, carried a cane, and felt himself superior to all kinds of labor" (Williams 1986, 251). It is difficult from the distance of two hundred years to determine what sort of character Peters had, because many evaluations of him might have been tainted with a racial slant. Whatever sort of person he was, Phillis's subsequent life was not a happy one. The couple had to evacuate Boston during portions of the American Revolution. There were several periods when Phillis was abandoned by her husband and was forced to support herself and small children by working as a scullery maid in a boardinghouse. Phillis's childhood companions, the twins Mary and Nathaniel Wheatley, both died as young adults and were unable to assist her. It appears that by the early 1780s, Phillis had been deserted by her husband and supported herself through menial labor. In 1784 Phillis died, abandoned and alone. Her youngest child died a few hours later. Phillis Wheatley was buried in an unmarked grave.

Phillis and her poems were largely forgotten in the decades after her death. There was a renewed interest in her when the abolitionist movement began to gather momentum in the early nineteenth century. Her remarkable linguistic ability, intelligence, and body of poetry were used as proof that blacks were capable of intellectual achievement and human dignity.

Further Reading

Applegate, Anne. "Phillis Wheatley: Her Critics and Her Contribution." *Negro American Literature Forum* 4 (1975): 123–126.

Davis, Arthur P. "Personal Elements in the Poetry of Phillis Wheatley." *Phylon* 13 (1953): 191–198.

Isana, Makhtar Ali. "The Contemporaneous Reception of Phillis Wheatley: Newspaper and Magazine Notices during the Years of Fame, 1765–1774." *Journal of Negro History* 85 (2000): 260–273.

Robinson, William H. *Phillis Wheatley and Her Writings.* New York: Garland, 1984.

Williams, Kenny J. "Phillis Wheatley." In *Afro-American Writers before the Harlem Renaissance*, ed. Trudier Harris. Detroit, MI: Gale, 1986.

Widowhood

Beyond the psychological stress associated with losing a spouse, women often faced the possibility of severe economic crisis upon the death of the family breadwinner. Most of the income in early America was generated through manual labor. Whether through farming, building, or manufacture, work usually depended on the physical strength of the head of the household. If a man in the prime of his life died, it is possible his widow would be unable to carry on his work. Law dictated that a widow was entitled to at least one-third of her husband's estate, although in practice husbands often gave more than the law required. Known as a dower right, or a "widow's thirds," this was to protect a widow from becoming a public charge or allowing greedy children means of getting control of the entire estate.

The severity of the economic consequences of widowhood was often dictated by the age at which a woman was widowed. If she was under age thirty, her likelihood of remarriage was high. Older women often had sons mature enough to fill the deceased father's shoes. Women in their middle years were most likely to find themselves in a difficult position. They were too young to have accumulated a substantial estate, too old to easily attract a new husband, and with children not yet ready to assume gainful employment. Most widowed women had four options for supporting themselves and children:

gainful employment, remarriage, dependence on kin, or reliance on charitable assistance.

Gainful employment was difficult, though not impossible, for a woman. In the seventeenth and early eighteenth centuries, division of labor between the sexes was not as pronounced as it would come to be in later times. Women hoed fields, tended crops and farm animals, and assisted with harvesting and preserving produce. They supplemented the family income by selling products such as cheese, candles, soap, or spun wool. Such ventures were merely supplemental to the family income and would never have been sufficient to support a household. Although virtually all women in colonial America worked, they were rarely paid wages that were sufficient to support a family. Studies indicate that women who received wages for work performed outside of the home were generally paid between 30 and 40 percent of a man's average wage.

Although it is unlikely that a sole woman would have been able to operate a farm without the assistance of an adult male, the widows of shopkeepers, printers, and craftsmen were often able to maintain the family business. Such women were usually middle class and living in an urban area. Widows became gunsmiths, leather tanners, shopkeepers, upholsterers, printers, and shoemakers. Skilled labor such as this would have taken years to learn and could not have been suddenly initiated upon the death of a husband. It is likely these women spent years closely associated with the daily operations of the shop. Women who inherited and were capable of operating such businesses were in the minority. Because most families were supported by agriculture, most widows were in working-class, rural communities. Such women would have to depend on the manual labor of sons, brothers, or extended kin to keep the farms operational.

Dependence on kin usually meant dependence on children. Because so much of a husband's estate was typically bound up in a family farm or business, it was often difficult to separate a portion for the support of the widow. Although the farm might be left to an oldest son, a certain number of rooms or a percentage of the annual harvest were typically set aside for the maintenance of the widow. In cases

---

Managing the Estate

In addition to the psychological burdens of widowhood, many women were confronted with the complex chore of serving as executor of their husband's will. This involved supervising the inventory of the estate, settling debts, and distributing property. Mary Willing Byrd (1740–1814) suffered an especially heavy burden. Her husband, William Byrd III, had committed suicide in the face of a mountain of debt. Byrd's plantations and investments had been immense, but his financial obligations were threatening to obliterate the fortune of one of Virginia's leading families. While caring for her eight young children, Mary Byrd took careful inventory of what could be sold or made more profitable. It took three years and the sale of most of the outlying property, but she was able to save the famous Byrd estate.

Source: Arthur, Mildred. "The Widow of Westover and Women's Rights." *Journal of Colonial Williamsburg* (Summer 1990): 28–34.

---

where children were not old enough to assume responsibility for the family business, a woman would either have to serve as a steward until her children came of age or turn to a trusted neighbor or relative for assistance.

Remarriage was surprisingly rare for widows. The exception to this rule was in the early decades of settlement or in frontier areas where women were scarce. After the sex ratio came into balance in the eighteenth century, only about one-third of widowed women remarried. Those who did remarry spent an average of five years in widowhood before finding another husband. The age at which a woman was widowed played a large role in her likelihood of remarriage. Eighty percent of those widowed before age thirty remarried, whereas about half of the women widowed between thirty and thirty-nine eventually remarried. Those widowed at later ages almost never remarried.

Statistics reveal that widows with no children were more likely to remarry than those who had children. This could be interpreted two ways: Either the presence of children made them less desirable to single men, or women who had children on the verge of becoming economically productive had no need of a new husband. Both scenarios were doubtlessly a major factor determining choices and varied widely depending on the unique circumstances of each case.

By far the least desirable option for a woman was to depend on the charity of the colony or church. Not until the twentieth century did the welfare state develop to the point at which it was a reliable safety net for women. A handful of widely scattered charitable institutions developed in the urban areas of colonial America. Reliance on charity was considered a shameful condition, believed to indicate laziness and moral weakness. Conditions at workhouses were made deliberately bleak in order to discourage the poor from taking advantage of charity. Poorhouses were intended only for adults, with separate facilities for destitute children and orphans. The lack of resources for women who wished to live with their children further discouraged widows from turning to public help.

Mourning Customs

Although rituals, specific dress requirements, and customs dictating remarriage all become quite elaborate during the Victorian era, there were few rules regulating how the dead were to be mourned in early America. If a woman owned a black dress, it is likely she would have worn it for a period of time. Although later tradition would insist that a widow mourn for two years, there were no such requirements during the colonial period. The necessity of re-forming a family unit was often necessary for the survival of the family, and there was little stigma associated with women who remarried within a few months of their widowhood.

Perhaps the most unique tradition surrounding death in early America was the mourning sampler. Beginning in the late seventeenth century, a common art form among women was the creation of elaborate embroidered works of art to commemorate the dead. Usually using silk thread, but sometimes the hair of the dead, the samplers might contain portraits of the deceased, the home where he lived, his gravestone, and some memorial verses.

See also Aging Women; Death and Funeral Customs; Wills and Inheritance

Further Reading

Smith, Daniel Scott. "Inheritance and Social History of Early American Women." In *Women in the Age of the American Revolution*, eds. Ronald Hoffman and Peter J. Albert. Charlottesville: University Press of Virginia, 1989.

Waciega, Lisa Wilson. "A 'Man of Business': The Widow of Means in Southeastern Pennsylvania, 1750–1850." *William and Mary Quarterly* 44 (1987): 40–64.

Walsh, Lorena S. "Till Death Do Us Part: Marriage and Family in Seventeenth-Century Maryland." In *The Chesapeake in the Seventeenth Century: Essays on Anglo-American Society,* eds. Thad W. Tate and David L. Ammerman. New York: W. W. Norton, 1979.

Wilkinson, Jemima
Utopian religious leader (1752–1819)

The extraordinary career of Jemima Wilkinson began in the most ordinary of circumstances. She was born into a large farming family in Cumberland, Rhode Island. Members of the Wilkinson family were devout Quakers, and Jemima embraced the teachings of her faith. When she was around twelve her mother died, and Jemima's interest in religion intensified. This coincided with the first Great Awakening, a time in which mainstream Christians became impassioned by ardent preaching and hope for the possibility of salvation. By her early twenties, Jemima was drinking deeply from the writings of George Whitefield, the Great Awakening's most illustrious preacher. She began to stray away from the plain, low-keyed doctrines of her Quaker church and was attracted to the New Light Baptists. Her increasingly radical opinions caused her to be ostracized by her fellow Quakers, but a serious illness a few months later was to have far more profound effect on Jemima's career.

In 1776 Jemima fell dangerously ill from typhus. She lingered in a comalike condition before making a swift recovery. After regaining consciousness, Jemima claimed to have died, experienced a vision of Heaven, and been sent back to preach to a sinful world. From this time until her death more than forty years later, she no longer acknowledged her name, Jemima Wilkinson, but insisted on being called "the Publick Universal Friend." She began an itinerant preaching ministry, moving throughout New England and the middle colonies. She was unusually successful in attracting followers of all races, classes, and genders. Among her supporters were a number of wealthy and prominent individuals. The most notable of her followers was Judge William Potter, who was inspired by Jemima to free his slaves and give up his political career. The judge built a fourteen-room addition onto his Rhode Island home, which Jemima used as her base of operations while preaching in the area. Other well-to-do supporters provided her with homes to use in Pennsylvania and Connecticut.

Jemima Wilkinson's popularity rested entirely on her magnetic charisma. Most of her teaching was drawn directly from traditional Quaker doctrine, and she offered little unique insight or interpretation. Her primary themes repeatedly drew from a handful of basic biblical tenets, such as repent sin and do unto others as you would have them do to you. Perhaps her most unusual quality was her androgyny. She wore her hair short and dressed in male clerical garb, usually flowing black or purple robes with a man's white cravat. She sometimes wore a Quaker-style, broad-brimmed hat. Contemporary observers acknowledged her to be a beautiful woman, with dark hair and eyes, and an eloquent way of preaching in which she rarely raised her voice.

Jemima's goal was to create a community where her followers could live free from the temptations of the world. In the mid-1780s her followers began scouting for land in western New York where her utopian community would take root. A spot was found and purchased west of Seneca Lake. Her followers spent years clearing the land and erecting structures, while Jemima continued her ministry throughout New England. She finally joined the "Friend's Settlement" in 1790, where close to three hundred people had relocated to be near the Publick Universal Friend.

It is certain that Jemima Wilkinson attracted large numbers of highly intelligent and successful follow-

ers, but she aroused deep mistrust as well. Rumors of sexual promiscuity followed her, possibly because of the deep friendships she had with wealthy men who donated homes to her mission. Many considered her to be a charlatan, and rumors that she used clever deceptions to trick her credulous flock were common. Although she never claimed to have clairvoyant or mystical powers, she did not discourage such rumors. One popular, possibly apocryphal, story relates to a group of skeptics who demanded she prove her powers by walking on water. She began to preach a sermon to the skeptics, asking if they believed faith was important to salvation. When they agreed it was, she closed the argument by declaring she had no need to walk on water, since faith requires no evidence to prove itself. Other stories claimed she had followers pretend to be dead, while she worked Lazarus-like resurrection charades. Many of the folktales of Jemima's exploits developed and were embellished long after her death. It is difficult to know if she ever indulged in such fraud or how she could have been successful in attracting such intelligent and successful converts if there was truth to the accusations.

A stately home was built for Jemima at her settlement. The home was always open to strangers and travelers. She freely provided education and medical care to any who visited her home. She was also an advocate for the rights of Native American tribes in the New York area. In 1791 and 1794 she participated in the signing of treaties to guarantee their rights. Her belief that all people share the same heavenly Father caused her to be a fierce anti-slavery advocate, and she believed women should obey God, rather than obeying men.

Jemima never married or had children. Her detractors accused her of promiscuity, but she never acknowledged any romantic relationships. Although she advocated celibacy as a superior state of life, she did not demand it of her followers. Jemima's utopian community was gathering momentum at the same time as the Shakers, also founded by a woman, Mother Ann Lee. Jemima's willingness to allow husbands and wives to cohabit might have drawn some followers away from the rigidly celibate Shaker communities. Despite their concurrent ministries in

New England, there is no evidence that Jemima Wilkinson ever met Ann Lee.

Jemima Wilkinson is a baffling historical figure. Her kindness to the poor and the oppressed is unchallenged. Although she lived a comfortable life, she could have exploited her wealthy followers to obtain far more luxurious amenities. Many of the hostile folktales of fraud circulated and grew more exaggerated long after her death. Yet her preaching of simplicity and humility are belied by her insistence on being referred to as "the Publick Universal Friend" and her strange choice of apparel. Biographer Herbert Wiseby suggests that although she was not a "conscious fraud," she fell victim to megalomania and encouraged rumors of supernatural powers to circulate on her behalf. She has been the subject of at least two historical novels, Robert St. John's *Jerusalem the Golden* (1926) and Carl Carmer's *Genesee Fever* (1941).

The success of Jemima's ministry was entirely dependent on her compelling personality. After her death in 1819 a few of her disciples attempted without success to sustain the ministry. There was nothing unique about her teaching, and without the force of her charisma, her following dispersed within a generation of her death.

Further Reading

Betcher, Sharon V. "The Second Descent of the Spirit of Life from God: The Assumption of Jemima Wilkinson." *Journal of Millennial Studies* 2 (Summer 1999), www.mille.org/publications/journal.html (accessed December 2001).

Juster, Susan. "Neither Male nor Female: Jemima Wilkinson and the Politics of Gender in Post-Revolutionary America." In *Possible Pasts: Becoming Colonial in Early America*, ed. Robert Blair St. George. Ithaca, NY: Cornell University Press, 2000.

Wiseby, Herbert. "Jemima Wilkinson." In *Notable American Women, 1607–1950*, ed. Edward T. James. Cambridge, MA: Belknap Press of Harvard University, 1971.

———. "Jemima Wilkinson: Historical Figure and Folk Character." *New York Folklore Quarterly* 20 (1964): 5–13.

———. *Pioneer Prophetess: Jemima Wilkinson, the Public Universal Friend.* Ithaca, NY: Cornell University Press, 1964.

Wills and Inheritance

Approximately half of all colonists died intestate (without leaving a will). In such cases, individual colonies had statutes that determined how estates should be divided among widows and other heirs. Most colonies granted one-third of the estate to the widow, often referred to as a "widow's thirds." If there were no children, the widow received half of the estate. Men who left wills were usually more generous to their widows than required by law. Prior to the early eighteenth century, approximately 75 percent of widows were awarded more than their widow's thirds. This percentage gradually declined throughout the century, until by 1790 only about 30 percent of men left their widows more than legal custom. Poor women were more likely to be granted a larger percentage of the estate than wealthy women.

Women's lives were greatly affected by the patterns of inheritance. The custom of primogeniture (leaving the majority of property to an eldest son) was common in the southern colonies. Although widows were entitled to their widow's thirds, the oldest son inherited the rest, leaving younger sons and all daughters dependent on the goodwill of their brother for financial settlements. Primogeniture was shunned in the New England states, where inheritances were far more equitably distributed among the children. Sons generally inherited the real estate, homes, and farm buildings. Daughters received movable goods, such as livestock, clothing, money, or household implements.

A widow might base her decision to remarry on the contents of her deceased husband's will. Some wills granted a widow use of the marital home or business only so long as she remained single. Men who left such wills were usually seeking to protect their children's inheritance from misappropriation by a second husband. Women who received property outright were more likely to remarry than women who stood to lose their inheritance. Likewise, if a husband was generous with his wife by leaving her the majority of the estate, she had more freedom to decide if she wished to remarry or not. Those who had comfortable fortunes might have felt no economic pressure to remarry. Conversely, a wealthy widow would have been a more eligible partner if she did seek to marry again.

The laws of coverture prohibited married women from writing their own wills. Single women over the age of twenty-one and widowed women regained *feme sole* status and were therefore able to enter into legal contracts, including writing a will. The choices made by women in their wills were distinctly different from those made by men. Women provided more generous bequests to their daughters. They were more likely than men to leave small offerings to friends, grandchildren, and distant relatives. It has been suggested that men were primarily interested in capitalizing their estate for future generations by preserving the bulk of the inheritance in a few large parcels, whereas women preferred to divide their estate among people who had been meaningful in their lives.

An important aspect in the division of an estate was the appointment of the will's executor. The duty of the executor was to take an inventory and set value on the estate, settle debts, and distribute the remainder according to the terms of the will. Executors needed to possess basic understanding of legal concepts, the valuation of property, and the common sense to administer the duty in a timely fashion. During the seventeenth and early eighteenth centuries, men usually appointed their wives to serve as their executors. Women with keen financial sense, such as Margaret Brent and Sarah Kemble Knight, were also called on to serve as executors of estates for friends and relatives. By the end of the eighteenth century only about half of the married women were appointed as executors of their husband's estate. This gradual exclusion of women from administering estates has caused much speculation regarding the apparent decline in confidence men had in their wives' ability to execute a will. Some historians claim that as infant mortality declined, men were more likely to rely on grown sons to administer their estate. Others claim that as estates grew more wealthy and complex, women were less capable of administering the estate. It is possible that the increased association of women with domesticity by the early nineteenth century made it socially inappropriate for women to dabble in complex business-related activities.

Perhaps the oddest feature of colonial wills to present-day observers is the choice of guardians for minor children. It was not assumed that a widow would retain custody of her children. Wealthy men were the most likely to appoint another individual as guardian of minor children. Although fathers' wills usually granted physical custody of the children to the mother, they often appointed another male relative to control the child's estate until sons reached the age of twenty-one, or until a daughter married. An impoverished man might make arrangements for his children to be put into service with another family.

See also Coverture; Widowhood

Further Reading

Grigg, Susan. "Women and Family Property: A Review of U.S. Inheritance Studies." *Historical Methods* 22 (1989): 116–122.

Speth, Linda E. "More Than Her 'Thirds': Wives and Widows in Colonial Virginia." *Women and History* 4 (1982): 5–41.

Walsh, Lorena S. "Till Death Do Us Part: Marriage and Family in Seventeenth-Century Maryland." In *The Chesapeake in the Seventeenth Century: Essays on Anglo-American Society and Politics*, eds. Thad W. Tate and David L. Ammerman. Chapel Hill: University of North Carolina Press, 1979.

Wilson, Sarah

Con artist (fl. 1770s)

The adventures of Sarah Wilson testify to the fact that women in colonial America were not immune from fraud and the temptations of an easy life. Born in Staffordshire, England, Sarah craved a more exciting life than could be found in her hometown. While still a teenager, she moved to London and headed directly toward the royal court. She found employment as a servant to Caroline Vernon, a lady-in-waiting to the queen. While at court, Sarah carefully studied the manners and accent of the aristocracy. She also began craving the trappings of wealth and started stealing from unattended rooms at court, including from the queen herself. Sarah stole a dress, a tiny miniature portrait of the queen, and some jewelry from the queen's private chamber. The queen noticed the disappearance of her possessions and ordered her rooms watched. Sarah was subsequently caught in the act of stealing and was sentenced to hang. The death sentence was commuted based on an appeal from the queen herself, and in 1771 Sarah was transported to the colonies to work as an indentured servant.

English convicts were often transported to the labor-hungry colonies, and Sarah's indenture was purchased by Mr. William Devall of Maryland. She was to work at Devall's rural plantation for several years of hard labor. Sarah did not linger in servitude long. She had managed to bring some of the stolen jewels and the miniature of the queen with her, and she used these to fund her escape. She fled to Virginia, where she dressed herself in fine clothes, prominently wore the stolen jewels, and passed herself off as Princess Sophia Carolina Matilda, the younger sister of the queen. She claimed that she had quarreled with the royal family, and they had sent her on a tour of the colonies as a punishment.

Sarah was eagerly embraced by the planters of Virginia, who were anxious for association with British royalty. She was invited to stay as a houseguest at a number of prominent plantations in Virginia and North Carolina. In return, she made promises of government appointments and promotions within the Royal Army and Navy. Although Sarah was able to mimic the manners of royalty, suspicion began to mount when she refused to speak German, the language of the country where the queen's family had been born and raised. When Mr. Devall heard reports of a suspicious royal princess who matched the description of his runaway servant, he posted advertisements of a reward for her return. His description of Sarah was precise, noting her rolled black hair and a blemish in her right eye. When Sarah's deception was revealed, she fled once again.

Sarah's subsequent history is unknown. Some reports claim that Mr. Devall succeeded in capturing his servant, but that she fled again two years later. According to this version, she married a British officer serving during the American Revolution. Another version claims she fled to New England, where she moved from town to town, always one step ahead of her pursuers. All that is known for certain is that she was successful in alluding punishment for her charade.

The interest in Sarah Wilson extends beyond mere curiosity at the audacity of an adventuress. Her story reveals much about the social needs of the planter class, who were still status conscious and eager for associations with British royalty on the eve of the American Revolution. It also speaks to the growing anonymity of town life in the eighteenth century. Early settlements in seventeenth-century America were suspicious of strangers, knowing they were liable to be spouses fleeing an inconvenient marriage or paupers in need of charity. Strangers were expected to arrive with letters of reference from respectable members of their home community before they received welcome. By the eighteenth century, towns were growing so large that personal knowledge of strangers was no longer the norm. As towns grew into cities, so did the opportunity for criminal intent.

See also Crime and Punishment

Further Reading

Hoxie, Elizabeth. "Sarah Wilson." In *Notable American Women, 1607–1950*, ed. Edward T. James. Cambridge, MA: Belknap Press of Harvard University, 1971.
Virginia Gazette, 3 June 1773, p. 2.

Witchcraft

The people of early America believed their world was influenced by supernatural powers. Most attributed inexplicable events such as epidemics, crop blights, strange sounds, lost animals, or mysterious deaths to the intervention of either God or the Devil. Many people believed in the power of the astrological influence of stars or some other unspecified pagan force. Religion contributed to colonists' willingness to believe in preternatural events. The

Puritans believed that women were more likely than men to succumb to the temptations of witchcraft. A common hypothesis claims that witchcraft accusations directed against abrasive women was an early form of sexism used to punish those who stepped beyond traditional female boundaries. (Library of Congress)

ministers told them the Devil was real, and he was looking for ways to tempt Christians into sin. It was believed a witch was a person who had surrendered to such temptations and subsequently had the power to use magic to bring revenge upon his or her enemies.

The debacle at Salem looms so menacingly over present-day perception of seventeenth-century America that it has created a distorted impression of communities where religious extremists vigilantly hunted for signs of satanic influence in their neighbors. In actuality, most people did not live in fear that they would be accused of witchcraft, nor in general was the rate of conviction anywhere near the anomaly of the Salem trials. Between 1620 and 1725 there were a total of 344 people accused of witchcraft throughout the New England colonies. If one removes the 185 people accused during the Salem trials from the equation, we are left with an average

of approximately one and a half serious witchcraft accusations per year. These accusations tended to be clustered around times of economic or social stress.

A distinction needs to be drawn between "cunning people" and the more sinister designation of "witch." Cunning people, usually women, were believed to be able to tap into a source of unique insight that allowed them to cure ill children, locate lost possessions, tell fortunes, or provide herbal remedies for ailments. A cunning woman was usually welcome in a community. Early America was a mysterious and dangerous world, full of unfamiliar territory, strange inhabitants, and primitive living conditions. The presence of a person who could bestow a good luck trinket or tell a reassuring fortune was a comfort to a large segment of the lower-class population.

Villagers who were willing to believe that a woman could manipulate forces for good were also likely to believe similar powers could be used for evil. Ministers frowned on anyone who claimed unique magical powers, and cunning people rarely sought any public recognition for their skills. Rather, it was whispered behind closed doors that a particular woman had special skills, such as the ability to brew an herbal potion to help a barren woman conceive. Unfortunately for the woman, if one of her neighbors took offense with her, or the community was blighted with a damaging natural phenomenon, she was liable to be suspect. If a person could use magic for good, they could use it for evil.

Powers of a Witch

A witch was believed to have the power of *maleficium,* the ability to manipulate supernatural forces to cause harm. Although this power could affect anyone, witches were usually charged with bringing harm to their neighbors or others with whom they had had angry dealings in the recent past. Children were believed to be the frequent targets of a witch's anger, and any sudden illness or misbehavior could be blamed on a witch. Witches were also blamed for causing crop failures, sickening animals, or causing the animals to wander away. Witches were viewed as unnatural beings who despised good, wholesome families. As such, they were especially likely to interfere in the reproductive process. They might be blamed for making a woman barren or miscarry a child. Birth deformities could be laid at their feet. An impotent man might even claim his troubles were caused by bewitchment.

Witches were believed to interfere in domestic chores. They could spoil beer, turn butter rancid, or prevent bread from rising. Cows might stop producing milk, or chickens cease laying eggs. One woman even claimed her inability to properly spin thread was the result of bewitchment.

One of the primary tools used by witches was the "familiar," an animal or imp who did the witches bidding. The familiar drew sustenance by nursing on the witch's body. The familiar could change shapes or be invisible. People claiming to be tormented by witches' familiars claimed to see these creatures floating through the air, seeking victims to harass. Witches could also recruit real animals to do their bidding, such as when a man claimed that early in the morning his horses had the appearance of having been ridden all night.

Dolls could be used to cause injuries to a witch's enemies. If the doll was dressed like the victim, it could then be stuck with pins, squeezed, held under water, or otherwise tormented to cause pain to the innocent victim.

Revenge appears to be a common theme among witchcraft accusations. People believed witches wanted the victim to suffer because of some insult or bad business dealing between the parties. It seems the majority of accusations were the result of unneighborly behavior, although some believed the witches were seeking converts. Witches were the Devil's tool, and as such, they attempted to recruit more witches from innocent members of society. Witches used both enticements and torments. Time and again accusers claimed the witch had tormented them into signing "the Devil's book." They claimed witches had the power to provoke convulsions, difficulty breathing or speaking, and to cause people to fall into deathlike comas. The girls of Salem repeatedly made vivid demonstrations of the torments they endured because of witches trying to coax them into temptation.

Characteristics of Accused Witches

The majority of people accused of witchcraft were women, with only one of four accusations being leveled at a man. This ratio underestimates the association of women with witchcraft, because most of the accused men were husbands or close friends of an accused female witch. Many theories have been offered to explain the correlation between women and witchcraft, because there was nothing in biblical scripture that implied women were especially vulnerable to witchcraft. A common hypothesis claims the charges against the accused women, who were often strong, outspoken individuals, was an early form of sexism used to punish women who stepped beyond traditional female boundaries. Although seventeenth-century America was undoubtedly a male-dominated society, there was little conflict between the sexes. Patriarchal authority was widely accepted, and an occasional assertive woman was hardly a threat to male power. Furthermore, the accusers were more often than not women themselves, making charges of outright sexism difficult to substantiate.

Puritans believed that women were more likely than men to succumb to the temptations of witchcraft. Women were physically weaker than men. The Devil could assault her body, looking for a way to breach her physical barriers as a means of getting at her soul. Thus, although a woman's soul was not believed to be any more evil than those of men, her weaker physical defenses left her more vulnerable to the Devil and his machinations.

When looking at the people charged with witchcraft in seventeenth-century America, no single, identifiable characteristic emerges. The accused came from every economic class, religion, race, age, and sex. Still, the majority of the accused meet the following criteria: abrasive or assertive personality; female; middle aged (between forty and sixty); married, but with few or no surviving children; midwife or healer; socially underprivileged.

What appears to be the most common feature among accused witches is the most difficult to decipher from the historical record. What were the character, comportment, and personality of these people? Were they sullen or reluctant to provide assistance when asked? Could their demeanor be interpreted as rude or blunt? We know that almost half of the women tried as witches had previously been brought to court for theft, assault, or slander. Less than 10 percent of the general population of women in seventeenth-century New England were ever brought to court, indicating that accused witches were at least five times more likely to have been accused of antisocial behavior. Many of the accused witches were disorderly people who failed to conform to the norms of their town.

An examination of the time and location of witch trials also reveals intriguing correlations. Villages that were under stress appeared to seek scapegoats by placing blame on members within their community. For example, a series of calamities struck Massachusetts and Connecticut in 1646–1647. War was simmering with the Pequot Indians, the crops were destroyed by an infestation of black worms,

and in 1647 an epidemic swept through the region. A series of accusations of witchcraft accompanied these disasters. The women were not accused of causing the crop failure or trouble with the Indians, but other frustrations were attributed to them. Margaret Jones was accused of sickening a neighbor's children in 1648, resulting in her execution as a witch. Mary Johnson was executed the same year for causing her employer's animals to weaken. In the following four years, more than a dozen other trials occurred in these two colonies. It appears that during periods of crisis, standard calamities were less likely to be tolerated as a normal part of life. Scapegoats needed to be found and punished. Accusations of witchcraft plummeted in times of peace and prosperity, although normal small-scale calamities still occurred.

Sporadic charges tended to be clustered around times of stress and tension. Such tension could occur at sea, as was seen in 1654, 1658, and 1659 during transatlantic voyages to the Chesapeake. In each case women were accused of putting the ship in danger by means of witchcraft. In 1658 the ship's crew was so certain Elizabeth Richardson had bewitched the vessel they threatened the captain with mutiny if she was not hanged. In all three cases the women were hanged at sea, and although the crew was subjected to an inquiry upon landing, there is no record of any punishment for these irregular executions.

A high percentage of accused witches were people involved in disputes. Ill temper, spiteful behavior, or quarrelsome demeanor all marked a person for exclusion from the community. Communities of size usually contain people who are not easily folded into the social fabric. Under normal circumstances these quarrels would remain localized between neighbors. When the community was under severe stress or threat, ill feelings could boil over. The abrasive neighbor, who had been merely an annoyance, now could become a scapegoat.

Witch Trials

Exodus 22:18 states "Thou shalt not suffer a witch to live." As with many aspects of theology, Puritans took a literal translation of the Bible. In 1641 Massachusetts enacted a law, "If any man or woman be a witch (that is hath or consulteth with a familiar spirit) they shall be put to death" (Drake 1968, 711). Other colonies followed suit, and the practice of witchcraft became a capital crime throughout the American colonies.

A person who wished to lodge a complaint of witchcraft needed to appeal to town authorities. Religious authorities might consult in the case, but all trials were secular. Most accused witches were vindicated early in the process. Although abrasive people were often the targets of accusations, the accusers also tended to be contentious people who carried little credibility. If there was no corroborating evidence, the accuser could even be punished for slander. If a combination of factors occurred, especially if respectable people lodged the complaint, prosecution of the case became more likely. If the accuser was of sound reputation and the "witch" was known to be a malcontent, the case would be examined more carefully. If the community was under pressure from forces over which they had little control, such as hostile Indians or an epidemic, people were more willing to pay heed to the threat of witches.

A typical case is that of Elizabeth Goodman of New Haven, Connecticut. In 1653 she was accused of knowing what had transpired in church, although she had not been in attendance. She was seen frequently muttering to herself and was accused of causing the sickness in Reverend Hooke's son, who had strange fits. After the accusations began circulating, others came forward to make complaints about Mrs. Goodman. She had quarreled with Mrs. Atwater, after which Mrs. Atwater's servant had become violently ill. Mrs. Bishop blamed her for causing fainting fits. Mrs. Thorpe claimed she had refused to sell chickens to the accused, because she knew of Mrs. Goodman's association with witchcraft. Later her chickens became ill with strange worms inside their intestines.

The court warned Mrs. Goodman they suspected her of witchcraft, but lacked the evidence to prove it. They released her with the warning that she must behave herself. She was brought up on charges twice again in 1655. After drinking beer with a neighbor, the two quarreled. The neighbor claimed that his beer was spoiled the next day and that Mrs. Goodman must somehow have been responsible. Once again, as soon as a charge was made, others came forward with inexplicable accidents they attributed to the contentious Mrs. Goodman. She was tried again, but not enough evidence could be found to warrant her execution. She was released from prison upon payment of £50 to ensure good behavior and was apparently never tried for witchcraft again.

The experience of Elizabeth Goodman is typical. She was a middle-aged woman with no children and had a reputation for abrasiveness. Evidence was presented against her, but nothing damning enough was produced to warrant a conviction.

Less than 15 percent of people tried for witchcraft were convicted. Conviction required the testimony of at least two witnesses who actually saw the accused engaged in witchcraft. Believing a woman had cursed your chickens and caused them to sicken was not enough to result in a conviction.

The introduction of *spectral evidence* into a trial was one means of overcoming the requirement of witnesses. Spectral evidence was testimony by a victim of witchcraft who claimed the ability to see invisible events in which the "witch" engaged in supernatural behavior. Because spectral evidence was invisible, it could not be refuted by onlookers who were unable to see the invisible behaviors. Most ministers opposed allowing spectral evidence to be admitted into court. They cited the cunning ability of the Devil to confuse innocent and virtuous people into believing they see things that do not exist. Spectral evidence was admitted at the outset of the Salem trials, resulting in the conviction of several women. As the accusations spread and more respectable individuals were charged on the basis of nothing but the testimony of teenage girls who claimed to see invisible forces at work, spectral evidence was disallowed. Without spectral evidence, the Salem trials quickly sputtered to a halt.

Other evidence of witchcraft was the inspection of the body for "witch's teats," which were flaps of skin, birthmarks, or other imperfections that were cited as places for Satan to suckle. It was believed that a witch's familiar needed to suckle at least every twenty-four hours in order to sustain itself. If the accused witch was fortunate, authorities would seek verification of her witchcraft by closely observing her for a full day. If her familiar did not appear, she was assumed not to have one. An unfortunate accused witch would be physically examined. It was believed such witch's teats would be near the breasts or vagina. Any mark or strange flap of skin could be considered a witch mark and used to bolster a prosecution case.

The water test was widely used in Europe, but used only on rare occasions in America as a means of exposing a witch. The theory was that if a pond or lake had been blessed, it would not accept the body of a witch. The suspected witch was bound with thumbs cross-tied to the opposite big toes, and dunked in a pool of water. Floating on the water was a sign the holy water rejected the individual as a witch, but if the accused sank, they were likely to be innocent.

Witchcraft was a capital offense, and the most common means of execution was hanging. Because authorities at Salem balked at hanging the dozens of people found guilty of witchcraft, they allowed people who confessed and repented the sin of witchcraft to live.

The Accusers

Although the majority of accused witches were women, so, too, were the majority of accusers. Accusers were of two types; those who showed signs of possession, and those who did not. The nonpossessed accusers merely suspected people as being witches. They noticed an inexplicable illness or accident and attributed it to someone who had wished them ill. Nonpossessed female accusers were more likely to complain of assaults on their children, whereas male accusers complained of attacks on cattle or spoiled property. Other than this, there was little to distinguish charges made by men or women accusers. Most of the nonpossessed women who lodged witchcraft complaints knew the suspected witch quite well. They usually lived in close proximity to the accused, with whom they had uneasy personal relationships.

Possessed accusers were those who claimed to be suffering from torments afflicted by the witch. Eighty-six percent of the possessed accusers were female. Most of these women were single and between the ages of sixteen and twenty-five. Almost all of them worked as servants. These were among the most powerless group of people in any town. Many of these girls were orphans, being raised in homes with caregivers who might not have provided them with the same loving attention a natural parent would have done. Unlike the nonpossessed accusers, these young women were rarely well acquainted with the people they accused.

Without husbands, a home of their own, and little means for attention, it has been suggested that these young women fed off the attentions and sense of importance they derived from their status as victims. The marriage prospects for these girls were far from certain. Few had dowries, and it was quite possible they would live their lives as servants or spinsters. Puritan society could be repressive and unforgiving of teenage rebellion. It is possible these girls had so internalized these norms that they dared not act out through overt rebellion, but found an outlet that was socially sanctioned. Dabbling in the witchcraft trials as an accuser garnered attention, power, and sympathy, something that would have been devoid in their ordinary lives.

The subsequent lives of these young women were rarely as positive as those untouched by witchcraft scandals. Many married late or not at all. The taint of diabolical possession clung to them. For people who did not believe in witches, such accusers were the worst sort of slanderer.

Ramifications of Witch Trials

Although most accused witches were not found guilty, the damaging accusation lingered for years over the person's reputation. Eunice Cole was repeatedly charged with witchcraft from 1656 to 1680. Eunice was no stranger to courts, having been brought up on charges of slander and other lesser crimes. She apparently taunted neighbors with her abilities as a witch, claiming she would sicken a neighbor's cows if he did not mind his animals. There is little doubt that Eunice Cole possessed an abrasive personality, and her willingness to imply she had special powers might have been a sign of mental illness. She spent much of her adult life imprisoned, and within a year or two of release was usually charged with witchcraft again. Other suspected witches were brought up repeatedly on charges, indicating there was lingering suspicion in people's minds that could not be cleared by a court acquittal.

After the horror of Salem, the momentum was taken out of the hunt for witches. Although there were a few sporadic cases early in the eighteenth century, belief in witches was on the decline. Increased education made people less credulous. Scientific experimentation was demystifying many aspects of the natural world. Most importantly, acknowledgment of the miscarriage of justice at Salem made people wary of condemning unpopular defendants based on the word of hostile neighbors or adolescent girls.

It was the testimony of the supposedly possessed young women at Salem who undermined belief in witches. When witchcraft accusations were lodged at social outcasts, the charges were credible. When young girls accused well-respected members of the community, people ceased believing the testimony in the absence of corroborating evidence. Women who had been accused but escaped execution began agitating for redress. In 1703 Abigail Faulkner petitioned Massachusetts authorities to exonerate her name, claiming she endured continuing anguish as a result of the accusations. In that same year other survivors of Salem requested and received public acknowledgment of their innocence.

See also Salem Witch Trials; Superstition and Belief in Magic; Tituba

Further Reading

Demos, John. *Entertaining Satan: Witchcraft and the Culture of Early New England.* New York: Oxford University Press, 1982.

Drake, Frederick C. "Witchcraft in the American Colonies, 1647–1662." *American Quarterly* 20 (1968): 694–725.

Hall, David D. "Magic and Witchcraft." *In Encyclopedia of the North American Colonies,* ed. Jacob Ernest Cooke. New York: Scribner's Sons, 1993.

———. "Witchcraft and the Limits of Interpretation." *New England Quarterly* 58 (1985): 253–281.

Karlsen, Carol F. *The Devil in the Shape of a Woman: Witchcraft in Colonial New England.* New York: Norton, 1998.

Wright, Patience Lovell
Sculptor (1725–1786)

Little is known about the early life of Patience Wright, other than she was raised in a devout Quaker family of farmers from Massachusetts. Her father insisted the family live as strict vegetarians, even shunning leather shoes in favor of wooden clogs. He required all his daughters to dress from head to toe in white, as a symbol of temperance and purity. Patience later claimed that her color-drained world prompted a sense of rebellion and love of color that was manifested in her later artistic endeavors. Perhaps to escape the severe formality of her family she married a cooper (a barrel maker) in Philadelphia, to whom she bore five children. Patience was a large, physically strong woman with a boisterous personality. People who knew her inevitably commented on her flamboyant personality.

When Patience was widowed in her mid-forties, she had no means of income and a large family to raise. Having talent in artwork, she took the unusual step of attempting to earn a living by creating lifelike images in molded wax. The eighteenth century was a time when professional sculptors in America were limited to producing tombstones and the figureheads for ships. Although she had virtually no training as a sculptor, Patience had an astonishing ability to create lifelike images. As a young woman she had played with creating figures from bread dough and clay. Her sister, Rachel Wells, had also dabbled in creating wax portraits, and the two began touring a collection of their work throughout the colonies.

Exhibits of wax figures had taken place in European cities, but the figures portrayed were usually limited to notorious criminals, famous people from history, or allegorical figures from the Bible.

Patience decided to specialize in creating images of prominent living individuals of the day. She colored the wax, used glass eyes, real hair, and clothing to dress her life-sized figures. The exhibits were well received, and her reputation as an eccentric artist began to grow. Tragedy struck in 1772 when a fire destroyed most of her work. Perhaps prompted by this event, she decided to move to England, where opportunities would surpass her limited career in the colonies. Bringing letters of introduction, she quickly made the rounds through the ranks of high society London. She called upon Benjamin Franklin and impressed the statesman with a head of his close friend Cadwallader Colden. Her work was generally considered to be superior to the only other notable wax sculptor in London, Mrs. Salmon.

Patience Wright's blunt, rustic demeanor was surprisingly popular in London. She mingled with the most powerful aristocrats, artists, and politicians in the city. She was commissioned to create life-sized images of famous people, including Prime Minister William Pitt. In 1773 she realized the ultimate honor, a request to reproduce likenesses of the king and queen. Her popularity increased when it became known she addressed them casually as "George" and "Charlotte." Little impressed with the social hierarchy of English culture, Patience delighted both aristocrats and commoners alike with her irreverent demeanor. Her habit of kissing members of the peerage on both cheeks and her stream of nonstop and humorous ramblings seemed to amuse the jaded and sophisticated social circles in London. Not everyone was universally impressed. Abigail Adams believed Patience to have a slatternly appearance and disrespectful manner.

Despite Patience's eccentric and rustic personality, she was a keenly intelligent and patriotic woman. At a time when tensions between England and the American colonies were heating to a boiling point, Patience deliberately inserted herself into politically active social groups. Having free access to salons and coffeehouses where political conversations ran rampant, Patience kept her ears open and scrupulously passed gossip on to Benjamin Franklin and other correspondents in America. In 1775 she gleaned information from various conversations about the deployment of troops, which she forwarded on to John Dickinson in Philadelphia.

Patience Wright is widely regarded to have been a spy during the American Revolution. It is said that she passed communications to members of Congress, concealed in wax effigies she sent to America. Although the value of the information she passed on rarely amounted to more than mere gossip, men such as John Hancock and John Dickinson praised her activities.

As the war progressed Patience indulged in some bizarre plotting. She hoped to coax Benjamin Franklin into leading a bloodless revolt of the poor and oppressed in England, causing the monarchy to be overthrown and a peace offering to be extended to America. Nothing came of her plotting, and it damaged her in Franklin's eyes. There is evidence he did not wholly respect her ability to be trusted with sensitive information, and this might have limited her usefulness as a spy.

Over time, Patience's welcome in England grew cold. One widely repeated story is that she personally scolded the king after the Battles of Lexington and Concord. It will probably never be known if this story is true, but it is known that she became increasingly strident at public gatherings where she espoused American superiority. Her decline in popularity coincided with a loss of fascination for full-sized wax figures. Small, wax portrait profiles were becoming the fashion, an art form that Patience did not practice. At the close of the American Revolution she briefly explored the possibility of opening a museum in France. When this venture failed, she made plans to return to America. Before she could accomplish this, she fell in an accident and died from her injuries.

Patience Wright's legacy owes more to her flamboyant personality, enormous talent for self-promotion, and her activities as an amateur spy than it does to her artistic talent. This does her a disservice, because the quality of her spying is dubious, but there is no doubt that her wax sculptures were magnificent.

Further Reading

Rubinstein, Charlotte Streifer. *American Women Sculptors: A History of Women Working in Three Dimensions.* Boston: G. K. Hall, 1990.

Sellers, Charles Coleman. *Patience Wright: American Artist and Spy in George III's London.* Middletown, CT: Wesleyan University Press, 1976.

Troop, Miriam. "Two Lady Artists Led the Way for Success and Fame." *Smithsonian* 8 (February 1978): 114–124.

Y

Young Ladies' Academy of Philadelphia

Founded in 1787, the Young Ladies' Academy of Philadelphia was the first chartered institution of higher learning for girls in America. The school was founded and administered by men, mostly from the ranks of Philadelphia's elite social class. These men believed that educated women made better wives and mothers. They were aware that their school was a grand experiment in providing a practical education for young women. Subjects included reading, writing, arithmetic, and geography. Noticeably neglected in the curriculum were "ornamental" subjects, such as music, art, and foreign languages. In the words of cofounder Benjamin Rush, mastery of such subjects was admirable, but too time-consuming to achieve. The number of hours needed to become truly fluent in a musical instrument or a foreign language would detract from the hours that could have been used to explore history, philosophy, or the practical arts.

Writing was considered the foremost skill the students should develop. Good writing reflected a well-rounded education, and the writer needed to possess a large vocabulary, a mastery of classical allusions, excellent penmanship, and the ability to express one's thoughts with clarity. Eloquent writing was considered a hallmark of social status, but the trustees of the school also considered mathematics important as a practical measure. A good wife should be able to assist her husband in his business endeavors, which often involved keeping accounts. Understanding arithmetic was also neces-

sary for a housewife to practice thrift, a quality admired even among the wealthy. Finally, it was acknowledged that a widow would need a good head for numbers when she assumed responsibilities for her deceased husband's affairs.

The Young Ladies' Academy was an immediate success. In the first year of operation it attracted more than one hundred pupils. Most were drawn from the ranks of Philadelphia's elite families, but a few came from Georgia, the Carolinas, Virginia, Maryland, and Massachusetts. The local girls resided at home, and the out-of-state students lived with friends or family members.

Six-hour examinations were given to the pupils at least twice per year. The girls read, spelled, answered questions, and submitted writing samples to a panel consisting of members of the board of trustees. A series of classes had to be successfully completed before a pupil could be awarded a diploma. A diploma from the Young Ladies' Academy was considered a mark of high distinction and was awarded in an elaborate and formal ceremony. A large audience of trustees, parents, and townspeople attended the events, and the valedictorian and salutatorian delivered orations. This commencement ceremony was one of the few times women outside of the theater delivered formal speeches to large crowds in early America.

The Young Ladies' Academy was a rare phenomenon. Educating women was an expensive luxury, and only a tiny fraction of Philadelphia's population could aspire to send their daughters to such a school.

Most young women needed to be profitably employed in household chores or had already embarked on marriage. The school was not designed to prepare women for employment anywhere except as a mother or high society hostess.

See also Education

Further Reading

Gordon, Ann D. "The Young Ladies' Academy of Philadelphia." In *Women of America: A History,* eds. Carol Ruth Berkin and Mary Beth Norton. Boston: Houghton Mifflin, 1979.

Nash, Margaret A. "Rethinking Republican Motherhood: Benjamin Rush and the Young Ladies' Academy of Philadelphia." *Journal of the Early Republic* 17 (1997): 171–191.

Savin, Marion B., and Harold J. Abrahams. "The Young Ladies' Academy of Philadelphia." *History of Education Journal* 8 (1957): 58–67.

Appendix I:
Household Chores Common to Early American Women

Churning Butter

Making butter was an easy task that most women who owned a cow would have performed. The milk was kept in large bowls until the cream rose to the top. After skimming, the cream needed to be stirred or churned in order to force the water to separate from the milk fat. Many household inventories reveal that owning a butter churn was not the norm, so those without a churn simply stirred the milk by hand using a flat paddle in a wide bowl.

The cream will begin to separate only if it is kept at a temperature of around 55–60 degrees Fahrenheit. During cold weather, the bowl needed to be set in a larger tub of warm water to achieve the necessary temperature. During the warmer months, a woman might try to use cold water to cool the cream, but butter making was often impossible during the hottest times of summer. After forty to fifty minutes of churning the cream, lumps of butterfat began to form. The churning would continue until it appeared that the amount of butter was no longer increasing. The butterfat was then removed from the bowl and squeezed through cloth to drain the water from it. Salt was often added to the butter at this point for flavor. The milk remaining in the bowl, known as buttermilk, could be used for cooking or drinking.

Making Cheese

The production of cheese was a difficult process that required more than a month of care and tending before the cheese was ready to eat. Making cheese required not only skill, but also a large number of cows. It took gallons of milk to yield a small round of cheese, and many women never even attempted to learn the skill. Women who made cheese could earn a substantial profit through the sale of the cheese, which was such a valuable commodity it was sometimes called "white meat." Cheese was one of the most nutritious and best means for preserving a perishable source of food.

The first step in cheese making was gathering rennet, an enzyme found in the stomach of calves that was essential to begin the curdling process. The calf stomach was rinsed, salted, dried, and cut into palm-sized squares. Each piece of stomach was soaked in a quart of lukewarm saltwater for at least twelve hours. The liquid that resulted was known as rennet water, and had to be stored in sealed jars until ready for use.

One cup of the rennet water was added to approximately three gallons of fresh, whole milk. It was covered and set in a warm place for half an hour, or until the mixture began to form into a firm curd. The curd was sliced into squares, crumbled with the fingers, and allowed to rest for a few hours. A thin liquid, known as whey, was then drained from the squares of curd. Whey could be used as a drink, so long as it was consumed immediately. If whey was not to the taste of any family members, it was used to feed pigs.

The crumbled curd was wrapped in cloth and hung to finish draining. After the draining was complete, the curds were wrapped in a damp cloth and pressed into a cheese mold (usually a small round tub) and placed under a vise to squeeze it tightly. After an hour of pressing, the cheese was removed, coarsely chopped, thoroughly salted, rewrapped in a damp cloth, and placed in the press again. The next day the cheese was turned over and the pressing began again. This process needed to be repeated on three consecutive days. Each time, the cheesecloth had to be dampened to prevent the cheese from sticking to the mold.

After the pressing was completed, the cheese round was rubbed with grease and placed in a clean, dark area. It needed to be wiped, greased, and turned each day for five to six weeks. Missing even a single day of turning the cheese would spoil it. During the process of rubbing and turning, the cheese began to form a natural rind that helped extend its longevity. An especially careful cheese maker might dip the completed cheese in paraffin to create an extra layer of protection. If a cheese was made properly and stored under suitable conditions, it could be kept for several years.

Making Cider

Making cider was much easier than making beer or wine, and most women who had access to apples and an apple press would have known how to do the chore. Cider was best made in the autumn, because as apples aged they became sweeter and made a more flavorful cider. Apples were washed, then ground into a "pommage," or apple pulp. This was heavy, physical work, and it is likely that the men of the household would have performed this part of the chore. The apples were placed in a large tub and pounded with a length of timber or a large stone until pulverized. The juice was squeezed from the pommage, and used to make cider.

Apples naturally contain a small amount of yeast and somewhat more bacteria. Two competing processes occur in stored apple juice: The yeast tries to ferment the juice into hard cider, and the bacteria works to turn the juice into vinegar. Keeping the juice cool was therefore essential to suppress the bacteria and allow the yeast to flourish and cause fermentation.

The juice was stored in jugs with some airspace left at the top, to accommodate the fermentation process. Kept at a temperature between 40–60 degrees Fahrenheit, fermentation would occur between two and ten weeks. Once the liquid was clear and had a slight bite to the taste, fermentation was stopped by pouring off the clear liquid and discarding the remaining sediment. The cider was stored in a cool place until ready for use. The cider remained good for four to six months, thus preserving the apples throughout the winter.

Brewing Small Beer

Small beer was among the most common beverages of early America. It was easy to brew at home and contained approximately 2 percent alcohol, compared with 5–7 percent for regular malted beer. Brewing malted beer usually required the services of a professional brewer. Making malt from barley was a difficult skill, requiring steeping, sprouting, drying, and cracking of the barley, which was beyond the skill of the ordinary farmer's wife.

Hops were a wild vine that grew plentifully throughout New England. Catkins are flowerlike tails that hops produce in the fall, which contain a flaky leaf essential to the brewing of beer. Catkins were gathered and separated, and the lightweight flakes that resulted were simply called "hops."

For small beer, an ounce of hops was added to a kettle with a gallon of water and heated until boiling. After two or three hours, another gallon of water and a half-pint of molasses were added, and the mix was allowed to cool. After the mixture reached body temperature, an ounce of yeast was added. After cooling, the beer was strained to remove any remaining debris from the hops. The beer was stored in a barrel, with a small bunghole left open until the fermentation process had halted, around four days later. Small beer needed to be consumed within a week.

Making Maple Syrup

Maple syrup was the only sweetener many settlers could afford. White sugar was an expensive import, and the Sugar Act of 1764 added additional taxes that placed sugar out of reach for many Americans.

The sap of maple trees contains 2–3 percent sugar, which needed to be boiled down to create concentrated sugar. Sugaring began in February or March, when daytime thaws induced the sap to begin flowing. Cuts were made into the trees, into which a notch or spout was inserted. Buckets were hung from the trees and collected by children when they were full. The sap was transferred to a large kettle, under which a fire was kept continually burning day and night. The boiling process usually took at least three days and required people to tend the flames throughout the night. The mix was then repeatedly boiled and strained until maple syrup resulted. The syrup could be sold for a healthy profit.

Preserving Meat

Colonists had three methods of preserving meat: salting, smoking, or pickling. Most families owned a large tub, known as a "powdering tub," for pickling and salting food. Drying meat in conjunction with these techniques further extended shelf life.

Pickling: Infusing meat with salt helped inhibit the growth of bacteria. It was the cheapest way of preserving meat, although it was only suitable for short-term preservation. A brine mixture was prepared, made of one pint of salt per gallon of water, a few ounces of sugar, and some seasoning. Many of the seasonings, such as clove, pepper, garlic, ginger, mustard seeds, and cinnamon, had antibacterial qualities that further helped preserve the meat. The brine mixture was boiled, then allowed to cool. Scum needed to be skimmed off the surface throughout this process. The meat was added to the cooled brine and weighted down with a board or stone. The meat needed to be exposed to the brine for three to four days per pound of meat. It was stored in a sealed container in the pickling solution.

Salting: This method used salt to remove liquid from the meat, creating an acidic environment that prevented decay. The meat was packed into barrels, with layers of salt engulfing each cut. The salt causes moisture to drain from the meat, mixing with the salt to create a brine solution. Meat preserved in this manner could keep for a year, although once a month the meat needed to be removed and resalted.

Smoking: Smoking was used for a variety of meat cuts, including venison, ham, beef, and mutton. The meat needed to be well salted before the smok-ing process could begin. This was done via the salting method described above. The meat was then hung above smoldering embers, and smoked for a period of time. The smoking process could take place in the kitchen, provided the fireplace was large enough to hang the meat well out of reach of the flames. Colonial kitchens often had fireplaces large enough for an adult to stand in for precisely this purpose. Normal cooking operations could take place over the fire, while meat was hung in distant corners for smoking. Some families had smoke holes or bacon shelves built into the sides of their brick chimneys. Other families might have had a smokehouse, a small building set away from the main home where the smoldering embers needed to be checked several times throughout the day.

It was important that the fire not be too hot, because that would melt the fat and cook the meat. The meat should be exposed to approximately 130 degrees Fahrenheit of heat. The fire was kept low by sprinkling it with water. The selection of wood influenced the flavor of the meat. Hickory, birch, or apple wood were thought to impart the best flavor. Near the end of the smoking, some women used pinewood to give a resinous tar finish to the meat. The result was distasteful, but it helped discourage pests.

The length of the smoking varied, depending on the size and type of meat. Beef might need only a day, but ham usually required three days. Smoked meat kept for up to a year.

Pickling Vegetables

Although the term *pickles* has become synonymous with pickled cucumbers, early American women pickled all sorts of foods, including peppers, grapes, lemons, cherries, beets, eggs, cabbage, walnuts, onions, and artichokes. Pickling was the most successful and popular means of preserving vegetables for use throughout the year.

Vegetables were cleaned, heavily salted, and allowed to rest for a few days in order for the water to be drawn out. The pickling solution was made by heating vinegar to the point just short of boiling for approximately five minutes. Anything longer or hotter weakened the vinegar. Into the heated vinegar was dissolved some seasonings, such as pepper, ginger, horseradish, or mustard seeds. The surface needed to be skimmed to remove any impurities that developed. Hot vinegar was poured over firm vegetables and the mixture was sealed in a container.

When pickling soft vegetables or fruit, such as peaches or cherries, the salting step was omitted and a heavy amount of sugar was used in its place. Many women preferred firm pickled fruit, and so used only cold vinegar in the preservation process. Those who liked the fruit softened used hot vinegar.

Infusing vegetables with vinegar created an acidic environment in which bacterial growth was suppressed. If the containers were relatively clean at the outset, pickled food lasted for at least a year.

Making Soap

Making soap was a disagreeable, but necessary, task. Fat was collected from beef and slowly boiled until it was rendered into liquid form. After straining any remaining scraps from the liquid, it was allowed to cool until it separated into tallow on the top and gelatin on the bottom.

Next came making lye. A barrel with small holes cut in the bottom was filled with ashes. Water was strained through the ashes and collected in a bucket beneath the barrel. The water was repeatedly strained through the ashes until the liquid developed into lye. The strength of the lye was tested by floating an egg on its surface. If the lye was too weak, the egg sank, if it was too strong, the egg sat on the top. The lye was just right when the egg floated so that only a coin-sized portion of egg could be seen above the lye.

Next, the tallow was collected and warmed to body temperature. The lye was also warmed, then slowly stirred into the warm tallow, two parts tallow to one part lye. The mixture needed to be stirred slowly for up to an hour. The smell was terrible, and this process was always performed outdoors. The liquid soap was then poured into a mold and required resting at room temperature for two weeks before it was ready for use.

Making Candles

Women of the colonial era had three materials from which they could make candles: tallow, beeswax,

bayberry wax, or a combination of any of the three. The most abundant but least agreeable to use was tallow. Tallow was harvested from any source of fat, such as deer, pork, or beef. The drippings from meat were boiled, then allowed to cool. As the drippings cooled, the rendering separated into gelatin on the bottom and tallow on the top. Tallow candles had the disadvantages of melting too quickly, sputtering while burning, and putting off a bad odor.

Bayberry wax was harvested from the bayberry bush, which grew abundantly in coastal areas. The bush produces small red berries speckled with white spots. Boiled in a pot of water, the berries yielded a greenish wax that was skimmed off and could be melted down for candle making. It took approximately fifteen pounds of bayberries to yield one pound of wax. Candles made from bayberries had a strong, sweet fragrance. Some found the fragrance overpowering, but others enjoyed the scent. The light shed from bayberry wax was brighter and longer burning than that from tallow candles.

Most desirable, but also most expensive, was beeswax. Taken from the comb upon harvesting honey, beeswax was the substance used to hold the walls of the hive together. It was very expensive, but made excellent candles. It burned the longest, had no odor, produced a bright light, and was the easiest of all the substances to work with.

Candles could be made either by dipping or by molds. Wicks were prepared by twisting pieces of cotton thread, although some women used the silken threads from milkweed plants. Candle molds were made of metal, with four or six tubes extending out from the frame. A tiny hole at the bottom of the tube allowed the wick to be threaded through. The mold was turned over, and the wicks secured to sticks laid across the opening of the mold. Hot wax was poured into the molds. The candles were removed when cool.

Dipping candles required a tall pot. The wax or tallow was heated just to the point of melting. To save time, a very long wick was usually dipped at both ends so that two candles could be made simultaneously. The wick was dipped, and allowed to soak for a few minutes on the first dipping to make sure the strands were infused with wax. The coated wick needed to cool for a few minutes before each re-dip. During the first few dips the wick tended to curl, and it needed to be tugged straight until the candle built up enough wax to prevent curving. The temperature of the wax pot needed to be kept even, because if it got too hot the wax would re-melt the previous layer of wax. After each dip, a small amount of wax slid down the candle, giving dipped candles a slight natural taper at the top. As soon as the candle was the proper width to fit in a candle-holder, the dipping stopped. Candles needed to cool for at least a day before use.

Laundry

Laundry appears to have been the chore most dreaded by colonial women. Time and again women spoke of the wretched discomfort associated with washday, and it was the chore most likely to be delegated to a hired servant if a woman could afford the luxury. Laundry was a physically strenuous and somewhat dangerous task. Washday involved hauling at least fifty gallons of water, weighing in at more than 400 pounds. The soap used had a heavy lye content, making the experience caustic and damaging to the skin. Struggling with kettles of scalding water over open flames while wearing a long skirt was not for the faint of heart.

For heavily soiled clothes, it was recommended to rub the soiled areas with a little soap, then soak them overnight in warm water. The primary means of cleaning the clothes was boiling. A large kettle of water was boiled to which the clothes and lye soap were added. They were stirred with a long, forklike paddle for only a brief period, then lifted out and placed in a basin of rinse water. Some women would have used an additional tub for water for a second rinsing.

Clothes were wrung out by hand. The heavy, wet clothes and bedding were then carried to a drying area. Some families had ropes strung to serve as clotheslines, but others would have spread the laundry on bushes or patches of grass to dry.

Because of the heavy labor involved in laundry, only undergarments, stockings, aprons, and baby diapers were washed regularly. Outer garments and bedding were seldom laundered, and blankets were usually washed annually.

Washday was at its worst in the winter, when most of the chore was done indoors. Even drying needed to occur inside, because wet items would freeze if placed outside.

Spinning Yarn and Thread

Almost all colonial women made their own yarn. It was an easy skill to learn, and literally any family could afford a simple spindle, a mere stick with weight on one end. Although not as efficient as a spinning wheel, the drop spindle could twist thread with the added momentum of the weight.

Wool from sheep or goats was used to make yarn. The fleece was soaked in warm water to remove dirt, but care was taken not to remove too much of the natural oils, because the oil aided in spinning. The fleece was squeezed dry, then "carded" by brushing the fleece between two flat wire brushes that straightened the fibers. The washed and combed wool was stored in a basket on the floor, and a single strand was plucked out, twisted, and pulled. The strand pulled up other strands of wool, which was twisted with wet fingers.

The initial strand was tied to a spindle, which was mounted on a spinning wheel. The spinning wheel was cranked by a foot pedal called a treadle. The purpose of the wheel was to keep the spindle spinning in a single direction, thus pulling more yarn from the bundle of raw wool. The tension and the twisting worked in harmony to create stronger and finer yarn. Early spinning wheels were quite small, but over time the wheel size expanded to as large as six feet. A small bowl of water was kept beside the wheel, and the spinner carefully wet the fibers as they twisted, helping create a tight, strong strand of yarn.

The process of spinning linen thread was similar to spinning wool, the only major difference being in the preparation of the raw material. Many farms grew a patch of flax plants, which were harvested in the autumn. The stalks of the plant were spread in the sun to dry. Then rippling, the process of combing the stalks to remove seeds and debris, was performed by hand. The most delicate part of the process, the retting, involved breaking the outer hull in order to extract the fibers within. It was these fibers that were used to spin into linen thread. After a thorough drying, the stalks were beaten in a process called "scutching," which rendered the fibers pliable. The fibers were then ready for spinning.

The natural fibers in wool and linen have a tendency to create small lumps in the thread, called "slubs." These slubs could be reduced by gently tugging on them with wet fingers, but some slubs were inevitable.

After making yarn, many women chose to knit it into stockings, blankets, or shawls. Almost all women knew how to knit, and would have made stockings for their families. Any remaining yarn was sold to local weavers, who used wool and linen to weave fabric on looms. Very few households possessed looms, and many professional weavers were men.

Filling and Maintaining a Mattress

Mattress covers were large sacks made from ticking, a tightly woven fabric. The most common stuffing for a mattress was cornhusks. Other scrap material could be used, such as bits of raw wool, straw, old rags, or even the leavings of hulls after threshing grain. Straw and cornhusk mattresses were typically placed directly on the floor and rolled away each morning.

Cornhusks were collected after harvest and dried in the sun. The tough ends were discarded, and the remainder was sliced into thin shreds, which were evenly spread throughout the mattress sack. A cornhusk mattress could last up to five years.

More substantial mattresses were used on bedsteads, which were the wooden frames used to raise mattresses off the floor. Rope was threaded through the frame, upon which a cornhusk mattress was placed. In the seventeenth century, only the head of the household was likely to have a bedstead, but as additional bedrooms became common in the eighteenth century, it was not unusual for bedsteads to be added for children.

Mattresses that were raised off the floor were often more comfortable. Straw or cornhusk mattresses were always used directly on top of the ropes, but featherbed mattresses were sometimes placed on top of the cheaper, cornhusk mattress. The featherbed mattress was filled with goose down and could be quite heavy. A well-filled featherbed mattress could weigh between fifty and seventy-five pounds.

Insects were a problem in bedding. Some women sprinkled a half-pound of cayenne pepper through the stuffing to prevent pests. If bedbugs infested a mattress, it needed to be emptied and the sack was boiled. Straw and cornhusks would be discarded, but feathers were more valuable. Thorough washing of feathers was usually attempted to salvage them. Bedbugs particularly liked hiding in the crevices of bedsteads. To prevent their infestation, crevices were to be sealed with lard or wax, which needed to be reapplied regularly.

From time to time, the stuffing of a mattress needed to be cleaned or replaced. If straw became damp, it could rot. Over time, straw and cornhusks became too matted to maintain comfort. It was an easy matter to replace straw, but goose down feathers were too valuable to replace. Feathers were periodically removed from the mattresses, washed, and dried in the sun or the attic.

Appendix II:
Documents

Necessary Equipment for Every Family Traveling to New England (1638), John Josselyn

The following list of recommended provisions for families immigrating to New England in the earliest decades of settlement reveals the spartan, labor-intensive world the early settlers inhabited.

Household Implements for a Family of Six Persons:

One iron pot
One great copper kettle
One small kettle
One lesser kettle
One large frying pan
One small frying pan
One brass mortar
One spit
One grid iron
Two skillets
Platters, dishes, and spoons of wood
Necessary Farming Equipment:
Bellows
Scoop
Great pail
Casting shovel
A sack
Lanthorn [lantern]
Tobacco pipes
5 broad hoes
5 narrow hoes

5 felling axes
2 hand saws
3 shovels
2 spades
2 broad axes
6 chisels
Nails of all sorts
3 locks and 3 pair fetters
2 curry combs
Hand vise
100 wt. spike nails and pins (120)
One whip saw
One file and wrest
2 hammers
2 augers
Wheels for a cart
Wheelbarrow
Canoe
Short oak ladder
Plough
Axle tree
Cart
3 gimblets [gimlets]
2 hatchets
2 frows [froes]
2 hand bills
2 pick axes
Chain and lock for a boat
Coulter
Pitch fork
Plough share

The Examination of Bridget Bishop, Salem Massachusetts (19 April 1692)

Bridget Bishop (c. 1640–1692) was one of the first women to be accused of witchcraft during the Salem hysteria of 1692. A number of personal characteristics made her a likely target of accusation. Her first marriage was cut short by the premature death of her husband, and her contentious second marriage to Thomas Oliver ended in divorce. Bridget and Thomas had a history of domestic violence, and Thomas eventually accused Bridget of practicing witchcraft. Some neighbors accused Bridget of raucous behavior, and she was put on trial during the winter of 1679–1680. Although she was acquitted, she continued to be a woman of suspicious reputation. She kept a tavern and dressed in a flamboyant manner.

The following transcript of her examination at her 1692 trial reflects the chaotic atmosphere during the hearings. Bridget repeatedly claims innocence, and reference is made of the hysterics that befell her accusers during Bridget's testimony.

Bridget Bishop's protestations of innocence were ignored. She was found guilty and executed on 10 June 1692.

The examination of Bridget Bishop before the Worshipful John Harthon and Jonathan Curren, esqs.

As soon as she came near all fell into fits.

Bridget Bishop, you are now brought before Authority to give account of what witchcrafts you are conversant in.

I take all this people (turning her head and eyes about) to witness that I am clear.

Hath this woman hurt you (speaking to the afflicted).

Elizabeth Hubbard, Ann Putnam, Abigail Williams and Mercy Lewis affirmed she had hurt them.

You are here accused by four or five for hurting them, what do you say to it?

I never saw these persons before, nor I never was in this place before.

Mary Walcot said that her brother Jonathan stroke her appearance and she saw that he had tore her coat in striking and she heard it tear.

Upon some search in the Court, a rent that seems to answer what was alleged was found.

They say you bewitched your first husband to death.

If it please your worship, I know nothing of it.

She shake her head and the afflicted were tortured.

The like again upon the motion of her head.

Sam: Braybrook affirmed that she told him today that she had been accounted a Witch these ten years, but she was no Witch, the Devil cannot hurt her.

I am no witch.

Why if you have not wrote in the book, yet tell me how far you have gone? Have you not to do with familiar spirits?

I have no familiarity with the Devil.

How is it then, that your appearance doth hurt these?

I am innocent.

Why you seem to act witchcraft before us, by the motion of your body, which seems to have influence upon the afflicted.

I know nothing of it. I am innocent to a Witch. I know not what a Witch is.

How do you know then that you are not a witch?

I do not know what you say.

How can you know you are no Witch, and yet not know what a Witch is?

I am clear: if I were any such person you should know it.

You may threaten, but you can do no more than you are permitted.

I am innocent of a witch.

What do you say of those murders you are charged with?

I hope, I am not guilty of murder.

Then she turned up her eyes, the eyes of the afflicted were turned up.

It may be you do not know, that any have confessed today, who have been examined before you, that they are Witches.

No. I know nothing of it.

John Hutchinson and John Lewis in open Court affirmed that they had told her.

Why look you, you are taken now in a flat lie.

I did not hear them.

Note: Sam: Gold saith that after this examination he asked the said Bridget Bishop if she were not troubled to see the afflicted persons so tormented. Said Bishop answered no, she was not troubled for them. Then he asked her whether she thought they were bewitched, she said she could not tell what to think about them. Will Good and John Buxton junior was by, and he supposeth they heard her also.

Excerpts from the Diary of William Byrd

William Byrd II (1674–1744) was a Virginia plantation owner and government official. Having been born into one of the most prominent families in Virginia, he owned immense estates and numerous slaves. In 1706 he married Lucy Parke, with whom he had a lively but turbulent relationship. Byrd chronicled his business and personal relationships in a coded diary, unusual for its frankness and detail. Although Byrd considered himself to have been a dignified and humane man, throughout the diary he makes casual reference to the beating of slaves. Byrd was a man of voracious sexual appetite, and his diary chronicled his sexual exploits with his wife and numerous other women. The fury that Lucy Parke vented on some of the female slaves makes it likely that Byrd's sexual exploitation extended to his slaves as well. The following excerpts provide a window into the life of Byrd's wife and slaves on an eighteenth-century plantation.

8 February 1709. I arose at 5 o'clock this morning and read a chapter in Hebrew and 200 verses in Homer's Odyssey. I ate milk for breakfast. I said my prayers. Jenny and Eugene were whipped. I danced my dance. I read law in the morning and Italian in the afternoon . . .

22 February 1709. I rose at 7 o'clock and read a chapter in Hebrew and 200 verses in Homer's Odyssey. I said my prayers and ate milk for breakfast. I threatened Anaka with a whipping if she did not confess the intrigues between Daniel and Nurse, but she prevented by a confession. I chided Nurse severely about it, but she denied, with an impudent face, protesting that Daniel only lay on the bed for the sake of the child. I ate nothing but beef for dinner.

7 April 1709. I settled my accounts and read Italian. I reproached my wife with ordering the old beef to be kept and the fresh beef used first, contrary to good management, on which she was pleased to be very angry and this put me out of humor. I ate nothing but boiled beef for dinner. I went away presently to look after my people. When I returned I read more Italian and then my wife came and begged my pardon and we were friends again.

10 June 1709. . . . I read some geometry. We had no court this day. My wife was indisposed again but not to much purpose. I ate roast chicken for dinner. In the afternoon I beat Jenny for throwing water on the couch.

27 August 1709. I rose at 5 o'clock and read two chapters in Hebrew and some Greek in Josephus. I said my prayers and ate milk for breakfast. I danced my dance. I had like to have whipped my maid Anaka for her laziness but I forgave her. I read a little geometry. . . . In the afternoon I played piquet with my own wife and made her out of humor by cheating her. I read some Greek in Homer. Then I walked about the plantation.

1 December 1709. I rose at 4 o'clock and read two chapters in Hebrew and some Greek in Cassius. I said my prayers and ate milk for breakfast. I danced my dance. Eugene was whipped again for pissing in bed and Jenny for concealing it.

3 December 1709. I rose at 5 o'clock and read two chapters in Hebrew and some Greek in Cassius. I said my prayers and ate milk for breakfast. I danced my dance. Eugene pissed abed again for which I made him drink a pint of piss. I settled some accounts and read some news.

17 June 1710. I set my closet right. I ate tongue and chicken for dinner. In the afternoon I caused L-s-n to be whipped for beating his wife and Jenny was whipped for being his whore. In the evening the sloop came from Appomattox with tobacco. I took a walk about the plantation. I said my prayers and drank some new milk from the cow.

15 July 1710. I said my prayers and ate milk and pears for breakfast. About 7 o'clock the negro boy that ran away was brought home. My wife against my will caused little Jenny to be burned with a hot iron, for which I quarreled with her.

5 February 1711. I rose about 8 o'clock and found my cold still worse. I said my prayers and ate milk and potatoes for breakfast. My wife and I quarreled about her pulling her brows. She threatened she would not go to Williamsburg if she might not pull them; I refused, however, and got the better of her, and maintained my authority.

27 February 1711. I rose at 6 o'clock and read two chapters in Hebrew and some Greek in Lucian. I said my prayers and ate boiled milk for breakfast. I danced my dance and then went to the brick house to see my people pile the planks and found them all idle for which I threatened them soundly but did not whip them.... In the afternoon Mr. Dunn and I played at Billiards. Then we took a long walk about the plantation and looked over all my business. In the evening my wife and little Jenny had a great quarrel in which my wife got the worst, but at last by the help of family Jenny was overcome and soundly whipped. At night I ate some bread and cheese. I said my prayers and had good health, good thoughts, and good humor, thank God Almighty.

30 April 1711.... my wife was melancholy. We took a walk in the garden and pasture. We discovered that by the contrivance of Nurse and Anaka, Prue got in the cellar window and stole some strong beer and cider and wine. I turned Nurse away upon it and punished Anaka. I ate some fish for dinner. In the afternoon I caused Jack and John to be whipped for drinking at John Cross all last Sunday. In the evening I took a walk about the plantation and found things in good order.

25 June 1711. My wife grew worse and after much trial and persuasion was let blood when it was too late.... My wife grew very ill which made me weep for her. I ate roast mutton for dinner. In the afternoon my wife grew worse and voided a prodigious quantity of blood. I settled some accounts till the evening and then took a walk about the plantation. Before I returned my wife sent for me because she was very weak and soon after I came she was delivered of a false conception and then grew better. I sent for Mrs. Hamlin who then came presently.

22 May 1712. It rained a little this morning. My wife caused Prue to be whipped violently notwith-standing I desired not, which provoked me to have Anaka whipped likewise who had deserved it much more, on which my wife flew into such a passion that she hoped she would be revenged of me. I was moved very much at this but only thanked her for the present lest I should say things foolish in my passion. I wrote more accounts to go to England. My wife was sorry for what she had said and came to ask my pardon and I forgave her in my heart but seemed to resent, that she might be the more sorry for her folly. She ate no dinner nor appeared the whole day.... I said my prayers and was reconciled to my wife and gave her a flourish in token of it. I had good health, good thoughts, but was a little out of humor, for which God forgive me.

Source: Wright, Louis B., and Marion Tinling. *The Secret Diary of William Byrd of Westover, 1709–1712.* Richmond, VA: Dietz Press, 1941.

About the Duties of Husbands and Wives (1712), Benjamin Wadsworth

The following essay by Reverend Benjamin Wadsworth is typical of the early eighteenth-century belief that a wife should be submissive to her husband. Like all prescriptive literature, this sermon did not reflect actual family life, but was a highly idealized vision of what the writer hoped to find in Puritan society.

Concerning the duties of this relation we may assert a few things. It is their duty to dwell together with one another. Surely they should dwell together; if one house cannot hold them, surely they are not affected to each other as they should be. They should have a very great and tender love and affection to one another. This is plainly commanded by God. This duty of love is mutual; it should be performed by each, to each of them. When, therefore, they quarrel or disagree, then they do the Devil's work; he is pleased at it, glad of it. But such contention provokes God; it dishonors Him; it is a vile example before inferiors in the family; it tends to prevent family prayer.

As to outward things. If one is sick, troubled, or distressed, the other should manifest care, tenderness, pity, and compassion, and afford all possible relief and succor. They should likewise unite their prudent counsels and endeavors, comfortably to maintain themselves and the family under their joint care.

Husband and wife should be patient one toward another. If both are truly pious, yet neither of them is perfectly holy, in such cases a patient, forgiving, forbearing spirit is very needful.

The husband's government ought to be gentle and easy, and the wife's obedience ready and cheerful. The husband is called the head of the woman. It belongs to the head to rule and govern. Wives are part of the house and family, and ought to be under the husband's government. Yet his government should not be with rigor, haughtiness, harshness, severity, but with the greatest love, gentleness, kindness, tenderness that may be. Though he governs her, he must not treat her as a servant, but as his own flesh; he must love her as himself.

Those husbands are much to blame who do not carry it lovingly and kindly to their wives. O man, if your wife is not so young, beautiful, healthy, well-tempered, and qualified as you would wish; if she did not bring a large estate to you, or cannot do so much for you, as some other women have done for their husbands; yet she is your wife, and the great God commands you to love her, not be bitter, but kind to her. What can be more plain and expressive than that?

Those wives are much to blame who do not carry it lovingly and obediently to their own husbands. O woman, if your husband is not as young, beautiful, healthy, so well-tempered, and qualified as you could wish; if he has not such abilities, riches, honors, as some others have; yet he is your husband, and the great God commands you to love, honor, and obey him. Yea, though possibly you have greater abilities of mind than he has, was of some high birth, and he of a more common birth, or did bring more estate, yet since he is your husband, God has made him your head, and set him above you, and made it your duty to love and revere him.

Parents should act wisely and prudently in the matching of their children. They should endeavor that they may marry someone who is most proper for them, most likely to bring blessings to them.

A Gardener's Calendar (1702–1779), **Martha Daniell Logan**

Martha Logan was a South Carolina housewife whose talent for gardening led her to market her own seeds and correspond with famous botanists of the day. In the 1750s she published A Gardener's Calendar, *a brief guide to tending kitchen gardens. Most colonial women kept kitchen gardens for providing their family with fresh produce, and Martha Logan's guide provides us with an excellent window into the character of gardening in the eighteenth century.*

January

Plant out all kind of evergreens, either from roots or slips. Sow late peas and beans. Sow summer cabbage and parsley; the last at the change of the moon, the first at the full, that the parsley may grow luxuriantly, and the cabbage head well. Sow spinach for seed, in a small bed of rich land; but let it never be cut, and it will yield a quantity of seed. Plant out artichokes, which will bear in the Fall after. Also plant rose and other trees, either for fruit, or ornament, except those of the orange tribe, as these are not to be moved till April. All kinds of flowering shrubs are now to be moved.

February

Sow all kinds of early melons, cucumbers, kidney-beans, squashes, asparagus, radishes, lettuce, and garden cresses, for seed. Sow late dwarf peas and onion seed; and at the full of the moon, carrots, parsnips, and red beets, in beds prepared before wanted, made as follows; lay a quantity of dung on the beds, and turn them up repeatedly with a spade, very deep; then make them up about two feet broad, trench them in shallow gutters, in which you drop your seed, cover them and let them lie. The middle of this month is proper for grafting in the cleft; if your trees have not been pruned, they must not be neglected now. Set out fig trees—plant out hops, and all kinds of aromatic herbs—set out cabbages, carrots, parsnips, turnips, etc., designed for next year's seed, but they ought to be hanging up in some dry cellar since December. Plant Irish potatoes. Sow oats, and reap in June.

March

What was neglected last month may be successfully done in this. Sow French and soy beans, all sorts of melons, etc. tomato seed, red pepper, for pickling—celery seed for next winter, which must be set out when of a proper size, and let grow all the summer, in gutters where it is to be blanched. Plant another crop of vines, rounceval peas, and transplant aromatic herbs. Now trim orange and lemon trees.

April

Sow cabbages, cauliflower, and savoys, for next winter, but let them remain in the nursery bed until August; when the rains set in, transplant them in good, rich land, laying their long stalks into the ground, up to the tops, leaving out only the leaves; from these you will have early cabbage and cauliflowers for winter. You may set out the savoy plants, when they are of a proper size, and let them grow all summer, as they will bear the heat without rotting, which neither of the others will do. You may sow carrots and parsnips, but let it be on the full of the moon, shade and water, to get up the seed. Plant out orange trees, but let it be done at the change of the moon, watering them well, until they have taken root.

May

This month is chiefly for weeding and watering, as nothing does well, either planted or sowed in it, unless you shade them. You may sow endive or cabbage for the fall.

June

Clip herbs for drying, and evergreens, if they are too much grown, but not otherwise, as the heat will be apt to dry them too much. If you have lost the last seasons for sowing carrots and parsnips, you may now sow them; but the beds must be watered, and then shaded to bring up the seeds; after the seed is in the ground, you may lay over the bed some long litter or wet straw, which must be taken off at night, and put on wet in the morning until it comes up, then shade them with crotches and boughs laid over, until they are strong enough to bear the sun—remember to make your bed according to the directions given in February.

July

This month is fit only for weeding and watering; if you have showers, plant late French beans. Early turnips, onions, and carrots may be sowed the full of the moon; but will require the same pains to bring them up as the last month; early salad will do with care. Be sure to water everything designed for seed, as much depends on it; but this must be done only in the evening, while the hot weather lasts.

August

At the full moon, sow parsnips, carrots, radish, turnips, onions, cauliflowers, cabbages, endive, and savoy; all in shady places, except for the two former, and these must be covered with boughs, to help their growth. Set out the plants sowed in April, as before directed, and be sure to water them constantly, if necessary, which will soon supply your garden.

September

As we may suppose showers of rain are frequent, sow the following seeds, spinach, lettuce, water and garden cresses, chervil, endive, parsley, late cauliflowers; all those on the increase of the moon. Cabbage, radish, and turnips, on the full; set out monthly roses, at the change, give them plenty of water and dung; you may also inoculate with the bud. Large onions may be set out for seed about the end of the month.

October

Dress your artichoke, taking away all their suckers, except three to each root, open their roots, lay about them a good quantity of untried earth and dung mixed, which method is proper in all cases where the roots are opened; if your plant suckers set them in places which have been dug out two feet square, and filled up with untried earth and dung. Trim and dress your asparagus beds, in the following manner: cut down the stalks, lay them over the bed and burn them; this done, dig up between the roots, and level it, then cover the bed, three fingers deep, with dung and earth mixed, and let it lie. You may plant celery, set it in gutters; as it grows, hill it up. Sow radish, and lettuce. Plant white and monthly roses, box, shallots, and evergreens.

November

Earth up celery, which was planted out in the spring. Tie up endive for blanching. Continue to sow spinach, radish, and lettuce seeds. Plant Windsor beans. (A liquor to steep Windsor beans, to give the first shoot strength, is prepared as follows: take three quarts of sheep dung, two quarts of pigeon's, four quarts of fowl's, and six quarts of well rotted horse dung from an old dung hill; pour eight gallons of water on it, stirring it well and frequently; after standing twelve hours, pour off the clear liquor, and let your beans lie twenty-four hours in it, then plant them out immediately.) Sow early peas. Trim your monthly roses; and, at the full moon, open their roots and dung them. Sow cabbage for the spring; but screen them from severe cold, while very young. Prune your vines; and plant out red and striped rose trees.

December

Prune and trim all kinds of vines and fruit trees, except the orange tribe. Transplant all sorts of evergreen and other trees; all kinds of roses and sweetbriars, honeysuckle, and jasmines. Sow late peas and Windsor beans, and set out onions for seed.

Source: Tucker, David. *Kitchen Gardening in America: A History.* Ames: Iowa State University Press, 1993.

The Green Corn Ritual among Native Americans (1765), William Bartram

Women played important ceremonial roles in many Native American spiritual celebrations, especially those dealing with agriculture. The following is a description of the Green Corn Ritual, an annual celebration to give thanks for corn, rain, and good weather. The passage was written by William Bartram, an explorer who witnessed the ceremony in 1765.

When a town celebrates the busk, having previously provided themselves with new clothes, new pots, pans, and other household utensils and furniture, they collect all their worn-out clothes and other despicable things, sweep and cleanse their houses, squares, and the whole town, of their filth, which with all the remaining grain and other old provisions, they cast together into one common heap, and consume it with fire. After having taken medicine, and fasted for three days, all the fire in the town is extinguished. During this fast they abstain from the gratification of every appetite and passion whatever. A general amnesty is proclaimed, all malefactors may return to their town, and they are absolved from their crimes, which are now forgotten, and they restored to favor.

Then the women go forth to the harvest field, and bring from thence new corn and fruits, which being prepared in the best manner, in various dishes, and drink withal, is brought with solemnity to the square, where the people are assembled, appareled in their new clothes and decorations. The men, having regaled themselves, the remainder is carried off and distributed amongst the families of the town. The women and children solace themselves in their separate families, and in the evenings repair to the public square, where they dance, sing and rejoice during the whole night, observing a proper and exemplary decorum; this continues three days, and the four following days they receive visits, and rejoice with their friends from neighboring towns, who have purified themselves and prepared themselves.

The Sentiments of an American Woman (1780), Esther DeBerdt Reed

Esther DeBerdt Reed published The Sentiments of an American Woman *as an anonymous broadside in Philadelphia. Written during a low point for American morale, the document was intended to rally women to the patriotic cause. The essay had a powerful effect on the women of Philadelphia, encouraging them to mobilize in an effort to collect funds and sew garments for the troops.*

On the commencement of actual war, the Women of America manifested a firm resolution to contribute as much as could depend on them, to the deliverance of their country. Animated by the purest patriotism, they are sensible of sorrow at this day, in not offering more than barren wishes for the success of so glorious a Revolution. They aspire to render themselves more really useful; and this sentiment is universal from the north to the south of the Thirteen United States. Our ambition is kindled by the fame of those heroines of antiquity, who have rendered their sex illustrious, and have proved to the universe, that, if the weakness of our Constitution, if opinion and manners did not forbid us to march to glory by the same paths as the Men, we should at least equal, and sometimes surpass them in our love for the public good. I glory in all that which my sex has done great and commendable. I call to mind with enthusiasm and with admiration, all those acts of courage, of constancy and patriotism, which history has transmitted to us: The people favored by Heaven, preserved from destruction by the virtues, the zeal and the revolution of Deborah, of Judith, of Esther! The fortitude of the mother of the Macchabees, in giving up her sons to die before her eyes: Rome saved from the fury of a victorious efforts of Volumnia, and other Roman ladies: So many famous sieges where the Women have been seen forgetting the weakness of their sex, building new walls, digging trenches with their feeble hands, furnishing arms to their defenders, they themselves darting the missile weapons on the enemy, resigning the ornaments of their apparel, and their fortune, to fill the public treasury, and to hasten the deliverance of their country; burying themselves under its ruins; throwing themselves into the flames rather than submit to the disgrace of humiliation before a proud enemy.

Born for liberty, disdaining to bear the irons of a tyrannic Government, we associate ourselves to the grandeur of those Sovereigns, cherished and revered, who have held with so much splendor the scepter of the greatest States, the Batildas, the Elizabeths, the Marys, the Catherines, who have extended the empire of liberty, and contended to reign by sweetness and justice, have broken the chains of slavery, forged by tyrants in the times of ignorance and barbarity. The Spanish Women, do they not make, at this moment, the most patriotic sacrifices, to increase the means of victory at the hands of their Sovereign. He is a friend to the French Nation. They are our allies. We call to mind, doubly interested, that it was a French Maid who kindled up amongst our fellow-citizens, the flame of patriotism buried under long misfortunes: It was the Maid of Orleans who drove from the kingdom of France the ancestors of those same British, whose odious yoke we have just shaken off; and whom it is necessary that we drive from this Continent.

But I must limit myself to the recollection of this small number of achievements. Who knows if the persons disposed to censure, and sometimes too severely with regard to us, may not disapprove our appearing acquainted even with the actions of which our sex boasts? We are at least certain, that he cannot be a good citizen who will not applaud our efforts for the relief of the armies which defend our lives, our possessions, our liberty? The situation of our soldiery has been represented to me; the evils inseparable from war, and the firm and generous spirit which has enabled them to support these. But it has been said, that they may apprehend, that in the course of a long war, the view of their distresses may be lost, and their services be forgotten. Forgotten! Never; I can answer in the name of all my sex. Brave Americans, your disinterestedness, your courage, and your constancy will always be dear to America, as long as she shall preserve her virtue.

We know that at a distance from the theater of war, if we enjoy any tranquility, it is the fruit of your watchings, your labors, your dangers. If I live happy in the midst of my family; if my husband cultivates his field, and reaps his harvest in peace; if, surrounded with my children, I myself nourish the youngest, and press it to my bosom, without being afraid of seeing myself separated from it, by a ferocious enemy; if the house in which we dwell; if our barns, our orchards are safe at the present time from the hands of those incendiaries, it is to you that we owe it. And shall we hesitate to evidence to you our gratitude? Shall we hesitate to wear a clothing more simple, hair dressed less elegant, while at the price of this small privation, we shall deserve your benedictions. Who amongst us, will not renounce with the highest pleasure, those vain ornaments, that she shall consider that the valiant defenders of America will be able to draw some advantage from the money which she may have laid out in these; that they will be better defended from the rigours of the seasons, that after their painful toils, they will receive some extraordinary and unexpected relief; that these presents will perhaps be valued by them at a greater price, when they will have it in their power to say: *This is the offering of the Ladies.* The time is arrived to display the same sentiments which animated us at the beginning of the Revolution, when we renounced the use of teas, however agreeable to our taste, rather than receive them from our persecutors; when we made it appear to them that we placed former necessaries in the rank of superfluities, when our liberty was interested; when our republican and laborious hands spun the flax, prepared the linen intended for the use of our soldiers; when exiles and fugitives we supported with courage all the evils which are the concomitants of war. Let us not lose a moment; let us be engaged to offer the homage of our gratitude at the alter of military valor, and you, our brave deliverers, while mercenary slave combat to cause you to share with them, the irons with which they are loaded, and receive with a free hand our offering, the purest which can be presented to your virtue.

Thoughts upon Female Education (excerpts) (28 July 1787), Benjamin Rush

Benjamin Rush (1746–1813) was a physician and social reformer whose progressive writing on social reform did much to shape attitudes in the late eighteenth century. He was an ardent opponent of slavery and capital punishment. He was one of the first physicians to recognize the development of physical dependence on alcohol and tobacco. Recognizing the importance of education, he was nevertheless critical of the education traditionally afforded the daughters of the elite. He believed that "ornamental arts," such as painting, foreign languages, and mastery of musical instruments, had little practical value. Rush helped found the Young Ladies' Academy of Philadelphia, a school that provided a rigorous education for women.

Addressed to the Visitors of the Young Ladies' Academy of Philadelphia

There are several circumstances in the situation, employments, and duties of women in America which require a peculiar mode of education.

I. The early marriages of our women, by contracting the time allowed for education, renders it necessary to contract its plan, and to confine it chiefly to the more useful branches of literature.

II. The state of property, in America, renders it necessary for the greatest part of our citizens to employ themselves, in different occupation, for the advancement of their fortunes. This cannot be done without the assistance of the female members of the community. They must be the stewards, and guardians of their husbands' property. That education, therefore, will be most proper for our women, which teaches them to discharge the duties of those offices with the most success and reputation.

III. From the numerous avocations to which a professional life exposes gentlemen in America from their families, a principal share of the instruction of children naturally devolves upon the women. It becomes us therefore to prepare them by a suitable education, for the discharge of this most important duty of mothers.

IV. The equal share that every citizen has in the liberty, and the possible share he may have in the government of our country, make it necessary that our ladies should be qualified to a certain degree by a peculiar and suitable education, to concur in instructing their sons in the principles of liberty and government.

V. In Great Britain the business of servants is a regular occupation; but in America this humble station is the usual retreat of unexpected indigence; hence the servants in this country possess less knowledge and subordination than are required from them; and hence, our ladies are obliged to attend more to the private affairs of their families, than ladies generally do, of the same rank in Great Britain.

The branches of literature most essential for a young lady in this country, appear to be,

I. A knowledge of the English language. She should not only read, but speak and spell it correctly.

And to enable her to do this, she should be taught the English grammar, and be frequently examined in applying its rules in common conversation.

II. Pleasure and interest conspire to make the writing of a fair and legible hand, a necessary branch of female education. For this purpose she should be taught not only to shape every letter properly, but to pay the strictest regard to points and capitals.

III. Some knowledge of figures and bookkeeping is absolutely necessary to qualify a young lady for the duties which await her in this country. There are certain occupations in which she may assist her husband with this knowledge; and should she survive him, and agreeably to the custom of our country be the executrix of his will, she cannot fail of deriving immense advantages from it.

IV. An acquaintance with geography and some instruction in chronology will enable a young lady to read history, biography, and travels, with advantage; and thereby qualify her not only for general intercourse with the world, but, to be an agreeable companion for a sensible man. To these branches of knowledge may be added, in some instances, a general acquaintance with the first principles of astronomy, and natural philosophy, particularly with such parts of them as are calculated to prevent superstition, by explaining the causes, or obviating the effects of natural evil.

V. Vocal music should never be neglected, in the education of a young lady, in this country. Besides preparing her to join in that part of public worship which consists in psalmody, it will enable her to soothe the cares of domestic life. The distress and vexation of a husband—the noise of a nursery, and, even, the sorrows that will sometimes intrude into her own bosom, may all be relieved by a song, where sound and sentiment unite to act upon the mind. I hope it will not be thought foreign to this part of our subject to introduce a fact here, which has been suggested to me by my profession, and that is, that the exercise of the organs of the breast, by singing, contributes very much to defend them from those diseases to which our climate, and other causes, have of late exposed them.

VI. Dancing is by no means an improper branch of education for an American lady. It promotes health, and renders the figure and motions of the body easy and agreeable. I anticipate the time when the resources of conversation shall be so far multiplied, that the amusement of dancing shall be wholly confined to children. But in our present state of society and knowledge, I conceive it to be an agreeable substitute for the ignoble pleasures of drinking and gaming, in our assemblies of grown people.

VII. The attention of our young ladies should be directed, as soon as they are prepared for it, to the reading of history, travels, poetry, and moral essays. These studies are accommodated, in a peculiar manner, to the present state of society in America, and when a relish is excited for them, in early life, they subdue that passion for reading novels, which so generally prevails among the fair sex.

VIII. It will be necessary to connect all these branches of education with regular instruction in the Christian religion. For this purpose the principles of the different sects of Christians should be taught and explained, and our pupils should early be furnished with some of the most simple arguments in favor of the truth of Christianity. A portion of the bible (of late improperly banished from our school) should be read by them every day, and such questions should be asked, after reading it, as are calculated to imprint upon their minds the interesting stories contained in it.

IX. If the measures that have been recommended for inspiring our pupils with a sense of religious and moral obligation be adopted, the government of them will be easy and agreeable. I shall only remark under this head, that strictness of discipline will always render severity unnecessary, and that there will be the most instruction in that school, where there is the most order.

I have said nothing in favor of instrumental music as a branch of female education, because I conceive it is by no mean accommodated to the present state of society and manners in America. The price of musical instruments, and the extravagant fees demanded by the teachers of instrumental music, form but a small part of my objections to it.

To perform well, upon a musical instrument, requires much time and long practice. From two to four hours in a day, for three or four years, appropriated to music, are an immense deduction from that short period of time which is allowed by the peculiar circumstances of our country for the acquisition of the useful branches of literature that have been mentioned. How many useful ideas might be picked up in these hours from history, philosophy, poetry, and the numerous moral essays with which our language abounds, and how much more would the knowledge acquired upon these subjects add to the consequence of a lady, with her husband and with society, than the best performed pieces of music upon a harpsichord or a guitar!

I beg leave further to bear a testimony against the practice of making the French language a part of female education in America. In Britain, where company and pleasure are the principal business of ladies, where the nursery and the kitchen form no part of their care, and where a daily intercourse is maintained with Frenchmen and other foreigners who speak the French language, a knowledge of it is absolutely necessary. But the case is widely different in this country. Of the many ladies who have applied to this language, how great a proportion of them have been hurried into the cares and duties of a family before they had acquired it; of those who have acquired it, how few have retained it after they were married; and of the few who have retained it, how seldom have they had occasion to speak it in the course of their lives! It certainly comports more with female delicacy, as well as the natural politeness of the French nation, to make it necessary for Frenchmen to learn to speak our language in order to converse with our ladies than for our ladies to learn their language in order to converse with them.

Let it not be said in defense of a knowledge of the French language that many elegant books are written in it. Those of them that are truly valuable are generally translated, but, if this were not the case, the English language certainly contains many more books of real utility and useful information than can be read without neglecting other duties by the daughter or wife of an American citizen.

It is with reluctance that I object to drawing as a branch of education for an American lady. To be the mistress of a family is one of the great ends of a woman's being, and while the peculiar state of society in America imposes this station so early and renders the duties of it so numerous and difficult, I conceive that little time can be spared for the acquisition of this elegant accomplishment.

I am not enthusiastical upon the subject of education. In the ordinary course of human affairs, we shall probably too soon follow the footsteps of the nations of Europe in manners and vices. The first marks we shall perceive of our declension will appear among our women. Their idleness, ignorance and profligacy will be the harbingers of our ruin. Then will the performance of a buffoon on the theatre be the subject of more conversation and praise than the patriot or the minister of the gospel. Then will our language and pronunciation be enfeebled and corrupted by a flood of French and Italian words. Then will the history of romantic amours be preferred to the immortal writings of Addison, Hawkesworth and Johnson. Then will our churches be neglected, and the name of the supreme being never called upon, but in profane exclamations. Then will our Sundays be appropriated, only to feasts and concerts. And then will begin all that train of domestic and political calamities. But I forbear. The prospect is so painful, that I cannot help, silently, imploring the great arbiter of human affairs, to interpose his almighty goodness, and to deliver us from these evils, that at least one spot on Earth may be reserved as a monument of the effects of good education, in order to show in some degree what our species was before the fall, and what it shall be, after its restoration.

I cannot dismiss the subject of female education without remarking that the city of Philadelphia first saw a number of gentlemen associated for the purpose of directing the education of young ladies. By means of this plan, the power of teachers is regulated and restrained, and the objects of education are extended. By the separation of the sexes in the unformed state of their manners, female delicacy is cherished and preserved. Here the young ladies may enjoy all the literary advantages of a boarding-school, and at the same time live under the protection of their parents. Here emulation may be excited without jealousy, ambition without envy, and competition without strife. The attempt to establish this new mode of education for young ladies, was an experiment, and the success of it hath answered our expectations. Too much praise cannot be given into execution. The proficiency which the young ladies have discovered in reading, writing, spelling, arithmetic, grammar, geography, music, and their different catechisms, since the last examination, is a less equivocal mark of the merit of our teacher, than any thing I am able to express in their favor.

To you, therefore, YOUNG LADIES, an important problem is committed for a solution; and that is, whether our present plan of education be a wise one, and whether it be calculated to prepare you for the duties of social and domestic life. I know that the elevation of the female mind, by means of moral, physical and religious truth, is considered by some men as unfriendly to the domestic character of a woman. But this is the prejudice of little minds, and springs from the same spirit which opposes the general diffusion of knowledge among the citizens of our republics. If men believe that ignorance is favorable to the government of the female sex, they are certainly deceived; for a weak and ignorant woman will always be governed with the greatest difficulty. I have sometimes been led to ascribe the invention of ridiculous and expensive fashions in female dress, entirely to the gentlemen, in order to divert the ladies from improving their minds, and thereby secure a more arbitrary and unlimited authority over them. It will be in your power, LADIES, to correct the mistakes and practice of our sex upon these subjects, by demonstrating, that the female temper can only be governed by reason, and that the cultivation of reason in women, is alike friendly to the order of nature, and to private as well as public happiness.

Women's Lives among the Delaware (excerpts) (1819), John Heckewelder

John Heckewelder (1743–1823) was a Moravian missionary who lived among the Delaware Indians of Ohio in the 1770s and 1780s. His observations on Indian culture were eventually published in 1819. In this passage, Heckewelder addresses the most common misconception held by Anglo society about Native American women, that of the overworked squaw. Heckewelder acknowledges the heavy physical labor performed by Indian women, but also notes their unusual level of personal autonomy.

There are many persons who believe, from the labor that they see the Indian women perform, that they are in a manner treated as slaves. These labors, indeed, are hard, compared with the tasks that are imposed upon females in civilized society; but they are no more than their fair share, under every consideration and due allowance, of the hardships attendant on savage life. Therefore they are not only voluntarily, but cheerfully submitted to; and as women are not obliged to live with their husbands any longer than suits their pleasure or convenience, it cannot be supposed that they would submit to be loaded with unjust or unequal burdens.

Marriages among the Indians are not, as with us, contracted for life; it is understood on both sides that the parties are not to live together any longer than they shall be pleased with each other. The husband may put away his wife whenever he pleases, and the woman may in like manner abandon her husband. Therefore the connection is not attended with any vows, promises, or ceremonies of any kind. An Indian takes a wife as it were on trial, determined, however, in his own mind not to forsake her if she behaves well, and particularly if he has children by her. The woman, sensible of this, does on her part everything in her power to please her husband, particularly if he is a good hunter or trapper, capable of maintaining her by his skill and industry, and protecting her by his strength and courage.

When a marriage takes places, the duties and labors incumbent on each party are well known to both. It is understood that the husband is to build a house for them to dwell in, to find the necessary implements of husbandry, as axes, hoes, &c.; to provide a canoe, and also dishes, bowls, and other necessary vessels for housekeeping. The woman generally has a kettle or two, and some other articles of kitchen furniture, which she brings with her. The husband, as master of the family, considers himself bound to support it by his bodily exertions, as hunting, trapping, &c.; the woman, as his help-mate, takes upon herself the labors of the field, as is far from considering them as more important than those to which her husband is subjected, being well satisfied that with his gun and traps he can maintain a family in any place where game is to be found; nor do they think it any hardship imposed upon them; for they themselves say, that while their field labor employs them at most six weeks in the year, that of the men continues the whole year round . . .

The work of the women is not hard or difficult. They are both able and willing to do it, and always perform it with cheerfulness. Mothers teach their daughters those duties which common sense would otherwise point out to them when grown up. Within doors, their labor is very trifling; there is seldom more than one pot or kettle to attend to. There is no scrubbing of the house, and but little to wash, and that not often. Their principle occupations are to cut and fetch in the fire wood, till the ground, sow and reap the grain, and pound the corn in mortars for their pottage, and make bread which they bake in ashes. When going on a journey, or to hunting camps with their husbands, if they have no horses, they carry a pack on their backs which often appears heavier than it really is; it generally consists of a blanket, a dressed deer skin for moccasins, a few articles of kitchen furniture, as a kettle, bowl, or dish, with spoons, and some bread, corn, salt, &c., for their nourishment. I have never known an Indian woman [to] complain of the hardship of carrying this burden, which serves for their own comfort and support as well as of their husbands.

The tilling of the ground at home, getting of the fire wood, and pounding of corn in mortars, is frequently done by female parties, much in the manner of those husking, quilting, and other frolics (which they are called), which are so common in some parts of the United States, particularly to the eastward. The labor is thus quickly and easily performed; when it is over, and sometimes in intervals, they sit down to enjoy themselves by feasting on some good victuals, prepared for them by the person or family for whom they work, and which the man has taken care to provide before hand from the

woods; for this is considered a principal part of the business, as there are generally more or less of the females assembled who have not, perhaps for a long time, tasted a morsel of meat, being either widows, or orphans, or otherwise in straightened circumstances. Even the chat which passes during their joint labors is highly diverting to them, and so they seek to be employed in this way as long as they can, by going round to all those in the village who have ground to till.

When the harvest is in, which generally happens by the end of September, the women have little else to do than prepare the daily victuals, and get fire wood, until the latter end of February or beginning of March, as the season is more or less backward, when they go to their sugar camps, where they extract sugar from the maple tree. The men having built or repaired their temporary cabin, and made all the troughs of various sizes, the women commence making sugar, while the men are looking out for meat, at this time generally fat bears, which are still in their winter quarters. When at home, they will occasionally assist their wives in gathering the sap, watch the kettles in their absence, that the syrup may not boil over.

A man who wishes for his wife to be with him while he is out hunting in the woods, needs only tell her, that on such a day they will go to such a place, where he will hunt for a length of time, and she will be sure to have provisions and everything else that is necessary in complete readiness, and well packed up to carry to the spot; for the man, as soon as he enters the woods, has to be looking out and about for game, and therefore cannot be encumbered with any burden; after wounding a deer, he may have to pursue it for several miles, often running it fairly down. The woman, therefore, takes charge of the baggage, brings it to the place of encampment, and there, immediately enters on the duties of housekeeping, as if they were at home; she moreover takes pains to dry as much meat as she can, that none may be lost; she carefully puts the tallow up, assists in drying the skins, gathers as much wild hemp as possible for the purpose of making strings, carrying bands, bags and other necessary articles, collects roots for dying; in short, does everything in her power to leave no care to her husband but the important one of providing meat for the family.

After all, the fatigue of the women is by no means to be compared to that of the men. Their hard and difficult employments are periodical and of short duration, while their husband's labors are constant and severe in the extreme. Were a man to take upon himself a part of his wife's duty, in addition to his own, he must necessary sink under the load, and of course his family must suffer with him. On his exertions as a hunter, their existence depends.

Source: Woloch, Nancy, ed. *Early American Women: A Documentary History, 1600–1900.* New York: McGraw-Hill, 2002.

Bibliography

Overviews of Colonial Life and Times

Cooke, Jacob Ernest, ed. *Encyclopedia of the North American Colonies.* New York: Charles Scribner's Sons, 1993. This is an outstanding, three-volume set that covers all aspects of life in colonial America. Each major topic, such as marriage, labor systems, festival traditions, or commerce, has chapter-length essays outlining the characteristics of the topic in the British, Spanish, French, and Dutch colonies. Special essays throughout deal with the unique experiences of Africans or Native Americans. Each essay has an outstanding bibliography for further research.

Deetz, James, and Patricia Scott Deetz. *The Times of Their Lives: Life, Love, and Death in Plymouth Colony.* New York: W. H. Freeman, 2000. One of the best studies of Pilgrim life in early America. The Deetzes recount the difficulties of the first years of the Plymouth settlement and also provide insights into the process of historical research.

DePauw, Linda Grant, and Conover Hunt. *Remember the Ladies: Women in America, 1750–1815.* New York: Viking Press, 1975. Originally designed to accompany a museum exhibit on women in early America, this highly readable book contains a survey of the period, covering topics such as motherhood, women at work, fashion, and marriage. Lavishly illustrated with full color photographs, it sheds light on many details and nuances of daily life in colonial America.

Fischer, David Hackett. *Albion's Seed: Four British Folkways in America.* New York: Oxford University Press, 1989. This book examines the cultural traditions of four distinct waves of English immigrants: the Puritans of New England, the aristocratic elite and their indentured servants who settled Virginia, the Quakers of Maryland, and the Scots-Irish immigrants who traveled to the backcountry. Fischer does an excellent job exploring how the differing economic, religious, and cultural traditions of each group influenced the development of American society. Special attention is given to speech patterns, marriage traditions, gender differences, food, dress, and recreation.

Hawke, David Freeman. *Everyday Life in Early America.* New York: Harper and Row, 1988. A breezy, light read, this book describes how early farms operated, what a typical home environment would have looked like, medical issues, contemporary manners, war, Indians, and superstitions.

Hoffer, Peter Charles. *Sensory Worlds of Early America.* Baltimore: Johns Hopkins University Press, 2003. A highly imaginative examination of what it felt like to live in early America. Hoffer examines issues such as how different races perceived and experienced the witch trials, the American Revolution, and the Great Awakening. He uses primary sources to explore how settlers experienced the scents, sounds, food, clothing, and work in the New World.

Holliday, Carl. *Woman's Life in Colonial Days.* Mineola, NY: Dover Publications, 1999. Reprint of 1922 edition. This is a dated and somewhat patronizing look at women in colonial America, which nevertheless provides information on daily activities, such as cooking, letter writing, visiting, and care of the home. The book focuses exclusively on upper-class women and lacks the objectivity of later research.

Nash, Gary B. *Red, White, and Black: The Peoples of Early America.* Englewood Cliffs, NJ: Prentice-Hall, 1974. This presents a nice combination of a narrative history of the earliest century of European settlement and a cultural exploration of Native American, African, and European settlers. Nash attempts to show how the actions of each group were perceived by the others, resulting in culture clashes and occasional cooperation. Nash addresses how European colonization impacted Indians and Africans, as well as the far-less-researched angle of how Africans and Indians shaped European culture and settlement in America.

Tate, Thad W., and David L. Ammerman, eds. *The Chesapeake in the Seventeenth Century: Essays on Anglo-American Society and Politics.* Chapel Hill: University of North Carolina Press, 1979. This book contains several excellent essays on the hardships of life in early America. Carville Earle examines how disease wreaked havoc on the early settlers. Two essays address how premature death disrupted traditional family patterns, which led to the prevalence of orphans, stepfamilies, and a sense of impermanence. Other essays explore settlement patterns, motivations for immigration, servitude, and the rise of an elite class.

Wolf, Stephanie Grauman. *As Various as Their Land: The Everyday Lives of Eighteenth Century Americans.* New York: HarperCollins, 1994. The book represents an excellent exploration of the daily rituals of everyday life, including topics such as the contents of a typical home, role of romantic love, and the nature of the work environment. Special attention is paid to how the diverse heritage of early immigrants manifested itself in the new environment of America.

Legal Aspects

Dayton, Cornelia Hughes. *Women before the Bar: Gender, Law, and Society in Connecticut, 1639–1789.* Chapel Hill: University of North Carolina Press, 1995. This comprehensive study examines various ways women were involved in legal actions, including debt, divorce, property and inheritance, rape, and slander lawsuits. The author uses the stories of dozens of women to illustrate her conclusions. She also examines how Puritanism provided women with greater access to the legal system, but as Puritan influence declined in Connecticut, the legal system took on the character of the traditional, patriarchal model inherited from England. Dayton concludes that women's legal standing declined throughout the eighteenth century as courtrooms moved to accommodate the commercial interests of men.

Grossberg, Michael. *Governing the Hearth: Law and Family in Nineteenth Century America.* Chapel Hill: University of North Carolina Press, 1985. This book covers all aspects of domestic law, including marriage and courtship issues, adoption, abortion, and custody rights. Most of this book is devoted to research in the later half of the nineteenth century and thus falls outside the scope of "early America." The author provides extensive background for each issue, making it relevant to the law of colonial society.

Hoffer, Peter, and N. E. H. Hull. *Murdering Mothers: Infanticide in England and New England, 1558–1803.* New York: New York University Press, 1981. This book studies the environmental factors that prompted some women to commit infanticide and the punitive factors that caused many women to conceal illegitimate pregnancies. The authors find that infanticide declined in the eighteenth century after the stigma of unwed pregnancy softened.

Hull, N. E. H. *Female Felons: Women and Serious Crime in Colonial Massachusetts.* Urbana: University of Illinois Press, 1987. This is an excellent overview of deviance in early America. Hull covers the characteristics of the female felon, the nature of crimes committed by women, the legal proceedings surrounding a court case, and the nature of punishment. Gender differences are revealed in the nature and circumstances of the types of crimes committed by men and women. Although female perpetrators usually accounted for no more than 10 percent of serious crime in colonial America, the nature of their crimes reveal much about domestic and societal pressures that shaped their world.

Pleck, Elizabeth. *Domestic Tyranny: The Making of American Social Policy against Family Violence from*

Colonial Times to the Present. New York: Oxford University Press, 1987. This book traces public policy and domestic violence beginning with the first laws passed by the Puritans of Massachusetts. The author asserts that through most of American history, laws and policy have been designed to strengthen the family, thereby preferring family reconciliation over punishment of abusers or protection of victims.

Salmon, Marylynn. *Women and the Law of Property in Early America.* Chapel Hill: University of North Carolina Press, 1986. Salmon examines how the law impacted women in their daily lives from 1750 to 1830. The author explores how contract law restricted women's access to property and how this might have influenced the choices a woman had in life. She also discusses the topics of divorce, separation, alimony, contracts, inheritance, and widowhood. Both case histories and the theoretical construction of the law are presented.

Sturtz, Linda L. *Within Her Power: Propertied Women in Colonial Virginia.* New York: Routledge, 2002. Although recent scholarship has documented the rise and power of propertied women in New England, Sturtz asserts this phenomenon to have occurred in the more patriarchal South as well. She studies examples of women who inherited farms, slaves, taverns, and other businesses and documents how these women played a limited role in the colonial economy.

Social Life and Customs

Baumgarten, Linda. *What Clothes Reveal: The Language of Clothing in Colonial and Federal America.* Williamsburg, VA: Colonial Williamsburg Foundation, 2002. This is a beautifully illustrated book richly embellished by hundreds of photographs and details of fabric. The author explores how clothing can be used to gain insight into the lives of Americans. The cut, fabric, and dimensions of the clothes give insight into status, occupation, functional needs, and aesthetic tastes of colonials.

Benson, Mary Sumner. *Women in Eighteenth Century America: A Study of Opinion and Social Usage.* New York: Columbia University Press, 1935. In this classic in the field, Benson examines the theoretical attitudes toward women as they were treated in religious litera-

ture, educational opportunities, and literary essays. She acknowledges that the reality of women's lives differed from the idealized views presented in prescriptive literature and includes chapters on legislation, commercial activities, and personal narratives of women in an attempt to reconstruct how women actually lived.

Berkin, Carol. *First Generations: Women in Colonial America.* New York: Hill and Wang, 1996. An excellent introduction to the period, this book offers a highly readable account of how European, Indian, and African women experienced issues such as marriage, work, health, and war. It also covers the rise of the upper class and the effect of the American Revolution on various groups of women.

Brown, Kathleen M. *Good Wives, Nasty Wenches, and Anxious Patriarchs: Gender, Race, and Power in Colonial Virginia.* Chapel Hill: University of North Carolina Press, 1996. This book covers an impressive collection of materials to portray the effect of race and gender on the formulation of legal and social codes that governed behavior in colonial Virginia. It provides a good analysis of how the rise of slavery transformed gender relations in the South.

Clinton, Catherine. *The Plantation Mistress: Woman's World in the Old South.* New York: Pantheon Books, 1982. Here Clinton offers an excellent examination of the life, work, and customs of elite white women of the plantation South. For the most part, the book concentrates on the nineteenth century, but some eighteenth-century women and their living conditions are addressed.

Crane, Elaine Forman. *Ebb Tide in New England: Women, Seaports, and Social Change 1630–1800.* Boston: Northeastern University Press, 1998. Much of this work focuses on how the maritime industries affected the lives of women left in harbor towns, but Crane also discusses how the supporting industries such as manufacturing and trade shaped women's legal and economic lives.

———. *Killed Strangely: The Death of Rebecca Cornell.* Ithaca, NY: Cornell University Press, 2002. Crane uses the death of an elderly woman in 1673 to examine complex family relationships, economic restrictions, and legal aspects of life in early New England. Rebecca Cornell's son was tried and ultimately executed for her death, despite strong evidence that the death was accidental rather than murder. The reasons how such a trial and verdict could have occurred provide excellent insight into family and village dynamics.

Gundersen, Joan R. *To Be Useful to the World: Women in Revolutionary America, 1740–1790.* New York: Twayne Publishers, 1996. A highly readable overview of women in the Revolutionary era. Special attention is paid to the experiences of women as they related to their children, servants, race relations, and the legal environment.

Hambleton, Else. *Daughters of Eve: Pregnant Brides and Unwed Mothers in Seventeenth Century Essex County, Massachusetts.* New York: Routledge, 2004. The author examines fornication and paternity court records from the 1640s through the 1690s, which reveal changing attitudes toward illegitimacy and premarital sex. She finds that women suffered disproportionate stigmatization after straying from Puritan ideals of chastity.

Kamensky, Jane. *The Colonial Mosaic: American Women, 1600–1760.* New York: Oxford University Press, 1995. Written for a young adult audience, this book is a highly readable survey of women in early America. Lavishly illustrated, with an engaging text and a mere 154 pages, it will appeal to adults who are looking for a quick read. It surveys the trials of frontier settlement, the variety of religious and work experience, the witchcraft trials, and the substantial transformation that occurred in the eighteenth century.

Kierner, Cynthia A. *Beyond the Household: Women's Place in the Early South, 1700–1835.* Ithaca, NY: Cornell University Press, 1998. Kierner focuses on the experience of upper-class, southern women as a lens through which to view the distinctive aspects of southern culture. She provides insight into the characteristics of gentility valued by southerners and how elite women's education became increasingly ornamental, emphasizing dancing, foreign languages, and decorative needlework over the practical activities of domestic farm life. Rather than concluding that this ornamental education was useless, Kierner argues that these hallmarks of gentility were used by southerners to secure their place in the social hierarchy.

Koehler, Lyle. *A Search for Power: The Weaker Sex in Seventeenth Century New England.* Urbana: University of Illinois Press, 1980. A classic text on sex roles in early New England. Koehler takes a highly critical position of the patriarchal aspects of Puritan culture, and supports his thesis with a rich variety of sources.

Premo, Terri L. *Winter Friends: Women Growing Old in the New Republic, 1785–1835.* Urbana: University of Illinois Press, 1990. This work focuses on how advancing age affected women's activities, societal obligations, family responsibilities, and economic well-being. It uses diaries and letters to capture women's attitudes as they shifted from middle age into old age.

Schenone, Laura. *A Thousand Years over a Hot Stove: A History of American Women Told through Food, Recipes, and Remembrances.* New York: Norton, 2003. The scope of this book moves well past the colonial era, but the early sections provide good insight into the colonial kitchen and women's labor.

Scherr, Arthur. *I Married Me a Wife: Male Attitudes toward Women in the American Museum, 1787–1792.* Lanham, MD: Lexington Books, 1999. The *American Museum* was a monthly periodical published for a predominantly male, middle-class audience. The author studied articles appearing in the magazine and concluded that most men were not misogynists and the laws that repressed women's rights lagged behind the prevailing social attitude of the times. Scherr asserts that the male attitudes reflected in the *American Museum* were favorable in respect to female intelligence. Although he acknowledges some stereotypical ideals of women in the pages of the magazine, he does not find women being described as inferior, unintelligent, or irrational.

Spruill, Julia Cherry. *Women's Life and Work in the Southern Colonies.* Chapel Hill: University of North Carolina Press, 1938. A classic in the field. Covers in exhausting, but very readable, detail the daily life of women in the early South. Included is information on running a household, recreations, courtship and marriage, education, and professional occupations open to women. Focuses primarily on middle- and upper-class white women.

Struna, Nancy L. *People of Prowess: Sport, Leisure, and Labor in Early Anglo-America.* Urbana: University of Illinois Press, 1996. An excellent survey of sports and leisure recreation. Although not specific to female sporting, Struna incorporates the experience of women throughout the text. "Sport" is broadly defined to include gambling, racing, card playing, boating, and attendance at horse races.

Thompson, Roger. *Women in Stuart England and America.* London: Routledge and Kegan Paul, 1974. Explores the differences in women's opportunities and social conditions in seventeenth-century England and America. The majority of seventeenth-century Americans were of English descent, but the environment of the American wilderness forced drastic changes in traditional gender roles. Thompson compares and contrasts the impact of differing sex ratios, economic opportunities, and material conditions in shaping the daily experiences of women in England and America.

Treckel, Paula A. *To Comfort the Heart: Women in Seventeenth-Century America.* New York: Twayne, 1996. This is a concise, narrative history of English, African, and Native American women as they adjusted to life in seventeenth-century America. The book covers marriage, fertility, work, religion, and legal issues as they affected each ethnic group.

Williams, Selma R. *Demeter's Daughters: The Women Who Founded America, 1587–1787.* New York: Atheneum, 1976. This is a readable, generally celebratory overview of women in early America, with chapters on Indians and African Americans. It contains many vignettes of individual women's accomplishments.

Wulf, Karin A. *Not All Wives: Women of Colonial Philadelphia.* Ithaca, NY: Cornell University Press, 2000. A small portion of colonial women never married, and there were limited opportunities for such women. Wulf's book outlines the options open to single women in early America and their disproportionate problems with poverty and scarce employment opportunities. She uses case studies to zero in on specific types of single women, such as spinsters, religiously motivated women, and widows. Also covered are issues of poor relief, political participation, and the role of women's work in urban and rural environments.

Marriage, Sex, and Family

Clinton, Catherine, and Michele Gillespie, eds. *The Devil's Lane: Sex and Race in the Early South.* New York: Oxford University Press, 1997. This is a collection of essays on the combined influence of race, gender, and class on sexual expression. Many essays focus on the legal aspects of miscegenation and coercive sex. The book includes some excellent studies on how gender shaped women's religious and economic choices.

Daniels, Christine, and Michael V. Kennedy, eds. *Over the Threshold: Intimate Violence in Early America.* New York: Routledge, 1999. This work contains several scholarly essays on domestic violence, especially as it relates to husbands, wives, and lovers. The relationship between parents and children is addressed in three articles, and three articles address violence between masters and slaves.

Demos, John. *A Little Commonwealth: Family Life in Plymouth Colony.* New York: Oxford University Press, 1970. This is the classic, groundbreaking work about the social history of families in early America. Demos reconstructs daily life among ordinary Pilgrims of the Plymouth Colony and finds they were not obsessed with the rigid morality often associated with early New England settlers. This slim, highly readable volume looks at child-rearing practices, courtship, marriage, and the material culture of early Plymouth settlers.

Fischer, Kirsten. *Suspect Relations: Sex, Race, and Resistance in Colonial North Carolina.* Ithaca, NY: Cornell University Press, 2002. Fischer examines sexual relationships that crossed boundaries among Europeans, Indians, and Africans, and how interracial sex resulted in increasing politicization of notions of racial difference.

Hodes, Martha, ed. *Sex, Love, Race: Crossing Boundaries in North American History.* New York: New York University Press, 1999. This collection of essays covers interracial relationships through to the present day. Early American essays focus on African-Indian relations, Anglo-Indian relationships on the frontier, and the dynamics of sexual relations between slaves and masters.

Lemay, Leo J. A. *Robert Bolling Woos Anne Miller: Love and Courtship in Colonial Virginia, 1760.* Charlottesville: University Press of Virginia, 1990. Robert Bolling was infatuated with Anne Miller, and his journal, letters, and poetry reveal the range of exuberance and bitterness he experienced from their brief, failed courtship. These documents provide unique insight into the male perspective of courtship among the elite class in Virginia.

Morgan, Edmund. *The Puritan Family: Religion and Domestic Relations in Seventeenth-Century New England.* Boston: Public Library, 1944. This is a classic text on the social life of the Puritans, dealing with marriage, parenthood, the relationships between masters and servants, and the social order.

Scholten, Catherine M. *Childbearing in American Society: 1650–1850.* New York: New York University Press, 1985. This is a fascinating study of all aspects of childbirth, including the training and regulation of midwives, the medical dangers of birth, customs surrounding pregnancy and labor, and the occupation of motherhood.

Smith, Merril D. *Breaking the Bonds: Marital Discord in Pennsylvania, 1730–1830.* New York: New York University Press, 1991. The author uses diaries, letters, probate records, newspaper advertisements, and court records to determine what factors contributed to the breakdown of marriages in colonial Pennsylvania. The scope of the book encompasses a time when patriarchal, businesslike marriages began to be replaced by expectations of a companionate marriage. Also covered are issues such as abuse, sexual dysfunction, alcoholism, and infidelity as precipitating factors for divorce.

Taves, Ann, ed. *Religion and Domestic Violence in Early New England: Memoirs of Abigail Abbot Bailey.* Bloomington: Indiana University Press, 1989. Taves edited the eighteenth-century diary of Abigail Bailey, a devout woman married to a brutal man, whose violence and sexual abuse extended to her servants and children. Her diary reflects profound anguish as she struggled to reconcile wifely obedience, her duty to protect her family, and her ultimate divorce.

Ulrich, Laurel Thatcher. *Good Wives: Images and Reality in the Lives of Women in Northern New England, 1650–1750.* New York: Knopf, 1980. Scholarly overview of women as wives, mothers, and members of a community. The book is rich with detail and fascinating stories.

Wilson, Lisa. *Ye Heart of a Man: The Domestic Life of Men in Colonial New England.* New Haven, CT: Yale University Press, 1999. This is one of the few books to focus on men and their domestic lives in colonial America. This study provides revealing insights into men and how they believed women fit into their lives. Wilson draws on men's letters, diaries, court records, and public statements to provide glimpses into the lives of ordinary men. Patriarchy was a major factor in colonial society, and an understanding of men helps put this cultural system into perspective.

Religion, Spirituality, and Witchcraft

Battis, Emory. *Saints and Sectaries: Anne Hutchinson and the Antinomian Controversy.* Chapel Hill: University of North Carolina Press, 1962. This work contains a good explanation of the antinomian controversy and how Anne Hutchinson's philosophy ran contrary to the prevailing Puritan views. This treatment is less sympathetic to Hutchinson than many other popular treatments, where she is often celebrated as a crusader for religious liberty.

Demos, John. *Entertaining Satan: Witchcraft and the Culture of Early New England.* New York: Oxford University Press, 1982. Demos examines the culture of the witchcraft phenomenon in New England and deliberately avoids focusing on Salem, which he believes has received disproportionate scrutiny. He uses demographic analysis to determine the sort of person likely to be accused of witchcraft and the psychological motivations that prompted people to believe witchcraft was a threat in their community.

Diner, Hasia R., and Beryl Lieff Benderly. *Her Works Praise Her: A History of Jewish Women in America from Colonial Times to the Present.* New York: Basic Books, 2002. This is a highly readable account of Jewish women in America. Although only the first few chapters address colonial women, it is one of the few sources that provide information on Jewish women from this era.

Karlsen, Carol F. *The Devil in the Shape of a Woman: Witchcraft in Colonial New England.* New York: Norton, 1998. Karlsen focuses on the gender aspects of witchcraft and why most of the accused were women. The primary focus is on the social system and gender assumptions within Puritan culture, but the author also examines the economic and demographic characteristics within seventeenth-century New England.

Larson, Rebecca. *Daughters of Light: Quaker Women Preaching and Prophesying in the Colonies and Abroad, 1700–1775.* New York: Alfred A. Knopf, 1999. This is an excellent summary of Quaker women, who are often neglected by historians who are fascinated with the Puritan culture that dominated early American history. Larson's highly readable book addresses the evolving role of Quaker women, whose seventeenth-century roots were uninhibited and zealous, leading their missionaries into confrontation with their Puritan neighbors. By the eighteenth century the character of American female Quakers was one of introspective Quietism. Larson contrasts the conservative social behavior of Quaker women in terms of dress, behavior, and language, with their unconventional views of women's spiritual equality and quest for social justice.

Levy, Barry. *Quakers and the American Family: British Settlement in the Delaware Valley.* New York: Oxford University Press, 1988. Levy contends that Quaker doctrines helped create the first truly child-centered families in America. This book examines how Quaker theology was reflected in the daily social and family life in colonial America.

Lindley, Susan Hill. *You Have Stept Out of Your Place: A History of Women and Religion in America.* Louisville, KY: Westminster John Knox Press, 1996. Lindley provides a comprehensive survey of women and religion in America from the colonial era to the present. The author includes sections addressing Native Americans, African Americans, the poor, and nonmainstream religions. The broad scope prevents in-depth analysis, but results in a readable survey of the topic. A handful of famous religious women such as Anne Hutchinson are profiled, but especially notable is the author's attention to the religious activities of ordinary women who never sought or achieved fame. Such treatment allows the reader to appreciate the role religion played in typical women's lives.

Reis, Elizabeth. *Damned Women: Sinners and Witches in Puritan New England.* Ithaca, NY: Cornell University Press, 1997. The book examines the witchcraft crisis in light of Reis's contention that Puritans believed women were more vulnerable to succumb to satanic temptation than men. Women were believed to be inherently weaker than men, which had far-reaching implications for the role of women in Puritan family and society.

Ruether, Rosemary Radford, and Rosemary Skinner Keller. *Women and Religion in America, the Colonial and Revolutionary Periods.* San Francisco: Harper and Row, 1983. Twelve separate religious traditions are addressed, including religion in Spanish America, black women's religion, revivalism, and utopian groups. After a short introductory essay, the bulk of each chapter is devoted to several lengthy excerpts drawn from contemporary diaries, letters, and essays.

Saxton, Martha. *Being Good: Women's Moral Values in Early America.* New York: Hill and Wang, 2003. Saxton uses three regions and time periods to explore what moral qualities were valued in early America. The Puritans of seventeenth-century Boston, the Anglicans of eighteenth-century Virginia, and African American women of nineteenth-century Saint Louis are the subjects highlighted. The author presents interesting conclusions about what factors were valued or downplayed among the three groups in defining what moral qualities an ideal woman should possess.

Work and Employment

Boydston, Jeanne. *Home and Work: Housework, Wages, and the Ideology of Labor in the Early Republic.* New York: Oxford University Press, 1990. The author does a fine job of documenting the labor performed by a housewife in the early nineteenth century. Although these women did not draw a wage, Boydston contends their labor contributed greatly to the material well-being and even survival of the household.

Clark, Alice. *Working Life of Women in the Seventeenth Century.* London: Routledge, 1919. The author focuses on available job opportunities and daily work of seventeenth-century women in Britain. Despite the

British focus, it is a classic in the field and provides excellent insight into the mind-set and cultural background of many early American immigrants.

Dexter, Elisabeth Anthony. *Colonial Women of Affairs: Women in Business and the Professions in America before 1776*. Boston: Houghton Mifflin, 1931. Overview of women involved in trade, medicine, education, publishing, and craftsmanship. Relies heavily on newspaper advertisements to document the activities of colonial women.

Gilgun, Beth. *Tidings from the 18th Century: Colonial American How-to and Living History*. Texarkana, TX: Scurlock Publishing, 1993. This book is written by a historical reenactor and provides a wealth of information on how colonial women worked in their domestic environment. Gilgun provides instruction in how clothing, baskets, mattresses, candles, soap, and quill pens were made. In every instance she uses only the materials that would have been available to colonial women. She provides valuable insight into which chores were easy, dangerous, or difficult. As a whole, the book serves as an outstanding example of the diversity of chores that made up an average woman's workday.

Hudak, Leona M. *Early American Women Printers and Publishers, 1639–1820*. Metuchen, NJ: Scarecrow Press, 1978. This is a landmark book on the history of women in the printing trade. Hudak has compiled an exhaustive list of female printers and provides insight into their lives, the quality of their printing, and bibliographies of works known to be printed by each printer.

Norling, Lisa. *Captain Ahab Had a Wife: New England Women and the Whalefishery, 1720–1870*. Chapel Hill: University of North Carolina Press, 2000. This fascinating study focuses on a subset of colonial women whose lives were defined by the extended absences of their husbands. The wives of colonial whale fishers created economic and social support structures to keep their families functioning during the yearlong whaling voyages. By the nineteenth century, some of the captains' wives elected to live aboard ship rather than have a life without male companionship.

Strasser, Susan. *Never Done: A History of American Housework*. New York: First Owl, 2000. An excellent summary of the nature of housework in the pre-industrial era. Most of the period Strasser covers postdates the colonial era, but this is one of the few resources that provides in-depth study of the actual chores that occupied the majority of a woman's day.

Tannenbaum, Rebecca J. *The Healer's Calling: Women and Medicine in Early New England*. Ithaca, NY: Cornell University Press, 2002. Tannenbaum persuasively argues that most of New England's goodwives served as their family's primary medical caregiver. Many women, including midwives and "doctoresses" also provided care on a professional basis. Such women were highly respected members of their community, although they were more vulnerable to charges of witchcraft. The author also traces the decline of women in the medical profession as college-educated male doctors gained ascendancy in the eighteenth century.

Arts and Letters

Bank, Mira. *Anonymous Was a Woman: A Celebration in Words and Images of Traditional American Art and the Women Who Made It*. New York: St. Martin's Press, 1995. This text explores folk art of women from the eighteenth and nineteenth centuries. Folk art was the product of "ordinary" people and was more likely to be reflective of the art a typical woman would have in her home, including quilts, samplers, paintings, and needlepoint.

Crowley, John E. *The Invention of Comfort: Sensibilities and Design in Early Modern Britain and Early America*. Baltimore: Johns Hopkins University Press, 2001. Crowley has created a sprawling, interdisciplinary work that examines how values, consumer culture, and technological developments were translated into the homes and design style of the seventeenth and eighteenth centuries. Crowley departs from many historians when he concludes that the stark simplicity of much early American life was not because they lacked the technology or wealth to have more luxurious material goods, but because comfort was not highly valued in early America.

Edmonds, Mary Jaene. *Samplers and Samplermakers: An American Schoolgirl Art, 1700–1850*. Los Angeles: Rizzoli, 1991. This text provides photographs of samplers, their patterns, and historical influences, and attempts to document the role samplers played in education and training in decorative arts.

Garret, Wendell. *American Colonial: Puritan Simplicity to Georgian Grace.* New York: Monacelli Press, 1995. This is a lavishly illustrated coffee-table book, the focus of which is on American residential architecture. It contains almost 200 color photographs of the interiors and exteriors of seventeenth- and eighteenth-century homes. Supporting text explains how culture, religion, and commerce influenced regional styles.

Hayes, Kevin J. *A Colonial Woman's Bookshelf.* Knoxville: University of Tennessee Press, 1996. This book seeks to answer the questions of what, why, and in what context did early American women read. Hayes firmly disputes the notion that most women could not read and examines the range of materials that women mentioned in the wills, letters, or surviving inscriptions on colonial books. He discusses conduct books, household manuals, religious texts, books on housewifery, and books of travel, biography, and novels.

Hull, Suzanne W. *Chaste, Silent and Obedient: English Books for Women, 1475–1640.* San Marino, CA: Huntington Library, 1982. Most books early American women read were printed in England, because American printing presses were primarily employed for newspapers and almanacs. Most books intended for a female audience were written by men, and therefore reflect the values men hoped to instill in women. Hull's book provides an overview of the types of books produced for women, primarily practical guidebooks, religious books, and literature. Particularly interesting is a chapter on books that discuss the innate virtue or corruption of the female sex, a topic that was hotly debated for centuries.

Krill, Rosemary Troy, and Pauline K. Eversmann. *Early American Decorative Arts, 1620–1860: A Handbook for Interpreters.* New York: Rowman and Littlefield, 2000. Compiled by the staff of the Winterthur Museum, this book provides comprehensive descriptions of various period styles in furniture, ceramics, paintings, glass, pewter, and clocks. Excellent photographs and explanations of period style provide insight into the material culture of upper-class Americans of the seventeenth and eighteenth centuries.

Kritzer, Amelia Howe. *Plays by Early American Women, 1775–1850.* Ann Arbor: University of Michigan Press, 1995. With the exception of Mercy Otis Warren, most early American female playwrights have faded from memory, and their works were unavailable outside of a few dusty archives. Kritzer provides the full text of eight early American women playwrights. Because most of these plays feature women in central roles, they provide fascinating insight into the daily concerns and attitudes common in their era. An annotated bibliography lists hundreds of other plays by female playwrights published in the nineteenth century.

Little, Nina Fletcher. *Neat and Tidy: Boxes and Their Contents Used in Early American Households.* Hanover, NH: Society for the Preservation of New England Antiquities, 2001. This book explores the special importance of boxes in early American households. Boxes were among the earliest furnishings in the sparse households, and they served purposes ranging from the storage of clothing to safeguarding valuable items, or simply as decoration. This is a charming book with illustrations and explanations of wooden, leather, needlework, and painting techniques.

Biographical Studies

Ashbridge, Elizabeth. *Some Account of the Forepart of the Life of Elizabeth Ashbridge.* Available at http://www.millersv.edu/~archives/archweb/manuscripts/manus031.htm. Elizabeth Ashbridge (1713–1755) emigrated from Ireland to New York in 1732 as an indentured servant. She became a Quaker, married a schoolteacher, and traveled among several colonies. Her memoir, though written in a sparse and simple style, reveals much about the life of an ordinary woman in colonial America.

Buel, Joy Day, and Richard Buel Jr. *The Way of Duty: A Woman and Her Family in Revolutionary America.* New York: Norton, 1984. The life of Mary Fish (1736–1818) is told through reconstruction of her letters, diaries, and court records. Married first to a minister, then to a lawyer who served as a general in the Revolutionary War, Mary's life provides a window into an average woman's daily activities in a close community. The Buels carefully reconstruct the details of her life, including the tragic death of a child, the turmoil of the American Revolution, the experience of aging, and the impact of the Industrial Revolution on family life.

Carlisle, Elizabeth Pendergast. *Earthbound and Heavenbent: Elizabeth Porter Phelps and Life at Forty Acres (1747–1817)*. New York: Charles Scribner's Sons, 2004. Based on the diary and letters of a colonial farmwife in Massachusetts, this biography provides good insight into the daily life of women, including chores, berry picking, quilting, financial concerns, and coping with illness. Elizabeth Phelps lived through and commented on three wars: the French and Indian War, the American Revolution, and the War of 1812.

Cleary, Patricia. *Elizabeth Murray: A Woman's Pursuit of Independence in Eighteenth-Century America*. Amherst: University of Massachusetts Press, 2000. Elizabeth Murray (1726–1785) was a thrice-married Boston businesswoman. Having been left a wealthy widow after her first marriage, she used her assets to pursue a thriving mercantile business. This biography chronicles her business, her mentorship of other young businesswomen, and her wartime experiences.

Crawford, Alan Pell. *Unwise Passions: A True Story of a Remarkable Woman and the First Great Scandal of Eighteenth Century America*. New York: Simon and Schuster, 2000. The story of Nancy Randolph, daughter of one of the most prominent Virginia families, who was accused of giving birth out of wedlock and killing her child. Although Nancy Randolph was found not guilty at trial, the scandal dogged her for decades. The author provides fascinating insights into the life of elite southerners and the story of how a family amassed land, power, and rank. The Randolph family was at the height of their wealth and power when the scandal broke in 1793, but as with almost all land-rich southerners, their facade of elegance masked rapidly declining fortunes and a way of life that could not be sustained. This is a highly entertaining read.

James, Edward T., ed. *Notable American Women, 1607–1950*. Cambridge, MA: Belknap Press of Harvard University, 1971. This classic, three-volume set provides brief biographical information for prominent women throughout American history, with bibliographies for additional study.

Ousterhout, Anne M. *The Most Learned Woman in America: A Life of Elizabeth Graeme Fergusson*. University Park: Pennsylvania State University Press, 2003. This work chronicles the life of the woman who hosted the premier salon in Philadelphia. Fergusson was at the center of the intellectual and cultural world in colonial America, and her journals provide valuable insight into the life of elite women during the Revolutionary era.

Sellers, Charles Coleman. *Patience Wright: American Artist and Spy in George III's London*. Middletown, CT: Wesleyan University Press, 1976. This is a lively account of an unconventional woman who had a talent for self-promotion and meeting all the right people.

Ulrich, Laurel Thatcher. *A Midwife's Tale: The Life of Martha Ballard, Based on Her Diary, 1785–1812*. New York: Vintage Books, 1991. Ulrich carefully scrutinized the apparently monotonous and mundane data in the diary of a New England midwife. Through careful analysis of the data she was able to draw conclusions about daily life, medical care, and conditions during the earliest decades of the national period. This book swept all the major awards for history writing, including the Bancroft and Pulitzer Prizes.

Withey, Lynne. *Dearest Friend: A Life of Abigail Adams*. New York: The Free Press, 1981. This is a highly readable account of the second first lady in U.S. history. Withey does an exceptional job of placing Adams in the context of the eighteenth century, with insights into the attitudes, customs, and personalities of the times.

African American Women

Elgersman, Maureen G. *Unyielding Spirits: Black Women and Slavery in Early Canada and Jamaica*. New York: Garland, 1999. Although the geographic scope falls outside of the continental United States, this book provides rare and valuable insight into black women's experience in the earliest centuries of American slavery. The author compares the domestic work of Canadian slaves with the agricultural labor on the sugar plantations in Jamaica. Despite the regional variations in work, these women developed similar coping techniques.

Gutman, Herbert G. *The Black Family in Slavery and Freedom, 1750–1925*. New York: Pantheon Books, 1976. Gutman examines how the slave family adapted to fractured families as parents were separated from their children because of death, sale, or relocation. He identifies a pattern of extended kin networks that developed in response to familial dislocation and the common slave culture that spread throughout the South as a result of this phenomenon.

Hine, Darlene Clark, ed. *Black Women in America: An Historical Encyclopedia*. Brooklyn, NY: Carlson Publishing, 1993. Hine offers a two-volume encyclopedia tracing the survival, progress, and culture of black women in America, from the earliest times through the twentieth century. The book includes excellent entries on slavery, attitudes toward beauty, "Mammy," religion, music, and other issues relating to black women in colonial America.

Horton, James Oliver, and Lois E. Horton. *In Hope of Liberty: Culture, Community, and Protest among Northern Free Blacks, 1700–1860*. New York: Oxford University Press, 1997. This is a highly readable survey of life among free African Americans in the North. Chapters address family arrangements, working conditions, political activism, and elements of spiritual culture that helped bind the community together. The Hortons discuss the sometimes-difficult transition from slavery into freedom. The text is richly detailed with dozens of examples of daily life among free men and women.

Jones, Jacqueline. *Labor of Love, Labor of Sorrow: Black Women, Work, and the Family from Slavery to the Present*. New York: Basic Books, 1985. This book explores black women's experience from the earliest days of slavery through the twentieth century. Jones contends that black women's experience has been distinctively different from those of white women and black men. The subculture she highlights shows black women have historically achieved respect within their family, but ongoing discrimination outside the home.

Morgan, Kenneth. *Slavery and Servitude in Colonial North America: A Short History*. New York: New York University Press, 2000. Morgan gives a brief overview of involuntary servitude, including convict labor and indentured servitude. The book includes topics on transportation of slaves, slave resistance, and a summary of how the evolving legal system impacted the living conditions of slaves.

Morgan, Philip D. *Slave Counterpoint: Black Culture in the Eighteenth-Century Chesapeake and Lowcountry*. Chapel Hill: University of North Carolina Press, 1998. Morgan examines the distinctive regional subculture among the slaves of the Carolinas and Chesapeake and how they helped forge an African American identity. Although women are not separately addressed, the author addresses women's role in family life, work, interactions between blacks and whites, and religion.

Native American Women

Anderson, Karen. *Chain Her by One Foot: The Subjugation of Native Women in Seventeenth Century New France*. New York: Routledge, 1990. Anderson believes that Jesuit missionaries targeted Indian women for their missionary activity, primarily because they disapproved of the egalitarian power enjoyed by Native American women. She argues that the process of conversion to Christianity resulted in Indian women's subjugation to men.

Axtell, James, ed. *The Indian Peoples of Eastern America: A Documentary History of the Sexes*. New York: Oxford University Press, 1981. Axtell provides excerpts of documents from eyewitness accounts to Indian life and culture. All excerpts relate to issues of gender. Topics such as puberty rites, marriage customs, and the rearing of children are all addressed. This book is one of the best sources for insight into early Native American women.

Demos, John. *The Tried and True: Native American Women Confronting Colonization*. New York: Oxford University Press, 1995. This brief overview was written for a young adult audience, but since there are almost no general books on Native American women during the colonial era, it might be a good choice for adults as well. Chapters cover the social and religious customs of the Pueblo, Iroquois, Cherokee, and southern Canadian Indian groups.

———. *The Unredeemed Captive: A Family Story from Early America*. New York: Alfred A. Knopf, 1994. Demos offers a comparative story of Anglo-American and Native American family life in the early eighteenth century. In 1704 the Williams family was captured and taken to Canada by Indians. After a two-year period of captivity, the family was returned to Connecticut, all except young Eunice Williams, who elected to remain with the Indians. Eunice learned the Mohawk language, married an Indian, and bore several children. Her identification with the Indians caused outrage among her former Anglo neighbors, who could not understand what caused a girl from a sound English family to "go native."

Devens, Carol. *Countering Colonization: Native American Women and the Great Lakes Missions, 1630–1900.* Berkeley: University of California Press, 1992. Devens examines the colonization process and how gender played a role in the cultural exchanges between the native population and European missionaries in the Great Lakes region. She believes the role of Indian women has traditionally been marginalized by scholars and seeks to highlight how the response of Native American women to colonization was distinctly different from the male experience.

Gutierrez, Ramon. *When Jesus Came, the Corn Mothers Went Away: Marriage, Sexuality, and Power in New Mexico, 1500–1846.* Stanford, CA: Stanford University Press, 1991. In this celebrated but controversial book, Gutierrez studies the intersection of race, power, and sexuality among the Spanish settlers and Pueblo Indians of the southwest. Although praised by historians, the book has been criticized by anthropologists, who claim the work carries overtones of racism and sexism and cite the author's neglect of the use of oral history and living Pueblos for insight into Pueblo history.

Plane, Ann Marie. *Colonial Intimacies: Indian Marriage in Early New England.* Ithaca, NY: Cornell University Press, 2000. Plane examines how the English perceived Algonquian gender, marriage, and family relations. As some Indians converted and moved into "praying towns," they made adjustments to conform to English norms. Their adaptation of European norms might have helped these Indians survive in the colonized lands.

Purdue, Theda. *Cherokee Women: Gender and Culture Change, 1700–1835.* Lincoln: University of Nebraska Press, 1998. Rather than focusing on how colonization changed Cherokee culture, Purdue concludes that most Cherokee women retained large portions of their traditional lives despite efforts to convert them to Christian-

ity. Although elite Cherokee women were more inclined to adopt aspects of Anglo culture, ordinary women sustained much of their traditional roles throughout the nineteenth century.

———. *Sifters: Native American Women's Lives.* New York: Oxford University Press, 2001. This book contains chapter-length essays on notable Native American women, including Pocahontas, Mary Musgrove, Molly Brant, Sacagawea, and others.

The American Revolution

Evans, Elizabeth. *Weathering the Storm: Women of the American Revolution.* New York: Charles Scribner's Sons, 1975. This work contains brief sketches of eleven women who lived through the American Revolution. It focuses on lesser-known women, such as Grace Galloway, a Tory who fought to keep her property from confiscation, and Sally Wister, a young girl coming of age during the war. Each essay contains historical context of the town and family circumstance of the woman depicted, as well as lengthy excerpts from diaries and letters.

Hoffman, Ronald, and Peter J. Albert, eds. *Women in the Age of the American Revolution.* Charlottesville: University Press of Virginia, 1989. A collection of scholarly essays on colonial women's property and legal rights, religion, widowhood, and the experience of black women during the American Revolution.

Kerber, Linda K. *Women of the Republic: Intellect and Ideology in Revolutionary America.* Chapel Hill: University of North Carolina Press, 1980. Kerber uses intellectual history to examine how the Revolution changed women's lives. The book pays special attention to the writings of Abigail Adams and Mercy Otis Warren to represent the views of women. Especially good is Kerber's treatment of "republican motherhood" as an outgrowth of the Revolution.

Kierner, Cynthia A. *Southern Women in Revolution, 1776–1800: Personal and Political Narratives.* Columbia: University of South Carolina Press, 1998. Kierner provides insight into the war's effects on women's lives. Following the war, southern states received almost 800 petitions from women seeking redress. The author provides the text of ninety-eight women's petitions, along with a brief biographical sketch of the woman who submitted the claim and the ultimate outcome of her petition. Petitions are assembled into five categories: Families at War; The Cost of Liberty; The Loyalist Legacy; Women, Allegiance and Citizenship; and The Limits of Revolution.

Mayer, Holly A. *Belonging to the Army: Camp Followers and Community during the American Revolution.* Columbia: University of South Carolina Press, 1996. This is an excellent survey of the social aspects of living with the army during the Revolution. Aspects of soldier life are covered, but the focus is on the thousands of camp followers who attached themselves to the military. Mayer discusses the motivations of these people, their legal constraints, and services they provided for the army.

Norton, Mary Beth. *Liberty's Daughters: The Revolutionary Experience of American Women, 1750–1800.* Boston: Little, Brown and Co., 1980. Norton documents the lives of women in prewar America and traces the effect of the Revolution on women's economic, legal, and social standing.

Ward, Harry M. *The War for Independence and the Transformation of American Society.* London: UCL Press, 1999. This is a brief survey of the war and its causes. It contains separate chapters on the experience of women, African Americans, and Indians during the conflict. Especially strong is the chapter on Revolutionary banditti and the terror they waged on the home front.

Primary Sources

Andrews, William L. *Journeys in New Worlds: Early American Women's Narratives.* Madison: University of Wisconsin Press, 1990. This work contains the writings of Mary Rowlandson, Sarah Kemble Knight, Elizabeth Ashbridge, and Elizabeth House Bridge. The unifying theme is that all of these women made extensive travels throughout America and were exposed to environments not normally experienced by early American women.

Berkin, Carol, and Leslie Horowitz, eds. *Women's Voices, Women's Lives: Documents in Early American History.* Boston: Northeastern University Press, 1998. The editors collected an assortment of excerpts from colonial diaries, letters, court records, sermons, wills, newspapers, and advice manuals. The material selected presents attitudes toward women and marriage, work, religion, law, and gender roles.

Forman, Elaine, ed. *The Diary of Elizabeth Drinker: The Life Cycle of an Eighteenth Century Woman.* Boston: Northeastern University Press, 1991. Few eighteenth-century diaries can compare with this one in terms of the number of decades chronicled and the detail of daily observations made. Drinker was from a wealthy Quaker family, and her diary discusses her courtship, years of raising young children, details about family illnesses, and the American Revolution.

Frey, Sylvia R., and Marian J. Morton. *New World, New Roles: A Documentary History of Women in Pre-Industrial America.* Westport, CT: Greenwood Press, 1986. This is a collection of documents from the seventeenth and eighteenth centuries that reflect on women's social, economic, legal, and religious lives. Documents include court proceedings, private letters, sermons, inventories, journals, wills, and newspapers.

Hoyt, Max E. *Index of Revolutionary War Pension Applications.* Washington, DC: National Genealogical Society, 1966. This is an index to hundreds of reels of microfilm, available from the National Archives Microfilm Rental Program. Thousands of veterans or their widows applied for pensions in the early nineteenth century, and these applications give insight into the nature of military service, material losses suffered during the war, and ongoing economic hardship endured by veterans and their families.

Woloch, Nancy, ed. *Early American Women: A Documentary History, 1600–1900.* New York: McGraw-Hill, 2002. This text provides a good overview of documents reflecting women's lives and attitudes. Woloch draws documents from a variety of sources, including those meant for personal use, such as letters and diaries. Also included are public documents that reflect the conditions in colonial America: laws, speeches, newspaper articles, advice manuals, court documents, and government reports.

Historical Fiction Featuring Women in Early America

Begiebing, Robert J. *The Strange Death of Mistress Coffin.* Chapel Hill, NC: Algonquin Books, 1991. Based around the actual murder of Kathrin Coffin in seventeenth-century New Hampshire. Primarily a murder mystery, the novel is rich with historical detail of the superstitions and living conditions of New England Puritans.

Bernhard, Virginia. *A Durable Fire.* New York: William Morrow, 1990. Temperance Yardley sails for Jamestown during its primitive, initial years of settlement. She survives widowhood, the brutal Starving Time, conflicts with the Indians, and various personal trials.

Bigsby, Christopher. *Hester.* New York: Viking, 1994. A prequel to the *Scarlet Letter.* Hester marries the eccentric Roger Chillingworth in England, but soon flees to America. Her initial meeting and love story with the Reverend Dimmesdale is retold in a manner that emulates Hawthorne's language and style.

Earhart, Rose. *The Diary of Dorcas Good, Child Witch of Salem.* New York: Pendleton Books, 1999. This work tells the true story of Dorcas Good, a four-year-old child who wore leg irons for nine months while she was imprisoned during the Salem witchcraft trials. Following her release, she endured a difficult life of abuse living on the fringes of society.

Edmonds, Walter D. *Drums along the Mohawk.* Boston: Little, Brown and Co., 1936. This is a fictional story of Lana Borst and her marriage to a young farmer. The couple moves to frontier New York at the outset of the American Revolution. The story recounts the years of struggle both must endure because of Indian raids, military duty, and raising a family on the frontier.

Hawthorne, Nathaniel. *The Scarlet Letter.* New York: Norton, 1988. Deeply influenced by Hawthorne's conflicted feelings toward the rigidity of his Puritan forefathers, the novel tells of the tribulations of a wise and brave woman accused of adultery in Massachusetts in the 1640s. This novel has been a major factor in shaping current attitudes toward the Puritans. It was originally written in 1850.

Johnston, Mary. *To Have and to Hold.* Boston: Houghton Mifflin and Co., 1900. Based around the 1621 shipload of women who were sent to the Virginia Colony to be brides to the settlers, the novel traces the adventures of a fictional character, Lady Jocelyn Leigh, as she marries and survives struggles in a new land.

Larson, Deborah. *The White.* New York: Vintage Books. 2003. Based on the real-life story of Mary Jemison, who was captured as a teenager and adopted by Seneca Indians. She ultimately chose to remain with her Indian family rather than return to white civilization.

Michener, James. *Chesapeake.* New York: Random House, 1978. Spans a four-hundred-year history of Maryland and its settlers. Much of the book concentrates on the early Catholics, Indians, and yeoman people as they settled the land and fought during the Revolution.

Miller, Arthur. *The Crucible.* New York: Chelsea House, 1996. Written in 1953, this play used the Salem witchcraft trials as veiled commentary on Senator McCarthy's anticommunist crusade. Despite its widely assumed parallels to the twentieth century, the play captures the sense of fear that engulfed Salem. A 1996 movie of the play brilliantly portrays the living conditions of New England in the 1690s.

Miller, Isabel. *Patience and Sarah.* New York: McGraw-Hill, 1972. This is an account of the life of Mary Ann Willson (active 1800–1825), a folk artist whose work was not widely celebrated until the 1940s. Research into Willson's life revealed her probable lesbian relationship with her housemate, Miss Brundage.

Petry, Ann. *Tituba of Salem Village.* New York: Harper-Collins, 1964. This is one of Petry's many novels focusing on the lives of African Americans and racial tensions. It tells the story of the Salem witchcraft trials through the eyes of Tituba. It begins with her life as a slave from the West Indies and speculates on her fate after the trials concluded.

Richter, Conrad. *A Country of Strangers.* New York: Knopf, 1958. Similar to Richter's *Light in the Forest,* this novel highlights the experiences of a young girl raised by the Indians since her capture at age five. Returned to her town in 1764, she meets with an unexpectedly cool reception.

Robson, Lucia St. Clair. *Mary's Land.* New York: Ballantine, 1995. This story describes life in 1630s Maryland through the eyes of an adolescent girl sold into indentured servitude and reveals the experiences of Margaret Brent, a wealthy Roman Catholic woman whose real-life encounters in primitive America make for an excellent novel.

Sedgwick, Catharine Maria. *Hope Leslie: or, Early Times in the Massachusetts.* New York: White, Gallaher, and White, 1827. Catharine Maria Sedgwick (1789–1867) was one of the most famous novelists of nineteenth-century America. Her best-known novel was *Hope Leslie,* a romanticized tale of Puritans in America. Hope challenges the restrictions placed on women, forms friendships with local Indians, and seeks to follow her heart in matters of love.

Seton, Anya. *The Winthrop Woman.* Boston: Houghton Mifflin, 1958. A novel based around the real-life story of Elizabeth Fones, niece of Massachusetts governor John Winthrop. The story chronicles her privileged position in the early Massachusetts Bay Colony, her turbulent marriages, and her conflict with restrictive Puritan society. Anya Seton has a passionate following among those who enjoy historical fiction, and this is one of her best.

Stone, Irving. *Those Who Love.* Garden City, NY: Doubleday, 1965. This is the biographical story of the courtship and marriage of John and Abigail Adams. It includes details of the war years and a large cast of historical characters.

Swerling, Beverly. *City of Dreams: A Novel of Early Manhattan.* New York: Simon and Schuster, 2001. Swerling provides a rich, sprawling epic beginning during the reign of the Dutch in New Amsterdam, following through the British conquest of New York and the American Revolution. The story begins with the adventures of Sally Turner, a young apothecary and her surgeon brother and traces the family history through several generations of medical healers, with keen insight into medical practices, epidemics, and political upheavals of New York.

Youmans, Marly. *Catherwood.* New York: Farrar, Straus and Giroux, 1996. Catherwood and her husband settle in the frontier town of Albany, New York, in 1678. She and her infant daughter become lost in the woods, and she must learn to survive in the primitive wilderness conditions for months until finding her way back to civilization. This book is suitable for young adults.

Zara, Louis. *Blessed Is the Land.* New York: Crown, 1954. Set during the years of Peter Stuyvesant, who ruled as the Dutch colonial governor of New Amsterdam, the novel traces the life of Jewish settlers as they wandered from Brazil to New Amsterdam. It contains good historical detail of Jewish customs, religious traditions, and experiences in early America.

On-Line Resources

American Memory. http://memory.loc.gov/

The Library of Congress has digitized a small portion of their immense historical collections. This site provides a searchable collection of digital images, maps, drawings, letters, manuscripts, and rare books that reflect unique aspects of American culture. It covers all eras of American history.

Colonial Connecticut Records Project, 1636–1776. http://www.colonialct.uconn.edu/

This is a fully searchable collection of public records, including court cases, laws, public announcements, wills, and probate inventories.

The Geography of Slavery in Virginia. http://www.vcdh.virginia.edu/gos/

This is an excellent, searchable database of advertisements relating to slavery published in Virginia between 1736 and 1790. It contains the full text and images of advertisements looking for escaped slaves or advertising a capture. The database is searchable by gender, age, geographic location, and skills of the person in question.

Martha Ballard's Diary Online. http://www.dohistory.org/

This site contains a rich collection of original documents in addition to the diary of midwife Martha Ballard (1735–1812). The Archive of Primary Sources has relevant newspaper articles, maps, letters, and public records. Most documents are digital images of the originals, plus text transcriptions.

The Plymouth Colony Archive Project. http://etext.Virginia.edu/users/deetz/

This is a collection of searchable texts, probate inventories, ground plans, court proceedings, grave art, and maps of the Plymouth Colony. The site also includes secondary sources such as lesson plans, research papers, and biographies of notable people.

Salem Witch Trials: Documentary Archive and Transcription Project. http://etext.lib.virginia.edu/salem/witchcraft/

This is an outstanding site created at the University of Virginia, which provides transcribed court records from the 1692 Salem trials. Photographic images of the documents are also available. The full text of several seventeenth-century books and pamphlets on witchcraft are available in photographic images. Supplementary materials include copies of old maps, letters, and biographical sketches of major people.

Virginia Gazette and Index. http://pastportal.org/browse/vg/

This archive consists of PDF-scanned images of all surviving copies of the *Virginia Gazette* from 1736 to 1780. An accompanying subject index makes it easy to identify topics by subject or named individual. The index also covers the copious advertisements and public announcements included in the newspaper, making it an excellent source to research social life and customs of the time. Provided by the Colonial Williamsburg Foundation, rarely has such a rich archive of primary source material been made freely available.

Index

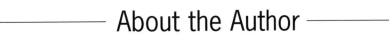 About the Author

Dorothy A. Mays is an assistant professor and librarian at Rollins College in Winter Park, Florida. She holds an MA degree in History from the University of Virginia and an MLS from Indiana University.